# THE COMP

# AR-15/M16 SOURCEBOOK

# THE COMPLETE AR-15/M16 SOURCEBOOK

What Every Shooter Needs to Know

REVISED AND UPDATED EDITION

Duncan Long

PALADIN PRESS • BOULDER, COLORADO

**Other books by Duncan Long:**

AK47: The Complete Kalashnikov Family of Assault Rifles
AR-15/M16 Super Systems
The AR-15/M16: A Practical Guide
Combat Rifles of the 21st Century
Hand Cannons: The World's Most Powerful Handguns
The Mini-14: The Plinker, Hunter, Assault, and Everything Else Rifle
Mini-14 Super Systems
Modern Combat Ammunition
Modern Sniper Rifles
The Poor Man's Fort Knox: Home Security with Inexpensive Safes
Ruger .22 Automatic Pistol: Standard/Mark I/Mark II Series
Streetsweepers: The Complete Book of Combat Shotguns,
Revised and Updated Edition
The Sturm, Ruger 10/22 Rifle and .44 Magnum Carbine
Super Shotguns: How to Make Your Shotgun Into a Do-Everything Weapon
The Terrifying Three: Uzi, Ingram, and Intratec Weapons Families

*The Complete AR-15/M16 Sourcebook:*
*What Every Shooter Needs to Know, Revised and Updated Edition*
by Duncan Long



ISBN 13: 978-0-87364-687-1
Printed in the United States of America

Published by Paladin Press, a division of
Paladin Enterprises, Inc.
Gunbarrel Tech Center
7077 Winchester Circle
Boulder, Colorado 80301 USA
+1.303.443.7250

Direct inquiries and/or orders to the above address.



Visit our Web site at www.paladin-press.com

# Contents

# Warning

Technical data presented here, particularly technical data on ammunition, rifles, and self-defense as well as the use and alteration of firearms, inevitably reflects the author's beliefs and experiences with particular equipment and tools under specific circumstances that the reader can not duplicate exactly. The information in this book should therefore be used *for academic study only* and approached with great caution. Neither the author nor the publisher assumes any responsibility for the use or misuse of information contained in this book.

# Acknowledgments

Thanks must go to the many companies and manufacturers that were especially helpful in supplying samples of the firearms, ammunition, and accessories listed in this book as well as photos, drawings, and other information. Without the help of these manufacturers, writing a book like this would be cost-prohibitive for an author.

Again, special thanks must go to Peder Lund, Jon Ford, Karen Petersen, and the other fine people at Paladin Press for producing this book; a nod must also be given to Virginia Thomas and Rose Marie Strassberg who respectively accepted and edited the first incarnation of this manual—one that was quite crude in retrospect, with Xeroxed and pasted-together drawings of firearms (the sort of thing that must give editors nightmares for years to come).

And, of course, my customary special thanks to Maggie and Nicholas, along with Chad and Kristen, for their continued patience with the in-house grouch who tinkers with AR-15s.

# Introduction

I can still remember the first time I held an AR-15. Remember it like it was yesterday. This was unlike any other rifle I'd ever held: there was no wood and blued metal as with the traditional guns I'd owned; this shooting machine resembled something from a sci-fi movie with its plastic and matte black metal and a pistol grip that might be found on a ray gun. Even the balance was different—in the center of the weapon instead of along the barrel somewhere. And the plastic handguard had ventilation holes in it. It wasn't just that the firearm's looks were weird. The AR-15 was foreign to my grasp, a new type of gun that seemed confusing to hands used to cradling a wooden stock.

Equally odd were the contrasting stories I'd read and heard about the AR-15. An army recruiting manual off a dusty high school library bookshelf told in glowing terms how a bullet fired from the M16, the military counterpart to the gun I now held, could pierce a car's engine block, travel through the passenger compartment, and exit through the back bumper with power to spare. Right. . . . At the other end of the scale were the "war stories" of GIs coming back from Vietnam about dead U.S. soldiers with M16s lying jammed beside them, as well as tales recounting the failure of this rifle's bullets to stop an enemy even though he was "pumped full of lead." Some of the stories, I would later learn, were true and could be attributed to the incompetence of military planners. However, I would also learn that the yarns about the bullets lacking potency were totally false and could be attributed to panic and poor marksmanship.

So there I was, holding this controversial rifle in my hands and wondering what it was really capable of. I shouldered the AR-15 and was pleasantly surprised at the clear picture presented by its peep sight and natural aim. (The safety under my thumb seemed to be at just the right place and worked with a positive feel.) I dry-fired the gun; the trigger pull was crisp and short. Nice. Shooting proved a revelation as well. The rifle seemed to put bullets right on target, about as far as I could see on the hilly Kansas field where I did this first test. And the 30-round magazines I'd bought along chugged ammunition like there was no tomorrow. Very quickly I fired several hundred rounds, and the barrel became scorching hot, oil smoking from it. Yet the handguard kept my fingers cool, and the point of impact didn't seem to wander despite the enormous heat buildup. Nor did the gun jam or malfunction, which would have happened with a hunting rifle had I put that much ammunition through it so fast.

I knew then that I was holding a very different firearm. And after that first session, I came home knowing that I had found *the* rifle that was everything I had ever hoped for. That feeling hasn't changed since then, even though I've traded, built, and tested more variants and models of this gun than anyone has the right to enjoy while I wrote one book or article or another about it. This amazing firearm will one day be bested, but it has set a standard that has so far proved impossible to beat and will remain the gun against which new weapons are measured for some time.

# Chapter 1

# Beginnings

Because of its checkered past, as well as a design very different from what Americans had carried in the past, the AR-15 sparked more controversy than any other rifle in recent history. It has inspired both hatred and love among those who have carried it on the battlefield, into the field to plink, or in the back of a patrol car.

In part, these emotional reactions stem from the rifle's design. Where walnut and polished blue steel normally are found, the AR-15 boasts waterproof plastics and an aluminum receiver. And even though the gun is becoming old (as military firearms designs go these days), its styling and good human engineering continue to give it a space-age appearance that traditionalists view with horror, even though the gun is now pushing the half-century mark.

The AR-15 was among the first firearms of the 20th century designed to take advantage of modern industrial methods. This allowed for streamlined production without a lot of special milling while also giving the shooter a lightweight, durable weapon that didn't look like it had been cobbled together by a plumber and sheet-metal worker. The use of plastics and aluminum in major assemblies along with castings and steel stampings allowed many machining operations to be done away with, which also made the gun less expensive to manufacture, an important factor in the marketplace.

At the same time, nothing was sacrificed in quality. Employing modern industrial machinery to fabricate rifle parts also allowed tight enough tolerances to permit ready substitution of parts when repair or replacement is necessary, a real plus for military users and a boon to gunsmiths. Likewise, the tight tolerances made off-the-shelf AR-15s as accurate as any highly modified target version of previous military rifles.

The AR-15 was conceived as a light and handy gun chambered for a cartridge that would produce a light recoil while shooting a bullet that took advantage of the high-velocity wounding potential of a small projectile. The overall result was a very potent battlefield weapon.

Despite the initial adverse reactions, it wasn't long before the excellence of the AR-15's design became apparent to everyone. In fact, its design features have been copied by manufacturers of many other military rifles, and more than a few knockoffs can be found in such diverse places as the People's Republic of China and the U.S. civilian market.

Like the rifle itself, the .223 Remington cartridge (also known as the 5.56x45mm and the 5.56mm NATO) that was developed for it has greatly influenced military thinking and has proven to be the most effective rifle cartridge ever created for combat. While the future will undoubtedly see the fielding of a more lethal round, the .223 Remington is going to be a hard act to follow. Little wonder, then, that many countries have adopted the round for their battle rifles and that the former Soviet Union switched to a very similar round for its AK-74 assault rifles. Little by little, the cartridge (or one virtually identical to it) has been adopted by all the major military powers of the world.

## ARMALITE'S BETTER IDEA

The lineage of the AR-15 can be traced to the 1950s. Interested in creating a small business, engineer and attorney George Sullivan, then the chief patent counsel for Lockheed Aircraft Corporation, initiated plans for creating rifles that departed radically from previous civilian firearms as well as those used by the U.S. military. Some brainstorming with firearms inventor and international arms broker Jacques Michault produced sketches and plans for rifles that would use aluminum receivers, fiberglass stocks, and straight-line, high sight layouts with a rear sight that doubled as a carrying handle—all of which later found their way to the AR-15.

Feeling that such firearms had a great potential in the civilian marketplace as well as with the U.S. military, Sullivan soon invested in a machine shop in Hollywood with the intention of fabricating experimental rifles

German rifles like this Sturmgewehr MP44, built cheaply by using modern industrial techniques, paved the way for later "assault rifles" that would be developed through the last half of the 20th century.

around the proposed designs. A short time later at a luncheon conference, Sullivan found himself sitting next to Richard S. Boutelle, president of Fairchild Engine and Airplane Corporation, and took the opportunity to tell the executive about the new rifle ideas and designs. Boutelle quickly became interested in the project, and on October 1, 1954, the Armalite Division of Fairchild Engine and Airplane Corporation opened its doors in California.

The first rifle created by the fledgling company was the AR-1 (Armalite Rifle number 1), based on a design of Sullivan and his brother-in-law, Charles Dorchester (who later became the plant manager for the new company). The two had actually started working on the rifle in 1947, so it was quickly completed once the new company started operation. The result was Armalite's Parasniper Rifle, a scoped, bolt-action sporting rifle that could double as a military sniper rifle. The rifle was chambered in .308 Winchester round (7.62mm NATO) and incorporated three features that would be seen in later rifles of the series: a fiberglass stock (filled with foam), an aluminum receiver, and an aluminum barrel with a steel lining.

Armalite's charter required that it develop prototypes and, when the designs were perfected, license the manufacturing rights to other companies. It was hoped this would quickly generate money for the fledgling company while minimizing capital outlays. Consequently, since there were no buyers for the design, the AR-1 never got beyond the prototype stage. The rifle did show the potential for creating a firearm with modern materials and techniques, however, and opened the door for the designs that would soon pour from the company.

### Eugene Stoner

A former marine and army ordnance technician,

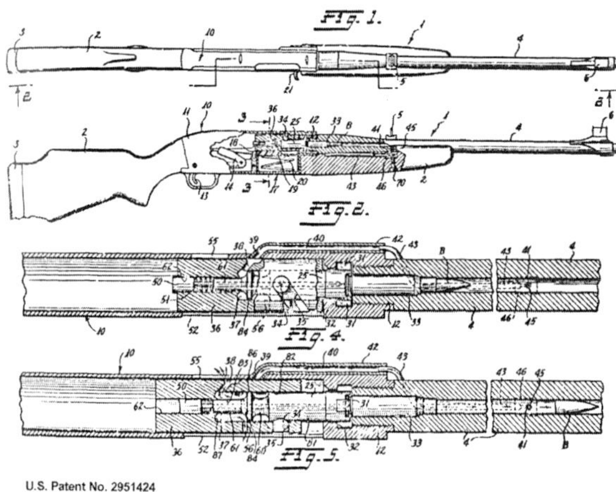


Stoner patent drawing for the rifle design he brought with him to the Armalite company.

Eugene Stoner is the man whose name most often comes to mind as the designer of the AR-15. And rightly so, since it is obvious the lion's share of features found on the guns leading up to the AR-15 were his ideas. Stoner was not with Armalite from the start but joined the fledgling operation as Armalite's chief engineer, winning this position with a semiautomatic rifle design he had brought with him to the business. Stoner continued working on this rifle, which would eventually become the company's AR-3.

So although the AR-3 never went into large-scale production either, it embodied many of the features that later found on the AR-15, including an aluminum body and a fiberglass stock. And it too demonstrated the practicality of Armalite's goals and blazed the path for subsequent rifles.

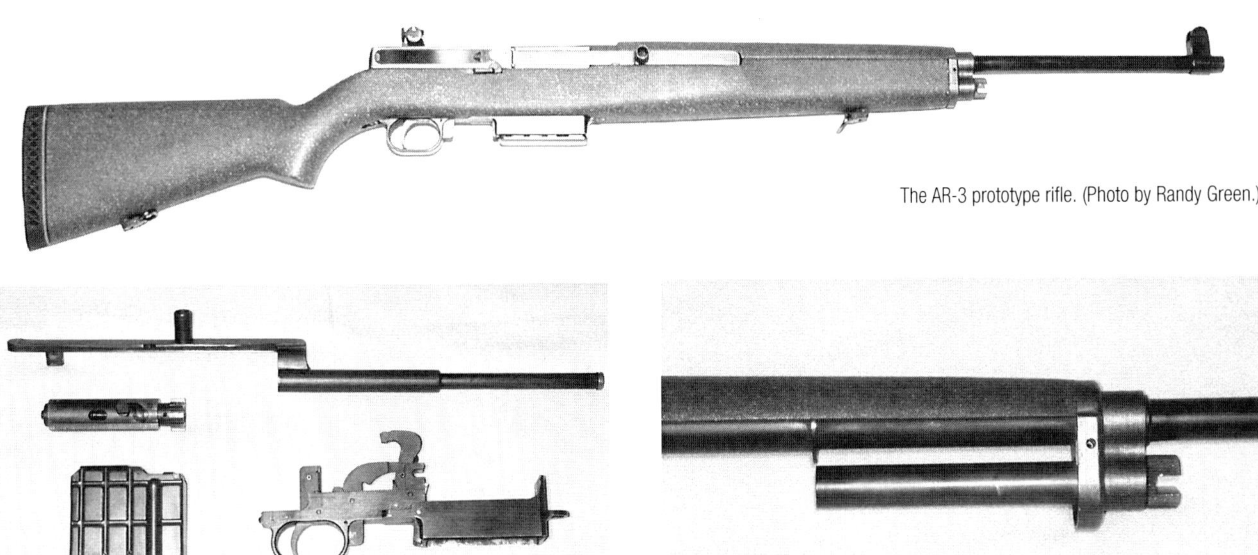

The AR-3 prototype rifle. (Photo by Randy Green.)

The AR-3 trigger group and bolt assembly. (Photo by Randy Green.)

AR-3 barrel and gas tube. (Photo by Randy Green.)

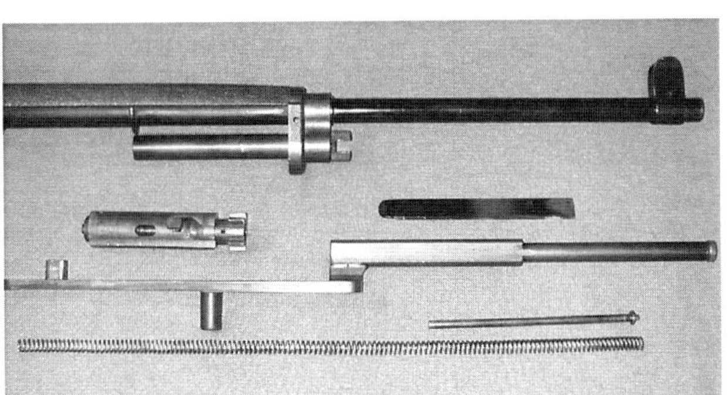

The AR-3 barrel, bolt assembly, and carrier above recoil spring. (Photo by Randy Green.)

"AR-3" stamp inside receiver. (Photo by Randy Green.)

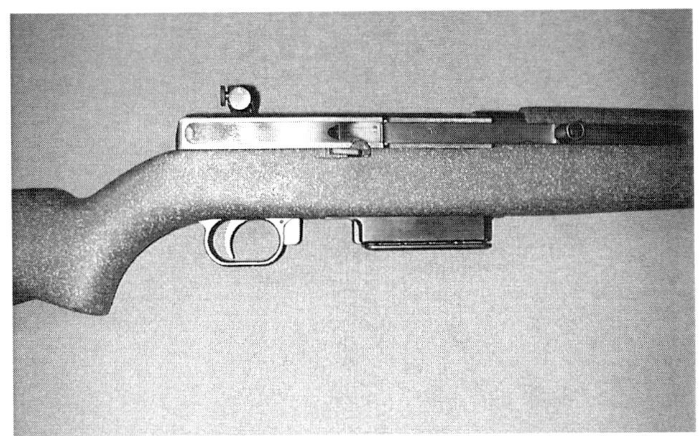

View of AR-3 receiver. (Photo by Randy Green.)

Two other talented workers were soon teamed up with Eugene Stoner: L. James Sullivan (no relation to George Sullivan), who worked as a designer/draftsman, and Robert Fremont, who supervised prototype manufacture and led studies that determined whether the tolerances needed for rifles would be practical from a mass-production standpoint. These three men worked on a number of the Armalite weapons and became the driving forces behind the company's design work (as well as such work worldwide in the decades to come).

Both Stoner and Sullivan would later go on to

**While working on this book, I was contacted by Randy Greenfield, who happened to have bought the AR-3 prototype. The pictures shown here are possibly the only ones ever to appear in print. The gun was well machined and looks like a production firearm. And while the layout and many of the components are not consistent with the design that would eventually be adopted for the AR-10 and AR-15, they point to the route the designers were taking that would eventually lead to these guns. As such, this makes this a very interesting bit of history. As Greenfield wrote,**

**I used a magnet to test the rifle and the following parts are non-magnetic and presumably were machined aluminum blocks:**

**Receiver**
**Trigger housing**
**Magazine housing**
**Front sight**

**The magazine itself has a stamped aluminum housing and machined aluminum follower block. The assembly is similar to the M14 with the barrel fitting into the stock and the trigger group locking it from the bottom. The trigger group is held to the stock with two screws, a machine screw forward of the magazine and a wood screw behind the trigger. I weighed the complete rifle on a reasonably accurate scale and it is in the 6-7 pound range.**

create a variety of new firearms and related products. Sullivan is credited with extensive work on such firearms and products as the AT-22, Ultimax 100 LMG, Hughes Chain Gun, Ruger Models 77 & Mini-14, and C-Mag, as well as many other designs that haven't met with as much success and recognition as these have enjoyed.

### By the Numbers

It should be noted that several Armalite firearms were being developed during the same period rather than just one after another as might be suggested by the numbers the company gave the various models. Apparently, such designations were assigned to rifles as new models were put into development, and so it's probable that several firearms were in various stages of development at any one time. The numbers only indicate to some extent the order in which the firearms were offered to licensing companies, but not when they actually went into production.

Many of the guns never even got into production—and some hardly got off the drawing boards. The AR-2, AR-4, AR-6, and AR-8 never went into production or were even offered for licensing as far as anyone knows. Exactly what these "missing" models might have been is unknown, and they may or may not have been similar to the company's other firearms (for example, the AR-13, according to company officials, was a "hyper-velocity aircraft gun"). And some of the models, such as the AR-16, were limited to prototypes because no manufacturers expressed interest in purchasing the rights to them.

## THE AR-5

Armalite's first brush with commercial success came in 1957 with the AR-5 rifle, which was designed for the U.S. Air Force's requirements for an aircrew survival weapon. Work on the AR-5 was apparently initiated by the friendship between Boutelle and Gen. Curtis LeMay, who headed the U.S. Strategic Air Command.

The AR-5 was a bolt-operated rifle chambered for the .22 Hornet. The rifle used a detachable magazine, designed for the Harrington & Richardson (H&R) M4 survival rifle being built for the air force, and a barrel that was held to the front of the receiver by a threaded ring; the rifle was 30 1/2 inches long when assembled and 14 inches when broken down, making it short enough to meet the air force's length requirements.

The rifle's receiver/action, barrel, and magazine could all be stowed in the A-5's hollow fiberglass stock when the firearm was broken down for storage. The materials used to make the rifle were so light that the rifle could float on water because of the buoyancy of the hollow stock (undoubtedly a strong selling point for a survival rifle, which might conceivably see use in a life raft or near the water). In addition to holding the rifle components, the hollow stock had a small storage compartment for a kit of matches, needles, fishhooks, and so forth, making it a survival package in itself.

Twelve AR-5s were fabricated for air force testing and, with some minor modifications, accepted for use on military planes. The AR-5 was designated the MA1 by the air force, but Armalite never saw any great monetary results from the rifle because the air force's large inventory of M4 and M6 Survival Guns precluded the purchase of significant numbers of the AR-5 (MA1).

Nevertheless, the experience of dealing with the military and the enthusiasm shown for the gun by those testing it suggested to those running Armalite that there might be a market for military firearms. Thus the company adjusted its initial marketing thrust, which

AR-5 survival rifle.

focused on civilian buyers while considering later advancement into military sales, and embarked on a two-pronged development course that would produce guns aimed at civilian as well as military buyers.

### THE AR-7

To take advantage of the work it had done on the AR-5 as well as create a viable moneymaker, Armalite created the AR-7 with an eye toward the commercial market in the United States. The rifle had the basic layout of the AR-5 but was chambered for the more popular .22 LR and changed to a semiauto blowback action (which was inexpensive to manufacture). The detachable aluminum barrel (with steel lining) was lengthened to 16 inches to conform to the U.S. Bureau of Alcohol, Tobacco, and Firearms (BATF) regulations for civilian rifles. The ability of the rifle to be broken down and stored in the hollow stock was retained, as was its ability to float on water.

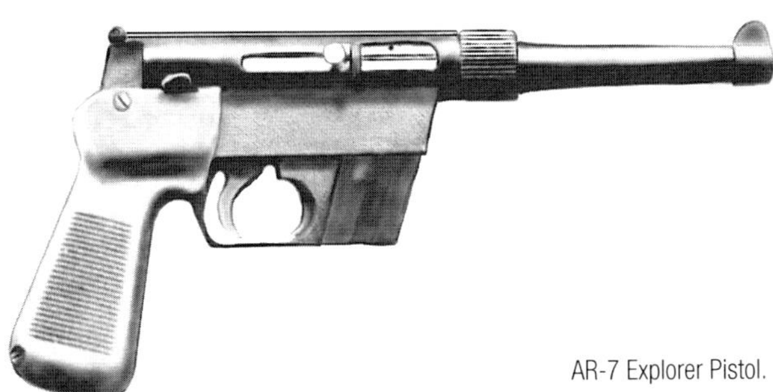

AR-7 Explorer Pistol.

Although Armalite actually produced a few of these firearms and sold them to the public, rather than tie up its production equipment with the rifle it sold the rights to the AR-7 to Charter Arms Corporation in mid-1973. Charter Arms produced the firearm for a number of years as the AR-7 Explorer and later sold a pistol version called the Explorer Pistol. (This pistol version may have been created earlier by Armalite, although Charter Arms has generally received credit for this design; a photo of Sullivan surrounded by Armalite's firearms shows him holding a Golden Gun shotgun in one had while holding what appears to be a pistol version of the AR-7 in the other.)

In 1990, Survival Arms, Inc. took over production of the AR-7, working under a license agreement with Charter Arms. In the late 1990s, AR-7 Industries, LLC also commenced production of the AR-7. In 1998, the design came full circle and was introduced into the product line of the newly reorganized Armalite company. (For a more detailed look at the AR-7 and its many variations, spin-offs, and accessories, see *AR-7: Super Systems*, available from Paladin Press).

### THE AR-17 GOLDEN GUN

Armalite's AR-9 was a semiautomatic shotgun with an aluminum barrel and body incorporating a number of design features that later found their way into the AR-10 and AR-15 rifles (including a rotating bolt design). Rather than market the 5 1/2-pound shotgun, Armalite decided in 1955 to shelve the design and instead exploit many of its features for a commercial shotgun that was

AR-7 Industry rifles.

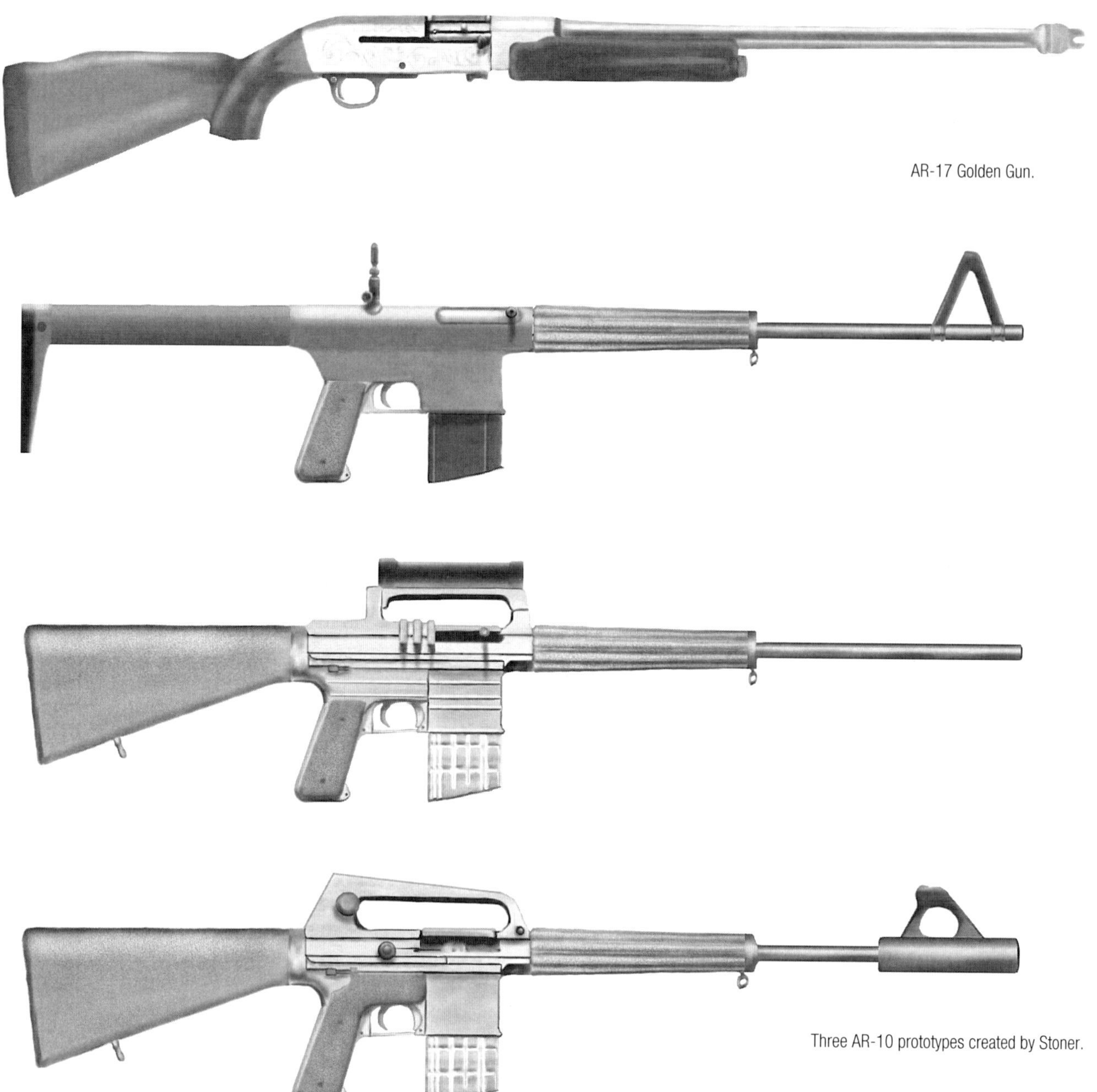

AR-17 Golden Gun.

Three AR-10 prototypes created by Stoner.

eventually marketed as the AR-17 Golden Gun. This two-cartridge semiauto shotgun met with limited success and was in many ways ahead of its time, with a polycarbonate stock and an anodized aluminum barrel and receiver (both of which normally had a gold-colored finish).

### THE AR-10

Development of the AR-10 can be traced back to 1953 to a design Stoner created before joining Armalite. Stoner's rifle was originally chambered for the .30-'06 cartridge (feeding off a Browning Automatic Rifle magazine) and was later modified for the new 7.62mm NATO cartridge, which appeared to be on its way to becoming the standard round for much of the free world.

As with most modern firearm designs, Stoner's work built upon earlier systems. Much of the bolt and receiver-mounted recoil tube of the AR-10 (and later the AR-15) can be traced to the original design of the Johnson light machine gun, which had been created at the end of World War II by American inventor Melvin M. Johnson Jr. While this automatic rifle saw only limited use during

World War II, it did prove to be a successful and forward-looking design, and it is obvious from a casual inspection of the AR-10 that Johnson's gun had a strong influence on Armalite's designers.

In fact, it's possible that Johnson himself had a hand in some of the developmental work with the AR-10 because he was on Armalite's payroll as "military rifle consultant and publicist"—perhaps one of the odder job descriptions of the century. At any rate, one of the most important features of the light machine gun to find its way into the AR-10 was the cam-controlled rotary bolt, which locked into the barrel, rather than the receiver, of the new gun. This made it possible to use a lightweight aluminum receiver with the firearm since the barrel supported all the gas pressure produced when the weapon was fired.

Another feature that enabled the AR-10's light weight was a simplification of its gas system. In lieu of a complex rod and spring assembly, a blast of gas was diverted through a gas port in the barrel and routed down a tube to unlock the firearm's chamber shortly after a round was fired. This, too, was borrowed from a previous firearm design, the Swedish Ljungman Gevar 42, which, in turn, was later employed with the 1944 and 1949 MAS rifles.

Even today, Armalite is a bit touchy about the suggestion that it built upon past designs, arguing that the AR-10 gas system is not the same as that of the Ljungman. In a sense this is true, since the gas system of the AR-10 and subsequent Armalite designs based on it employ a camming bolt and carrier, which are unlocked by gas pressure pushing against the bolt carrier key. However, it should be noted that the Ljungman system, like the later AR-10, has a tube that ports gas from the barrel to a cavity in the bolt carrier, thereby causing the gun to cycle. This in no way takes away from the genius of Stoner in building on the past to assemble a system that was greater than the sum of the parts borrowed from past firearms.

### Trials and Tribulations

A version of the AR-10, the AR-10A, was submitted to the U.S. Springfield Armory in 1956 for testing as a possible replacement for the M1 Garand rifle. The AR-10 was able—unlike the M14—to shoot in the automatic mode while remaining easy to control due to its straight-back design and a special titanium muzzle brake. The rifle met with success, and soon the army expressed an interest in more rifle trials with the new weapon.

Unfortunately, Armalite switched from the first prototype guns with their had steel barrels to a new design that used a steel liner surrounded by an aluminum jacket (similar to that developed for the earlier Armalite survival guns); during military tests early in 1957, the barrel burst just ahead of the soldier firing the weapon. Even though no one was injured, the potential for harm to testers was obvious, and the rifle was immediately pulled from the trials.

Stoner—with the assistance of armorers at the U.S. Springfield Armory—quickly fabricated an all-steel, conventional-style barrel for the rifle so the testing could be resumed. Ironically, it was later discovered that milling longitudinal cuts into the steel barrels allowed the rifles to remain as light as those with aluminum-and-steel barrels.

One of the main features of the rifle, an efficient muzzle brake that had originally been made of "duralumin," was replaced by an equally efficient but more durable—and also more expensive—one made of a titanium alloy. This added considerably to the expense of the firearm. And the "Buck Rogers" look of the rifle undoubtedly met with some negative reaction from conservative forces in the military. Add the minor malfunctions, part breakage, and the barrel failure, and the U.S. Army's enthusiasm for the new Armalite rifle quickly dropped off. A short time later, the army chose the M14 rifle over the Belgian Fabrique Nationale (FN) FAL and the AR-10.

### The Dutch AR-10

Even though the AR-10 was still being redesigned by Stoner and L. James Sullivan, Fairchild had actively promoted the rifle worldwide. In 1957 Armalite licensed the government-owned arsenal of Artillerie-Inrichtingen of Hembrug, Holland, to manufacture the new rifle with an eye toward sales to the Dutch military as well as to other buyers around the world.

For a time the Dutch military seemed poised to purchase large quantities of the AR-10; Artillerie-Inrichtingen quickly invested $2.5 million to tool up for producing the new rifle, undoubtedly with a hope of some large initial sales at home. During this period the AR-10A design was modified, with the gas tube being moved from the side of the barrel to run instead from the front sight/gas port assembly and down along the top of the barrel to a "gas key" coupled to the bolt carrier.

Since the Dutch military wanted the capability to launch rifle grenades from any rifle it adopted, the efficient muzzle brake of the original AR-10 was sacrificed for a more conventional flash hider that could accommodate a rifle grenade. This was an unfortunate trade-off because it sacrificed much of the lightweight rifle's ability to handle full-auto fire without loss of control by the shooter.

Because Fairchild executives expected large sales of the AR-10, the Artillerie-Inrichtingen arsenal was licensed to build, but not sell, the new rifles. Worldwide sales rights were broken down and sold by Armalite to Interarms (which was to handle sales to Norway, Sweden, and

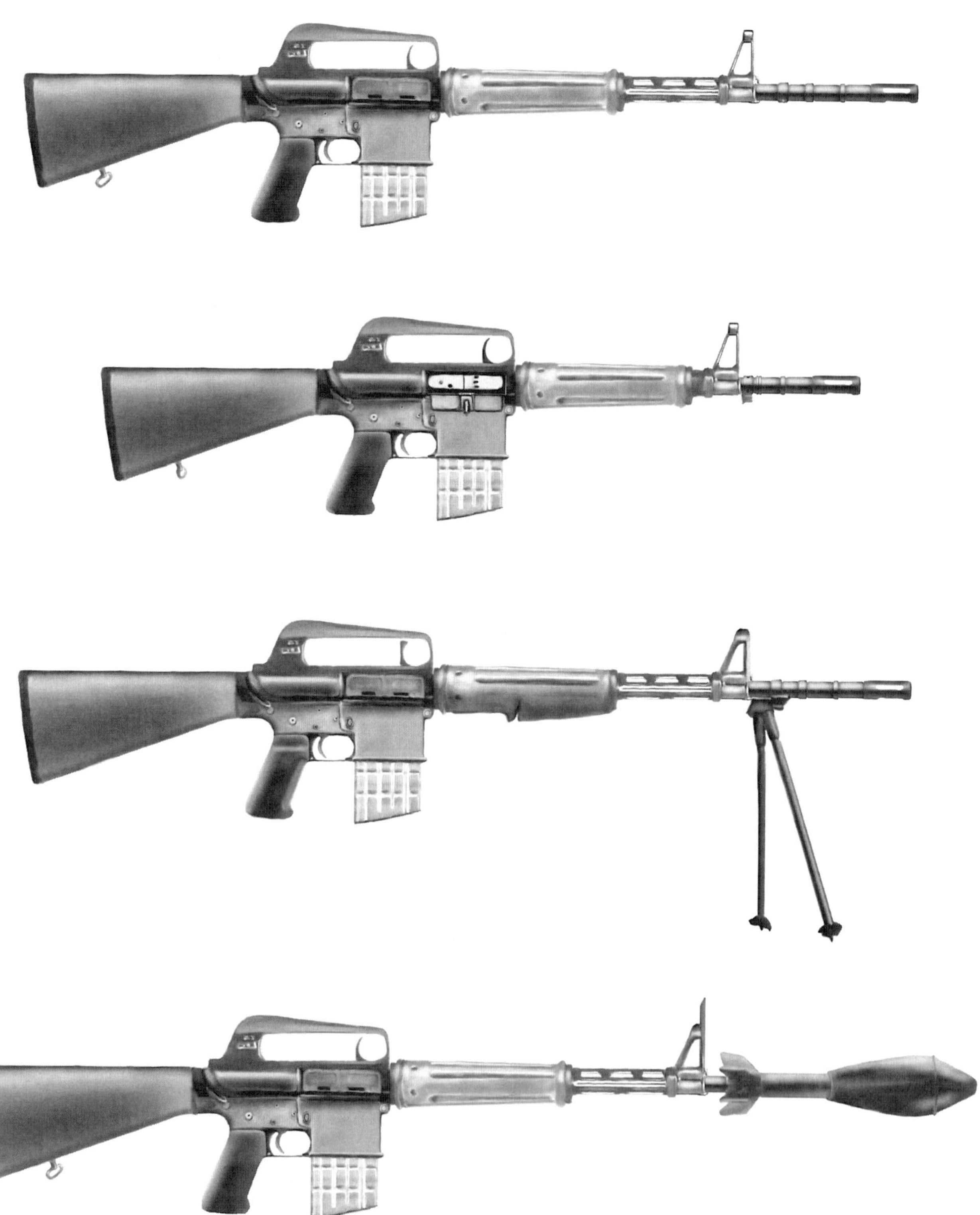

"Family" of AR-10s created by Artillerie-Inrichtingen.

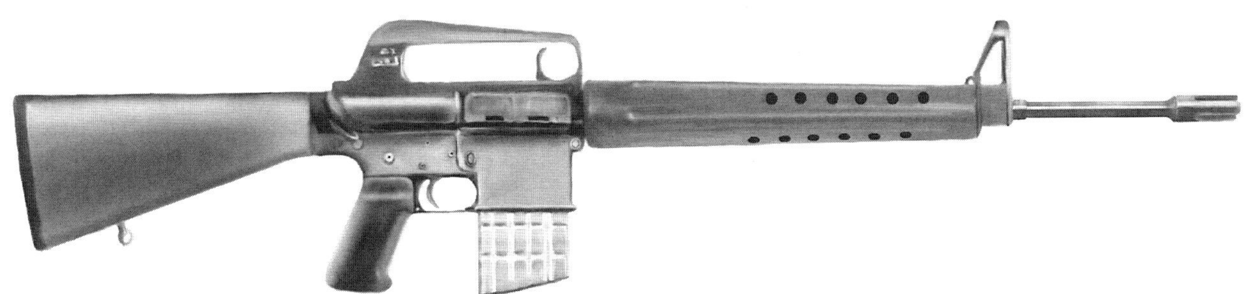

The Cuban-Sudanese version of the AR-10.

Finland, as well as all South American sales and African sales south of the Sahara) and Cooper-Macdonald, Inc. (which was to handle Southeast Asian sales).

The first AR-10s Artillerie-Inrichtingen produced were plagued with problems, including poor accuracy due to improper heat treatment of the cold-forged barrels. By the time these problems were solved, countries shopping for a 7.62-caliber battle rifle had adopted the FN FAL or weapons offered by other manufacturers. The nail in the coffin for the AR-10 came when the large Dutch contract that had been expected fell through.

In the end, Artillerie-Inrichtingen manufactured fewer than 6,000 AR-10s. Cuba, Mexico, and Panama purchased only a handful of the guns for testing; Venezuela chose to buy only 6; Finland asked for 10, and Guatemala purchased from 200 to 500. The "large numbers" went to Sudan, which acquired from 1,500 to 1,800; Portugal, which procured from 800 to 1,000; and Nicaragua, which bought 7,500.

In short, the AR-10 was a commercial failure.

Artillerie-Inrichtingen finally halted production of the rifle in 1959, and Colt's Patent Firearms was licensed to manufacture the improved version of the AR-10A. By this time the weapon had seen major improvements in the form of a stronger extractor, a more reliable magazine system, and a cocking handle that had been moved from inside the carrying handle to the rear of the receiver. It had become an excellent weapon with no interested buyers, since both the Fabrique Nationale and Heckler & Koch now were offering similar rifles in the same chambering that had had the advantage of extensive military testing by some of the major armies of the world. In short, no one wanted to take a chance on the AR-10 when there were other "safe" choices that had been adopted by Germany, Britain, and other large military powers.

### AR-10 Innovations at Armalite

While developing designs for the Artillerie-Inrichtingen, Armalite devised several innovative versions of the AR-10, including a short-barreled carbine, several light machine gun (LMG) variations, and a sniper model. Included were belt-fed guns as well as a clever high-capacity magazine that utilized a spring-lifter that enabled a standard AR-10 to feed hundreds of cartridges without the need to reload or modify the gun for belted operation. Later, Colt's went on to modify the gas tube and spring-load it for use with quick-change barrels and developed a belt-fed model of the rifle. But, as with later firearms families, none of the variations attracted much interest among military buyers.

Today most authorities see the AR-10 as an excellent weapon that missed its place in history because of poor timing and marketing. And despite rumors of manufacturers tooling up to construct a version of the AR-10 for the public, such civilian models have all been AR-15 variants chambered for the .308 round. A true AR-10 built to the specs of the original design has never materialized. The problem with creating a new AR-10 is one of economics; it will always be cheaper to produce an AR-15 chambered for the .308 than to completely retool for a true AR-10 rifle that is not much different and has little to offer other than historic interest to the buyer.

While exact figures aren't known, it appears that the numbers of AR-10 rifles sold by Armalite and its contracts during this original organization of the company (not to be confused with the current operation covered later in this book) were quite small. Among these were a few apparently chambered for the Soviet/Russian 7.62x39mm cartridge, which were tested by Finland as a possible alternative to its AK-47-style Valmet rifles.

Most of these AR-10s were simply for testing and evaluation. Additionally, Nicaragua ordered 7,500 AR-10s but canceled the order when one of the test weapons allegedly blew up. The total numbers produced are as follows:

| Country | Quantity |
|---|---|
| Cuba | 1 |
| Finland | 6–10 |
| Guatemala | 200–500 |

The "family" of AR-10s created by Armalite.

| | |
|---|---|
| Mexico | 1 |
| Panama | 1 |
| Portugal | 800–1,000 |
| Sudan | 1,500–1,000 |
| Venezuela | 1 |

## LESS WELL-KNOWN ARMALITE RIFLES

Armalite also created the AR-11, which boasted a conventional stock and resembled the AR-3 (and was chambered for the .222 Remington cartridge that eventually would be modified to become the round used in the AR-15). The company's AR-12 was a steel-stampings version of the AR-10, the basic design of which was modified to make it easy to mass-produce in Third World countries; the AR-12 was chambered for the 7.62mm NATO and might have been made at about half the cost of the AR-10 but never went beyond the prototype stage. The AR-14 was the sporting version of the AR-10 with a conventional Monte Carlo stock (without a pistol grip) and iron sights. It was chambered for .308 Winchester/7.62mm NATO, .243, and .358.

The AR-16 rifle appeared during 1959 and was notable because it exploited the inexpensive manufacturing techniques pioneered by the AR-12. Chambered for the 7.62 NATO/.308 Winchester, the AR-16 wasn't commercially successful; only three of the guns were ever made. But the rifle did break ground for the development of the AR-18, which would eventually become a competitor with the AR-15 for use among the militaries of the free world.

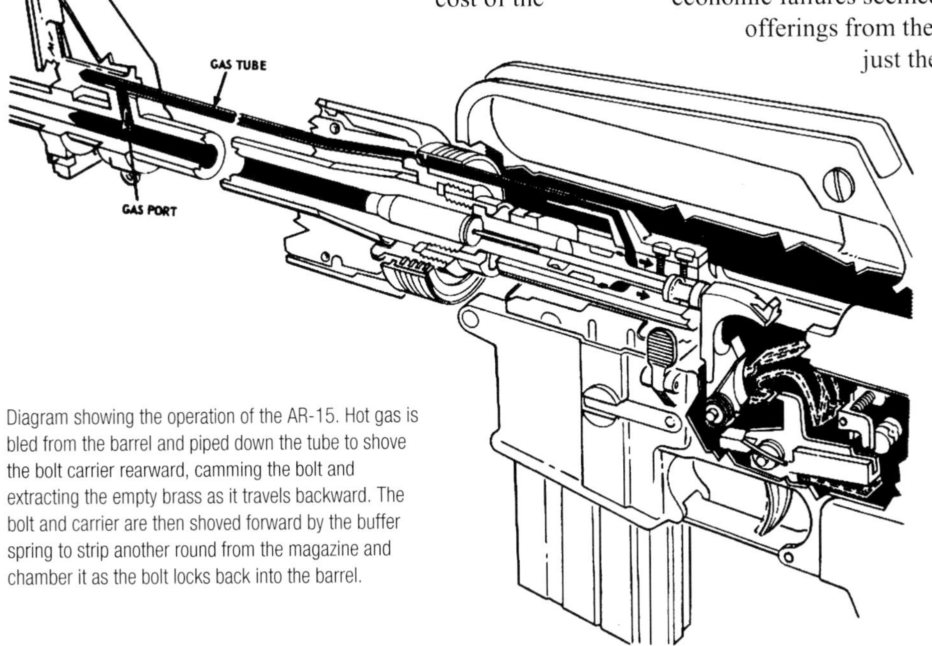


Diagram showing the operation of the AR-15. Hot gas is bled from the barrel and piped down the tube to shove the bolt carrier rearward, camming the bolt and extracting the empty brass as it travels backward. The bolt and carrier are then shoved forward by the buffer spring to strip another round from the magazine and chamber it as the bolt locks back into the barrel.

## THE AR-15

Whereas Armalite's timing had been all wrong and economic failures seemed to be the norm for previous offerings from the company, the AR-15 enjoyed just the opposite. The rifle captured the imagination of buyers and had several lucky breaks that made the sales of the gun skyrocket.

One could conclude that this was to be expected, however, considering all the work Armalite had put into the design of the guns that led up to the AR-15. Add to that the fact that company officials, salesmen, and other personnel had by now created a lot of good contacts within the industrial-military complex as well as becoming more savvy marketers of firearms in general. Having gained valuable experience with

The XAR1501 prototype that would eventually lead to the AR-15 design.

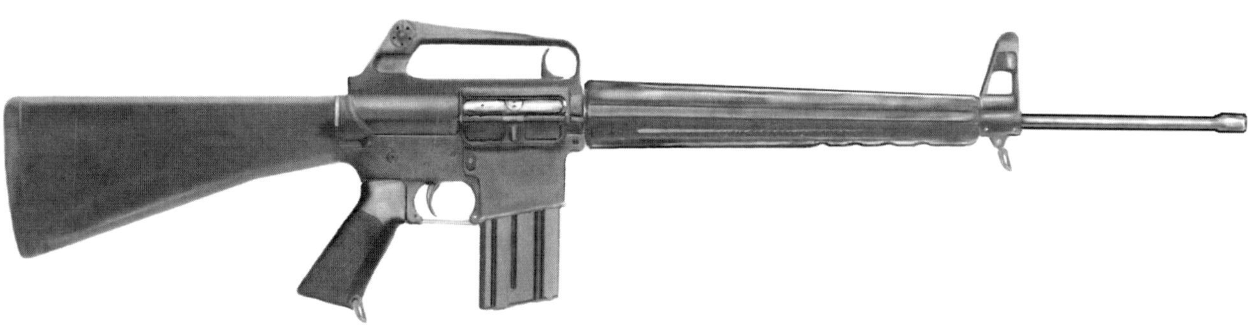

Early AR-15, identifiable by its lack of flash hider.

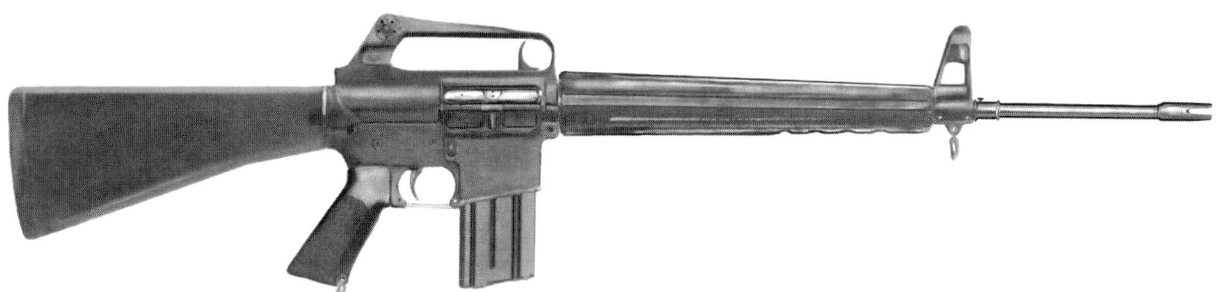

Armalite's AR-15.

previous rifles, the company now had an excellent weapon as well as the ability to laud its capabilities to potential buyers.

Developed from 1956 to 1959, the AR-15 made use of a number of principles and features of the AR-10 and in many ways was simply a scaled-down AR-10. Like the AR-10, it used the same type recoil/buffer system in the stock, a gas tube to unlock the chamber and operate the bolt of the rifle, and lightweight aluminum receiver halves with the bolt locking into a barrel extension.

Placing the recoil spring in the stock of the rifle and dispensing with the heavy gas rod found in most similar guns shifted the balance of the rifle toward the stock. While traditional shooters may dislike this arrangement, many shooters find the rifle even easier to carry than might be the case with another firearm of its weight because of this shift in balance toward the rear of the gun. And many also find it easier to hold on target because of this.

The basic design of the AR-15 is generally credited to Stoner because he headed the AR-10 project, but the actual work on the AR-10 was started before he joined the company, and some features date back to the rough sketches created by Jacques Michault and George Sullivan. However, because Stoner perfected and debugged the AR-10 and later picked out and refined the cartridge that would be used in the AR-15, he is generally credited with the AR-15, even though his contributions were only a part of the developments that eventually led to the rifle.

Much of the actual scaling down of the AR-10 to create the AR-15, as well as the perfection of the new rifle, was done by Robert Fremont and L. James Sullivan, while Stoner apparently worked to perfect the AR-10 for Dutch manufacture. "Scaling down" a firearm is no minor task, since it involves changing the parts of the rifle to accommodate a smaller cartridge while retaining the length and size of the grip, stock, and barrel to fit the human body. Adding to the complexity of the process was the fact that the pressure of the gases that would be contained in the smaller chamber were actually higher than with the large 7.62mm cartridge, so some parts of the firearm actually had to be scaled up somewhat.

Because the new smaller cartridge of the AR-15 had a flatter ballistic arc than the AR-10's round had enjoyed, Fremont and Sullivan adopted a simplified two-position "L" rear peep sight to replace the complicated screw mechanism of the AR-10. The new system moved the elevation adjustments to a spring-loaded detent on the screw-in front sight.

Perhaps to stay within the later military weight requirements, the first AR-15 prototypes had fluted barrels under the handguard and dispensed with the foam reinforcement inside the stock and handguard in favor of simply using fiberglass shells with an aluminum heat shield under the handguard. The greatest change in the new design was in the trigger group, where the disconnector was replaced by a completely new design and modified trigger and hammer layout (the auto sear design and selector remained pretty much the same).

## A MORE POTENT ROUND

The cartridge created for the AR-15 was the result of many years of testing by the U.S. military and varmint hunters alike. The military work dates back to the 1920s when army ordnance personnel created a lightweight .22-caliber bullet for the M1 rifle cartridge with an eye toward a long-range machine gun round. This work was revised in the 1950s when the army started sifting through information garnered from ALCLAD.

The ALCLAD study had started out to learn the requirements for better body armor (some of which had proven highly effective when tested in the field during the Korean War). But the study got into areas of interest to small-arms experts when it examined such things as the range at which casualties occurred, the effects of bullets or shell fragments on the human body, the frequency and distribution of wounds, and so forth. To obtain these data, The army's Continental Army Command Operations Research Office (ORO) conducted a large statistical study involving the 3 million casualty reports from the first two world wars and the Korean conflict.

The results of this study flew in the face of most military thinking. It found the following:

- In combat, nearly random shots produced more casualties than did aimed fire.
- Rifle fire was seldom used effectively at distances greater than 300 yards.
- The majority of rifle casualties were produced at ranges of 100 yards or *closer*.
- Even expert marksmen could seldom hit targets beyond 300 yards because of terrain features or the marksmen's need for cover.

This study was buttressed by research done by the military writer and historian, Gen. S.L.A. Marshall, who discovered that nearly four-fifths of all foot soldiers in World War II never fired a round in any given battle—with one exception. The soldier charged with carrying the Browning Automatic Rifle (BAR) almost always fired his weapon, apparently because he could dominate his enemy through automatic fire. And to some extent his firing also encouraged the soldiers next to him to engage the enemy as well. This finding also laid the groundwork for development of the AR-15 as the U.S. military searched for a lighter alternative to the BAR—a rifle capable of controlled automatic fire that would enable troops to fight aggressively in battle.

## SALVO

The above facts led to the Operations Research Office SALVO project in the early 1950s. In turn, the project made a number of findings that would affect later small-arms design and basically send military small-arms development in the United States in two very different directions. The two major points made by SALVO were these:

- A lightweight projectile was adequate for a soldier's needs at normal combat ranges.
- Long bursts of fire tended only to waste ammunition, while three- to five-round bursts were the most effective automatic fire in small arms.

The principal thrust of the SALVO project was to outline the requirement for a small-caliber rifle that was capable of automatic fire. To achieve these ends, designers took two routes. One was toward the use of smaller bullets in more compact cartridges, the route that would finally prove to be most effective. The other was the basis of the Special Purpose Individual Weapon (SPIW) project, carried out during the early 1950s with the aim of creating a weapon with a superfast projectile that would satisfy the requirements for an effective weapon put forth by the ALCLAD and SALVO research. SPIW was principally directed at producing a weapon that could create a multiple projectile pattern of shots through the use of flechettes packaged in one round, similar to a shotgun shell. (Later the thrust of the program shifted to single flechettes packaged in separate cartridges and fired serially or several at a time in multibarreled guns.)

After some experimentation, flechette configuration was more or less settled: a small rocket-shaped steel dart weighing only around 10 grains (0.65 gram). This permitted packing a number of the darts into one payload package without producing excessive recoil, while putting a number downrange on the target to increase the chances of hitting it, even if the shooter's aim was somewhat off the mark. Generally this basic configuration is credited to Irwin Barr, who commenced work toward perfecting the flechette as a modern weapons projectile in 1950. His Cockeysville, Maryland, company, Aircraft Armaments Incorporated (AAI), handled much of the work and eventually landed a number of government contracts to develop the flechettes and weapons to fire the projectiles.

Barr conducted his early project without funding, contacting the Department of Defense (DOD) to let it know what he was doing in the early days of his project. His work was received with great interest, and in 1952 AAI was offered a contract to produce some demonstration shotgun shells loaded with Barr's flechettes.

Work progressed, and in May 1956 AAI received another contract to study the effectiveness of flechettes. Nine months later, AAI concluded that the 10-grain flechette was the optimally sized flechette and that a speed of 4,000 fps would make it as effective as the much larger but slower 150-grain bullet in a .30-'06 cartridge fired from the M1 rifle.

By now it seemed like flechettes were the fast track to the future, so the U.S. Army awarded a contract to AAI to carry the concept forward with a test gun that would be employed in a variety of tests. Toward this end, AAI employed 10 Winchester Model 70 bolt-action rifles, which were rechambered to accommodate flechette ammunition. Tests with these guns further suggested that the flechette load held promise, so in October 1962 the army asked for rifles that could both fire at specific targets like a rifle and hit a large area with a barrage of projectiles.

This time AAI had some competition, with bids being submitted not only by AAI but by nine other firms as well. Of these, AAI, Harrington & Richardson, and Winchester received development contracts early in 1963, with work to also be done at the U.S. Army's Springfield Armory. These three companies and Springfield Armory each presented 10 test rifles in March 1964 for evaluation. Army test personnel decided that the Springfield Armory and AAI prototypes had the most going for them and provided more funds to develop each system, hoping one or the other would prove viable.

The Springfield Armory design was quite futuristic for its day and in many ways blazed the trail for the modular systems that more or less became the norm in the last decades of the 20th century. The gun could be converted into several configurations, including a bullpup rifle or standard rifle. The AAI design was more conventional in its layout, departing from the basic rifle concept only in its use of a flechette payload.

Springfield Armory and AAI each submitted 10 rifles in August 1966 to the U.S. Infantry Board at Ft. Benning, Georgia, for testing. Things didn't go well in the tests, with both systems proving faulty; however, it was felt that AAI rifle showed promise, so the company received more funding to continue development of its system through a 35-month research-and-development program.

Although by this time the AR-15 had made its way to the scene and voices were calling for its adoption (more on this story in a bit), some felt the flechette gun was the best bet. One of these was General Electric's Armaments Division, which submitted a proposal to refine and perfect Springfield Armory's modular design. The company was issued a contract for this in January 1969, and AAI again had competition.

To carry out its work, General Electric leased the Springfield Armory complex from the government (the armory having recently been closed) and hired Richard Colby, who had been working at the armory on SPIW. Ultimately, the work would reach a dead-end: no practical system was ever developed from the project before funding ran out.

Meanwhile, AAI had four different projectile packages in the works by mid-1969. But the work toward perfecting its rifle had reached an impasse: the gun was far from reliable. Hoping to get the bugs out of the rifle system so that work with the flechette testing could go forward, the U.S. Army transferred the work to its Small Arms Systems Agency at the Rock Island Arsenal in Illinois.

The latest version of the AAI design at this point was the XM70, which went through many modifications and design changes to make it reliable, as well as testing its ammunition as the work progressed. This continued through the early 1970s, with the rifle ultimately becoming viable.

But there was a growing realization that the flechette concept itself was far from promising. In fact, the projectiles weren't nearly as effective as had been hoped. The fin stabilization proved to be very inaccurate over long ranges, and the area coverage afforded by groups of the projectiles was haphazard at best, with a large percentage often hitting the ground well before the target range, thereby being totally wasted. Additionally, there were some doubts about how effectively it would actually wound a soldier, the fear being (apparently based on animal tests) that the wound would be small and penetrating but perhaps not debilitating in many instances.

In addition the AR-15 was by then becoming established in the U.S. military—the army having decided to adopt the rifle as its M16— so the decision was made to pull the plug on all funding for SPIW.

This wasn't the last of the flechette, however; AAI would be submitting a gun chambered for a flechette round in the mid-1990s for consideration by the U.S. military. But today the program is generally seen as a technological failure. Ultimately, military planners decided to stick with conventional but scaled-down rifle ammunition rather than adopt the shotgun-shell-style or single-flechette cartridges created by SPIW.

### Conventional Bullets

Running counter to SPIW were several programs that would actually lead to viable weapons systems. Some of the tests involved were conducted using necked-down M1 carbine cartridges firing .22-caliber bullets. These proved that such weapons were practical and effective (and the rifle was liked by the troops due to its low recoil and light weight). The end result was the suggestion that an ideal combat weapon would fire a conventional, but smaller than currently employed, .22-caliber bullet weighing 55 grains and traveling at 3,300 fps.

Armalite learned about the army tests and proposed switching to the smaller caliber during the AR-10 testing. Much of the AR-10's failure had been due to the new system's not having been tested long enough to uncover all the bugs. Thus, Armalite set out to make a new rifle that would conform to the military's needs by building on the AR-10 system, which had by then seen a lot of refinements and was close to being perfected.

The new AR-15 was originally chambered for the .222 Remington used in the AR-11, since it came closest to the type of cartridge the army would be asking for. This round was then topped with a 55-grain boattail bullet developed for Armalite by the Sierra Bullet Company. Because the original cartridge case was not large enough to create the velocity desired, it was lengthened slightly, and the new round was named the .222 Special.

The first ammunition manufactured for use in testing was made by Remington and bore the head stamp of .222 Special. Later, when Remington began marketing the .222 Magnum, which was very similar, Armalite renamed the .222 Special the .223 Remington to avoid confusion (the .223 round would fit and fire in rifles chambered for the .222 Magnum — with potentially disastrous results). Ironically, the bullet for the .223 Remington is .224 inch in diameter, making the ".223" label misleading to many novices.

The gas system of the AR-15 was tied into the basic design of the rifle and the military's velocity requirements. Through experimentation, Armalite engineers discovered that for the gas system to work properly, a fast-burning powder had to be used; a slow-burning powder would not be completely burned by the time it entered the gas system to propel the bolt open and to operate the reloading mechanism. In fact, repeated firings with a slower powder created major fouling in the bolt of the rifle until jamming finally developed. Because of this, one of original design specifications for the new rifle was for fast improved military rifle (IMR) powders rather than the slower ball powders traditionally used by the U.S. military.

As will be noted later, the specifications for this cartridge would later create problems for the AR-15, due to bureaucratic blundering and lack of proper training of troops in Vietnam.

## THE CONARC TRIALS

As Armalite had expected, the U.S. Continental Army Command (CONARC) announced that it was searching for a lightweight, small-caliber weapon to replace some or all of its rifles and submachine guns. Interested manufacturers and individuals submitted their proposals, and in 1957 the Infantry Board in Ft. Benning officially asked Winchester-Western (a division of the Olin Mathieson Corporation) and Armalite to develop candidate rifles and ammunition to be tested as possible replacements for the M14 and 7.62mm NATO round. These had been developed by the military itself and were failing to perform as well as had been hoped. A third rifle was to be created "in house" by the U.S. Springfield Armory to compete against the two commercial designs and serve as a standard against which the other two rifles would be compared.

The requirements set forth by the Infantry Board for a small-caliber high-velocity rifle were as follows: (1) the rifle would weigh less than 6 pounds when fully loaded; (2) the rifle would need to be capable of automatic fire; (3) the round the rifle fired would be capable of penetrating body armor, a steel helmet, or a 10-gauge steel test plate out to 500 yards; (4) the round would be equal in lethality to the M1 Carbine within 500 yards; (5) the weapon would have a detachable 20-shot magazine; and (6) accuracy and trajectory would be equal or better than the M1 rifle out to 500 yards.

The range requirements in two of these specifications were 200 yards greater than the ranges ALCLAD had shown were needed. Those privy to the requirements have admitted that the range was raised from 300 to 500 yards simply to make the specifications look better to superior officers. Later, when the military decided to use meters rather than yards to conform to other NATO countries, the specifications were changed to 500 meters, making the final cartridge have to perform at twice the range ALCLAD had found was actually needed. Some of this added range might have been justified if the army ever mounted a scope offering magnification of distant objects on its rifles so that the longer range potential might be utilized by troops. But as long as rifles are going to be issued with iron sights, range requirements greater than 300 yards are unsupported by any known studies (and there is no sign that other research or testing to prove otherwise has ever taken place).

On March 31, 1958, Armalite delivered 10 AR-15s, 100 magazines, and 100,000 rounds of ammunition to the Infantry Board for the trials. Because no manuals had been created for the new rifles, Eugene Stoner accompanied the guns and served as a "living manual,"

Lightweight rifle candidates: the gun submitted by Winchester-Western (top), the gun created by Springfield Armory (center), and Armalite's AR-15.

The M1 carbine in many ways served as the yardstick against which the AR-15 was measured. Like the AR-15, the M1 carbine was light and handy, firing a cartridge that produced little recoil and was easy to manage during automatic fire.

showing army personnel how to operate the firearm and helping with minor repairs necessitated by the wear incurred during the tests.

The tests at Aberdeen Proving Ground in Maryland and Ft. Greely, Alaska, suggested a number of modifications and improvements to the AR-15, most of which were subsequently made. The barrel was strengthened (to allow for firing with small amounts of water in the bore of the rifle) and a flash hider was added to it; the cocking handle was moved from the inside of the carrying handle to the rear of the receiver (probably due to problems with the lever becoming overheated with extended firing and to allow those wearing arctic mittens to operate the mechanism); the single-piece handguard was replaced with a clamshell design held in place with a knurled (later ribbed) spring-loaded ring; a rubber butt was added to the plastic stock (probably to help prevent the stock from breaking); the rear sight's size was increased; the selector was modified so that the safe setting was forward rather than the original setting pointing upward (since dragging the rifle could set it to the fire position); and the trigger pull was reduced to 7 pounds and its return spring strengthened.

Additionally, to improve the mechanism's tolerance for dirt, the clearance between the magazine and receiver was increased, the clearance around the buffer increased, and the bolt carrier's lands reduced. Since the dust cover had a tendency to come loose, a cam was added to it. To increase reliability of the rifle, the feed ramp angle was also altered and the capacity of the magazine reduced from 25 to 20 rounds. All these changes made the rifle about a pound heavier than the original specifications of the Infantry Board but resulted in a better rifle as far as the military testers and Armalite were concerned.

Winchester's rifle, designed by Ralph Clarkson, proved to be very similar to the M1 carbine and sported a traditional walnut stock coupled with the look of a miniaturized M14 rifle. By fluting the rifle's barrel, Winchester was able to keep the weight of the gun to only 5 pounds with an empty magazine. However, the Winchester rifle had a major problem: in order to beat Armalite in delivering rifles for testing with the army, the company had started chambering its rifles for the .222 Remington before the range requirements for the new rifle were upped from 300 to 500 yards. Winchester made some frantic efforts to modify the gun and cartridges, but the end result was less than ideal reliability of both rifle and ammunition, so the AR-15 came out looking better after the trials than might otherwise have been the case.

## BIGGER IS NOT BETTER

During 1959, the army conducted tests involving the AR-15 and Winchester's .224 Lightweight Military Rifle but reached no decision on adopting the Armalite cartridge or either of the rifles for actual military use. However, during the tests one thing became very apparent: the lighter weight of the AR-15 coupled with its more controllable recoil made it popular with troops testing it as well as highly effective in putting aimed fire on target. During the trials the soldiers noted how the smaller rifles (the Winchester and especially the AR-15) handled. Nearly all preferred the smaller caliber weapons to the heavier M14 rifles.

During this same period, the Combat Development Experimentation Center (CDEC) discovered that a 7- or even 5-man squad armed with AR-15s could do as well or better in hit-and-kill potential in combat-style tests than the traditional 11-man squad armed with M14 rifles—something that undoubtedly didn't sit well with military planners because the U.S. Army had just elected to arm its soldiers with the M14.

During the tests, it also became very clear that the heavy recoil of the M14 rifle was almost impossible for an average soldier to control under actual combat conditions (as opposed to target-style shooting). And the AR-15 proved to have an overall malfunction rate of only 6.1 per 1,000 rounds fired. This was amazingly good for a nonproduction gun and outperformed the M14, which was averaging a failure rate of 16 per 1,000 during these same tests.

The army CDEC's report concluded that the army should develop a lightweight, reliable rifle "like the AR-15" to replace the M14 and also suggested that the increased firepower afforded by such a weapon would allow a reduction in squad size—all of which undoubtedly displeased more than a few generals in the Pentagon. No contracts were offered to either company for new rifles; the military "stuck to its guns," keeping the M14.

The M14 rifle proved heavy and awkward at best and was almost unmanageable when fired in the automatic mode.

### Changing the Results

What happened next during U.S. military tests involving the AR-15 is clouded in controversy. Supporters of Armalite would later claim that efforts had been made to sabotage the AR-15. Certainly this appears to be the case, though as with most historic occurrences that are less than open to public scrutiny, it may be that a series of blunders and mishaps created the problems. Whatever the cause, the outcome was that the AR-15 came out of the tests looking bad.

The problems started when three of the AR-15s the U.S. military was employing in testing were sent to Ft. Greely to check their functioning under arctic conditions. (Today the need for a standard weapon that functions in all climates may be questioned; however, in the middle of the Cold War the need for this capability was not far-fetched. Although the United States had never really seen battlefield conditions as extreme as those at Ft. Greely, with Soviet territory just a few miles from Alaskan shores, there was serious concern about the potential need for such a rifle. In addition, considering the stalemate of the Korean War and the growing tensions in Vietnam, having to repel an invasion of Alaska by Chinese or Soviet troops was seen as a possibility if not a probability.

It wasn't until Armalite officials received a call for replacement parts from Ft. Greely that they even knew some of their firearms had been sent to the base. Unsure of what was going on, the company sent Stoner with the parts, both to replace the parts himself and to determine what exactly was behind the somewhat unusual breakage problems, since the parts called for were normally not subject to failure.

What the inventor found was later described as appalling: some of the guns had been improperly disassembled. Worse, parts had been lost and replaced—with handmade parts of dubious quality.

After repairing the rifles, Stoner test-fired them and found that the AR-15s functioned well in the arctic conditions at the base. Thinking the problems were cured and knowing that the firearms were functioning properly, Armalite officials undoubtedly heaved a corporate sigh of relief and figured the testing would again give their rifle high marks.

Only months later did the shock come. The rifle appeared to be the proverbial "jammatic," with numerous failures, according to the data that emerged from Ft. Greely. As company officials looked into the matter, they discovered what must have been infuriating: the problems created by the substitute parts were included in the test results and conclusions, with no mention of the alterations or near flawless performance after Stoner had placed the proper parts in the guns.

The M16A2 functions reliably in temperature extremes. Here a U.S. Marine uses his ski poles to steady his M16A2 rifle in preparation for a live-fire exercise. (Courtesy of U.S. Department of Defense.)

## DIVESTING THE AR-15

Although it is hard to know what insiders at Armalite and Winchester thought of the testing done by the U.S. military, many historians feel that the army had intended to use the tests as a vehicle to show off its own designs while giving the illusion of the tests' being open and fair. As more than one critic of the trials has suggested, the U.S. military had a long history of creating its own firearms designs. The thought of a civilian operation's developing a weapon that would be adopted as the standard-issue rifle was not one that many military leaders cared to entertain. The key criteria for the tests, as this argument goes, were that rifles from outside sources be rejected by the military while in-house designs received every benefit of the doubt. Given the Ft. Greely tests, as well as subsequent rigged tests that would come, this argument seems plausible. If so, then the tests were all just window dressing designed to justify the army's selection of the M14 rifle as its new firearm.

After army brass announced the decision to adopt the M14 rifle, officials at both Armalite and Winchester realized they had invested a lot of time and money in the military trials of their rifle with little to show for it. Soon Winchester discontinued work on the weapon and the model was shelved, never to go into production.

Likewise, Armalite (whose parent company, Fairchild, was having financial difficulties keeping the firearms branch going) found itself struggling because of the lack of any military contracts and the black eye given by the Ft. Greely tests. What had looked like a promising start on a major sale to the U.S. military had fallen flat. Thinking it was simply throwing away good money after bad if it continued to market the design, Armalite sought to divest itself of the AR-15. What had appeared to be a goose that would lay golden eggs was, as far as company officials at Armalite could tell, dead. The firearm that had looked so promising was placed on the auction block.

By now, having failed to generate any significant revenue despite creating so many excellent rifle designs, Armalite saw key personnel leaving the company, headed for greener pastures. Fremont left for a more secure job with Colt's in 1959 and was followed by Stoner two years later. Sullivan left in 1960. Thus the firearms team that had created so many innovative designs disintegrated.

# Chapter 2

# Colt Firearms

Too many times, excellent firearms designs have gone into the dustbin of history simply because there was no market for the gun. This might easily have been the case with the AR-15 had Colt's Firearms Corporation not also been having economic problems at the same time that Armalite was. Instead, what appeared to be the death knell for the AR-15 became the chain of events that would make this firearm one of the success stores of the 20th century and put it into the hands of troops around the world (as well as those of numerous civilian and police users).

Colt's Firearms Corporation was created in the mid-1800s by Samuel Colt, who secured a patent for the first successful revolver mechanism in 1836. Although his business was not as successful as sometimes pictured (in part due to the intense competition for business from Smith & Wesson and other gunmakers), Colt guns have always captured the imagination. They even inspired the post-Civil War slogan, "Abe Lincoln may have freed all men, but Sam Colt made them equal." Colt guns did just that, doing away with the brawn that was often called for when a single-shot weapon failed to do its work, instead giving a shooter several follow-up shots to deal with a single enemy, or even a band of outlaws or renegades.

Colt died at the early age of 47, but his business continued, flourishing in large part through military sales of firearms created by and licensed from John Moses Browning. Business was especially good during World War I, World War II, and the Korean War, thanks to the military contracts needed to win these conflicts.

Following the Korean conflict, the company began doing some serious belt tightening. Although civilian sales were a major part of Colt's operation, its bread and butter often came through major sales to the U.S. government. The firm had seen money roll in from military contracts almost from the day Samuel Colt had started his firearms operation. At one time or another, Colt had made Gatling guns, single- and double-action revolvers, various automatic pistols (including the 1911 adopted by the U.S. military), the BAR, and several styles of Browning machine guns.

This came to an abrupt halt when the U.S. Army decided to adopt the M14 rifle and Colt failed to obtain the contract to make the new guns. Meanwhile, orders for the weapons it had been making were cut back with an eye toward phasing in guns like the BAR. Colt undoubtedly realized it was hurting and things were only going to get worse if it didn't add a new product that could add military sales to its lineup.

In September 1955, Colt's management had formed a conglomerate with Leopold D. Silberstein's Penn-Texas Corporation, becoming a wholly owned subsidiary of the holding company based in New York. This arrangement continued until 1959, when a group of investors gained control of the company, dismissed Silberstein, and renamed his company Fairbanks Whitney.

When it learned that the license to build the AR-15 was up for grabs in 1959, Colt's management jumped at the chance to obtain the rights and, in the process, secured the rights for manufacturing the AR-10 as well.

## SELLING THE PRODUCT

After Colt signed the contract with Armalite, its aggressive sales techniques enabled it to sell a number of the rifles to several small Southeast Asian countries. (The rifle was much easier for Asian soldiers to control since it was lighter and offered less recoil—both important considerations for the smaller physique of the average oriental trooper.)

Eugene Stoner, who was soon working for Colt in marketing, accompanied gun exporter Bobby Macdonald through Southeast Asia, demonstrating the AR-15 and AR-10 to potential governmental buyers in Burma, India, Indonesia, Malaya, Australia, and the Philippines. While none of those who saw the AR-10 were much interested, the AR-15 was loved by nearly every government representative who fired it. When word of the AR-10's failure to attract a potential buyer reached Colt, the company suspended all plans to produce the larger-caliber rifle, even though more than $100,000 had been spent in tooling for it.

(NOTE: The AR-10 nearly got another lease on life as the U.S. Army's sniper rifle when it was one of six rifles tested at the Aberdeen Proving Ground in 1977. The Rock Island Arsenal modified the rifle, removing the front sight assembly and the rear sight/handle and incorporating a scope base and ART scope. But the tests were inconclusive and only pointed to the need for a better ranging system and more accurate ammunition. Again, the AR-10 failed to be adopted for military use.)

In December 1959, Colt produced its first run of 300 AR-15 rifles, which was broken into small lots and sent for testing to many of the countries Stoner and Macdonald had visited. Some of the governments expressed interest, but sales were blocked to most of them because the mutual-aid funds the U.S. government was offering required that firearms be standard issue with the U.S. military. The AR-15 wasn't issued to U.S. troops, so the U.S. government wouldn't provide funds for its purchase. With funds running low and a lack of actual buyers, Colt was getting close to serious problems and Armalite was not receiving the royalties it had been hoping for from AR-15 sales.

Then both companies had a stroke of luck.

## RIVALRY TO THE RESCUE

Boutelle, president of Fairchild, had maintained his friendship with General LeMay during the years since the development of the AR-5 survival rifle. During a skeet shoot on his farm, Boutelle demonstrated an AR-15 to the general, firing at a ripe watermelon, which exploded spectacularly when struck by the burst of high-velocity bullets. LeMay was very impressed with what he saw, thus setting in motion a chain of events that would eventually bail both Armalite and Colt out of their financial woes.

Problems had been brewing between the air force and the army since the former had rejected the latter's M14 as too heavy and awkward. The army then turned around and refused to supply parts for the M1 Garand the air force had retained, claiming the spare parts for the World War II-vintage rifle had been scrapped when the M14 was adopted. Consequently, air bases with nuclear weapons were being guarded by security forces armed with the outdated M1 carbine, a weapon never noted for the effectiveness of its cartridge or reliability with automatic fire. Thus the air force was forced to either make due with the M1 carbine or adopt a rifle it viewed as being no great improvement on World War II-vintage rifles.

And then LeMay saw the demonstration of a rifle that fit the bill for the air force's needs, firing a potent little bullet while still being almost as lightweight as the M1 carbine and pounds lighter than either the M1 Garand or the M14.

At LeMay's prompting, the U.S. Air Force started its own tests of the AR-15 at Lackland Air Force Base in Texas. The tests suggested the new rifle was everything the service had hoped for. In 1960, the air force asked for an analysis of the weapon by the Army Ordnance Corps in order for the AR-15 to be granted candidate rifle status for more air force tests.

The army's test and evaluation was conducted at Aberdeen Proving Ground, and the AR-15 proved nothing short of phenomenal. The rifles fired by army personnel proved capable of 10-round groups of 1.5 inches at 100 yards using iron sights and 10-shot groups of 1.1 inches with scopes—as good as many target rifles.

It didn't end there, however. The rifle not only was accurate, it was tough and reliable. During endurance tests of 18,000 rounds fired, only 10 parts broke and the average malfunction rate was only 2.5 rounds per 1,000—an excellent figure for a gun that had hardly gone into production. Of course, the "not-invented-here" syndrome appears to have been alive and well during the tests; the army final report begrudgingly concluded that the AR-15 was "reasonably satisfactory"—an understatement if ever there was one.

The air force followed up with more tests of the AR-15 at Lackland, this time comparing it with the M14 (perhaps to show the army how well a reasonably satisfactory gun would do in contrast to the army-designed M14). When the smoke cleared, 43 percent of the shooters firing the AR-15 could qualify as expert marksmen, whereas only 22 percent of those shooting the M14 could reach this level of skill.

The air force had found its rifle.

But there were hurdles to be jumped before the acquisition process could be started to get the rifles. Most important was the need for appropriations from Congress, which routed funds to what it felt were more urgent needs (at least in terms of constituents). Only after fighting for 2 years to get approval for the purchase was the air force finally able to procure 8,500 AR-15s in 1962.

## GOOD NEWS, BAD NEWS

Ironically, the air force order for the firearms would pave the road for future sales of the guns to both the air force and foreign countries but would fail to bring financial success for Colt and Armalite employees involved in laying the groundwork for the deal. During the 2-year wait for the deal to be finalized, both Colt and Fairchild were taken over by larger corporations. During the

Although the AK47 family of weapons are tough and reliable, the cartridge they were chambered for was definitely second best when compared with the .223 Remington.

reorganization of the two companies, Boutelle got fired, and both companies' personnel who had been involved in marketing sample guns to foreign companies, which would soon be buying quantities of the rifles, were also laid off.

Yet a few AR-15s continued to be sold to various military users around the world; and those guns were gaining users who had nothing but good words for what was becoming known as "the little black rifle." Limited testing in Asia, especially in the South Vietnamese combat arena, showed just how lethal the lightweight rifle and the .223 bullet it fired were (and proved the ALCLAD requirements for an ideal combat rifle had been on the mark). Wanting to put the best weapon possible in the hands of its troops, Army of the Republic of South Vietnam (ARVN) placed an order for 1,000 AR-15s in December 1961, and, since the rifle had been approved for use by the air force (even though it hadn't been funded), the way was cleared for sales to Vietnam.

Meanwhile, U.S. army troops were slugging it out with communist guerrillas in Vietnam. And just as the its tests had suggested in 1959, the army was finding that the M14 was too heavy for easy handling and that automatic fire was so haphazard that most guns were being modified to fire only in the semiauto mode. Compounding the problem was an occasional blowup of an M14 receiver that had apparently been improperly

The AK47 was heavier and less user friendly than the M16; it also had inferior sights, but most important, its ammunition was inferior ballistically to that of the AR-15.

heat-treated. Although the latter event was rare, soon Colt representatives were pointing out such problems to potential buyers and paving the way for the future sales of the AR-15 and rejection of the M14.

## PLAYING THE GOLDEN ARPA

Perhaps recognizing the problems the M14 would present in jungle warfare, the U.S. Army purchased 8,500 AR-15 rifles to test in 1961. In 1962 Colt persuaded the DOD's Advanced Research Project Agency (ARPA) to test an additional 1,000 in its Project AGILE, which was aimed toward finding a better weapon for use in Vietnam.

The ARPA tests again silenced many critics of the AR-15. Among the findings were the following:

- A squad armed with AR-15s had five times the level of overall kill potential than a squad armed with M14s.
- AR-15s could be produced at a lower cost and with a higher degree of quality control than the M14.
- The AR-15 was more reliable, durable, rugged, and easier to care for than the M14 under the adverse conditions often found in combat.
- Soldiers learned to shoot better and more quickly with the AR-15 (than with the M14).
- Three times as many rounds could be carried by a soldier with an AR-15 (in contrast to the M14) when the weight of both the weapon and the ammunition was taken into account.

Equally arresting findings came from the AGILE tests involving Vietnamese troops and U.S. advisors who used the rifles in actual combat. Here again, the AR-15 proved extremely durable and reliable. Not only that, the round used by the rifle showed itself to be highly potent against enemy targets.

Up until the time the AR-15 was fielded in Vietnam, the wounds created by small-arms fire tended to be through-and-through wounds resulting from the bullet's momentum and stability. This was true of the AK47 and SKS used by the Vietcong and North Vietnamese as well as the M14 and M1 carbine. Such penetrating wounds were the most common unless bullets were deflected somewhere in their paths by obstacles or through a collision with hard tissue in the target.

This situation changed with the AR-15, whose bullet was light, fast moving, and unstable—a combination that proved deadly in the battlefield.

One of the U.S. advisors who had seen the AR-15 used in combat wrote,

> At a distance of approximately 15 meters, one Ranger fired an AR-15 full automatic, hitting one VC with 3 rounds with the first burst. One round in the head took it completely off. Another in the right arm took it completely off, too. One round hit him in the right side, causing a hole about 5 inches in diameter.

Another soldier in the field gave an equally graphic account of the effectiveness of the new rifle:

> On 9 June a Ranger Platoon from the 40th Infantry Regiment was given the mission of ambushing an estimated VC Company. . . . Back wound, which caused the thoracic cavity to explode. . . . Stomach wound, which caused the abdominal cavity to explode. . . . Heel wound; the projectile entered the bottom of the right foot, causing the leg to split from the foot to the hip. . . . These deaths were inflicted by the AR-15 and all were instantaneous except [for a] buttock wound. He lived for approximately five minutes.

As another reported, “Range was 50 meters. One man was hit in the head; it looked like it exploded. A second man was hit in the chest, his back was one big hole.”

But it didn’t end there. Troops in Vietnam also discovered that rifle grenades fired from the AR-15 enabled them to lay down what was similar to their own mortar fire. Furthermore, troops cared for the weapon and treated it more carefully than the M1 carbine because they had greater respect for it.

In short, the little black rifle fielded in Vietnam was everything its designers had promised—and more. The troops not only liked the rifle, they also were chalking up serious body counts with it. The weapon enabled those using it to “own the battlefield,” not only becoming deadly opponents to Vietcong troops, but also becoming more aggressive as they learned the capabilities of the rifle they carried.

## CHANGES AT COLT

Colt continued to do well turning out AR-15 rifles for the U.S. military as well as reviving a number of older guns, such as its black-power revolvers and Sharps rifle, as Western movies and TV fueled the civilian market for guns of the Old West. However, changes came again in 1964 when the company reorganized under the name Colt Industries and the firearms section became a subsidiary called Colt’s Inc., Firearms Division.

Colt aggressively sought to broaden its market by continuing to sell revolvers of all and the .45 semiauto 1911 pistol to the public through the 1960s and 1970s and into the 1980s. In addition, it created its Colt Custom Gun Shop, which made special target handguns as well as offering engraving on all of its firearms. Nevertheless, the company’s bread and butter continued to be sales of its AR-15 rifle to military, police, and civilian buyers around the world.

The M16 rifle version of the AR-15 proved popular among U.S. troops—when it functioned properly—not always a given due to ammunition that wasn’t formulated for it and lack of cleaning kits. (Courtesy of U.S. Army.)

## MEANWHILE, BACK AT ARMALITE

With its engineers gone and large sales of the AR-10 and other rifles failing to materialize (except for the AR-15, the rights to which Armalite had sold to Colt’s Firearms without realizing as much profit as could have been, given later sales), Armalite and its parent company, Fairchild, were in financial trouble in 1961. This led Sullivan and the other original owners of Armalite to buy the company back from Fairchild along with the rights and title to all firearms designs except the AR-10 and AR-15, which had been licensed to Colt. The goal of this reorganized company was still to create firearms, but with an eye toward actually making some serious money in the process; finding financial backing was not impossible due to the track record of Armalite. Funding was supplied by Capital Southwest Corporation of Dallas (with Charles Dorchester and Richard Klotzly later acquiring the majority common stock position in Armalite by buying out Capital Southwest Corporation late in 1971).

This new business entity became "Armalite, Inc." and except for the change of ownership was run by the same key personnel. Armalite worked from 1962 through 1971 without meeting with any great financial success.

Since Armalite had failed to experience any great wealth flowing in from its deal with Colt, the company needed a new rifle that might gain acceptance by those not interested in the AR-15 and thereby bring in much-needed capital. Since Colt now owned the rights to the gas system used on both the AR-10 and AR-15, this new rifle also could not employ this or other features found on the AR-15.

This task wasn't as daunting as it might otherwise have been because a rifle design meeting this criterion was actually on the shelf at Armalite. All that was needed was some modifications to the design. Thus, from 1962 to 1964, engineers at Armalite worked on modifying the AR-16 rifle to the .223 Remington cartridge in much the same way that the AR-10 had been modified to create the AR-15. This new rifle was designated the AR-18, and Armalite pinned nearly all of its hopes for financial success on the new gun. (Although the AR-18 was marketed after Stoner had left the Armalite Company, according to Burton T. Miller, who was the vice president of Armalite during this time, Stoner was nevertheless responsible for much of the development of the AR-18 before its introduction, having taken part in the development of the AR-16.)

Due to its being chambered for the more compact .223 cartridge, the AR-18 was slightly shorter than the AR-16. But it continued the overall construction design of mostly sheet-metal stampings that were easy and cheap to produce. Internally, the gun employed a gas piston similar to that of the Soviet Tokarev to move the bolt and its carrier rearward, in the process keeping the trigger group clean of powder residue, a fact that gave the AR-18 the potential to be slightly more reliable than the AR-15, and most certainly making cleaning and maintenance of the rifle easier. Unlike the AR-15, which had a large recoil spring in the stock, the AR-18 used twin recoil springs and guides located within the rear of the receiver; this made possible a folding stock (and later bullpup designs when this system was adopted by other rifles).

Soon this new rifle was in competition against its AR-15 sister in military trials around the world. Although it is arguable whether the AR-18 was a better rifle than the AR-15, one thing is almost certain: the AR-18 never really got a fair trial against its competitor during U.S. military trials. This was because of a disastrous business arrangement Armalite made in selling the manufacturing rights of the new rifle to the Howa Machinery Company of Nagoya, Japan.

Sadly for both companies, this coincided with the Japanese government's efforts to force an end to the war in Vietnam. To bring pressure on those involved with the conflict, the Japanese government refused to grant an export license to Howa for the shipment of AR-18s to any country even remotely involved in the fighting. What appeared to be a lucrative market was suddenly out of reach to those wanting to sell and demonstrate the AR-18.

This problem was compounded when the U.S. Army started searching for a gun that would be even more reliable than the AR-15. One potential choice was the AR-18. The Japanese government's refusal to allow the guns out of the country left Armalite no choice but to supply the army with hand-built AR-18s from the Armalite factory, which were undoubtedly less reliable than those produced at the Howa plant. Thus both firms both missed yet another chance. The U.S. Army became committed to purchasing the more expensive—but readily available—AR-15 manufactured by Colt. (And by the time the Vietnam War was over, the U.S. military was fully committed to the AR-15, which pretty well had all the bugs worked out of its design and was as reliable as anyone could ever have hoped for, far outperforming most similar rifles that were available.)

### Testing the AR-18

Exactly why the few AR-18s produced by hand at Armalite for limited testing by the U.S. military failed to live up to expectations is a matter of some debate. Armalite had earlier arranged for exhaustive tests by the independent H.P. White Laboratory in Belair, Maryland, which verified Armalite's claims that the AR-18 was both tough and reliable. Yet this wasn't the result seen in the military tests subsequently conducted by the U.S. Army. What was going on?

Some Armalite officials later claimed these tests were less than fair, again suggesting that the army was protecting its new rifle just as it had earlier done with the M14. According to Burton T. Miller, some tests the army conducted with the 10 available AR-18s employed the wrong type of ammunition and a defective magazine. If so, this undoubtedly resulted in failures of the rifle because ammunition was fed poorly into the chamber.

To make matters intolerable, the Japanese

government outlawed export of the rifle even to nations that weren't tied to the Vietnam War. This unfortunate turn of events occurred when the Irish Republican Army was found to have illegally acquired a number of Howa AR-18s made in the early 1970s. Thus, in 1973 the Japanese government halted all rifle exports. In all, Howa produced only 3,927 semiauto and selective-fire AR-18s between October 1970 and February 1974.

### The British Ministry of Defence

Added to the growing list of Armalite's near misses was its experience with the British Ministry of Defence, which was looking for a compact rifle for its elite troops and perhaps even its entire military. With an eye toward potentially large sales, Armalite submitted sample AR-18s to the British in March 1966.

The tests found the firearm to be lighter and more compact than the currently issued FN FAL. Additionally, it was concluded that the gun would be considerably easier to manufacture, needing far fewer machining operations in the creation of its receiver assembly. However, British testers felt the rifle had some key, albeit minor, weaknesses as well, including lack of a gas adjustment valve, weak stock hinge, less than ideal accuracy in automatic fire, and the lack of a buffer system (which might cause excessive receiver breakage over the long term). Finally, and perhaps the greatest drawback, there was unsatisfactory performance when the AR-18 was exposed to mud and sand.

Armalite quickly made a series of modifications to the gun to deal with the majority of these problems. Key changes were a beefed-up hinge, addition of an ejection port cover, and creation of an improved muzzle brake/flash suppressor. These were incorporated into new test rifles submitted to the United Kingdom in August 1966 for more testing.

The modified rifles did well but still failed the sand and mud tests. And the lack of a buffer (which Armalite had not added to the gun for some reason) was also a point of contention. In January 1969 Howa versions were submitted for evaluation. Again, the guns failed the mud and sand tests.

Armalite officials came to feel that the Ministry of Defense tests were far from objective. Like their U.S. counterparts, British testers were representatives of the government arms factory. Not only was the Royal Small Arms Factory the source of the FN FAL rifles used by the British military, but it also had some rifle designs of its own that were contenders for adoption by the British military. As if this weren't bad enough, there was bad blood between the Royal Small Arms Factory and Armalite's British representative company, the Sterling Armament Company in Dagenham, England.

(NOTE: This rivalry and possible lack of objectivity would take another amazing twist years later when the new 5.56mm battle rifle the United Kingdom adopted would actually be based on the AR-18. Although it has a much different layout and exterior, the SA-80, which became the British L85 rifle, lifted such features as the gas system, bolt carrier, and others directly from the AR-18 design. Equally ironic is that the British gun has come to be known as one of the worst designs of the 20th century. Generally unreliable and prone to breakage, it is often found in the field held together with wire and duct tape.)

### The AR-180

With the rights to the military markets closed because of its contract with Howa and the actions of the Japanese government, Armalite next tried to gain sales of rifles to the police and civilian markets. It modified the AR-18 for semiauto fire only and designated the model the AR-180. This semiauto rifle was intended for law enforcement and sporting use, especially for shooters in the United States.

The guns were manufactured in the pilot plant Armalite opened in mid-1968 in Costa Mesa, California. During the time the plant was in operation, it produced 1,171 AR-18s and 4,018 A-180s from July 1969 through June 1972. In addition to the standard rifle, Armalite experimented with carbine and "submachine gun" versions of the AR-18, though, like the parent rifle, these never saw any financial success and never went much beyond the prototype stage.

With the usual misfortune in timing that seemed to plague Armalite, the Japanese government picked this time to ease it restrictions on Howa, allowing it to export semiauto versions of the AR-18 (as the AR-180) to the United States. Production of these guns continued into the late 1970s before the gun was finally discontinued.

The Japanese government had dealt Armalite a terrific blow. On one hand it had permitted AR-180s to be sold in the United States in direct competition with Armalite; on the other it continued its restrictions on export of the AR-18, making it impossible for the company to have a supplier should it find a military buyer for the gun. Having worked with the Sterling Armament Company in England earlier during the military trials of the AR-18, Armalite entered into a business agreement in 1974 to move its production machinery to England and licensed Sterling to produce the firearms.

With the moving process sapping resources, it was nearly 15 months before a single firearm could be

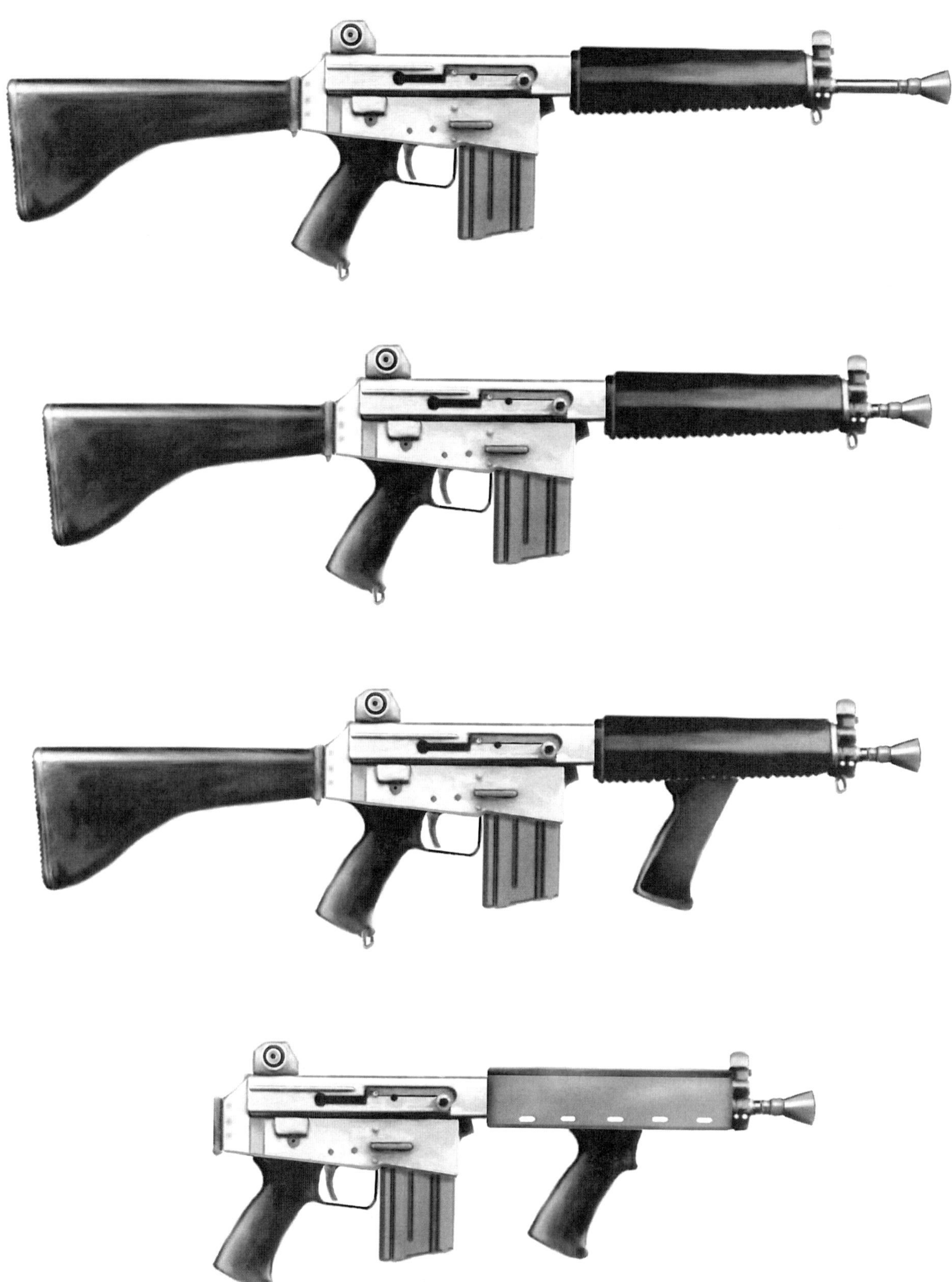

The AR-18 family of guns, including experimental carbine and a stockless "submachine gun" version of the rifle.

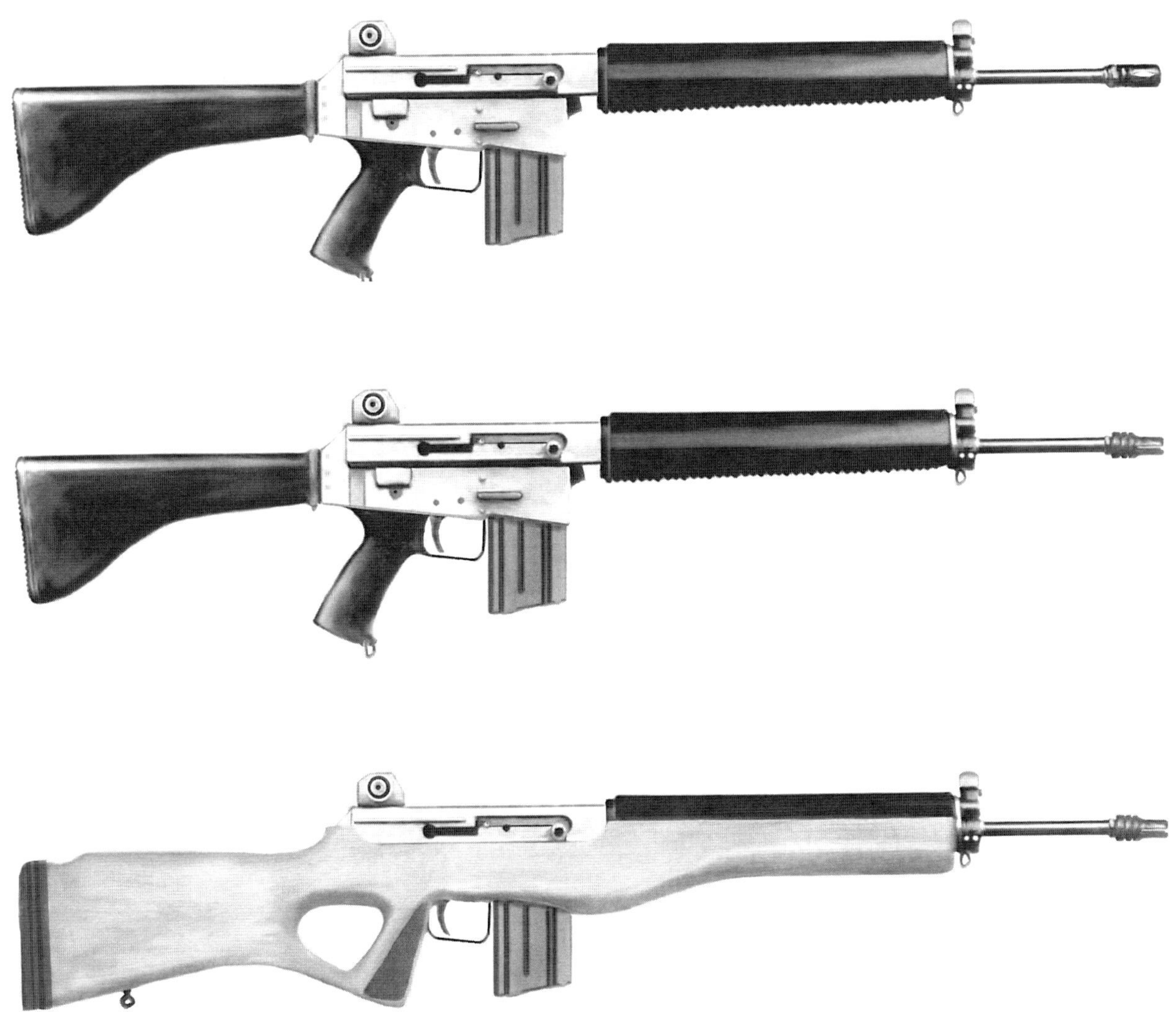

The AR-18 (top) was modified into a semiauto version that was marketed as the AR-180 (center). Sterling designers also created (and advertised) a prototype wooden-stocked version that was eventually nixed by Armalite.

produced. Once production commenced, Armalite imported the Sterling rifles into the United States for civilian sales. Both Sterling and Armalite attempted to market the firearms worldwide but met with little success. Sterling is believed to have produced 12,362 AR-180s between the 1975 and 1983, exporting some 10,946 of these to the United States.

It should be noted that during the late 1970s, Sterling advertised a wooden-stocked version of the AR-180 for police and other buyers. Although a prototype was made and apparently a number of the stocks were produced by Sile (Italy), the "home office" in Costa Mesa would eventually veto this variant. Thus, even though advertising for this gun appeared and more than one gun writer assumed it was available (this writer included), the variant was never actually produced in any numbers; most likely only the original prototype was actually assembled. What happened to the wooden stocks is somewhat of a mystery, though it appears they were destroyed shortly after the order was given to quit marketing this version.

In addition to nearly producing this unauthorized version of the AR-18, the Sterling Armament Company also seems to have had quality control problems, with many guns apparently being less than ideal in terms of fit and finish. When Sterling ceased its production in 1983, Armalite next offered the manufacturing rights to companies in the Philippines. However, by this point the market for the AR-180 had all but dried up as more and more buyers flocked to the AR-15 offered by Colt as the semiauto AR-15 Sporter, which had captured the American police and civilian markets.

The final irony of Armalite's tale of woe is that it was eventually purchased by the Philippine conglomerate that was manufacturing the AR-180s for the American company. Having failed to see any military sales of the AR-18, and considering the growing preference of police and civilian shooters for the AR-15 over the AR-180, Armalite's owners sold the rights and machinery to Elisco Tool Manufacturing Company in the Philippines in 1983.

### Elisco Tools

The Armalite Division of Elisco Tool brought the original Armalite to a rather inglorious end. The operation was headed by Bruce Swain, an Englishman brought in by Elisco to run the operation. He was later replaced by John Ugarte, with Joe Armstrong acting as vice president of marketing.

Elisco Tool had been producing M16 rifles for the Philippine government under a license issued by Colt's Firearms. However, when Colt and Elisco failed to reach an agreement on renewing this license, Elisco needed another rifle to sell. Its solution was to buy Armalite and thereby gain the right to manufacture the AR-18, which was arguably a better gun than the AR-15.

Initially Elisco didn't actually manufacture its AR-18s; instead the guns were simply assembled from parts made by Sterling earlier and sold to Armalite. Thus, the tooling and machinery sent from Sterling's plant to the Philippines with the sale of Armalite was never actually used in making any of the guns being sold.

At this point, the government of Ferdinand Marcos was overturned and the president went into exile. With his exit went Elisco's connections for selling firearms to the Philippine government. Actual production of the AR-18 never took place in the Philippines other than through the assembly of parts that came with the inventory shipped from Sterling. U.S. branches of Armalite were closed in 1987, and for all practical purposes the company ceased to exist except on paper, its machinery sitting idle, slowly deteriorating in the humid Philippine climate.

## FLYING HIGH

If Armalite and the AR-18 are a tale of woe, Colt and the AR-15 make for a success story unlike few others in the history of gun manufacturing, marked by good fortune at every turn.

In 1962 the U.S. Air Force finally got the go ahead to purchase some AR-15s. After conducting additional tests, it suggested some minor design modifications and then ordered 1,000 AR-15s from Colt for further testing, which proved the AR-15 to be very reliable. During one test in which 27 of the rifles were fired with 6,000 rounds apiece, the malfunction rate averaged only once per 3,000 rounds fired, and part breakage occurred only once per 6,200 rounds fired. Following these final tests, the U.S. Air Force chose the AR-15 as its standard-issue rifle, designating it the M16 Rifle.

Meanwhile, the U.S. Army was under pressure from President Kennedy and Defense Secretary McNamara's "whiz kids" to buy the high-tech gun that appealed to those wanting to remake the U.S. military into an efficient operation modeled after corporate America. Thus, it began purchasing more AR-15 rifles in limited numbers for use by special forces in Vietnam. (It should be noted that "special forces" is a rather generic term that generally encompasses several elite groups in the U.S. military, including the Army Rangers, Marine Force Recon, and Navy SEALs, as well as the Green Berets and lesser known groups.)

As mentioned earlier, when the first 1,000 AR-15s reached the ARVN in 1962, the reports that came back couldn't have been better if they'd been written by Colt's advertising staff itself. The rifles had a fantastic record of reliability in the hands of the Vietnamese and continued to be very lethal in combat.

Yet the U.S. Army was still dragging its heels, apparently for mostly political reasons. The M14 rifle had been produced by the army for the army, and a number of officers had vested interests in keeping it as the standard weapon. Furthermore, in developing the rifle, U.S. Army personnel had virtually ignored all the U.S. and British military studies showing that the battle rifles from World War I through the Korean War had too much power for the job they were called upon to do. Flying in the face of such facts, army designers had created the T65 cartridge, a shortened version of the old .30-'06 round. The round was more powerful than necessary for the limited range at which ALCLAD studies suggested most combat occurred; this too powerful cartridge made the weapon nearly uncontrollable, unlike other lightweight automatic-weapons' rounds.

One can only surmise that many of the officers involved in creating the M14 didn't want to admit their mistakes and possibly ruin their careers in the process. (This is not to say that this was the case with all those involved. Many also had legitimate concerns that the ALCLAD conclusions might somehow have been flawed. The ideal rifle that could hit anything as far as the eye can see seems logical enough and was at odds with the idea that combat almost always took place within very short ranges.)

## TALES OF WOE

With the Soviet Union and communism becoming a

growing menace following World War II, the push was on for NATO to adopt a standard round in order to simplify supplying troops in the field. More than a few problems had arisen during World War II because of the hodgepodge of cartridges the Allied troops had required. With the possibility of yet another world war in Europe, military leaders were calling for one cartridge that could be used in rifles, light machine guns, and squad automatic weapons—hand-held machine guns similar to the World War II vintage BAR carried by U.S. troops.

The British .280/30 was undoubtedly a superior round. It was light and fired a bullet that—as would later be shown by the .223 cartridge in the AR-15—might have become super deadly on the battlefield.

Friction between the militaries of various NATO countries started to become apparent during the Comparison Test of United Kingdom and U.S. Lightweight Rifles at Aberdeen range on February 16, 1950. Here the British EM2 bullpup rifle and the new Belgian FN FAL, both chambered in .280/30 were tested side by side with the U.S. Army's prototype T25 rifle chambered for the new T65 cartridge. Despite the T25's performing miserably in the tests, the final report concluded (with what many suggested was a painful twist of logic) that the T25 was superior, even though the powerful cartridge was in large part what had made the rifle nearly impossible to control during automatic fire.

Had the U.S. Army been realistic about testing and the needs of soldiers on the battlefield, the FN FAL might have become the rifle that U.S. soldiers would carry for the next few decades. And had the army adopted the .280/30 cartridge or one like it rather than the T65, it seems likely that the M14 and M16 rifles might never have been created (or of course seen action in Vietnam).

That scenario wasn't to be, however, because the United States browbeat its NATO partners into adopting the T65 round.

Doing this wasn't easy. The British Parliament, perhaps smarting from the idea that the Yanks had bailed the Brits out of World War II, wanted to demonstrate the country's ability to arm itself and create an effective rifle from a domestically produced design; Defence Minister Emanuel Shinwell announced that the EM2 and the .280/30 cartridge would be adopted as the official British military rifle and cartridge.

Washington cried foul, pointing to an agreement among the United States, Canada, and Britain that there would be a standardization of rifles and ammunition in an effort to bring a large segment of NATO under one umbrella. Britain, U.S. politicians claimed, couldn't adopt its own rifle and ammunition. It would have to adopt the same cartridge and weapon that the United States and Canada did.

Both sides trotted out their "experts" in an effort to gain the upper hand in what was seen as a choice market for the company holding the manufacturing rights to the firearm adopted. British military experts claimed that while the U.S. round was effective to 1,000 yards, the British .280/30 cartridge was effective to 2,000. U.S. experts scoffed at the idea that the puny British round could be nearly as effective as the larger, more powerful cartridge.

### Churchill Returns

Long a proponent of strong U.S.-British ties, Winston Churchill became the new prime minister in 1951. And one of his first tasks was to undo the wrangling between the United States and Britain over NATO rifles and ammunition. He immediately countermanded the adoption of the EM2 rifle and .280/30 cartridge as the official British round, thereby putting an end to much of the squabbling between British and U.S. NATO leaders.

The Americans didn't accept the olive branch, and not without reason. More than American or British pride was now on the line. The Korean War was heating up and more rifles were needed. Since no one had demonstrated a rifle that was as reliable as the old M1 Garand, orders for that gun were placed with International Harvester as well as the Springfield Armory.

Following the Korean conflict, NATO leaders knew they were facing a formidable enemy in Cold War communism. The need was greater than ever for standardized equipment against a foe that might—without any great stretch of the imagination—soon be invading NATO member countries.

The U.S. military held demonstrations for the press showing the ability of older weapons like the BAR, 1919A4 Browning LM, to chamber and operate on the new .308 cartridge it had created. Included in these demonstrations were the T47 and T44 rifles. The army, the press was told, was on the verge of selecting one of these guns to replace the M1 rifle.

Things weren't quite that simple. Soon the British and Belgians were presenting versions of their rifles, chambered for the T65, and asking for more ordnance trials per their NATO agreements. More trials took place, and with them came new controversy.

### Trials and Politics

The trials pitted the new U.S. rifles against the Belgian FN FAL and British EM2 rifles late in 1952. The FN FAL had gone from being a so-so contender to a robust firearm, while the EM2 had been all but abandoned by the British and did poorly in the tests. That left only two players in the game: the United States with its T25, T44, and T47 rifles and Belgium with the FN

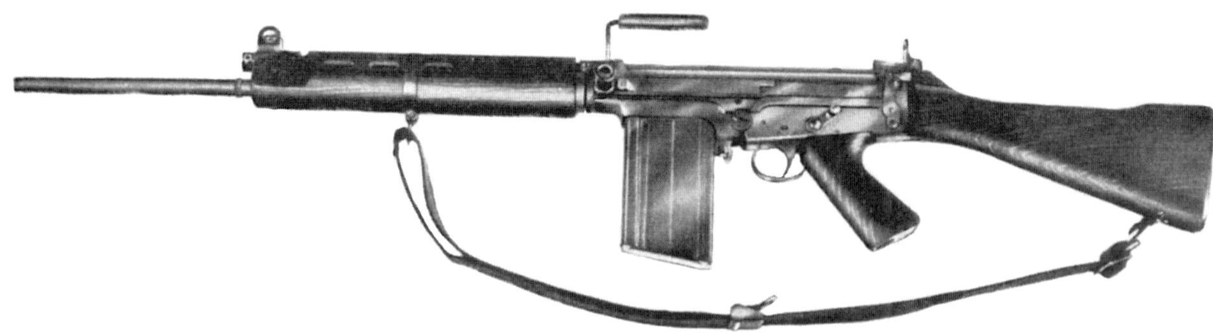

U.S. T48 rifle.

FAL. During these trials the T25 and T47 both did poorly. But the T44 displayed the reliability and robustness needed in military rifles, as did the FN FAL.

The U.S military decided to put the FN FAL rifles under an extended test, ordering a small quantity of the guns. By 1953, the tests had gone so well that the military ordered work on the M44 and recommended that the FN FAL be adopted as the new U.S. rifle. The army ordered 3,303 of the rifles from the Fabrique Nationale, designating them the Rifle Caliber .30 T48 FN.

At this point the FN FAL/T48 appeared to be a shoo-in. But it still had a few more trials to go, including the torturous Arctic conditions testing.

In December 1953, the rifles were sent to Alaska for tests under arctic conditions. Unfortunately for supporters of the FN FAL, the tests appear to have been somewhat rigged.

Perhaps this should not come as a surprise. Army designers at the Springfield Armory weren't happy that their T44 hadn't been adopted as the next U.S. rifle. Even though their work on the rifle was supposed to have been discontinued, workers secretly kept refining the design, hoping the FN FAL would somehow fail, thereby giving their in-house gun another shot at being chosen as the next U.S. rifle.

The Alaskan tests gave the U.S. designers their chance (just as the same type of tests would later be employed to blackball the AR-18). Working in the "cold chamber" at the armory, the designers tuned their guns so they would work with the low pressures created when the cartridges were fired in extremely cold conditions. The catch, of course, was that these guns would be horribly unreliable, if not dangerous, should they be fired in a hot climate. This was not a standard battle rifle that would work in all climates, but rather a highly modified design created solely to prevail in the upcoming tests in cold-weather conditions. Once the guns were modified to operate at peak efficiency in such conditions, the magazines and other parts were polished by hand to improve their operation even further.

The T48 had the ability to be loaded from a clip that could recharge an empty magazine.

The tests began as the Springfield Armory's "standard" rifles were submitted to compete against unmodified FN FAL/T48 rifles. Not surprisingly—to those who knew what was going on, at least—the tuned T44s functioned reliably and the standard-issue FN FALs had troubles.

With the modifications made to the T44 kept hidden from those conducting the tests, early word was leaked to military decision-makers that the T44, though only the equal of the FN FAL in previous tests, was definitely the better gun in arctic conditions. In the

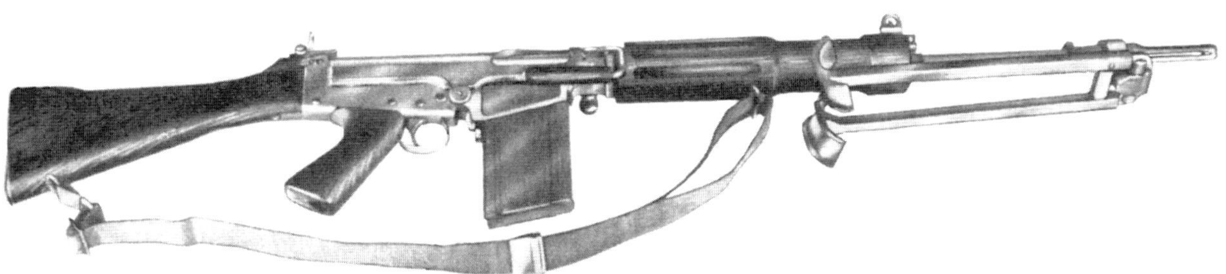

U.S. T48E1.

meantime, representatives of the Fabrique Nationale sent their designer, Ernest Vervier, to Alaska hoping the engineer could solve the problems that arose by modifying the rifles.

His solution was less than elegant. He simply opened up the gas ports of the FN FAL rifles to improve functioning with the low gas pressure produced by the ammunition in cold weather. This made the rifles function a bit better but also caused excessive wear and tended to tear the rims off cartridges, leaving the empty behind to jam the gun. This latter effect caused new functioning problems to crop up.

As the trials were completed, the sure-fire winner was not the FN FAL/T48 (which many had expected), but rather the T44. Those in command would not learn about the secret fine-tuning of the test guns until much later.

### Problems in NATO

Despite the apparent failure of the FN FAL to match the T44 in arctic conditions, there was pressure on the United States to adopt the FN FAL since it was the rifle that the other NATO allies were choosing one by one. This demand grew more vocal as NATO members pointed out that the United States had more or less agreed to adopt the same rifle that other NATO members chose.

Knowing that the politicians might soon be adopting the FN FAL as the standard U.S. rifle, and perhaps having recently learned of the Springfield Armory's adjustments to the rifles involved in the Alaska tests, the U.S. military hired High Standard (a large U.S. manufacturer that made a variety of small arms) to create drawings of the FN FAL calibrated in inches rather than in metric dimensions (used by the Belgian designers). The goal of this project was to enable the U.S. government to make its own FN FALs should the rifle be adopted by the army. Additionally, the military contracted with High Standard to fabricate 12 rifles from the English measurement drawings.

After testing the High Standard rifles and finding them reliable, the U.S. Army contracted for more guns, this time to be built by Harrington & Richardson (H&R) under the supervision of the Boston Ordnance District (by now it was felt that the Springfield Armory wasn't the place to have these guns built—no doubt because the word was out about how the Alaska tests had been rigged).

The contract awarded to H&R called for 500 FN FALs, designated T48s, while Springfield Armory created 500 T44 rifles it had been promoting.

When H&R designers started examining the drawings created by High Standard, they found them to be less than perfect. Realizing that the Canadian government had already produced drawings for their manufacture of the FN FAL, H&R worked through various channels to take advantage of the fact that both countries were NATO allies. Soon the H&R team had access to the Canadian drawings as well.

This was important because these new drawings contained changes dictated by Canadian, British, and Australian testing. U.S. designers incorporated these into the T48 design to create a more reliable weapon without spending a cent on actual research or field trials.

Not surprisingly, these guns proved to be extremely reliable and passed a new round of arctic-conditions tests, which took place from 1953 through 1954. Only now there was a new problem: the guns were built to such close tolerances that they failed to do well in the desert conditions conducted by the army early in 1955. However, this proved a minor problem; U.S. engineers conferring with British learned of a simple modification that would overcome it. After a small debacle caused by oversizing the bore of test rifles (causing poor accuracy), the H&R rifles were fitted with new barrels, modified for desert use, and once again proved themselves to be of excellent design.

The catch was that by now the army had tooled up to produce its T44 rifle. Creating the tooling and buying the right to manufacture the FN FAL would put a big dent in the U.S. budget, not to mention its loss of face in having to arm troops with a foreign-designed rifle for the first time since the Revolutionary War.

Not surprisingly, then, despite the fact that the FN FAL was most likely a superior rifle, the United States decided to adopt the Springfield Armory's T44 instead. Only later was it discovered that the T44 would also require new tooling and, as would be shown in a series of mishaps, wasn't as "debugged" as designers had thought. However, by then the die was cast. The T44 soon was being carried by U.S. soldiers as the new M14 rifle with a heavy-barrel version, the M15, that proved so unreliable during automatic fire that it was rarely if ever seen in the field.

### Angry Politicians

If American pride had won the day with the selection of the T44, in Britain national pride was not faring so well. First the British military, still smarting from having to import U.S. weapons during World War II, had been forced to adopt the 7.62mm NATO cartridge instead of the arguably superior round created by British designers. Then the British EM2, although excellent in concept, proved to be vastly inferior to both the U.S. and Belgian contenders for standard-issue rifle.

Now, to add insult to injury, after the British had swallowed their pride and adopted the FN FAL, the Americans announced that they would not do the same. This was added to the fact that the Americans had, by some accounts, verbally agreed that if NATO adopted the T65 cartridge they would go along with the gun chosen by U.S. allies.

How firm this agreement was varies by who tells the story. U.S. politicians would claim it was just casual, not at all firm. And they pointed out that there were no formal written agreements between the United States and its allies that the FN FAL would be adopted by all parties involved.

But things got worse. Before long, the 7.62mm NATO cartridge the United States had forced everyone to adopt would soon be put aside by the U.S. Army in favor of the smaller, more effective round the AR-15 was chambered for.

### The M14's Tale of Woe

One of the arguments presented by supporters of the T44, adopted as the U.S. Army's M14, was that it would be cheaper to produce than the FN FAL. The theory behind this was that M1 Garand tooling left over from World War II could be converted to manufacture the similar M14.

In fact the machinery was so outdated as to be useless. Furthermore, the new rifle had so many design specification changes that most of the tooling would have required replacement even if it could have been employed to make the new rifle. Thus, the savings promised by the adoption of the M14 evaporated once actual production was under way.

Nor was the M14 able to act as the do-it-all weapon that army salesmen had contended it would. While the rifle was supposedly a lightweight replacement for the BAR as well as the standard M1 Garand, in actual use it was not. The M14 wasn't light in weight, not at 12.75 pounds. Yet even with that much mass, it still proved to be nearly uncontrollable in auto mode thanks to the powerful recoil of the 7.62mm NATO round. With egg on their faces, military designers attempted to create a new version of the rifle with a pistol grip and straight-back stock design coupled with a muzzle brake. This "new" rifle was designated the M14E2 and later adopted as the M14A1. In theory, these modifications made the rifle more controllable in automatic fire, but in practice the improvements were marginal.

In addition, because the gun lacked a detachable barrel and only held 20 rounds in its magazine, it lacked the firepower to handle many machine gun roles. And even if the magazines could be inserted fast enough to do the job, then there were problems with the barrel overheating.

However, the United States was now committed to the M14 rifle, and manufacture of the gun went ahead despite the need for new tooling. As with most weapons, the design was gradually perfected as actual use revealed minor flaws that could be fixed with internal changes and parts modifications. Gradually the gun became easier to manufacture, and greater design tolerances made the gas piston less apt to lock up and bend if it became fouled.

But these changes did little to overcome the basic problems the rifle had in terms of both its weight and its inability to handle automatic fire, even in the M14A1 configuration.

At this point the AR-15 appeared on the scene, with glowing reports coming back to the United States about its use in Vietnam.

## AR-15 ARMY TESTS

Under pressure to adopt the AR-15 (and perhaps mindful of the sleight of hand that had enabled the M14 to win out over the FN FAL), those in the U.S. military who thought the M14 was a good rifle proposed—what else?—a series of tests conducted by the Army Materiel Command that would pit the AR-15 against the M14.

Not surprisingly, even though the AR-15 had done very well in previous tests and had an amazing record in the hands of Vietnamese troops using it in combat, when the smoke cleared U.S. military trials "proved" the M14

Even with a modified stock and bipod, the M14E2 proved unsuitable for military use due to its weight and poor control during automatic fire.

to be notably *superior* to the AR-15.

With the questionable procedures used in previous testing having become common knowledge, the secretary of the army smelled a rat and had the army's inspector general look into the Materiel Command's tests to be sure they were aboveboard. The inspector general found that, far from being fair, the tests had indeed been all but rigged. Among his findings were the following:

- Those involved in the testing had handpicked target-grade M14 rifles, whereas AR-15s were chosen at random without consideration as to how well they shot.
- Ranges of 800 yards were used in the tests, even though 500 yards had been established as the maximum range for combat rifles (and the ALCLAD studies suggested 300 yards was a more realistic maximum).
- Testers had conducted a "dry run" before the official tests to see how the two models would do. They then conducted the official test, omitting any parts in which the AR-15 had done well during the dry run.

So the results of the rigged test were ignored by military decision-makers, and by 1963 large numbers of AR-15 rifles were finding their way into the hands of U.S. troops. The Green Berets purchased 85,000, and army airborne units purchased large numbers as well, as did CIA. The air force purchased an additional 19,000.

Secretary of Defense Robert McNamara continued to be impressed with how well the AR-15s were working on the battlefield and in January 1963 announced the suspension of M14 production. This was done with the understanding that the AR-15 would only be a stopgap until the SPIW program bore fruit—something the army kept promising was on the horizon but in fact would never materialize.

Then, just as the superdependable AR-15 was gaining acceptance, it suddenly became a rifle that was consistently *un*reliable.

# Chapter 3

# Failures, Problems, and Solutions

Even as the U.S. military was purchasing the AR-15 in greater numbers, rifles in the field were mysteriously proving to be less and less reliable. Much of this appears to have resulted from the push at Colt to produce enough rifles to keep up with the sudden demand, and quality control seems to have been marginal during peak production. Possibly, too, Remington faced the same problem in producing ammunition.

During one army test of three AR-15s, sales representative Bobby Macdonald was horrified to see up to 31 failures to fire in rifles going through a 600-round test. Some of the failures were unusual and could only be blamed on the ammunition. In other cases at the time, even though poor ammunition may have been the reason primers often fell out of ammunition, bullets lodged in barrels, and cartridges failed to chamber, the blame went to the rifle. Nevertheless, U.S. Army personnel were impressed with the basic layout of the rifles—but suggested that work was needed to make the AR-15 more reliable before it could be adopted as an issue weapon.

Another problem with these AR-15s could be traced to the rifle's early magazine design. The original 25-round magazine was abandoned at the suggestion of army testing personnel (for unstated reasons; it's possible the 25-round magazine had problems of its own). In the hurry to bring a 20-round magazine into production to replace the 25-round design, Colt created a steel "waffle pattern" magazine similar to that of the AR-10. This functioned very poorly and was soon replaced by an aluminum 20-round magazine that wasn't much better, either.

The first 20-round aluminum magazines that reached U.S. troops were prone to jamming if an extra round was pushed into the magazine. Soon instructors, as well as soldiers who had become familiar with the firearm, were telling other troops to place only 18 or 19 rounds into each magazine (the logic being that if a soldier lost count, he'd be less apt to put 21 cartridges into the magazine if he was only aiming for 18 or 19). Needless to say, the few magazines that did become jammed did little to help the image of the AR-15.

Colt also began work on a plastic disposable magazines designed to be shipped prepackaged with ammunition and used once or twice and then discarded. These might have been issued to Special Forces and Ranger units for evaluation in the field during combat in

Armalite's 25-round magazine, shown here, was soon abandoned for a 20-round version.

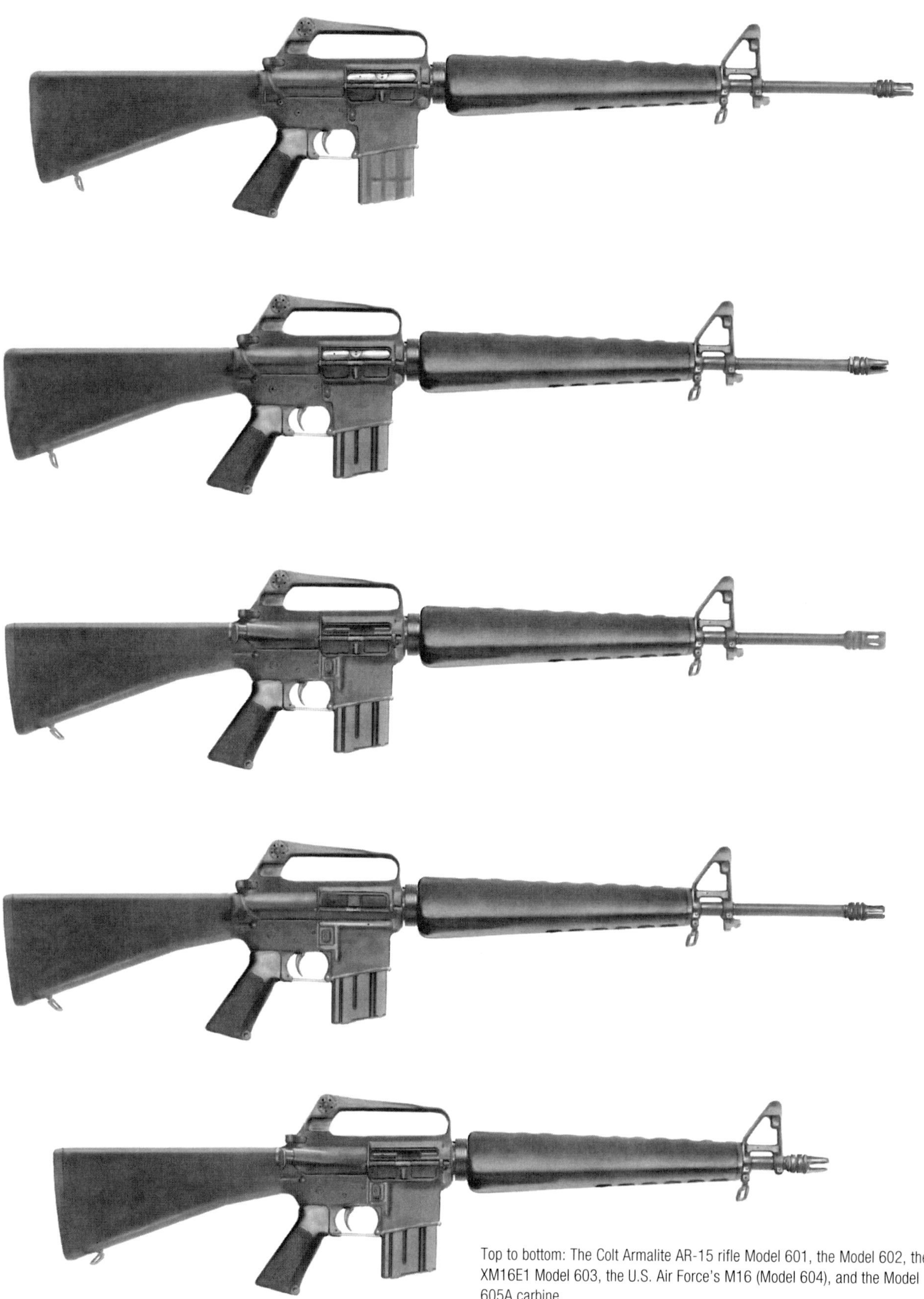

Top to bottom: The Colt Armalite AR-15 rifle Model 601, the Model 602, the XM16E1 Model 603, the U.S. Air Force's M16 (Model 604), and the Model 605A carbine.

Vietnam, but this is uncertain. The U.S. military tried to secure the rights to manufacture the magazines from Colt, but the company was afraid the deal might interfere with the royalty agreement it had with Armalite. For a time the army considered "reverse-engineering" the magazines, which is a polite term for stealing the dimension information and design of a device and manufacturing it without the original specifications), but eventually it abandoned this plan. (The idea of plastic—but not disposable—magazines for the AR-15 was revived in later years, with both the Israeli and Canadian militaries as well as commercial companies in the United States producing several excellent designs. These will be covered in detail later in this book.)

Later a similar concept was created in the form of plastic sealed packs into which U.S. troops could place loaded 20-round magazines. In the humid jungle environment this undoubtedly helped prevent the corrosion of brass as well as keeping debris out of the magazines. But the time taken to remove the magazine from the packet could be disastrous in combat, and eventually the plastic bags were all but abandoned.

## THE TCC

In an effort to eliminate the problems with the AR-15, Secretary of Defense McNamara formed a Technical Coordinating Committee (TCC) comprising personnel from the four branches of the military (probably assisted by personnel from Colt and Remington as well as Eugene Stoner himself). The TCC was to work on changing the AR-15 design to improve reliability. Apparently still smarting from the army's attempt to rig tests against the AR-15, and perhaps to speed things up (though some maintain it was to prevent sabotage of the rifle), McNamara gave his representatives from the Office of Secretary of Defense (OSD) veto powers over any changes the TCC suggested.

Due to the rush to get the AR-15 into testing and then into production, there were many minor flaws in dimensions that needed to be corrected to refine and strengthen the AR-15. Additionally, it was discovered that the chamber of the gun was being reamed to slightly different dimensions than the ammunition Remington had been fashioning. Eventually the TCC recommended 130 modifications (a number that apparently nearly sent Secretary McNamara into a tizzy when he first heard the committee's recommendations).

Most of these changes were very minor, but several provoked controversy when things got down to the wire and the TCC was debating the merits of the modifications. The TCC generally viewed the AR-15 as a new weapon that needed improvement, while the OSD took the position that Stoner and Armalite had refined the system to near perfection and believed the military should adhere to the old adage, "If it ain't broke, don't fix it." Also, the various military services represented on the TCC each wanted the rifle configured in slightly different ways and apparently fought rabidly to keep their own proposals on the table while dismissing those of the other services.

One major problem the air force had discovered had to do with the 1-in-14 twist of the barrel. This twist had been used in varmint rifles firing the .22-caliber bullets, and Armalite simply adopted it when designing the AR-15 around the .222 Remington. As it turned out, the .224-caliber, 55-grain bullet fired from the rifle was only stable in warm weather; when the gun was fired in extremely cold conditions, the bullet became very unstable and accuracy went down the tubes.

But some ballistic experts maintained that the lethality of the rifle, as seen in Vietnam, was due to the slow twist that allowed the bullet to upset upon impact with a flesh-and-blood target. Changing the twist, they argued, would ruin the rifle as a combat weapon. To confuse things even more, the army couldn't seem to duplicate with ballistic gelatin the same type of wounds being reported in the field. Critics of the army argued that the army ballistic experts weren't mixing their gelatin properly or maintaining it at the correct temperatures during their tests (and dropped hints that the army was trying to sabotage the rifle).

Finally, McNamara approved the change in rifling, but this would come to haunt him later when authorities, including Stoner, appeared before congressional hearings and testified that this change lowered the wounding potential of the rifle. In fact this was probably not the case. Later studies suggested that much of the effect of the bullet was created by its fragmenting, which, coupled with its speed, created several large wound channels with one impact.

A proposed change that the army desired and the air force declared detrimental was a bolt-closing lever of some type. The army's argument was that a round couldn't be silently chambered the way the rifle was, and if a bolt failed to close, a forward assist would get the cartridge chambered and the bolt locked over it. The air force argued that an oversized or corroded round caught in the mouth of the chamber of the rifle would have to be extracted if the rifle were left as it was. Furthermore, it maintained that with the capability of forward assist, a soldier would likely jam a defective round halfway into the chamber, thereby making it impossible to either fire the weapon or extract the defective round to chamber a good one. (Those who have worked with an AR-15 without a bolt assist know that a round can be quietly

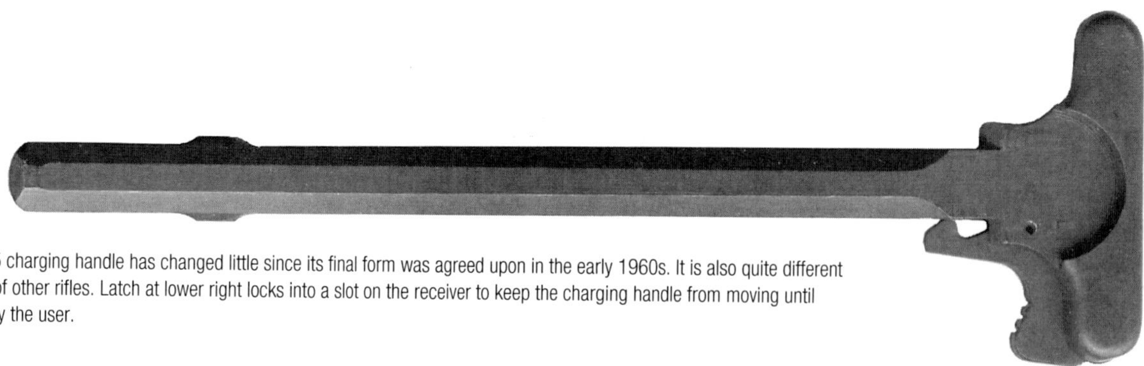

The AR-15 charging handle has changed little since its final form was agreed upon in the early 1960s. It is also quite different from that of other rifles. Latch at lower right locks into a slot on the receiver to keep the charging handle from moving until released by the user.

chambered by easing the charging lever forward and carefully sliding the bolt carrier forward by placing the finger through the ejection port and pushing the small scalloped cut on the bolt carrier forward. This will chamber all but badly corroded ammunition, making it a technique that is less apt to get the shooter into trouble if poorly sized or dirty cartridges are encountered.)

The army and air force could not agree, and representatives from the navy and marines were more or less passive, stating that a forward assist would be all right if it didn't mar overall performance but that they also didn't consider the device essential. To further complicate matters, McNamara had demanded that only one version of the rifle be created for all the services. Meanwhile, Colt was facing financial ruin if the rifle design wasn't adopted.

To prove the practicality of a forward assist, army personnel created several systems for bolt closing the Springfield Armory. Among them was a modified charging lever with a wide heel and a leaf spring over the bolt carrier, which, when coupled with a detent placed on the top of the receiver, allowed the charging lever to engage the carrier and shove it forward.

Meanwhile Colt personnel labored to create a forward-assist assembly of their own. They eventually came up with two versions of a basic pattern, one on the left side of the upper receiver and the other on the right. These had a ratchet that engaged small grooves cut into the sides of the bolt carrier to shove it forward.

## THE XM16E1

Eventually McNamara gave up on the "one rifle" concept. The air force was allowed keep its version of the rifle (which would remain designated the M16), whereas the army, marines, and navy would have a forward-assist variant with Colt's forward-assist design on the right upper receiver. The army's model would become the XM16E1 (eXperiMental rifle number 16, modification 1) when first issued to be tried by troops in the field.

The original forward-assist knob was simply a rounded stud, subsequently modified into a round knob. Eventually the forward assist would be given a "teardrop" shape when the design of the XM16E1 was modified slightly to become the M16A1. Oddly enough, the round shape was adopted again years later when the rifle was updated to its M16A2 configuration.

Colt wasn't out of the woods yet. Production of the rifles was held up by the TCC's discovery that some AR-15s were slam-firing ammunition, especially if a round was chambered with the bolt locked open and then released to go crashing forward. At first Colt officials suspected that shooters must be having problems with ammunition with high primers, but quick tests proved this was not the problem.

The slam-fires occurred with perfect ammunition. In fact, the free-floating firing pin had enough momentum when the bolt slammed forward—especially if it didn't have to strip off a cartridge from the magazine—to fire the primer without the hammer's dropping on the firing pin.

The Springfield Armory created a complicated locking firing pin with four ball detents around the head of the firing pin (and which would undoubtedly have been expensive to make and sensitive to dirt and lubrication conditions of the rifle). Colt came up with two more practical ideas. One was to create a spring-loaded firing pin, and the other was to simply thin the head of the firing pin, reducing the pin's mass so it wouldn't have enough inertia to fire a cartridge during bolt closing. This last modification was the simplest and cheapest and was therefore quickly adopted.

The other major modifications that the TCC agreed on and the OSD approved were quickly incorporated into the rifle with the approval of all parties involved. These included changing the chamber dimensions (to fit Remington's ammunition); modifying the charging handle so it was easier to grasp; reworking the bolt carrier release lever (making it stronger and more reliable); strengthening the flash suppressor (the open prongs were retained but made thicker to prevent bending); changing from a steel to aluminum magazine to prevent corrosion;

adding a captive detent to keep the front receiver takedown pin from being easily lost; coating the front sling swivel with plastic (to keep the swivel quiet in the field); and impregnating the stock, grip, and handguard with black dye (rather than retaining the brown fiberglass with a green-paint coating that flaked off over time).

By November 1963 the modifications were officially adopted and Colt was finally back in business, narrowly avoiding a financial crisis again. DOD number 508 procured 104,000 of the new AR-15s, with 85,000 to go to the army and marines as the XM16E1 with bolt forward assist at a price of $121.84 each. The air force received the remaining 19,000 for $112 each and kept the old designation of M16, since the modifications of the rifle didn't change its outward appearance. To simplify the paperwork involved in obtaining large numbers of the rifle, McNamara put the U.S. Army in charge of procurement.

### Westmoreland Weighs In

General W. C. Westmoreland, the commander of all the U.S. Army forces in Vietnam, was so impressed with the effectiveness of the AR-15s in the field that he issued an urgent request for additional weapons for the infantry in Vietnam. When his request went unanswered for some time, Westmoreland told visiting congressmen that the M14 just wasn't doing the job. In an end run around the secretary of defense, Westmoreland finally contacted the chairman of the Senate Armed Services Committee and asked him to get the rifles into the hands of the U.S. ground troops in Vietnam. Sen. Richard Russell then told Secretary McNamara that Westmoreland would either get the rifles or the press would learn about the inadequacies of the M14s being issued to the troops. Abruptly, the request for 100,000 AR-15s for the army ground troops in Vietnam was approved and fulfilled in 1965, and another 100,000 followed the next year. While all U.S. Air Force units in Vietnam were armed with the M16, most of the rifles purchased by the ground forces went through a trickle-down process that started with the U.S. Army Special Forces and airborne troops. As more rifles became available to all branches of the military, the AR-15s slowly filtered to marines and helicopter crews, then the 1st Cavalry Division and the 173rd Airborne Brigade, before finally being fielded in large enough numbers to get into the hands of the "grunts" in Vietnam. Once the army committed itself to adopting the AR-15, the gun's deadly abilities were soon realized, and the gun became the standard-issue weapon.

As it turned out, the changes in the basic AR-15 design instigated by the TCC proved beneficial or, in the case of the army's bolt forward assist, didn't hurt the reliability of the weapon much. But this wasn't the case with the modifications to the ammunition that were soon proposed.

### A Disastrous Change

As the lots of DuPont's improved military rifle (IMR) 4475 powder ran out (because Olin had picked up the contract for the military's 7.62mm ammunition and was using a different powder to load it), Remington discovered it couldn't purchase the special runs of the powder that DuPont had been producing for loading .223 rounds. All other powder substitutes created dangerous pressure levels at the amounts needed to attain proper bullet velocity (especially in arctic conditions).

Stoner and others wanted to redesign the bullet of the cartridge so it would stay within the army's original specifications for velocity without creating excessive pressures. Others wanted to simply lower the required velocity because the need to hit targets at 500 yards was unrealistic, especially in Vietnam where the troops were often unable to engage targets beyond 100 yards. But both proposals were rejected by the OSD, and instead the decision was made to adopt the ball propellant being used in the 7.62mm cartridges.

On June 1963, ball powder that had been used in other rifle ammunition in the past without problems and—on paper at least—would work equally well in arctic areas or in the heat of a jungle was specified as an alternative powder for newly manufactured .223 cartridges for the AR-15. Since the army set the procurement policy for the U.S. military, its decision to use the ball powder forced the air force to follow suit. Whatever small advantage was gained in using the ball powder was countered by two very disastrous disadvantages that soon came to light.

First, the ball powder burned slower than the IMR, which meant that burning particles could enter the gas tube of an AR-15 and move down it into the chamber/bolt area of the rifle. This gradually created deposits that would foul the weapon enough to cause functioning and chambering problems (which, when coupled with the forward assist and the poor fire discipline among the troops, could jam a rifle in a short time). The second problem was that the recoil created by the ball powder increased the cyclic rate of the rifle to the point that it could not extract and chamber rounds consistently. In addition, parts wore out prematurely as a result of the added momentum the bolt, carrier, and buffer assembly experienced during cycling.

In 1965, Colt conducted its own tests of the AR-15 and found that the rifle was not likely to fail using IMR powder, but that the rate of malfunctions was on the order of 50 percent for any given group of AR-15s when ball powder was used. (Out of group of rifles fired for a given period, half would malfunction at least once during a test.) Stoner complained that he had not designed his weapon for use with anything other than IMR powders. Tests at Frankford Arsenal found that AR-15s had 3.85 malfunctions or stoppages per 1,000 rounds fired with cartridges using IMR powder, whereas the same rifles produced 23.7 failures per 1,000 rounds fired when using ball powder. In an effort to keep production of the rifles going, the required cyclic rate of the rifles was raised from 850 rounds per minute (rpm) to 900 rpm—and the failure rate was ignored for the time being.

### More Ball Powder Woes

Late in 1967, the U.S. military made another horrifying discovery about its ball powder. Testing at Frankford Arsenal showed that both ball powder and IMR powders left residues in the gas tube and action of the AR-15s after extensive firings of 4,000 to 6,000 rounds. The residues left by IMR powders didn't harm the functioning of the rifles, but ball powder residue was a different story. It tended to clog the gas tube to the point that the rifle failed to function. Continued investigation of the problem by Frankford Arsenal and Winchester-Western Powder Company found that the residue was created by calcium carbonate mixed with primer residue and fragments from bullet jackets.

From here a search was begun to determine why ball powder was causing this buildup. The reason was simple: too much calcium carbonate was being placed in the powder in its manufacture. Also, some of the ball powder apparently some of the ball powder was remanufactured from World War II–Korean-War vintage artillery powder into which excessive amounts of calcium carbonate were added to neutralize the acid created by the deterioration of the chemicals in the powder. Thus, in 1968, the amount of calcium carbonate added to powder was lowered by 50 to 75 percent to prevent excessive fouling of the gas tube.

At this time the army created a "technical data package" to standardize the design and parts measurements of the AR-15, since the rifles in the field were now functioning well and the failure rate had actually dropped to less than 1 round per 1,000 (given proper cleaning and maintenance), even with the dirty ammunition being fired in them. With the completion of this work, the rifle was finally judged to be perfected for all practical purposes, and the TCC, deemed no longer necessary, was abolished in mid-1968.

McNamara also shut down the majority of the military's research and development facilities by closing the Springfield Armory and moving much of its equipment to the Rockford Armory. This brought to an end to the many innovations (in terms of new silencers, flash hiders, and other test vehicles) the U.S. Army had been achieving, often in conjunction with ammunition and firearms manufacturers. And although the technicians at the Springfield Arsenal had arguably failed to produce a viable rifle for the army during the 1960s, the operation had created a lot of spin-off technology. And experiments it conducted generated information that was ultimately utilized by commercial manufacturers, including those at Armalite and Colt.

### The "Self-Cleaning" Rifle

Other problems were growing, unnoticed by the TCC. Because perhaps overenthusiastic copywriters at Colt had suggested that the AR-15 was easily maintained and needed less cleaning than any other rifle, the army pushed this promise to its maximum limits. No cleaning brushes were manufactured to clean out the locking area of the barrel, and the cleaning rods issued to troops were flimsy and broke easily. Additionally, many troops got little if any training on maintaining and cleaning their weapons since the aluminum magazine and receivers and plastic furniture (handguard, pistol grip, and stock) made the exterior of the gun practically impervious to the elements.

Late in 1964, testing at Aberdeen Proving Ground also revealed that the guns being issued were slightly less accurate than earlier production models (shot groups were now at around 3.5 inches at 100 yards rather than slightly over 1 inch). Most important, the report issued stated that "adequate cleaning equipment needs to accompany the rifles." The testers found that for peak reliability, the AR-15 needed to be cleaned every 1,000 rounds.

This and other suggestions that cleaning the rifle was important fell on deaf ears. Little by little, guns in the field in Vietnam were becoming dirtier and dirtier, and no one in charge seemed aware of the mounting problem.

In 1965 another test, this time conducted at Frankford Arsenal, revealed that while the new WC846 ball powder used in the cartridges manufactured for the AR-15 was producing the correct ballistics, the powder caused excessive fouling, and after 1,000 rounds a rifle would repeatedly fail to operate. This report recommended a switch to DuPont's EX820, but that powder wasn't going to be available to the cartridge manufacturers until mid-1966. With the action in Vietnam heating up, the military couldn't afford to wait for the cleaner burning powder. The decision was made to continue loading cartridges with WC846.

In 1966, McNamara learned that the SPIW program was bogged down with no end in sight (an assessment that was to remain true for over a decade); McNamara decided that the AR-15 (XM16E1) would have to become the standard issue rifle for the U.S. military. Once he

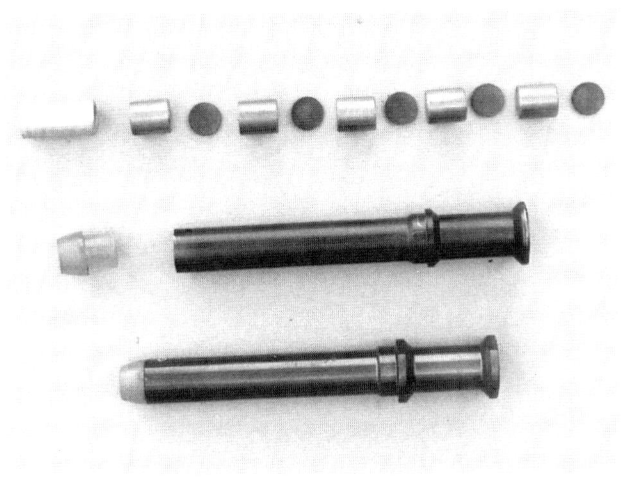

The buffer of modern AR-15s is a collection of steel weights coupled with rubber pads that ride between each weight. Coupled with the plastic bumper at the end of the buffer, these lower the cyclic rate of the rifle to increase its reliability.

made that call, a total of 419,277 M16s and XM16E1s were ordered from Colt.

At about this same time, Colt engineers, who had been working to overcome the fast cycling the new powder created with the weapons, devised a new buffer assembly that incorporated steel weights coupled with rubber pads inside its body rather than the hollow spring rings that had been used previously. This new assembly, coupled with a polyurethane bumper on the end of the buffer, lowered the cyclic rate of the rifle to 850 rpm even with the new ball powder and had the added benefit of lowering the abuse to the action from recoil. It also improved the chambering of cartridges due to the rebound of the plastic off the rear of the buffer tube, making automatic fire more reliable.

This change improved the performance of the Colt AR-15; during an extended test during which 102,000 rounds were fired, Colt found the malfunction rate had dropped to only 0.25 per 1,000 shots. And it undoubtedly also lowered the wear of the rifles, making them more durable. But the modification that was adopted by the TCC for new AR-15s didn't decrease fouling problems. Unfortunately many TCC and military members were apparently unaware of the poor cleaning practices in the field and therefore concluded that the new buffers would do away with jams caused by excessive fouling.

Even those who knew of the fouling problem saw little that could be done. The powders slated to replace WC846 were not available, and the discontinuance of the M14 and adoption of the AR-15 made it impossible to change to another weapon. The official stance was that WC846 produced fouling but "not to an unacceptable degree" as one memo put it.

### Let the Troubles Begin

As more and more XM16E1s were issued to troops on the ground, the rifles were subjected to both heavy fire and poor maintenance under grueling environmental conditions. Soon reports were filtering back of excessive failures of the rifle and loss of confidence in it by troops in the field. This was in sharp contrast to earlier reports of the weapon in the hands of Special Forces and the South Vietnamese army (when the IMR powders were used in the cartridges).

Colt sent one of its representatives, Kanemitsu Ito, to Vietnam to see what the rifles in the field were like. He later told the Ichord Subcommittee in Congress the following:

> I was shocked. I never had seen equipment with such poor maintenance. . . . I spoke to many enlisted personnel as to why they did not maintain their rifles. Some of them didn't know how. Many of them said they were never taught the maintenance of this rifle or had not seen this rifle until they had arrived in Vietnam. . . . [With some rifles] you could not see daylight through the barrels [which were] rusted and the chambers were rusty and pitted.

When Ito asked a platoon leader what was done to clean the rifles, he got the reply, "Nothing."

Early in 1967, the army finally woke up to the critical situation in the field. It started securing brushes (including a chamber brush, which had been missing from the few cleaning kits that were issued), stronger cleaning rods, and squabs that were sent to the troops in Vietnam along with a hastily printed maintenance card. (The card also cautioned against using damaged magazines, addressing another problem that most autoloading rifles often face, since magazines are easily damaged and even a minor ding or bent lip invariably causes functioning problems.)

Even as it was taking these steps, the army officially adopted the XM16E1, its new M16A1 designation signaling the rifle's change in status from experimental to standard issue. Cleaning rods continued to be in short supply for some time, many troops gave rifles little care, and malfunctions due to the excessive fouling continued. In an effort to encourage troops to clean their rifles properly, the army went so far as to hire *Mad Magazine* comic artist Will Eisner to create a cartoon book showing how to properly clean and maintain the rifle. Many old-timers felt this was a sad commentary on how seriously some troops took the conflict. (Despite its comic book format, this booklet is full of excellent information and continues to be printed commercially; a reproduction is available from Sierra Supply for $6.)

Young men were writing home begging for cleaning kits, and tales of whole squads found dead with jammed M16A1 rifles by their sides were spreading, even though many of these were only rumors. The U.S. House of Representative appointed Richard Ichord, Speedy O. Long, and William Bray to form a subcommittee chaired by Ichord with a dual mission of getting to the bottom of problems with the M16A1 rifle and making recommendations for alleviating the problem.

The hearings produced much information that will undoubtedly be sifted through by various firearms enthusiasts for years to come. Although the committee members were woefully lacking in technical expertise and often followed the most persuasive arguments offered by the experts paraded in front of them, they were able to draw logical conclusions about the obvious problems with the AR-15 rifle—especially after going to Vietnam to visit troops in the field. The committee found that the decision to switch to ball powder had been almost criminal, as had the lack of adequate training and scarcity of field cleaning kits. It further recommended a restructuring of the methods used to test and procure firearms.

## PRODUCT IMPROVEMENTS

At the same time, genuine efforts had already been under way both at Colt and in the military to upgrade the AR-15 design. Testifying before the Ichord committee, a Col. Harold Yount told of 10 major changes that would be made to the basic rifle (along with 149 minor ones), most designed to make the gun more reliable. Among these were the following:

- Change in bolt hardness to improve its life
- Stainless steel gas tube to prevent corrosion
- Chrome plating to the interior of the bolt carrier key
- Increase in the size of the bolt catch mechanism to reduce wear to the lower receiver
- Replacement of the machined firing pin retaining pin by a cotter pin
- Redesign of the disconnector to increase life expectancy of the part
- Placement of a thick rim around the magazine release to prevent its accidental release
- Replacement of the duckbill-style flash hider (which seemed prone to wicking water into the bore as well as getting caught in foliage) with a birdcage-style hider
- Strengthening of the bolt to increase its life
- Addition of the already approved new buffer assembly created by Colt

In an effort to prevent chamber erosion and cartridge extraction problems, the army had also launched a program to develop a cheap, reliable way to chrome the chamber and bore of AR-15s. By the time this technique was perfected, it was no longer needed, just as Stoner had argued earlier. When the army finally instituted proper maintenance, chamber rusting and pitting stopped being a problem—even as the new chroming process was perfected and the more expensive chromed barrels were added to the M16A1s coming off the assembly line.

In 1966 the air force also agreed to accept M16A1-style serrated bolt carriers. Although these were no better than the standard bolt carriers in the M16s that lacked the forward assist, they did allow Colt to produce just one style of carrier. They also prevented the occasional problem of having a smooth bolt carrier show up in the M16A1 rifle where it would make the forward assist nonfunctioning.

### The 30-Round Magazine

The same year saw the introduction of the 30-round magazine developed for the "submachine gun" versions of the AR-15 (more on these variations later). This magazine turned out to be somewhat flawed. The reason for this was that to feed the tapered .223 cartridge through a 30-round magazine, the whole magazine needed to be slightly curved, and the AR-15s had been designed with only the 20-round, straight-walled magazine in mind. When Colt engineers made some curved magazines, the new design worked perfectly in new rifles—but wouldn't fit in some old ones. They discovered that the wells of some AR-15s were too tight to accommodate the gentle curve needed for a 30-round magazine designed for optimal feeding.

So that specifications would not have to be changed from the original rifle, the top of the final magazine was straight like the 20-round magazine until it got past the magazine well section, where it then started to curve. This arrangement worked, but not as flawlessly as the all-curved version. And this situation continues to this day, compounded in other rifle designs, as the AR-15 magazine becomes the standard model for NATO users as well as other gun designers worldwide. (A quick look at the Stoner rifles designed immediately after this period shows that their forward magazine well is noticeably short; apparently the designer wasn't about to make the same mistake twice.)

### Non-Colt AR-15s

By 1967, Colt was having trouble making rifles fast enough to maintain its end of the contracts with both the

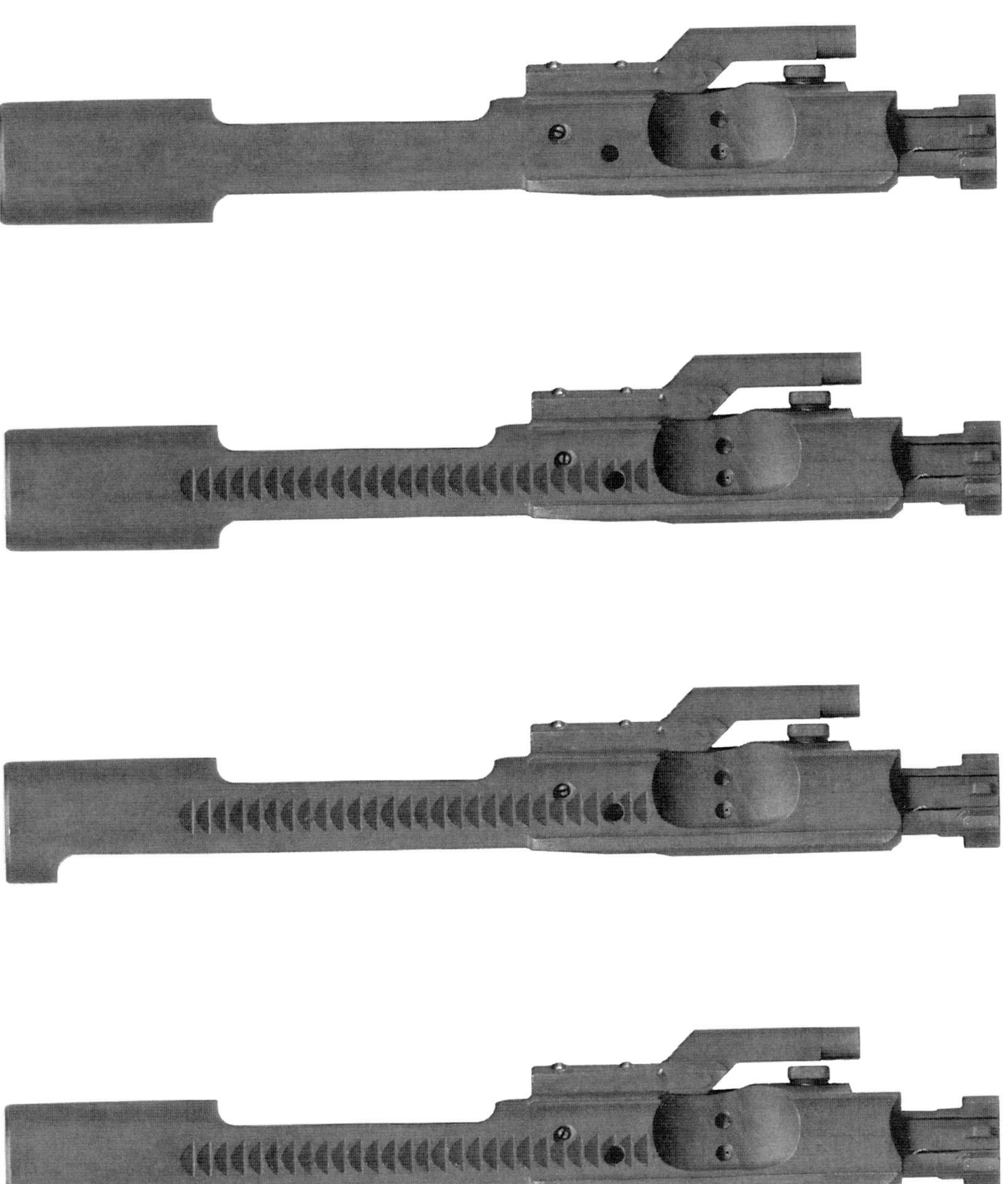

The AR-15 bolt carrier has gone through several changes. Top carrier is the original style created for the rifles without a forward assist. Second from top is the M16 carrier with forward-assist cuts. Third from top is carrier designed for the AR-15 semiauto "Sporter." Bottom carrier is late model for Colt semiauto rifles with lower rear completely milled away to prevent any chance of auto conversion.

U.S. and Singapore governments. And several other countries were also interested in purchasing the firearms. Suddenly Colt was facing the problem of having too much business; it offered the U.S. government the chance to purchase the right to make AR-15s under the license the company had secured from Armalite.

Upon learning that Colt was going to have trouble supplying enough rifles on time, the U.S. government starting looking for other companies that could build rifles under license with Colt. Soon the military had entered into contracts with General Motors' Hydramatic Division and H &R for approximately 240,000 rifles each.

This received a less than enthusiastic response from workers at Colt, who immediately went out on a two-month strike to protest the management's decision. This decision to have other contractors make the rifles was not

The Colt Model 703 (top) was, at the company, designated the M16A2. Shown below it is the M16A2 "Enchanced" model with a flip-up front sight; it also failed to capture U.S. military sales.

without its congressional detractors as well, since Colt had been selling AR-15s at $104 each, while H&R was asking $250 per gun and General Motors (GM) $316. Furthermore, H&R had come under a cloud since its previous production of M14 rifles had been plagued with poor quality control. Adding to the furor, of the 12 firms that initially bid on the contracts several had come in lower than GM but had not been chosen.

The army argued that part of the reason GM had received the contract was that it could quickly go into production with the AR-15s, something the lower bidders couldn't guarantee. Nevertheless, many in congress remained doubtful—especially those who were against having U.S. troops in Vietnam in the first place—so it is difficult to see where politics left off and actual concern began.

GM managed to get its first production run of AR-15s assembled ahead of time, and the weapons functioned well. H&R had problems getting its assembly line going, and quality control appeared to be poor in some instances. Some feel these latter weapons also did little to help the AR-15's battered reputation.

## THE M16A2 THAT NEVER WAS

In an effort to get around the problems that still remained with the use of ball powder, Colt engaged in another line of experimentation in conjunction with the Rock Island Arsenal and Olin/Winchester, which had developed a gas piston system that could replace the gas tube of the AR-15.

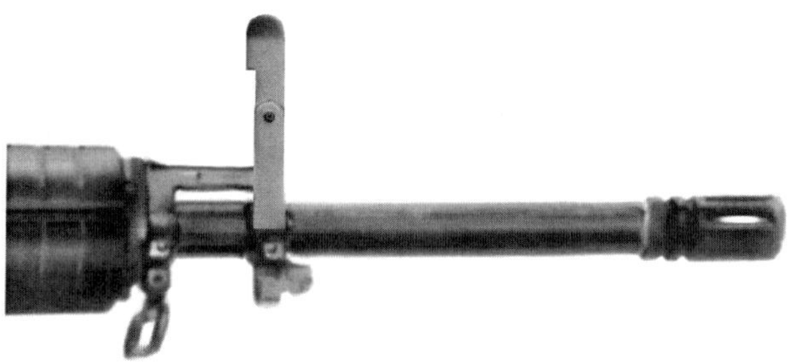

Detailed view of the M16A2 "Enhanced" front sight.

Soon Winchester delivered 25 working prototypes with this system to Colt, each rifle having a standard AR-15 lower receiver mated to a redesigned upper one, gas system, and barrel with lowered sights. The front of the gas system was uncovered to help in heat dissipation, and the gas regulator near the front sight had three positions so it could be adjusted to different types of ammunition (probably a prime consideration for Colt at this point). The handguard design did away with the delta ring and used two spring clips to secure it in place, making removal quick and easy. The gas piston extended along the top of the barrel and connected to a modified bolt carrier with a cross pin so the assembly could be taken apart during field stripping.

Overoptimistic Colt personnel designated the new gun the M16A2 and assigned it a stock number of 703 (both of these would cause a bit of confusion later, since the military's M16A2 developed years later would have a standard gas tube system, as would the even later 700 series rifles). It shipped 10 prototypes to the Rock Island Arsenal for tests. After putting the rifles through their paces while using M16A1s as controls to compare performance against, the army found that the guns didn't work much better than standard M16A1 rifles. So the project ended up being shelved, though Singapore and South Korea eventually used a similar system for their knockoff versions of the AR-15 (more on these later).

Two features of the M16A2 rifle would eventually make their way into general use, however. One was a trapdoor assembly on the stock, which turned it into a storage compartment for a cleaning kit. The other was the burst selector. The new stock was soon incorporated into the M16A1 design, but nearly two decades would pass before the U.S. military finally adopted the burst control, strangely enough on what would eventually be designated the real M16A2.

The new trapdoor stock had another feature that appears insignificant but can make a big difference in the field: a small drain hole in the screw holding the stock to the buffer tube. This hole effectively lets a small amount of air through from outside the rifle into the buffer tube. The plus of this is that should the rifle be dropped into the water and the buffer tube become filled, the water will quickly drain out. Thus it is possible for the rifle to operate properly even under such dire circumstances (assuming the user has the sense to drain the water from the bore before firing).

### Pulling the Plug on the FRP

In 1968 the U.S. government again exercised its contract options with Colt and ordered more than 700,000 M16A1s; this was followed by an order for 458,435 M16A1s from Colt and 229,217 from Hydramatic for 1969.

With the U.S involvement in Vietnam coming to an ignoble end and the AR-15 working dependably, the perceived need for a combat rifle that might replace it was less intense than it once had been, and antiwar members of Congress were calling for reduced military spending. Consequently, by the time the United States pulled out of Vietnam in 1973, programs like the Future Rifle Project (FRP), designed to create a replacement for the M16/M16A1 rifles, came to an abrupt halt, leaving inventors like Eugene Stoner and the ARES company he had created high and dry after spending huge sums to create experimental rifles for the military.

Although Colt was hurt by the falling demand for the AR-15 rifle as the U.S. military reduced its troop strength, it also was left in the catbird seat in that it held the manufacturing rights to the weapon the military was committed to. And failure of the military to pursue the FRP could only help Colt, giving it time to develop new models of its already debugged rifle, which was becoming more and more reliable.

In 1975 Frankford Arsenal finally concluded another program that had been going on since 1967. The purpose of the research had been to create a reflexive sight capable of locating targets in twilight conditions and producing target acquisition faster than that with iron sights during the day. The tests involved more 60 sighting systems that varied in design from self-illuminating scopes to occluded eye "dot" scopes to sight blades with glow-in-the-dark inserts. Among the oddities tested was a gyrostabilizer-scope combination, whose gyrostabilizer hung under the rifle, attached to the pistol grip; in theory this helped prevent barrel wobble to keep the rifle on target as the trigger was squeezed.

In addition to the promethium night sight that grew out of this study and was finally adopted by the army, the military came up with a reflex collimator sight (RCS) developed by AAI and Frankford Arsenal. This device increased the chances of a shooter hitting his target by 30 to 50 percent over those with iron sights by using a Y-shaped reticle that glowed a bright yellow. To hit a target, a soldier simply needed to bracket it and pull the trigger on his rifle.

Despite some favorable results in the RCS program, the end of the Vietnam War and decreased funding apparently placed this program on hold. (A similar program was initiated in 1990, with some elements from this study being resurrected, when the U.S. Army announced the need for a scope to create a new M16A3 version of the AR-15. And again, at the time of this writing, it appears that this program will be placed on hold as military spending is decreased.)

## THE SEARCH FOR MORE LETHAL BULLETS

From the mid-1960s through the 1970s, a number of schemes had been devised to give the .223 cartridge extra punch so that it could be used both in rifles and light machine guns. Among the more impressive of these was by the Industrie Werke Karlsruhe AG (IWK) for Cadillac Gage, which was marketing the .223 firearms family of guns Eugene Stoner had developed for it, generally known as the Stoner 63.

The IWK ammunition had a hard tungsten-carbide core and a long 77-grain bullet that maintained its momentum out to 1,000 yards. Cadillac Gage boasted that where the standard .223 bullet penetrated ten 1-inch boards and the 7.62mm NATO bullet 16 boards, the new IWK bullet went through 46. Unfortunately for the company, no countries purchased its Stoner 63 weapons, so the expensive cartridge was soon dropped from the company's offering as well.

Colt also produced a more conventional 68-grain bullet for the .223 machine guns it had been trying unsuccessfully to market. This new bullet performed well but demanded a 1-in-9 or faster twist; adopting it would force the United States and other countries using the AR-15 to rebarrel all their guns — something the U.S. Army was not interested in pursuing at that point.

The army also experimented with a long 55-grain bullet that would remain accurate in the standard 1-in-12 twist of the AR-15. Rather than having a bullet with a pure lead nose like the standard bullet, this projectile had a steel penetrator in its nose. The bullet delivered increased range and penetration; the standard version was designated the XM777 cartridge, and its sister tracer version the XM778.

Meanwhile, the Fabrique Nationale also devised a penetrator bullet that fell halfway between the U.S. military and the IWK designs. This 61.7-grain bullet had a steel penetrator, but its weight required a faster twist rate of at least 1-in-9, and its extralong tracer version required an even faster 1-in-7 twist. This pair of cartridges became known as the SS109 (standard bullet) and L110 (tracer).

Since the effectiveness of the AR-15 in Vietnam had been noted by most militaries worldwide, a race was by many to develop or adopt rifles chambered for the cartridge. Many smaller countries simply espoused the AR-15, either buying the rifle directly from Colt or obtaining a license to manufacture the weapon themselves. A few countries produced knockoff versions that incorporated some or all of the AR-15's features into "original" designs, often differing from the Armalite rifle only in minor points (these variations are examined in a subsequent chapter).

Larger countries developed their own .223 rifles, which often failed to operate on the level of the now-perfected AR-15 design but which undoubtedly were necessitated by national pride. France, Italy, Switzerland, Austria, and others were soon fielding .223 rifles of varying degrees of reliability, while Britain and West Germany were working on rifles chambered for smaller cartridges. Soon the various NATO members were exerting pressure on each other to adopt a .223 standard round that would work in all the member countries' rifles, ideally with the long-range capabilities of the IWK and Fabrique Nationale rounds—despite the fact that most military studies showed such range was normally not needed in combat.

Since the United States had more or less bullied other NATO members into adopting the 7.62mm cartridge it had developed and then had switched to the .223 cartridge shortly after, the other NATO members were not prepared to see the same thing happen again. So when trials were initiated for the selection of a second NATO cartridge between April 1977 and the spring of 1979, they were complicated, and no mention was even seriously made of adopting a standard rifle (though the AR-15 magazine was adopted as a standard by many of the NATO members).

After arctic-condition tests in Canada as well as extensive tests in Germany, Britain, and France, the end result was the adoption of Fabrique Nationale's SS109 cartridge as the new 5.56mm NATO. The U.S. military quickly decided to adopt the new cartridge (perhaps to stay in step with NATO this time around), even though it meant replacing the barrels on its entire inventory of AR-15 rifles. The new round, designated the M-855, officially weighed 62 grains (even though it is actually a tad under this weight due to the metric units used by its Belgian inventors) and featured a solid-point/boattail design. It proved capable of greater long-range penetration than the older 7.62mm NATO at 1,000 meters. But since the new 62-grain bullet would require a much faster twist rate to maintain its stability and accuracy (though it could still be used in the M16Al with its 1-in-12 twist, accuracy was poor), the U.S. military at first wanted to look for a replacement for the AR-15.

### The SS109 Ballistic Surprise

There was a surprising asset from this faster twist in addition to improved accuracy in the new M16A2. The torque placed on the bullet by the faster spin caused it to break apart more easily when hitting a flesh-and-blood target. Although for years the lethality of the .223 cartridge had been attributed to the instability of the bullet, it was soon apparent that in fact the important wounding property was the.223 bullet's fragmenting along its cannelure. As the twist rate increased, this fragmenting was enhanced, making the 1-in-7 twist extremely lethal. This was a somewhat ironic "twist," since many ballistics experts had expected the faster twist to create less serious wounds, and some "humanitarians" even embraced the new twist because they thought it would be less lethal.

The three-round burst had a few quirks that shooters sometimes found exasperating: it was possible to fire only one or two rounds in the three-round burst position when the trigger was quickly released, and then, when the trigger was pulled again, the remainder in the group (only one or two rounds, depending on how many shots were fired previously) would fire, regardless of how long the trigger was held.

Another oddity was that the weight of pull of the

trigger varied, even when fired in the semiauto mode. This can be especially distracting to target shooters who encounter a different trigger pull in a series of shots.

Although the heavier barrel helped in the M16A2's accuracy and lowered heat buildup to a small degree, many critics suggested it had been placed "in the wrong spot." The heavier section was ahead of the front sight, while the area under the handguard, where weight might be better used to prevent heat buildup and barrel flex) was the same diameter as it had been before.

In fact, placing the thin portion of the barrel under the handguard was necessary for several reasons. One was that in order to accommodate the M203 grenade launcher, the section of the barrel under the handguards had to remain as thin as the M16A1's, or all the grenade launchers in the U.S. inventory would all have to be reworked. The second reason was that bayonet practice and the hard-to-break practice of troops' using the rifle as a pry bar to open crates often bent the end of the barrel ahead of the front sight. So even though bayonets are rarely used in combat and crates are ideally opened with a pry bar, the M16A2 didn't have the tendency of the older model to end up with a bent barrel when abused by troops. (Furthermore, some shooters prefer having the balance of the rifle shifted forward slightly by this added weight.)

### THE PIP

The tests to determine the new NATO ammunition had also brought up another interesting point: although the trials were not designed to select a standard NATO rifle (only a .223 cartridge), the malfunction rates of the various countries' rifles had been recorded. And when the AR-15 was compared with the Belgian FNC, the French FAMAS, the Israeli-made Galil (submitted as the he Dutch MN1), and the British XL65E4 and XL65E1, the U.S. rifle proved to be much more reliable.

So rather than procure a new system and go through the headaches of debugging it, U.S. military planners decided to stick with what had become "old reliable" and instead consider modernizing the rifle at the same time the switch was made to new 1-in-7 twist barrels that accommodated the new SS109/M855.

Since the U.S. Marines had aging AR-15s as well as BARs (chambered for the World War II-vintage .30-'06 round) that needed to be replaced, the marines had started searching for an updated replacement for their inventory of weapons. After testing other small arms they had collected from around the world, they had quickly reached the conclusion that the AR-15 was the best system available. Thus, from 1978 to 1979 they had already been working in conjunction with Colt to produce an "M16 PIP" (Product ImProved M16) and now had a gun ready to be purchased "off the shelf."

Many of the changes in the M16 PIP were in fact changes Colt had devised on its own to offer to foreign buyers. Many of these modifications had also been offered to the U.S. military, but they were rejected because the M16A1 had been adopted. (After the air force-army squabbles over just a forward assist assembly, it is likely that no one really wanted to tackle anything as momentous as completely revamping the rifle.)

At any rate, when the Joint Services Small Arms Program (JSSAP) set about looking at changes to be made in the M16 rifle, Colt had its M16 PIP waiting in the wings. The JSSAP ordered 50 of the M16 PIPs delivered for testing in November 1981. The military testing was done by marines at Quantico, Virginia, and when the smoke cleared the PIP model had proved itself superior in all respects to the standard-issue weapon. As an added plus, it could be used with the.223 cartridge as well as the new M855 cartridge, so the ammunition already purchased would not have to be scrapped in the changeover process. The rifle was designated the M16A1E1 and its configuration finalized with the following changes from the older M16 standard-issue rifle:

- The front sight was a square stationary post.
- The windage and elevation adjustments to the sighting system would both be on a new rear sight assembly having easily operated dials.
- The birdcage-style flash suppressor lacked lower slots in order to reduce the upward movement of the barrel during burst firing and reduce dust problems during prone shooting.
- The barrel was heavier from the front sight forward, with the 1-in-7 twist.
- The handguards were round-ribbed, with the two halves interchangeable. (Although this seems pretty straightforward, the catch was creating a design that would allow both the triangular A1 handguards as well as the new round stocks to fit onto a rifle without modifying the handguard-retaining assembly at the front of the barrel. This was achieved by Seth K. Bredbury and Harold J. Waterman with patent number 4,536,982, and Colt Industries Corp. was named as the assignee in the patent.)
- The slip ring was tapered to make it easier to take off the handguards.
- The buttplate of the stock was checkered to reduce its tendency to slip off the shoulder during firing.
- The stock was lengthened 5/8 inch to increase the ease in holding the rifle in the firing position (old stocks would be retained for use by shorter soldiers).

Staff Sergeant Solomon fires an M16/A2 rifle at a range in Bosnia and Herzegovina. (Courtesy of U.S. Army.)

- The plastic stock would be 10 times stronger than the old fiberglass.
- The lower receiver was strengthened in spots that had been prone to cracking.
- The pistol grip was reshaped to better conform to the user's hand and had a finger-grip ridge and grooves to improve retention.
- The forward assist was changed from the teardrop shape to a round button.
- A brass deflector hump was added to the upper receiver just behind the ejection port (a welcome boon to left-handed shooters).
- The rifle had a three-round burst selection rather than a full auto option on the selector (thus having three positions: safe, semiauto, and three-round burst).

The marines soon designated the new M16A1E1 the M16A2 and placed orders with Colt for the new rifle. The new model had its detractors, both in the army and civilian sectors. Many of these people focused on the faster twist used with the gun, suggesting that it would wear out quickly and that the tiny bullet when stabilized to such a great extent would have decreased performance in terms of wounding ability.

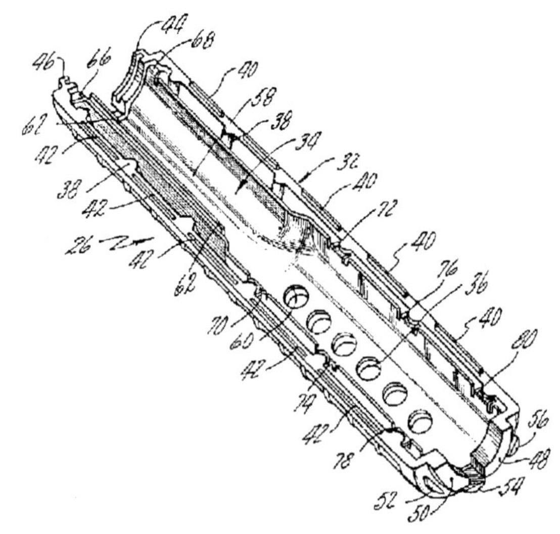

Patent drawings for Colt's round A2 handguard.

Certainly the faster twist did become fouled with copper plate after extensive firing—but this was in the 6,000-round range. And barrel erosion did not become a problem, despite the prediction by some that it would (perhaps because of the chrome bore, which finally may be serving a real purpose).

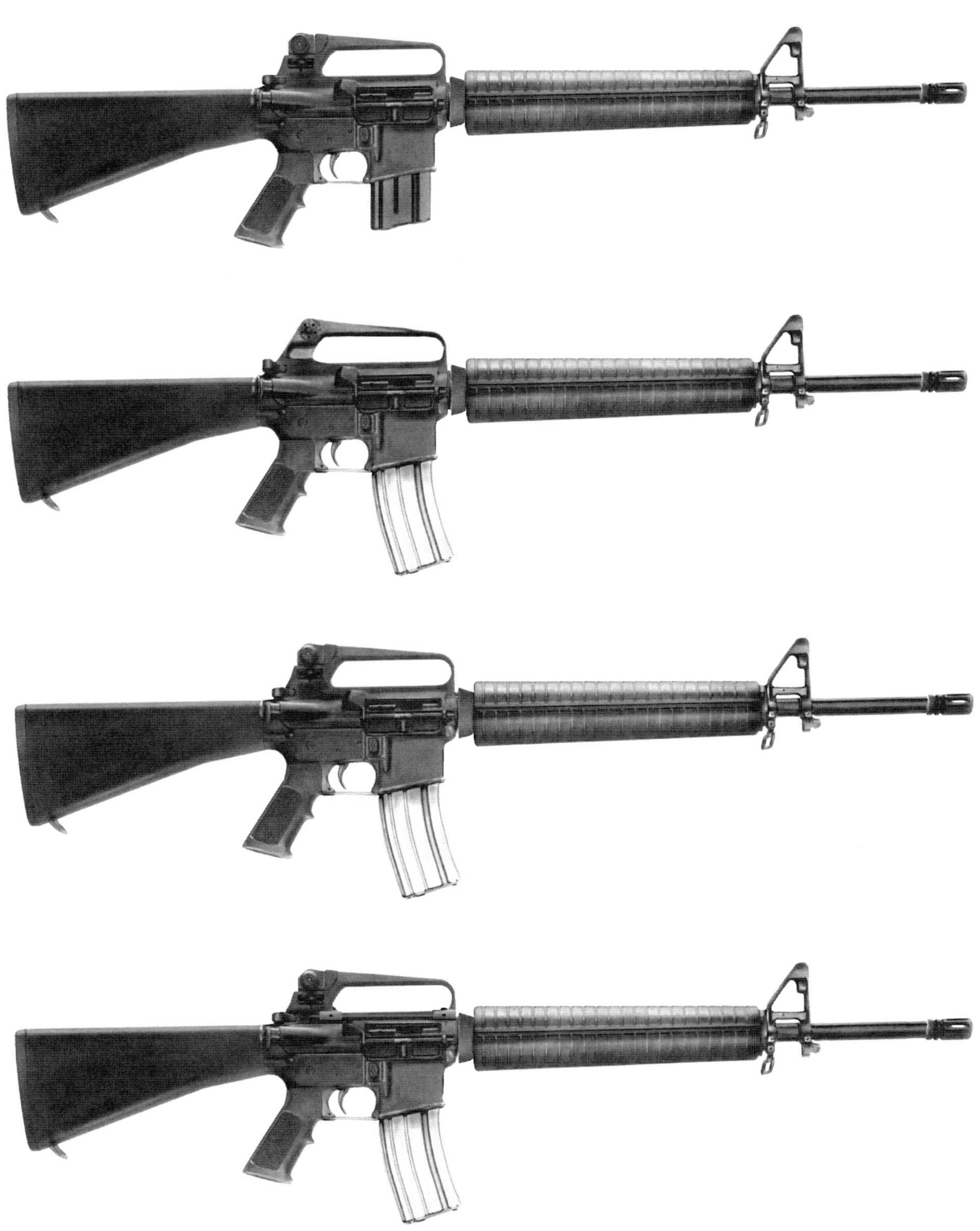

Top to bottom: The first M16A2 (Colt's Model 645), export version of the M16A2 with A1 sights (Model 711), the standardized M16A2 (Model 719), and the M16A3 with "flat-top" and detachable carrying handle (Model 905).

### M16A1 to M16A2 Conversion Kit

It should be noted that Colt offers a conversion kit for transforming the M16 into the M16A2 configuration. The kit has continued to see service, from the time the first U.S. military M16A1s were to be upgraded to the M16A2 configuration right up to the present, as foreign nations owning A1s decide to upgrade them. The "Kit, Mod, M16 (Rifles and Carbine Team, AMSTA-LC-CSIR)" consists of the following:

- A2 handguard
- Rifle stock
- Pistol grip
- A2 flash hider
- Three-round burst mechanism
- Adjustable rear sight-upper receiver assembly
- A2 square front sight post
- A 1-in-7-twist A2 barrel with the standard A2 increase in diameter ahead of the front sight post

This kit upgrades an A1 to the A2 configuration but also creates significant confusion for those attempting to identify these guns, since the lower receiver markings will show the rifle to be an older weapon while it has the configuration of a newer model. Just to keep things even more confusing, a rifle so converted is sometimes designated an M16E1-A3.

### The Enhanced M16A2

With the CAWS program coming to a dead end, meeting much the same fate as the earlier SPIW program, the U.S. Army decided in 1985 to start its own program to "enhance" the M16A2, the principal thrust being to place an optical sight on the weapon, possibly completely doing away with the carrying handle in the process. It should be noted that although the carrying handle on the AR-15 has always been greatly appreciated by the soldier in the field, it is often despised by high-ranking military officers, who prefer to have the soldier carry weapons in a manner that makes them quicker to bring into action, rather than bearing the firearm the way a yuppie carries a briefcase. Those in favor of the carrying handle often point out that its greatest critics are the people who don't carry a loaded firearm all day long and therefore don't know how strenuous it is.)

The army's enhancement program soon encountered a number of obstacles, the principle one being that although there were good optical systems available, none was tough enough for extended use in combat, all were very expensive, and improvements over the peep sight were not as substantial as had been hoped for even with expensive systems (this was especially true with troops who were experienced in using the standard iron sights).

Finally in 1986, the army begrudgingly announced a procurement contract with Colt to purchase the new model of rifle with the placement of an order for 100,176 new M16A2 rifles. Since then the rifle has seen combat in Panama and the Middle East, proving that it is one of the best (if not the best) combat rifles yet devised.

## THE CAWS

The army monitored the marines' testing of the M16A2 but was not as quick to adopt the new rifle, partly because its inventory of weapons was newer and partly because it was still hoping for a breakthrough in the various weapons programs it had been conducting in an effort to create an even better weapon than the AR-15. One of the lines of endeavor was the Close Assault Weapon System (CAWS) project. Started in the early 1980s, the program's goal was to produce an updated selective-fire shotgun that would shoot a salvo of pellets over almost twice the range of conventional shotgun ammunition. The ammunition itself was to be carried in detachable magazines to allow for quick reloading of the CAWS, and the automatic mode would allow troops to supersaturate an area with projectiles if the need arose.

Late in 1983, two CAWS contracts were given to the AAI Corporation and Heckler & Koch (H&K). Olin Corporation produced ammunition for the CAWS, and for a time it looked as if the new weapon would become a viable alternative to the rifle. But in the end, all the project had to show for the time and money spent was what amounted to a dead end. The weapon was too heavy for easy carrying, and even with its excessive weight it had abusive recoil due to the range requirements of the project. Additionally, the ammunition was heavy and automatic fire proved impractical both because of recoil as well and speed with which it exhausted the amount of ammunition a soldier could carry comfortably.

The new M16A2, by contrast, was capable of more controlled bursts of fire, was considerably lighter, and didn't create enough recoil to threaten to pound its user to death. Also, it now had a maximum workable range of out to 800 meters (compared with the CAWS' 150 to 200 yards—short even by ALCLAD standards). (For a look at the exotic weapons created by the project along with other military shotguns, see *Streetsweepers: The Complete Book of Shotguns*, available from Paladin Press.)

## FABRIQUE NATIONALE STEPS IN

By the late 1980s, Colt had produced at least 10 million rifles based on variations of the original AR-

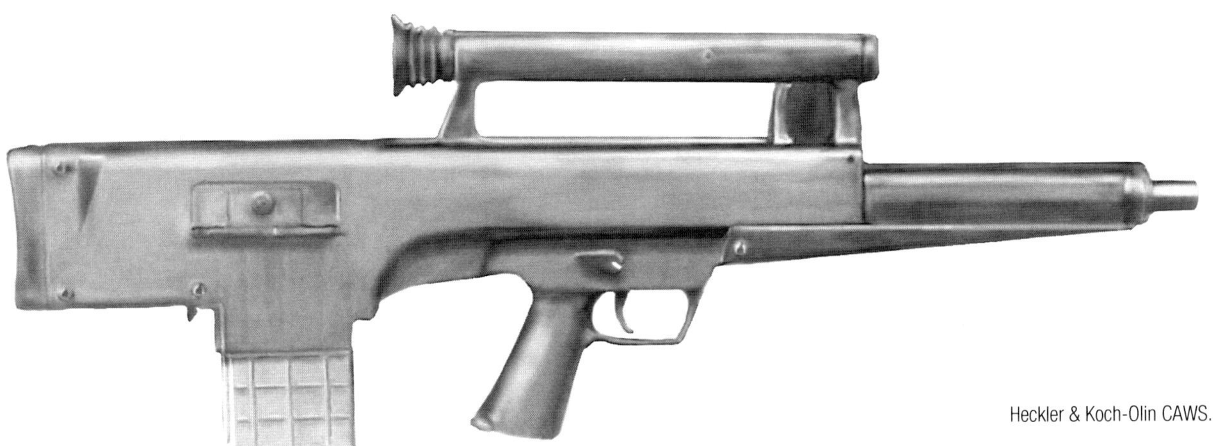

Heckler & Koch-Olin CAWS.

15 it bought the rights to from Armalite. But the company continued to receive its share of financial hard knocks and suffered through a workers' strike starting in 1987 and continuing into 1989. This raised the company's operating costs, forcing it to raise its bid on the new M16A2 contract being offered by the U.S. government following the successful work of the M16PIP program.

Colt's rival, Fabrique Nationale (which as far back as the early 1900s had been buying Browning's firearms inventions about as fast as Colt, creating a rivalry between the two businesses that continues to this day) had been competing for the American manufacturer's customers since the beginning of the 20th century. No doubt there was more than a little crowing in the FN offices when the company beat out Colt's bid and received a contract to produce the military's Squad Automatic Weapon (SAW).

The Belgium-based manufacturer had set up a plant in Columbia, South Carolina, gaining a foothold in the United States. With the new plant producing the Minimi SAW as well as the MK19 40mm grenade launchers, it was soon set to tackle other projects and already had met the U.S. government requirement that any guns made for the U.S. military had to be manufactured in the United States.

When the government announced a call for bids for building the M16A2 rifles, the Fabrique Nationale was ready and bid $420 per rifle compared with Colt's bid of $477.50. So late in 1988, the Fabrique Nationale was awarded the $112 million contract to produce 267,000 M16A2 rifles over the following five years.

## COLT FOR SALE

After Colt lost the contract, its parent company, Colt Industries, announced the discontinuation of civilian sales of the AR-15 (which many saw as a political move to placate the assault-rifle hysteria being generated by members of Congress and liberal elements in the press and perhaps to curry favor among antigun senators in Washington). But none of these criticisms helped; soon Colt Industries had put its firearms division up for sale.

Colt Firearms was sold to an odd coalition of private investors, including the state of Connecticut (where Colt's plants were based), and the union employees who worked for the company. This new corporation was renamed Colt's Manufacturing Company, Inc. (See below.)

Although this brought an end to the United Auto Worker (UAW) strike that had just about put the nail in the coffin of Colt Firearms (the strike ending as the workers became part owners of the reorganized company), things didn't improve much. The company continued to hurt for money and by 1992 had entered into Chapter 11 bankruptcy; litigation between Colt's Manufacturing Company, Inc. and C. F. Intellectual Properties then took place with an eye toward salvaging the business, rather than discontinuing the manufacture of firearms and closing Colt's doors for good.

Things appeared hopeless for Colt. In 1994 the Hartford Armory portion of the company was closed, with workers relocated to the West Hartford facility, which had just been completed with new equipment.

Then the break Colt needed arrived. The company secured the sole-source contract to supply nearly 19,000 M4 carbine variants of the AR-15 to the U.S. Army and joint special forces. By September, a new group of investors, suspecting that the company was now coming out of the doldrums, purchased it.

At this point things still looked a bit precarious for Colt. However, this was actually the turning point for the company, with 1997 bringing a second government contact for 6,000 more M4 carbines and 1998 a third contract for more than 32,000 M16A2s, along with a contract for updating the U.S. Air Force's 88,000 M16A1 rifles to A2 configuration. These contracts were capped with one for the exclusive production of the M4 carbine through the year 2010, as more of these carbine versions of the AR-15 were employed as replacements for the U.S. Army's aging supply of pistols, rifles, and submachine guns.

### The ACR Program

Although Colt had turned a financial corner, those at the company, lacking crystal balls, didn't know this. But they did have another ray of hope in addition to renewed military contracts they had just landed: the company's Advanced Combat Rifle (ACR) was now slated to be part of the U.S. Army's testing aimed toward the development of a possible replacement for the M16A2 rifle (more on this process and the actual rifles involved in this test in a later chapter). The carrot on the stick in this case was the thought that if the ACR proved to be a replacement for the M16A2, the manufacturer holding the rights to the gun could make a financial killing, especially if it was set up to build the rifles as well.

Colt's candidate product for the program, which had been submitted early on, had made it through the first safety evaluations and tests to put it in the running with three other ACR candidates in the $300 million battery of army tests. Derived from the standard AR-15 system, Colt's ACR was a mature design without any of the bugs that had already disqualified a number of the other weapons in the test (including the one submitted by Eugene Stoner through ARES).

So Colt had an edge: unlike the other firearms in the test, the Colt gun was basically an AR-15 with some new improvements. As such, the gun was familiar to army personnel and had established a long record of success and a reputation for reliability. Additionally, Colt had an entire weapons family to go with its ACR, from the M203 grenade launcher (which had proven itself to be highly effect and was being adopted in ever greater numbers by the army) to short commando versions of the gun (already adopted as the M4 by the military) to compact 9mm version of the AR-15 that fired the NATO pistol cartridge. More on all of these versions appears in a subsequent chapter. Again, these were ready to use right off the shelf, and many were already in the military's inventory. Adoption of Colt's ACR would not entail a lengthy development program or extraordinary expense, aside from simply purchasing the weapons or parts, upgrading the current inventory, and issuing the firearms to the troops.

Another plus of the Colt ACR was that both Fabrique Nationale and Colt had the machinery to manufacture the M16A2 rifle; the tooling costs of producing the ACRs would thus be minimal, far less than if one of the totally new candidates from other companies were selected. Selection of an ACR produced by H&K, Steyr, or AAI, on the other hand, would entail building entire plants, training new workers, and exorcising the bugs from the firearm and the machinery used in manufacturing it—an expensive and time-consuming proposition. From an economic standpoint, Colt's ACR had a lot going for it.

While the testing of the ACR was in progress, January 1990 saw the sale of Colt Firearms by its parent company, the CF Holding Corporation, by a group of investors that had been put together by Colt executive Anthony Autorino. Autorino secured two foreign investors, borrowed money through an Australian bank, and persuaded the Connecticut State Pension Fund to invest $25 million in the company in exchange for a 47-percent stake in the profits. The firearms operation was purchased and quickly reorganized, opening officially in March 1990 as Colt's Manufacturing Company, the name originally given the firm by Samuel Colt and under which it had operated from the end of World War II until it was reorganized in 1955.

### Unique Features of the Colt ACR

Colt's candidate rifle in the ACR tests concentrated on making the rifle as user friendly as possible. It featured a recontoured handguard with enlarged vent holes and an improved heat shield as well as a front-end restricting ring to help prevent a shooter's hand from sliding past the handguard to touch a hot barrel, a "barrel rib" running along the top of the handguard to improve quick aiming at close ranges (though this capability is negated when the scope is attached to the rifle rather than iron sights), and a pistol grip reshaped to fit a shooter's hand more comfortably. Additionally, the ACR had a muzzle brake compensator coupled to its "birdcage" flash holder to help reduce recoil and barrel climb to give smaller dispersion.

The stock was patterned after the telescoping Commando stock but had a longer heel for greater comfort when shouldering the rifle; the locking mechanism on the stock also had several positions, making it possible to adjust length of pull from shooter to shooter or according to the weight of clothing being worn. (The latter is no small consideration with a firearm that might be used by both tall and short shooters or by the same shooter, sometimes in warm-weather gear and sometimes in bulkier cold-weather gear.)

As with the M16A2, the 20-inch barrel on the ACR had a 1-in-7-inch twist to give optimal performance with a wide range of bullet sizes and shapes. The rifle accepted an

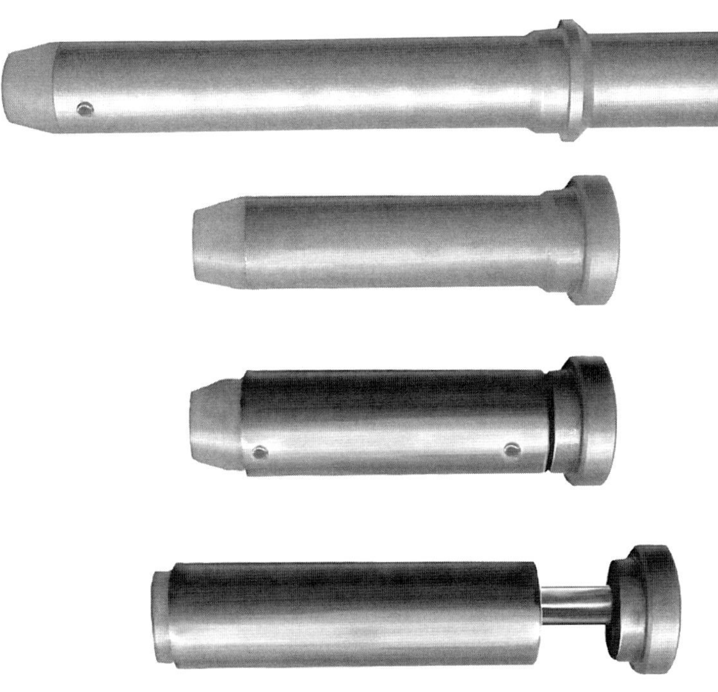

An amazing variety of buffers have been created for the AR-15, and these can have a profound effect on reliability as well as the cyclic rate of the gun. Top is the standard AR-15 buffer, two center models are designed for the shorty Commando, and the lower is an oil-spring hydraulic buffer.

optical sight or a special iron-sight assembly that included a carrying handle with a flat top to aid in snap shooting.

An "oil-spring hydraulic buffer" (borrowed from the Colt heavy-barrel machine gun) replaced the M16A2 buffer and lowered the rate of full-auto fire as well as reducing felt recoil. This buffer coupled with the muzzle brake made felt recoil 40 percent less than the M16A2's.

The ambidextrous selector had a surprise: its three positions were safe, semiauto, and auto. Apparently the switch back to the automatic setting was dictated by both the simpler M16 trigger mechanism and the increased practicality of control due to a slower rate of fire and reduced recoil. This made it practical for shooters to control burst lengths by limiting the time the trigger was pulled—or so the theory went. It seemed likely that some troops might "freeze" and clutch the trigger during actual combat with such a system unless their training was very efficient in instilling habits to prevent this.

### The AR-15 "Assault Weapon"

During this time, antigun elements in Washington, D.C., as well as the mainstream press were pushing for a ban on so-called assault weapons, including the AR-15. Since nearly all the hoopla was from people who knew almost nothing about firearms, Colt and other companies took the expedient measure of making minor changes in firearms and renaming them to produce "safe" rifles that were no longer "assault weapons" (even though they were virtually identical to the "dangerous" guns they replaced in the company's lineup). Thus 1990 saw the reintroduction of the AR-15 for civilian sales that was only slightly different from the previous model. This gun was no longer sold as the AR-15 Sporter II, but rather simply as the Sporter.

The only outward difference between the Sporter and the AR-15 Sporter II was a missing bayonet lug. Although this was something most shooters would not notice was missing, it was one of the features that the antigunners had got it into their heads that criminals were going to use. (This even though cases in which "assault weapons" employed by criminals made up only around 1 percent of all crimes; those involving a bayonet on a rifle were virtually unheard of.

Internally, the new Sporter had a slightly modified lower receiver, and the changes apparently came as older parts in Colt's inventory were exhausted. Thus, one can find several variants of these guns, depending on when they were made.

By the same token, various company markings may be found on these guns, reflecting the transition from Colt Firearms to Colt's Manufacturing.

The first change to come along was a lower receiver that was nearly identical to that of the M16A2, with a few guns even having the same front push pin that had previously been missing on the AR-15, replaced instead by a double screw. This created a stronger receiver and a generally better gun, thanks to the shielded magazine release that made inadvertent dropping of the magazine less likely.

By the end of 1990, again as a concession to the antigun crowd, Colt started milling the whole rear of the bolt carrier away and adding a lower receiver block, secured by a roll pin, to make it more difficult to add an auto sear to the gun. Although it is doubtful that this would have prevented illegal conversion to automatic by those intent on such modification, it again appeased those who knew little about such things (and who assumed that converting the AR-15 was easier than converting other semiauto rifles, many of which lack the internal safety features of the AR-15 trigger group that actually make such conversions more difficult).

### Colt's Troubles Continue

Colt faced many problems, with more than 1,000

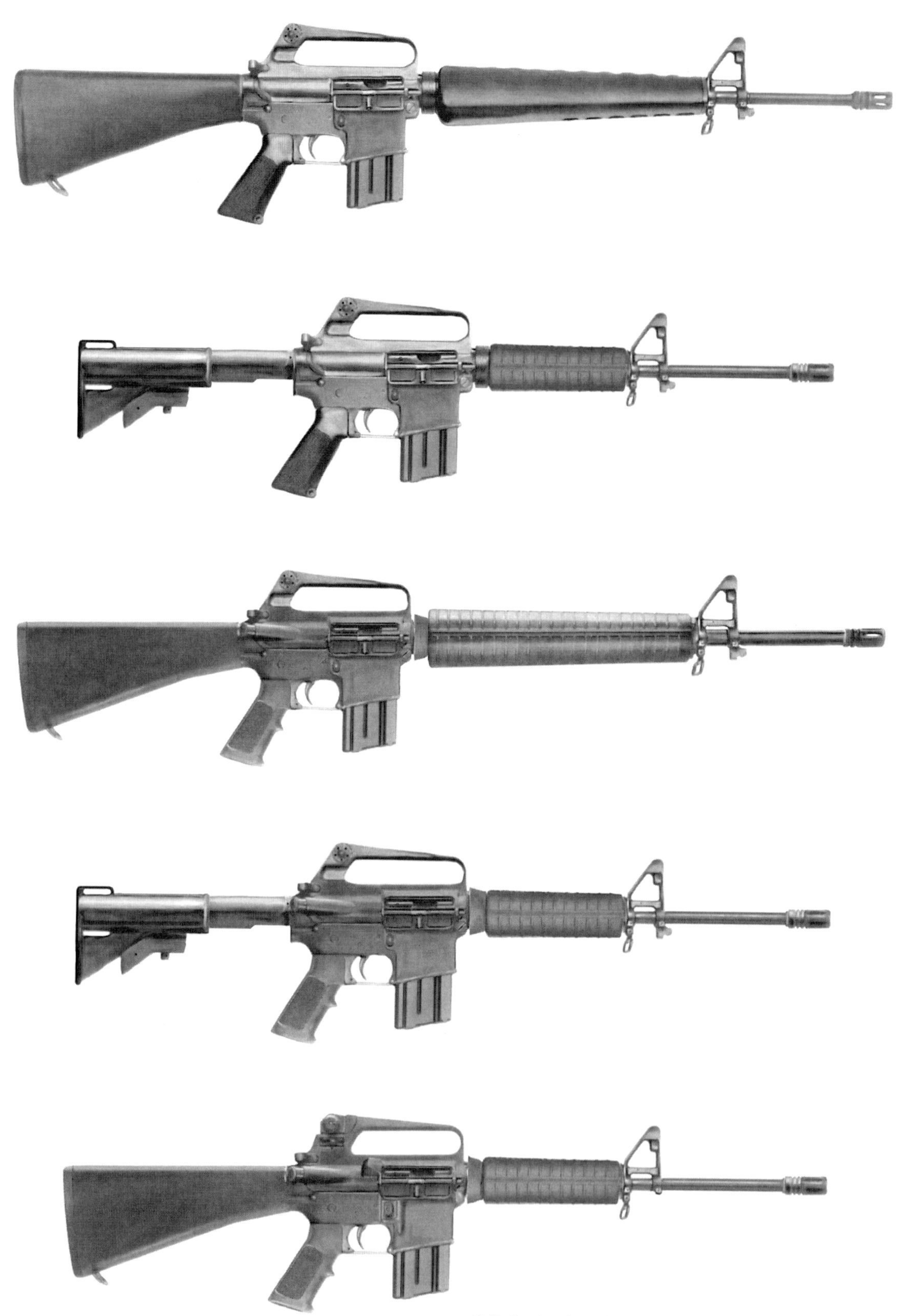

Colt's Sporters (top to bottom): AR-15 Sporter Model 6000, Sporter Carbine 6001, Sporter II 6500, Sporter II Carbine 6520, and Sporter Carbine 6530.

workers in the powerful UAW having been laid off during the course of strikes. The previous management had replaced striking workers with nonunion workers, and many were not as skilled as those they replaced. Plus, the company's two manufacturing plants were sadly outdated, with equipment that was far from high-tech by any stretch of the imagination and Colt's yearly sales had dropped below the $100 million mark, suggesting that the operation was about to sink into financial ruin.

As the new man at the helm, Autorino's first order was to fire the replacement workers and instigate a $13 million back-pay settlement with the UAW strikers, rehiring more than 700 skilled workers that the company had lost. He then gave the UAW three seats on the 11-member board of directors, thereby giving the workers a say in how the company was run and bringing Colt into the current trend of allowing workers to have an interest in whether a manufacturer fails or succeeds.

While these steps were seen by many as a gamble, they had often paid off with other companies and seemed likely to do so with Colt. Autorino went one step future and created a stock plan that gave workers shares amounting to 11.5 percent ownership of the company—another move that would allow those doing the work to reap the benefits of a job well done or suffer the consequences of shoddy workmanship. Autorino later told the press, "I want everyone to share equally in the growth and success of Colt. Management and workers have to be absolute equals and agree to constructively try to work out any disagreements. Otherwise, you end up with the constant picking at each other that is so destructive."

Early in 1991, after the reorganization of the company and some behind-the-scenes lobbying, Colt finally received good news: The U.S. Army would award it a $9.5 million contract for the production of 12,000 M16A2 rifles plus spare parts for the guns. This contract was not nearly as large as that awarded to FN nearly 2 years before, but it was a hopeful sign that Colt was at least back in the running. Furthermore, Colt's sales to police departments had picked up thanks to the fact that unionized departments no longer had qualms about dealing with the company once it had settled with the UAW.

The ACR testing came to an end, producing little new knowledge. None of the candidate rifles did noticeably better than the standard M16A2. The bottom line was that buying a new rifle would do little to improve the abilities of troops in the field. So instead the focus shifted to improving the abilities of the shooter rather than trying to make improvements to a firearm that was already functioning at near perfection and boasted accuracy that had been only obtainable with select target-grade, bolt-action firearms just a few decades earlier. (The ACR rifles including those produced by Colt are covered in more detail later.)

## IMPROVING ON THE M16A2

The results of the ACR program, and its failure to better the performance of the M16A2 rifle in any of the tests, led to the call for an M16A3 model, which would be identical to the M16A2 in most respects except that it would have the detachable carrying handle-rear sight assembly similar to that of Colt's ACR. The sight assembly would then normally be removed, and a scope, night-vision device, or laser sight (as well as other types of aiming systems that might be developed in the near future) mounted on it for troops in combat.

Getting rifles for testing was easy, because the tooling to produce the new model had already been done for Colt's ACR program as well as a similar new style of upper receivers the company was marketing on one version of its civilian rifles. So the assembly was available to the army at a nominal cost. (Although technically this rifle model was classified as the M16A2E2, in fact most army personnel close to the tests generally referred to it as the "M16A3.")

Another advantage such a system had was that expensive sights wouldn't have to be mounted on "behind-the-lines" rifles issued to noninfantry personnel, since an A2-style iron sight detachable assembly was available for these rifles. An additional plus was that, as with Colt's ACR, the standard M16A2 could be operated in the same manner as the new M16A3 model, with only the new optical system differing from the earlier firearm. (However, some consideration was given to adding features from the ACR model Colt had produced, since the logical time to incorporate such changes would be with the adoption of a new model of the rifle. Talk among company insiders at that time also suggested they were considering a change to a four-pronged "Vortex"-style flash hider as well as decreasing the twist rate to 1-in-9 to minimize barrel plating by copper bullet jackets during the life of the firearm.)

Furthermore, most of the scopes available for mounting on the A3 model could have been mounted on M16A2 rifles with the addition of a scope mount, making it possible to buy the scopes and mount them on rifles that had already been purchased if funds weren't available for a completely new rifle. Thus, for only a little more, the new receiver might be purchased with the scopes and M16A2 rifles converted to the new configuration. And new scopes were to be designed so they would also work on the M249 SAW with the addition of a modified stock and a scope mount rail on the top of the machine gun's receiver. So, all in all, the idea of upgrading the capabilities of the AR-15 (and M249) by adding a new sight system made a lot of sense.

Six companies originally expressed interest in submitting sights for the tests: Gun South, Inc., Hughes, OEC, Pioneer, S-Tron, and Trijicon. All six were judged to be technically equal, so the contracts for samples of the scopes for testing were awarded to Hughes, OEC, and S-Tron.

In addition to being capable of blocking laser light—laser weapons capable of blinding troops being under development in several countries that might be hostile to the United States—the scopes were required to offer 3X to 4X magnification. This, it was hoped, would enable soldiers to identify enemies more readily at greater distances, thereby finally making it possible to engage foes at greater than 300 yards (and justifying the need for the range requirements made in the past).

Optics of high enough quality to gather light in the early dawn or at dusk were needed, as was a tritium-lit reticule. Both could make it possible to engage an enemy in near darkness when iron sights were useless. A built-in bullet drop compensation system that allowed for changes in point of impact out to 800 meters was another requirement. Finally, the scopes had to have a wide field of view so targets could be located quickly, and they had to be tough enough to survive the rigors of combat, including parachute missions.

The event of 1991 was the crumbling of the Soviet Union. While this might have been good news to free people everywhere, it didn't present a rosy picture for Colt, which would be less apt to sell arms during a time of declining military tensions. Furthermore, with downturns in the U.S. economy and calls from President George Bush and Congress for reduced military spending or even freezes in weapons procurement, both the ACR and M16A3 models were put in jeopardy.

Eventually the M16A3 rifle was adopted while the ACR program ground to a halt, the latter due to lack of funding as well as the obvious fact that none of the contenders were much better than the M16A2 currently in the military's arsenals. In the end the military recognized that simply improving the M16A2 through the addition of sights and other accessories, coupled with issuing more carbine versions of the gun, would do as much good as introducing a whole new system—and with a lot less expense, retraining of troops, and general confusion.

### The M16A3, M16A4, and MWS

For a time there was a bit of confusion regarding the designation for this model, since the M16A3 and M16A4 were identical for all intents and purposes. Today the A4 designation is generally used with the version that has a safe/semi/auto selector rather than the safe/semi/burst selector found on the M16A2 and the M16A3.

Addition of a floating integrated rail mounting system similar to that originally created for the M4 carbine is also available for current versions of the M16 rifle; this transforms the weapon into the Modular Weapon System (MWS), rifle version, and permits mounting the scopes, forward grip, lasers, and other accessories on the Picatinny rails of the unit.

## THE NEXT LOGICAL STEP

As will be noted later, the leapfrogging in technology that might make the AR-15 obsolete has not yet materialized, despite very promising guns that appeared to outshine the aging rifle. Time and again, as the AR-15 has continued to be refined and redefined, it has proven to be as good or better than the firearms proposed as replacements. Eventually something a quantitative step above the AR-15 will come into being. But exactly when is hard to predict. If history proves anything about predicting history, it is that those in the game of prophesizing are generally mistaken. Even minor gains in technology and new materials, let alone actual technological breakthroughs, can result in rapid and unforeseen improvements.

In the meantime, it seems likely that Colt will continue to produce and sell versions of the AR-15 worldwide, and it is certain that the AR-15 family of weapons will be used by soldiers, police officers, and civilians well into the 21st century. And regardless of choices by the militaries of the world, the number of AR-15 rifles and accessories for it on the commercial market guarantees that—like the Mauser bolt-action "combat" rifle of the previous century—the AR-15 will see more than a century of use by sportsmen before being retired as an antique.

## THE END OF AN ERA

The1997 death of Eugene Stoner, the former marine most often credited with the AR-15 as well as many other firearms and their improvements, marked the end of an era. Arguably, this one inventor has done more to make U.S. soldiers safer, more aggressive, and more likely to win on battlefields around the world thanks to the variants of the M16 they've carried over the past decades. Stoner had the distinction of having not one or two of his guns considered as the battle rifle of the United States, but at least five, including the AR-10, AR-15, AR-18, Stoner 62 and 63, and ARES ACR candidate.

Furthermore, at one point the AR-15, AR-18, and Stoner rifles were all being considered. Only John

Browning came close to this record, and even he didn't have three completely different systems competing against each other at any given time.

This unsung hero's passage was little noted except in a few military and gun magazines. Most notable was the succinct obituary in *Soldier Of Fortune,* August 1997:

**Eugene M. Stoner 1922 – 1997**

Gene Stoner, well-known designer of such weapons as the M-16 rifle and the Stoner 63 Weapons System, died of cancer at his home in Palm City, Fla., at the age of 74. Born in Gasport, Ind., in 1922 and educated in Long Beach, Calif., Stoner worked for Vega Aircraft, which became Lockheed Corporation. A veteran of WW II Marine Corps' service in the South Pacific and North China, Stoner held some 100 patents at the time of his death. His most recent association was with Knight Manufacturing Company, where he worked on the development of the SR-25 precision rifle.

# Chapter 4

# Colt's AR-15 Variations

During the relatively short time that Armalite and Colt have made the AR-15, they have come out with a variety of models. This is due partly to their innovative staffs and partly to the varying requirements specified by the military and government purchasers of different countries. Additionally, Colt has sought to augment sales through creating sporter versions of the AR-15. Often these must have specific barrel lengths or semiautomatic-only modifications that transform a selective-fire version of the rifle into a very different model externally as well as internally and also make it harder to create a selective-fire rifle from it.

By far, the largest numbers of these various models of the AR-15 can be found among the rifle versions. Carbine, "submachine gun," machine gun, and other renderings of the firearm have been manufactured in much smaller numbers. In some cases, perhaps, fewer than a dozen actual firearms were made for government trials or even in-house testing by engineers but never went into production due to lack of capabilities or interest. Additional variations of sorts have been created through the use of "bolt-on" devices such as 40mm grenade launchers and scopes.

New versions of the rifle will undoubtedly be seen in the future as everyone from garage tinkerers and inventors to major manufacturers create modifications and refinements on this basic design.

### RIFLE VARIANTS

Being prototypes, the first AR-15s Armalite built showed no model type as such. But surprisingly, they had nearly all the features that would eventually find their way onto the first M16 models that Colt produced for the U.S. Air Force. The principal areas where these prototypes differed from Colt's first actual models were these:

- A tapered, round one-piece handguard that lacked a "delta ring" spring assembly for quick removal (it being necessary to remove the front sight to free the handguard)
- A trigger-shaped charging lever located inside the carrying handle rear sight rather than at the rear of the receiver
- A 25-round magazine
- A "compressed" front sight that wasn't as large as the final version
- Lack of a flash hider or, later, a flash hider that was thinner than the final Colt version (the latter dictated by the need for rifle grenade launching capabilities)

Additionally, the fiberglass furniture on the gun was brown, and many of the parts were slightly different in size or shape from those of the production design. Nevertheless, the first AR-15 models Armalite produced were surprisingly "finished" for experimental prototypes.

When Colt finally went into production with the first M16 rifles for the U.S. Air Force, the company had switched to the beavertail handguard, apparently in an effort to control heat buildup under the handguard. Except for the forward assist and other minor modifications made by the TCC (as noted previously), the M16 and the forward-assist M16A1 remained pretty much as they were with changes in the flash hider, addition of ridges around the magazine release button, and addition of a trapdoor in the stock (which made its appearance late in the 1960s). These were the only outwardly noticeable modifications of the two models during their tenure.

In 1967, the U.S. military decided to start using select AR-15s to supplement the M21s (accurized M14s) that were being already in use as sniper rifles in Vietnam. Colt created two basic versions of the M16A1 for this purpose using select barrels. One model (Model 655) was nearly identical to the issue M16A1 with a scope block mounted in its carrying handle; this was usually equipped with the Leatherwood Realist 3–9X power ranging scope and often fitted in the field with an

Colt created two snipers for use in the Vietnam War. Top rifle is a Model 655; lower rifle, the Model 656.

army Human Engineering Laboratories (HEL) M4 or Sionics sound suppressor (more about scopes and sound suppressors later.

Colt's second sniper rifle, the Model 656, had a lowered front sight and an upper receiver with very low iron sights and a milled rail forming the top receiver without any carrying handle. This created a better cheek weld for the shooter than did the "heads-up" configuration of the carrying handle scope mount. This model, too, was often seen with a HEL M4 or Sionics suppressor. Unlike the Sionics suppressor, the HEL M4 required a bolt modification to deal with the increased gas pressure that the suppressor created and a gas deflector mounted over the charging lever to keep the extra gas from coming into the face of the shooter. Consequently the Sionics model soon won the favor of those using the sniper rifles.

The Sionics suppressor was designated the MAW-A1 and could be placed on an unmodified AR-15 by simply unscrewing the rifle's flash hider and adding the narrow tube to the muzzle of the gun. Even though the unit didn't silence the sonic crack of the bullet by any means, it did tame the muzzle blast so that enemy soldiers at some distance couldn't locate the sniper by the sound of his firearm's discharge.

Although the AR-15 equipped with a suppressor and scope had the potential for being a very demoralizing device for the enemy, the U.S. military never really took full advantage of the system. In the end, fewer than several hundred of the special guns, scopes, and suppressors appear to have ever been put to any great use during the Vietnam War.

### The 703

In 1968, in an effort to get around the fouling problems of the ball powder being used in the military's cartridges, Colt produced the Model 703 rifle, which utilized a gas system similar to that of the Stoner rifles. This rifle used mostly standard parts with a gas port and long piston above its barrel, along with an upper receiver lacking a carrying handle and a lower front sight. A triangular handguard specially made for the model surrounded the piston and barrel, though the front of the gas system was left exposed to prevent heat buildup. These rifles failed to perform any better than the standard AR-15s being used as a control group. The military didn't express interest in this modification, and Colt never added the design to its product line.

A number of patents have been taken out for a variety of methods of modifying the AR-15 gas system with an eye toward keeping it from blowing burned powder residue into the trigger group and bolt areas of the rifle. Among the more notable are the systems created by Michael C. Morris (U.S. Patent 4,765,224, August 1988) and Walter J. Langendorfer Jr., with David W. Coffin Sr. (U.S. Patent 4,244,273, January 1983). Few of these have had any commercial success, however, for the simple reason that the AR-15 system

Inventors: **Walter J. Langendorfer, Jr.,** Lansdowne; **David W. Coffin, Sr.,** Prospect Park, both of Pa.

Assignee: **Langendorfer Plastics Corporation,** Lansdowne, Pa.

Appl. No.: **965,983**

Filed: **Dec. 4, 1978**

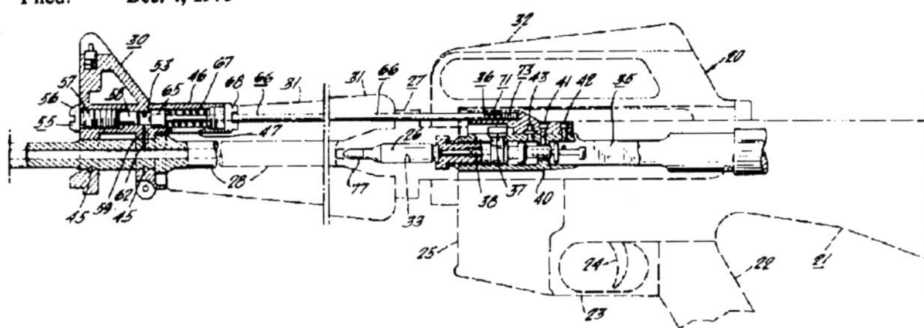

Patent drawing for system that replaces AR-15 gas tube with an operating rod.

Inventor: **Michael C. Morris,** Rte. 202 and County Line Rd., Chalfont, Pa. 18914

Appl. No.: **897,150**

Filed: **Aug. 15, 1986**

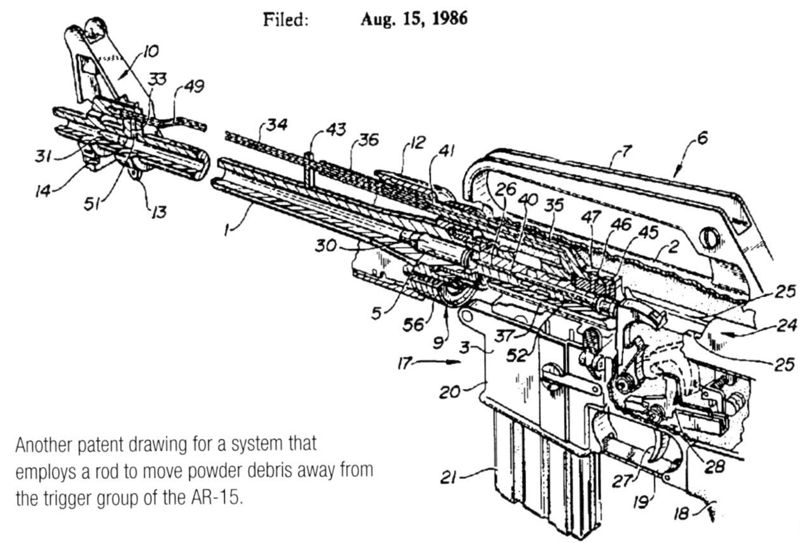

Another patent drawing for a system that employs a rod to move powder debris away from the trigger group of the AR-15.

has proven so reliable that few buyers are willing to risk modifications that might have unforeseen detrimental effects over the long haul. Better to have users do a little extra cleaning, the thinking goes, than monkey with a system that is nearly 100-percent reliable when employed with quality ammunition.

### Aftermarket Improvements

One system that did go into production during the early 1980s was Rhino International's retrofit gas system for civilian and police AR-15s. This system required only the replacement of the front sight assembly having a large gas port, a gas piston under the handguard, and a modified bolt carrier key having small plastic inserts that softened the rearward force to prevent shearing off the bolts holding it in place. Standard handguards were modified near the front sight to accommodate the enlarged gas port. Like other improvements to the AR-15 gas system, this one was destined for economic failure with the few guns converted now being collector's oddities rather than sought after shooting rifles.

In 1975 when the army was searching for a reflexive optical sight system, several M16A1 rifles were modified by having their front and rear sights chopped off and a scope rail attached to the upper receiver. Many of these guns were rebarreled to fire a .17-caliber (4.3mm) "microbullet" and had a special muzzle brake that dropped recoil almost to nothing. Eventually this line of development failed to produce any improvements over the standard AR-15 and was dropped.

### The AR-15 Sporter

In an effort to capture the civilian market, Colt introduced a semiauto-only AR-15 in the mid-1970s. The company's designers used the standard M16 design but replaced the front push pin with a double screw, changing the receiver dimensions slightly so military and commercial receivers couldn't be joined together easily. They also modified the hammer and bolt carrier so removal of the sear would jam the gun rather than cause slam fires, and altered the trigger group and bolt carrier so an automatic sear couldn't be installed.

This semiauto sporter version was originally marketed under the name Colt Comanche, but that name was later dropped because a commercial aircraft had been marketed as the Comanche just before Colt introduced its new rifle. Thus the rifle became simply the AR-15 Sporter. These rifles are easily distinguished from selective-fire versions of the rifle by their two-position selectors and lack of a front pushpin and their "flat" right receiver lacking the protective ridges around the magazine release.

The experimental handguard created by HEL permitted rapid snap shooting and also helped cool the barrel during extended firing.

### The HEL

Another little-known variant of the AR-15 was the army's HEL. This rifle had a new handguard that had a long, ventilated rib passing between the front and rear sight. A white line was inscribed down the top of this rib. Experimenters using the rifle discovered that rapid "snap" shooting, much like that used by shotgunners on clay pigeons, was possible with this handguard. This rapid engagement of close targets was never pursued, though a similar handguard was eventually incorporated into Colt's ACR candidate weapon, with a flat-topped iron sight/carrying handle undoubtedly enhancing this effect.

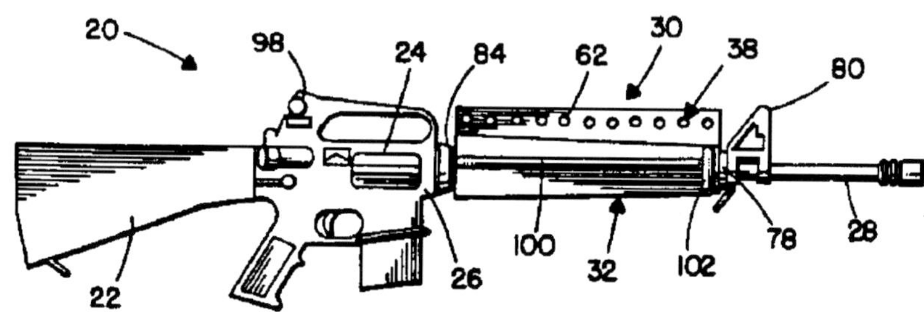


Patent drawing of convection-cooling, high-rib handguard invented by Paul G. Kennedy. This system was eventually used on Colt's ACR.

This quick-aiming device fell to the wayside, perhaps a victim of the electronic age when a dot scope made quick aiming even easier. However, one has to wonder whether a handguard that makes aiming quick—and needs no batteries or comparatively fragile optics to operate—doesn't still have merit. It may be that we have not seen the last of this rib aiming system.

Such a rib could have an additional plus, as revealed in the specifications of U.S. Patent 5,010,676 in 1991 (secured by inventor Paul G. Kennedy, with Colt named as the assignee). It shows that in addition to giving a quick-aiming system to the firearm, a rib incorporated into the upper handguard creates a convection chimney over the barrel, causing it to cool more rapidly than with a regular handguard. Thus, in addition to creating an instinctive sighting system, a ribbed handguard like that of the Colt ACR also creates a barrel that can withstand the heat created during sustained firing.

### The M16A2 and the Sporter II

The adoption of the M16A2 rifle resulted in several new models of the semiauto civilian version of the AR-15. These were generally marketed as the AR-15 Sporter II and were first seen with standard A1-style sights coupled with a forward assist and the furniture of the M16A2. Later models were offered with the adjustable A2-style sights.

Like the Sporter, these AR-15s had their trigger groups, bolts, and receivers modified to prevent easy conversion to automatic fire. A heavy-barrel (H-BAR) version of the Sporter II was also offered in 1986; it has adjustable A2 sights and was generally identical to the standard Sporter II except for a heavy barrel. Also seen was the Sporter Competition with detachable rear sight/carrying handle in 1991.

### Rumors of the M16A3

As mentioned earlier, the U.S. Army had been experimenting with a scoped version of the AR-15, designated the M16A3. As originally proposed, this rifle was basically identical to the M16A2 except for a scope mount upper receiver, that can be traced to the Colt's ACR, though whether this was actually a spin-off from the ACR or whether both guns had a common

Colt's Model 606B M1 H-BAR (top), the belt-fed M2 (center), and the open-bolt fire Model 741.

ancestor is not clear. (The ACR is discussed fully in the previous chapter.)

As work continued toward the selection of an M16A3, rumors abounded about the final configuration of the gun. Some suggested that a "duckbill"-style flash hider (manufactured by Western Ordnance International Corp.) would be added to the final model along with a 1-in-9 twist that would lower the amount of fouling produced by copper jackets. In the end, the M16A3 turned out to be pretty much a standard gun with just the addition of the detachable carrying handle/rear sight and the Weaver-style flat top on the receiver that permitted easy mounting of scopes and other equipment.

### Colt's AR-15 Machine Guns

Since Colt always looked to improving its products as well as making foreign sales, its designers were soon at work creating an Military Weapons System family of variations on the AR-15 after securing the manufacturing rights from Armalite. Like the Stoner "family" of weapons, the several types of Colt guns could easily be operated by troops familiar with just one of the weapons because all the firearms in the group had common controls and the same general handling characteristics.

Colt marketed the rifle and submachine gun versions of this family with both the beavertail handguards and the round, ribbed handguard the company had developed around 1965 (and that would eventually find its way onto the M16A2). The guns in this group that most closely resembled the AR-15 were referred to in company literature as "CAR-15s" (Colt Automatic Rifle version 15), while the heavier versions were dubbed "CMGs" (Colt Machine Guns).

Like other systems rifles, all of the guns in the CAR-15 family had many interchangeable parts, and all used the same type of ammunition. These features offered definite logistical and operational benefits to military purchasers, who could exchange parts or modify their weapons according to their needs.

Early CAR-15s generally used the three-position selector of the standard M16. However, Colt engineers soon discovered it was possible to create a cam system that allowed two-, three-, or five-round bursts of fire. These were often seen on these rifles, generally with a four-position selector (safe, semi, auto, and burst), though sometimes the burst position was substituted for the auto position for a three-position configuration. (Several other manufactures apparently "borrowed" this mechanism, since it showed up later on some European rifles.)

In addition to the Commando (XM177), Survival Rifle, and grenade launcher variants (listed below), as well as the basic AR-15/M16 rifle variants (above), the Colt military weapons systems group included a number of different light machine guns (LMGs). The first LMGs listed in Colt catalog were the H-BAR-M1 (Heavy-Barrel Model 1), the Heavy Assault Rifle-M2, and the CMG-1.

The H-BAR-M1 fed from the regular magazines and weighed 7.6 pounds (empty); it was designed for use as a squad heavy automatic rifle and fired from a closed bolt. The Heavy Assault Rifle M2 weighed 8.3 pounds (empty) and was also designed for use as a squad heavy automatic rifle. The M2 could be fed from regular 20- and 30-round magazines or converted without tools to use a disintegrating belt.

The M2 was usually seen in its belt-fed configuration, which used a lightened bolt carrier with a spiraling cam cut toward its front left side. When the bolt carrier cycled rearward, the cam connected to and powered the belt feed mechanism. A 50-round ammunition box and a larger 120-round box were created for the CAR-15 M2. These had a false magazine that locked into the receiver's magazine well, held in place by a ringed cross pin that went through the lower receiver and bottom of the feed mechanism assembly that extended into the well. (The cross pin was necessary because the weight of the belted ammunition and box were too much for the magazine release latch.) The belted ammunition fed from the left into the mechanism of the machine gun, with brass ejected out the port of the weapon while the links were caught in a chute on the right side of the ammunition box, saving them for later use.

An M2 was sent to the Springfield Armory for evaluation by the army in late 1964, apparently for

Jonathan Arthur Ciener converted a number of AR-15s to the M2 configuration. Shown here is the ammunition pack; the chute below the ejection port was designed to collect ammunition links so they could be reused, a boon to do-it-yourselfers. (Courtesy of Jonathan Arthur Ciener.)

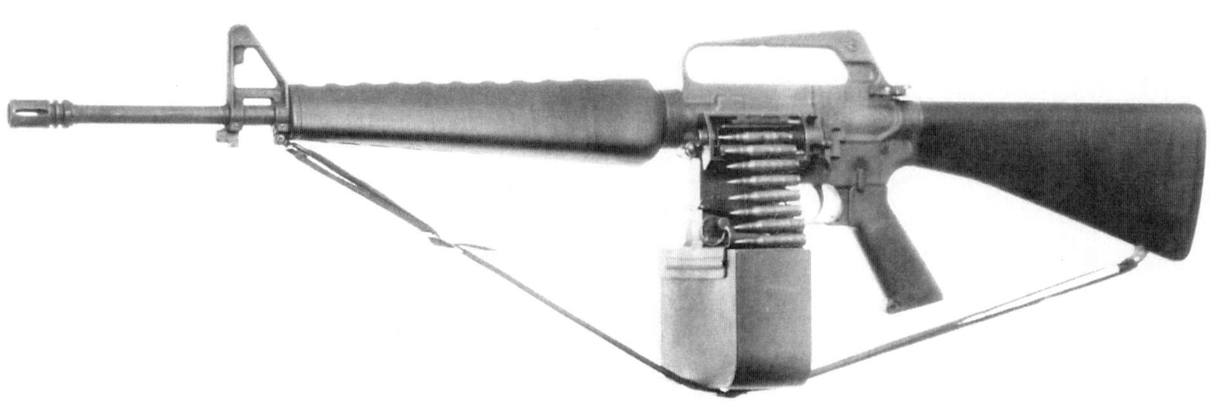

Side view of a Jonathan Arthur Ciener M2 conversion. (Courtesy of Jonathan Arthur Ciener.)

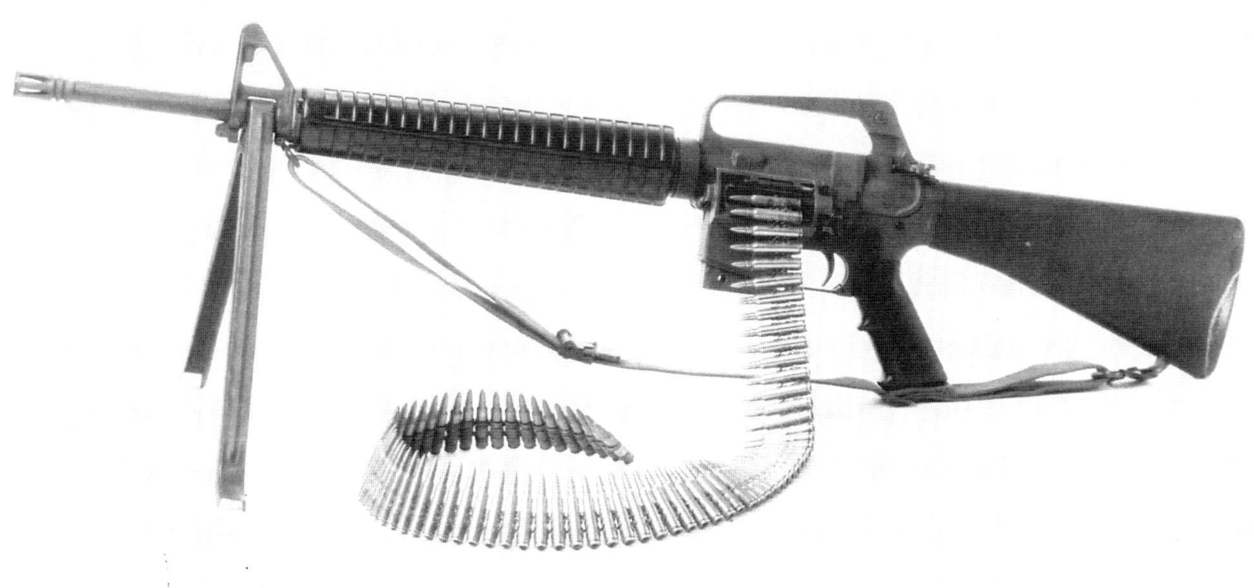

The M2 (shown here is the Jonathan Arthur Ciener conversion) could also feed from an external belt in addition to the integral belt carrier designed for it. (Courtesy of Jonathan Arthur Ciener.)

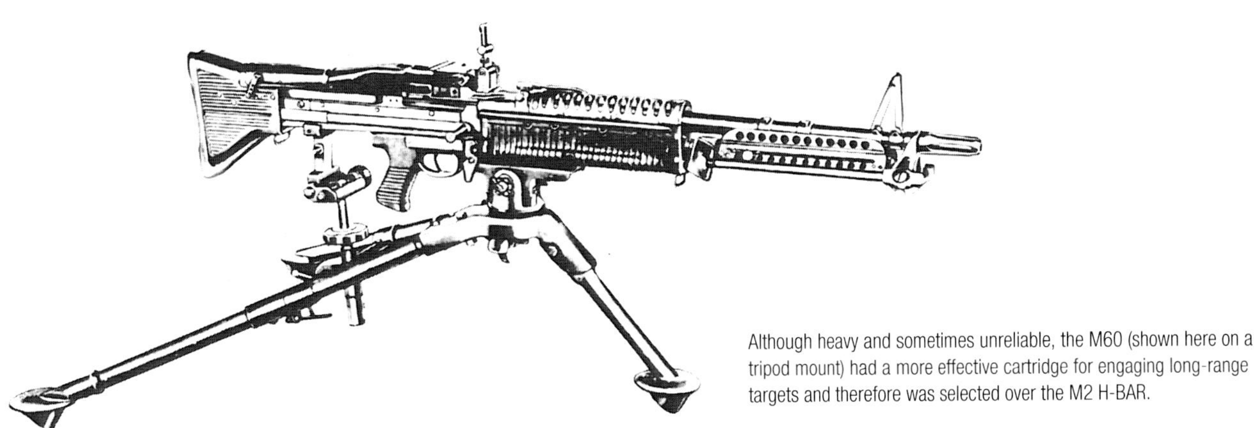

Although heavy and sometimes unreliable, the M60 (shown here on a tripod mount) had a more effective cartridge for engaging long-range targets and therefore was selected over the M2 H-BAR.

consideration as a helicopter door gun. This was rejected in favor of continuing with the M60 7.62mm machine guns already in use, and in the end fewer than 20 of the CAR-15 M2s were ever made because there just didn't seem to be much interest in them among military purchasers. (The design would later be revived by Jonathan Arthur Ciener, however.

The CMG-1 weighed 11.5 pounds with its light barrel or 12.5 pounds with a heavy barrel. The first CMG-1 was designed using the gas tube and bolt/bolt carrier of the AR-15 rifle; later models used a different system that improved the capability of the gun while lowering its ability to exchange most major parts with other members of the CAR-15 family.

In addition to the tripod mount of the original CMG-1, a pintle, bipod (with stock), and solenoid accessories pack allowed the machine gun to be transformed into a variety of configurations to handle different tasks. The end result was a machine gun that used many AR-15 parts; and most non-AR-15 parts were steel stampings that could be easily manufactured. The belt could be fed from either the right or left side of the gun for added versatility. Cyclic rate was 650 rpm or 650–850 rpm with solenoid operation. But apparently no government ever expressed interest in the CMG, and only two or three prototypes were ever fabricated.

### New Rounds for the CMG-1

The CMG-1 was conceived early in the 1960s by a design team headed by Robert E. Roy. This group developed the lightweight machine gun with an the idea of using as many of the AR-15 parts as possible to enhance the ability of the weapon to be serviced with standard parts already in the military inventories. To get around the

Top to bottom: early "thin-barrel" CMG-1, and later stock, pintle, and solenoid mounts and versions.

inherent limitations of the current .223 cartridge, Colt engineers worked to develop special ammunition to extend the range of the machine gun. Working with Frankford Arsenal, the company created an experimental 68-grain bullet during the mid-1960s that, coupled with the 1-in-9 twist they developed for it, probably worked nearly as well as the 7.62mm NATO round.

The bullet itself was based on the heavy .22-caliber bullets made in 1954 by Sierra for experiments at the Aberdeen Proving Ground. Colt started with this 68-grain bullet and changed the ogive from a 7-caliber tangent radius (like that of the old military .30-'06 M1 bullet) to a 10-caliber secant radius (like that of the 7.62mm NATO bullet). Just as the 7.62mm ballistics were improved over the .30-'06 by the change, so, too, was the new 68-grain bullet's performance improved over the older version originally made for the Aberdeen experiments. These new bullets were manufactured and loaded into rounds by the Federal Cartridge Corporation during 1965 and 1966 for Colt to use in its machine guns.

The CMG-1 could also be mounted on a tripod—perhaps a bit optimistic in view of the 5.56mm NATO chambering.

The adoption of the M249 as the U.S. Army's squad automatic weapon was the result of the SAWS. (Courtesy of U.S. Army.)

The round was later modified by the Frankford Arsenal and designated the XM287. It was used for a time in the Stoner 63 system when the U.S. military was evaluating it for possible adoption. The XM287 was manufactured for the tests by Valcartier Industries of Canada and had a muzzle velocity of 2,960 fps, which—coupled with its mass—made it perform as well as the 7.62mm NATO round when it came to the flatness of trajectory, accuracy, penetration, and ability to resist wind deflection.

Of all the services, apparently the U.S. Marines were the most interested in adopting the 68-grain bullet—and possibly some of Colt's machine guns. But the service finally returned to the standard .223 ammunition because a change to Colt's new cartridge would entail replacing the barrels on all of the 50,000 M16 rifles in the Marine Corps inventory.

### H-BARS to the Rescue

So even though the Colt family of weapons did offer many advantages, it was never accepted for actual combat use except for the Commando carbines, the AR-15 rifle (that was already in use as the M16 rifle), and the H-BAR with a 1-in-12 twist and standard ammunition, for limited use in some U.S. Marine squads. The H-BARs that saw combat were used as automatic rifles, with two H-BARs issued to a squad. In theory, the other members in the squad were to use their M16s in the semiauto mode

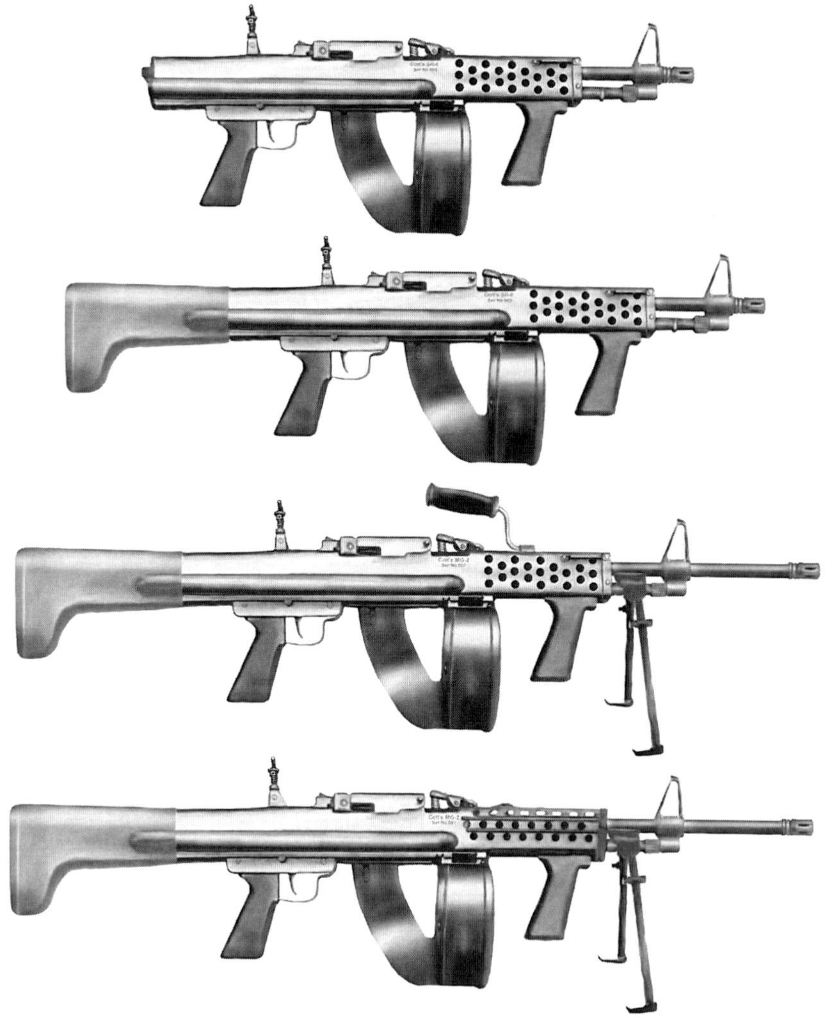

Colt's CMG-2 family of firearms had a lot going for it, but lacked the high rate of fire that the U.S. military was looking for.

only while the H-BARs were fired in the automatic mode. (This idea was good on paper, but convincing some squad members not to ever fire in automatic mode was not always very successful in actual combat.)

One development of the systems work that quickly found its way to the battlefield was the 30-round magazine developed for the Commando. The AR-15 was first issued with a 20-round magazine (mostly because the original specifications given by the military called for a 20-round magazine), but the CAR-15 machine guns demanded 30-round magazines for increased firepower.

At this point the Stoner system used a 30-round magazine, and the Vietcong were armed with the AK-47 assault rifle that boasted a 30-round magazine. So when Colt perfected the 30-round magazine for its CAR-15 family of guns, it was not surprising that the U.S. military decided to adopt the new magazines and soon introduced them in Vietnam.

The larger 30-round magazine was first seen in the field on the Commando and the H-BAR and eventually filtered down to those using the M16A1. Special LC-1 web gear was designed to hold three 30-round magazines and became standard issue.

### SAWS

Starting in 1966 with the Small Arms Weapon Study (SAWS), the U.S. Army had been working with the idea of producing a lightweight machine gun for the squad level and fire the standard .223 rifle cartridge. Two of the requirements the military decided on for such a machine gun were that it weigh less than 22 pounds with 200 rounds of ammunition and be capable of delivering fire

Front view of Colt CMG-2. (Courtesy of Colt Firearms.)

effectively beyond 800 yards.

Given the ammunition of the time, these two requirements were in direct conflict with each other, since a machine gun that weighed 22 pounds with 200 rounds would have to fire 5.56mm ammunition, which wasn't effective out to that range! (Many authorities attribute the range requirement to those who favored the 7.62mm NATO, though it may have been designed to encourage the development of more effective .223 ammunition. At any rate, the need for that long a range again flew in the face of the ALCLAD research showing that nearly all rifle casualties were produced within 300 yards, the majority at less than 100 yards.)

Eventually, those involved in SAWS decided to first upgrade the .223 ammunition used in the rifle so it would have the desired range while creating a minimum of change with the standard weapon in the U.S. arsenal. Strangely enough, Colt's CMG-1 machine gun was never submitted to SAWS because all work on it had been stopped in the late 1960s in favor of developing a completely new design that would not necessarily use the same parts or design features as the AR-15.

This second version of a .223 machine gun was designated the CMG-2 and was developed by a team under the direction of George F. Curtis and Henry J. Tatro. It was created with virtually no parts interchangeable with the AR-15 and was fed from a belt of 150 cartridges encased in a drum below its receiver.

The Colt CMG-2 was tested during 1969 but was rejected because it didn't have a high enough rate of fire and because of the SAWS 800-plus yards requirement.

## The Stoner 63

The Stoner 63 system was also tested from 1968 through 1972 and was turned down for many of the same reasons that the CMG-2 had been. Later, both the CMG-2 and Stoner 63 machine guns were submitted to the U.S. Navy SEAL team trials that took place at about the same time. Colt submitted a short-barreled version of its CMG-2; it was beat out by the Stoner, which became the MG MK23 MOD O (and saw very limited use in Vietnam).

Oddly enough, this was the only real acceptance the Stoner 63 weapons system would see. Worldwide, Stoner's rifle system was competing with Colt or those developed by the countries searching for a .223 rifle. Nevertheless, it is interesting to note that during this period the three most popular rifles in the West—and arguably the best—were the AR-15, AR-18, and the Stoner 63—all of which Eugene Stoner had helped to develop.

After leaving Colt, Stoner had worked at Cadillac Gage Corporation on developing a family of weapons (perhaps an idea he'd picked up from Colt's extensive modification of the AR-15). At Cadillac Gage, he secured his two coworkers that had been with him at Armalite: Robert Fremont and James Sullivan. Together they created the Stoner 62 system for the 7.62mm NATO round, and later his two coworkers modified the system to create the Stoner 63, which chambered the smaller .223 cartridge (much as had been done in transforming the AR-10 into the AR-15).

Stoner 63 "family" of weapons. The modular design of this gun made it possible to quickly change its configuration to suit the task at hand.

The Stoner 63 family consisted of 15 assemblies that could be interchanged to create a number of configurations to suit a number of purposes, from creating carbines to LMGs, with each gun's basic control layout being identical.

The firearms that could be assembled from a parts kit included a short carbine with folding stock, a full-size assault rifle, an LMG (belt/magazine feed), a medium machine gun, and a tank machine gun. This system was evaluated by the U.S. Army for some time (as the XM22 Rifle, XM23 Carbine, and XM207 Machine Gun), and the Stoner LMG was field-tested in Vietnam by the marines (as the MK23 Belt-Fed Machine Gun).

Even though the Stoner System had a lot going for it, the basic assault rifle was too heavy (7.75 pounds unloaded) because it needed rugged receiver for its use as an LMG. Consequently, only the MK23 saw much use, and then only in the hands of the navy SEAL teams.

### The Army's SAW Search

Meanwhile, the army found no weapon that could meet its SAW requirements, so in 1972 it decided to hire American manufacturers to develop candidates for possible adoption as the new SAW. The military originally hired only two companies, the Maremont Corporation (creating the XM233) and Ford Aerospace (responsible for the XM234). Oddly enough, no attempt was made to upgrade the Stoner or Colt machine guns that had already been developed. But soon a third company in the running when Rodman Laboratory added its XM235.

The U.S. Marines decided to produce their own "interim SAW" rather than wait for the results from the long, drawn-out army test. Rather than use Colt's H-BAR M1 or Heavy Assault Rifle M2, which were already available, the marines decided to try to create a version of their own and experimented with an H-BAR M16 that had been modified by WAK, Incorporated, with a special buffer (that permitted firing from an open bolt) and a new muzzle compensator to prevent muzzle climb with the lightweight gun. This project didn't work out well, however, and was abandoned in 1977.

Meanwhile, the army's work on the SAW program continued. The Rodman Laboratories XM235 was modified to become the XM248, and three more weapons were submitted by other companies to the trials: the

Early (top) and later model of the XM106 candidate SAW.

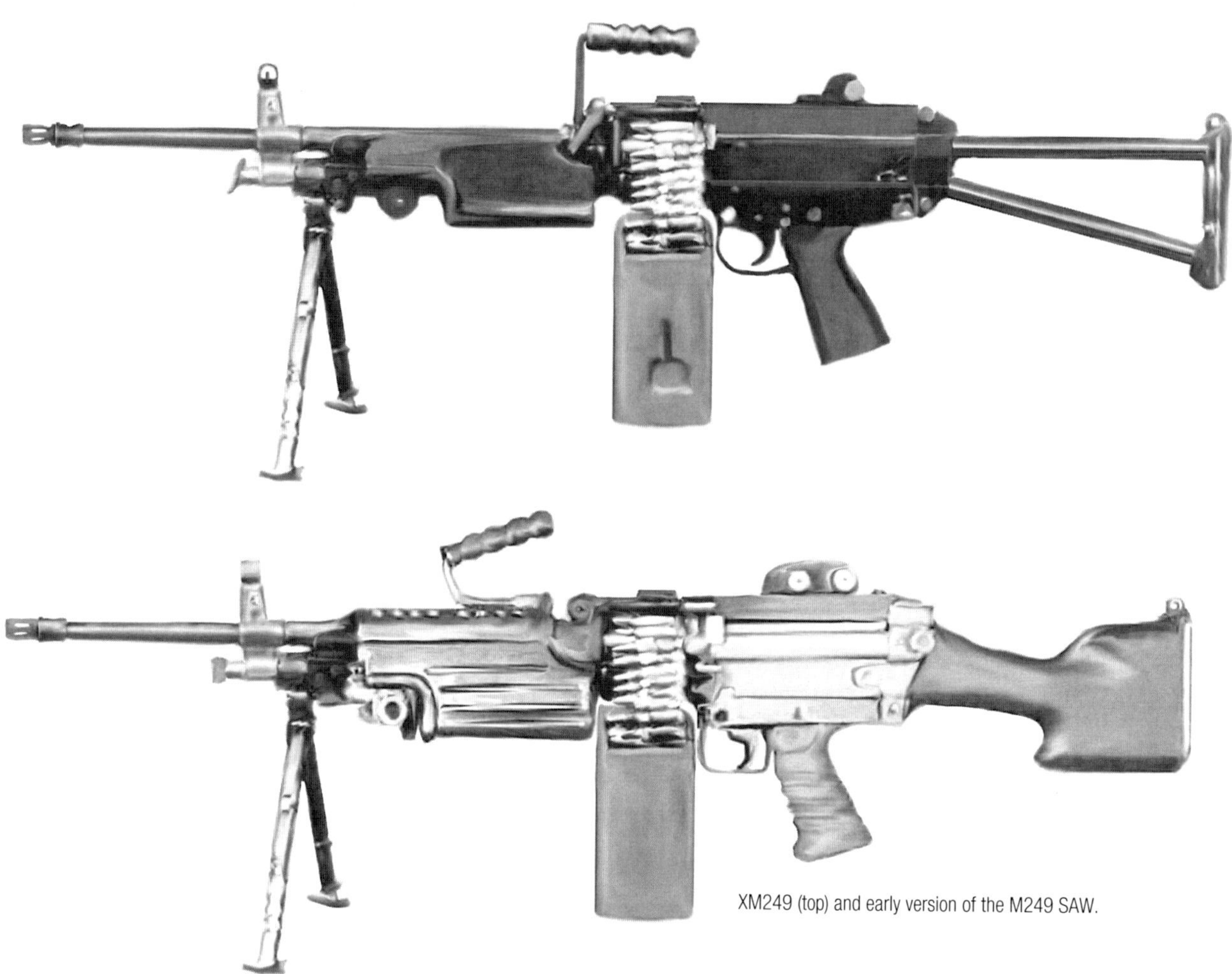
XM249 (top) and early version of the M249 SAW.

Fabrique Nationale's Minimi, designated the XM249; H&K's 23, designated the XM262; and an H-BAR AR-15, designated the XM106.

The AR-15/XM106 was created in 1978 by the Ballistic Research Laboratory at the Aberdeen Proving Ground and was apparently the end result of the marines' work toward developing an H-BAR rifle for use in their squads. Consequently, the XM106 was nearly identical to the army's standard M16Al but had the handguard permanently mounted in place, while a quick-change, detachable barrel unit was encased in it.

Some versions of the XM106 had the front sight base moved forward on the barrel to create a longer sighting radius; others had the sight at the normal position. A standard M14 M2 bipod was added to the center of the handguard with a pistol grip mounted under the barrel à la the Thompson submachine gun. The rear sight was originally a modified M60 machine gun assembly but was replaced with a leaf sight, which had settings for 300, 500, 800, and 1,000 meters.

The XM106 fed off regular 20- or 30-round magazines, though an 83-round drum magazine was created for it along with special "tri-mag" assemblies developed as a part of the WAK H-BAR project of 1977 (the tri-mag was simply three 30-round magazines joined together). With a cyclic rate of 750 rpm and a weight of 10.6 pounds (empty, with bipod), the XM106 was one of the lightest candidates in the trials.

Throughout the tests, the XM106 was used more as control against which the other machine guns were measured than an actual candidate, since it lacked the belt-feed mechanism that U.S. military tacticians maintained was essential for the SAW. In the end this was apparently one of the deciding factors against the XM106. Since all the entrants were required to have magazine wells for standard magazines—apparently so other members of the rifle squad could "feed" the machine gun with the magazines they carried—it has been argued that a belt-feed mechanism was not all that necessary. But it would seem that this was a moot point among the decision-makers involved in the project.

Another problem with the XM106 was the excessive modification necessary to make a quick-change barrel. Since the AR-15 design makes it quick and easy to simply remove the whole upper receiver, bolt carrier, and barrel assembly, it might have made more sense to use a modified standard receiver/barrel assembly and simply change the barrel and the upper receiver when the barrel overheated.

Given the lighter weight of the XM106, such a system would have created a lighter machine gun than the other candidates even with the added weight of a spare bolt, bolt carrier, and upper receiver. Even with an extremely heavy barrel assembly, the AR-15 would have weighed only in the neighborhood of 10.5 pounds. The 3-plus pounds saved over a system like the FN Minimi translates into 90 rounds of extra ammunition packed in magazines for a soldier carrying the SAW.

Furthermore, the only modification to speed up the release of the upper receiver would have been to weld knurled knobs to the front and rear push pins so that they could be quickly grasped and pulled free. Such a system would have also allowed the barrel to be sighted in beforehand—unlike the quick-barrel-change systems used for the other candidate weapons.

Although the Soviet Union and other former communist countries' weapons don't provide the best examples, it should be noted that their counterpart to the U.S. SAW, the RPKS-74, was generally fielded with a standard 40-round magazine or a 75-round drum magazine. This system continues to be used in armies of nations that were formerly part of the Soviet bloc. The RPKS-74 fires from a closed bolt and operates in the same manner as the standard rifle, so that little time is lost in training troops to operate the weapon. And most versions of the weapon don't have a detachable barrel. Likewise, Britain, England, Australia, Taiwan, and other countries have adopted similar weapons that feed from magazines, most based on a version of their rifles. All these systems seem to work quite well.

Two of Colt's H-BAR designs, with the most apparent change being from the earlier pistol-style vertical handguard (top) to the rounded grip shown on the lower rifle.

Colt's H-BAR guns proved to be good target rifles. Shown here are (top to bottom) the Model 6551 Match H-BAR, the Model 6600 Match H-BAR, the Model 6600DH Sporter Match Delta, the MT6551 Match Target Rifle, and the MT6601 Match Target H-BAR.

In the end, the detachable barrel and belt-feed capability won the day. The winner of the contests was the Fabrique Nationale Minimi, which became the M249 SAW in 1982 and was soon being issued at army squad level.

### Colt's H-BAR

During the 1980s, Colt modified its H-BAR design, increasing the size of the gas tube (to help prevent damage to it from overheating), as well as adding an FN FAL-style carrying handle on top, an M60 bipod, and a large square handguard with a pistol grip placed below it (the latter apparently coming from a molding created for the CMG-2). Internally, the gun had a hydraulic buffer system, and the trigger group was modified so that the H-BAR fired from an open bolt. Finally, the company added an adjustable sight, capable of compensating for bullet drop to 800 meters (this sight was later used on the M16A2 version of the AR-15).

In an effort to give the H-BAR machine gun more firepower, Colt purchased MWG's Ninety Round Magazine to add to the firearm. The MWG snail drum would give the gunner 90 shots before the magazine had to be changed and, unlike a belt system, was less apt to pull dirt or debris into the action of the machine gun during use. This system gave the firepower of an LMG coupled with only slightly greater weight than that of their standard rifle while enabling anyone who knew how to operate the standard rifle the ability to handle the H-BAR.

The 700-series of Colt firearms, which generally uses the M16A2 configuration, has several versions of the H-BAR as well; one fires from the closed bolt and is virtually identical to the "A2"-style guns in the 700 series except for the heavier barrel. Early sales literature on this family shows this H-BAR with an M60-style bipod; it seems likely that Colt's new bipod developed for the LMG version of the H-BAR will replace this. This standard handguard model of the H-BAR is often seen without any bipod. Since the heavy barrel also lends itself to a bit more accuracy than the standard rifle barrel, Colt offers this H-BAR as a target and sniper rifle. Colt even "dressed up" one semiauto version of the H-BAR with a Cherokee cheek rest, ARMS scope mount, and Tasco 4X-power scope intended for police, civilian, and military users. This rifle was marketed as the Delta.

Colt has also created another version of the H-BAR, working in conjunction with Diemaco of Canada, which manufacturers the Canadian military's AR-15 rifles. This version was designed to be used as an SAW and is based on Colt's H-BAR originally developed for the U.S. Marines. It has all M16A2 parts (rather than just the A2-style rear sight of the earlier version), retains the square handguard and heavy gas tube and front sight, replaces the M60 bipod with a lighter one of Colt's design, and has a ribbed vertical grip that is considerably more comfortable to use than the original angled grip. (Later models are often seen with a ribbed rather than smooth carrying handle, suggesting that this minor change will be present on future models in this series.)

This Colt-Diemaco version of the H-BAR was adopted by the Canadian army as the C7 machine gun (not to be confused with the C7 rifle), and the U.S. Marines are purchasing it in limited numbers to replace and upgrade their assortment of earlier M16A1-style H-BARs. Like the earlier version of this gun, it is often seen with MWG's 90-round magazine, and the Canadians have an extended 45-round magazine that can be used in pairs with the system. The Brazilian and El Salvadorian militaries have also purchased small quantities of this H-BAR LMG.

### Colt's Commando Submachine Guns

When Colt started adding to its CAR-15 military weapons systems, many in the company felt that a carbine version of the AR-15 would make an ideal weapon for personnel manning vehicles and crew-served weapons. The first attempt to create such a weapon was a modified rifle with a 16-inch barrel, with its front sight assembly moved back on the barrel, and a shortened set of beavertail handguards placed on it. This apparently worked well but wasn't pursued, possibly because it would have entailed tooling up for a new handguard assembly.

Instead, the engineers struck upon the idea of simply cutting the barrel of a standard rifle off just ahead of the front sight and threading the now-15-inch barrel so a standard flash hider could be placed on it. This was a simple process and gave the company a short, 6-pound carbine with a minimum of fuss. This firearm performed well once the gas port leading from the barrel was reamed to the same diameter of the gas tube to allow extra gas to travel rearward to cycle the bolt assembly; for even better reliability, parts were milled off the bolt carrier to lighten it. Despite its handy size, the carbine never sparked any interest among military buyers, and apparently only a few prototypes were ever made.

Perhaps taking off from the unsuccessful carbine project, Colt engineers working in 1965 produced the first AR-15 with both a shortened barrel and a telescoping stock. With a 10-inch barrel, this rifle weighed 5.3 pounds empty and was designed to replace pistol-caliber submachine guns—and indeed is often classed by firearms experts as a "submachine gun" even though it uses rifle ammunition rather than pistol ammunition as a true submachine gun does. Small numbers of this short AR-15 were soon being

Other H-BAR target rifles produced by Colt include the Model 6700 Sporter II H-BAR (top), Competition Sporter Model 6701 (center), and the CR6724 Colt Accurized Rifle.

sent to special forces troops in Vietnam for evaluation in the field.

The first version of this submachine gun had a standard-shaped handguard and stock that, when the stock was in its short position, made it look as if it were a regular rifle somehow scaled down to child size. It was 26 inches long with the stock closed and 28.7 inches long open. Handguards were usually chopped beavertail rifle handguards, with grip thickness determined by whether the original handguards were cut down from the front or rear.

Much the same was done with the stock, which had its release mechanism in the buttplate of the small carbine. Early models of this submachine gun had the pistol grip cut slightly short and were built around the M16 pattern and lacked a forward assist. These generally used the standard duckbill flash hider. Later versions had a full-size pistol grip.

The first experimental models Colt produced suffered from excessive muzzle flash and noise with the standard flash hider. It soon became obvious that a special flash/noise suppressor was called for, and one was soon designed for the short-barreled CAR-15, greatly improving the operation of the weapon. The big drawback to this muzzle attachment was its tight exit hole, which tended to become coated with copper and often "snuffed out" tracers so that they failed to burn when exiting. The suppressor also had a tendency to get clogged up with extended firing, so it eventually failed to lower muzzle noise to any great extent. Eventually these devices were replaced by a design that would remain effective for a longer period.

This weapon had a very handy length, but the short barrel produced several problems. Since the regular-length AR-15 had been designed to have its powder mostly consumed when it reached the gas tube, the shortened barrel of the submachine gun CAR-15 created excessive blast when unburned powder exited the barrel. This reduced the velocity of the bullet to 2,750 fps rather than the normal 3,000-plus fps of the regular rifle (which wasn't too great a problem at close ranges where a submachine gun is normally employed).

A more serious problem was that the unburned gases entered the gas tube and caused excess fouling in the chamber area. This, coupled with the faster cycling of the action because of the shorter gas tube, meant that if the gun wasn't cleaned rigorously, it would often suffer from jamming problems. Nevertheless, the handy length of the submachine gun made it attractive for personnel working in vehicles or operating equipment, so Colt continued developing the rifle.

In 1965 Colt also introduced a 29-inch survival rifle, which was designed to be taken down into two parts and stored on U.S. Air Force planes for emergency use. Although the stock on the 4.75-pound rifle is shaped like telescoping stocks that later appeared on Colt's Commandos, in fact it was a fixed stock. To save space, the standard pistol grip on the survival rifle was cut to a shorter length to make it fit into the tight space provided for it. The gun was to have been stored with one 20-round magazine in place and three more 20-round magazines in reserve.

Two models of the survival rifle were created, one with a very stubby pistol grip and a cone-style flash hider, the other with a slightly longer (but not full-size) pistol grip and a more conventional flash hider. Both had 10-inch barrels. No military group ever expressed interest in the Survival Rifle, and fewer than 10 were ever manufactured.

Applying the lessons learned with these two cut-down versions of the CAR-15, Colt introduced the Commando submachine gun in 1966, and the military ordered 2,815 of these for testing. As part of the CAR-15 weapons system," these guns had the round ribbed handguard that Colt had developed for its family of firearms rather than the wide beavertail handguard then on the M16 rifles.

Since Colt was pushing the short submachine gun as a member of its CAR-15 weapons system, the company designation eventually led to a rather confusing mix-up when the compact gun was being tested by the U.S. special forces. Its official designation of CAR-15 Commando Model Submachine Gun was a mouthful that few in the military wanted to go around saying day in and day out, and soon army personnel were simply calling it the CAR-15 even though technically that could mean any of six or more versions of the AR-15 that Colt had created. The confusion about the correct name for the Commando has persisted, with many shooters, writers, and even manufacturers of non-Colt versions of the AR-15 adopting the CAR-15 misnomer in reference to short Commando-style carbines.

### Birth of the XM177

The Commando guns were delivered with standard open-front flash hiders, and testing at Aberdeen suggested the noise level of these guns was excessive and should be lowered to prevent injuring the firers' hearing. Colt quickly went to the drawing board and developed a slightly longer flash hider/noise suppressor with internal baffles capable of reducing the muzzle blast to nearly the same level that the AR-15 rifle had with a barrel twice as long. These new devices met with approval, and the Commandos were refitted with them and delivered. This model was designated the XM177E1 by the U.S. Army. ("XM" stood for "eXperiMental," and the "177" was used to take it out of the M16, XM16E1, and M16A1 series of development numbers to prevent confusion. "E1" showed that the system had a forward assist like the army's rifle.)

The air force was also interested in purchasing these guns and soon had an almost identical gun—without the forward assist on the receiver (just as the air force's AR-15 rifle didn't have a forward assist). The air force version was designated the XM177.

Both the XM177 and XM177E1 had 10-inch barrels, and each had an empty weight of 5.5 pounds and a cyclic rate described in Colt's sales brochures as "650 to 850 rounds per minute." (The speed differences most likely were attributable to the type of ammunition used with the rifle.) This new carbine had a telescoping stock that looked similar to the fixed stock of the Colt survival rifle (Model 608) and was built on an earlier short barreled, telescoping gun, the Model 607 (which at first glance might easily have been mistaken for a toy version of the rifle). With the stock in its short position the Commando was 28.3 inches long; with the stock extended it was 31 inches long.

During this same period Colt produced several experimental models of the Commando, which no major buyers expressed an interest in purchasing. These models were created with a four-position selector (safe, semi, auto, and burst) and sometimes had ribbed barrels hidden under the handguards—apparently in an effort to dissipate heat, since barrel temperatures become excessive after extended firing with the short barrels.

In 1967, the Commando was modified slightly by giving it an 11.5-inch barrel that allowed the use of a grenade launcher—and, more important, made it more reliable; the short barrel seemed to produce malfunctions in cycling, especially in automatic fire. Colt upgraded its flash/noise suppressor at this point as well. This new version was redesignated Colt's Commando XM177E2; the army ordered 510 of these new guns for use by the Military Assistance Command-Study and Observation Group (MAC-SOG). The air force version of the

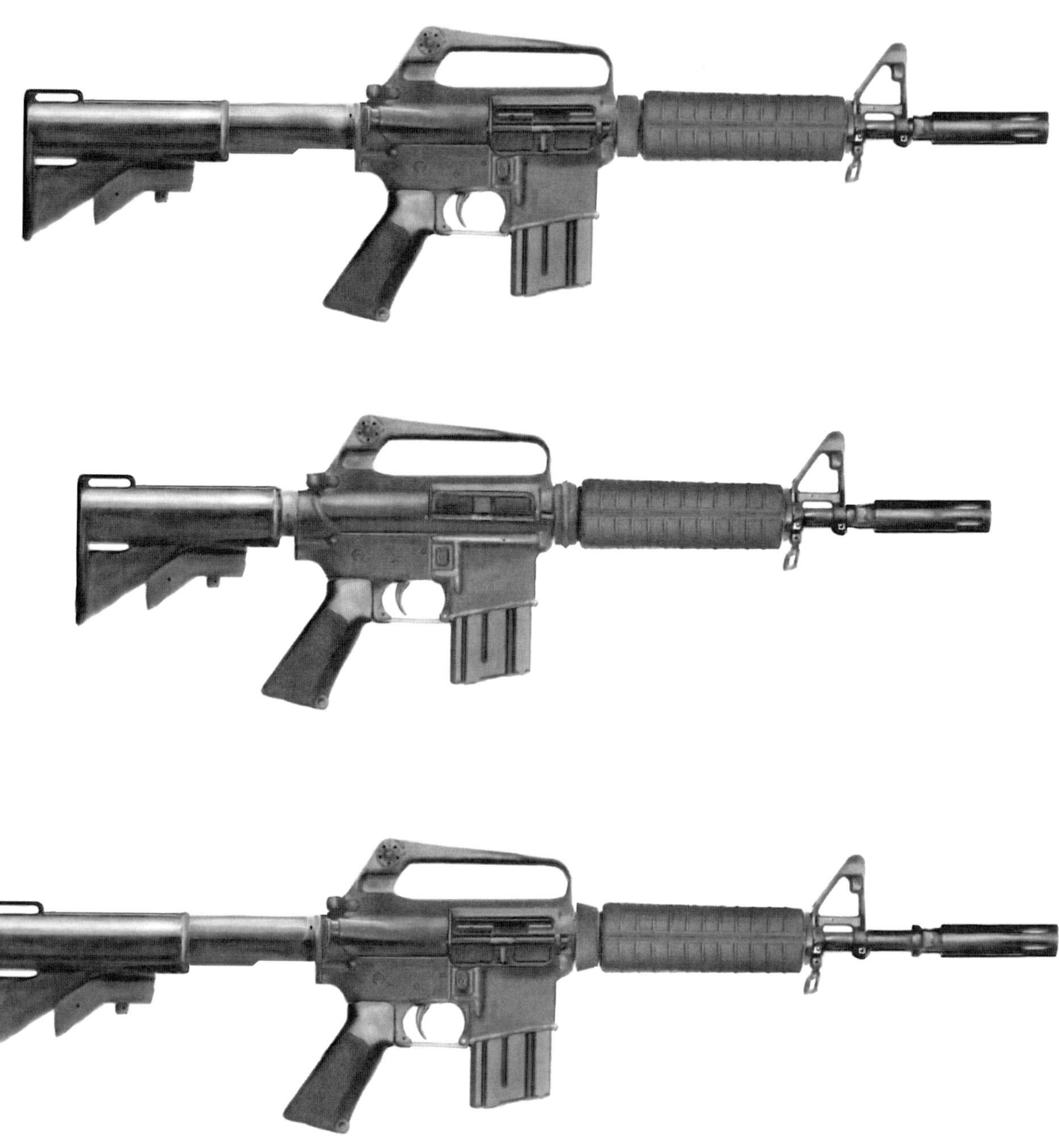

The Commando (top) XM177E1 (Colt Model 609), the Model RO610B (center) with a four-position selector, and the XM177E2 (Model 639).

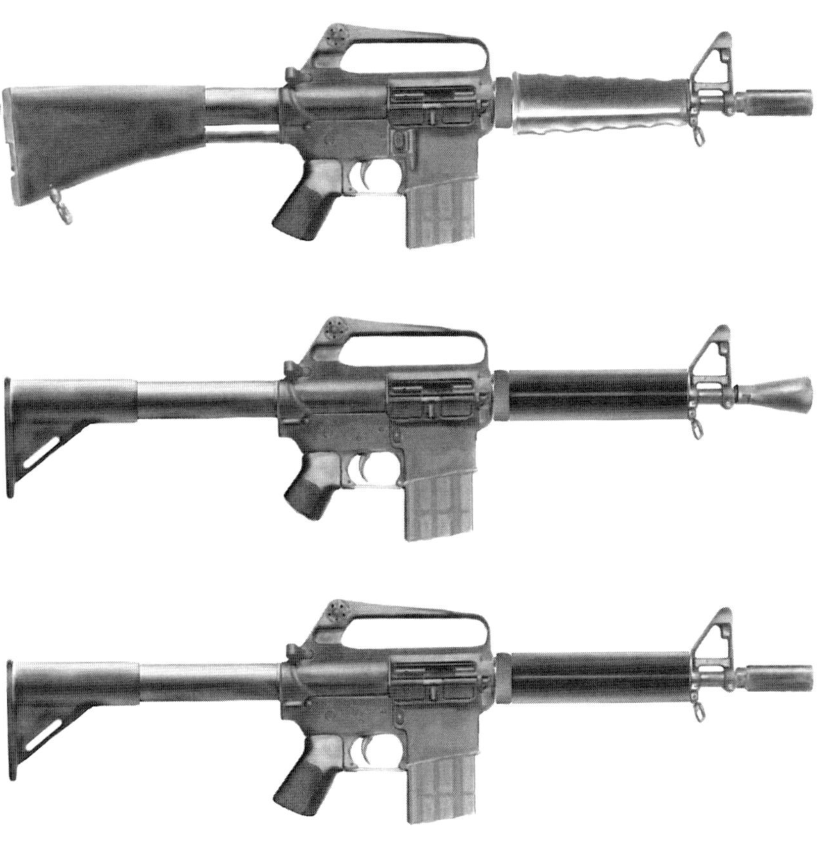

The telescoping stock Model 607 (top) and two versions of the Model 608, which would eventually lead to the XM177 "submachine gun" versions of the M16 rifle.

The Colt 607A proved that the basic concept for the Commando was sound. This version had a forward assist and a special "low-noise" muzzle brake.

Commando was also modified with a barrel 1 inch longer barrel at this time, but still without the forward assist. It is generally seen with its original designation, though it sometimes is referred to as the GAU-5/A/A.

With U.S. involvement in Vietnam winding down, military planners did not see the Commando as a priority weapon, and the buying programs proposed to purchase more of the submachine guns were placed on hold. Oddly enough, while military leaders considered the Commando ineffective because of its short barrel and low muzzle velocity, those in the field who actually carried the weapon, including Special Forces, SEALs, and LRRP units, were generally very pleased with it. The short firearm was seen in the hands of Special Forces during the 1983 invasion of Grenada and was apparently used by air force security units, army Special Forces, and the Rangers for some time until the M4 carbine officially replaced it.

Interestingly, in the mid-1970s the suppressors on the Commandos were classified by the BATF as silencers because they lowered the muzzle blast. This quite possibly made the Commando's suppressor one of the noisiest "silencers" ever created: its muzzle noise was equal to that of a standard AR-15—hardly quiet by any stretch of the imagination. Surplus units were ordered destroyed when the Commandos were retired from the U.S. inventory.

The "silencer" situation on the Commando would have been funny if not for the fact that the Carter administration, in what many saw as a mood of sanctimony, issued an edict that silencers were not to be exported from the United States on the grounds that such devices were

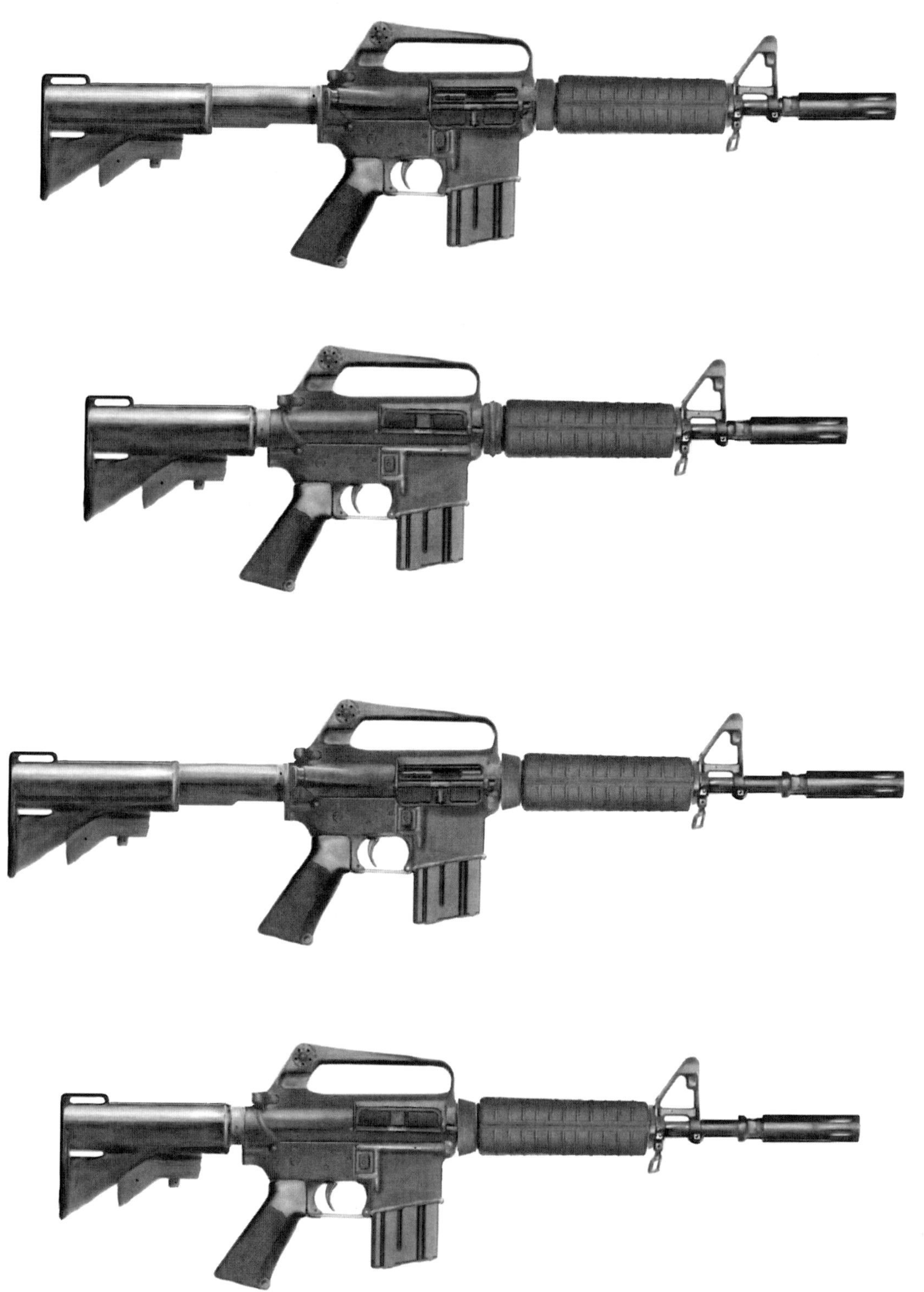

(Top to bottom) Colt's Commando 609, 610B, and the 639, which would become the U.S. Army's XM177E2. Bottom gun is the Model 649, adopted by the air force as the GAU-5/A/A.

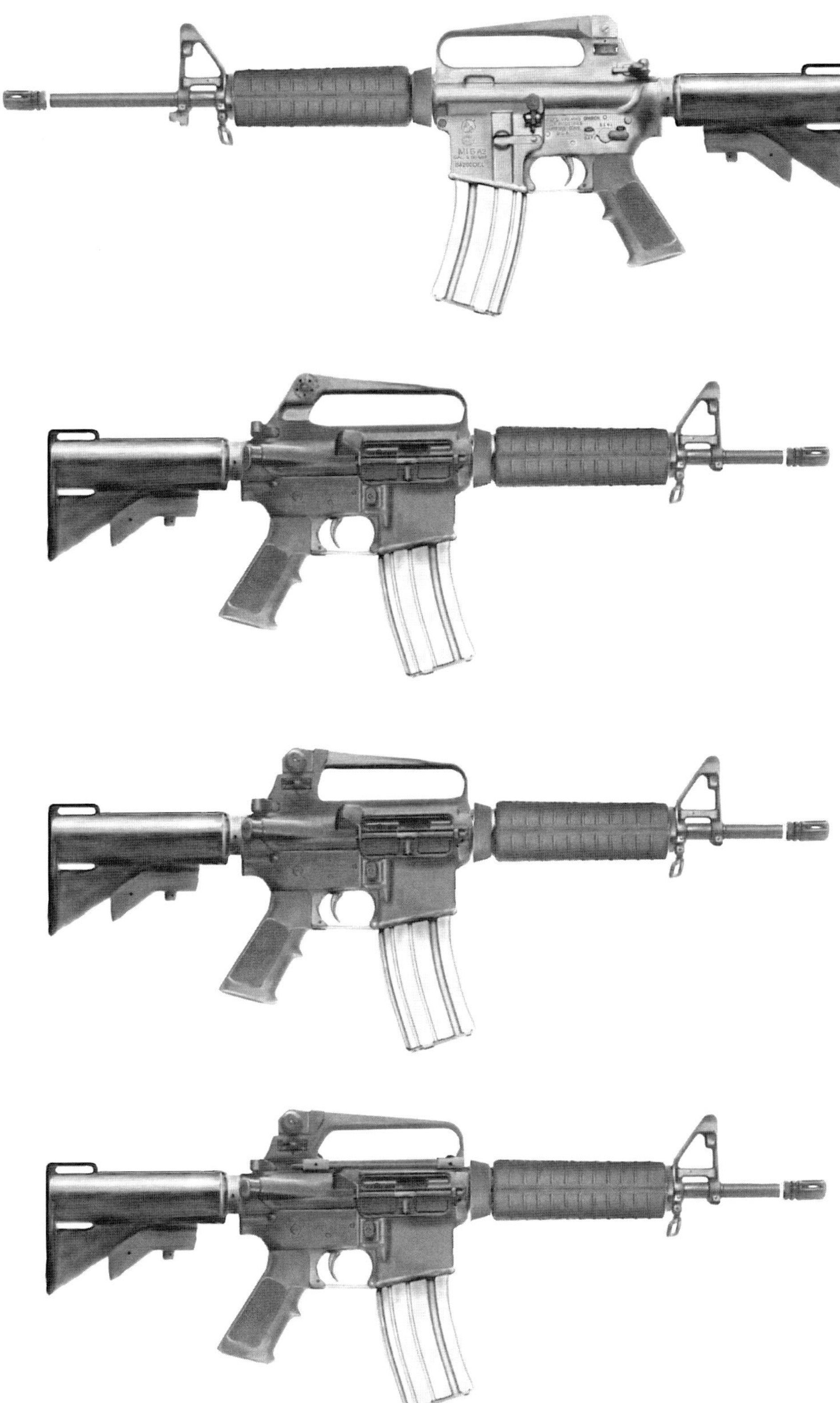

The Commando continues to be in the Colt product lineup. Shown here (top to bottom): Export Model 723 with built-on A2 receiver, Model 733 (A1 receiver), Model 735, and Model 933 with a flat-top receiver.

immoral (something that no doubt came as a surprise to those using them in Vietnam). This meant that Colt was no longer able to export the Commandos with the "silencers" required to tame the short-barreled weapon's muzzle blast.

Because the military wasn't placing orders for the Commandos and Colt could no longer export them, the company was forced to discontinue manufacturing the suppressors, and that brought foreign military sales to a near standstill, since the guns were brutally loud without the muzzle attachment. The result was an end to what many thought was the handiest carbine ever issued to U.S. military personnel.

### Improving on the Commando

Fortunately, Colt didn't abandon the basic idea behind the design. Soon selective-fire Commandos, less the effective suppressor, were being marketed with 11.5-, 14.5-, and 16-inch barrels along with a semiauto version aimed at the civilian market, which was sold as the Sporter Carbine.

While the 11.5-inch barrel was too noisy and the 16-inch too long for most military users, the telescoping stock coupled with a 14.5-inch barrel on an M16A1 or M16A2 receiver proved to be as popular as the original Commando, with the U.S. military as well as in Israel and elsewhere. Even with a regular flash hider, muzzle blast is not excessive with the 14.5-inch barrel, and the added length increased the muzzle velocity, allowing the weapon to be more effective at greater ranges than the 10- and 11.5-inch-barreled guns had ever have been. In addition to being sold with the telescoping stock, some of these guns are also available with the standard M16A1 or even the long M16A2 stocks; all models have the ribbed, round handguard.

In the civilian market, Colt offered the 16-inch version of the Commando with a semiauto-only receiver similar to their Sporter rifle series. This carbine had a standard flash hider and a telescoping stock. Later the company withdrew this version and reworked it by modifying the bolt carrier, removing the bayonet lug, and replacing the telescoping stock with a fixed stock; and reintroduced it to the American public as the Sporter Lightweight Rifle.

Colt had been experimenting with 9mm versions of the Commando for some time, possibly in an effort to cut into the markets that H & K's MP5 series of guns and the Israeli Uzi had almost totally divided between themselves. With the growing acceptance of the 9mm cartridge among law enforcement personnel in the

Although civilian sales of the telescoping stock version of the Sporter Carbine have ceased due to the federal assault weapon ban, Colt still offers the gun to law enforcement buyers as the Model 6520 Government Carbine (top) and the detachable carrying handle/flat-top Model 6721 Tactical Carbine.

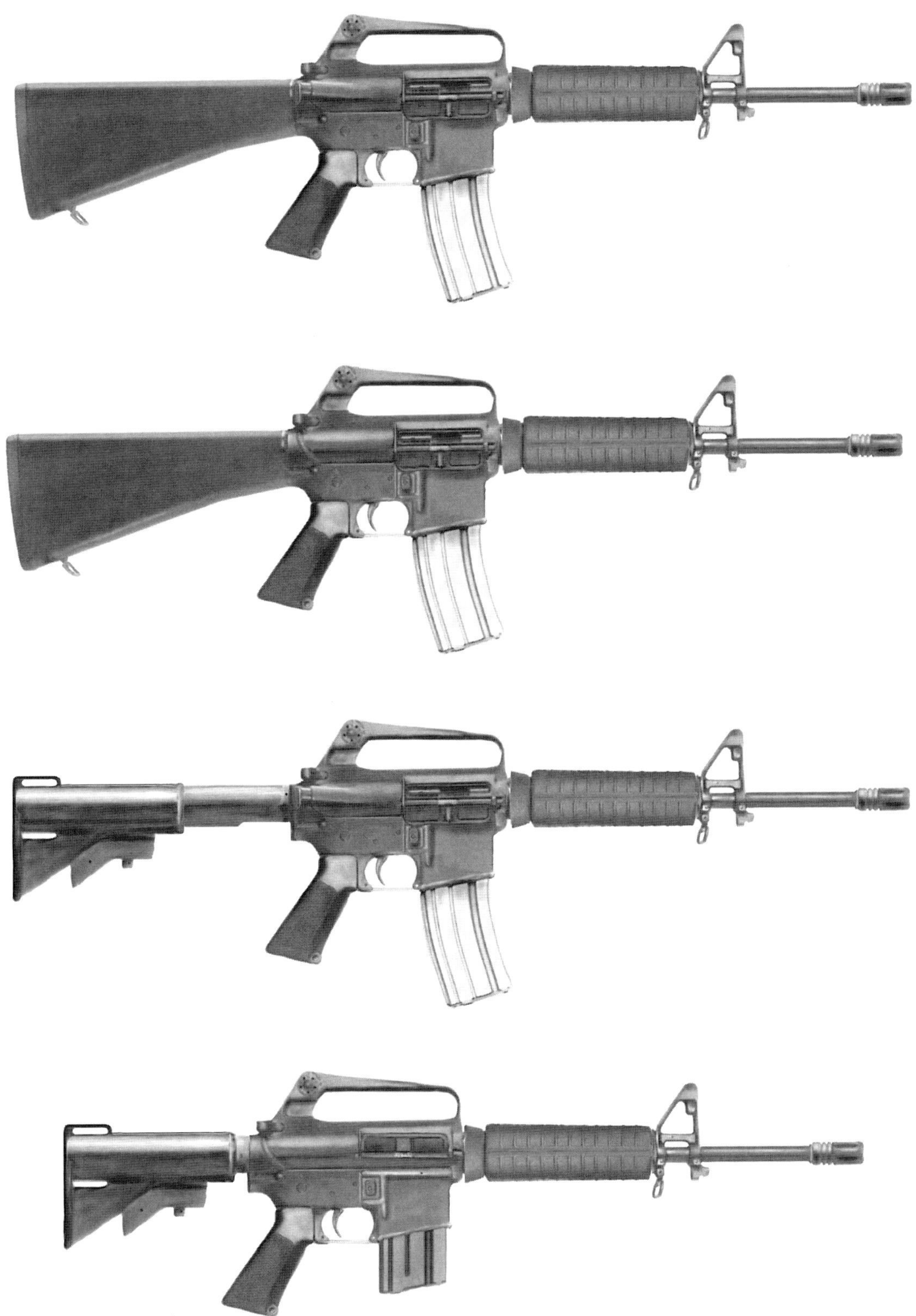

Colt markets carbines with both standard and telescoping stocks with a variety of barrel lengths. Shown here (top to bottom): The Models 651, 652, 653, and 654, all with 14.5-inch barrels.

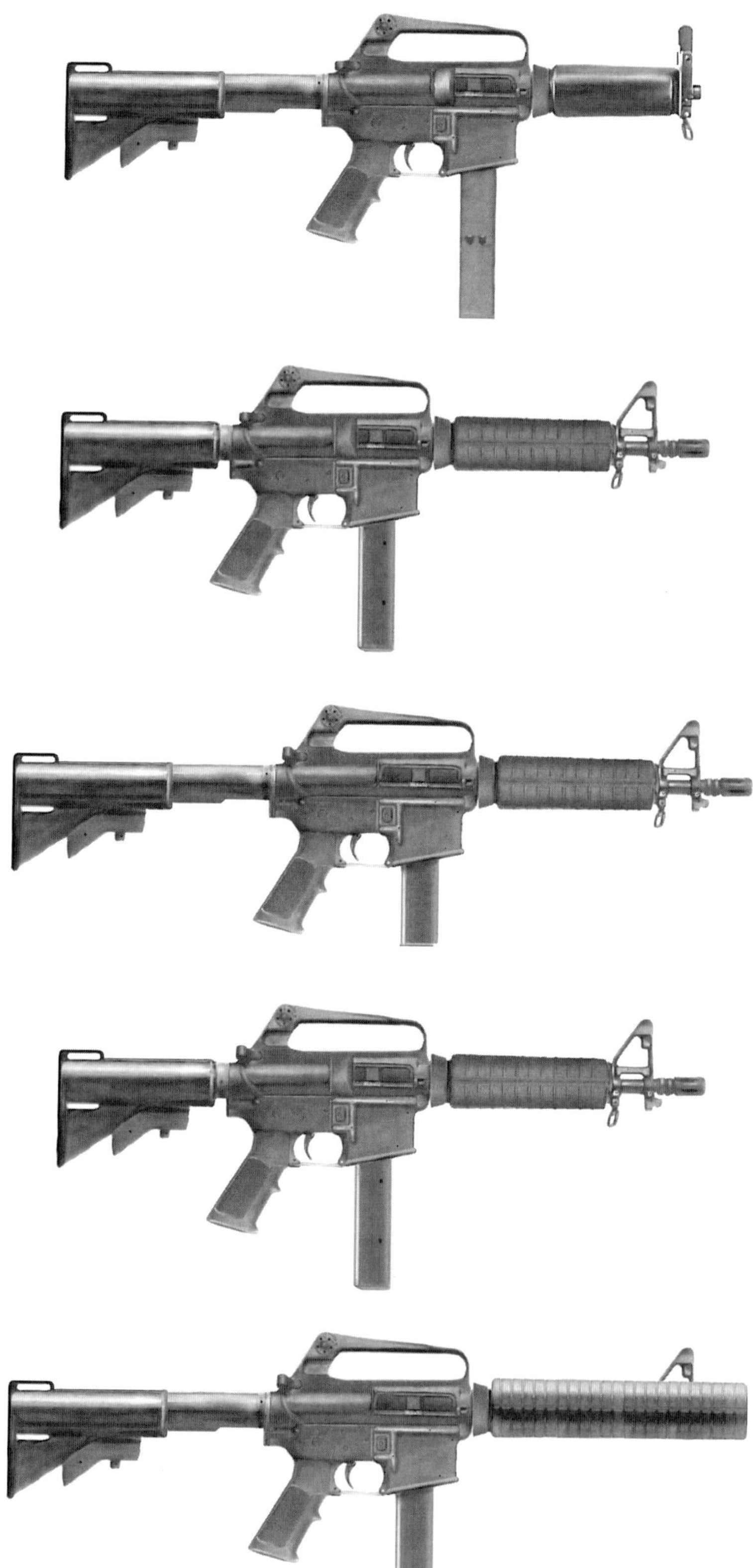

Colt's 9mm submachine guns (top to bottom): Models 633, 634, 635, and 639, and the DEA model.

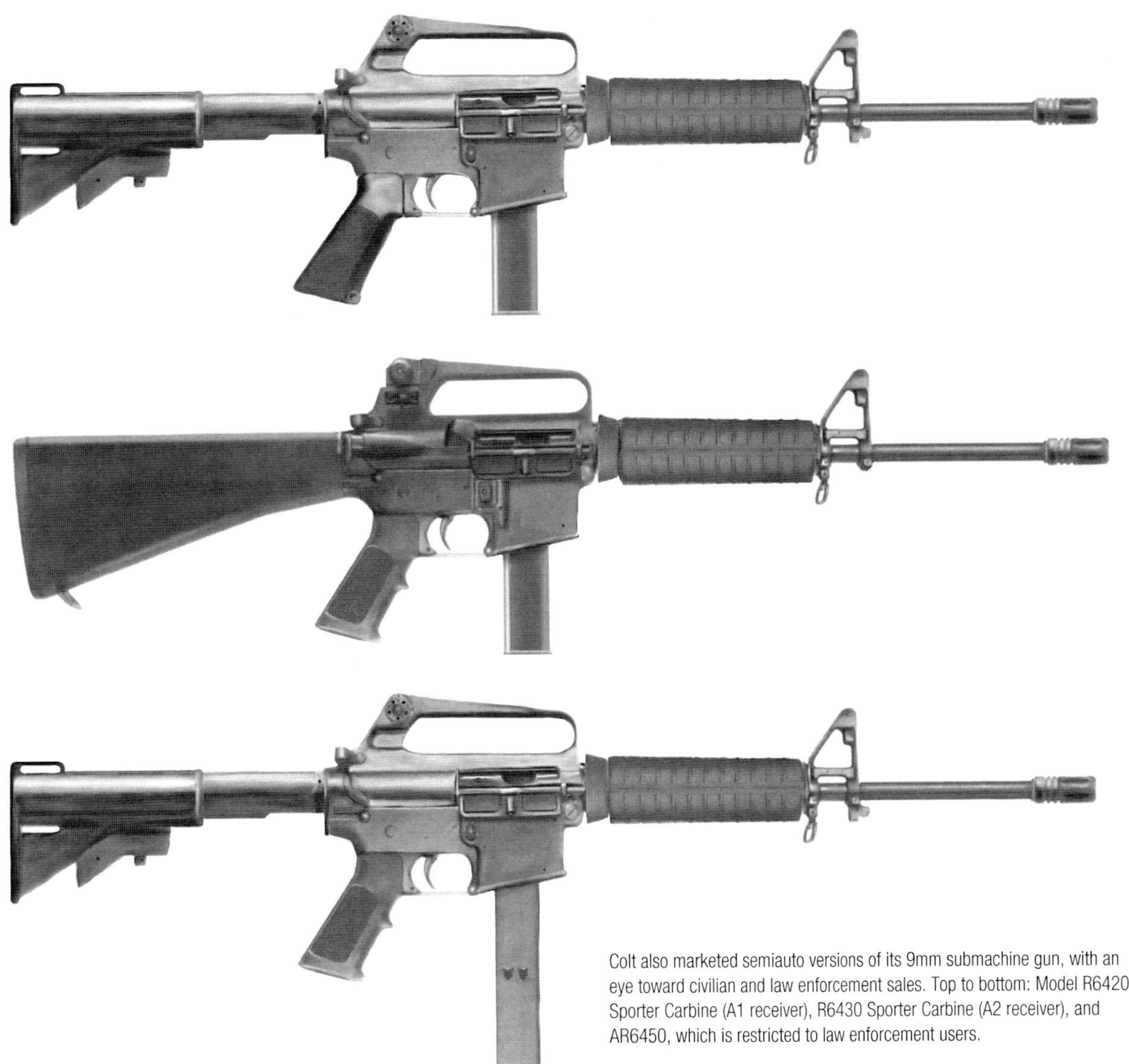

Colt also marketed semiauto versions of its 9mm submachine gun, with an eye toward civilian and law enforcement sales. Top to bottom: Model R6420 Sporter Carbine (A1 receiver), R6430 Sporter Carbine (A2 receiver), and AR6450, which is restricted to law enforcement users.

United States as well as the switch to the cartridge by the U.S. military, it wasn't surprising in 1985 when Colt introduced some 9mm Commando-style guns, which were true submachine guns since they fired a pistol cartridge, operating by blow-back with the bolt never locking. This design dispensed with the gas system of the firearm as well as with the need for an expensive bolt assembly.

Colt's 9mm submachine gun used a regular M16A1 upper receiver with a large cartridge deflector behind its ejection port (which necessitated cutting off the rear portion of the ejection port cover). The lower receiver and many of the internal parts were standard AR-15 assemblies with only the barrel, magazine (a modified Uzi design), parts of the trigger group, and bolt being of a slightly different design. A lower receiver insert adapted the magazine well to the narrower 9mm magazine. The gun used the standard telescoping stock and handguard of the Commando and was first seen with a 14-inch barrel, although the 10-inch barrel has become the one often seen in actual use. All of these barrels sport an AR-15 birdcage flash hider.

The 9mm submachine gun offered a distinct advantage for those used to the AR-15, since its sights, selector, magazine release, charging handle and general handling characteristics were all identical to its parent rifle. In addition to the submachine gun, Colt also produced a very limited number of ribbed silencer/handguard 9mm submachine guns, giving an option of reduced recoil and much quieter operation.

A third model, a 16-inch barrel semiauto version, was also produced for the civilian market. Two magazines were available for this gun, with 20- and 32-round capacities.

In the early 1990s the U.S. Drug Enforcement Agency (DEA) adopted both the standard and silenced versions of the 9mm submachine gun for its agents, and at the time of this writing the firearm is under evaluation by several military contractors at home and abroad. (Sources at Colt are uncertain whether the silenced version of the 9mm AR-15 will see more than very limited production.)

In the late 1980s Colt withdrew the semiauto civilian version of the 9mm carbine from the from the marketplace, perhaps to placate the antigun legislators in the U.S. Congress who apparently thought the gun "looked like a submachine gun" because of its telescoping stock. In 1992, a "sanitized" version of the 9mm semiauto carbine was reintroduced with a standard stock, rather than the telescoping stock that many in Congress apparently thought only criminals should own. This wholesome model also lacked a bayonet mount on its front sight assembly (which had been useless on the earlier model because of the 16-inch barrel) and was sold as the Sporter Carbine.

M4 carbine fired during a joint training session at a firing range in Lazarevica, Republika Srpska, Bosnia, on December 8, 1999. (Courtesy of Department of Defense.)

Although Colt has a pistol-caliber 9mm carbine version of the AR-15 available, it seems unlikely that it will follow the lead of other manufacturers and create a .45 ACP, .40, or 10mm version of its own (of these the .40 is the most likely, given its use by some law enforcement agencies and police departments). From a ballistic standpoint, the .223 seems to do much better than these other cartridges, so there is really little reason from a tactical standpoint to employ another cartridge or create conversions of the basic AR-15 system.

### The Abu Dhabi Carbine

In the military market, 1987 saw Colt's introduction of the "Abu Dhabi" carbine, which has since become very popular. This gun had a heavier than usual (for carbines) 14.5-inch barrel with a small groove around the barrel just ahead of the front sight, allowing the weapon to accept the M203 grenade launcher while still keeping the barrel heavy enough to combat quick heat buildup. The total weight of the gun was increased to only 6 pounds, keeping it a very handy weapon.

The Abu Dhabi carbine used the A2-style sights and was generally seen with a four-position selector (with both burst and auto positions). With the 14.5-inch barrel and SS109 ammunition, the muzzle velocity was 3,020 fps, giving it a more respectable range than had been enjoyed by the 10- or 11.5-inch Commando submachine guns.

This new barrel length yielded a happy compromise between range and weight and created a compact firearm that, like the M1 carbine before it, a user could fall in love with (especially if the gun had to carried all day or in the field). The capacity for a grenade launcher was the frosting on the cake, weighing less in comparison with a full-size rifle carrying the ungainly M203 launcher.

### The M4 Carbine

The U.S. military soon purchased some of the Abu Dhabi models for tests as the XM4 carbine and was favorably impressed. Soon the marines requested modifications to the basic layout and adopted it as their M4 Carbine. The army initiated its own tests of the system and soon followed the marines' lead.

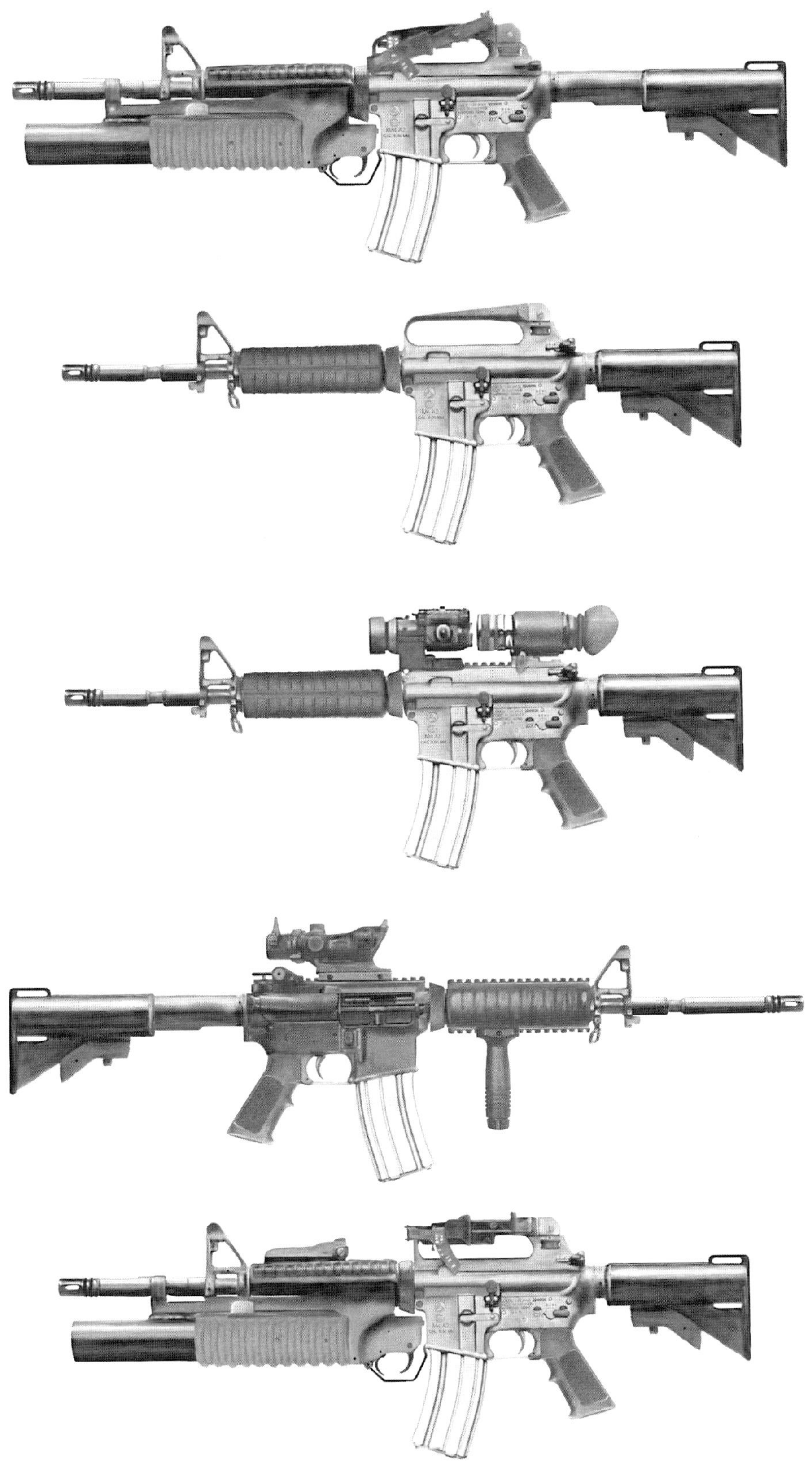

Top to bottom: XM4 (with modified grenade launcher), M4A1, M4 (shown with dot and night vision scopes), M4 with Special Operations Peculiar Modification (SPOMOD) accessories, and M4 with grenade launcher designed for it.

In 1994 the U.S. Army officially adopted the M4, technically making it the carbine in the hands of GIs during the 20th century, though in reality the Commando or one form or another of the shorty was seen in the hands of special forces or others from Vietnam on. With this adoption the M3 "grease gun" submachine gun (which fired the .45 ACP cartridge) was officially retired, replaced by the M4. Interestingly, the army also noted that the M4 would be replacing some of its M9 semiautomatic pistols as well as M16A2 rifles among those who had formerly been issued these weapons.

The adoption of the M4 after so much questioning of the effectiveness of earlier "submachine gun" and other shorty versions of the gun may seem like an odd shift in logic. However, a look at the muzzle velocities produced by various lengths of barrels and with old and new cartridges shows why the M4 carbine with the new SS109 ammunition is considerably more effective than earlier guns with shorter barrels.

**Muzzle Velocities and Energy by Barrel Length**

| Barrel Length (inches) | Muzzle Velocity (55- grain bullet – fps) | Muzzle Energy (55-grain bullet – foot-pounds of energy) | Muzzle Velocity (52- grain bullet – fps) | Muzzle Energy (62-grain bullet – foot-pounds of energy) |
|---|---|---|---|---|
| 10 | 2,739 | 916 | 2,627 | 950 |
| 11.5 | 2,872 | 1,007 | 2,738 | 1,032 |
| 14.5 | 3,064 | 1,146 | 2,907 | 1,163 |
| 16 | 3,132 | 1,198 | 2,989 | 1,230 |
| 20 | 3,259 | 1,297 | 3,095 | 1,318 |

As can be seen from this table the M4 carbine, coupled with the new SS109 bullet, operates at about 125 percent of the older shorty versions and, when compared with the older M16 firing a 55-grain bullet, comes very close to the older performance that proved so effective in Vietnam. Added to this is the greater support foot soldiers can expect from aircraft, artillery, and smart munitions in general, making them even less dependent on long-range engagements than in the past. All in all, the adoption of the lighter, shorter M4 over its larger rifle counterpart makes good sense, especially for soldiers already overburdened with equipment.

Little wonder, then, that at the time of this writing the M4 is also displacing the M16A2 in the hands of some soldiers. Both the 82nd Airborne and 101st Airborne Divisions are generally issuing the carbine rather than the rifle to soldiers, a factor that undoubtedly makes parachute jumps a bit less hazardous due to the more manageable size of the carbine. Use of the M4 instead of a pistol by officers makes a heavier bundle to carry; however, it also provides a better weapon and, perhaps more important, makes it harder for snipers to spot and single out officers.

The only question that remains is whether the M4 will become the general-issue weapon, with the full-size rifle becoming a special-purpose gun similar to the M203 and SAW. This might make sense, yet it seems likely that the old idea of soldiers being armed with full-sized rifles will die hard.

An army assessment of the rifle and carbine in mid-1990 found that soldiers shooting at targets at 300 meters actually scored 11 percent better with M4s than they did with the M16A2 (a surprise, given the shorter sighting radius of the carbine). Scores were 43 percent with the M16A2 in contrast to 54 percent with the M4. However, the picture is a bit muddied because the army conducted another test with shooters firing at 500 meters, with the M16A2 scoring hits 26 percent of the time, compared with 16 percent for the M4 in this test. The catch? Some suggest that the army was up to its old tricks in the latter test, skewing the results by using shooters unaccustomed to firing from 500 meters (and the extreme range would give the rifle an edge).

More tests conducted by the army in 1992 concluded that the M16A2 (and M16A4, which was also tested) only outperformed the M4 at extreme ranges; their rounds were able to penetrate helmets out to 567 meters, whereas the M4 could do so only out to 505 meters. Against flak vests, the rifles performed to 1,785 meters while the M4 did so at 1,725 meters, making the latter test somewhat moot.

As noted earlier, since the majority of combat takes place within 150 meters and rarely beyond 300 meters, the M4 is every bit as good as a rifle in terms of actual combat conditions. And it does this while weighing in at more than a pound lighter and with a shorter, easier to handle length. All the reasons are there for the M4 to replace its sister weapon, but old ideas die hard.

The air force and navy adopted their own versions of the M4 carbine shortly after the army did. These guns are nearly identical to those of the army and marines, but early versions employed M16A1 rear sights; this version was also designated the M4 (Model 723). Consequently there were three distinct versions of the M4, including one with A1 sights, the other original M4 carbines, and one with A2 sights and (what appears to have become more common) a subvariant with the detachable carrying handle/flat-top rail mount on the upper receiver.

Little by little, however, the A2 sight system has replaced the A1 configuration. It seems likely that fewer of the A1 sights on M4 carbines will be seen as time goes on, with the detachable-sight/flat-top version the one the U.S. military is now purchasing because it permits the easy mounting of a variety of accessories on the weapon.

The A2 sights on the M4 are a bit different from the M16A2 as far as calibration is concerned. Generally, the

M4 has elevation adjustments to 600 meters, while the M16A2 permits adjustments out to 800.

As is often the case, more than a little confusion on the naming of the M4 carbine arose before its adoption, with early guns being called M16A2 carbines (usually the Model 720) as well as XM4 carbines. In the meantime, the U.S. Army also adopted an M4A1 version in 1994, and (just to keep things a bit confusing) this gun has A2-style sights (generally with a flat-top receiver like the M4). The only difference between the two guns being that the M4 has the three-position burst selector, while the M4A1 has a three-position selector that has safe, semi, and auto positions without a three-round burst mode.

Ironically, Colt lost one of the contracts to build the M4 to Bushmaster Firearms/Quality Parts when the small company underbid Colt and received a contract to build 3,000 of the new carbines for the navy SEALs and army Special Forces in 1991.

Other variants of the shorty carbine are seen in the hands of military users worldwide, with Colt still offering the 11.5-inch Commando in what is otherwise an M4 configuration. Another likely substitute is the M4-style gun with a four-position selector offering a three-round burst as well as full-auto positions in addition to safe and semiauto fire.

The M4 and its spin-offs have a large number of accessories, made practical by the removable carrying handle/rear sight. Removing this handle gives the user what has come to be known as the flat-top receiver, which has a built-in Weaver-style rail that can be employed to mount a telescopic site, dot scope, night-vision scope, and laser site, as well as (there's always one more accessory to be sold) a flip-up iron sight (which, in fairness, is more useful than the carrying handle assembly, since it can be mounted in conjunction with a scope to serve as backup should the device fail).

Currently the U.S. Special Operations Command has issued a special operations peculiar modification (SOPMOD) kit for the M4 carbine. This kit includes the following:

- Rail interface system
- Four-power scope
- CQB reflex sight
- Infrared and visible laser sight/designator
- Suppressor (aka "silencer")
- Modified M-203 grenade launcher
- Night vision scope
- Carrying case for the above accessories

Since the Fabrique Nationale has secured several M16A2 contracts, it is not surprising that the firm has also developed several key accessories that are often found on the U.S. military's M4 carbines. These have become known as the floating integrated rail mounted (FIRM) system, made possible through the use of a sleeve that mounts around the handguard of the carbine. Once in place, this sleeve has a series of rails to which a laser sight, forward grip, or other accessories can be secured. This gives the shooter the ability not only to customize the weapon but also to add otherwise unattachable accessories. The FIRM has become standard issue for the M4, with kits of accessories generally being issued to squads carrying the weapon.

The FIRM system is also sometimes referred to as the modular weapon system (MWS). The MWS was the brainchild of Knight's Manufacturing Company (which is also well known for its silencers, as well as for being the marketer of the Stoner S25 rifles). Having taken nearly 10 years of research and development to perfect, the MWS was adopted by the U.S. Army, type classified, and thereafter quickly deployed to Special Forces for use

M4 carbine with some of the SOPMOD attachments, including rail interface, dot scope, and vertical forward grip.

on the M4 carbine. The key feature of the MWS is its precision machined aluminum Picatinny rail that permits scopes, lasers, or other accessories mounted on it to maintain their bore alignment. A side benefit is that the unit acts as a heat sink, thereby cooling the barrel of a carbine that has a lot of rounds put through it in a short time. While the conventional handguard is able to handle this, often it comes close to the proverbial "too hot to handle" condition, making the MWS a welcome addition for this reason as well.

For special operations users, a suppressor is sometimes also issued with the M4. This unit became standardized in 1997 and is currently being built by Knight's (Gem-Tech is offering a similar unit with a view toward other military users and civilian sales). Currently designated the M4-96D suppressor, this unit has a diameter of 1.5 inches with an overall length of 6.2 inches and a weight of 20 ounces. It is attached to the firearm with the threading that normally holds the flash hider on the M4.

Provided that special subsonic ammunition is employed in conjunction to the M4-96D, these units are capable of reducing the noise signature by 30 decibels (dB), thereby bringing it down to the report of a .22 LR. True, this is far from quiet (unlike in the movies where silencers generally live up to their name), but the reduction is enough for those wishing to operate more or less covertly.

Heat buildup during extended automatic fire is sometimes a problem with carbines, including the M4; handguards can become uncomfortably hot. To address this, Colt and other manufacturers have developed a

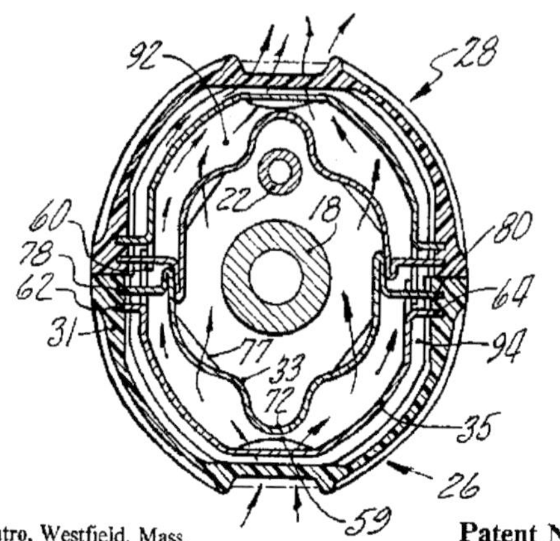


Patent drawing of Colt's double-liner handguard system.

Colt also offers versions of the M4 carbine to the law enforcement community. Shown here is the Model LE6920 (top) with a profiled, 16-inch barrel, and the LE6921 with 14.5-inch barrel. Both guns fire in semiauto mode only.

(Top to bottom) XM231, first M231, second without rear sight, and final M231, which lacks sights and stock.

variety of systems to help cool the barrel. One solution is the double heat shield patented by Colt. Another is the simple expedient of using an aluminum free-floating handguard or aluminum rail attachment, either of which tends to soak up and dissipate heat.

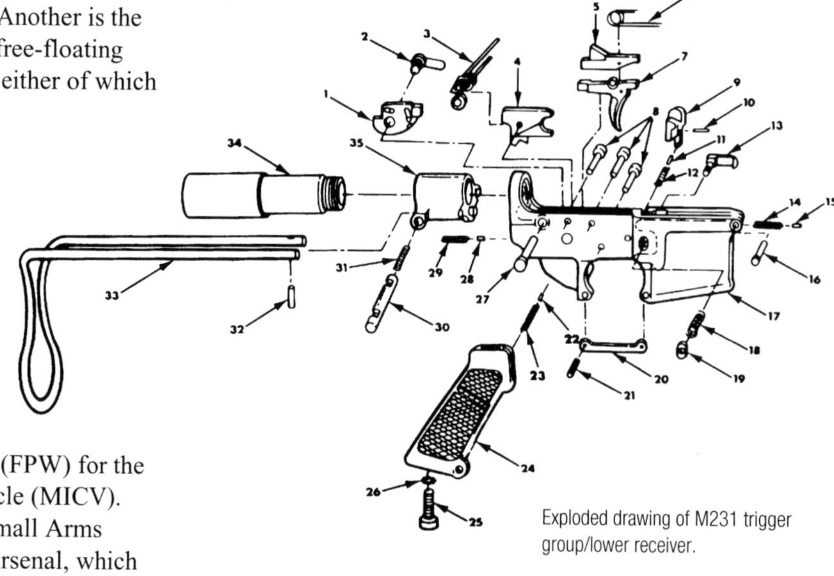

Exploded drawing of M231 trigger group/lower receiver.

### M231 Port Firing Weapon

The mechanization of the infantry during recent decades has created the need for a weapon that can be fired from the cramped quarters of an armored personnel carrier. Work was started on creating a modified AR-15 for U.S. military vehicles in 1972, when the army started experimenting with a firing port weapon (FPW) for the XM72 mechanized infantry combat vehicle (MICV). Much of this work was handled by the Small Arms Systems Laboratory at the Rock Island Arsenal, which ran tests involving the M3A1 "grease gun" chambered in .45 ACP, the H&K 33 chambered in .223 Remington, and a modified AR-15 chambered in .223.

The modified AR-15 proved most promising. It was designated the XM231 in 1974, and Colt was offered a contract for further development of the weapon. Firing from an open bolt, the original XM231 had an 11-inch barrel and an extremely high cyclic rate of 1,050 cycles per minute.

Working with the FPW, Colt engineers determined that the cyclic rate needed to be dropped to 200 cycles per minute to obtain the best probability of making hits on a target (since the weapon was aimed via tracer rounds

INSTALLING

1 With weapon upright, insert barrel thru firing port hole until BARREL COLLAR engages threads of firing port and PIN GROOVE aligns with QUICK RELEASE PIN.

2 2. Rotate weapon one full turn (360°) clockwise until QUICK RELEASE PIN locks into place.

REMOVING

1 Pull out on mount QUICK RELEASE PIN and rotate weapon one full turn (360 degrees) counterclock-wise so QUICK RELEASE PIN alines with pin groove.

2 Remove weapon.

WARNING
ALWAYS REMOVE MAGAZINE AND BE SURE WEAPON IS CLEARED BEFORE INSTALLING OR REMOVING FROM VEHICLE.

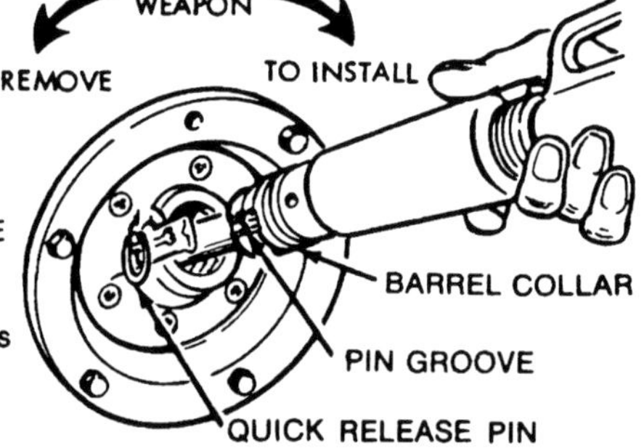


Field manual showing how the M231 can be "screwed into" its firing port.

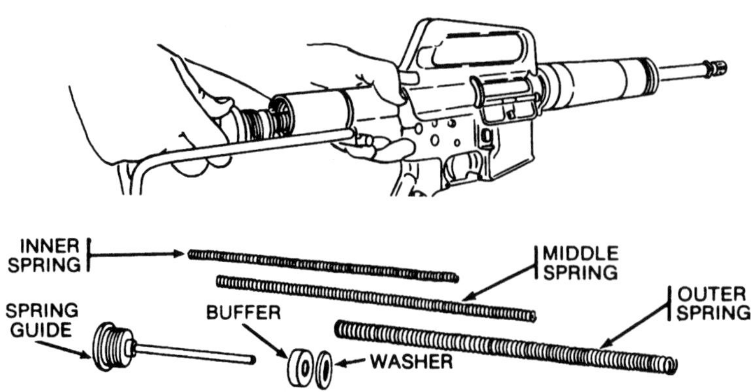


The M231 uses three recoil springs nestled inside each other.

necessitated by the tiny firing port and view ports). The engineers found they could do this with modifications to the spring and buffer assembly.

By 1976, all tracer-round magazines were being fired in the automatic-fire-only XM231. A telescoping wire stock and flip-up front sights had been added to the weapon so it could be removed from the port and used by soldiers in the armored personnel carrier when they left the vehicle. Many of those in authority felt that the sights were unwarranted, since the troops in the MICV were to have their own rifles, which they were to retain when they left the vehicle (and some might also have feared that troops would be tempted to abandon their rifles for the lighter and handier XM231).

So, in an odd compromise, the version agreed upon at the end of 1979 was to have a stock but no sights, and the barrel length was extended to 15.6 inches to increase the potential range of the weapon. Oddly enough, the cyclic rate in the final version of the M231 was raised from the accurate 200 rpm back to the less accurate 1,100 to 1,200 rpm, making it likely that troops would exhaust the firearm's magazine before they could hit a target (though the rate of fire would certainly devastate any targets that were hit).

Soon it was discovered that the high cyclic rate made the weapon dangerous to fire when it wasn't fastened into the ball swivel mount of its firing port due to the rapid barrel rise caused by the gun's recoil. The decision was made to dispense with the stock for reasons of safety.

This version of the M231 was designated the Submachine Gun, 5.56mm: Firing Port Weapon, M231 (Rifles and Carbine Team, AMSTA-LC-CSIR) in December 1979, concurrent with the standardization of the M2 Bradley Infantry Fighting Vehicle. Many of the M231 parts are interchangeable with those of the AR-15, some 65 percent being identical. The major departures from the parent firearm are in the M231's recoil spring/buffer system that has been shortened through the use of three nestled springs, which also power the striker. The gun fires from an open bolt, which, coupled with a heavy barrel, helps avoid overheating.

The handguard ends in a large set of threads that allow a soldier to screw the weapon into its firing port. The total weight of the short, 28.5-inch weapon is 8.5 pounds, empty.

### Colt's AR-15/M16 Model Numbers

Listed below are all the AR-15 models produced by Colt with their principal feature, from model number RO601 through AR7650, including all the weapon's configurations.

"RO" models are designed for military sales; "R" models are semiauto models with flash suppressors (and usually bayonet lugs) from before the assault weapon ban (1994); "LE" are postban guns for law enforcement sales only; "MT" (match target) models are postban without bayonet lugs or flash hiders; "CR" (Colt-accurized rifle)—only one to date—is the top-of-the-line target gun. The "DH" suffix is the Delta H-BAR; the "DC" suffix denotes a conversion kit (usually consisting of an upper receiver/barrel assembly with the appropriate magazine); an "S" suffix denotes a scope. "B" is for burst, and the "K" suffix is either for early Korean export guns or for the later .22 LR conversion kits.

NOTE: **Question marks in the features list denote conflicting information provided by various sources, with some claiming a model has this feature and others claiming it does not. It might also mean that this feature was transitional, i.e., Colt changed the model's configuration over time.**

RO601 M16-style without forward assist, 20-inch barrel with 1-in-14 twist, beavertail handguards, brown furniture painted green, Type 1 duckbill flash hider, chromed bolt and bolt carrier. A few of these appear to have been made with a mottled "wood" pattern in the furniture. Marked "Colt Armalite AR-15."

RO602 M16-style without forward assist, 20-inch barrel, beavertail handguards, Type 2 duckbill flash hider. Marked "Colt AR-15."

R0603 XM16E1 and M16A1 with forward assist, 20-inch barrel, 1-in-12 twist, beavertail handguards, Type 2 duckbill or birdcage flash hider. Marked "Colt AR-15."

R0603K Identical to RO603 but manufactured under contract in Korea.

RO604 U.S. Air Force M16 without forward assist, 20-inch barrel, 1-in-12 twist, beavertail handguards, Type 2 duckbill or birdcage flash hider. Marked "Colt AR-15."

| | |
|---|---|
| RO605 | Carbine with standard M16A1 rifle parts but a 15-inch barrel, without forward assist, with Type 2 duckbill flash hider. Marked "Colt AR-15." |
| R605A | Carbine with standard M16A1 rifle parts but a 15-inch barrel, with forward assist. Marked "Colt AR-15." |
| R0605B | Same as Model RO605 but with four-position burst selector (semi/safe/auto/burst), no forward assist, Type 2 duckbill flash hider. Marked "Colt AR-15." |
| RO606 | H-BAR version of RO604 without forward assist, 20-inch barrel, Type 2 duckbill flash hider. |
| RO606A | H-BAR version of RO603 with forward assist, 20-inch barrel. |
| RO606B | H-BAR version of RO603 with forward assist, 20-inch barrel, burst selector, Type 2 duckbill flash hider, usually with bipod and chrome bolt carrier. |
| RO607 | Colt's first Commando-style offering, in .223 with beavertail handguard, twin-tube telescoping stock, 10-inch barrel without forward assist, standard or abbreviated grip, no bayonet lug, low-noise muzzle brake. Marked "Colt AR-15." |
| RO607A | Similar to RO607, with beavertail handguard, twin-tube telescoping stock, 10-inch barrel with forward assist, standard or abbreviated grip, no bayonet lug, low-noise muzzle brake. |
| RO608 | Survival rifle with 10-inch barrel; round, nonribbed handguard; abbreviated pistol grip; no forward assist; no bayonet lug; cone or low-noise muzzle brake. Marked "Colt AR-15." |
| RO609 | Commando, which became the army's XM177E1, with forward assist, 10-inch barrel, no bayonet lug, low-noise muzzle brake with flash hider, round and ribbed handguard. Marked "Colt AR-15." |
| RO610 | Commando, U.S. Air Force XM177, without forward assist, 10-inch barrel, no bayonet lug, low-noise muzzle brake with flash hider, round and ribbed handguard. Marked "Colt AR-15." |
| RO610B | Commando with four-position selector (safe/semi/auto/burst), no bayonet lug, low-noise muzzle brake with flash hider. Marked "Colt AR-15." |
| RO611 | H-BAR with forward assist, 20-inch barrel, beavertail or round handguard. Export model. |
| RO611P | H-BAR with forward assist, 20-inch barrel, made under license in the Philippines by Elisco. |
| RO613 | Export version of RO603 (Israel and Great Britain). |
| RO613P | Version of RO603 made under license in the Philippines by Elisco. |
| RO614 | Export version of RO604 (Great Britain). |
| RO614S | Version of RO604 made in Singapore under license by Chartered Industries. |
| RO615 | H-BAR version of RO604, without forward assist, with beavertail handguard. |
| RO616 | U.S. government H-BAR without forward assist, with 20-inch barrel, round handguard. |
| RO619 | Export version of RO609. |
| RO620 | Export version of RO610. |

RO621 U.S. government (marine) H-BAR version of RO603 with forward assist, 20-inch barrel, beavertail handguards, generally with M60 MG bipod.

RO629 Commando with 11.5-inch barrel, forward assist.

RO630 Commando with 10-inch barrel, without forward assist.

RO633 9mm Luger submachine gun version with 7-inch barrel, short triangular handguard, telescoping stock, without forward assist, no bayonet lug (U.S. Department of Energy).

RO634 9mm Luger semiauto version of "submachine gun" with safe/semi selector, 10.5-inch barrel, A2 flash hider, A1 sight, telescoping stock.

RO635 9mm Luger "submachine gun" with 10.5-inch barrel, A2 flash hider, A1 rear sight, safe/semi/auto selector, no forward assist, telescoping stock, bayonet lug (U.S. DEA).

RO635S Silenced version of RO635 (U.S. DEA).

RO639 Commando with 11.5-inch barrel, forward assist, U.S Army's XM177E2, special noise-reducing flash hider. Marked "Colt AR-15." (Some of these may have been made with standard birdcage flash hiders.)

RO640 Export version of RO630.

RO645 First M16A2-style production rifle with rear sight "wheels," reinforced barrel, forward assist, round stock, safe/semi/three-round burst selector. Marked "Colt M16A1."

RO649 Commando with 11.5-inch barrel, no forward assist, large flash hider, telescoping stock, M16A1 receiver. Marked "Colt M16."(U.S. Air Force.)

RO650 Carbine with M16 stock and 14.5-inch Commando barrel/handguard, forward assist, M16A1 receiver, birdcage flash hider.

RO651 Carbine with M16 fixed stock and 14.5-inch Commando barrel/handguard, with forward assist, M16A1 receiver, birdcage flash hider, bayonet lug.

RO652 Carbine with fixed stock, M16A1 receiver, 14.5-inch barrel, without forward assist, birdcage flash hider, bayonet lug.

RO653 Carbine with telescoping stock, 14.5-inch barrel, forward assist, birdcage flash hider, M16A1 receiver, bayonet lug (exported to Israel and Great Britain and used by U.S. Navy and Air Force).

RO653P Philippine version of RO653, manufactured by Elisco.

RO654 Carbine with telescoping stock, 14.5-inch barrel without forward assist, birdcage flash hider.

R0655 Sniper rifle built around M16A1 with scope mount in carrying handle, H-BAR, and Leatherwood/Realist ranging scope on quick-detach mount.

R0656 Sniper rifle with hooded, low front sight assembly; milled scope block on receiver; no carrying handle; and Leatherwood/Realist scope.

RO701 Export M16A2 with 20-inch barrel, 1-in-7 twist, round handguard, safe/semi/auto selector, A2 windage/elevation adjustable rear sight. Marked "Colt M16 A2."

RO702 Export M16A2 with 20-inch barrel, 1-in-7 twist, round handguard, safe/semi/burst selector, A1 rear sight.

(703) M16A1 with gas piston (for a time mistakenly designated the M16A2 but never adopted by the U.S. military), unique upper receiver/gas system and handguard, bayonet stud, forward assist. Marked "Colt M16 A2."

RO703 Export version of M16A2 and A1-contour 20-inch barrel (but with 1-in-7 twist). Marked "Colt M16 A2."

RO705 Export version of the M16A2 with safe/semi/burst selector; A2-contour barrel. Marked "Colt M16 A2."

RO707 M16A2 with 20-inch A1 contour barrel, 1-in-7 twist, safe/semi/burst selector.

RO711 Export version of M16A2 with A1 sights and 20-inch A1-contour barrel, 1-in-7 twist, A2 flash hider, A2 stock, safe/semi/auto/burst selector. Early production lacked brass deflector; later versions had it. Marked "Colt M16 A2."

RO713 Export version of M16A2 with A1 sights and 20-inch A1-contour barrel, 1-in-7 twist, A2 flash hider, A2 stock, safe/semi/burst selector.

RO715 Canadian armed forces C7 with M16A2 parts except safe/semi/auto selector and A1-style rear sight.

RO719 Standard M16A2.

RO720 M4 carbine with M16A2 receiver, 14.5-inch stepped barrel (contoured to accept M203 grenade launcher), telescoping stock, A2 flash hider. Marked "Colt M16 A2."

RO723 Export carbine with 14.5-inch Commando barrel, telescoping stock, A1 sight assembly, standard flash hider, A2 grip, safe/semi/auto selector. Marked "Colt M16 A2."

RO725 Canadian armed forces C8 carbine with 14.5-inch barrel, A1 sight assembly, safe/semi/auto selector.

RO726 Another export version of RO723.

RO727 XM4 during tests (aka Abu Dhabi carbine), with 14.5-inch stepped barrel (grooved to accept M203 grenade launcher), telescoping stock, A2-style sights, four-position (safe/semi/auto/burst) selector.

RO733 Commando with A1 sights, 11.5-inch barrel, 1-in-7 twist, telescoping stock, M16A2 flash hider, safe/semi/auto selector. Marked "Colt M16 A2."

RO733A Commando with A1 sights, 11.5-inch barrel, 1-in-7 twist, telescoping stock, M16A2 flash hider, safe/semi/burst selector.

RO735 Commando with A2 sights, 11.5-inch barrel, 1-in-7 twist, telescoping stock, and safe/semi/burst selector.

RO737 M16A2 20-inch H-BAR, A1 rear sight, safe/semi/burst selector, M16A2 flash hider.

RO741 Export H-BAR 20-inch barrel, M16A2-style stocks and sights, safe/semi/auto selector with heavy barrel, 1-in-7 twist, and M60 bipod. Marked "Colt M16 A2."

RO750 Colt/Diemaco H-BAR LMG with 20-inch barrel, M16A2 parts, and heavy gas tube/rectangular handguard with carrying handle and forward vertical grip. Fires from open bolt, two-position semi/auto selector. Issued with a variety of magazines, including Beta C Mag. Marked "Colt M16 A2."

| | |
|---|---|
| RO777 | M4 carbine with stepped barrel, 1-in-7 twist, A3 flat-top detachable rear sight/receiver rail scope mount, telescoping stock, safe/semi/auto selector. |
| RO779 | M4 carbine with stepped barrel, 1-in-7 twist, A3 flat-top detachable rear sight/receiver rail scope mount, telescoping stock, safe/semi/burst selector. |
| RO901 | M16A2, 20-inch A2 barrel, 1-in-7 twist, A3 flat-top receiver, safe/semi/burst selector. |
| RO905 | M16A2, A3 flat-top receiver, safe/semi/burst selector. |
| RO925 | M16A3 Commando, 14.5-inch barrel, A3 flat-top receiver with detachable carrying handle, telescoping stock, safe/semi/burst selector. |
| RO927 | M4A1 carbine, A3 flat-top receiver with detachable carrying handle, 14.5-inch stepped barrel (contoured to accept M203 grenade launcher), telescoping stock, A2 flash hider, side-sling adapter, safe/semi/auto selector. |
| RO933 | Commando, A3 flat-top receiver, safe/semi/auto selector, telescoping stock, 11.5-inch standard barrel, 1-in-7 twist. |
| RO935 | Commando, A3 flat-top receiver, safe/semi/burst selector, telescoping stock, 11.5-inch standard barrel, 1-in-7 twist. |
| RO941 | M16A3, 20-inch H-BAR, A3 flat-top receiver, A2 flash hider, probably with safe/semi/burst/auto selector. |
| RO942 | M16A3 SAW, 20-inch H-BAR, A3 flat-top receiver with detachable carrying handle, safe/semi/auto selector. |
| RO950 | M16A3 SAW, 20-inch H-BAR, A3 flat-top receiver with detachable carrying handle, safe/semi/burst selector. |
| RO977 | M4 carbine, A3 flat-top receiver, telescoping stock, safe/semi/auto selector, 14.5-inch step-cut barrel, 1-in-7 twist. |
| RO979 | M4 carbine, A3 flat-top receiver with A3 detachable rear site, telescoping stock, safe/semi/burst selector, 14.5-inch step-cut barrel, 1-in-7 twist. |
| R6000 | AR-15 Sporter, 20-inch barrel with 1-in-12 twist, beavertail handguard, bayonet lug, without forward assist, A1-style rear sight. |
| R6001 | Sporter Carbine, 16-inch barrel with 1-in-12 twist, round handguard, bayonet lug, without forward assist, A1-style rear sight. |
| R6002 | Model R6000 with 3X-power Colt's combat scope. |
| R6003 | Model R6001 with 3X-power Colt's combat scope. |
| R6004 | Model R6000 with Colt's Reflex Sighting System (red-dot scope) and Colt's carrying bag. |
| (R6222) | .22 LR conversion kit for rifle—not actually a rifle model. |
| R6420 | Sporter Carbine in 9mm Luger with 16-inch barrel, round handguard, bayonet lug, without forward assist, A1-style rear sight. |

| | |
|---|---|
| R6430 | Sporter Carbine in 9mm Luger, rifle stock, 16-inch barrel, A2 adjustable sights and forward assist, without bayonet lug. |
| R6430-DC | 9mm carbine conversion kit. |
| R6450 | Sporter Lightweight, 9mm Luger, standard stock. |
| AR6450 | AR-15 9mm carbine, 9mm Luger, 16-inch barrel, semiauto only, telescoping stock, A2 flash hider, A1 receiver, law enforcement sales only. |
| R6500 | Sporter II with round handguard, forward assist, 20-inch barrel with 1-in-7 twist, bayonet lug, A1-style rear sight. |
| R6520 | Sporter II Carbine with telescoping stock, 16-inch barrel with 1-in-7 twist, forward assist, bayonet lug, A1-style rear sight. |
| R6520-DC | Sporter II Carbine conversion kit with 16-inch barrel in .223. |
| AR6520 | AR-15A2 Government Carbine with telescoping stock, 16-inch barrel with 1-in-7 twist, forward assist, bayonet lug, A2-style rear sight, semiauto only. Law-enforcement sales only. |
| R6530 | Sporter Carbine with rifle stock, 16-inch barrel with 1-in-7 twist, A2 sights, forward assist, no bayonet lug. |
| R6530-DC | Sporter Carbine conversion kit with 16-inch barrel in .223. |
| MT6530 | Match Target Light Weight with 16-inch barrel, 1-in-7 twist, no flash hider, A3 flat-top receiver/rear sight, no bayonet lug, A2 stock, handguard, and grip, semiauto only. |
| R6550 | Target Government with A2 rear sight, match H-BAR 20-inch barrel with 1-in-7 twist, round handguard, forward assist, without bayonet lug. |
| R6550-CC | Model R6550 with camouflage finish. |
| R6550-K | Model R6550 with .22 LR adapter kit. |
| R6551 | Sporter Target or Target Model with A2 rear sight, 20-inch barrel with 1-in-7 twist, round handguard, forward assist, without bayonet lug, with flash hider. |
| R6551-DC | Target conversion kit with A2 sight and 20-inch barrel in .223. |
| MT6551 | Match Target Rifle with 20-inch barrel; 1-in-7 twist; no flash hider; A3 flat-top receiver/rear sight; no bayonet lug; A2 stock, handguard, and grip; semiauto only. |
| R6600 | Match H-BAR with A2 rear sight, 20-inch barrel with 1-in-7 twist, round handguard, forward assist, without bayonet lug. |
| MT6601 | Match Target H-BAR with 20-inch heavy barrel; 1-in-7 twist; no flash hider; A3 flat-top receiver/rear sight, no bayonet lug; A2 stock, handguard, and grip; semiauto only. |
| R6600-DH | Sporter Match Delta with A2 rear sight, scope, cheek pad, H-BAR 20-inch barrel with 1-in-7 twist, round handguard, forward assist, without bayonet lug. |
| R6600-K | R6600 with R6222 .22 LR conversion kit. |

| | |
|---|---|
| R6601 | Sporter II with A2 rear sight, match H-BAR 20-inch barrel with 1-in-7 twist, round handguard, forward assist, without bayonet lug. |
| R6601-DC | Upper barrel/receiver kit with H-BAR 20-inch barrel. |
| R6601-DH | Sporter Match Delta H-BAR, 20-inch barrel, 3–9X Tasco scope, ARMS mount, cheekpiece, hard carrier. |
| R6700 | Sporter II with A3 flat-top rear sight, H-BAR 20-inch barrel, round handguard, 1-in-9 twist, no bayonet lug. |
| R6700-CH | Competition Sporter H-BAR with A2 sight, scope block mount, H-BAR 20-inch barrel, round handguard, 1-in-9 twist, forward assist, without bayonet lug, 3–9X power scope. |
| R6700-DC | Upper receiver/barrel conversion kit; H-BAR 20-inch barrel. |
| R6700-S | R6700 with 3–9X Tasco scope. |
| MT6700 | Postban Match Target Competition H-BAR with 20-inch heavy barrel; 1-in-9 twist; no flash hider; A3 flat-top receiver/rear sight; no bayonet lug; A2 stock, handguard, and grip; semiauto only. |
| R6701 | Competition Sporter limited edition (2,000 made) with flat-top receiver (scope block mount included), H-BAR 20-inch barrel, round handguard, 1-in-9 twist, forward assist, without bayonet lug, with flash hider. |
| R6721 | AR-15A3 Tactical Carbine 16-inch H-BAR, 1-in-9 twist, flat-top A2 flash hider, bayonet lug, telescoping stock (only 134 believed to have been manufactured prior to ban). |
| AR6721 | AR-15A3 Tactical Carbine with 16-inch H-BAR barrel, 1-in-9 twist, flat-top receiver, A2 flash hider, bayonet lug, telescoping stock, semiauto only. Law enforcement sales only. |
| R6724 | Sporter Competition H-BAR with 24-inch, 1-in-9 twist barrel; flat-top receiver; "shaved" front sight. |
| R6724-DC | Upper receiver/barrel conversion kit, H-BAR 24-inch barrel, A3 receiver. |
| CR6724 | Colt accurized rifle with 24-inch stainless steel heavy barrel, 1-in-9 twist, semiauto only, no sights, flat-top receiver, floating barrel handguard. |
| R6731 | AR-15A3 Competition 16-inch H-BAR, 1-in-9 twist, flat-top receiver with A2 flash hider. |
| R6731-DC | AR-15A3 16-inch barrel/receiver conversion kit. |
| MT6731 | Match Target Competition H-BAR II with 16-inch heavy barrel; 1-in-9 twist; no flash hider; A3 flat-top receiver/rear sight; no bayonet lug; A2 stock, handguard, and grip; semiauto only. |
| MT6731-DC | Conversion kit for upper receiver/barrel in MT6731 configuration. |
| R6750 | Sporter Competition H-BAR with 20-inch "extra heavy" barrel, 1-in-7 twist, bipod, and special handguard. |
| R6821 | Sporter 16-inch H-BAR, 1-in-12 twist, flat-top receiver, A2 flash hider. |
| R6821-DC | Upper receiver/barrel conversion kit in 7.62x39. |
| R6830 | Sporter Lightweight, 7.62x39, 16-inch barrel, 1-in-12 twist, A2 flash hider. |
| R6830-DC | Upper receiver/barrel conversion kit in 7.62x39. |

| | |
|---|---|
| MT6830 | AR-15A2 Government Carbine with telescoping stock, 16-inch barrel, chambered for 7.62x39mm, forward assist, bayonet lug, A2-style rear sight, semiauto only. Law enforcement sales only. |
| R6850-DC | Sporter 16-inch H-BAR, 1-in-12 twist, flat-top receiver, A2 flash hider. |
| R6851-DC | Sporter 16-inch H-BAR, 1-in-12 twist, flat-top receiver, A2 flash hider. |
| R6900 | 20-inch H-BAR, 1-in-9 twist, A2 flash hider. |
| R6900-DC | 20-inch H-BAR upper receiver/barrel assembly conversion kit. |
| MT6900 | Postban upper conversion kit with 20-inch H-BAR, 1-in-9 twist. |
| LE6920 | Semiauto M4 carbine with 16-inch stepped barrel, 1-in-7 twist, flat-top receiver, A2 flash hider, bayonet lug, telescoping stock, side sling adapter. Law enforcement sales only. |
| AR6920-DC | M4 upper conversion kit with 16-inch stepped barrel (LE6920). |
| RO6920-DC | M4 upper conversion kit with 14.5-inch stepped barrel (upper similar to LE6921). |
| LE6921 | Semiauto M4 carbine with 14.5-inch stepped H-BAR, 1-in-7 twist, flat-top receiver, A2 flash hider, bayonet lug, telescoping stock, side sling adapter. Law enforcement sales only. |
| AR7650 | AR-15A3 Tactical Carbine with 16-inch H-BAR barrel, 1-in-9 twist, flat-top receiver, A2 flash hider, bayonet lug, telescoping stock, semiauto only. Law enforcement sales only. |

## AR-15 MAGAZINES

Working on the theory that a little miscellaneous data must fall here and there within a book, the following section is a partial list of AR-15 magazines made by a variety of companies, including Colt. It is doubtful that this list is complete or totally accurate with those magazines listed. But it is hoped that it will give the reader some idea of the variety of magazines that have been produced for this rifle and perhaps help some collector as well—not to mention making a few experts feel all the more superior when they find a gap in the list.

It should be noted that often a company will use parts up when possible rather than discarding them when a new product is introduced. For this reason, one might see transitional magazines with previous floor plates on new models, markings from a previous owner, and so on. No attempt has been made to cover these transitional variations or even guess as which might be "out there" in the hands of collectors or squirreled away in corners of drawers and bins in old warehouses. Generally Colt magazines made before 1969 marked "Cal. .223," and those made after this date are marked "Cal. 5.56mm," though there might be some overlap here as well.

Military/law enforcement magazines made after the high-capacity ban that went into effect on September 13, 1994, will have a date stamp or be marked "For Law Enforcement Use Only" (or something similar). Currently there are enough preban magazines available to make counterfeit preban magazines only a gleam in a bootlegger's eye. But as the stock of preban magazines dries up, illegal postban magazines may become a problem. At that point, buyers will need to exercise caution to avoid breaking the law and committing a felony by purchasing such contraband, assuming the ban is still in effect at that time. (The specifics of many of these magazines are covered in more detail in the accessories chapter of this manual.)

## Magazines Produced for the AR-15/M16 Rifle

NOTE: **Question marks denote conflicting information from sources regarding precise numbers or dates.**

| Type | Capacity | Characteristics |
|---|---|---|
| Armalite waffle-sided | 20-round | Gray finish, pre-1963 |
| Air Force | 20-round | Colt Parts Manufacturing Co. Inc., 1963 to 1968 |
| Army and Air Force | 20-round | Colt Firearm Division, 1969 to 1971 |
| Army and Air Force | 20-round | Simmonds, 1966 to 1971 |
| Army and Air Force | 30-round | Colt Cal. .223, 1968 to 1969 |
| Army and Air Force | 20-round | Adventureline, 1966 to 1971 |
| Army | ? | Cooper – generally agreed to be of poor quality |
| Army and Air Force | 30-round | Colt Cal. 5.56mm, 1970 to present |
| U.S. Government | 30-round | Misc. Manufacturers: Adventureline, Center Industries, Cooper Industries, Fabrique Nationale, Labelle Industries, Okay Industries, Parsons Precision Products, Sanchez (DSI); 1975 to 1994 |
| U.S. Civilian Market | 20-, 30-, 40-round (for AR-180 or AR-15) | Sterling |
| Colt – Civilian Market | 20-round | Colt, 1980 to 1989 |
| Colt – Civilian Market | 5-round (in 20-body) | Colt, 1989 to around 1991 |
| Eagle/Armalite | 5-, 30-round | 1986 to present |
| Colt – Civilian Market | 5-round (in 20-body) | Colt, rivet in floor plate, 1991 to 1994 |
| Israeli Government | 30-round | Orlite plastic magazines, ? to 1994? |
| Canadian Government, Civilian Market | 30- , 45-round | Thermold |
| Colt – Civilian Market | 5-round (in 20-body) | "Colt," permanent spacer, 1994 to present |
| Civilian and Government Market | 30-round | Labelle Industries, no date stamp, Bushmaster or BFI, June 1994 to September 13, 1994 (preban) |
| Government Market | 30-round | Labelle Industries, date stamp, "Cal. 5.56mm, Made in USA," September 13, 1994 to present (postban) |
| Civilian and Military | 90-round | MWG |
| Chinese Military, US Civilian | 90-, 100-round? | |
| Law Enforcement and Military | 100-round | Beta "C-Mags" |
| Colt – Law Enforcement | 30-round | "Colt's Mfg. Co. CAL. 5.56," 1995 to present |

## MANUFACTURER STAMPINGS

Some key parts of the AR-15 have Colt's or another manufacturer's stamp or proof mark on them. Often these can tell a shooter whether he has the original parts on his gun or whether they have been "mixed and matched." That said, it should be remembered that some parts, especially with guns assembled by smaller manufacturers, will have parts subcontracted out; a few large manufacturers even do this from time to time. So if you have a gun that has, say, a barrel made by Colt but the gun is sold by company X, this is not necessarily a bad thing—and could even be a sign of quality since the manufacturer decided to let someone else handle a job that couldn't be done as well in house.

Markings will usually be found along the top of the barrel, on the bolt, on the bolt carrier, and perhaps on trigger parts or other components. Some of these are simply a letter or two and are easy to miss, with most owners undoubtedly totally unaware of what "those little letters" stand for.

Barrels often have a wealth of additional information on them, including the twist rate, whether the barrel is chromed, and when it was made, in addition to the manufacturer stamp marking (listed in the above table). With barrels, "MP" stands for magnetic particle tested; "C" for a chromed chamber; "CB" for a chromed bore; and "H-BAR" for heavy barrel. The chambering will be self-evident (usually.223 or 5.56 NATO) and the twist rate will be shown as a fraction; for example, "1/7" would be a twist rate of 1 turn per 7 inches of barrel length.

**Manufacturer Marks**

| | |
|---|---|
| B | Bushmaster |
| C | Colt |
| D | Diemaco |
| FNMI | Fabrique Nationale |
| M | Global Sales marines version, produced by Smith Enterprises |
| MPC | Colt |
| MPN | Bushmaster |
| N | Global Sales navy version, produced by Smith Enterprises |
| NM | Global Sales National Match version, produced by Smith Enterprises |
| SAK | SACO |
| SE | Smith Enterprises |

# Chapter 5

# Grenades, Launchers, Ammunition, Miscellany

## GRENADES

Grenades are nothing new on the battlefield. Hand-held bombs date nearly as far back in history as firearms. Although the hand grenade is successful within short ranges, the throwing ability of the average soldier limits its range; therefore, most grenades are more suited as defensive weapons. Grenades launched from rifles are a more recent development. From the time troops were at an impasse on the Western Front during World War I, inventors have been trying to create a way of delivering a compact "warhead" over several hundred yards by using a rifle and various attachments.

World War II-vintage rifle grenades were placed over the muzzle of a rifle barrel and launched with a powerful blank cartridge, transforming the firearm into a miniature mortar. But these grenades were awkward, and a blank cartridge charge powerful enough to deliver the device to a target any great distance away created excessive recoil, making it impossible to fire grenades from the shoulder. Prolonged use soon turned a rifle into a broken pile of scrap metal and splintered wood.

World War II saw only a slight improvement in U.S. rifle grenades, with the introduction of the Mills Bomb Mark 2. Developed for the M1 Garand, this grenade that looks like a rocket was mounted on the barrel with a special adapter (the M7 launcher) and was propelled by firing a blank, just as the World War I version had been. Regular ball ammunition could not be used to launch the rifle grenade, and the Garand couldn't fire ball ammunition with the launcher in place.

The rifle grenade did give troops a needed option, and by the time the U.S. military was fielding the M14 rifle, many types of rifle grenades were available (including the M1A2 grenade projection adapter, which allowed regular hand grenades to be mounted and fired as rifle grenades). The U.S. grenade inventory at the time included the M31 antitank grenade, smoke grenades (in several colors for marking and signal purposes), star clusters, white phosphorus grenades, and practice grenades. The effectiveness of the rifle grenade had been improved since World War I; the M31 antitank grenade, for example, was capable of defeating 20 inches of reinforced concrete or 10 inches of armor.

### The Energa

When the AR-15 flash hider was being revamped for the U.S. military, the army specified that it should be capable of accommodating a rifle grenade. One of the most popular rifle grenades seen with the AR-15, especially in the early days of the Vietnam War and later with Israeli troops, was the Energa, which could be fired from any of the AR-15 rifles except for carbine versions with 10- or 11.5-inch barrels. The Energa was launched with a special blank cartridge just like the rifle grenades of World Wars I and II and had a maximum range of 350 meters.

The Energa grenade proved effective in actual combat. During the ARPA's AGILE program in 1962, a

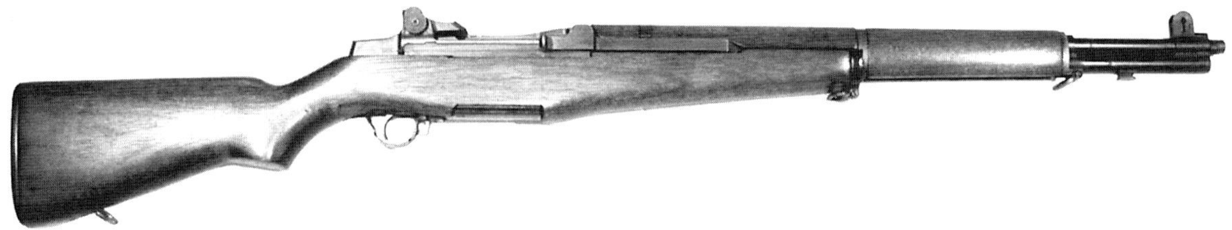

M1 Garand. (Courtesy of Randy Green.)

U.S. soldier in the 7th Infantry Regiment wrote about the AR-15 and its capabilities: "Grenades were used [by us] for the first time and were very effectively employed at ranges of 100–500 meters. They served as the real artillery support as we could not get the artillery to fire any closer than 400 meters. About 36 grenades were utilized in the heavy action, all propelled from the AR-15."

Unfortunately, the rifle grenade was not actively pursued by the U.S. military for several reasons. One was that the devices required special range finders to achieve any real degree of accuracy at longer ranges. Although Colt did create a sight made by steel stamping that could be clamped onto the front sight of the AR-15 to fire grenades, it was never adopted by the military. (And the idea of loading up a rifle with a special blank cartridge so the rifleman had to either launch the grenade or remove it before he could fire bullets may have been abhorrent to tacticians.)

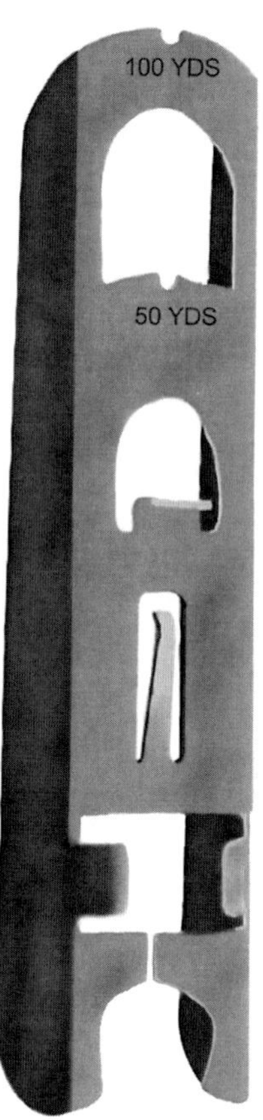


Armalite created a simple stamping that could be attached to an AR-15 sight to act as a grenade launching sight for the Energa or similar grenades.

### New Rifle Grenades

Although the United States has pretty well abandoned the use of grenades launched from rifles in favor of grenade launchers, some countries have not embraced the launcher and have worked toward producing updated rifle grenades. Among the more innovative of these are produced by the French firm Luchaire and the Belgian Fabrique Nationale.

Luchaire produces rifle grenades that will work on the AR-15 since some of their potential customers use the rifle and many other .223 firearms have adopted the same diameter flash hider assembly to accommodate grenades

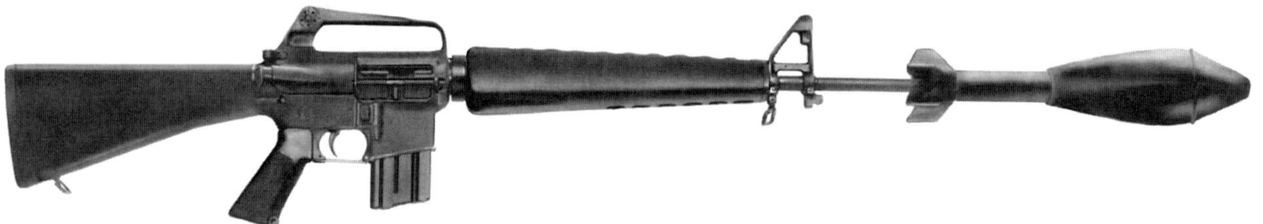

Energa grenade mounted on AR-15 rifle.

Spring system used to secure grenade to AR-15 barrel.

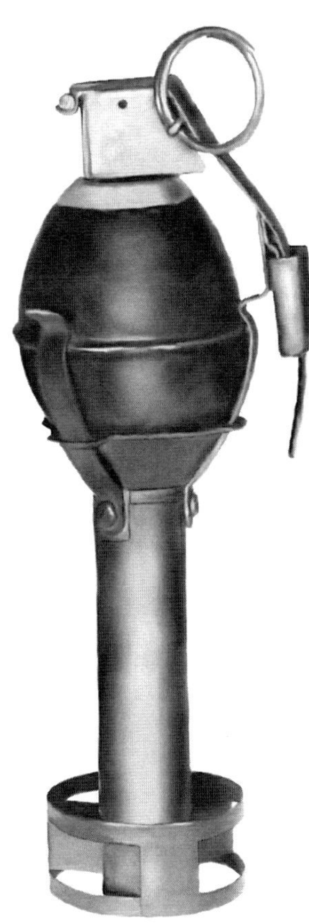

Standard grenades could also be launched from the AR-15 using this attachment. Grenades were armed by pulling the pin; the grenade fuse was then set off when the grenade hit its target, releasing the grenade handle.

designed for the AR-15. The big selling point of the Luchaire grenades is bullet traps in the base of the projectiles, which make it possible for troops to launch grenades with regular rounds rather than having to chamber a special blank.

Luchaire claims that with a little training a soldier using its special range finder can easily place grenades through a window-sized opening at 150 meters. The company offers both antipersonnel and antiarmor grenades, with the latter capable of defeating the side or rear of tank armor (250–300mm, or 10- to 12-inch penetration of rolled homogeneous armor). The antipersonnel grenades offer 60mm (24 inches) of armor penetration and a lethal radius of 11 meters (12 yards).

### The FN Bullet-Thru

Another interesting rifle grenade concept that permits firing standard ammunition is the Bullet-Thru rifle grenade pioneered by the Fabrique Nationale. This design allows the bullet to pass through the rifle grenade while still harnessing the gas produced during discharge of the firearm to propel the grenade. Recoil is not excessive, so the grenade can be fired from the shoulder, and armor-piercing bullets won't damage the grenade.

The FN grenade places the explosive of the grenade along the body of the projectile rather than just in its nose (as is the case with most earlier rifle grenades), making the projectile more compact (only 7.5 inches long) and light (only two-thirds of a pound). Its tail fins are protected by a metal ring so they aren't easily damaged.

### The Raw Deal

Another innovation along the lines of the rifle grenade is the rifleman's assault weapon (RAW). It looks somewhat like a rifle grenade but in fact is a rocket. The 6-pound RAW was meant to be mounted on the barrel of an AR-15 by locking the base onto the front sight assembly and bayonet lug. When a regular bullet was fired, an integral bullet trap caught it and the bullet's gas set off a percussion igniter, which in turn started the rocket motor. Unlike a grenade, which has a very steep trajectory (and is therefore difficult to aim at long ranges, the RAW had a flat trajectory due to both a downward and forward thrust of its rocket that kept it parallel to the aim of fire for 200 yards.

For hitting more distant targets, a ballistic arch was necessary. With a special aiming sight, the rocket was capable of phenomenal 2,000-yard shots. In addition to the downward and rearward rocket exhaust, two tubes diverted another portion of the rocket's thrust along the circumference of the projectile to create a stabilizing spin that maintained accuracy over such long ranges.

Since the rocket created minimal recoil, there was no firing strain on either the rifle or the rifleman, which also aided in accuracy and would have been much appreciated by most troops who find rifle grenades somewhat rough to fire (with much the same being true for the M203). Unlike many rockets, the RAW had a very low noise signature; its launching was slightly quieter than a regular rifle shot with almost no backblast, so it could be fired from indoors or from vehicles.

Manufactured by Brunswick Corporation during 1980 for evaluation by the Advanced Systems Concept Office, U.S. Army Missile Command, in Huntsville, Alabama, the RAW had an explosive warhead that made it effective against armor, bunkers, walls, or vehicles. But the 6-pound weight of the weapon also made it similar to the light antitank weapon (LAW) and other rocket launchers already in production, so it was tabled to divert funds to tank and helicopter research, which the military considered a more urgent need at the time. Given the success of the M203, it's doubtful that the RAW will be used by U.S. troops in the near future,

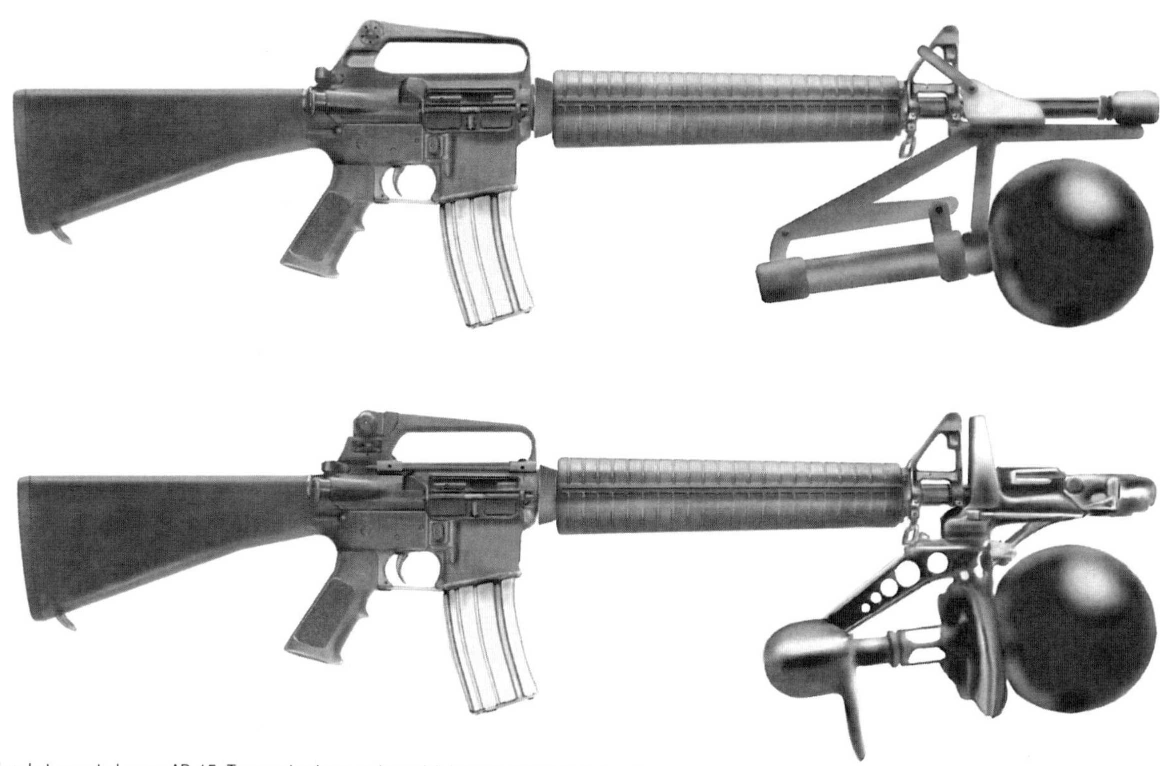

RAW rocket mounted on an AR-15. Top version is an early model; lower is the perfected system.

though it seems likely that this promising concept will someday be revived.

## LAUNCHERS

### The SPIW That Never Was

Perhaps a bigger incentive to disregard the rifle grenade was the program the U.S. military had cooking at about the same time the Energa was proving itself on the battlefield. This was the push to create a special-purpose individual weapon (SPIW) capable of launching small projectiles similar to bullets as well as grenades comparable to rifle grenades—with both features available at any time. The SPIW project had factions in the military supporting it, including those who had been behind the M14 and who were unhappy with the AR-15 because it had been developed outside the U.S. military establishment (where careers were made by creating weapons systems, thereby justifying the large research and development programs). Most likely, the fewer capabilities the AR-15 had the better as far as some members of the army were concerned.

This is not to say the SPIW wouldn't have been an excellent weapons system; it would have been, had it been technically possible. And although the flechette part of the SPIW program never really met with much success, it did create one useful spin-off: the 40mm grenade, which would be matched to the M79 launcher.

### The M79

The SPIW program had envisioned the 40mm grenade launcher as a multishot system (and thereby created many heavy and ungainly prototypes that were more like field pieces than rifles), and the 40mm cartridge, though somewhat limited, was capable of delivering an explosive charge over extreme combat ranges. However, once designers found that a multishot system was out of the question, they "dropped back and punted," creating a light, single-shot grenade launcher, the M79, that was similar to a giant-bore single-shot shotgun. The weapon and cartridge were quickly put into production and fielded in Vietnam, where they proved highly successful despite the limited reloading speed of the weapon.

Perhaps the biggest drawback of the M79 was that its user had no way to defend himself because of the weapon's single-shot capability and the 30 yards' range needed to arm the explosive rounds (a distance that was necessary to keep the shooter from killing or wounding himself and those around him if he accidentally fired into the ground or hit a nearby obstacle when launching a grenade). One solution was to arm the grenadiers with a

M79 40mm grenade launcher.

pistol, but this was far from the long-range weapon often called for in defense and demanded drawing the pistol and dropping the M79 or holding it in a free hand.

There were a number of attempts to overcome the shortcomings of the single-shot launcher. For instance, a special 12-gauge adapter was made to allow the launcher to fire shotgun shells. This took care of the close combat problem—in a one-shot sort of way—but made it impossible to fire regular M79 grenade rounds quickly since the adapter had to be slipped out of the barrel to do so. Next, a special 40mm buckshot round was created that could be fired without an adapter, but the single round wasn't any more potent than a regular shotgun shell, and the large cartridges were awkward to carry. Finally, modified SPIW multishot grenade launchers with three-round 40mm launchers were tried as substitutes for the M79, but these proved to be too heavy for dragging through the fields on extended patrols.

### The M16-Mounted Grenade Launcher

Troops in the field had other ideas about how an M79 might be deployed. A few cut down the stocks of their M79s and wired the launcher to the underside of AR-15 barrels, giving them the option of delivering rifle fire or grenades on enemy positions. But this was far from ideal because there was no practical sighting system for the M79, making its accuracy marginal at best, and the recoil of the M79 soon shook lose any but the most permanent of improvised mounts. Soon military designers were following the lead of the soldiers in the field. In mid-1963, the U.S. military requested a 40mm grenade launcher that could be attached to the AR-15. Colt's agreed to tackle the task.

Rob Roy devised the first grenade launcher at Colt's that consisted of a very simple mechanism based on a sliding sleeve that went around the launch breech. The military rejected this system. Eventually Roy and Karl R. Lewis created the CGL-4 (Colt Grenade Launcher 4), which was based on the original design but modified with a spring-powered striker at its rear that was released by a small button on its underside.

However, the U.S. Army was interested in creating its own launcher, so it dismissed this design while engineers at the Springfield Armory worked toward adapting an SPIW prototype to the AR-15. The end result was an AR-15 mated to AAI's Disposable Barrel and Cartridge Area Target Ammunition (DBCATA). An innovative concept, the DBCATA used only the base and mechanism of a launcher on the AR-15, and each cartridge held not only a grenade but its own a disposable barrel. This kept the weight on the rifle low and made it very quick to reload a new cartridge-barrel to the launcher after the previous one had been fired.

The catch to the system was that it didn't fire the standard 40mm grenade but rather a brand-new DBCATA cartridge created by AAI. Since the 40mm grenade was already being fielded for the M79, the prospects of introducing yet another type of ammunition to the battlefield was a logistics nightmare for military planners. There already was a hodgepodge of cartridges for each chambering of gun being used, including the .45 ACP, .223 Remington/5.56mm, 7.62 NATO, .50 BMG, and 40mm grenades, along with a smattering of .38 Special, .30 carbine, 9mm Luger, and other odds and ends thrown in for security personnel, special forces, and CIA agents. So, finally, rather than introduce a new round into the procurement process, the military decided to drop the DBCATA, despite the apparent success of the design. In 1965, the army signed a contract with Colt's to further develop its CGL-4, which the army designated the XM148 Grenade Launcher.

Top to bottom: AAI DBCATA and Philco-Ford's Aeronutronics Division's GLAD, Aero Jet General's GLAD, Colt's CGL, and the XM148.

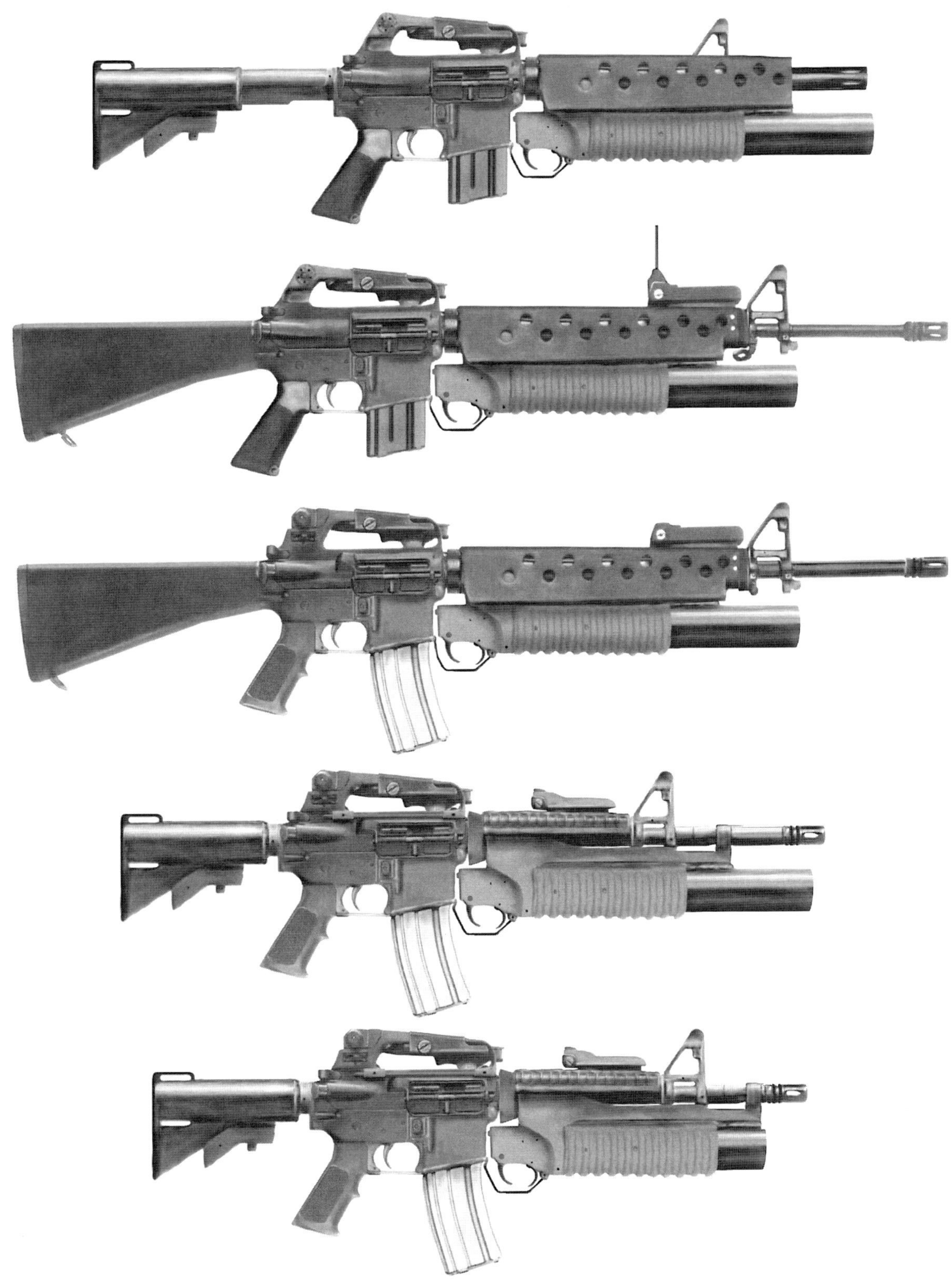

Top to bottom: AAI prototype XM203, early M203 on M16A1, current M203 (on M16A2), M4 carbine with M203, and Knight's abbreviated version of the M203, mounted on a shorty.

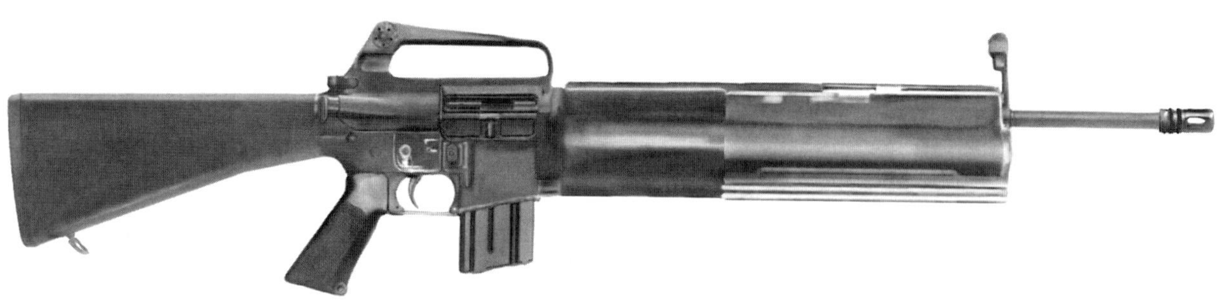

The U.S. Army's Human Engineering Laboratory (HEL) created this multishot, 30mm grenade launcher prototype. However, the system was never developed, the 40mm M203 fulfilling its role well enough to put the need for the 30mm HEL in doubt.

### The XM148

The new launcher looked promising. Whereas the M79 weighed 6.45 pounds loaded, an AR-15 with the launcher attached tipped the scaled at a bit under 10 pounds while giving a soldier the firepower of the rifle coupled with the capabilities of the launcher, either of which could be fired according need.

But the XM148 was a fragile system from the start and was plagued with parts breaking during tests. Colt's worked at overcoming these problems and by 1966 had a more durable system that was of interest to both the air force and army. The army initially purchased 10,500 and later increased its order to 19,236. In spite of initial problems with the barrel forgings, XM148s were headed toward Vietnam at the end of 1966.

In the field, the concept of the combination rifle-launcher was well liked and highly effective. But the XM148 itself was still having problems with parts breaking—and an error made in calibrating the sights during manufacture had doomed the launcher to be less accurate than it should have been. Additionally, cocking the weapon required 20 to 30 pounds of force, and the trigger was easily damaged if disassembled incorrectly during field stripping.

The 27,400 XM148s the military had already purchased were soon slated for disposal because they were becoming too unreliable. However, the concept of the launcher had proven valuable and, after again rejecting the DBCATA (along with AAI's proposal to convert the M79 to use the DBCATA ammunition), the military announced that it needed a new grenade launcher that could be attached to the AR-15 rifle. This project became known as Grenade Launcher and Ammunition Development (GLAD).

### GLAD and the M203

Three companies won contracts to work on GLAD: AAI, Aero Jet General, and Philco-Ford's Aeronutronics Division. The initial tests of the prototypes were scheduled for mid-1968. Colt's engineers also went back to the drawing board in an attempt to devise a new design of their own. The result was the CGL-5, but this version was dismissed during initial army tests.

Not that all the other GLAD candidates were much better. Aero-Jet General created a monstrosity that worked with delayed-blowback inertia. The result of its endeavor was what one onlooker described as "the poorest thing imaginable." It's doubtful that anyone attending the tests argued with his statement.

Philco-Ford's Aeronutronics Division's better-designed candidate featured a pivot action and was not so unwieldy. But it proved second best to the simple and reliable "slide action" system AAI had developed. The AAI model won the tests hands down and was designated the XM203 grenade launcher.

By the end of 1968, testing of the XM203 had gone successfully, and after a few design changes (and the rejection of an adapter that could be used to turn the launcher into a single-shot system similar to the M79), the XM203 was redesignated the M203. Somewhat ironically, AAI wasn't set up to handle the volume of manufacturing required to supply the military's needs, so Colt's won the final contract, purchasing the manufacturing rights from AAI.

Over the next two decades, Colt's manufactured nearly a half-million M203s for the U.S. military and foreign customers. In addition to being mounted on the standard military AR-15, the launchers could be accommodated on many of the Commandos. On the submachine gun, the launchers were often seen with special handguards or even with just the top half of the carbine's handguard left in place to protect its gas tube from damage. This created a potent but small-weapons system that, in many ways, was capable of delivering the firepower that the SPIW experimenters had been trying to create without success by using flechettes and multishot grenade launcher assemblies.

Whether on a Commando or the more common AR-15 rifle, it seems likely that the M203 will remain in service for some time. Although work continues to develop a multishot launcher and a more compact grenade cartridge continues, the creation of such a weapon seems unlikely given today's technology.

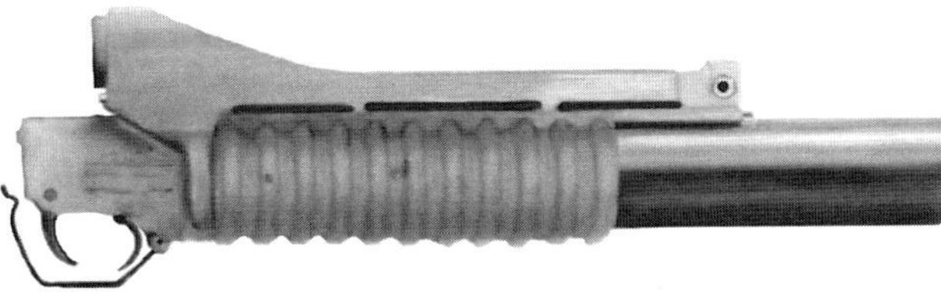

M203 launcher assembly.

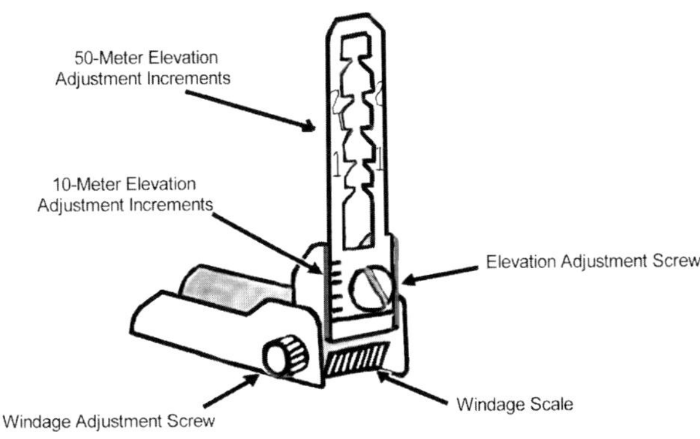


M203 "quick-sight" leaf assembly. This sight is normally mounted on the handguard of the rifle and used in conjunction with the front sight of the rifle.

The sliding action of the M203 makes the weapon quick to reload, with the release found on the left side, just above the barrel. When released, the barrel slides forward, extracting any empty cartridge. The user then loads a new round in the breach and pulls the barrel rearward into its locked position. This also cocks the internal striker. The safety inside the trigger guard is then shoved forward, and the grenade is ready to fire with a pull of the launcher's trigger.

During their fighting in Lebanon during the 1980s, the U.S. Marines discovered that it was possible to treat the weapon like a crew-served gun, with one man handling the reloading while the other aimed and fired. This enabled the two to lay down a heavy barrage almost as with a small artillery piece.

The M203 is normally issued with a battle sight mounted on the handguard along with a quadrant sight that mounts on the rifle's carrying handle. The battle sight is graduated for 50 to 250 meters (54 to 271 yards) on a "ladder" system that rotates upward. The more accurate quadrant sight is graduated from 50 to 400 meters (54 to 433 yards). These systems are generally calibrated somewhat differently from some rifle and carbine assemblies, so the two aren't always interchangeable in the field.

The sight on most M203s has the 50 meters/50 yards in older guns) marked in red for a reason. This range is dangerous to the firer because fragments from a shell can travel this far and create injury. Therefore, firing at 50 meters is done only in extreme circumstances or from a sheltered position. Shells fired at extremely close ranges will generally fail to explode because the projectile is spin-armed to protect the user. Rounds are generally

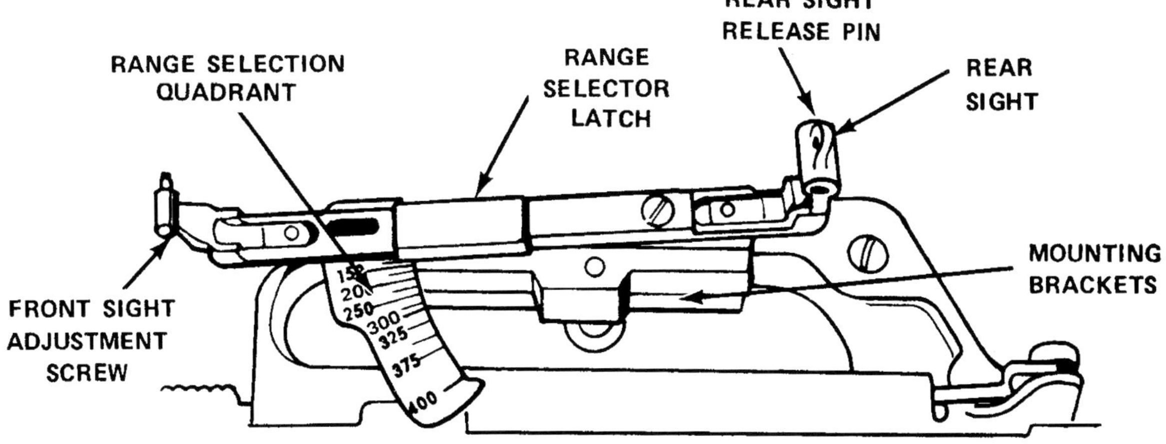


The tangent sight mounts on the carrying handle/rear sight of the AR-15 rifle. Though not as quick as the leaf sight, it offers greater potential accuracy, especially when firing at longer ranges.

armed only after traveling 14 to 38 meters (15 to 41 yards). Obviously, a direct hit by a round this heavy and traveling at speed is lethal. However, failure to explode does away with the shrapnel normally responsible for the casualties produced by this weapon.

### M203 Specifications

| | |
|---|---|
| Length of rifle and grenade launcher | 39 inches |
| Length of barrel (grenade launcher) | 12 inches |
| Length of rifling (grenade barrel) | 10 inches |
| Number of lands (grenade barrel) | 6 |
| Weight of launcher unloaded (without rifle) | 3.0 pounds |
| Weight of launcher loaded | 3.5 pounds |
| Weight of rifle and grenade launcher (both fully loaded) | 11.0 pounds |
| Chamber pressure | 35,000 psi |
| Muzzle velocity (grenade) | 250 fps |
| Maximum range | 400 meters (433 yards) |
| Maximum effective range (fire-team-sized area target) | 350 meters (380 yards) |
| Vehicle or weapon point target | 150 meters (163 yards) |
| Rate of fire | 5 to 7 rpm |

The M203 has proven highly reliable and become one of the mainstays of the U.S. military arsenal. It is especially popular with the infantry because it fires the same rounds as the M79. Like the M79, its maximum range is 400 yards with a 30-yard arming range for explosive rounds.

### The M203 PI

In the mid-1980s, J.C. Manufacturing, Inc. introduced a modified version of the M203 called the M203 PI ("product improved"). A key selling point of the launcher was a universal mounting system that adapted it to all NATO rifles as well as many Kalashnikov rifles and AR-15 variants. The mounting system also permitted swift

M203 PI grenade assembly. (Courtesy of J.C. Manufacturing.)

Inventor: **Joseph C. Kurak**, Fridley, Minn.
Assignee: **R/M Equipment, Inc.**, Miami, Fla.

**Patent Number: 4,733,489**
**Date of Patent: Mar. 29, 1988**

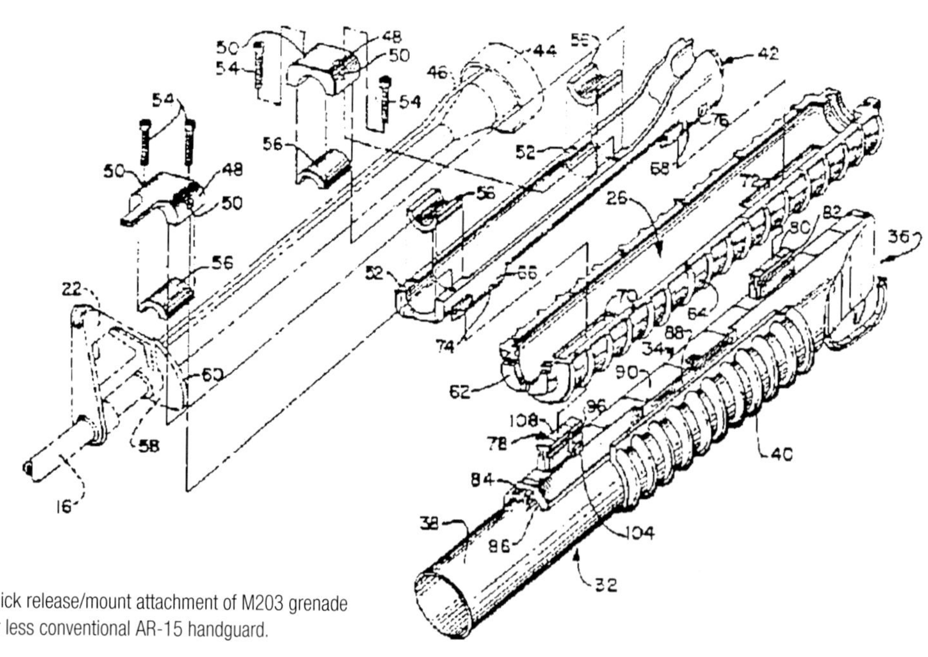

Patent drawing for quick release/mount attachment of M203 grenade launcher to a more or less conventional AR-15 handguard.

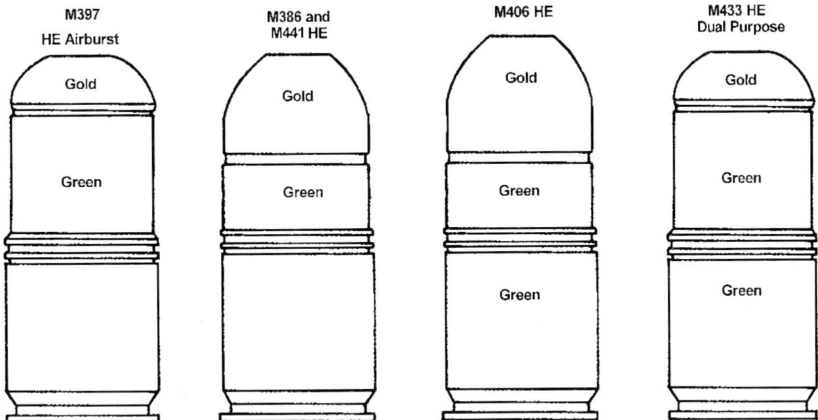


Standard 40mm HE cartridges.

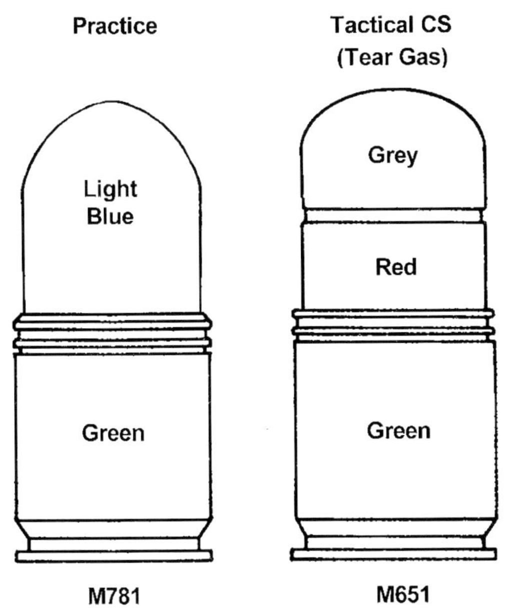


Special 40mm cartridges.

removal or replacement of the launcher, allowing a rifleman to quickly modify his rifle or move the unit from one firearm to another.

The M203 PI has a longer breech opening so that longer cartridges can be chambered, allowing a wide range of special-purpose ammunition to be created for the weapon in the near future. (This creates a potential problem, however, since the more powerful 40x53mm SR developed for automatic grenade launchers can be chambered in the M203 PI; firing such a cartridge in a hand-held weapon would be disastrous to both the shooter and the launcher.)

J.C. Manufacturing also manufactured 12-gauge, 37mm, and 38mm versions of the M203 PI to capture police and military markets worldwide: the 12-gauge shotgun cartridge and 37mm tear gas cartridge have become standards in North and South American law enforcement communities, while European police agencies use the 38mm cartridge. The company also created devices that could be mounted on the rifle's carrying assembly when the M203 PI was removed, including a laser aiming device, a flashlight, and a special compact shotgun.

Considering the U.S. military's limited budget and the general satisfaction with the standard M203 and its ammunition, it seems likely that militaries will begin to adopt the M203 PI only gradually. All the same, the new units have been appearing among police departments, and, if the company can persevere, it seems possible that this improved version of the M203 may eventually supersede the original.

## AMMUNITION

### 40mm Cartridges

Ammunition for the M203 includes high explosive (HE), various colors of smoke (for ground use or by parachute), CS gas, flares of various colors for signaling and illumination, multiple projectile rounds, and practice rounds. These all add up to a lot of options for combat, and since most rounds weigh approximately 8 ounces each, a soldier can carry a number of these cartridges without becoming overburdened.

Among the most common 40mm rounds currently found in the U.S. military are the following:

- *High-explosive dual-purpose (HEDP) round.* This round has an olive-drab aluminum skirt with a steel cup attached, white markings, and a gold ogive; it penetrates at least 5 cm (2 inches) when fired straight at steel armor. It is armed at between 14 and 27 meters, and causes casualties within a 5-meter radius.

- *HE round.* This round has an olive drab aluminum skirt with a steel projectile attached, gold markings, and a yellow ogive. It is armed between 14 and 27 meters (15 and 29 yards), and it produces a ground burst that causes casualties within a 5-meter (16-foot) radius.
- *Star parachute round.* This round is white or bar alloy aluminum with black markings. It is used for illumination and signals and is lighter and more accurate than comparable hand-held signal rounds. The parachute attached to the round deploys upon ejection to lower the flare at 7 fps, burning for about 40 seconds of illumination.
- *White star cluster round.* This round is white or bar aluminum alloy with black markings. The attached plastic ogive presents a raised "W" for night identification. The round is used for illumination or signals; individual stars burn for about 7 seconds during free fall. The round is lighter and more accurate than comparable hand-held signal rounds.
- *Ground marker round.* This round is light-green impact aluminum with black markings. It is employed for aerial identification and for marking the location of soldiers on the ground being armed between 16 and 49 meters. If a fuse fails to function on impact, the output mixture provided in the front end of the delay casing backs up the impact feature, eventually igniting the projectile.
- *Practice round.* This round is blue zinc or aluminum with white markings. It is used for practice and produces a yellow or orange signature on impact.
- *CS ("tear gas") round.* This round has a gray aluminum base with a green casing and black markings. It produces a white cloud of CS gas on impact.

Currently in the U.S. military, high explosive (HE), high explosive dual purpose (HEDP), and training/practice (TP) grenades are generally packed in a can with 6 bandoleers of 12 rounds each, for a total of 72 rounds. Smoke and cluster ammunition are generally issued in wire-bound boxes containing 2 cans with 22 rounds each, for a total of 44 rounds. CS ammunition is packed in boxes containing 2 cans with 4 bandoleers of 6 rounds each, for a total of 48 rounds.

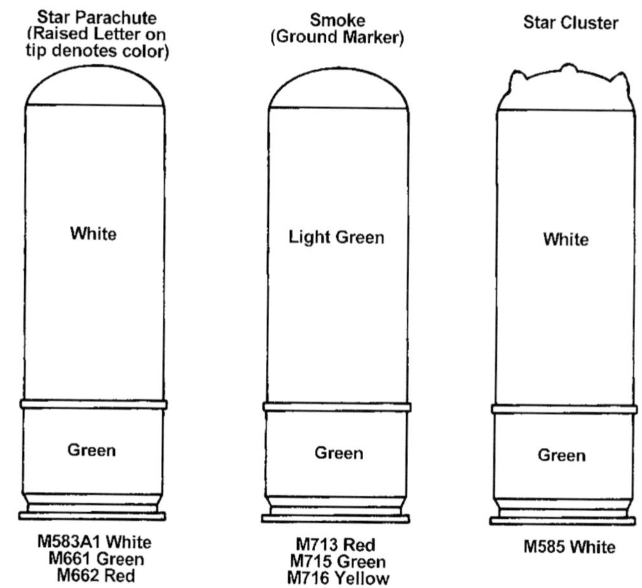


40mm star and smoke cartridges.

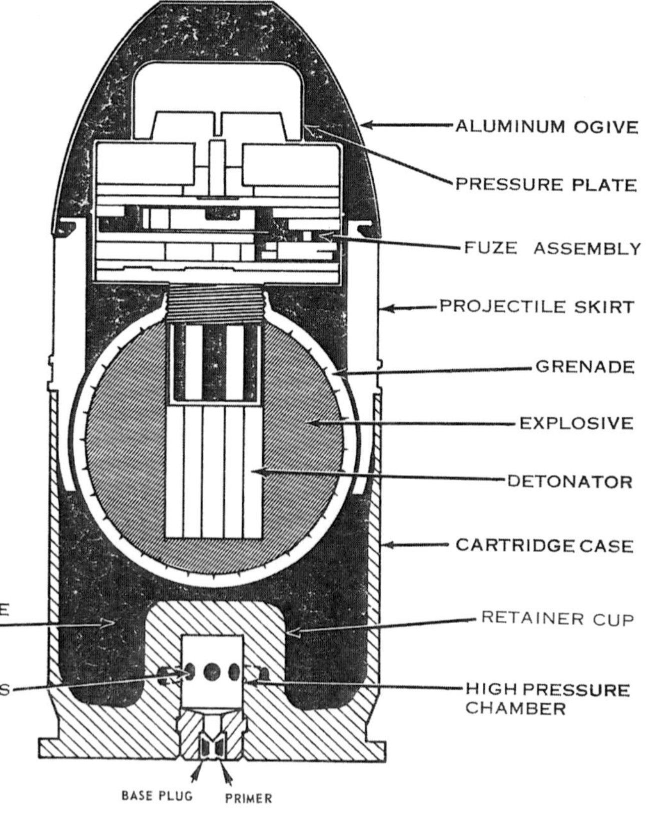


Cross-section of 40mm cartridge.

Among the various Western militaries, the 40mm cartridge—officially designated the 40x46mm SR—has more or less become the standard. Israel, Germany, Belgium, South Africa, and Argentina have all adopted the U.S. cartridge for their own grenade launchers and also created additional types of ammunition in this chambering.

Nearly all of these rounds have a high-pressure charge that is ignited inside a small container (actually a blank pistol cartridge in many cases), which lies in a larger chamber in the base of the cartridge. This container is ruptured, and the pressure drops as the gas moves into the larger chamber. In the process, the gas pressure also drops, pushing the grenade's payload down the tube and leaving an empty casing in the chamber of the launcher. This roundabout method of launching the grenade makes the recoil much lighter than with a conventional cartridge the size of a 40mm grenade.

It should be noted that the U.S. 40mm grenade may not explode when it falls into snow or water, thereby creating what amounts to a land mine that can be set off when stepped on or driven over. For this reason, great care needs to be exercised when employing it in such conditions, especially during training and practice.

## MISCELLANY

### The DMPS

DMPS offers a 37mm flare launcher kit that swaps directly with the upper of an AR-15, thereby transforming the lower into a single-shot flare launcher without any modification to the AR-15 assembly. In just moments, a shooter can switch from a rifle to a 37mm gun capable of launching a variety of flares and pyrotechnics from its smooth-bore barrel. The barrel drops open for loading like the M79 grenade launcher. The upper has an aluminum receiver, breech, and barrel. A (recommended) option for this kit is an M203 leaf sight assembly that makes aiming considerably more accurate. Cost of the adapter kit at the time of this writing was $389.

### Riot Control Devices

At the other end of the scale are riot control devices, which seem to be growing in popularity among those who want to disperse crowds while reducing the chances of actual casualties (though any of these devices might be lethal under certain circumstances, especially at close range). Israel Product Research Company has created a grenade-style projectile for riot/crowd control rather than combat. This unit can be fired from an AR-15 or a Galil rifle (which has the same size flash hider as the AR-15). Called the Rubberhead Projectile M-809, it has a large rubber ball atop a conventional rifle grenade style launcher.

The grenade can be used to hit a troublemaker from 160 yards and gives a knockout punch that is less apt to injure the person than are plastic bullets, rubber projectiles, or fired batons. The Rubberhead Projectile is also filled with 80 grains of tear gas so other members in a crowd will be affected by the grenade and be more apt to disperse than continuing to cause discord.

As with earlier grenades, the Rubberhead Projectile has to be fired with a special blank, but this is probably less of a problem in crowd control than in combat, since troops generally will not have cartridges chambered in their weapons (though such situations can quickly escalate into major confrontations that lead to bloodshed).

In the 1980s the U.S. military introduced the M234 riot control launcher (Rifles and Carbine Team, AMSTA-LC-CSIR), a lightweight assembly that attaches to the muzzle of a rifle. Once in place, a ringlike, open-centered 64mm projectile can be inserted into the launcher and fired with a blank cartridge. Thanks to its open design, the projectile travels in a very flat trajectory to deliver a stinging blow when its forward rim connects with the target. Aiming is done with integral sights on the unit. The system is not recommended for use below 20 degrees Fahrenheit.

### Flare Launchers

While the M203 is classified as a destructive device and cannot be purchased by civilians in the United States without a lot of paperwork, there nevertheless has been a lot of interest in the grenade launcher. Several companies offer the device, as well as 37mm flare-launcher versions.

For those willing to go through the federal, state, and local red tape to obtain a destructive device, Jonathan Arthur Ciener, Inc. offers the real McCoy in the form of a finished, working M203. (Prices vary, and it's best to get in touch with the company to see what is available and how to wade through the paperwork to qualify for one of these units.)

Parts for the M203 can also be found in the surplus market. Although the receiver and barrel are restricted or hard to find, do-it-yourselfers wanting to build a "wall hanger" will often discover that enough parts are available to create such a conversation piece. Those interested in obtaining parts will generally have best luck with SARCO and Gun Parts.

Frankford Arsenal, Inc. marketed 40mm, 37mm flare, and nonfunctioning versions of the M203 during the mid-1980s, but the company has since gone out of business, having made only a few of the units. In 1991, TAPCO, Inc., introduced its own version of the M203 as

Ciener's Remington 870 mounted on an AR-15. (Courtesy of Jonathan Arthur Ciener, Inc.)

the CM-2037. This model uses the standard handguard and barrel assembly of the M203 with a striker/receiver of the company's own design. The barrel is 37mm, so it can accommodate only flares and tear gas grenades; thus it can be sold to the general public because the purchase of flare launchers is not restricted in most areas of the United States. Cost of the CM-2037 is $220 with flares also available from $7 each (Bushmaster and others also market this accessory for about the same price).

Another route a commercial manufacturer could take is to offer a one-shot, black-powder grenade launcher look-alike. Since black-powder weapons are not restricted by caliber or barrel lengths, it is perfectly legal for anyone who can normally obtain a firearm to own one. The M203-style weapon could even be loaded with black-powder substitutes to create a legal—though awkward to reload—short-range shotgun.

A flare launcher (or black-powder) version of the M203 has to be viewed more as an "adult toy" or collector's piece rather than a weapon suitable for anything but the most limited combat, but it would no doubt be sobering to any criminal who breaks into a house and is confronted by a homeowner carrying an AR-15 with one of these mounted under its barrel. The 37mm barrel leveled at the crook would undoubtedly have a nice deterrent effect.

Do-it-yourselfers may wish to try constructing their own M203-style firearms (*after* securing the proper paperwork). Ragnar Benson's *Homemade Grenade Launchers* (available from Paladin Press) gives step-by-step instructions for creating a launcher for the AR-15. Although this unit is rather crude, it works and might be refined with a better striker system and mounting assembly for a more "professional" look. It's important to note that a working M203-style assembly is a restricted device and should not be constructed without first obtaining BATF approval; care must be taken to adhere to local and state laws as well.

### Shotgun Attachments

It's possible to mount a shotgun under the barrel of the AR-15 in much the same manner as an M203. Jonathan Arthur Ciener, Inc. will custom fit a Remington 870 shotgun to the owner's AR-15. "Chopped" versions of the shotgun are available to those who have the paperwork to purchase a shotgun with a barrel shorter than 18 inches. Although a shotgun isn't really more effective in combat than the AR-15 rifle, some shooters may have a need for the capability—or simply want to own a unique attention-getter for the field or target range.

The U.S. military apparently has fielded a very limited number of shotgun assemblies that have been mounted on AR-15 rifles. Known as the Masterkey, this system, believed to have been introduced in 1992, consists of a Remington Model 870 pump shotgun with its barrel cut back to 10 inches to match the length of the M4 carbine it is usually mounted on. Capacity of the shotgun is only three rounds in the magazine plus an additional one in the chamber. Its name suggests that its intended role is to provide instant access to a locked building by breaking locks or severing door hinges.

C-More has also fielded a shotgun system, the Lightweight Shotgun System (LSS), that rides under an AR-15 barrel. This unit has a two-round detachable magazine (with a five-round magazine on the drawing table) and accommodates standard as well as 3-inch shotgun shells.

### The Frankengun

Do-it-yourselfers can create their own combination

Ciener's Remington 870 mounted on an AR-15 carbine. (Courtesy of Jonathan Arthur Ciener, Inc.)

Masterkey mounted on M4 carbine.

guns coupling the Ruger 10/22, AR-7, Marlin .22s, or other firearms to the AR-15 in a style similar to that of the M203. Attaching the secondary gun to the AR-15 sometimes takes a bit of experimentation, but generally the double clamps designed for reinforcing extended tubular magazines under a shotgun barrel work well. (These are available from Choate Machine and Tool and other companies for around $10.)

If the barrel diameter permits it, adapters designed to attach miniflashlights to the barrel of an AR-15 may also be employed for this purpose.

While such Frankenstein creations are arguably sort of iffy in their utility, they can be a lot of fun for plinking or simply eliciting stares from those around you at the rifle range. Shotguns are also iffy in this way, it should be noted, given that the AR-15 bullet is much more effective in almost every respect than the storm of pellets thrown from a shotgun, save for blasting away a door lock—and even in this I wouldn't place any bets without prior experimentation.

### XM303

The Fabrique Nationale's XM303 was apparently developed to meet the U.S. armed forces' requirements for nonlethal weapons set forth during the Clinton administration. It is aimed at the market that's developing in both the law enforcement and military communities as more and more government workers find themselves confronting angry mobs—with international TV cameras rolling. In the past, soldiers or policemen in situations where injuries from flying bottles, bricks, or Molotov cocktails are a serious threat would have been justified in using lethal force to protect themselves. But today, with mounting political pressure from politically corrcct folks who are critical of such actions, governments are developing effective but less dangerous ways to deal with

FN's XM303 mounted on an M4 carbine.

mobs. (Whether this will succeed in controlling such crowds or simply embolden them due to decreased risk of death remains to be seen.)

The XM303 employs a compressed-gas tank on its right with a barrel and "ammunition" system on the left. Once in place on an AR-15 rifle or carbine (or any of a number of popular military rifles), the XM303 can propel what is basically a paintball filled with anything from stinking liquids to dye to tear gas, depending on what is most likely to have the desired effect on a crowd. The basic XM303 can also be mounted on its own separate stock assembly, which is perhaps a safer way, given that a soldier or policeman might conceivably pull the wrong trigger during the confusion of a riot and escalate a situation from nonlethal to lethal.

The XM303 weighs 5 pounds with its own stock, or 4 pounds when mounted on a rifle. The stand-alone version is 29 inches long, and the undercarriage version is 16.7 inches. The air gun will hold 15 projectiles, and its gas canister will fire 65 shots before needing to be replaced; the muzzle velocity remains constant as the pressure in the canister drops. The effective range of the XM303 is 109 yards, giving the user a standoff range beyond that of most bottles and rocks. The ammo pellets currently available, described by Fabrique Nationale as "impact" (designed to create a stinging blow), "marking," "malodorant," and "illuminating," weigh around 8 grams (.3 ounce).

Given the high cost of the XM303, along with the fact that similar riot control rounds are available from MK Ballistic Systems, Combined Tactical Systems, and others for the shotgun, M203, and 37mm tear gas guns, it seems unlikely that this system is going to see a lot of sales. On the other hand, the Fabrique Nationale has invested a lot of money in it and has close ties with government military users. Time will tell.

### M203-IMP

The M203-IMP, marketed by Firequest International, is very similar in appearance to the M203, but has a slightly different trigger system, including a large cocking knob. It tends to be marketed as a low-cost alternative to the M203 (with an eye toward civilian or police sales rather than military). Mounted on its own stock/pistol assembly, the grenade launcher is marketed as the M-79 LF; on an AR-15, it is the M203-IMP. Firequest offers 40mm and 37mm versions of the M203-IMP, and both will handle a variety of cartridges including, 7.5-inch smoke grenades. (Firequest also offers 37mm reload kits for those wanting to fire "on the cheap.")

### Shivak 37mm M203

At the other end of the cost scale from cheaper M203 look-alikes is the 37mm version of the M203 built by Randall R. Shivak, a Class II manufacturer that actually makes the standard 40mm M203. Shivak's 37mm version isn't cheap, but it is a real military-style launcher right down to the last part. And it can be purchased by almost anyone who can own a standard firearm, since the Bureau of Alcohol, Tobacco, and Firearms classifies launchers with a 37mm barrel as tear gas guns rather than destructive devices requiring special permits to own. Shivak also offers a 9-inch-barrel version of the M203 for mounting on Commando carbines with 11.5-inch barrels.

### Odds and Ends

As with M203 parts, some types of nonexploding rifle grenades and flares are also seen on the commercial market. Many of these, too, are generally legal to own even without a special destructive devices permit from the federal government.

Most common on the commercial market are parachute flares and practice grenades that can be launched by an AR-15. Often these can be purchased through military surplus equipment suppliers, although they've been a tad hard to find of late.

It's also feasible to launch things other than grenades with the AR-15. The Mach V Sport Launcher created by Arizona Ballistics (now, sadly, out of business) is similar in concept to the tear gas launcher H&K developed for its rifles. The Mach Launcher, which screws right onto the threads of a preban AR-15 (after removing the flash hider), is designed for launching hand-thrown tear gas or smoke grenades and propels regular tear gas grenades to 300 yards (range being determined by the angle of the trajectory and the power of the blank used to launch the grenade).

This launcher can also be used to fire cans of *uncarbonated* liquid or other similarly sized objects; the possibilities are seemingly endless for those with a little imagination. Grenade launcher blanks are ideal for this purpose. When the grenade launcher is empty, standard bullets can be fired through the assembly, though its size and weight makes this a bit awkward except when engaged in prone firing. The original cost of the basic launcher was $80 (and once in a while these can still be seen for sale in *Shotgun News* or elsewhere).

For the uninitiated, it's important to remember that the recoil in launching most rifle grenades (or cans of juice) is greater than that produced by a standard cartridge. Whenever possible, the firer should place the stock against the ground—and keep his head clear of the grenade. It's good to remember that a steady diet of rifle grenades is a bit hard on the rifle. Also, ordinary blanks shouldn't be used to launch rifle grenades: the grenade will travel to only a few feet away—which may have unexpected results!

Whether for launching carbonated cans or deadly Energa rifle grenades, a variety of devices have been created to enhance the abilities of the AR-15 rifle, many of them capable of converting the rifle into a miniature one-man field piece.

### Fake M203s

Sometimes folks just want to *look* like they have an M203. I must say that I can see the fun in this even though it's a good way to create a stir or even panic that might result in a law enforcement official's challenging you to prove that you legally own what appears to be a destructive device. This is more legal hassle that I would care to tackle.

However, for those brave souls who need the look if not the actual bang of an M203 launcher, DPMS offers a fake kit for $200. The kit includes some actual M203 parts, including the handguard and liner, leaf sight, and a mounting bracket for the barrel. To prevent illegal conversion, the inside diameter of barrel is undersize with no rifling, though it moves forward and back like an actual M203 barrel. The receiver is an aluminum alloy casting with nonfunctional trigger group.

Because it looks like the real thing but isn't, you need no license to purchase it (though some state or local laws may apply to real-looking, nonfiring replicas, so it's wise to check beforehand). DPMS is also a good parts source for those owning and maintaining the real thing.

# Chapter 6

# Armalite Rises Again

If there were a fictional account of an endeavor such as Armalite—last seen with its production equipment rusting away in crates in the Philippines—a businessman on a figurative white horse would ride to the company's rescue, plucking it and its firearms from ruin and raising them to new heights of financial success.

In this case life would imitate art. A business group did ride in to resurrect the Armalite name and produce guns that carried the old company logo and that were similar in concept.

The chain of events leading to this resurrection began in 1986 when Karl Lewis and Jim Glazier formed Eagle Arms of Coal Valley, Illinois. Lewis had been manufacturing a wide variety of commercial and military parts for M16 rifles through his company, Lewis Machine and Tool. Originally, Eagle Arms was to assume the sale of parts that Lewis Machine and Tool had produced, but company officials soon realized that with the expiration of the Stoner patents on the AR-15, Eagle Arms could produce the guns by itself rather than simply selling parts, thereby cutting out a middleman and increasing its profit potential. So, in 1989, Eagle began producing AR-15-style rifles carrying the Eagle logo and built from Lewis Machine and Tool parts. As might be expected, these guns were of a very high quality, being made by a company that had long met the needs of those selling guns to both military and commercial buyers.

Although the patent rights on the AR-15 had expired, Colt still had the trademarks AR-15 and M16. This prohibited other manufacturers, including Eagle Arms, from using these names for their own firearms. However, it didn't prevent companies from choosing names that left little doubt about the kind of rifle. Eagle Arms called its AR-15-style gun the EA-15.

### THE AR-10B RIFLE

Eagle Arms was sold in January 1994 to Mark Westrom, a former army ordnance officer and later a civilian employee of the Weapons Systems Management Directorate of the U.S. Army's Armament Materiel and Chemical Command located at nearby Rock Island Arsenal. While the company continued to produce the EA-15, Westrom planned to add several more products to the Eagle Arms line, including night scopes.

In November 1994, Westrom started work on a version of the EA-15 chambered for the .308 caliber round. With a nod toward the AR-10 rifle that the new gun resembled, Eagle Arms designated it the M-10. The task of engineering this rework of the EA-15 went to Lewis Machine and Tool, where a quality assurance expert, David Dorbeck, did the major redesign work.

The company slated to produce the rifle sights to be marketed by Eagle Arms was owned by Dr. John Williams, who had worked for Armalite many years earlier. Upon learning about Eagle Arms' design work on a gun chambered for the .308 cartridge, Williams introduced Westrom to former Armalite Production Manager John McGerty.

In talking to McGerty, Westrom learned that the Armalite trademark had been purchased by John Ugarte, a man whose father had worked for Armalite (and who appeared in a TV ad produced by Lava soap, telling viewers that after a hard day at the rifle range test-firing the AR-10, "only one soap can get these hands clean").

Seeing a chance to place the Armalite name and logo on the new M-10 rifles, Westrom purchased the rights to the trademark and was again free to market an "Armalite rifle," complete with the old logo.

But it got better from a marketing standpoint. By now American shooters were familiar with Armalite's past reputation, and the AR-10 had a following all its own in the United States based on the few guns that had been built from imported Dutch parts and other sources. There was a growing market for the gun. All that was needed was a manufacturer.

Thus, the timing of Westrom's purchase of the company trademark was impeccable, and production of guns was soon under way at the Eagle Arms plant. Since the new rifle so closely resembled the old AR-10, Westrom, with marketing genius, changed the name from M-10 to AR-10—actually the AR-10B. (The original Armalite company had created an improved version of the AR-10 in the 1960s, designated the AR-10A, so AR-10B fit perfectly into the basic nomenclature and eliminated any confusion over whether this was a new gun or one of the originals.) In addition, because the Armalite name had considerable weight with potential buyers of the AR-10B, the corporation was reorganized under the name of Armalite, and Eagle Arms became one of its divisions.

The AR-10B is of interest in more ways than just its name. For starters, the gun was designed from the ground up by computer, with all testing done in computer simulations. The gun was never prototyped, although subcomponents were tested on aluminum slabs that acted as a lower receiver while mounted to a Stoner SR-25 upper receiver assembly (the Stoner SR-25 is discussed elsewhere in this book).

This design process was somewhat risky: had the computer simulations been off the mark, the tooling might easily have been in need of expensive changes. However, given that the Eagle EA-15 on which the gun was based was a thoroughly debugged system, perhaps it was not as risky as it might seem. Both the skill of the designer and the sophistication of today's computer technology proved to be real time and money savers in this project. The full prototype AR-10B was the first rifle off the production line, and it worked almost perfectly.

First shipments of the new AR-10B commenced in January 1996, and the only glitch was that production rifles in the field sometimes had problems with surplus ammunition. Fortunately, the fix was simple. The original gun plans had included a firing pin retarding spring to handle such problems. Although this part was omitted initially because it was thought unnecessary, designer Dorbeck had the foresight to leave space for it in the bolt carrier should the spring be needed. The part was quickly made, sent to AR-10B owners, and added to production guns. Since then, other adjustments to dimensions and tolerances have been made to improve the gun's durability, but all these changes have been minor, again demonstrating the skill of Dorbeck and the usefulness of computer design.

The AR-10B also employs a modified M14 rifle magazine, which is reliable, plentiful, and inexpensive to own—important pluses since current U.S. law prevents the manufacture of new 20-round magazines for civilian use. Fortunately there are plenty of M14 magazines available, and it seems unlikely that they would become too scarce for shooters to buy and use n the near future. (That said, Armalite is currently selling rifles that have only a 10-round magazine capacity, while making 20-round magazines available as accessories.)

Since its introduction the AR-10B has had brown-finished handguards, grip, and stock created for it that mimic the original AR-10 furniture. With these and an in-the-handguard "trigger"-style charging handle, the gun appears to be one of the original Armalite AR-10 rifles.

AR-10T (Courtesy of Armalite.)

AR-10TC. (Courtesy of Armalite.)

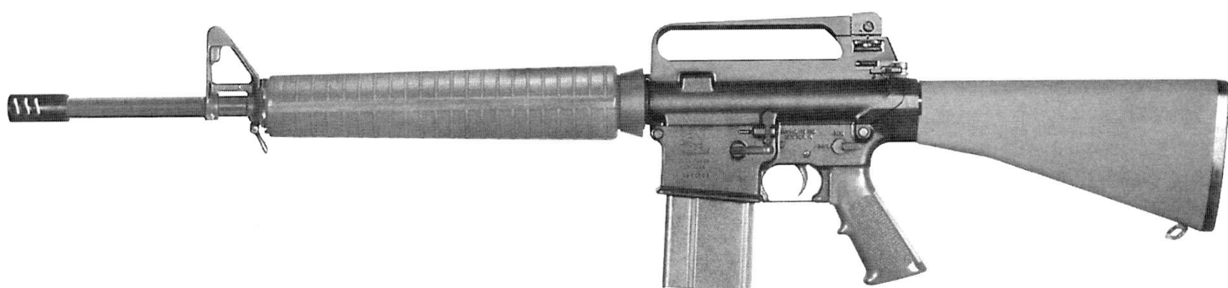

AR-10A2. (Courtesy of Armalite.)

AR-10A2C. (Courtesy of Armalite.)

### AR-10T and AR10A2 Series

Although Armalite has reserved the AR-10B designation for the model that mimics the original AR-10A, the company has expanded the system into several lines. These new guns are sold in a variety of barrel lengths with either carbine- or standard-length handguards (Armalite's carbine handguard is 2 inches longer than Colt's Commando handguard).

The AR-10T series comprises target rifles with scope mounts or target sights, and that generally lack the standard AR-15- style carrying handle and sight assembly and without a front sight assembly (with the gas block just forward of the handguard). The handguard on this model is unattached to the barrel; this permits the barrel to "float" inside the handguard, thus eliminating any barrel flex that might otherwise result from the sideward pressure exerted by a shooter's hold or a sling. Barrels are available with or without a muzzle brake with these models. The AR-10TC is the carbine version, with a 16-inch barrel.

The AR-10A2 series is similar in appearance to the AR-15A2, with the A2-style handguards and carrying handle/rear sight assembly. The AR-10A4 series splits the difference between the target and A2 models, having a flat-top scope mount on the receiver and no front sight assembly and using standard A2 handguards. The A2 and A4 series both generally have a muzzle brake. The AR-10A4C is the carbine model of this rifle.

In addition to the standard .308 Winchester chambering, Armalite also offers the AR-10T and AR-10A4 series in a .243 chambering for those hunters who believe this round is superior to the .308. (This change of caliber dictates some modification of the gas system, something for kitchen table gunsmiths to keep in mind before trying to "mix and match" parts between the two versions of the gun.)

Oddly enough, there is also an EA-10, which is basically the AR-10A2 without a flash hider. This gun is marketed by the Eagle division of Armalite and is designed to be a sister to the EA-15. However, it accepts most of the accessories of the AR-10A2, and the only major difference between the two models is the EA-10's lack of a muzzle brake.

The original Armalite rifles made until the company's demise under Elisco Tool Manufacturing are marked with "Armalite Costa Mesa, CA" on the receiver. Models made by the newly reorganized Armalite have a receiver marked "Coal Valley, IL," whereas current and later models reflect a change of address, with "Geneseo, IL" on the receiver. (At the time of this writing, the Armalite Web site at <www.Armalite.com> has a search engine that enables users to locate information about specific rifles based on their serial number.) The AR-10As made by Dutch Arsenal Artillerie are so marked on their receivers.

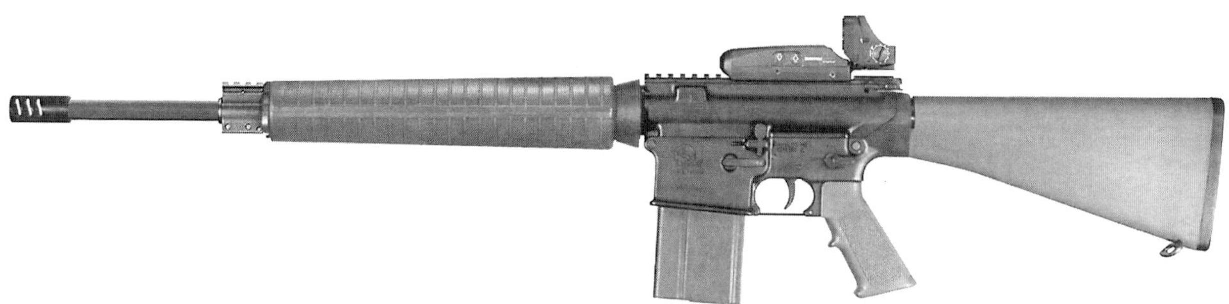

AR-10A4. (Courtesy of Armalite.)

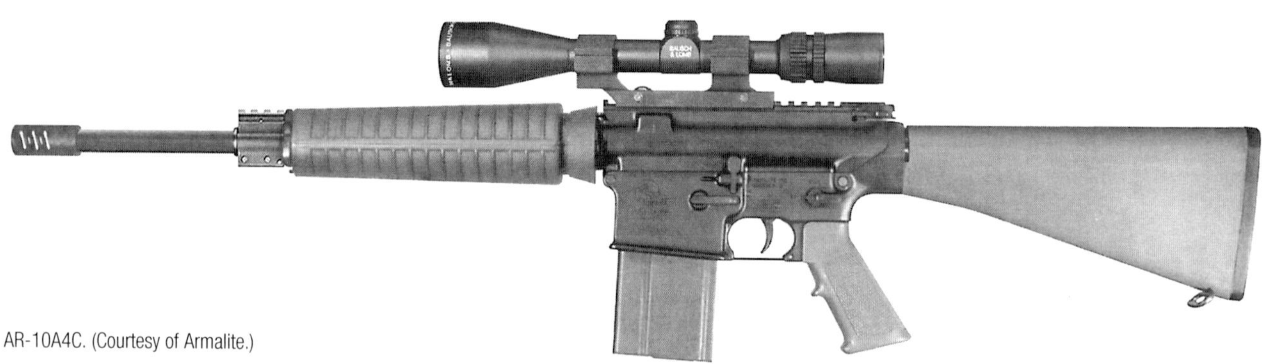

AR-10A4C. (Courtesy of Armalite.)

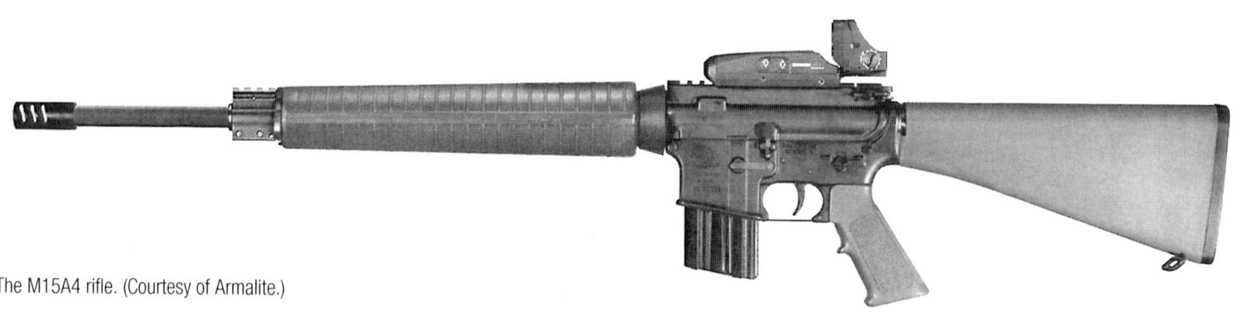

The M15A4 rifle. (Courtesy of Armalite.)

The M15A4C carbine. (Courtesy of Armalite.)

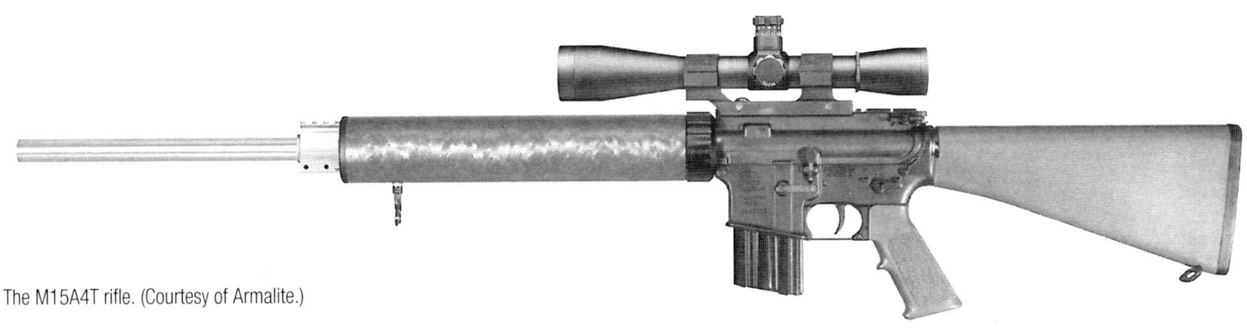

The M15A4T rifle. (Courtesy of Armalite.)

The M15A4TC carbine. (Courtesy of Armalite.)

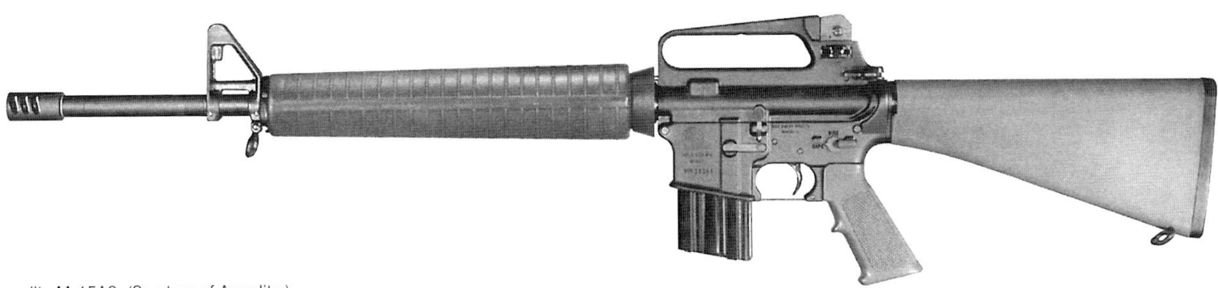

Armalite M-15A2. (Courtesy of Armalite.)

## M15 SERIES

Since the introduction of the AR-10 series of guns, Armalite has created a sister group of models chambered for the .223 Remington. Designated the M15 models, these are nearly identical in many ways to the Eagle Arms EA-15 series (and undoubtedly use most of the same parts) but have the Armalite logo on their receivers—a plus in the eyes of many buyers.

The M15A4T models (available in 16-inch carbine or with a 24-inch barrel) have flat-top receivers for scope rings and telescopic sights and lack a front sight. These guns have a free-floated barrel for maximum accuracy and a stainless-steel heavy barrel. The M15A4 models have flat-top receivers for scope mounts but have standard Armalite carbine or full handguards on 16- or 20-inch barrels.

The M15A2 has the standard M16A2 configuration but, like all other models, is semiauto only and employs a muzzle brake rather than a flash hider (due to the restrictions of the federal assault weapon ban). The M15A2 Match Rifle is nearly identical in appearance to the standard M15A2, but has a heavy stainless-steel barrel; the M-15A2C is the carbine version of the rifle.

All models are also available in "law enforcement" models; these are basically the same as the standard models outlined above, with a flash hider (legal for law enforcement use) added to the barrel of some.

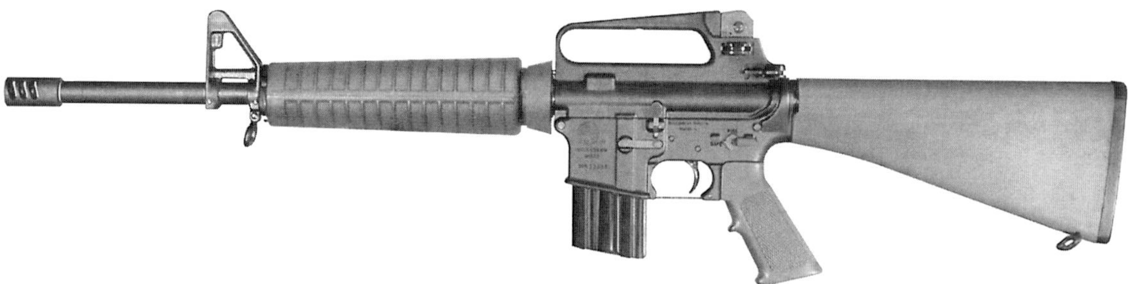

Armalite M-15A2C carbine. (Courtesy of Armalite.)

Armalite offers a choice of black or green plastic furniture with all these models.

## AR-50

Successful gun manufacturers are ever on the lookout for products that will fill niche markets. A case in point is the AR-50, created by Armalite late in 1997. As the name of the gun suggests, it is chambered for the Browning machine gun (BMG) .50-caliber cartridge, a rimless round that looks like an overgrown .308 or .223 cartridge. This rifle is single shot and, unlike most other .50-caliber rifles, designed strictly for recreational shooters. The brainchild of Westrom and his design team of brothers George and Paul Reynolds, it went into production in 1999. (George Reynolds joined Armalite in 1997, bringing with him the designs for a blank-firing system and a subcaliber device, either of which could be employed in the U.S. military's Mark 19 Mod 4 grenade machine gun. These projects soon joined the Armalite line of products, designated the AR-22 and AR-23.)

Unlike previous Armalite guns that were noted for their light weight, the AR-50 is a massive firearm, weighing 41 pounds empty and measuring 59 inches long with a 31-inch barrel. The gun has a magnesium phosphated finish on steel parts and anodized aluminum at other points. Recoil is kept in check largely by the weight of the firearm. However, it also has a multiflute muzzle brake and a Pachmayr shoulder rest to further reduce felt recoil. The bolt sports a triple front locking lug and has a Sako-style extractor. A spring-loaded plunger on the ejector automatically tosses empties for a fast reload when it is called for. A single-stage trigger mechanism helps shooters wring the last bit of accuracy from this rifle.

## AR-30

The AR-30 is a bolt-action rifle that is basically a spin-off of the AR-50. Like the AR-50, the AR-30 is built around an aluminum stock that merges a machine rest with a rifle stock for the maximum stability needed for target shooting or varmint hunting (with the potential for use as a countersniper rifle by law enforcement buyers).

The machine rest/stock has a V-shaped channel that, coupled with a recoil wedge, secures an octagonal receiver in place with action screws that draw the action down into the stock for a tight fit. The result is superb accuracy without the need of hand fitting or bedding.

Unlike the AR-50, the AR-30 is slated to have two options for its action. One is the conventional turnbolt action more or less like that of most bolt-action

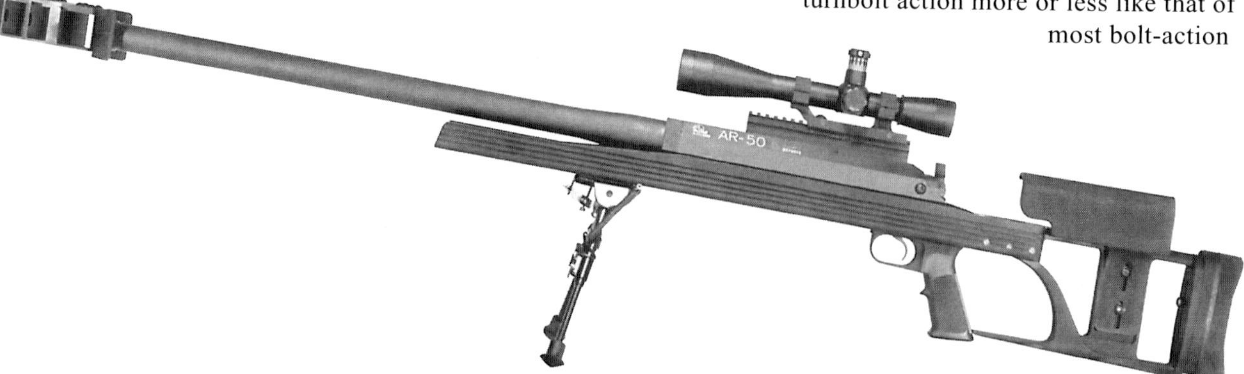


AR-50 rifle.

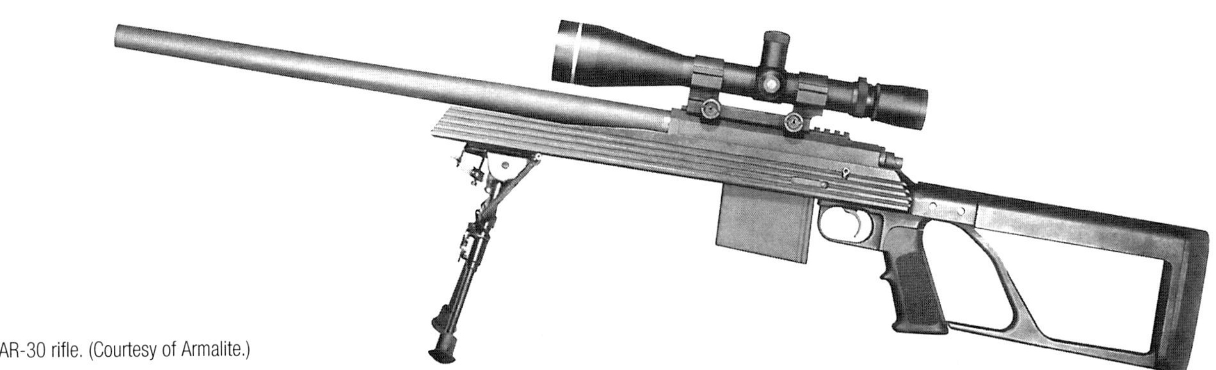
AR-30 rifle. (Courtesy of Armalite.)

rifles. The other is a straight-pull action that will permit faster reloading.

AR-30 receivers will accept conventional scope mounts as well as Armalite's special sight bases, which are designed to minimize recoil to the scope mounted on it. The AR-30 will also be available with optional integral bases. Stainless-steel barrels will be available in a variety of lengths out to 24 inches; initial chamberings will be .243, .308, and .30-'06, with more scheduled to follow.

### EAGLE ARMS EA-15

In the first edition of this book, Eagle Arms was given a minor heading and a little attention; its rifles merited only three short paragraphs, ending with, "These rifles are very well made and surprisingly accurate. This young company would appear to be one of the 'up and coming' marketers of the AR-15-style guns that are aimed for a clientele of police and civilian customers."

Talk about understatements! With the addition of the parent company's AR-10 series of guns and accessories to its line, along with the EA-10 .308 chambering, this company has become a major contender among marketers of excellent, trouble-free rifles.

The original Eagle Arms rifles were based on several main model groups. The R series models have the general appearance of the U.S. Army rifles but fire in semiauto only. The E1 versions have sights like those of the M16A1, while the E2 models have sights like those on the M16A2 versions (which can be adjusted easily with the elevation and windage knobs). Before the company became a subdivision of Armalite, its lineup was broken into the following models:

- EA-15E1 was the standard rifle (with M16A1-style sights).
- EA-15R3 was the H-BAR.
- EA-15R4 Carbine had shorty-style telescoping stock, E1 sights, and 16-inch barrel.
- EA-15R5 Carbine has E2 sights, telescoping stock, and 16-inch barrel.
- The R7 Golden Eagle is an H-BAR with a Douglas target barrel.
- Earlier models of the EA-15 will generally be seen with a receiver marked "Coal Valley, IL" whereas newer models will reflect a change of address, with "Geneseo, IL" on the receiver.

### THE "NEW" AR-180

In 2001, Armalite announced that it would again introduce the AR-180 to the U.S. market. The new version of this gun appears to have a few design changes but overall has the same distinctive look of its forebears. It will be interesting to see whether this new gun succeeds where the old one did not.

### M-15P

Arguably this is more of a training aid (or even a toy) than a rifle, but the M-15P is an interesting air rifle that seems to be headed for inclusion in the Armalite line. The air rifle operates like a selective-fire M16 rifle and has the overall look and feel of an Armalite firearm. Not regulated by firearms laws, the M-15P fires in both semi- and auto mode, and its recoil can be increased to mimic that of a real AR-15, apparently with an eye toward selling the air rifle as a trainer.

The M-15P fires a small .22-caliber ball fed from a 25-round tubular magazine located along the barrel; the gun can also fire pellets that are loaded into a revolving cylinder system. Most AR-15 accessories and scopes will fit on the M-15P flat-top receiver. The retail cost is not cheap: the air rifle is slated to sell for $899.

## MODELS PRODUCED BY ARMALITE

It seems likely that almost any list of guns produced by Armalite over the years will have some gaps in it that probably represent little-known prototypes, or even drawings, that never went into production. That said, there are probably very few (and hopefully none) in the following list, which was compiled based on information from reliable sources. Production dates, where shown, are the years when a firearm was actually produced by Armalite; some of these guns were produced in other years by manufacturers licensed by Armalite.

| | |
|---|---|
| Parasniper | Military sniper rifle or sporting gun. Several chamberings, .308 Winchester being most common; bolt action. |
| AR-1 | Foam-filled fiberglass brown stock; anodized aluminum barrel with steel liner. Few of these guns were actually made. |
| AR-5 | Produced from 1954 to 1955. Bolt action; four-round magazine; chambered for the .22 Hornet; 2.75-pound weight; could be taken down with barrel and action stored in hollow stock; became the air force's MA-1 survival rifle (few sales were actually made due to the air force's failure to offer a contract for the rifle). |
| AR-7 Explorer | Produced from 1959 to1960; reintroduced to Armalite product line in 1999. Semiauto action; chambered for .22 LR; barrel and receiver could be stored in hollow stock; 8-round magazine; 2.75-pound weight. |
| AR-10 | Produced 1955 to1956; .308 Winchester chambering; aluminum receiver halves; fiberglass furniture; 20-round magazine; titanium flash hider/recoil reduction assembly. |
| AR-10A | Improved version of the AR-10; conventional flash hider. |
| AR-10B | Produced 1996 to present; EA-15-based version chambered for .308 Winchester or .243; employs AR-15 parts wherever practical but has many parts unique to the rifle; brown plastic furniture designed to mimic look of original AR-10, as well as an in-the-carrying-hand charging lever. |
| AR-15 | Produced 1956 to 1959; .223 Remington chambering; aluminum receiver halves; fiberglass furniture; 20-round magazine; no flash hider on early guns; standard flash hider on majority of guns produced. |
| AR-16 | Produced from 1959 to 1960; folding stock; chambered in .308 Winchester; grenade launcher flash hider; sheet-metal receiver; and trigger group parts. |
| AR-17 Golden Gun | Produced from 1956 to 1962. Semiauto 12-gauge shotgun; two-round capacity; anodized receiver and barrel; brown wood-grain plastic furniture; 2,000 made but only 1,200 initially sold. |
| AR-18 | Produced 1963 to 1965 (may be brought back into production); folding stock; chambered in .223 Remington; grenade launcher flash hider; sheet-metal receiver and trigger group parts; 6.9-pound weight. |
| AR-20 | New firearm under development at Armalite at the time of this writing. |
| AR-22 | Produced 1998 to —; blank-firing device for Mark 19 Mod 4 40mm grenade launcher (using 7.62mm NATO blank). |
| AR-23 | Produced 1998 to —; subcaliber training device for Mark 19 Mod 4 40mm grenade launcher (using special tracer designed to simulate grenade trajectory). |

| | |
|---|---|
| AR-30 | Currently under development; machine-rest stock target rifle; bolt- or straight-pull action; variety of chamberings planned, up to and including .338 Lapua. |
| AR-50 | Produced 1998 to—; .50 BMG chambering (with 12.7mm chambering available; aluminum stock; weight 41 pounds. |

# Chapter 7

# Bushmaster

When Bushmaster Firearms underbid Colt to win the contract to build the M4 carbine in 1991, the company put itself on the map in the eyes of many in the armaments business. Although the turn of events was a tad unexpected, this company had been gearing up and producing quality guns for some time. Considering the innovations from Bushmaster over the few decades it had been in operation, this contract was just one more stepping stone in its line of successes.

Although many people know Bushmaster best from the parts-supply side of the business, Quality Parts, the company offers a number of rifles and carbines, including an XM15E2 rifle series with A2-style rear sights, available with standard 20-inch barrel or heavy National Match barrels in 20-, 24-, and 26-inch lengths. It also offered a preban carbine with a choice of 16- or 11.5-inch barrels (the latter with a flash hider permanently pinned and welded to it to keep the barrel within federal requirements). The carbines are offered both with A2- and A1-style rear sight assemblies.

Essential to winning the contract with the government was Bushmaster's ability to add a durable chrome lining to a rifle barrel. Like Colt and a few other major manufacturers, Bushmaster mastered this technique, and nearly all the company's rifles and carbines have this feature. In 1989, the firm moved to a larger 44,000-square-foot facility, enabling it to tackle large contracts like that for the M4 carbine.

### BUSHMASTER COMMEMORATIVES

In addition to standard guns, Bushmaster has produced some limited series of commemorative AR-15s. Collectors' guns have made for lucrative business with other types of firearms in the past, and it is probable that such AR-15-style commemoratives will be seen in the future. Most of these guns are shootable, but firing them too much can ruin their value as collectors' pieces. Commemoratives are often specially engraved, have special pictures engraved in their receivers to commemorate special events in which the firearm played a key role, and may have gold plating and a gloss.

One recent commemorative gun was issued by Bushmaster on its 20th anniversary in 1998. This rifle has a 20-inch barrel with a modest amount of engraving on the upper and lower receivers (most notably on the right side under the rear sight and over the magazine well) as well as an inset stock medallion and gold plating on key components of the rifle. Most of these guns were sold with a hardwood presentation case. One such gun was raffled off at the July 15, 2000, meeting of the U.S. Army Special Forces Association, after being donated to the group by Bushmaster.

### THE CMP

The CMP is the top-of-the-line rifle offered by Bushmaster in conjunction with the U.S. Civilian Marksmanship Program (CMP). Under this contract, specially marked Bushmaster (DCM) Competition Rifles introduced in 1997 were sold to CMP-affiliated state associations and clubs throughout the United States. These rifles had a large "CMP" engraved on the right upper receiver half just below the rear sight and a large eagle seal of the CMP on the lower right receiver halve on the magazine well. The program subsidized the production of the guns, which were built around the Bushmaster target version of the company's AR-15-style rifles. For purchase eligibility, the CMP required that affiliate clubs have a Junior Rifle Program in place.

While retaining the basic look of an M16A2 to stay within CMP regulations, the DCM sports a 20-inch barrel with competition modifications to the trigger group, sights, barrel, fore end, and buttstock for increased accuracy. A few of the CMP receivers went to Compass Lake Engineering, which built target rifles around them; these, too, were sold through the CMP.

This rifle has a modified A2 rear sight that can

accommodate interchangeable microaperture sights. Additionally, the windage and elevation mechanisms are available in either 1/2- or 1/4-minute adjustments for each click of the windage knob or elevation dial. The heavy barrel is "floated" inside the handguard for additional accuracy, with the sling swivel attached to the leading edge of the tube rather than the barrel itself. Several front sights are available; These include .052-, .062- (the standard width), or .072-inch diameter posts and can be screwed into place like regular front sight posts.

The stock contains more than 3 pounds of lead, giving the rifle added mass to help keep it on target as well as totally erase any felt recoil (this weight can be adjusted downward by those users wanting a lighter rifle or a different balance).

## THE M17S RIFLE

The M17S is very similar to the AR-15 and therefore merits mention. The rifle was designed by the Australian company Edenpine. This firm had invested time and money in developing the rifle, only to discover that new Australian regulations effectively outlawing civilian ownership of such firearms virtually robbed it of its market. So Edenpine sold its manufacturing rights, tooling, and three prototype rifles to Bushmaster. Bushmaster further refined the rifle and marketed the new gun as its M17S.

Early-production Bushmaster M17S rifles are easily identified by their flat-black finish on the receiver as well as short-throw, captive pins that connect the receiver's halves. These were produced for about a year.

The second model was produced with a matte-black Teflon coating. The third year of production saw a third refinement of the rifle, this time in the form of long-throw captive pins that united the upper and lower as well as modifications in the upper receiver to reduce its weight; a steel cam pin track in the upper receiver was also added to reduce the wear in this area. Outwardly, receivers introduced after year two can be identified by their four Allen screws on the left side of the top receiver.

All these models were produced before to the 1994 assault weapon ban. After the law was passed, Bushmaster created a fourth version of the rifle to conform to the new regulations, this one easily identified by its lack of a flash hider. At the same time, some other modifications were made to the gun, including the following:

- Shortening its barrel
- Installing a lock nut at the muzzle (replacing the flash hider)
- Removing the firing pin spring
- Adding emergency iron sights to the carrying handle
- Incorporating a new scope mount design
- Refining the trigger link
- Adding a chromed bore (not present in previous versions of the rifle)

Other minor changes have undoubtedly been made since that time and will most likely continue to be made to improve the life of the rifle and ease its manufacture, as is the case with most firearms. However, this last version appears to be working well and is likely to be the "final" configuration for some time. That said, except for the lack of flash hider this last version is arguably the best

Bushmaster M-17S, shown here without a scope mounted on the integral Weaver rails on its carrying handle. (Courtesy of Bushmaster.)

version for those interested in firing the rifle rather than collecting guns.

It should be noted that the barrel lock nut threading is too shallow to permit the secure mounting of a flash hider, which is therefore discouraged by Bushmaster. The nut is a necessary part that retains the barrel shroud. This sheath increases the tension between the two ends of the barrel as it heats up when fired, thereby keeping the point of impact consistent and improving accuracy. For this reason, the extension tube is an essential part that should not be removed even though the firearm may function without this part in place.

The M17S' carrying handle has a see-through base with a top surface that has molded-in Weaver rails so it can easily accept any scope or night-vision device that uses Weaver clamps or rings. The base also has emergency sights, which are somewhat limited given the short space between them; these are roughly zeroed at 25 meters.

The heavy profile match competition barrel coupled with the integral scope base offers a lot of accuracy. The trigger pull on these guns is not as ideal as that of a standard rifle (true of most bullpup designs due to the coupling needed with the sear's being in the receiver while the trigger is far ahead). Nevertheless, the gun has a good feel, and many target shooters undoubtedly appreciate the compact package offered by the bullpup configuration.

The lower receiver/pistol grip and carrying handle are made of 43-percent glass-filled nylon, making them lightweight but very durable. The upper receiver is constructed of aircraft-quality aluminum, identical to that used on the AR-15 models the company makes. In addition to supporting the scope, the carrying handle has a rear section that acts as a charging handle. Pulling it to the rear and releasing it cycles the action, just as pulling on the charging handle does on an AR-15.

Cleaning is also quite easy, thanks to a hinged pushpin that releases the top of the gun from the lower receiver/stock assembly. Once these are separated, the user can then clean all parts of the firearm without problem.

**M17S Specifications**

| | |
|---|---|
| Barrel | H-BAR, 21.5 inches, crowned, hard-chrome lined |
| Overall length | 30 inches |

## THE BUSHMASTER PISTOL AND RIFLE

Although today Bushmaster is best known for its M17 and AR-15-style guns, it started out with a very different sort of weapon, albeit one that incorporated many AR-15 parts into its design. This weapon was in turn very loosely based on a gun Colt had started work on in the 1960s, which at that time appeared to be the stepping stone in small arms development in the United States, especially in the area of submachine gun and pistol replacements.

Colt's firearm used very few AR-15 parts. The design was radical, a modified bullpup that placed the pistol grip in front of the magazine. Unlike the standard bullpup, this gun didn't have a stock and was more of an "arm gun," which Colt described as a "lightweight rifle/submachine gun" for lack of a better term.

Colt .221 IMP arm gun.

The shooter using the stockless arm gun would hold the weapon straight out in front, using his free hand to hold the butt of the weapon against his upper arm. He would then aim, resting his head against the upper part of the arm holding the weapon and sighting down a small scope or the moveable sight (which swiveled to accommodate right- or left-handed users).

The arm gun was originally chambered for pistol ammunition, but the recoil was so mild that the 5.5-pound weapon was soon chambered for rifle ammunition and, according to those who fired it, the recoil even with 7.62mm NATO ammunition was minimal because the hand and arm absorbed the recoil rather than the shoulder, as with regular rifles.

In 1969 the U.S. Air Force tested the arm gun for possible adoption as a survival weapon or a 5.56mm "submachine gun." The arm rifle used in the tests was chambered for the .221 IMP cartridge (and the weapon itself is sometimes called the IMP due to this chambering). Although the arm rifle apparently worked well, no contracts were forthcoming, and the design was shelved.

Bushmaster came up with a slightly modified version of the arm rifle idea that actually did go into production. This new design, created by Mack W. Gwinn Jr., utilized the basic concept of the original but incorporated many more of the AR-15 parts, keeping the tooling costs of

Bushmaster pistols. Midproduction model (top) and late production design.

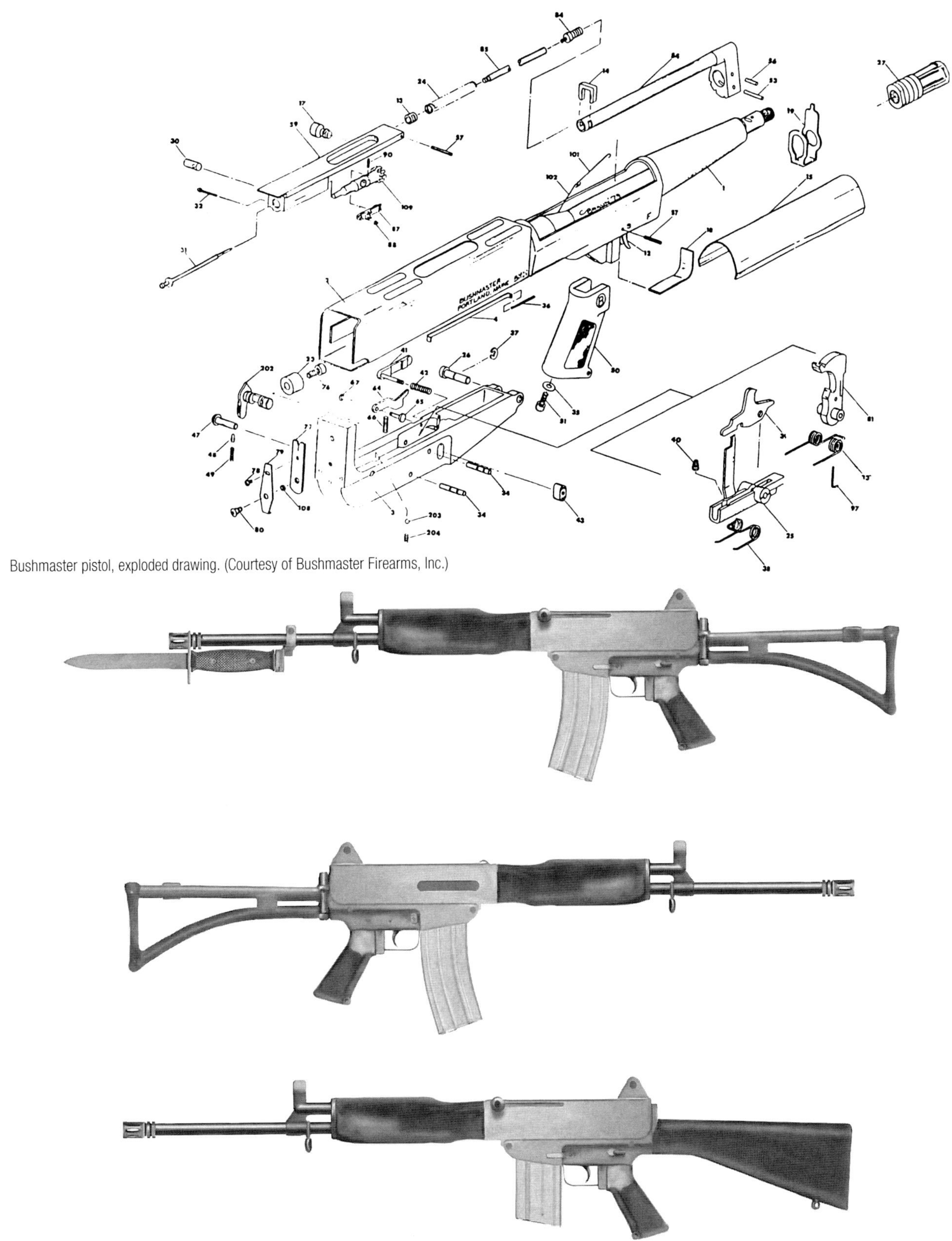

Bushmaster pistol, exploded drawing. (Courtesy of Bushmaster Firearms, Inc.)

Bushmaster rifles with side-folding and wooden stocks. Top rifle has optional bayonet lug attachment.

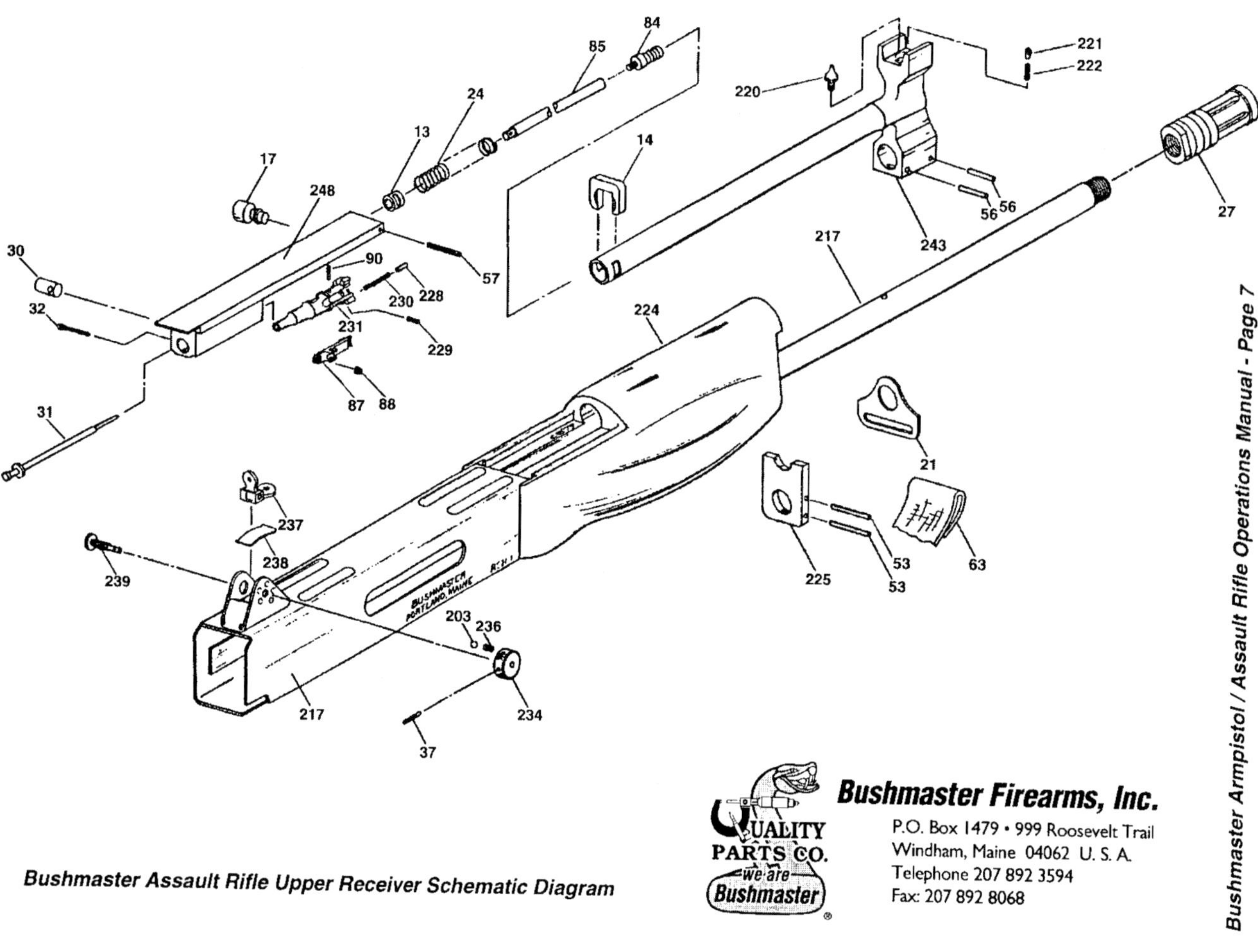


Exploded drawing of Bushmaster rifle's upper receiver. (Courtesy of Bushmaster Firearms, Inc.)

manufacturing the firearm down. Because the firearm lacked a conventional stock, the BATF ruled that it was a pistol, which allowed Bushmaster to mount a short barrel on it without running into legal problems or red tape. It was eventually sold as the Bushmaster Pistol.

In the rush to get the first Bushmaster pistols produced, the company that was created to manufacture and sell them suffered from quality control problems and soon went bankrupt. The early guns it produced can be identified by a safety located on the right of the pistol, just above the trigger guard; late production models had a safety inside the trigger guard, ahead of the trigger.

In 1982 a new manufacturing company was created, and the quality of the Bushmaster pistols was vastly improved. These models were revamped in many key areas, with production becoming more refined. This design dispensed with the trigger safety, retaining only the selector/safety on the left of the receiver to the rear of the magazine well.

At about this time Bushmaster also created a second model of the firearm. Also designed by Mack W. Gwinn Jr., this model brought the weapon full circle: a stock was added along with a longer barrel, and the pistol grip was moved back into a conventional position. Since the internal parts of the Bushmaster were already mostly identical to those of the AR-15, the end result was a stamped-steel receiver version of the AR-15 with a piston/recoil spring assembly over the barrel rather than a gas tube with a recoil/buffer assembly in the stock.

The Bushmaster pistol weighed 5.25 pounds and was 20.5 inches long with an 11.5-inch barrel. The rifle weighed 7.5 pounds (empty) and was 37.5 inches long. In addition to the fixed wooden stock, Bushmaster also made a folder that shortened the rifle to 27.5 inches when folded. The barrel on both versions of the Bushmaster was welded to the steel receiver and had a twist of 1 turn to 10 inches.

Unfortunately, the very first production

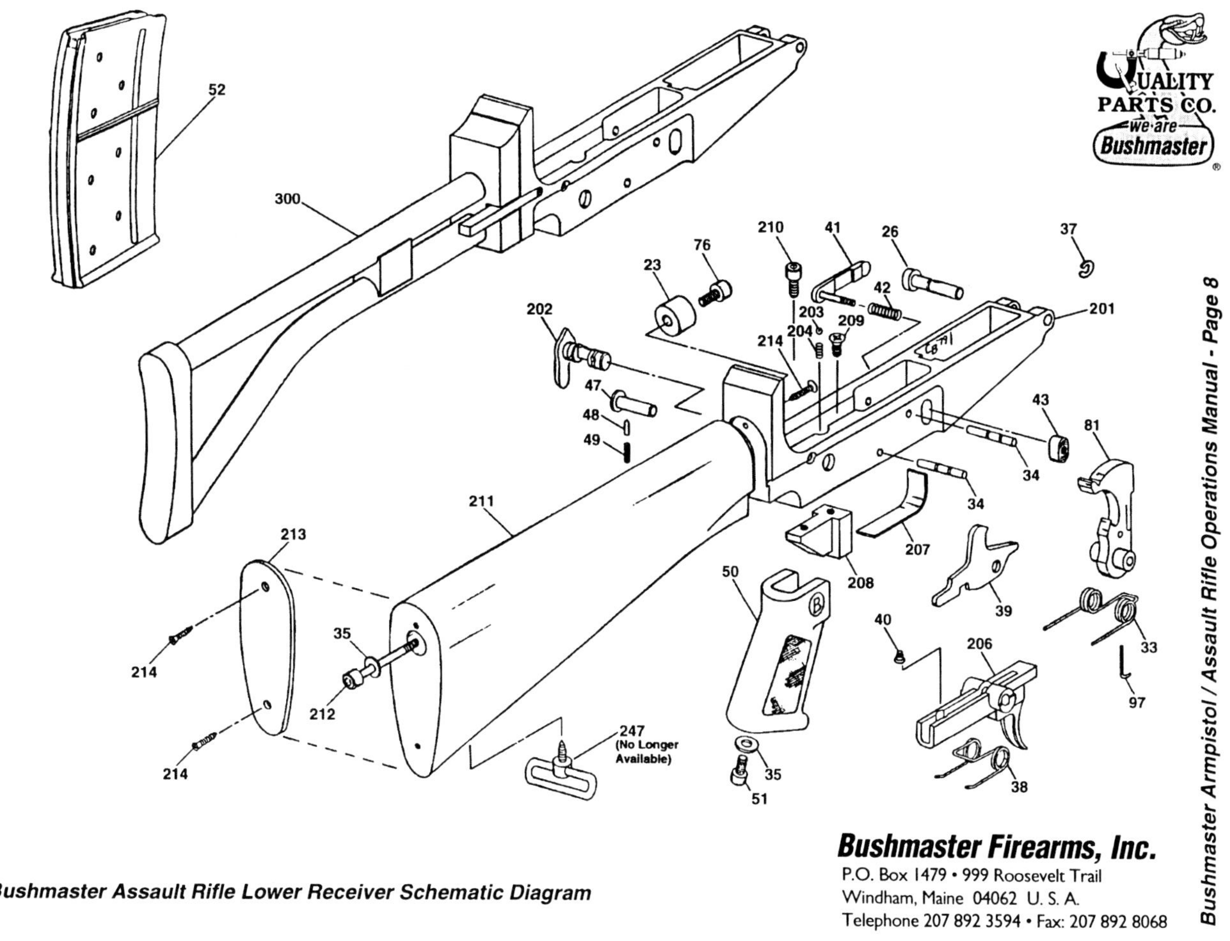


Exploded drawing of Bushmaster rifle's lower receiver. (Courtesy of Bushmaster Firearms, Inc.)

Bushmasters had tarnished the image of the newer pistol and rifle (much as had happened with early AR-15s). Eventually, production of the rifle was discontinued, and even though sources at Bushmaster remark from time to time that management toys with the idea of producing the gun again, to date this has not occurred and it seems doubtful that it will, given the success of the company's AR-15 and M17 rifles. (At the same time, the pistol remains on the company's logo and, from a mechanical standpoint, the M17 is actually a Bushmaster pistol in bullpup rifle clothing.)

In the meantime, a few Bushmaster pistols and rifles are still seen on the used gun market. These are becoming collector's guns but they also make good shooters. Both selective fire and semiauto-only versions of the firearm were manufactured with both blued-steel and nickel finishes. Since the basic design of these guns is sound, any of them (whether of early or late production) can be "tuned" to work flawlessly. For those wanting the very best, the later pistols of better quality-control runs have a "J" prefix on the serial number, and the later rifles have an "F" prefix on their serial number.

### Preban Bushmaster AR-15s

The preban Bushmaster AR-15-style rifles and carbines were pretty much like those built by Colt, with a basic 20-inch rifle and a 16-inch-barrel carbine being the main guns offered. However, Bushmaster went one better on Colt, selling a variety of barrel lengths for its rifle as well as complete upper receiver/barrel kits that gave a buyer the ability to create a shorty from his own full-sized rifle simply by replacing the upper assembly with a secondary kit bought from Bushmaster.

Additionally, Bushmaster offered the Dissipator

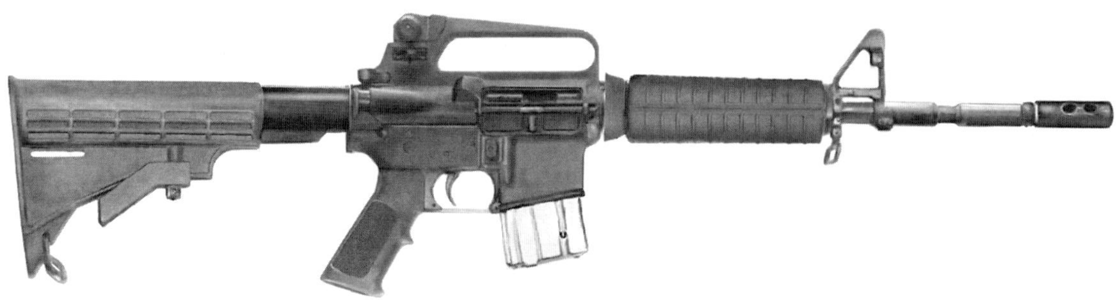

Bushmaster M-15E2S M4 is a compliant postban rifle, thanks to a muzzle brake and a fixed, noncollapsible stock.

Bushmaster XM15 E2S. (Courtesy of Bushmaster Firearms, Inc.)

upper receiver/barrel kit (as well as an assembled Dissipator carbine), which was quite unlike any other system available at that time. The pertinent feature of this model was a 16-inch barrel coupled with gas block that lacked a front and a secondary front sight placed on the barrel ahead of it. This permitted placing a full-sized handguard over the gas block, giving it the feel of a full-sized rifle with the length of a carbine—arguably the best of both worlds, especially for larger shooters who find the carbine handguard too short for a comfortable hold.

### Postban Bushmaster Rifles

The postban Bushmaster line is basically the same as the preban one, but an even greater variety of models are now available. These postban guns generally have a crowned barrel, sans flash hider or muzzle brake, and are missing a bayonet lug; however, a few models have a muzzle brake permanently welded on. Most also come with a politically correct10-round magazine.

Receivers on the Bushmaster guns are forged from 7075T6 aircraft-quality aluminum, are given a nonreflective phosphate finish, and are hard-anodized, just like the guns Bushmaster sells to the military. The receivers have the M16A2 design improvements, including cartridge case deflector and raised ridges around the magazine release button. Although most rifles are sold with 20-inch barrels, Bushmaster also offers 24-inch barrels on rifle models (which often yield greater accuracy and a bit greater velocity with some slower powders while lowering the report of the gun). Bushmaster manufactures its own barrels in 11.5-, 14.5-, 16-, 20-, and 24-inch lengths and also offers standard as well as lighter but still rigid fluted barrels with many of its target guns (in the 20- and 24-inch lengths).

Although the "shorty" telescoping stock would normally make a postban gun illegal, Bushmaster designers have simply employed the basic layout of the telescoping stock—which does not contract but rather is permanently pinned to its "out" position—to create a shorty look-alike. Most models have a 1-in-9 twist, cutting down on barrel wear and stabilizing larger bullets while (well, perhaps; this is a matter of debate among experts). Bushmaster also offers rifles with the telescoping stock, flash hider, bayonet lug, and/or other

Bushmaster Dissipator Carbine. (Courtesy of Bushmaster Firearms, Inc.)

Bushmaster XM15 E2S Shorty AK. (Courtesy of Bushmaster Firearms, Inc.)

preban features to military and law enforcement users. Both civilian and government models are currently shipped in a hard plastic case that can be locked.

Most Bushmaster models have an upper receiver/barrel kit counterpart that permits a buyer to transform his AR-15 into one of the Bushmaster configurations. That said, the following are the basic Bushmaster models at the time of this writing.

Bushmaster XM15 E2S V-Match Carbine. (Courtesy of Bushmaster Firearms, Inc.)

| | |
|---|---|
| XM15 E2S M4-Type Carbine | Lightweight 14.5-inch barrel machined to M4 profile with permanently attached Mini Y Comp muzzle brake (16-inch barrel overall); fixed telescoping stock. |
| XM15 E2S A2 Shorty | 16-inch crowned barrel, standard rifle stock, A2 sights. |
| XM15 E2S Shorty | A3 16-inch crowned barrel, standard rifle stock, flat-top receiver with detachable rear sight/carrying handle |
| XM15 E2S Shorty AK | 16-inch barrel with AK-style flash hider welded onto muzzle, standard rifle stock, A2-style sights |
| XM15 E2S Shorty AK A3 | 16-inch barrel with AK-style flash hider welded onto muzzle, standard rifle stock, flat-top receiver with detachable rear sight/carrying handle |
| XM15 E2S Dissipator | 16-inch Dissipator barrel with crowned muzzle, standard rifle stock, A2-style sights |
| XM15 E2S Dissipator A3 | 16-inch Dissipator barrel with crowned muzzle, standard rifle stock |
| XM15 E2S V Match Carbine | 16-inch crowned barrel without front sight assembly, V Match knurled aluminum handguard and free-float barrel, flat-top receiver, standard stock |
| XM15 E2S A2 Rifle | 20- or 24-inch crowned barrel, A2-style sights, standard stock, flat-top receiver with detachable rear sight/carrying handle |
| XM15 E2S A3 Rifle | 20- or 24-inch crowned barrel, flat-top receiver with detachable rear sight/carrying handle, standard stock |
| XM15 E2S V Match | 20- or 24-inch crowned barrel with or without front sight assembly, V Match knurled aluminum handguard and free float barrel, flat-top receiver, standard stock. |

Bushmaster XM15 E2S PCM. (Courtesy of Bushmaster Firearms, Inc.)

Bushmaster XM15 E2S Target Rifle with a 24-inch barrel. (Courtesy of Bushmaster Firearms, Inc.)

Bushmaster XM15 E2S V Match Carbine. (Courtesy of Bushmaster Firearms, Inc.)

Bushmaster XM15 E2S law enforcement carbine. (Courtesy of Bushmaster Firearms, Inc.)

Bushmaster M4A3-style law enforcement carbine with fixed stock. (Courtesy of Bushmaster Firearms, Inc.)

Bushmaster M4A3-style law enforcement carbine. (Courtesy of Bushmaster Firearms, Inc.)

Bushmaster XM15 E2S law enforcement Dissipator carbine. (Courtesy of Bushmaster Firearms, Inc.)

Bushmaster XM15 E2S Target Model (law enforcement version). (Courtesy of Bushmaster Firearms, Inc.)

Bushmaster XM15 E2S V-Match Competition Rifle (law enforcement version). (Courtesy of Bushmaster Firearms, Inc.)

In addition to its rifle lineup, Bushmaster offers the M203 grenade launcher, shown here mounted on the company's XM15 E2S rifle. (Courtesy of Bushmaster Firearms, Inc.)

## LAW ENFORCEMENT MODELS

After landing the contract with the U.S. military, the way was paved for other U.S. agencies to purchase Bushmaster guns. The company now boasts of sales to the U.S. Border Patrol, Department of Defense, Department of Energy, Department of Parks and Recreation, Customs, Drug Enforcement Agency, Marshal Service, and Secret Service, as well as the SEALS, Rangers, and Green Berets who got the carbines purchased with the original contract. Not surprisingly, this has also resulted in more than a few state and local law enforcement agencies purchasing Bushmaster carbines or rifles for use by special units.

In addition to the rifles and carbines listed below, Bushmaster offers its own M203 grenade launcher that is virtually identical to that manufactured by Colt. Like other M203 assemblies, this can be mounted on the company's M4 carbine or any of its nontarget rifles with standard handguards and barrel configuration.

All of the following are included in the current line offered by Bushmaster to government buyers (these models all are sold with the A2-style flash hider and bayonet lug).

| | |
|---|---|
| M4 Carbine A2 | 14.5-inch barrel machined to M4 profile, A2 receiver, telescoping stock |
| M4 Carbine A3 | 14.5-inch barrel machined to M4 profile, A3 flat-top receiver with detachable carrying handle/rear sight, telescoping stock |
| XM15 E2S | Lightweight 16-inch barrel, A2 receiver, telescoping stock |
| XM15 Shorty A3 Model | Lightweight 16-inch barrel, A3 flat-top receiver with detachable carrying handle/rear sight, telescoping stock |
| XM15E2S Dissipator | Lightweight 16-inch barrel, A2 receiver, Dissipator system with full-size rifle handguard, telescoping stock |
| XM15 A3 Dissipator | Lightweight 16-inch barrel, A3 flat-top receiver with detachable carrying handle/rear sight, Dissipator system with full-size rifle handguard, telescoping stock |
| XM15 E2S Patrolman's Carbine | 16-inch barrel cut to M4 profile, A2 receiver, telescoping stock |
| XM15 A3 Patrolman's Carbine | 16-inch barrel cut to M4 profile, A3 flat-top receiver with detachable carrying handle/rear sight, telescoping stock |
| V Match Carbine | Heavy16-inch barrel, A3 flat-top receiver (detachable carrying handle/rear sight is an option with this model), free-float handguard, standard rifle stock |
| XM15 E2S Rifle | 20-inch standard barrel, rifle stock, A2 receiver, A2 handguards and grip |
| XM15 A3 Rifle | 20-inch standard barrel, rifle stock, A3 flat-top receiver with detachable carrying handle/rear sight, A2 handguards and grip |
| XM15 PCM Target Rifle | 20-inch match barrel, rifle stock, A3 flat-top receiver with detachable carrying handle/rear sight, A2 handguards and grip |
| V Match Rifle | Heavy 20- or 24-inch barrel, A3 flat-top receiver (detachable carrying handle/rear sight is an option with this model), free-float handguard, standard rifle stock. |

# Chapter 8

# Innovations, Spinoffs, and Copycats

Because the Armalite/Colt original patent on the AR-15 design has long since expired, there are a number of companies, both foreign and domestic, that build one form or another of the AR-15 (although none can legally use the trademarked "AR-15" as part of its own model name). Some of these guns are even built on equipment originally licensed by Colt to other countries; others are made on equipment created by reverse-engineering AR-15s. Some of these rifles differ substantially from the basic AR-15 design, others are outright copies, and more than a few "new" rifles have incorporated the AR-15 trigger group, bolt, or other subassemblies into their designs. Add these up and you have almost endless variations on the AR-15 theme.

Some of the most innovative of these are the semiauto versions of the gun created to meet the huge demand for firearms in the U.S. civilian marketplace, where police, target shooters, varminters, and homeowners intent on protecting themselves have all embraced the AR-15, in one form or another, as the rifle to own.

Many of the basic parts and receivers for these guns are marketed by Western Ordnance International Corp. (and apparently manufactured by Smith Enterprises) and Defense Procurement Manufacturing Services, Inc., among others. These components are then sold to large dealers, which in turn offer parts, kits, and assembled rifles to smaller dealers as well as the general public. Barrels, especially target barrels, are offered by other wholesalers, and other small businesses manufacture many accessories and parts, including grips, stocks, and so on, that are purchased by individuals and companies to create the many "custom" versions of the AR-15.

Several companies have even grown to the point of challenging Colt in securing military contracts. For instance, Rock Island Armory (a commercial company, not a military entity) secured a contract with El Salvador. Although the details are not available to the public, it appears that a lawsuit brought against Rock Island Armory by Colt (apparently for trademark or patent infringement) brought this deal to an end. In the process, Rock Island was nearly wrecked financially and has since stopped producing AR-15-style firearms. (Receivers with the Rock Island logo are still seen on U.S. civilian AR-15-style rifles sold on the used gun market.)

This lawsuit also resulted in most manufacturers' avoiding the use of the AR-15 name or trademark in their sales literature. Designations such as "XM-15," "XM-16," "EA-15," and so on abound because of this (and add to the confusion in model designations already created by the wealth of variations that can be concocted with various styles of barrels, grips, receivers, and so forth).

A more successful challenge to Colt was mounted by Bushmaster Firearms, which won a contract to produce the U.S. military M16A2-style M4 carbine and secured several foreign contracts. The company currently has the distinction of being one of the few to produce most of its rifle parts (including magazines) and has mastered the hard-chrome process required by the military for the chamber, bore, gas key, and inside of the bolt carrier of its rifles. Additionally, Bushmaster is one of the few companies that actually finishes its receivers with the hard-anodized film and final nickel acetate coat required by the U.S. military.

In addition to its military rifles, Bushmaster offers a line intended for U.S. civilian and law enforcement markets, along with parts sold through its Quality Parts division. For a time the company also manufactured the Bushmaster pistol and rifle (more on these later), but it discontinued them, choosing to focus on the more profitable marketing of AR-15-style firearms.

Several smaller operations also purchase parts from the larger suppliers and then build AR-15-style rifles on a custom basis, usually more or less to the specifications of the purchaser. Most of these guns are expensive and one of a kind, but as the major dealers create more and more target, carbine, and specialty versions of the AR-15 and accessory makers create unique parts that enable rifle owners to make many changes to a rifle's configuration on their own, the custom builders find the going gets tougher and tougher.

Besides the U.S. domestic manufacturers and custom gunsmiths offering variations on the AR-15 design, a number of foreign companies are busily churning out similar rifles. Many of these companies started out licensed by Colt to manufacture AR-15s for their own countries and then decided to quit paying royalties and monkeying with the U.S. government's red tape and instead create and market similar rifles of their own design. The export and foreign manufacture of the rifles, plus the large stocks lost during the fall of South Vietnam that are found around the world on the black market and through Communist giveaway programs of the 1980s, have made the AR-15 one of the most common rifles in the world, rivaled only by the much older AK-47.

Israel had a running experiment going as to whether its Galil would replace the AR-15s received or bought from the U.S. military and Colt. From the mid-1970s to about the mid-1990s, its troops used both rifles to varying degrees. In the end, the AR-15 proved to be the better gun. Although the Galil was arguably tougher, it was also more cumbersome and prone to receiver cracks after prolonged use. Although rumors abounded that Israel might produce its own version of the AR-15, possibly with single plastic molding that would form the lower receiver, grip, and stock/buffer tube, in fact the final result, the TAR, is more like the Steyr AUG with its bullpup design and AUG-style pistol grip.

Whether it's possible to create a single plastic molding for the lower receiver assembly, the answer has been affirmative, not only with one of the companies listed below, but also back when Colt created several experimental rifles with molded-plastic lower receivers for testing by the U.S. military in the 1960s. These were built around a single molding that incorporated the stock, pistol grip, and lower receiver into one unit. Although finally rejected by the army, in part because the plastics of the day weren't as tough as those of today, those rifles laid the groundwork for the plastic-receiver versions of the AR-15 that would first make their appearance in the late 1990s—a trend that will most likely only grow through the 21st century (perhaps with metal receivers getting the same looks of scorn now reserved for revolvers by fans of semiauto pistols).

## CHAMBERINGS

New types of cartridges are redefining the roles played by the AR-15 and its spin-offs in the civilian and police arenas, and these cartridges may also create new versions of this firearm in the near future. Already, SWAT teams and similar special personnel have discovered that varmint cartridges like Federal's Blitz, coupled with faster twists, result in a round that has one-shot stopping power but only the penetration of building materials seen with a pistol bullet or shotgun pellet. Thus, a change in cartridges has enabled law enforcement personnel to use the AR-15 in its carbine or Commando version, giving them the advantage of heavy firepower without the overpenetration problems. Likewise, many homeowners have given up the traditional shotgun for a more effective and faster firing semiauto AR-15-style rifle loaded with this varminting cartridge.

Other experimenters and ammunition companies are creating cartridges based on the .223 that will ultimately increase the number of tasks the AR-15 can handle. The research goes in two directions, one toward .17-caliber bullets and the other toward 6mm or even .30-caliber bullets to create greater momentum at longer ranges, perhaps coupled with wind-bucking capabilities.

Hunters in those regions that allow the .223 cartridge for hunting report good results with deer and antelope with the round (often fired from an AR-15), the typical comment being something like, "When the bullet hit, the animal dropped like a rock."

There's obviously nothing wrong with the .223 cartridge, provided the hunter places the bullet in a vital area of the animal. But some states have made it illegal to use any .22-caliber cartridge for hunting animals larger than a coyote. As is often the case with laws perceived as being out of line, this resulted in a flurry of inventive genius focused on enabling shooters to do what they were able to in the first place. Consequently, in 1966 the 6x45mm (also known as the 6mm/.223) was introduced as a wildcat (hobbyist-designed) cartridge that was simply a .223 cartridge necked up to accept a 6mm bullet. Changing the barrel to one chambered for this cartridge transformed an AR-15 or other .223 rifle that was formerly illegal for hunting deer or other medium-sized game into a firearm perfectly suitable for the purpose as far as the law was concerned. As one might expect, this cartridge proved as effective as the .223 in short-range hunting.

The 6mm (PPC) round was introduced a few years later. This cartridge was even more powerful than the 6x45 and was short enough to fit into a standard AR-15 magazine. But it failed to feed reliably and also required a major change in the bolt face of the rifle because the cartridge head diameter was nearly as great as that of the .30-'06.

In 1990, Ray Wheeler, owner of Peace River Arms, set out to produce a new cartridge that would boost the power of the AR-15 while remaining reliable in the rifle's action. After studying reloading manuals, he discovered an almost forgotten cartridge, the .30 Remington, that had a small head only slightly bigger than the .223 and that was short enough to fit into the AR-15's magazine. Phone conferences with Hornady produced reloading dies and reamers needed to construct the new cartridge Wheeler envisioned. Calls to Schuetzen Gun Works (SGW) and Clymer Manufacturing produced the barrel blank and special reamer to chamber the cartridge, which would be topped with a 75-grain, 6mm bullet. The new round became the 6x44mm Wheeler in honor of its inventor.

As Wheeler experimented, he discovered he had a potent cartridge that produced a muzzle velocity of 3,200-plus fps. Compared with the .223's standard 55-grain bullet, which produces a muzzle energy of 1,282 foot-pounds of energy, the 6x44 Wheeler had 1,674. And at 500 yards, the heavy bullet retained 497 foot-pounds of energy—more than twice the energy of the .223 bullet at that distance. Currently, SGW plans to offer a barrel and bolt face for this new cartridge, making it a viable alternative for those interested in transforming an AR-15 into a potent hunting rifle.

The .30 Apache (created by Joe Apache in the mid-1980s) is another interesting wildcat that might be adapted to the AR-15. The cartridge is created by necking up a .223 case to .30 caliber and placing a 150-grain or larger bullet into it. Normally, this cartridge has the bullet seated too far forward to feed through an AR-15 magazine; however, it works to switch to a lighter bullet and seat it deeper into the case to create a working shell that fits the magazine. Whether there are advantages to such an arrangement will have to be determined by the experimenters, but the idea of creating greater power and firing a .30-caliber bullet from an AR-15 is fascinating.

An interesting proposal by John Whitworth Engel involves placing a 6.5mm bullet into a renecked .223 brass (or at least in a cartridge 45mm long so it would function in the standard AR-15 magazine). For various reasons, the 6.5mm diameter has historically performed well in longer cartridges; Engel's thinking is that it might also do better than one might otherwise expect in a shorter cartridge—and that it would obviously maintain greater energy and sustain a flatter trajectory than can be achieved with a 5.56mm bullet. Whether his contentions prove valid will be interesting to see. If so, it may just boost the effectiveness of the AR-15 a little more.

A similar cartridge sometimes used in AR-15 rifles is the .300 Whisper, which generally employs a 220-grain, 6mm or 6.5mm bullet in modified .221 Remington Fireball cases. The result is a slow-traveling, heavy bullet that has a very soft report, making it ideal for silenced rifle use. This round appears to be gaining popularity. One small ammunition company, Quality Cartridge, even offers it in its catalog, and SSK Industries sells an upper conversion kit for the AR-15.

SSK Industries has recently created several variations on the Whisper theme in the form of the 6.5 Whisper (which uses bullets weighing from 85 to 160 grains) and the 7mm Whisper (with 100- to 185-grain bullets). Both these new cartridges work in AR-15 conversions as well as other type guns.

## AR-15 KNOCKOFFS AND VARIANTS

Several cartridges have already led to versions of the AR-15 that extend the capabilities of the rifle, creating a niche between the rifle cartridge and pistol in terms of speed while retaining much of the power of the rifle. It seems likely that these and similar cartridges will be seen more in the future, perhaps with shorter barrels, special silencer barrel/tube combinations, and other features to give the user an extra edge in one situation or another. Interestingly, the smaller companies scrambling for a share of Colt's market have been the first to offer such new chamberings. (It seems that in the firearms industry, innovations still come from the little companies or even individuals tinkering in their spare time.)

That said, the following is a list of the most notable non-Colt knockoffs of the original AR-15 design. Some of these firearms have been discontinued after a brief flurry of activity in the marketplace. Others are going strong and appear likely to hold their own against their competitors for some time.

### Advanced Armaments

This small operation is now out of business. But while in operation it produced some AR-15 rifle variants, apparently built around receivers machined in house. These guns were sold as "M-15" rifles.

### American Spirit Arms

American Spirit Arms specializes in AR-15-style rifles for competition shooters and varminters. Launched in 1998, this company has established a reputation for producing rifles with good fit and finish. Its guns are built around stock rifles that have (for the most part) a bull barrel free-floated inside a handguard along with match triggers, target grips, chromed bolt, chromed bolt carrier, and other niceties to increase their accuracy and the shooter's ease in connecting bullets with the target.

American Spirit rifles.

American Spirit Arms has also produced a .308 match rifle that appears to be built around a Stoner 25 aluminum upper/lower receiver and is marketed as the AS-308. The rifle, aimed at the target-shooting market, has a stainless-steel Harris match barrel. The charging handle is mounted to the right for use with a scope.

Following are the basic AR-15 models in the company's lineup.

| | |
|---|---|
| Open Match Rifle | 16-inch fluted and ported stainless-steel match barrel, 2-stage match trigger, special target grip, A2 rear sight. |
| DCM Service Rifle | 20-inch stainless steel match barrel, 2-stage match trigger, DCM service free-float handguard, A2 rear sight. |
| Bull Barrel Rifle | 20-, 22-, or 24-inch Wilson stainless-steel barrel, free-float handguard, flat-top receiver. |
| Bull Barrel A2 Rifle | 20-, 22-, or 24-inch Wilson stainless-steel barrel, free-float handguard, A2 sights. |
| Invader | 16-inch Harris stainless steel barrel, free-float handguard, A2 sights. |
| 20-inch Rifle | 20-inch Wilson heavy match rifle; overall A2 configuration with furniture and sights, no muzzle brake or flash hider. |
| C.A.R. 16-inch Rifle | 16-inch Wilson heavy match rifle; A2 rear sight, noncollapsible shorty-style stock, muzzle brake. |

### A.R.C. Weapons System

This was a conversion kit that was often placed on a new, stockless lower receiver to create a legal AR-15 pistol. This conversion kit was marketed by A.I.I. (Prescott Valley, Arizona) as the A.R.C.Weapons System. Although the company has gone out of business, guns made around these units are still seen (chamberings in 9mm Luger and .45 ACP have apparently been marketed, and .22 LR and .380 ACP versions may have been as well). The kits had one unique feature: they fed from the side of the upper receiver rather than through the lower receiver, making it unnecessary to modify the lower receiver in any way to accommodate the conversion assembly.

### Armscor/Squires Bingham M-1600

For a short time, the Philippines-made Armscor/Squires Bingham M-1600 was imported into the United States. The name itself was probably this firearm's biggest similarity to the AR-15 (or in this case the M16 rifle). It was actually a Squires Bingham Model 20 .22 rifle, and an AR-15-ish carrying handle and pistol

A.R.C. Weapons System 9mm conversion mounted on a carbine lower.

grip tacked onto it to gave a first-glance impression that it was akin to the AR-15. However, this mimicry didn't fool many for long, especially given that the carrying handle was too far forward, giving it a warped look in the eyes of most AR-15 fans. Most of the Armscor/Squires Bingham guns, which were generally marketed as the M16 or M1600 in the United States, have wooden stocks and grips that are generally painted a flat black.

Ironically, its menacing look in the eyes of gun grabbers would lead to the rifle's being banned from import into the United States even though it was just a .22 rifle in wolf's clothing, not unlike the plinkers that have been made and sold in the United States for many years.

### Armstech

Armstech is a small operation run by gunsmith Mike Jackson, who makes major modifications to the FN FAL and AR-10, as well as to AR-15-style rifles. Armstech sells these products to the public and to law enforcement groups. Much of the work appears to be done on a custom basis to suit the buyer's needs.

Although most of the company's AR-15 modifications are more or less "standard" as far as military-style rifles and carbines go, its Compak 16 may be of interest to some police users since this version of the Commando creates one very short weapon, especially with its telescoping stock retracted. This modification consists in part of cutting the barrel down to 10.47 inches and then adjusting the gas port for reliable functioning, giving the user a gun similar in layout to the original XM17 carbine of the Vietnam era.

### Australian Automatic Arms

During the 1970s, an Australian version of the AR-18 that used the AR-15 lower trigger group and magazine was created in an effort to gain military contracts; a semiauto version marketed as the Leader saw limited sales in the United States. This rifle lacked the quality control to appeal to either military or civilian shooters, and the company that created it soon failed. The basic rifle design was sound, however, and in the early 1990s Australian Automatic Arms reworked and debugged the firearm and remarketed the weapon. The company created three distinct models, each having a semiauto-only and selective-fire version, to appeal to a wide range of buyers.

The rifle model, available in SAR (semiautomatic rifle) and AR (automatic rifle) versions, weighed 7.5 pounds with a 16.25-inch barrel; the SAC (semiautomatic carbine) and AC (automatic carbine) weighed 6.9 pounds with a 10.5-inch barrel; and the stockless SAP (semiautomatic pistol) and AP (automatic pistol) weighed 5.9 pounds with a 10.5-inch barrel. In addition to the .223 versions of all these firearms, 9mm Luger chambers were also made.

The compact SAP and AP pistol versions of these guns fill a gap not met by other .223 rifles (though the tAP pistol version of the AR-15 does as well and weighs less); the other models are actually heavier than their AR-15 counterparts due to their steel, rather than aluminum, receivers. This makes them a second choice to the AR-15-style guns for most potential buyers.

### Bohica

Bohica (arguably an unfortunate name for a company—if you don't know why, don't ask) is now out of business. The AR-15 variants, marketed as the M16-SA, are notable in that they had stainless-steel lower receivers. The company also made a few AR-15 pistols.

### Century Arms

Century Arms has marketed several AR-15 rifle variants as the CIA. These appear to have been built by SGW/Olympic Arms, and the receivers were stamped with the Century Arms CIA logo.

### Chartered Industries SAR 80 and SR 88

After developing the AR-18, Armalite licensed the manufacturing rights first to the Japanese and then, after revoking the Japanese license in 1973, to Sterling Arms of England in 1976. Sterling had quality-control problems that never improved and also created a rifle of its own.

Meanwhile, Chartered Industries of Singapore (CIS), an enterprise chartered and owned by the Singapore government, had been licensed by Colt to produce the M16A1 rifle. CIS went through endless frustration in trying to sell the rifles it manufactured (permission had to be obtained from Colt, which in turn went through U.S. government red tape, before any of the rifles could be sold). After CIS manufactured 200,000 M16A1s, the delays and the high overhead costs involved in making the rifles according to the Colt specifications finally were too much; the company decided to try to manufacture a rifle of its own design that wouldn't have all the red tape tied into its production.

Sterling and CIS combined their efforts to develop a new rifle loosely based on the AR-18, with a trigger group nearly identical to that of the AR-15 (apparently made on the tooling originally used for the AR-15 parts). The designer in charge of perfecting the blend of these two rifles was Frank Waters, originally from the Sterling plant. By 1978, prototypes were being sent to the Singapore Military School of Infantry Weapons for testing. The Singapore government was interested in the design, so CIS went to work on the bugs that still plagued the basic design.

By 1980, the weapon was pretty well debugged and rifles were undergoing another series of tests. Actual manufacture of the rifle was slated to begin at the end of the trials. The new rifle was designated the SAR 80 (Singapore Automatic Rifle 1980)—although it was occasionally referred to as the Sterling Assault Rifle.

Early models of the SAR 80 had wooden furniture; later rifles sported plastic stocks, grips, and handguards. Like the AR-18, the SAR 80 had two recoil springs inside its receiver and used a gas piston system. Upper and lower receivers were steel stampings so the high-tech tooling needed for the AR-15's aluminum receivers wasn't called for (an important consideration, since the weapon might be licensed for manufacture by other countries). The trigger, disconnector, selector, and hammer are forgings nearly identical to those of the AR-15, and front and rear sights were similar to those of the M16A1. Likewise, SAR 80 had the AR-15 flash suppressor, magazines, and bayonet. Since these had become more or less the standard worldwide, CIS had a wide range of accessories readily available for its rifle and didn't have to manufacture them; this also made it possible for a country to easily switch from the popular AR-15 to the SAR 80 with a minimum of fuss, which, at the time, was undoubtedly an important marketing consideration. With an 18-inch barrel, the SAR 80 weighed 8 pounds empty.

CIS also created an SAW to accompany its rifle. This became the Ultimax 100, which many see as being one of the best light machine gun designs ever made and a direct competitor with the SAW version of Colt's H-BAR. The Ultimax 100 used elements of the AR-18 and an extralong recoil spring to soften recoil. Like many of the AR-15 H-BARs, the Ultimax 100 fired from an open bolt and used a drum magazine as well as standard rifle magazines (but not a belt-feed system). L. James Sullivan, original coworker of Eugene Stoner at Armalite and later Cadillac Gage, did the major design work on the new gun, and it couldn't have been handled by a better person.

In 1988 the SAR 80 was reworked and the new version introduced as the SAR 88. This new rifle boasts an aluminum receiver, ability to accept the M203 grenade launcher, three-round burst option, and plastic handguard, stock, and grip—all selling points of the AR-15 design. The rifle also has an FN FAL-style carrying handle.

As this is written, it appears that the SAR 21, which is the brainchild of STKinetics (the reorganized CIS), may be the rifle that ultimately replaces the aging M16A1 rifles still in service with Singapore's army. Unlike the previous rifles produced for consideration by the military, the SAR-21 takes the bullpup configuration and bears more than a passing resemblance to the Steyr. The basic gun will have both an optical 1.5X sight built into its carrying handle and a built-in laser aimer (operating on AA batteries).

Other configurations that are likely be fielded include the following:

- An LMG that fires from the open bolt, rather than a closed bolt like the rifle version, and is equipped with a heavy barrel and integral folding bipod
- A 40mm grenade launcher with a laser aiming device mounted on the launcher quadrant
- A Picatinny rail variant (with a MIL-STD-1913 for mounting an optical sight, most likely for night-vision scopes and the like)
- A Sharp Shooter sniper rifle with a 3X sight in its carrying handle

The SAR-21 specifications are as follows:

| | |
|---|---|
| Caliber | 5.56x45mm |
| Weight | 5.07 pounds (empty) |
| Length | 31.6 inches |
| Barrel | 20 inches, cold-hammer forged, 1-in-12 or 1-in-7 twist optional |
| Cyclic rate | 450–650 rpm |

### Dalphon

This small company offers several AR-15 rifles as well as kits that permit converting rifles to several pistol cartridges, including the .50 AE, .45 ACP, .40 S&W, and 9mm Luger. The company also offers silencers for these kits as well as for AR-15s chambered in .223 or 7.62x39.

The .50 AE version (available as a kit as well as a complete rifle) employs a gas system with an adjustable gas block to tune the gun to the ammunition being used (.50 AE varying somewhat in power from one manufacturer to the next, as well as according to how the cartridge is reloaded). The gun uses a standard AR-15 magazine shell with an insert spacer coupled with a replacement follower and spring; the result is a magazine that fits in the standard magazine well.

### Defense Procurement Manufacturing Services

Defense Procurement Manufacturing Services, Inc. (DPMS) is well known to many AR-15 owners who have purchased special AR-15 parts or accessories from the company. DPMS was incorporated in 1986 as a U.S. Department of Defense (DOD) consulting agency and initially served as somewhat of a go-between for the U.S. Army and various machine shops across the country selling parts. Over time, time this company also began marketing the same MIL-SPEC AR-15 parts to civilians and gunsmiths.

In addition, DPMS has also started marketing several AR-15-style rifles of its own under the Panther Arms trademark. These vary from more or less standard rifles to target guns, to a "pump-action" AR-15 rifle and pistol designed by Les Branson (which can have a bayonet lug and flash hider, since the assault weapons ban only applies to semiauto guns). Among the models is also a rifle chambered for 7.62x39mm. Perhaps the most amazing model for those of the lefty persuasion is a "true southpaw" gun with the ejection port on the left of the receiver. The company also markets government-only versions of its rifles, including a selective-fire shorty, M4 carbine, and M16 rifle models.

The DPMS guns generally have barrels with a 1-in-9 twist, although there are some with different twists. Stocks and receivers are generally A2 style with rifles or the standard plastic telescoping stock for shorties and carbines.

The current DPMS line includes the following:

| | |
|---|---|
| Panther Classic | M16A2-style rifle without flash hider and bayonet lug, crowned 20-inch barrel, A2 stock and handguards. |
| Panther 20-inch A-3 Classic | A3-style flat-top receiver, crowned 20-inch barrel, A2 stock and handguards. |
| Southpaw Panther | Left-side ejection port, bolt modified for left-hand ejection, M16A2-style rifle without flash hider and bayonet lug, crowned 20-inch barrel. |
| A-15 Panther Pump Rifle | M16A2-style rifle with a "pump" handguard, flash hider, bayonet lug, 20-inch barrel, standard A2 stock. |
| Single-Shot AR Rifle | No magazine well, single-shot, 20-inch crowned barrel; no bayonet lug or flash hider; standard A2 handguard, grip and handguard (legal in California). |
| DCM Panther | M16A2-style appearance, but with floating handguard and target sights for competition use, crowned 20-inch barrel, no bayonet lug. |
| Panther 7.62x39 | M16A2-style appearance, but with floating handguard, crowned 20-inch barrel, no bayonet lug, chambered for 7.62x39mm. |
| Bull A-15 | Target rifle with 20-inch bull crowned barrel, trimount on flat-top receiver, floating-barrel handguard, standard A2 stock. |
| Bull A-15 with Hi-Rider | Target rifle with 20-inch bull crowned barrel, Hi-Rider scope mount that permits a more "heads-up" scope picture, floating-barrel handguard, standard A2 stock. |
| Bull A-15 with A3 Lo-Rider | Target rifle with 20-inch bull crowned barrel, A3 flat-top receiver, floating-barrel handguard, standard A2 stock. |
| Panther Bull Classic | Target rifle with 20-inch bull crowned barrel, A2 flat-top receiver with front sight assembly on barrel, floating-barrel handguard, standard A2 stock. |
| Bull Classic with SST Lower | Target rifle with 20-inch bull crowned barrel, A2 flat-top receiver, front sight assembly on barrel, floating-barrel handguard, standard A2 stock, stainless-steel lower receiver. |
| Arctic Panther | Target rifle with 20-inch bull crowned barrel, flat-top receiver, floating-barrel handguard, standard A2 stock, white-finish receivers and handguard, black Teflon finish on barrel. |

| | |
|---|---|
| Deluxe Bull Twenty-Four Special | Target rifle with 24-inch bull crowned barrel, A3 flat-top receiver, floating-barrel handguard, adjustable A2 stock. |
| Extreme Super Bull Twenty-Four | Target rifle with 24-inch bull crowned barrel with extra-large 1.5-inch diameter, Hi-Rider flat-top receiver, floating-barrel handguard, adjustable skeletonized stock. |
| Panther Race Gun | Iron Stone adjustable stock, JP detachable front and rear sights, fluted 24-inch barrel, JP adjustable trigger. |
| Panther Classic Sixteen | M16A2-style receiver, 16-inch crowned barrel, carbine handguard, no bayonet lug, A2 stock. |
| Carbine A-15 | 11.5-inch barrel with 5.5-inch flash hider, M16A2-style receiver, selective fire, telescoping stock (law enforcement sales only). |
| Panther M4 - M4A | Selective fire, M4 carbine configuration with telescoping stock (law enforcement sales only). |
| A-2 Tactical 16 inch | A2-style receiver, 16-inch crowned barrel, no bayonet lug, A2 stock, A2 rifle handguard, front sight assembly. |
| A-2 Tactical 16 inch (preban) | A2-style receiver, 16-inch barrel, flash hider, bayonet lug, A2 stock, A2 rifle handguard, front sight assembly (law enforcement sales only). |
| A-3 Tactical Carbine | A3 flat-top receiver, 16-inch crowned barrel, no bayonet lug, A2 stock, A2 rifle handguard, front sight assembly. |
| Panther 16 inch A-3 Classic | A3 flat-top receiver, 16-inch crowned barrel, no bayonet lug, A2 stock, carbine handguard, front sight assembly. |
| Panther Lo-Pro Classic | Flat-top Lo-Pro scope mount, 16-inch crowned barrel, no bayonet lug, A2 stock, carbine handguard, no front sight assembly. |
| Bull Sweet Sixteen | Target rifle with 16-inch bull crowned barrel, A3 flat-top receiver, floating-barrel handguard, standard A2 stock. |
| Bull Sweet Sixteen Lo-Pro | Target rifle with 16-inch bull crowned barrel, Lo-Pro flat-top receiver, floating-barrel handguard, standard A2 stock |
| A-15 Panther Pump Pistol | M16A2-style receiver, "pump" handguard, flash hider, bayonet lug, 10.5-inch barrel, no stock |

Chinese CQ Rifle.

### Chinese CQ

From the mid-1970s, the People Republic of China's state-run NORINCO (Northern Industries Corporation) arsenals have produced a wide range of firearms, from copies of the Soviet SKS and AK-47 rifles to copies of the U.S. .45 automatic pistol and M14 rifle. Not surprisingly, then, NORINCO introduced a knockoff of the M16A1; this rifle is nearly identical to the original AR-15, right down to a 1-in-12 twist and 20-round magazine. When this rifle was first created is uncertain, but it was first seen in the West during the mid-1980s.

The rifle is designated the CQ, a Chinese transliteration of the number 16, translated back into English. About the only distinguishing departures from the original Colt's forebears are the grayish plastic furniture and the modified shape of the handguard, pistol grip, and stock. Perhaps with an eye toward police sales and maybe even sales to U.S. civilians, NORINCO also offers a semiauto version of the CQ as its Type 311.

### Daewoo K1A1 and K2

The Republic of South Korea manufactured the AR-15 in its M16A1 configuration under license to the company that would eventually become the Pusan Arsenal. In 1983 Daewoo Precision Industries, Ltd. took over the operation of the plant and soon started work on a derivative rifle, both to avoid having to pay royalties to Colt and to sidestep U.S. government interference in the selling of firearms.

The first rifle developed by the company was the K1, which had the trigger group, sights, lower receiver, and gas system of the AR-15. Only the recoil system and charging handle were noticeably different from the parent rifle, and suspiciously like that of AR-180, at that. This gun was created to serve the role of a carbine with 10-inch barrel and telescoping "grease gun"-style stock.

The original 6.4-pound carbine had a four-position selector (safe/semi/auto/burst) and soon had a semiauto-only, 16-inch barrel version known as the K1A1 that was created with a view to exporting it to the United States and other areas where selective-fire weapons were hard to obtain. As might be expected, the rifle used the AR-15 magazines, which are becoming the standard for the free world.

Daewoo next introduced the K2, which was quite similar to the K1 but had an 18.3-inch barrel and weighed 7.5 pounds empty. It featured a gas system similar to that of the AR-18 and a side-folding stock (also similar in concept to the AR-18 but with the locking mechanism of the Galil rifle). In other respects the rifle was almost identical to the K1.

Stoeger Industries imported the semiauto versions of each rifle into the United States, redesignating the K1A1 as the MAX I and the K2 as the MAX II. During the late-1980s witch hunt involving military-style rifles imported into the United States (even though such rifles were seldom used by criminals), President George Bush issued an executive order that outlawed the importation of the Daewoo guns (along with 44 other firearms). But, in 1991, the Springfield Armory reintroduced the K2 with a "sporter" thumbhole stock rather than its original folding assembly, dubbing it the DR-2000. This new stock has apparently transformed it from a "drug pusher's weapon of choice" into a sporting rifle in the eyes of the BATF. The gun grabbers eventually won out in this story, changing the law so that even this version could no longer be imported.

### Diemaco

In addition to having a contract with Colt to produce firearms for the Canadian military, Diemaco secured the rights to sell its rifles to markets in Southeast Asia. The two biggest potential markets, New Zealand and Australia, both selected the Steyr AUG bullpup rifles over

The "sporterized" U.S. import version of the K2. (Courtesy of the Springfield Armory.)

Canadian C7 rifle.

the Diemaco AR-15s during the military trials in these countries. And the Taiwan T65, Chinese CQ, Daewoo K1 and K2, and Singapore SAR 80 series of guns all threaten to capture any Southeast Asian market with products that are more competitively priced due to less expensive labor. So whether any real sales will be realized in this arena by Diemaco remains to be seen.

Diemaco has been creating several interesting experimental versions of the AR-15, suggesting that it has an active research and development department. This may eventually pay off for the company by enabling it to offer models of the rifle that are unavailable elsewhere. Among the modifications seen outside the company's walls was a standard rifle with its rear sight/carrying handle milled off and a scope mount base actually glued on (a process that the company claims creates an effective mount if it is done properly). These rifles were used during the Canadian military's experiments with optical systems—which were finally rejected in favor of A1-style iron sights. These iron-sight versions are nearly identical to the M16A2 except for the A1-style sights. The Canadian military adopted the rifle version as its C7 rifle and the carbine as its C8.

In addition to .223 rifles, Diemaco has created the C10 training rifle chambered in .22 LR. Because the 1-in-7 twist of the C7 and C8 tears up .22 LR bullets when the rifles are fired with adapters, creating excessive leading in a short time, the Canadian military needed a dedicated .22 rifle or a new type of training ammunition. The Canadians decided to go with the C10, a firearm that uses 83 percent of the standard C7 rifle parts with 14 non-AR-15 components and 7 modified parts. The training rifle has a 15-round magazine, a barrel with 1-in-16 twist, and sights adjusted to 30- and 100-meter ranges with the standard .22 LR ammunition.

### Elisco Tool M16A1

Elisco Tool made Colt-licensed versions of the M16A1 and 14.5-inch barreled Commando for the Philippine government in the mid-1960s. In the late 1980s, it purchased what was left of the failed Armalite Company and transported the operation to the Philippines. At the time of this writing, it appears that the company will produce its own .223 rifle based on elements of the AR-18, though it seems likely that it may also incorporate the AR-15 trigger group or other assemblies and will undoubtedly use the AR-15 magazine.

**Essential Arms**

Essential Arms created several AR-15 rifles and carbines, as well as selling parts for these guns. The company went out of business in 1993 and apparently sold much of the operation to DPMS.

**Federal Engineering XC-220, XC-900, and XC-450**

These carbines were made in .22 LR, 9mm, and .45 versions as the XC-220, XC-900, and XC-450, in both carbine and pistol configurations. They all used the trigger group and pistol grip of the AR-15, with the center-fire versions also making use of the AR-15 firing pin, extractor, and ejector system.

If anything, these guns were overengineered, with steel receivers that made them considerably heavier than they needed to be. This extra weight, their high price tags, the appearance of the Colt and SGW carbines, and the availability of military-style stocks for less expensive .22 rifles undoubtedly contributed to the demise of these rifles. The Federal Engineering firearms are generally well made, but they offer little that can't be found with the AR-15 family and weigh too much for carbine- or pistol-style guns.

**Frankford Arsenal 9mm**

Before it went out of business in 1987, the privately owned Frankford Arsenal (not to be confused with the U.S. government arsenal of the same name) manufactured several more or less conventional AR-15s in .223.

One of the more innovative designs to come from the company was a 9mm Luger conversion unit for the AR-15. This kit consists of a 16-inch, 9mm barrel mated to a standard receiver with a special blowback-operated bolt. To accommodate the Sten magazines used with this conversion, an adapter fits into a standard receiver's magazine well. The upper receiver then mates to the lower receiver with military-style front and rear push pins.

In operation, the AR-15 buffer system became the recoil spring for the conversion unit and a new magazine release lever extended out of the lower receiver just behind the Sten magazine. Except for the magazine release that was behind the magazine well (with the regular release holding the adapter in the well), the rifle operated in the standard manner; safety, charging handle, and point of aim were all like those of the standard rifle.

The Frankford Arsenal 9mm conversion was also offered with a 10-inch barrel for those who had selective-fire rifles. An internal and an external suppressor were offered as well. The internal suppressor was interesting in that it occupied what appeared to be a standard handguard (a concept apparently pioneered by Colt).

**Fulton Armory**

Fulton Armory offers several target rifles built around the AR-15 system, as well as bolt-action and M14 rifles. The company also offers upper receiver kits that a buyer can use to basically transform a standard AR-15 into a target gun, a practical proposition given that most accuracy with the AR-15 is derived from free-floating a match barrel on the upper receiver.

The Peerless Grade AR-15 Match Rifle was first offered in 1998 and comes with a variety of features desired by most match contestants, including a Krieger bull barrel, Lipski adjustable rear and front sights (with a bubble level to prevent canting), a rectangular handguard that floats the barrel, adjustable hand stop, tactical charging handle latch, and extended bolt catch release. The lower receiver sports a Royal Arms pistol grip and a fully adjustable butt plate.

The Peerless Grade AR-15 Varmint Rifle (as its name suggests) has a Krieger barrel in a free-float handguard but dispenses with the sights so a user can mount a scope atop its flat-top receiver.

The Millennial AR-15 Tactical Rifle has the standard A2 layout with a full-size handguard and a choice of 20-

Fulton Armory's AR-15 Peerless Grade Match Rifle.

or 16-inch barrels. Crowned muzzle, muzzle brakes, and (for law enforcement buyers or with preban lowers) flash hiders are also offered.

Fulton Armory also offers its Peerless Grade AR-15 CMP/DCM-Legal National Match Rifle, which couples a match target barrel with the looks of an A2 rifle to keep it legal in DCM contests.

### Gunsmoke Enterprises, Inc.

Gunsmoke Enterprises, Inc. was founded in 1971 by Ed Basile, who was a gunner's mate on a U.S. Navy destroyer during the 1960s. After having been trained on the M1 Garand and using an M14, Basile claimed it was "love at first sight" when he first got his hands on an M16. He transferred to become an M16 armorer and never quit working with the gun, even after leaving the service.

For a time, Gunsmoke Enterprises offered an AR-15 pistol kit that permitted a shooter to build his own AR-15 around new parts that had never been assembled into a rifle (thereby making it legally a pistol according to federal law). The assault weapon ban put an end to this product. However, Gunsmoke Enterprises has been able to take up the slack with a variety of products from guns produced by Bushmaster (including the M17, as well as AR-15 variants) along with parts for the AR-15. However, the most interesting aspect of the business is the variety of target and custom guns it produces.

These are seen in a variety of configurations, with the Varminter, International High Power Match, Competition, and an M15 M4 Tactical carbine making up the line (though the variations in these groups according to the needs of the buyer make the offering a lot larger than just four basic models). The target/competition/varminter guns have or have had the option of a Douglas XX Premium barrel for premium accuracy with barrel lengths ranging from 16 to 26 inches, with a choice of chrome molybdenum or stainless steel; twists include 1-in-7, 1-in-8, 1-in-9, 1-in-10, 1-in-12 and 1-in-14 to accommodate a wide range of needs and bullet weights. Chrome bolt carriers and free-floating barrels in stiff handguards complete the picture at the front of the rifle, while RPA rear micrometer sights boost accuracy on those guns not employing a scope.

Gunsmoke Enterprises has also started offering similar custom work based on the new AR-10 rifles, offered with a variety of features and available not only in the .308 Winchester but also in .243, 6.5mm.08, and 7mm.08.

Many of these guns are most easily recognized by the stock Gunsmoke Enterprises employs, a buffer tube with a buttplate assembly without the usual stock. This gives it a bit of a shorty stock look while allowing it to be modified to a variety of positions for better head and cheek placement when aiming.

### Hesse Arms

Launched late in 1997, this small operation makes a number of different AR-15-style guns, with an emphasis on quality rather than quantity.

All rifles are postban and, except for law enforcement models, therefore, do not have bayonet lugs or flash hiders (though many do have muzzle brakes that maintain the flash hider look). The "shorty" model has a telescoping stock that is "fixed" so it is permanently extended.

The company makes its HAR-15 series in .223; barrel twists are generally 1-in-9. These rifles are also available by special order in the following chamberings: .17 Remington, 6mm PPC, 6x45mm (6mm x 223), 300 Fireball, and 7.62x39mm. The HAR-25 series is chambered for .308, generally with 1-in-10 twists.

Among the models offered are the following:

| | |
|---|---|
| HAR-15A2 | Standard A2 layout in semiauto only; law enforcement buyers can get guns with flash hider and bayonet lug. |
| HAR-15A2 Carbine | A2 Carbine layout with 16-inch, M4 profile barrel; fixed telescope-style stock to conform to assault weapon law. |
| HAR-15A2 Dispatcher | Standard A2 rifle layout but with 16-inch barrel. |
| HAR-15A2 Bull Gun | A2 styling with 20-inch stainless-steel bull barrel; no muzzle brake. |
| HAR-15A2 National Match | A2 styling with DCM legal free-float handguards, stainless-steel barrel with 1-in-8 twist, chromed bolt carrier. |
| HAR-15A2 .50 Action Express | .50 AE chambering, A2 Carbine layout with 16-inch, M4 profile barrel; fixed telescope-style stock to conform to assault weapon law. |

| | |
|---|---|
| HAR-15A2 Omega Match | Free-float handguard, match barrel with 1-in-8 twist, Choate E2 stock, flat-top receiver. |
| HAR-15A2 X-Match Rifle | A3 flat-top layout with free-float, ventilated handguards and no front sight. |
| HAR-15A2 LMG | Semiauto version of Canadian armed forces H-BAR with square handguard and carrying handle, 1-in-8 twist, forward grip under handguard, muzzle brake. |
| HAR-25 Bull Rifle | 26-inch stainless-steel bull barrel, aluminum free-float handguard, STANAG front gas block that accepts removable front sight, flat-top receiver. |
| HAR-25 Target Rifle | 24-inch stainless-steel bull barrel, aluminum free-float handguard, STANAG front gas block that accepts removable front sight, flat-top receiver. |
| HAR-25 Standard Rifle | 20-inch heavy barrel, A2 handguards, STANAG front gas block that accepts removable front sight, flat-top receiver. |

Holmes' variation on the AR-15 theme, with a 9mm carbine. (Courtesy of Bill Holmes.)

### Holmes 9mm and .45 AR-15 Kits

Inventor Bill Holmes created two pistol-caliber conversions of the AR-15, one with a sheet-metal upper receiver and the other with a steel-tubing assembly; these fit the standard AR-15 lower (with the round-tubing model requiring removal of the bolt hold-open lever). The kits used an integral pair of recoil springs to cycle the large bolt of the conversion unit (in a manner similar to operation of the recoil springs/bolt in an AR-180 rifle).

Holmes' design did away with the need for the slip ring, weld spring, and so on, with the barrel simply screwing into the front of the receiver with a one-piece handguard held between the barrel and front sight assembly. The conversions are available in 9mm and .45 ACP versions.

Since the recoil springs are in the upper receiver, the regular AR-15 buffer and buffer tube were not needed for these units to function, making possible the creation of a carbine with a folding stock or even an AR-15 pistol.

Holmes didn't manufacture any great number of these firearms, though his sales literature advertised a 9mm or .45 kit with 16-inch for $250 and a 6-inch barrel 9mm unit for $300 in the late 1980s.

That said, he has written an excellent how-to guide that enables the reader with a little skill to build a do-it-yourself carbine that resembles his commercial guns. These guns are unique in that they duplicate the look of an AR-15 while comprising a large number of home-built parts that make them quite different from the AR-15 in many ways. Yet the design also incorporates a lot of the AR-15's layout and even parts. For those wanting to build a gun that will attract some stares at the rifle range, this is it. (And being able to say, "I built it myself" has a lot of pull with fellow shooters as well.) The book, *Home Workshop Guns, Vol. V*, is available from Paladin Press for $20.

### Insight Systems Kits

Although technically a conversion kit, the free-floating upper receiver/barrel assembly offered by Insight Systems is often seen permanently mounted on an AR-15 lower and, in effect, creates a version of the rifle in and of itself. The assembly offered by Insight gives fantastic accuracy: those who own one consider a 3/4- to 3/8-inch shot group at 100 yards normal.

The most common configuration of the Insight Systems rifle kit is with the carrying handle milled off and a scope rail mounted to the top of the

Field-stripped Holmes 9mm carbine. (Courtesy of Bill Holmes.)

receiver (though a version with an AR-15 carrying handle/rear sight is also offered). The sightless system is coupled with a special barrel nut and gas tube designed by the mastermind behind Insight Systems, gunsmith Lee Mosher. A Douglas premium barrel is free-floated inside an injection-molded handguard (also designed by Mosher), and detachable sling mounts on the lower edge of the handguard are located at the front and the rear of the handguard, allowing attachment of slings or Harris bipod according to the shooter's desires. Insight Systems kits are available in two receiver styles—one that mates to Colt "Sporter"-style receivers and another for military-style front push pin receivers.

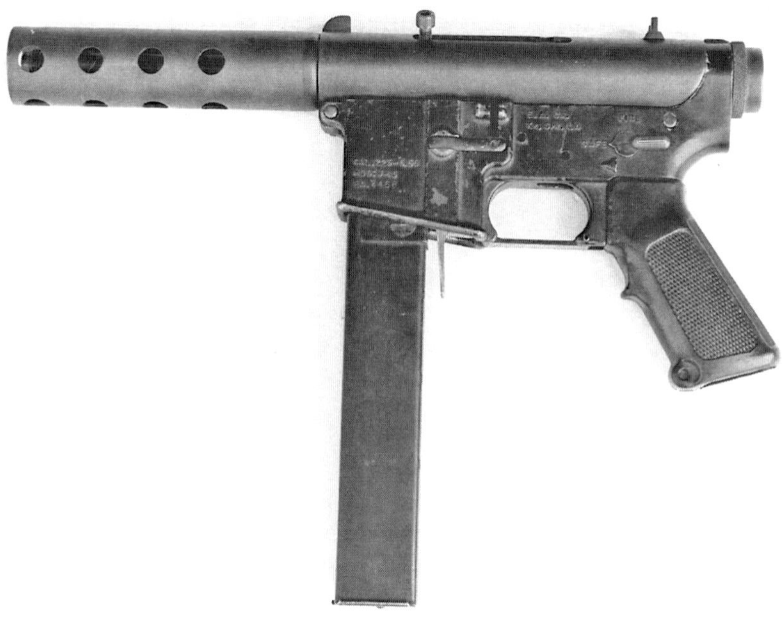
Holmes' design also permits a pistol version of the AR-15. (Courtesy of Bill Holmes.)

Among the options for those purchasing one of their units are a choice of barrel lengths (16-, 18-, 20-, 22-, and 24-inch), chamberings (.223, 5.56mm NATO, or 6mm/.223 among others), and twist rates (1-in-12, 1-in-9, 1-in-7). Prices vary according to the options.

### Iver Johnson

Some might argue that technically this gun doesn't belong in this chapter since there is little in common between the M1 carbine and the AR-15 other than the basic concept of a light, handy firearm that employs a cartridge with low recoil. However, mention must be made of the odd firearms created by Iver Johnson a few years before the company went out of business. The concept behind these seemed to be of the "if you can't beat them, join them' school of thought.

Designers took the M1 carbine operating system and then basically tacked on AR-15-style sights and stock,

A pair of AR-15s with Insight Systems handguard and match barrels. (Courtesy of Insight Systems.)

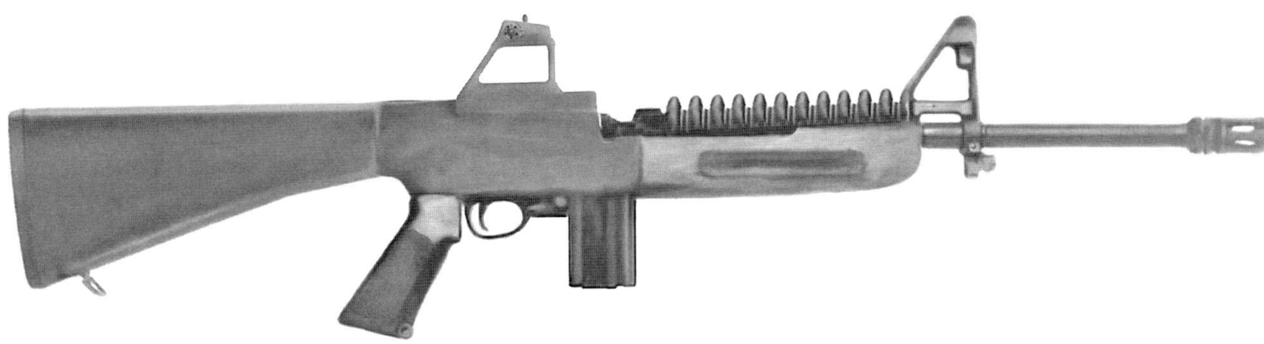

The M1 carbine in AR-15 clothing.

giving it the appearance of the more popular rifle. Much the same was also done with a 9mm pistol version of the M1 carbine. Neither gun went into production, though prototypes were apparently built.

### JLM & Sons

This small business produces AR-15 rifles and carbines on a custom basis. The serial numbers on these guns suggest that the total number produced is in the range of several hundred. Since the business is a Class III dealer, it seems probable that it may have produced some automatic versions for law enforcement use as well (though this is pure speculation).

### Jonathan Arthur Ciener

In addition to creating excellent silencers for a variety of firearms, Jonathan Arthur Ciener, Inc. has been altering AR-15s into several unique configurations. Among these are an under-the-barrel shotgun assembly for use on AR-15 rifles and carbines and a belt-feed conversion of the Commando and rifle.

A converted Remington 870 shotgun (advertised as the ultimate over/under) with the hardware to place it on an AR-15 costs $449 as of this writing and requires a special permit because the shotgun's barrel is under the 18-inch minimum of most federal and state laws. For those who want to avoid the paperwork, it's also possible to purchase the Ultimate Over/Under 870 with an 18-inch barrel and a 26-inch overall length (which makes it a legal shotgun in most areas of the United States).

The Ciener Ultimate Over/Under fastens to the bayonet lug of the AR-15 with the rear of the shotgun's receiver fastening around an extended front pushpin that replaces the original. This makes it possible to quickly detach or reattach the shotgun.

Jonathan Arthur Ciener also offers belt-fed semiauto AR-15s. These are built on Colt rifles, and, at the time of this writing, a Sporter version runs $1,995, a Sporter Match H-BAR $2,170, and a carbine $2,110. The modified links necessary to feed the ammunition through these firearms costs $35 per hundred, and an ammunition carrier/link catcher like that created by Colt for its belt-fed machine guns runs $250. Jonathan Arthur Ciener will also convert a Colt AR-15 for $1,250 (semiauto) or $1,750 (for selective-fire versions). For those wanting an M203, the company also offers these to qualified buyers for $995.

### Knight's Armament Company

Knight's Armament Company brought the AR-15 design full circle with its SR-25 (Stoner Rifle number 25). Chambered for .308 Winchester, it is the caliber-equivalent of the AR-10. The rifle is designed for hunting or target shooting (with readily apparent potential as a police or military rifle), with a free-floated (originally Douglas, now Obermeyer) barrel and a scope block atop its receiver.

As might be expected, the principal difference between the SR-25 and standard AR-15s is a lengthened magazine well, necessitated by the longer .308 cartridge. Oddly enough, some of the first photos of this rifle show it with what appear to be old waffle-style AR-10 magazines.

The SR-25 was the brainchild of Eugene Stoner himself. Knowing that tooling up to make gun parts is an expensive proposition, Stoner utilized as many AR-15 parts as was practical in his new gun; some 60 percent of the SR-25 are interchangeable with AR-15 parts. From there he created a "floating" barrel inside the rifle's handguard, thereby doing away with one of the problems that has detracted from AR-15 accuracy.

Stoner SR-25 Match Rifles.

One of Stoner's goals in designing the rifle was to create a weapon that might be pressed into service by the U.S. military to replace the bolt-action systems that snipers seemed to always return to throughout the 20th century, despite the out-of-the-box accuracy of the AR-15 (the more powerful cartridge always seeming to make the difference—at least in the minds of those choosing sniper rifles for the military). The result was the SR-25, which, in its 24-inch version, is sold by Knight's with the guarantee of sub-1-inch groups at 100 yards (with the norm being 3/4-inch groups).

The accuracy of Stoner's design has not gone unnoticed, although Stoner didn't live long enough to see it bear fruit. The U.S. Navy SEALs adopted the SR-25 as its official sniper rifle in May 2000. Type-classified as the Mk 11 Mod 0, the weapon comprised not only the rifle but also the Leopold scope, emergency iron sights, and a suppressor.

The silencer created some design problems for Knight's, since it made the 24-inch barrel normally used on the most accurate SR-25s too long. Mounting a suppressor on such a rifle turned it into a very awkward 50-inch-long device; a 20-inch barrel was essential.

But designing an *accurate* 20-inch rifle entailed more than just exchanging barrels, because to achieve the accuracy that Knight's offered, the mechanism had been modified for the vibrations produced by a 24-inch barrel. Thus, the company had to rework the firing pin, ejector, extractor and buffer to duplicate the level of accuracy achieved with its 24-inch-barrel target rifles. But the changes did the trick.

Knight's SR-15 rifles.

This may seem like a lot of work to sell 300 rifles to the SEALs. However, the status gained from having an elite military group choose one's rifle is something money can't buy; undoubtedly Knight's was more than happy to do the work in exchange for the glory. And no doubt more than a few shooters have already bought an SR-25 with the knowledge that the SEALs selected it as their sniper rifle.

The NRA has included the SR-25 in the service rifle competition in the national matches. This will undoubtedly result in higher sales of the rifle, since the heavier .308 bullet has some wind-bucking abilities that AR-15 does not enjoy, and unlike the M14 rifle, the SR-25 would not necessitate extensive reworking, glass bedding, and other tricks necessary to make an M14 accurate. Although the AR-15 knockoffs continue to rule the range at the National NRA Service Rifle Championship Matches, G. David Tubb showed that this situation may be changing when, using an SR-25, he won at Camp Perry in 1997.

The SR-25 is ideal for mounting a scope. The top of the standard gun has a Picatinny/Weaver-style base machined into its upper receiver, making mounting a scope quite simple and also placing the line of sight along the stock, thereby doing away with the need for a cheek rest. Another plus is that this also permits using iron sights designed for the M16A3 as well as dot scopes, night-vision scopes, and so forth.

Bringing the design process full circle, Knight's added several AR-15-style models to its lineup. All chambered in .223, they include the following:

| | |
|---|---|
| SR-15 Match Rifle – 98070 | Target 20-inch barrel, free-floating handguard, Picatinney Rail, flat-top receiver, two-stage match trigger. |
| SR-15 M5 Rifle – 98071 | Modular rail system with flip-up rear sight, standard 20-inch barrel, flat-top receiver, two-stage match trigger. |
| SR-15 M4 Carbine – 98072 | Modular rail system with flip-up rear sight, 16-inch light barrel, flat-top receiver, two-stage match trigger |

Knight's also offers a semiauto .50-caliber rifle as its SR-50 Rifle – 98074. Even though this system doesn't have a lot to do with the AR-15 design, it is historically interesting because it is another gun that Stoner designed, and it also makes use of a few AR-15 parts. The gun weighs 31 pounds and is 58.5 inches in overall length.

### La France M16K

La France modifies firearms for use in Hollywood movies as well as for law enforcement officials. As one might expect, the company has produced exotic-looking versions of a number of familiar firearms.

One of the company's more interesting AR-15 variants is the M16K, which goes a bit beyond the Commando by cutting the barrel back to 8.39 inches. The gas tube couples into a large block and secondary tube, allowing gas to be compressed in the system thereby spreading out its pressure buildup curve. In addition to slowing the rate of fire to below 600 rpm, this modification also makes the compact gun somewhat more reliable and creates slightly less fouling.

Because of the noise and flash inherent in such short-barreled rifles, La France also offers a suppressor for use with the M16K.

### Leitner-Wise Rifle Company

The Leitner-Wise Rifle Company has created several interesting variations on the AR-15 theme, including the LW-15.22, which is available either chambered for the .22 LR or .22 WMR while being styled like an M4 carbine or AR-15 rifle. With an eye toward sales in areas that have banned "assault weapons," Leitner-Wise also offers versions of the LW-15.22 that conform to laws in California and elsewhere.

The upper assembly is also sold separately in both 20-inch rifle and 4.5-inch carbine versions with a choice of flat-top or A2 layouts. The rifle feeds from modified AR-15 magazines with an insert that provides 25-round capacity—at least as these are available—for civilian sales. Unlike most other .22 versions and adapters, these guns have bolt-hold-open ability on the last round along with a functional forward assist. According to the company, the U.S. Army has purchased a number of these, apparently for use in training recruits.

Leitner-Wise also offers a conversion kit chambered for the 12.5x40mm cartridge (which fires a 0.499-inch-diameter, 400-grain bullet with a muzzle velocity of 1,600 fps). This proprietary cartridge feeds through standard AR-15 magazines but sits in a single column due to its girth, giving the user 14 rounds in a standard 30-round magazine. Rifles and kits in this chambering are available with flat-top receivers and 16.5-inch barrels.

The company has also introduced the 7.82Sx24mm cartridge for use in its LW7.82Sx24 System conversion kit. This is available only for law enforcement and military sales due to its ability to penetrate armor. The .30-caliber bullet weighs 50 grains and travels at 2,400 fps.

Leitner-Wise also offers the LW-15.5 carbine, which is also specifically designed for the 7.82S x 24 cartridge. With a very short 7.5-inch barrel and telescopic stock, the LW-15.5 is the submachine gun league and has the ability to defeat most ballistic armor out to 200 yards.

### Military Manufacturing

Also known as M2, this company creates AR-15-style guns only for military or law enforcement buyers. Its guns are generally selective fire with semiauto only as an option.

One of the more intriguing shorty guns Military Manufacturing produces is its M16SP (special purpose), which sports a barrel only 8.38 inches long (1/100 inch shorter than rival company La France's similar shorty).

Perhaps wanting to make sure there would be no contest as to who had the shortest barreled shorty, Military Manufacturing has also introduced two even

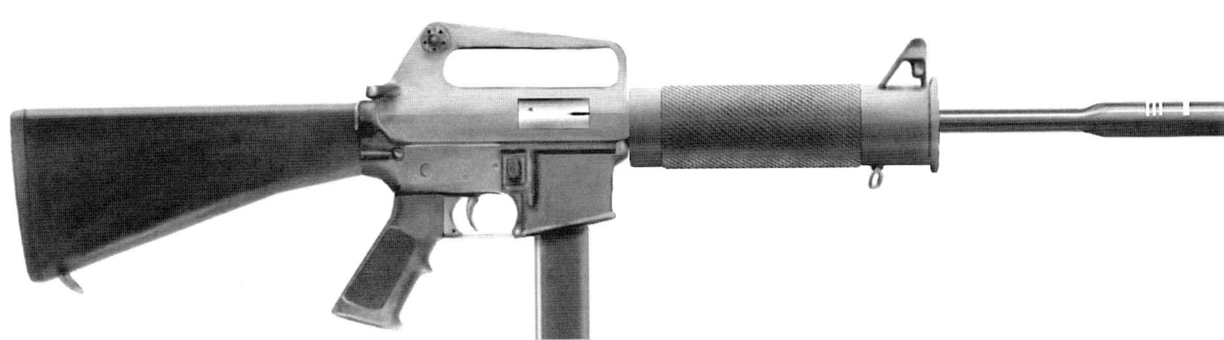

La France M16K-45.

Two very short shorties: the M16X (top) and M16SP.

shorter guns, the M16C, which has a barrel only 6 inches long and an overall length of just 22.13 inches, and the M16X, with a barrel only 4 inches long. With specially designed handguards and telescoping stock, these make for very compact guns that seem ideally suited as entry weapons for SWAT teams or hostage rescue work, albeit with undoubted noisiness in operation (which might be an asset in close-quarter combat).

### Mitchell Arms M16A1/22 and CAR15/22

For some time Mitchell Arms has imported several .22 LR firearms into the United States. These rifles are designed to mimic the appearance of more expensive (and, of late, sometimes hard-to-purchase) firearms, including a PPS "submachine gun" look-alike, a simulated Galil rifle, and several imitation AK-47s.

Included in the company's offerings is an Italian-made Armi Jager AR-15. This look-alike was first modeled on the M16A1 and marketed in the United States by EMF as the AP-74 in both a .22 LR and a .32 ACP version. Although EMF no longer imports the AP-74 into the United States, when the U.S. military adopted the M16A2, Mitchell Arms soon added an updated Jager rifle decked out with an A2-style pistol grip and handguard to its offerings in the United States. Oddly enough, this model was dubbed the M16A1/22, even though it had A2, not A1, styling. Mitchell Arms also created the CAR15/22, which has a telescoping Commando-style stock and a 16-inch barrel.

Although the magazine release, 18-round magazine, and safety of these rifles are not very similar to those of the AR-15, the weight, point of aim, and overall feel of the rifle are nearly identical, making these firearms ideal for cheap practice and shooting at ranges that don't allow the use of full-power rifle cartridges.

Additionally, since the new 1-in-7 twist rate creates excessive leading when .22 LR bullets are fired with .22 adapters through newer AR-15 barrels, having a Mitchell Arms M16A1/22 or CAR15/22 makes sense for those wanting to engage in some inexpensive practice. In fact, one of these guns (with a price tag of around $325) can pay for itself through the use of inexpensive .22 LR ammunition rather than .223 centerfire cartridges in a short time.

### Nesard and Sendra

Nesard was a small operation that was a sister company to Sendra, both names being created with different arrangements of the same letters. This company is one of the few that produced AR-15-style parts that I could never get to function properly, apparently due to uneven quality control (which has earned it a reputation that causes most knowledgeable buyers to go elsewhere).

Some shooters have rifles built around the Nesard or Sendra receivers that work fine, and some gun builders buy parts from these firms and— although they send some back for exchange—end up with usable pieces. Perhaps others I've talked to and I have just had bad experiences that are the exception to the rule; but my advice is that a person would do well to steer clear of

Professional Ordnance Carbon 15 pistol and Type 20 rifle.

guns built around these receivers and also avoid buying parts from these two companies or other operations connected to them.

### Pacific West Arms

Pacific West Arms was a small operation that is now out of business. The company sold receivers and also made a rifle and carbine, both with A1-style uppers.

### Professional Ordnance

Professional Ordnance has taken the AR-15 design forward to incorporate plastic moldings for the upper and lower receiver and other key components in the Carbon 15 series (the "carbon" referring to the carbon-fiber composite plastic used in manufacturing these guns). In addition to producing a rifle and pistol that depart from the AR-15 as far as looks, this has also made possible a much lighter firearm. Internally, however, these guns are pure AR-15, with the magazine, trigger group, and other components identical to those used in other guns in this chapter.

Because of the light materials used in these guns, it has also been possible for Professional Ordnance to produce a pistol version of its gun that is light enough to avoid the limitations of the assault weapons ban, something that undoubtedly galls the gun grabbers no end.

Another interesting feature of these guns is that, because the carbon fiber composite plastic tends to be self-lubricating and the hard-chromed bolt carriers slick, the manufacturer recommends using the gun without lubrication in these areas and notes that the guns generally function best when "run dry." At the same time, the plastic is highly chemical resistant, making it practical to clean these guns with standard solvents like CLP.

Currently Professional Ordnance offers the following models:

| | |
|---|---|
| Carbon 15 Rifle – Type 97S | Iron sights and Weaver rail extending down top of receiver and handguard, muzzle brake, 16-inch stainless steel barrel, 1-in-9 twist, weight of 4.3 pounds. |
| Carbon 15 Rifle – Type 97 | Weaver rail on top of receiver, muzzle brake, 16-inch stainless-steel barrel, 1-in-9 twist, detachable stock, weight of 3.9 pounds. |
| Carbon 15 Rifle – Type 20 | Weaver rail on top of receiver, muzzle brake, light profile 16-inch stainless-steel match barrel, 1-in-9 twist, detachable stock, weight of 3.9 pounds. |
| Carbon 15 Pistol – Type 97 | Ghost ring rear sight, muzzle brake, 7.25-inch stainless steel barrel, 1-in-9 twist, detachable stock, weight of 46 ounces. |
| Carbon 15 Pistol – Type 20 | Ghost ring rear sight, muzzle brake, 7.25-inch stainless-steel barrel, 1-in-9 twist, detachable stock, weight of 40 ounces. |

### Ramo Defense Systems

Ramo Defense Systems is currently marketing the USAS-12 shotgun, a firearm that utilizes several key features of the AR-15. The history of the current model can be traced back to the late 1980s, when the U.S.-based Gilbert Equipment Company created a shotgun design that incorporated a number of the AR-15 rifle features, apparently as a sort of close assault weapon system (CAWS) that might be easily employed by troops, police officers, or civilians familiar with this gun. Since Gilbert Equipment wasn't set up to manufacture a firearm, it worked with South Korea's Daewoo to put the shotgun into production.

The final gas-operated model was to be made in both semiauto-only and selective-fire models. Unfortunately for Gilbert Equipment Company, the rifle was listed as one of the firearms that couldn't be imported into the United States just as the guns were coming off the assembly lines in South Korea. Including the USAS-12 in the list of banned guns was especially odd. The ban was supposedly to halt the importation of firearms used by criminals, an impossibility given the fact that this gun wasn't in production. In a further ironic twist relating to this "criminal use" classification, some U.S. government agencies purchased small numbers of the USAS-12.

This was followed by the BATF's unprecedented

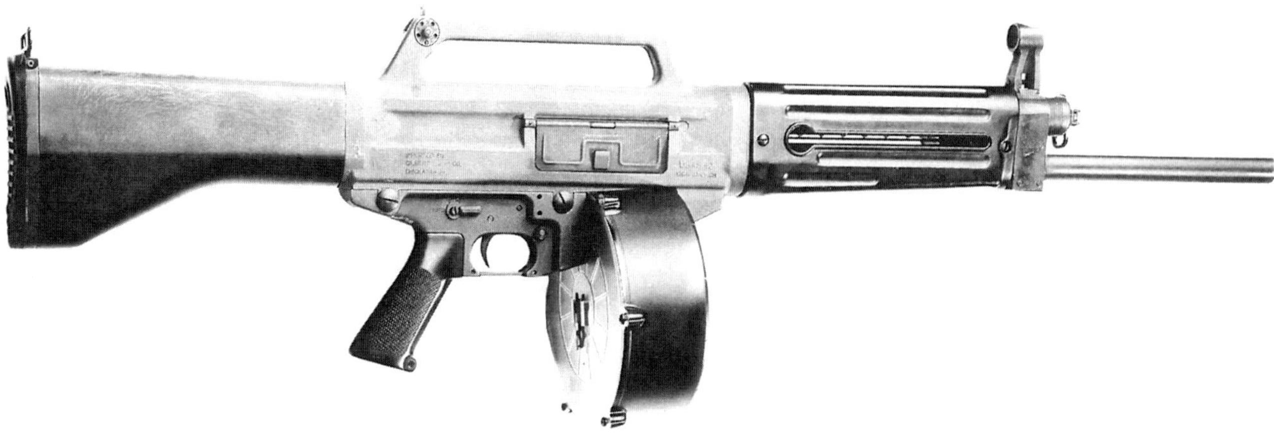

The USAS-12. (Courtesy of Gilbert Equipment Company.)

classification (apparently with the urging of Clinton's appointee to the Treasury, Lloyd Bentsen) of the USAS-12 as a "destructive device" in 1994 under the National Firearms Act, 26 U.S.C. Chapter 53. This classification was made with no legal authority, since the USAS-12 conforms to all federal regulations covering a shotgun. Nevertheless, it went into effect and has remained unchallenged in court. The only ray of hope in all this is that the BATF classified this (as well as two other shotguns) as a destructive device after previously approving it. Thus, owners were permitted to register the weapons without paying the $200 tax required for destructive devices under federal law. (The applications to register these firearms had to be posted no later than midnight on May 1, 2001. Any of these not so registered is now considered contraband.)

These unfortunate events have effectively removed a very innovative shotgun from the U.S. marketplace. While the external controls of the USAS-12 are similar to the AR-15 and the shotgun looks like an AR-15 on steroids, internally the two are quite different. The USAS-12's long recoil spring, coupled with the 12-pound weight of the firearm, absorbs the recoil of 12-gauge shells; the gas piston/bolt carrier more closely resembles the Kalashnikov rifle than anything else does. The USAS-12 has two magazines available for it, including a 10-round box magazine and a 20-round drum.

In 1990 Gilbert Equipment Company obtained a permit from BATF to import parts for the USAS-12, which the company planned on assembling on an American-made lower receiver. Shortly after spending more than a million dollars in tooling up, Gilbert Equipment Company received notification from BATF that if the rifle were assembled in the United States, the company would be in violation of a ruling that prohibited the USAS-12 from being imported in the first place. This odd decree (especially in light of the earlier permit to import parts) more or less dealt the deathblow to any chance of U.S. citizens' owning one of these shotguns. Ironically, this AR-15-style shotgun will likely enjoy sales worldwide, including those to U.S. government agencies and possibly special military units in the United States.

After buying the rights to the USAS-12 from Gilbert Equipment Company, RAMO Defense Systems, Inc. started marketing the firearm in the United States again in 2001. With more than three decades of engineering and manufacturing under its belt, RAMO turned an eye toward sales to foreign military customers as well as the U.S. military, to which it supplied ordnance systems and components. Even with the apparent targeting of the military and law enforcement market, it is doubtful that there will be many USAS-12 sales. A promising system that was killed with red tape and regulations before it ever had a chance to succeed, this gun will most likely drop into obscurity.

### Rock Island Armory, Inc.

Rock Island Armory (not to be confused with the U.S. government's arsenal) was a sister corporation to Springfield Armory, with the former marketing a line of

AR-15 style rifles. These guns were in the A1 rifle and carbine configuration. As noted earlier, Rock Island Armory crossed swords with Colt by undercutting it in bids for sales to El Salvador. This led to a lawsuit in which Colt contended that Rock Island Armory was infringing on some of its patents. This was followed in the 1980s by a lawsuit brought against the company by BATF, in which the government claimed that Rock Island Armory possessed machine guns that were illegally manufactured under the 1986 ban against such weapons for civilian sales. Between these two court actions, Rock Island Armory was pretty much forced out of business.

Even though these guns haven't been made for some time, a few Rock Island guns from the 1980s are still floating around. These rifles and carbines are generally well made and reliable. The company also sold lower receivers and other parts, so guns assembled from parts on the lower receiver are also undoubtedly circulating; these guns will be as good—or bad —as the parts used in their assembly and the skill of the hobbyist or gunsmith putting them together.

**Rock River Arms**

Rock River Arms makes several models of AR-15 rifles covering everything from law enforcement and military-style rifles to target guns. The company also makes use of its intermediate handguard to create models halfway between carbines and rifles in appearance; furniture is available in green as well as the standard black. With a few exceptions (as noted below), the guns have chrome moly barrels with a 1-in-9 twist. The shorty stock used on some models is the company's own design, with a lower toe than is found on the original telescoping stock, which makes for a much more comfortable fit when shouldering the gun. This stock is permanently fixed in its open position to conform to the assault weapon ban, except for law enforcement models, which have a fully functional stock. The Rock River Arms AR-15 line includes the following:

| | |
|---|---|
| CAR A2 | 16-inch barrel, choice of mid- to short handguard and standard or telescoping stock, muzzle brake optional. |
| CAR A4 Flat-tops | 16-inch barrel with front sight, choice of mid- to short handguard and standard or telescoping stock, flat-top receiver, Weaver rail gas block and muzzle b rake optional. |
| Le Tactical CAR | Flat-top carbine, 16-inch barrel, A4 collapsible stock, A2 flash hider, match trigger, Commando handguards, law enforcement sales only. |
| Elite Le Tactical CAR | Flat-top carbine, 16-inch barrel, telescoping stock, A2 flash hider, match trigger, mid-length handguards, law enforcement sales only. |
| Standard A2 | 20-inch barrel, standard semiauto A2 receiver, muzzle brake optional. |
| Standard A4 Flat-top | 20-inch-barrel, flat-top receiver, match trigger, muzzle brake, carrying handle, Weaver rail gas block and detachable front sight optional. |
| Varmint Rifle | 16-, 20-, or 24-inch stainless-steel barrel, 1-in-8 twist, flat-top receiver, A2 stock and pistol grip, floating handguard, match trigger, optional carrying handle and front sight. |
| NM A2 – DCM Legal | 20-inch stainless-steel barrel, 1-in-8 twist, fine-adjust A2 sight, match trigger. |

### Rocky Mountain Arms, Inc.

This company manufactured upper and lower AR-15 receivers and also marketed the Patriot pistol. Like most other pistols made before the assault weapons ban, this one is now out of production. Its weight was above the legal limit, which, coupled with the magazine placement gave it two of the no-nos that define the dreaded-by-leftists-everywhere "assault weapon." Patriot pistols still appear in the market for used guns from time to time. At the time of this writing, it appears that Rocky Mountain Arms may get back into the AR-15 manufacturing business, but the company has no line of these rifles yet.

### SGW/Olympic Arms

SGW is a small, U.S.-based company that also markets products under the name of Olympic Arms, Inc. In addition to a wide range of parts and accessories for the public, SGW offers AR-15-style rifles and upper receiver/barrel assemblies. The latter make it possible to convert lower receiver assemblies with military-style front push pins to carbines capable of firing 9mm Luger, 10mm (both the reduced FBI round and the full-power version), .40 S&W, .45 ACP, 6mm PPC, 6mm-.223, .17 Remington, .300 Fireball, or 7.62x39mm, among other chamberings. These various chamberings are often seen as complete rifles rather than just conversion kit assemblies; however, it isn't unusual to find shooters who use just the conversion parts to transform their standard .223 rifle to another chambering for special-purpose work such as hunting or for varminting.

The rifle-caliber versions of SGW's guns have locking bolts that are gas operated just like the .223 versions of the rifle. The pistol-caliber versions are of the straight blowback system, so bolts lack locking lugs and, with some calibers (like the .45 ACP), a weight is added to the rear of the bolt carrier to slow the cycling rate and guarantee reliable chambering. With both systems, the standard buffer/recoil spring cycles the action.

The SGW conversion units are quick for exchanging in the company's standard AR-15 models, since all use military-style receivers with front and rear push pins. The owner just snaps out the front and rear push pins, exchanges the SGW receiver/barrel upper receiver for the original, closes the assembly, slaps a magazine into the firearm, and it's ready to go. The retail cost of each SGW assembly is around $595 at the time of this writing. Rifle-caliber conversions use magazines that are latched into the receiver with the standard magazine catch. With pistol-caliber conversion units, a slightly different system is used.

With early SGW conversion units, an extension on the spine of the magazine allowed the standard release button to latch onto the magazines. The newer conversion units have an adapter that fastens into the rear of the magazine well with the rifle's magazine catch; a thumb toggle on this adapter then latches the magazine into place. (Some critics claim that this system could cause a person in the habit of releasing magazines with the side-mounted button to drop the empty magazine *and* the conversion adapter in the magazine well. Those using one of these firearms for self-defense can avoid this problem by simply placing a small cap over the original magazine button and then taping or even gluing the cover into place. Thus the user can avoid inadvertently releasing both the adapter and magazine.)

SGW has also fielded 9mm and .40 S&W conversion kits that can use Glock, SIG, or Beretta pistol magazines; these magazines have to be modified to work in both the AR-15 and the pistol, a task SGW does for $5 per magazine. The cost for this conversion is $649 at the time of this writing.

The rifles offered by SGW vary from more or less standard rifles and carbines to target rifles capable of greater accuracy than most shooters can appreciate. Among the company's offerings are the Ultramatch (with steel handguard and scope mount block without front or rear sights and with 20-inch stainless steel, 1-in-10-twist barrel); International Match (with target sights, aluminum or steel handguards, and 20-inch stainless-steel, 1-in-10-twist barrel); Service Match (with the M16A2 layout and furniture with 20-inch target barrel and trigger job); Multimatch (free-floated match 16-inch barrel, thumbhole or telescoping stock); CAR-15 (Commando-style carbine with 16-inch barrel); and 20-inch Semiauto Heavy Match Rifle (standard military-style rifle with A1 sights and match barrel).

A wide range of other models can be created, with various options for each model, including barrel lengths, chamberings, stocks, and handguards. Additionally, the company offers Pacs, with one lower receiver and several upper assemblies, so the owner can alter his rifle for several different purposes.

SGW has also offered one commemorative rifle as part of the Bill of Rights 200th anniversary. The Bill of Rights rifle was part of a set including a .45 ACP Safari Arms Matchmaster pistol (to which SGW owns the manufacturing rights). Only 201 of these guns were produced, with serial numbers form 1791 to 1991. The AR-15-style rifles had upper and lower receivers milled from gold-colored beryllium-and-copper alloy; steel parts were of a highly polished blue steel. A scroll representing the Bill of Rights was engraved on the receiver along with other "flowers and curlicues." The furniture on the rifle was a special composite plastic, colored brown to simulate wood. The dealer price was $4,950, and prices are likely to climb as the years pass.

After the federal assault weapons bill was passed in the mid-1990s, Olympic modified most of its products to conform to this law, though most of the original configurations are still available to law enforcement users. The new "civilian" versions of the guns that conform to the law are virtually identical to the previous models except for no flash hider, bayonet lug, and/or telescoping stock (on shorty versions). These new models generally have a PCR ("politically correct rifle") prefix on their model numbers to reflect the change. The exception to this is the CAR-97 model. It has the appearance of a preban shorty but actually has the stock modified so it remains in the extended position and has a muzzle brake rather than a flash hider permanently welded to its barrel. Thus, on all but the casual inspection, it is politically correct under the assault weapons law.

Another interesting carbine offered by Olympic is the PCR-7 Eliminator, a carbine that mimics the original Vietnam War-era Colt carbine with a 16-inch barrel coupled with a full-sized rifle handguard, giving the sight radius of a full-sized rifle coupled with the handiness of a carbine. Like most of the other guns in Olympic Arms' current lineup, the PCR-7 has a barrel with a 1-in-9 twist; a muzzle brake completes the picture on this model along with an A2 rear sight assembly.

SGW has also recently started making titanium lower receivers. These are as strong as steel but about the same weight of aluminum, giving the user a much stronger lower that is also more resistant to corrosion. Although arguably most AR-15 lower receivers hold up just fine, in some environments titanium might offer some more useful capabilities.

### SSK Industries

SSK offers a conversion kit for adapting a standard AR-15 rifle to the Whisper .300 cartridge as well as other wildcat rounds. The company also sells complete rifles in this chambering. These generally have a flat-top receiver with a match-grade, free-floated barrel.

### tAP Rifles, Pistols, and Kits

Gunsmith Tom Provost created a number of AR-15 accessories and built AR-15-style target rifles for customers before leaving the business for an easier job. (Gunsmithing being an arduous task that often takes its toll on patience as well as physical health.) He created a variety of target rifles, often utilizing the free-floating barrel system he designed. This system employed standard rifle handguards, giving the gun the appearance of a standard rifle when, in fact, it was a target gun (a consideration in some matches).

In addition to these, Provost created two innovative pistol designs based on the AR-15; these function with standard .223 ammunition and use mostly standard AR-15 parts. One employs a short buffer tube—without buffer assembly; the other cuts the bolt carrier short and places a recoil spring behind it, all within the length of the receiver, a screw cap replacing the buffer tube in the lower. These are offered in kits that permit the transformation of an unassembled, new AR-15 parts set into a pistol (since federal law prohibits creation of a pistol from parts that had previously been assembled as a rifle).

Both of these pistols are very compact, and Provost has produced an 8-inch- barrel version (and believes a 5-inch barrel to be possible). Needless to say, such guns are fire-breathing, ear-shattering firearms—which produce some spectacular fireworks with unburned powder when fired at night.

Even with a 10-inch barrel, these pistols are very compact and lighter than any similar firearm offered by any manufacturer at that time, though several have since met this challenge.

Kits of only the components needed to transform a new, standard parts kit into a pistol sold for as little as $80 for the receiver extension and for possibly as much as several hundred dollars for the over-the-carrier version when it is developed and ready for sale. Only some of these kits have been sold. Step-by-step procedures for building an AR-15 pistol using the basic Provost design and all-new AR-15 parts was covered in my *Making Your AR-15 into a Legal Pistol*, available from Paladin Press for $14; it should be noted that guns assembled at the time of this writing must conform to the assault weapon ban).

### Type 65 Rifle

Taiwan produced its own version of the AR-15, which its military adopted as the Type 65 rifle. This version of the AR-15 has a lowered front sight, altered swivels, a lowered rear sight, reshaped stock, and redesigned handguards. The Taiwan design also did away with the carrying handle and used the AR-18 gas system rather than the AR-15's gas tube. This rifle weighs 7 pounds (empty) and is 39 inches long; no carbine version or SAW variations of this gun seem to have been built.

The basic design was revamped and given an AR-15-style gas tube, apparently partly to mitigate the heat buildup in the handguard and partly to simplify and lighten the firearm. Virtually identical to the AR-15 except for the furniture and sights, the new model, designated the Type 65K2, has had its barrel twist increased to accommodate the SS109 cartridge.

### Victor Arms .22 Conversion

Victor Arms has marketed a dedicated .22 LR upper that can be fitted to the AR-15. The receiver is a flat-top

Some of the possible configurations of guns built around the two different Provost recoil spring/buffer systems.

with a 16-inch barrel; magazines are designed by the company. There is also an M16 conversion kit that operates in selective-fire weapons, with 30-round magazines available only for government and law enforcement users. The semiauto kits sell for $389, while the selective-fire version retail for $439.

**Wilson Combat Tactical Rifles**

Wilson Combat's line of Tactical Rifles, assembled on more or less a custom basis, are built around CNC machined 7075 T6 forged-aluminum receivers coupled with Wilson Combat's own match-grade 1-in-9-twist barrels. Most guns are sold with a single-stage target trigger (with a pull of around 3 pounds) and a flat-top

Wilson UT-15 Urban Tactical carbine.

Zitta's Master Blaster manually cycled pistol laid the groundwork for later Z-M Weapon guns. (Courtesy of Allan Zitta.)

upper receiver. The company offers three basic versions: the UT-15 sports a 15-inch free-floated premium match-grade barrel with a permanently installed muzzle brake to bring it to a legal 16.5-inch length; the TPR-15 has an 18-inch fluted, medium-weight barrel and is available with an optional bipod and a Leupold Tactical; and the M-4T has a 16.25-inch M4-style heavy barrel topped with a muzzle brake.

### Z-M Weapons

Gunsmith Allan Zitta's guns have a lot of special features, including several handmade wooden pistol grips, machined handguards, and often one-of-a-kind parts and features. When the first edition of this book was printed, Zitta had created a number of custom-made AR-15s, including manually operated ones for target shooters (sold as the Master Blaster) and various types of free-floated barrel target guns. Since that time, Zitta's innovative designs have blossomed, expanding into a while array of products, including an AR-15 design that departs enough from the original that one might easily argue that it is an entirely new system.

The secret behind Zitta's semiauto pistol designs is the placement of the recoil spring and its hollow guide around the gas tube of the AR-15. This is a complex proposition and entails the creation of special handguards to accommodate the extra parts above the barrel, but it works well and creates a very compact firearm with no need of a buffer assembly behind the receiver. This system might also be adapted to a bullpup stock for those interested in such a system (or a carbine—which is what eventually happened).

The various models custom guns Zitta created were quite reasonably priced as custom guns go, running about $1,300 to $2,000 each, depending on the various features incorporated into the firearm. Zitta also did (and does) trigger tuning (to 3 1/2-pound pull on a standard AR-15) and custom stock and receiver/scope mount work, as well as offering unique tube sights, muzzle brakes, and other products, operating from his Cycle Dynamics, Inc. motorcycle shop (which caters to his other great interest in life).

Since those first pistols were run out of the Cycle

Zitta's beautifully crafted rifle. The inventor's over-the-barrel recoil spring was later incorporated into Z-M Weapons guns. (Courtesy of Allan Zitta.)

Z-M Weapons carbines.

Dynamics shop, a few things have changed. First, the business became good enough that Zitta created Z-M Weapons to handle a whole line of guns based on his forward spring design. Second, the assault weapon ban put many of the innovations out of the reach of the public. However, Z-M Weapons appears to have taken this major obstacle in stride, now selling those verboten guns to law enforcement buyers and offering conversion kits to owners of preban guns as well as fixed-stock/compensator guns and kits to civilians.

The basic rifle design is designated the LR 300 and it makes a compact, light carbine in both its military, LR 300ML configuration and its LR 300SRF civilian version. The system is built around a refinement of Zitta's older interconnecting operating-rod gas system that permits both the short barrel and folding stock, making the LR 300ML ideal as a police entry weapon as well as a compact sporter in its LR 300SRF form.

The LR 300 has a flat-top receiver that accepts all Weaver-type mounts, electronic sights, and scopes, so it is readily equipped with a variety of accessories. The unit also has an ARMS military rear sight so the shooter can use the gun without a scope or use the sight as a backup. Furthermore, because the ARMS unit is attached with a Weaver system, it can be moved forward or backward across the upper receiver rail to accommodate a variety of accessories (as well as older eyes that have trouble focusing on near objects—though this isn't a great problem with the peep sight, it is a consideration for some shooters).

Although it is different from most other AR-15 systems, the LR 300 still retains the AR-15 trigger group, charging handle, and other parts, making it easy to maintain. And it also accepts the standard AR-15 magazine, again giving the user a variety of magazines to choose from according to his needs.

The LR 300 has the slightly different grip designed by Zitta. The angle is the same as that of the 1911 .45 pistol, an angle that many feel is superior to that of the AR-15. Consequently many shooters may discover they prefer it (and the grip can be replaced with the standard AR-15 grip is this is not the case).

The LR 300ML is available in semiautomatic or select-fire configuration and sports an 11.5-inch barrel with the company's Phantom flash hider. Zitta has designed a new handguard for his rifle that permits fastening a pistol grip in one of five positions as well as easy mounting of slings and other accessories, Accessories include a full-length rail mount that runs from the rear of the receiver to over the front gas tube as well as a Tri-mount that has a Weaver mount fitting around the lower and right/left sides of the front gas block, to which lasers, flashlights, or other devices may be fastened (making this one great carbine for those who are into gadgets).

At the tail end of the gun the buyer has a choice of two stocks. One is the company's unique folder, which incorporates a shorty-style latch system into a side folding design. The result is that the user can adjust the length of pull to five different positions as well as fold the stock to the left side of the rifle for more compact storage.

The other folder is the spitting image of that offered by Fabrique Nationale for its rifles, but adapted to the AR-15 system. This, too, folds to the left of the receiver, leaving the ejection port and magazine release clear if the gun needs to be fired with the stock folded.

Overall length when folded is only 21.5 inches; unfolded it's 31 inches. The gun weighs in at 7 pounds and fires at a cyclic rate of 950 rpm on select fire using the Zitta system.

The LR 300 SRF has the FN-style folder but with the stock permanently set in its open position coupled with a crowned 16.5-inch barrel to keep the whole system in line with federal laws regarding minimum rifle lengths and assault weapons. Despite these features, the carbine is still very short and handy and capable of using most AR-15 accessories as well as those offered by Z-M Weapons. Additionally, the barrel is offered with the option of having a very effective muzzle brake permanently attached, a feature that reduces the recoil to an almost unnoticeable level.

The LR 300 SRF weighs a half-pound more than its military counterpart (due to the longer barrel), tipping the scales at 7.5 pounds with an overall length of 36 inches. For those owning preban AR-15s, a conversion kit with the 16.5-inch barrel and either of the folding stocks is also available. With the stock folded, these guns are 26.5 inches long.

The LR 300 system is an interesting weapon that joins the best of the AR-15 with elements of other rifles to the creative genius of Zitta. It will be interesting to see what other inventive accessories and firearms may flow from Z-M Weapons in the future.

# Chapter 9

# Replacing the Warhorse

There have been pushes to replace the AR-15 as a military rifle almost from the time the U.S. Army officially adopted the gun as its M16 rifle. One by one, programs that promised to develop new technology as alternatives to (if not outright replacements for) the AR-15 have come and gone, from the SPIW and CAWS to the systems covered in this chapter.

Sooner or later there will be some innovation, some breakthrough that will lead to a viable replacement for the AR-15. In the meantime, seeing how and why various contenders have failed and what is currently on the back burner as a possible replacement is both entertaining and instructional. It may even give some reader the spark of an idea that will become the next leap forward in the creation of a new, more effective battle rifle—or a weapon so different from anything yet dreamed of today that it can't even be considered a rifle.

The most recent push to find a replacement for the M16A2 and M16A3 versions of the AR-15 was in the mid-1980s, when the Joint Services Small Arms Program (JSSAP) was in charge of the Rifle Successor Program (RSP), which was tasked with finding an eventual replacement for the M16A2 rifle. The JSSAP broke the RSP into three parts:

- A program that would further optimize the M16-A2 so it could remain effective until it was replaced
- The advanced combat rifle (ACR) program, whose goal was to see whether it was technologically feasible to create a firearm twice as effective as the M16A2 in creating enemy casualties
- In-depth research into the possibility of other technologies or alternatives to conventional firearms designs (the qualifying factor being that any such technology must be practical to field in the near term)

With a nod toward the family-of-weapons concept, the U.S. military also wanted to create a sister weapon to the ACR. This would consist of an advanced combat support weapon (ACSW) similar in concept to the SAW or a light machine gun using the same ammunition as the ACR. Additionally, the military wanted a personal defense weapon (PDW) that would at fire the same ammunition as the ACR (ideally, this would be of pistol proportions, but it's plausible that it could end up being a short-barreled version of the ACR). According to the military's original Small Arms Master Plan, the ACR, ACSW, and PDW, if they proved viable, would be implemented by the armed services during the 1990s, along with a crew-served weapon similar to the Mark 19 grenade-launching machine gun (GMG) that fired 40mm grenades. (Obviously, these goals were not met, though they have influenced some changes in the M16A2/M16A3/and M4 carbine.)

Along with these weapons development programs, the military instituted ongoing research to create a thermal-imaging sight capable of use on anything from a rifle to a GMG. This would enable troops to "see" and engage targets day or night, and through smoke and fog. (This goal was achieved, and limited numbers of these scopes are now seen among U.S. troops.)

### THE ACR PROGRAM

By the beginning of 1985, the U.S. Army's Training and Doctrine (TRADOC) had created an operation and organization (O&O) plan to formally set the requirements for the new ACR so manufacturers could create test rifles for army trials. The initiation of this O&O plan officially launched the search for an ACR. While the ACR program was not charged with finding an actual replacement for the M16A2 (officially it was only to test new technologies and concepts), the "feel" among contenders and many involved in the testing was that they might be working with the weapons that would become the new standard-issue firearm for American soldiers in the 21st century.

ACR testing used the M16A2 rifle as a benchmark or control against which ACR candidates were judged; this made it prove—or disprove—that a proposed replacement for the M16A2 would actually be a better gun. To reduce errors in comparing the various rifles, each soldier involved fired a different ACR candidate as well as the M16A2 under a variety of conditions.

A wide selection of troops was involved in the tests to give a viable "cross section" of the various types of soldiers expected to actually employ the firearm. The test groups included male and female soldiers, skilled marksmen, and "average" shooters. It was also determined that unless the new ACR performed significantly better than the M16A2, the military's money would be better spent in developing new technologies or sighting systems to enhance the M16A2 rather than simply exchanging one good system for a comparable one.

Since the foremost problem of the M16A2 is that a rifleman in battle seems unable to exploit the range or accuracy of the reliable weapon to the fullest, part of the research was aimed at studying how stressful shooting conditions in combat modify the performance of a shooter.

Among the other requirements for the ACR were a sighting system that would enable the soldier to locate targets at night or in conditions of limited visibility due to fog or smoke and projectiles that would penetrate body armor at a range of over 600 meters. Finally, it was felt that the ACR should be quieter and produce less muzzle flash than the M16A2.

As outlined in the TRADOC O&O paper, the four basic weapons in the family, which the army now seemed intent on getting, were these:

- A basic ACR
- An Advanced Close Support Weapon (ACSW) similar to the current SAW in concept
- An Advanced Personal Defense Weapon (APDW) similar to a submachine gun in size
- An Advanced Grenade System (AGS)

The ACSW was to be capable of using the same ammunition as the ACR and sustaining heavy rates of fire without "cook-offs" (a situation where ammunition is ignited and fired by the high barrel temperatures produced by excessive firing) or the need to change barrels. It was also to be modular, with many parts being interchangeable with the ACR. In addition, the O&O paper stipulated that an alternative "kill mechanism" (a bureaucratic term for ammunition) was to be available to enhance the weapon's ability to attack armored vehicles, bunkers, or buildings. The overall weight of the ACSW was to be no greater than the U.S. M249 Minimi SAW (i.e., 14.5 pounds).

The APDW specs called for it to be light enough so that it wouldn't detract from the carrier's normal duties—such as commanding troops, driving a vehicle, operating a radio, and so on. While the APDW was to use the ACR's ammunition, the range requirements for the APDW were reduced to 200 meters—perhaps to accommodate a shorter barrel. (It seems doubtful whether such a weapon derived from an ACR would actually be capable of replacing the pistol, as the O&O seems to propose, though it's conceivable that a chopped ACR might come close to realizing these requirements if iron sights, a short barrel, and very short overall length could be obtained.)

The proposed AGS was to replace the M203 rifle/grenade launcher. The O&O specifications called for far greater lethality, range, and hit probability than the M203 has. The real catch was that the standard for performance was not the M203 but the Soviet RPG-16 rocket-propelled grenade, making these specifications tough to meet with current technology.

### SAS2000

At about the time the O&O specs came out, another military paper also had a great impact on the army's push for future weapons systems. Released by the Infantry School at Ft. Benning late in 1986, the Small Army Strategy 2000 (SAS2000) document argued that combat rifles had reached the technological limits of gun design. Therefore, it reasoned, further development work toward perfecting a rifle was basically wasted effort, since the pinnacle of the current technology had very nearly been realized with the AR-15. The SAS2000 concluded that whole new system was needed—one that fired something other than flechettes or bullets, an HE warhead being the most practical of possibilities.

The ACR program ignored the SAS2000's arguments, going full speed ahead with its attempt to create a better rifle, even though tests showed that the M16A2 was about as rugged and accurate as one might ever hope for in a firearm. In the end, the ACR program pretty much proved the Infantry School's argument. In the process time and resources were perhaps squandered, even though this may have been necessary to prove to any doubting Thomases that SAS2000 was correct.

As the ACR program got under way, there were two candidate rifles, one produced by AAI and the other by Heckler & Koch, developed under an earlier army program. Both guns used caseless ammunition. Realizing that caseless ammunition was a somewhat iffy proposition, Undersecretary of the Army James R. Ambrose decided to hedge his bets and widened the ACR

ACR candidate rifles from (top to bottom) AAI, Heckler & Koch, and Steyr.

trials to include rifles supplies by other manufacturers—a move that would seem justified because AAI soon abandoned its caseless ammunition for more conventional cartridges in its ACR candidate weapon.

With this widening of the trials, the Armament Research Development and Engineering Command granted funds to Colt Firearms ($3.1 million), ARES ($3.5 million), and McDonnell Douglas Helicopter Company ($4 million) to develop alternate ACRs. Additionally, the ARDEC granted Steyr-Daimler-Püch a $4 million contract to produce a modular ACR that could be expanded into a family of small arms for use by the military. During this time AAI abandoned its caseless ammunition, adopting new ammunition that could be topped with a flechette projectile or bullet and resubmitting it for consideration in the ACR program.

The Colt and Steyr ACRs met with approval in the initial test and evaluation phase of the ACR trials and thus entered the running. The McDonnell Douglas and Stoner-designed ARES guns were both disqualified in 1987, however, largely because the guns submitted were still pretty much prototypes and, as such, not as reliable as they should have been. Furthermore, Stoner's gun took a different route to the goal of hitting the target, arguing that sighting systems were seldom used in combat and should be replaced with tracer ammunition.

The rejection of the other contenders left four guns in the running, produced by H&K, Steyr, Colt, and AAI.

### The Heckler & Koch G11

The G11 is perhaps the most noteworthy of the guns involved in the tests, if for no other reason than its unique operating system and ammunition—oddities in an age when most firearms are refinements and combinations of earlier designs.

The basic system was powered by caseless ammunition. This was hardly a new concept, the German military experimenting with it during World War II, and the U.S. Frankford Arsenal working with it in the 1950s, but this was not an easy way to go. There were the technological hurdles of making ammunition stable and impervious to moisture and dealing with the heat produced during firing: a brass cartridge wasn't available as a "heat sink" when powder was ignited. These hurdles were overcome, making the G11 the first combat rifle with ammunition that actually worked as efficiently as its brass cartridge equivalent.

Caseless ammunition offers a number of advantages to the design of a rifle. In theory, such a rifle can be simpler since there is no mechanism to extract or eject fired cases (except when the cartridge fails or the weapon is unloaded). This makes it possible to seal the system against dirt because the ejection port doesn't offer a large entrance to dust, sand, or mud every time the weapon is fired. The lack of a metal case also makes the ammunition lighter, allowing a soldier to carry a greater quantity without becoming overburdened.

Because rounds are not extracted during its operation, such a gun can also cycle very quickly. This was certainly the case with the G11, which cycles up to 2,000 rpm. When the rifle is fired in an automatic or burst mode, recoil is a steady push rather than successive jumps—and barrel climb is nonexistent. This means a burst of small-caliber bullets can improve the chances of hitting the target as well as the wounding potential of the weapon via multiple hits.

Problems with making the ammunition tough enough to stand up to moisture and the mechanism of a rifle as well as withstand the heat generated in a chamber without igniting prematurely kept the caseless ammunition concept from working for decades. But in the late 1980s, Dynamit Nobel and H&K finally managed to perfect a system in the form of the G11 rifle and its ammunition. The rounds designed for the rifle are small rectangular chunks of solid "powder" molded into a body around the bullet with the primer located in the center of the tail end of the round. The bullet is 4.7mm in diameter, and the entire round is about half the length of a 5.56mm NATO round.

The gun proved viable, and, after extensive tests, the German government was on the verge of issuing the weapon to its infantry troops along with a light machine gun based on the cartridge and a pistol system created around a smaller version of the caseless round that was also in the works at H&K.

But there was a catch.

With the collapse of the Soviet bloc nations and the reunification of Germany came unforeseen costs because of East Germany's having become an economic basket case under communist rule. Furthermore, there was the news that guns wore out earlier than hoped, resulting in Germany's tabling the decision to rearm troops with the new G11. Only special forces were ever issued G11s for actual use outside of field testing. But when the G11 went to the U.S. trials, it still appeared that it would be adopted by the German military, and many felt it might also ace the ACR trials.

The model employed in the ACR trials was somewhat different from the German army version. On the original G11 design there is an integral 1X scope that doubles as a carrying handle. Because the scope doesn't magnify the target, the shooter can use it with both eyes open. The scope has a battery to illuminate the reticle in low-light conditions, and the reticle itself is of a quick-to-use circular pattern, similar to that used on the Steyr AUG.

With H&K's ACR candidate the scope offered both the 1X setting and a second setting for targets at 300 to 600 meters, with 3.5X magnification and a range reticle in the scope picture to aid in hitting targets.

The G11 is easy field-strip, and a cleaning kit is handily located in its hollow pistol grip. The weapon is only 29.53 inches (75 cm) long and weighs 8.6 pounds (3.9 kg) with an empty magazine. The ammunition is light; 50 rounds weigh only a little over half a pound (220 g), making it easy for a soldier to carry more than twice as much ammunition than if he were limited to the same weight in standard 5.56mm NATO cartridges.

### The Steyr ACR

Steyr's ACR candidate borrowed much of its layout and modular conception from the company's AUG. Like its parent rifle, the ACR made use of plastic in a wide array of parts normally made of steel. Added to this were the futuristic appearance of both rifles, their bullpup design, and the normal use of an optical scope mounted high over the barrel of the rifle.

The stock, pistol grip, and handguard of the ACR were made of polycarbonate plastic moldings, with the rear stock assembly being removable during field-stripping. As with the AUG, the ACR's pistol grip/trigger guard wrapped around the entire hand so that the rifle could be easily operated even with mittens on. The magazine release was a plastic lever just behind the magazine well and, by virtue of its central position, could easily be reached by left- or right-handed shooters.

Unlike the AUG, the Steyr ACR had a forward handguard rather than a forward pistol grip that protected the shooter's off hand from the barrel when it became hot. The barrel was free-floated in the handguard and had an M16-style flash hider on it with a number of small holes added along its top to help counter barrel rise during firing.

The shooter could select semiauto or three-round burst fire by the position of the square push-through safety located on the side of the rifle above the pistol grip. The far-left position of the push-through button was safe, the center position was semiauto, and the far right position was three-round burst.

Unlike the burst-fire mode of some rifles, the Steyr system reset itself to cycle again if the trigger was released after only one or two rounds were fired. This prevented short-cycles of only one or two shots from being fired during a successive burst.

The Steyr ACR had a detachable Swarovski scope that was normally mounted on the carrying handle/scope base of the rifle; this design permitted use of night-vision equipment or other gear in possible military use. With the scope detached, iron sights were also available for use. In this mode, the long rib running down the top of the handguard had the potential to improve a soldier's ability to quickly engage targeted in "snap" shooting.

The scope had two settings: 1.5X for shooting within 300 meters and 3.5X for 300 to 600 meters. The scope had a ring reticle similar to that of the AUG, which gives a very quick sighting under battle conditions. The reticle ring could also be used to give rough range estimates based on how much of the ring an enemy soldier's image filled, although the high speed and flat trajectory of the Steyr ACR's projectiles (which had an amazing muzzle velocity of 4,900 fps) made such considerations immaterial except at longer ranges. Consequently, the 3.5X scope on the Steyr ACR didn't even have range markings; the flechettes had such a flat trajectory that the drop could be ignored for any shooting inside 600 meters. (With a 600-meter zero, the trajectory rises only 13 inches at midrange, making adjustments for range generally unnecessary for this as well: most shooters would be simply aiming at the mass of the target rather than a specific part of the body at such ranges). The speed of the flechette also decreased the need to lead moving targets, thereby also increasing hit probability with aimed fire.

Semitransparent magazines designed for the rifle allowed the shooter to visually check the amount of ammunition remaining. Magazine capacity was small compared with the other ACR candidates: the Steyr ACR magazine held only 24 rounds.

The charging handle was similar to that of the AR-15/M16 and was located at the rear of the scope mount/rear sight assembly. Spent cartridges were ejected from a port on the lower side of the receiver just ahead of the magazine well. This downward ejection made it possible for the shooter to safely adopt either a right- or left-handed hold with the rifle, thereby doing away with one of the major shortcomings of many other bullpup designs.

Internally the Steyr ACR was gas operated. But the weapon didn't have a bolt as such. Rather, it employed a unique rising feeding arm attached to the gas cylinder; the gas cylinder assembly acted as a sleeve to cycle along the barrel, which acted as a fixed piston. This arrangement simplified the overall design and helped keep it light.

During the operation of the rifle, the feeding arm shoved an empty cartridge—if one was present in the chamber—out the ejection port; the arm then stripped a new round from the magazine and thrust it into the moving chamber of the weapon. The chamber next rose with the cartridge to align with the barrel. As the round was lifted to align with the bore, a fixed firing pin extended through a hole in the chamber to strike the cartridge on its side. This ignited the primer resting inside an internal aluminum ring encircling the plastic-cased cartridge.

Each cylindrical cartridge for the ACR was 3/8 inch in diameter and 1 3/4 inch long, and the only opening at the front of the cartridge was lacquered to make it completely waterproof. Each cartridge weighed approximately half that of a standard .223/5.56mm cartridge, thereby making it possible for a soldier to carry twice as much of the Steyr ammunition without increasing the weight of his load.

Inside, the cartridge contained a carbon-steel flechette that was 1 5/8 inch long and weighed only 9.85 grains. The front of the finned projectile was surrounded by a four-piece sabot that dropped away after the flechette left the barrel. The sabot was made of liquid-crystal polymer, similar to that used by AAI for its sabots. The sabot was held in place by a small plastic boot on the shaft of the flechette.

The bore of the ACR had a twist of only 1-in-10. This twist was needed only to give enough centrifugal force to the sabot to cause it to quickly fall from the projectile after leaving the barrel; the flechette was stabilized in flight by its fins. The light weight of the flechette-sabot combination made recoil of the Steyr ACR very gentle and easy to control.

The overall length of the Steyr rifle was 30.7 inches (78 cm), and it weighed 7.12 pounds (3.2 kg). The rifle's design was very simple and had only 100 parts; the weapon could be disassembled to armorer maintenance levels without any tools.

### The AAI ACR

The final AAI ACR candidate rifle was more conventional than its previous ACR candidate, which had employed caseless ammunition that was not without its problems. The new ACR used standard M16 (SS109/M855) brass cartridges with standard primers and a modified propellant to fire the company's favorite projectile, the saboted flechette. Weight of the cartridge was about 75 percent of the standard M855 cartridge, giving a slight increase to the total ammunition load a soldier could carry as well as reducing recoil as compared to the M16A2.

The flechette itself weighed 10.2 grains, was about 1/16 inch in diameter and 1 5/8 inch long, and had a sharpened point at its front and fins at its rear. A four-piece sabot fit around the flechette to trap gas from the cartridge and propel the flechette out of the barrel. A special O-ring secured the sabot in place around the flechette until the assembly exited the barrel, at which point air resistance separated the flechette from its sabot.

With a muzzle velocity of around 4,600 fps, this flechette also offered a very flat trajectory. Dispersion of three-round bursts was roughly in a circular pattern. All these features gave this round a lot of potential for military use.

The gas-operated rifle operated with ported gas that forced a piston to the rear to unlock the bolt in the manner of many other such rifles. To allow the rifle to operate properly with flechette loads, the gas port was positioned toward the chamber; chambering and firing standard M16 ammunition in the rifle would undoubtedly damage it. Therefore, a special block was added to the magazine well so only the AAI magazines could be inserted into the rifle.

The magazine of the AAI ACR was nearly identical to the standard AR-15 30-round magazine in size but used a constant-force spring that had a greater potential for reliable feeding. The magazine release was a toggle located on the lower side of the receiver behind the magazine well.

An efficient muzzle brake/compensator helped prevent muzzle rise during recoil, bursts remaining closely dispersed on the target. The rifle fired from a closed bolt. A selector on the right side of the receiver allowed the shooter to "dial" either semiauto or three-round burst mode. The safety was positioned forward of the trigger so it was easily moved off safety by right- or left-handed shooters.

The AAI rifle was seen in the ACR trials with an ACOG 4X scope (developed for Trijicon with an eye toward the ACR program). The scope had a quick-detach feature allowing a rapid changeover to iron sights. Additionally, the rifle was designed to accept other standard scopes and night-vision equipment.

The ACR's lower receiver, pistol grip, and stock were all a single plastic molding; the upper receiver, fore grip, and barrel shroud were another unified molding. This simple design made the rifle easier to manufacture; created strong, integral assemblies; and simplified assembly or repair. Field-stripping the AAI rifle was similar to that for the AR-15/M16: the upper receiver/barrel assembly was released and rotated downward to allow for removal of the bolt carrier/bolt, recoil spring, and gas tube.

The AAI ACR candidate was 40 inches long and weighed 7.78 pounds without its magazine or sights. Iron sights weighed about 1/4 pound, while the optical sights were almost 3/5 pound. A loaded 30-round magazine brought the weight of this ACR to 8.2 pounds with the optical sight; the iron-sighted loaded rifle weighs 7.9 pounds.

### The Colt ACR

The Colt ACR was derived from both the rifle and carbine versions of the AR-15/M16. However, Colt had made several notable changes in the furniture of the rifle after doing "human engineering" tests to determine what best fits the human body.

Among these changes were a recontoured handguard that had enlarged vent holes and an improved heat shield, as well as a front-end restricting ring to help prevent a shooter's hand from sliding past the handguard to touch a hot barrel. The most readily apparent change to the new handguard was the "barrel rib" running along its top surface; this rib improved a shooter's ability to engage targets at close ranges (though its potential was somewhat negated when the scope was attached to the rifle) and also acted as a chimney of sorts to draw heat away from the barrel. The pistol grip was longer and recontoured to fit a shooter's hand more comfortably.

The barrel of the Colt ACR had a muzzle brake compensator coupled to its birdcage flash holder to help reduce recoil and muzzle climb, thereby reducing the dispersion during three-round bursts. The 20-inch barrel had a 1-in-7 twist to give optimal performance with a wide range of bullet sizes and shapes.

The barrel and upper receiver of the Colt ACR departed noticeably from the M16's traditional look, with both the triangular skeletal front sight and "carrying handle" rear sight base missing. In their places were a vertical front sight base that extends up to barely top the

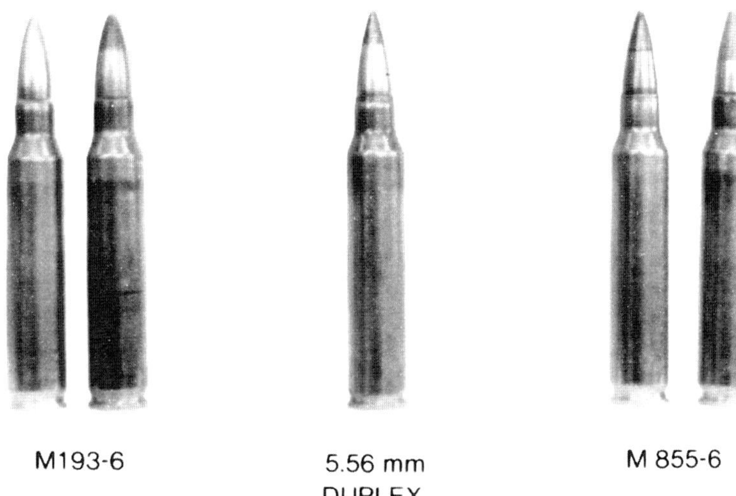


In addition to using the older M193 and new SS109 (M855) cartridges, the Colt ACR could also fire the duplex ammunition created by Olin/Winchester. Each of the duplex rounds had a 35-grain bullet that rode above a 33-grain bullet, putting two projectiles on target with each round fired.

rib's surface on the handguard and a detachable rear sight assembly that can be replaced by a scope. However, a more traditional-looking iron sight/carrying handle was available to replace the scope assembly if necessary. At the left side of the front sight was a sling swivel that allowed the rifle to be easily carried in the "assault position" by threading a sling through the swivel at the front and the molded-in swivel slots in the stock. The gun weighed in at 8.66 pounds empty with its optical scope.

The stock borrowed heavily from the telescoping Commando carbine version of the AR-15/M16. The most notable change in the telescoping stock was a lower toe of the butt plate; this enabled the gun to be shouldered more comfortably than the original Commando stock. Rather than merely being rounded, the new-style stock had cheek rests molded into both its left and right sides for added comfort. When the stock was retracted, the rifle was 36.75 inches long; with the stock extended, the total length was 40.63 inches.

Additional locking slots were drilled into the bar running down the underside of the buffer tube on the ACR (today this is a standard feature with most telescoping stocks). This made it possible to telescope the stock in or out for a longer or shorter length of pull. This feature made the rifle more compact for storage or vehicular use as well as "customizing" its length of pull to six different positions according to the clothing bulk or different statures of various shooters.

Inside the stock/buffer assembly, an "oil-spring hydraulic buffer" replaced the old plastic, washer-filled buffer. This new buffer was borrowed from Colt's SAW work and lowers the rate of full-auto fire to an optimum rate as well as reducing felt recoil. This buffer, coupled with the MBC on the muzzle, made the felt recoil 40 percent less than that of the M16A2 rifle.

The selector had three positions: safe, semiauto, and full auto. The selector was ambidextrous, with a control lever on the right and left of the lower receiver in the standard AR-15/M16 position. (The simpler M16 trigger mechanism had apparently been used in the ACR rather than the three-round burst trigger assembly of the M16A2; in theory, the lower cyclic rate of the ACR made it practical for the shooter to control burst lengths by limiting the time he pulls the trigger. Whether this would prove true in actual combat or whether a shooter's finger might "freeze" in place to empty the whole magazine in the gun in a long string of fire remains to be seen.)

The Colt ACR mounted a 3.5X scope manufactured by Ernst Leitz of Canada on its rifle. This scope had a tritium illuminating device for periods of reduced light. Other standard optical equipment, such as high-power scopes or night-vision devices, could also be easily mounted on the ACR's Weaver-style sight base, as could the emergency iron sights.

Working closely with Olin/Winchester, Colt created a new cartridge for its ACR. The round was similar to the duplex cartridge developed during early SALVO work and based on the 5.56 NATO cartridge rather than the 7.62mm NATO, however.

Olin/Winchester's duplex cartridge had two bullets, one nestled below the other (and held in place by the powder filling the brass) inside a standard 5.56mm cartridge. This arrangement allows a 35-grain bullet to ride above a 33-grain bullet. Upon firing, the front bullet travels toward the point of aim, while the rear bullet slightly dispersed. Given the requirement for an ACR candidate to show a 100-percent greater hit ability than the M16A2, the Duplex cartridge likely increased the Colt ACR's chances by quite a margin. (These special cartridges have a yellow-lacquered tip for identification.)

In addition to using the duplex cartridge (which shows best results within 300 meters), the Colt ACR also shot standard 62-grain M855/SS109 NATO cartridges.

Left and right view of the Colt ACR.

Additionally, Olin/Winchester had recently created a 62-grain Penetrator cartridge that outperformed the already potent M855 cartridge.

One asset of the Colt ACR was that the M16A2 could have been retrofitted into the ACR configuration had the go ahead to do this been given. Simply replacing the flash hider, forward sight assembly, hand guards, safety/selector, upper receiver/sights, pistol grip, stock, and buffer would have transformed the standard M16A2 into a close approximation of the Colt ACR. All this could have been done at a fraction of the cost involved in adopting a totally new ACR candidate. Army training manuals, target ranges, and so on would only have needed slight modifications to handle a changeover from the M16A2 to the Colt ACR.

Since the Fabrique Nationale, Bushmaster, and Colt's Manufacturing all had the machinery and know-how to manufacture the M16A2 rifle to U.S. military specifications, the tooling costs of producing the ACRs would have been minimal for any one of them, with plenty of competition for bids. On the other hand, had the H&K, Steyr, or AAI candidate been selected, it would have entailed building entire plants, training workers, and working bugs out of new systems and machinery—a comparatively expensive proposition at best.

These are moot points, however, since the ACR program didn't provide any clear direction toward a replacement for the M16A2 except, perhaps, in pointing out ways that the new M16A3 model might be created from elements of the Colt ACR.

## AND THE WINNER ISN'T

The ACR trials brought home a fact known but never fully addressed since the ALCLAD studies: the problem in hitting the target isn't that the weapons are incapable of enough accuracy over long ranges. Rather, the problem is that troops firing in combat have little time to aim, have trouble seeing targets, and are likely to miss a target even when aiming.

If anything this was painfully clear in the ACR trials, where several of the candidate rifles, as well as the M16A2 control weapons were capable of accuracy found only in custom-built sniper rifles of just a few decades earlier. Although some of the ACRs were capable of minute-of-angle shots (i.e., placing a group of aimed fire inside a 1-inch space at 100 yards), the soldiers carrying the guns came nowhere near to realizing this accuracy with the rifles or even using them in a highly effective manner anywhere beyond a very short distance.

Eventually, these facts would provide the impetus for the U.S. Army's next step toward finding a replacement for the M16, the objective individual combat weapon (OICW) program. But in the meantime, the Germans took another stab at creating a firearm to replace the expensive G11 that would also find its way into the OICW program.

### THE G36: CONTENDER FOR THE THRONE

For several decades, H&K has attempted to capture chunks of the market that Colt might otherwise hold or once held. Currently, it appears that H&K's G36 system might well oust the AR-15 from its almost universally accepted position as the best battle rifle available (a view shared somewhat by nations that have opted for a variant of the AK-47).

The G36 is largely an outgrowth of earlier H&K guns, including the G3 and MP5. However, the work on creating this system is generally traced back to 1990, when Project 50 was initiated by the German Bundeswehr in a search for a combat rifle following the realization that the promising G11 had flaws that weren't apparent at its outset.

The Bundeswehr wanted a group of guns built around a common receiver that could be used with a variety of configurations, from a 9mm submachine gun to a 7.62mm NATO belt-fed machine gun. This said, some of these have not been realized with the G36, including the 9mm and 7.62mm ammunition versions. However, considering the growing numbers of troops with body armor and the advances in 5.56mm ammunition, these two chamberings may become not only unnecessary but also less than ideal, given the complications they pose for supply lines during a protracted war. Other requirements were that the gun be lightweight, inexpensive, and (perhaps with the memory of the expense of the G11) of a more or less conventional design without blazing any new trails in technology.

The original gun was designated the HK50 at Heckler & Koch, but since its adoption by the German army, the gun

Two versions of the G36K (one with a vertical grip attached and the other with folded stock); bottom rifle is the standard G36 rifle.

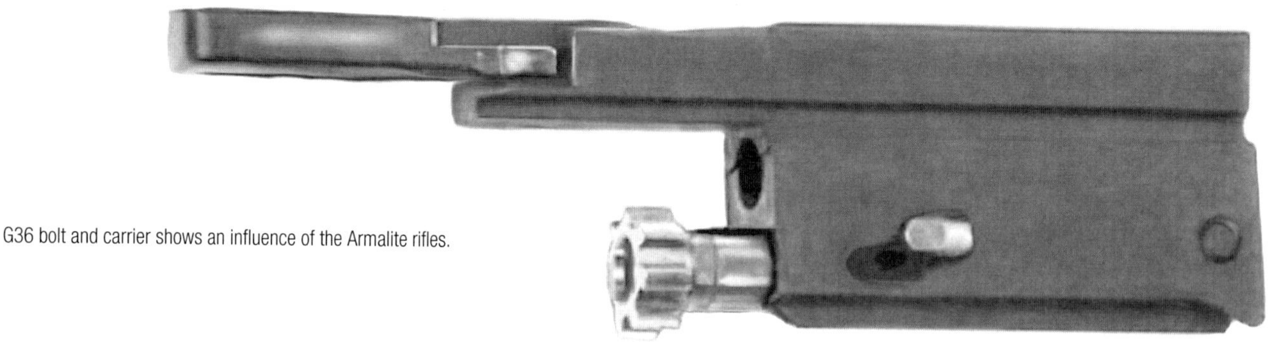
G36 bolt and carrier shows an influence of the Armalite rifles.

now is generally known by its military designation, Gewehr model 36, or G36.

It isn't hard to see why the Bundeswehr has adopted the G36 for nearly all its troops. Building on the basic idea of a modular system, this weapon has a folding stock, thanks to a recoil system in its receiver rather than in a buffer tube behind the receiver, as is the case with the AR-15. Chambered for the now universally accepted 5.56mm NATO cartridge, the gun is available in a variety of configurations, from the diminutive G36K carbine with a 12.5-inch barrel up to a heavy-duty SAW machine gun. All are based on the same receiver assembly, and most parts can be exchanged easily to reconfigure the gun.

If aluminum castings were the high-tech gun construction material of the 20th century, it seems certain that plastics will be the material of choice in the 21st. Indeed, this trend has already gained a firm foothold, beginning with the Glock pistol and continuing to the "plastic" receivers of a variety of other pistols and rifles as well as the stocks, pistol grips, and handguards of most modern battle rifles. The G36 takes this to its logical next step, with a huge number of its parts constructed of tough, carbon-fiber-reinforced polymer. The gun also boasts a simple, self-regulating gas system (permitting up to 15,000 rounds to be fired without cleaning in tests), which makes it reliable with a variety of ammunition, from the best to the grungiest. These features make the G36 lightweight, dependable, and inexpensive to build and maintain. The polymer parts can be cleaned with a variety of materials, from standard cleaning fluids used on firearms to good old soap and water.

An armorer can easily exchange the barrel on this gun to create a rifle, carbine, or SAW around the same basic receiver, making a variety of configurations possible as needed, given the proper spare parts. In addition, the G36 system includes a variety of accessories, scopes, stocks, and the like that are part of the modular concept. Thus, troops can quickly modify a rifle for the need at hand.

Among the G36 parts is a 30-round translucent polymer magazine that permits the shooter to see how much ammunition is in it and also locks together without a magazine clamp. The plastic construction makes it tough yet 30-percent lighter than a metal magazine. The gun also has a 100-round dual-drum magazine available; though this is designed for SAW use, the large magazine fits all G36 models, making it ideal for antiterrorist work, among other such things.

All the controls on the rifle are for ambidextrous operation, including the safety/selector lever. The catch button enables the shooter to lock the bolt open when the magazine is empty; there is also the option of disabling it without tools so that the bolt closes when the magazine is empty. Like other recent H&K firearms, the G36 has a variety of trigger groups, from a semiauto system to a variety of selective-fire configurations. The stock folds to the right with cutouts and placement that avoid covering any key controls or the ejection port. An integral mounting rail system permits tactical lights, lasers, or other accessories.

G36 weapons are available with two sighting options. One is a single 1.5X optical sight integrated into a detachable carrying handle with backup iron sights located on the top of the sight and carrying handle. The other is a dual sighting system that couples a 3.5X optical sight and an electronic red-dot sight; these are independently adjustable, making it possible to use one or the other at different ranges or to meet other specific needs. To conserve battery power, the dot sight can be used during the day with available light.

The G36 rifle weighs 7.28 pounds (3.3 kg) with an 18.9-inch (48 cm) barrel. The overall length is 39.28 inches (100 cm) with the stock extended or 29.84 inches (76 cm) with the stock folded. The G36K weighs 6.62 pounds (3 kg), thanks to its 12.52-inch (39 cm) barrel. It is only 24.21 inches (62 cm) long with the stock folded and 33.78 inches (86 cm) long with the stock unfolded. The machine gun configuration weighs 7.87 pounds (3.9 kg) and has the same dimensions as the standard G36.

U.S. soldier models complete Land Warrior gear. (Courtesy of U.S. Department of Defense.)

Business end of a Land Warrior soldier's AR-15. Monocle receives picture from infrared scope mounted on the rifle. (Courtesy of U.S. Army.)

## LAND WARRIOR

At this point it is necessary to take a side trip in the history of the AR-15 and the U.S. military's search for its replacement. As is often the case, the low are brought high in this story, the low in this case being those in the military who thought the M16A2 (and M4 carbine) were excellent systems and all that was needed was to mount a few good accessories to make the weapons fit the needs of the user. The positive in this line of endeavor is that such a course isn't very expensive because the rifles are already in the inventory. It also lets manufacturers do most of the research and development in creating many off-the-self accessories, with only small expenditures necessary for those that aren't readily available. All said, it offers a lot of bang for the buck, even though it isn't as glamorous as producing a state-of-the-art (but often impractical) weapons system.

This process, which became the U.S. Army's Land Warrior project in 1991, started with an unusual recommendation by a group that was studying soldiers in combat. It suggested that the military should treat soldiers as if they were a *part* of a complete weapon system that could be enhanced by adding the right accessories. Although such recommendations might easily have been dismissed as nonsense, the army took them seriously and set out to see if their implementation would improve the performance of troops in combat.

In the end the Land Warrior concept has proved a huge success. The U.S. military has bought $2 billion worth of accessories, issuing the first lot of a total of 45,000 in 2001 as part of a program that will continue to field the equipment through 2014. The cost is not low, with a pricc tag of around $70,000 per complete set of gear for the individual; however, the prices is likely to come down as production increases and electrical components become less expensive. And complete kits aren't issued to every soldier but only those actually engaged in combat.

In starting with this line of research, the army set three priorities for the Land Warrior project:

- To increase the lethality of troops
- To improve the survivability of soldiers
- To improve the command and control communications between troops and those in charge of them

From the first, the proposed systems created for Land Warrior have been tested in the field, with input from soldiers being part of the program. Most testing has taken place at the U.S. Army Infantry Center at Ft. Benning. Direct feedback from soldiers allowed the equipment designers to quickly spot flaws and make the gear more usable and reliable in ways that might otherwise have been overlooked.

The end result is a collection of equipment that breaks down into several subsystems comprising a wide range of gear and accessories for the M16A2 or M4 carbine as well as the soldier himself. For instance, there is an integrated helmet assembly with communications equipment and an optical system that connects to other equipment to create a TV-screen-like view over the soldier's eye. Among the systems are protective clothing, a mobile computer/radio system, and the software to run some of this equipment.

There are several key modules that can be employed with the weapon (these generally aren't used at once, due to their combined weight), including the following:

Land Warrior optical sight system permits a soldier to stay under cover while searching for an enemy. (Courtesy of U.S. Department of Defense.)

- Combination laser range finder-digital compass
- Daylight video camera/sight system
- Laser aiming device
- Thermal sight

Most of the electronics development for this program was handled by Raytheon Systems Company, with subcontractors that included Motorola, Honeywell, Omega, GENTEX, and Battelle (all of which are most likely to be involved with the continued development and upgrading of the systems).

For those using the M16A2 or M4 in combat, the integrated sight (IS) promises to help them hit more targets while reducing the likelihood of their being targeted by those they are attacking. The IS integrates an uncooled thermal imager, eye-safe laser range finder, electronic compass, TV camera, and infrared laser pointer into a single lightweight sight that mounts atop the receiver of a rifle (and can also be hand-held or tripod-mounted). The IS provides the soldier with the ability to acquire targets during daylight, darkness, adverse weather, and through battlefield obscurants such as fog or smoke. It also provides target position data (azimuth and range) so that indirect fire can be employed to hit targets.

In addition to acting as a sight, the TV camera or thermal image can be transmitted via the Land Warrior radio system to higher echelons so that commanders and

Once thought impossible to build, thermal imagers small enough to mount on an M4 carbine are not only possible, but being fielded by U.S. forces.

others can know what is going on in the battle, thereby making more informed decisions that may be decisive. The IS thermal imager is a marvel of miniaturization thought impossible a few years back, as was the range finder a few decades ago. Now they are in a unified system. Besides being used as a more or less standard sighting system, the TV or thermal sight can be coupled to the user's helmet eyepiece. This makes it practical for the shooter to maneuver the gun around a corner, over an obstruction, and so on so that he can not only "see around a corner" but also engage an enemy in a gunfight without exposing himself to enemy fire. (The pistol grip of the M16A2 coupled with the FIRM forward grip mounted on the gun makes holding the weapon and firing it without a shoulder hold very practical.)

The integrated helmet assembly subsystem uses advanced materials to provide ballistic protection at less weight than the current helmet shell. So despite its having a sight monocular and electronics incorporated, it is actually lighter than the Fritz helmet it replaces. In addition to the monocular display that connects into the gun sights and other systems, the helmet has a laser detection module (important if troops are to be aware that they may be a target of someone with a laser system), a visor that provides ballistic and laser eye protection, and a microphone and ear piece for communications.

The protective clothing includes modular armor that can stop many small-arms projectiles and shrapnel as well as protect the wearer from chemical and biological weapons. The outfit includes an integrated load-bearing frame and rucksack. A computer/radio subsystem attaches to the load-bearing frame, and the rucksack carries personal gear. The computer processor contains the radio as well as a global positioning system (GPS) and is operated with a handgrip attached to the soldier control module on the soldier's chest. The SCM is a device similar to a computer mouse that can be operated with a finger to change screens, key on the radio, select radio frequencies, and so on. Some critical functions of the system are controlled with two buttons located near the trigger guard of the weapon so that the soldier can send and receive data while maintaining a firing position. Embedded in the load-carrying frame are the antennas for the GPS and soldier radio.

Squad leaders and others in command have a dual radio. The main system is based on an improved Single Channel Ground and Airborne Radio System (SINCGARS) and will be fully compatible with the U.S. military's SINCGARS System Improvement Program (SIP) communications; this section will have a flat panel display/keyboard. The second radio system is based on a repackaged commercial hand-held system marketed by Motorola that will allow command to communicate to the soldiers as well as permitting communication between squad members.

All this gives the soldier the ability to communicate on the digitized battlefield with others in his squad as well as be appraised of the situation on a battlefield by his commander (or vice versa), greatly improving awareness and survivability through increased command and control. Video images from weapons can also be feed into the system to give commanders a view of the battlefield. Software in the Pentium-based computer includes tactical and mission support modules and maps with tactical overlays. (Currently this system is being built by Raytheon and is expected to be updated and miniaturized.)

The two differences in the radio system have led to

the fielding of two major types of the Land Warrior system—a "standard" and a "leader" version. Other versions, with special provisions for use by medics, combat engineers, and forward observers, will be fielded as well.

The only technological hurdle that has not been cleared (at the time of this writing) is the ability to provide long-lasting power for the system. With all the systems a soldier has available with the Land Warrior running at once, battery packs only last around an hour and a half. Although the soldier can extend this time by using equipment intermittently, the limitation is still unacceptable. However, battery packs being developed by the army's Communications Electronics Command are to increase the battery life to as much as 30 hours, making the system viable for troops being supplied regularly.

That said, some of the sights and other systems have their own battery packs—and of course the rifle itself has iron sights, so a soldier will never be worse off than without the system in the first place. If the computer fails, many of the subsystems (e.g., helmet display, radios, camera, thermal scope) are "smart" in their own right and will continue to function.

At around 80 pounds (the original maximum weight goal when Land Warrior was first proposed), the system is on the heavy side, but this is expected to drop as smaller and lighter versions of the systems constituting it come on line. In the meantime, the backpack has quick-detach straps so troops can quickly shed their radio and gear to operate with rifle and helmet only.

Because it is modular, the Land Warrior system is likely to become lighter and more reliable and have additional capabilities as time goes on, thanks in part to a science and technology program, Force XXI LW, that is charged with developing key technology upgrades for the system through 2015.

As the equipment that makes up the Land Warrior becomes more practical, new tactics are being developed to exploit its capabilities in the context of urban warfare which soldiers are now more apt to face than battles in open terrain. It's already been discovered that squads can spread out more because they can

Various components of the Land Warrior system in use during exercises at the U.S. Army Infantry Center, Ft. Benning. (Courtesy of U.S. Department of Defense.)

remain in communication with their radios, improving survivability considerably because the troops involved present fewer targets in the event of an ambush. When the troops start firing this spreading out also gives the appearance of a much larger force that can demoralize an enemy as well as cause responses that might leave other areas of an enemy's line inadequately protected from indirect tactical approaches.

Training at Ft. Polk, Louisiana, and elsewhere with this equipment has proven that it has a lot to offer in improved capabilities and confidence building to encourage the aggressive action that wins battles. "We own the night" seems to be the phrase most often heard during the first encounters troops have in using the Land Warrior helmet displays: they can actually see what goes on at night. In addition, they are able to look and fire at the enemy from cover while exposing only their rifles and hands—a factor that promises better aiming because it removes most of the fear of becoming a casualty.

Several U.S. military programs are conducting such training, including the Marine Corps Warfighting Laboratory's Urban Warrior program, conducted by the Special Purpose Marine Air-Ground Task Force (Experimental) from Quantico, VA, with troops from various elements of the marines. As these studies go on, developments by Land Warrior will undoubtedly lend themselves to increasing the capabilities of soldiers already carrying the M16A2 or M4 carbine and the program's high-tech equipment.

## C$^4$I

At the turn of the 20th century the U.S. Army launched another program that promises to enhance the capability of its soldiers carrying an M16 rifle or M4 carbine. Known as C$^4$I (command control, communications, computers and intelligence), it is charged with creating a variety of systems that enable troops to operate more efficiently while allowing the supply system to almost simultaneously add new hardware and software to fielded equipment without reconfiguring systems in the entire network. While some of the descriptions of this system sound bureaucratic, in truth it promises to greatly advance the way the U.S. military operates while increasing the efficiency of troops.

Among the key features of interest to those carrying one of the AR-15 variants are the following:

- A system that permits rapid identification of a soldier spotted on the field as a U.S. trooper, an enemy, or a noncombatant. This not only increases the ability of troops to engage an enemy without hesitation or doubt, but also prevents unnecessary friendly fire and noncombatant injuries.
- Powered optics for all individual and crew-served weapons, with the ability to give depth perception at night.
- An intelligence collection/dissemination unit that may be, for all intents and purposes, a robot issued at the platoon or squad level. This unit will explore possible routes and do reconnaissance, relaying information by audio/video link. The unit will ideally have modular sensors so it can see through standard walls, spot where sniper fire is coming from, and the like.
- A hand-held, through-the-wall sensor to rapidly determine whether a building or the next room in a house-to-house search is empty or occupied by friendly, enemy, or noncombatant personnel.
- A small detector to spot sniper locations and fire from hidden positions.
- A hand-held target designator to guide munitions from airborne, artillery, mortars, or other large munitions onto enemy targets very precisely.
- A position location device to indicate to other friendly troops precisely where they are located, thereby allowing troops to more easily reinforce themselves while spreading to optimal distances from each other.
- A remote delivery marking system to place both visible and nonvisible distinguishing systems to show areas of buildings, walls, people, and vehicles to troops.
- A system that rapidly detects and disarms booby traps and mines inside buildings.
- A hands-free sling for the M16 (and SAW) that permits soldiers to remove one or both hands from weapon and still have it remain pointed toward a probable enemy location and ready to fire.
- A "soft round" that penetrates an enemy and then stops either in the body or in a wall, thereby preventing friendly fire injuries during house-to-house combat as well as in antiterrorist operations.
- Nonlethal weapons and munitions offering a "family" of effects for users to choose from.
- A "man-sized hole" produced by a modular explosive kit to breach concrete walls, ceilings, or floors.
- A nonlethal, blunt-trauma training round for use in MOUT (military operations on urban terrain) that can be fired from the M16, SAW, 9mm, and M60.
- A nonlethal "stun" grenade that incapacitates enemy personnel inside a room but doesn't send lethal fragments through thin, adjoining walls.
- A much lighter mask that provides

nuclear/biological/chemical protection while offering a wide field of view and is compatible with night-vision devices and hands-free communications devices and firearms. This is augmented by a small disposable mask that provides protection against smoke, dust, and the like.

- Hearing protection that permits troops to hear normal voice communications while filtering out rifle reports and other concussive waves produced on a battlefield.
- A man-portable ballistic shield that stops rifle and small-arms projectiles, with vision ports and an infrared source to illuminate areas to night-vision equipment.

A few of these devices are already being fielded in limited numbers as this is written. Others are in testing—and some might prove impractical. But the bottom line is that little by little the rifleman, armed with a variant of an AR-15 or similar weapon, is going to become more capable and more lethal to enemy forces as time goes on. Furthermore, another area of the $C^4I$ program is charged with producing an easily portable antiarmor system. Should this become practical, it might quickly turn the battlefield into an area where foot soldiers, capable of downing helicopters, low-flying planes, or tanks, are the main players and all others are effectively banned from an area.

## THE OICW

The Land Warrior program showed that the efficiency of a soldier armed with an AR-15 can be enhanced and extended. And the $C^4I$ program promises to further extend the soldier's capabilities through the addition of technology. Yet there is the realization that the plateau beyond which little will be achieved with a system based on a rifle has been reached. The ACR tests seemed to confirm this, with the guns never achieving potential capabilities when they are fired under combat conditions. Mechanically, firearms technology has for all practical purposes peaked, with human operators unable to efficiently utilize the accuracy offered by the weapon. Accordingly, improvements can come only in the form of new and lighter materials, cheaper manufacturing processes, and the like, but without added lethality on the battlefield. The rifles are already superdependable and highly accurate. It's the soldier's inability to hit his target that is the problem; troops still have trouble connecting with their targets in actual combat conditions, just as suggested by studies following World War II. Firing without seeing an enemy, and perhaps without even aiming, is the norm on the battlefield.

The conclusion is that a new rifle is not needed. Rather an entirely new system is required to contend with the actual combat conditions. This new system, it is hoped, would enable troops to score more hits on enemy targets during combat. There are two routes that can be taken to improve the situation. One is to make sighting systems that permitted locating and hitting a target even under fire. The other is to develop a wholly new weapon unlike the rifle with munitions that should improve the chances of hitting an enemy soldier.

With these two courses in mind, the JSSAP launched the OICW project, its stated objective being to provide U.S. troops with a double-capability weapon comprising an abbreviated rifle to deal with targets at close quarters or when pinpoint accuracy was called for and a 20mm multishot grenade launcher with "smart" warheads that explode after aligning themselves with a target. The key component of the 20mm grenade part of the OICW is to be an HE charge that propels a blast wave and projectiles to create casualties. Fragments are to be capable of penetrating body armor and standard-issue helmets at close range.

To further improve the hit probability (as well as guide the smart grenade to its target), the OICW are to have a high-tech sighting system that includes a laser range finder, a thermal imager, and a close-combat optical sight. With such a sight a soldier should finally be able to effectively engage targets out to 1,000 meters and hit them with grenades. Additionally, the thermal vision capabilities should permit picking out the infrared image of enemy personnel even if they hide in the dark or behind smoke screens, fog, or light vegetation.

The new specs for the OICW to go into development include the following:

- A 500-percent increase in probability of incapacitation over that of the M16A2
- Capability to defeat targets in defilade (e.g., hidden behind objects)
- Effective range to 1,000 meters
- Day/night fire control
- Wireless weapon interface with the soldier
- Substantial weight reduction
- Ergonomic design

The program guidelines for the OICW originated with the Small Arms Master Plan and Joint Service Small Arms Master Plan. The JSSAP also put forth the following time schedule for the development of the new weapon:

- *Phase 1:* Study of the feasibility of the OICW to be completed by December 1994.

This experimental grenade launcher, tested during the 1990s, helped pave the way for the grenade-launching half of the OICW.

- *Phase 2:* System design and subsystem demonstration to be completed by December 1996.
- *Phase 3:* Prototype system demonstration in fall of 1997 through January 1998.
- *Phase 4 – 5:* Hardware assembly and live-fire simulation beginning in April 1998.
- The first unit is to be fielded in 2005.

The specs and timetable are obviously hard to meet. But two companies have stepped up to give it a shot: AAI and H&K (working in conjunction with Olin).

### The First Round of OICWs

Having perhaps learned its lesson with its XM70 SPIW and new ACR rifles, AAI opted this time to simply modify the M16A2 to create the rifle half of its OICW. This logical step brought the AAI engineers a long way toward achieving their goal because the M16 was thoroughly debugged and reliable. This still left the engineers with the formidable task of creating the optics and a 20mm grenade launcher that would not make a weapon too heavy to be carried easily in the field.

Structurally the engineers were somewhat hamstrung by the AR-15 buffer tube, which was a necessity if the M16A2 was not to be extensively modified. The solution was to place the 20mm section of the new weapon atop the M16 section, then mount the thermal imager and sighting system on top of the grenade launcher. In the process AAI created what resembled a weapon from a sci-fi movie, with the AR-15 somewhat hidden by its structure so as to be easily mistaken for an entirely different weapon.

The H&K/Olin prototype was a fairly conventional design with a thumbhole stock. Somewhat unconventionally, H&K's solution to placement of the grenade launcher was to run it alongside the rifle barrel, then mounting the sighting system atop the weapon.

While neither the H&K/Olin gun nor the AAI version was seen as potential replacements for the M16A2, they did demonstrate that the whole idea was viable.

### Round Two

With the initial AAI and H&K guns proving the OICW concept feasible and laying the groundwork for the development of a high-tech weapon that might actually serve as the battle "rifle" for U.S. soldiers in the 21st century, the decision was made to move forward with the program. A new $8.5 million contract was awarded to Alliant Techsystems Integrated Defense Company (Hopkins, Minnesota) and H& K. The contract covered the building of a new OICW candidate that would combine some of the more successful elements of the earlier demonstration guns with new technologies that might be developed. These would then be incorporated into seven prototype OICWs with 4,700 rounds of ammunition for testing at Picatinny Arsenal in New Jersey.

This phase of testing went well; next Alliant and H&K were awarded a total of $95,426,483 to continue their research and development of their OICW, with a completion goal of 2004. After a lot of hard work, a replacement for at least some AR-15 rifles and all M203 grenade launchers in the U.S. military inventory seemed to finally be on the way.

### The Final OICW Design

Although it is likely that many minor changes in the OICW will take place before it is fielded, the basic system seems to be established as of this writing. Even though the rifle portion of this new OICW appears, upon casual examination, to be an AR-15 because of the AR-15-style grip, this is not the case. A closer look reveals the gun to be a modified G36 with its barrel cut back to 10 inches and its overall layout modified so that it can be attached to the grenade-launcher section of the weapon. The rifle unit fires in semiautomatic or two-round burst mode.

Sitting atop the rifle portion of the gun is the 20mm grenade launcher, which has an 18-inch barrel. Interestingly, a single trigger mechanism operates both systems, thanks to an internal linkage between the trigger and both sections of the OICW, with a selector determining which will fire.

Because the grenade half of the OICW is in a bullpup configuration with the ejection port on the side opposite the shooter's cheek rest, provision has been made for a user to select which side empties will be ejected from. To do this, he simply partially field-strips the weapon, rotates the grenade bolt 180 degrees, and then reassembles the weapon. That said, firing a grenade with the bolt in the wrong position could conceivably cause injuries, so this is a point users have to keep in mind. It could also potentially cause problems in urban warfare where troops have always had a slight advantage when they can fire a weapon around the corner of a building from either shoulder, thereby avoiding exposing their bodies to enemy fire. However, the capability of the OICW to "see" around corners may offset this shortcoming to a large extent.

### OICW Fire Control System

The brains of the OICW is a fire-control system (FCS) that combines a video camera, a laser range finder, a 6X rifle scope, and a fire control and aiming computer system into one unit atop the OICW, where it is powered by a modified BB2847 lithium battery. Currently, this entire unit weighs 5 pounds, which is expected to decrease as technology advances.

The video camera, which at first might seem out of place, actually is good for several purposes; in addition to being capable (with the right hardware) of relaying data from the battlefield, it has a more practical purpose. Coupled with a helmet-mounted viewer or a rotating viewer at the rear of the gun, it makes it possible for the operator to look around corners while keeping his body safe from enemy fire. This capability will help soldiers aim and engage targets without the worry of being hit themselves.

The weapon's sight automatically defaults to the 3X optical "dot" scope (with an 11-degree field of view); during the day this scope operates without the need for battery power, giving a soldier a way to aim and fire his weapon even if a battery fails unexpectedly, the electronics of the weapon are damaged, or the unit otherwise malfunctions.

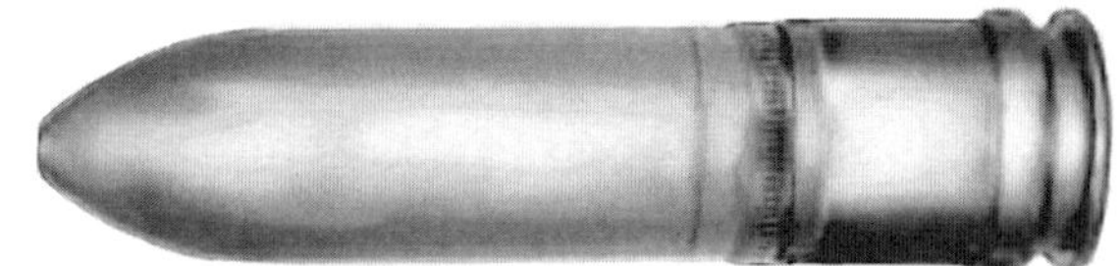

The OICW uses two types of ammunition, one a conventional .223 cartridge and the other a "smart" 20mm grenade.

The ability to use a right- or left-hand hold on a weapon can be an important plus in urban combat. (Photo by S.Sgt. David J. Ferrier, U.S. Marine Corps, courtesy of U.S. Department of Defense.)

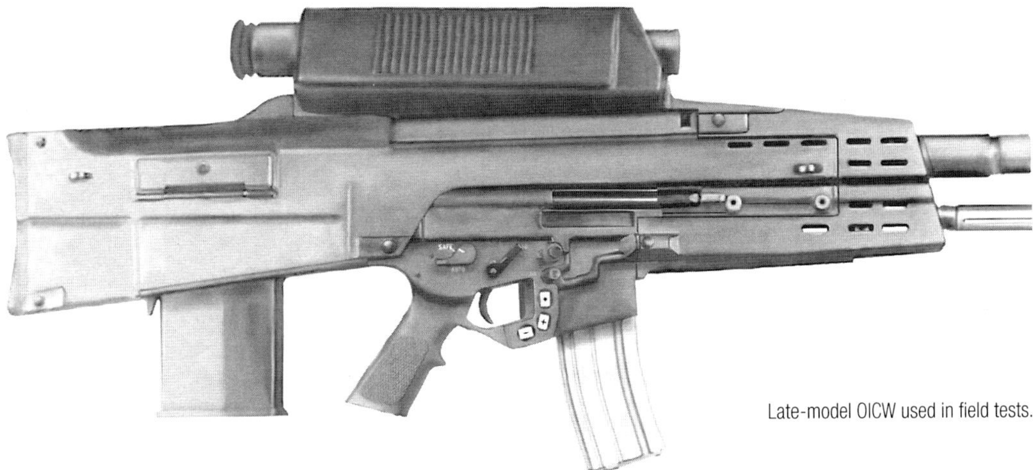


Late-model OICW used in field tests.

Field-testing of the OICW. (Courtesy of U.S. Army.)

If the OICW works as promised, soldiers will be able to engage an enemy out to 1,000 meters, day or night, in rain, fog, or smoke. (Courtesy of U.S. Army.)

From this "fail-safe view" of a target, the operator of the OICW has a number of other options. He can select the TV mode, which gives him a view from its screen and offers a standard view or 2X setting. Switching to a night mode gives a thermal imaging view that spots heat sources, thereby making it possible to "see" a man hidden in thin vegetation, a smoke screen, or darkness. Additionally, this system may give clues to such things as whether a vehicle is running or the chimney in a building is giving off heat—which, in combat, might be important tip-offs to dangers that are otherwise easily missed, if not totally invisible to the unaided eye.

There are groups of touch pads on the OICW that permit a user to interact with the computer brain of the FCS. One set is on the trigger guard; the top button activates the laser range finder with the plus or minus buttons moving the detonation point of a grenade forward or rearward in 1-meter increments.

Another set of controls is recessed in the left side of the FCS. These select viewing options, fuse settings, viewer magnification, and scope dot brightness according to the needs of the user.

A third set of controls is on the rear of the FCS below the eyepiece. These permit the user to actually interact with the microprocessor in the unit through a series of menus that appear on the TV screen. Currently, these options deal with the laser and video systems and other adjustments but also include compass heading information, modifications of response by ammunition type being used with the OICW, and other functions. The remaining modes include self-diagnostic tests, bore sighting information, and calibration of the sights. (It seems that the capabilities of the on-board computer might be expanded in the future and conceivably handle other useful processes, such as global positioning satellite data or other communications.)

The laser range finder uses an erbium laser with a very narrow beam that does not damage the eye. It sends out pulses a few microseconds apart so that the signal won't be confused with that from other weapons. Once the range to a target has been determined (a process all but instantaneous to the user), the red dot in the weapons site is adjusted for a first-round hit. Perhaps one of the more amazing features of the sight is that it also attempts to compensate for the gunner's wobble as well as the cant of the weapon, thereby increasing the likelihood that the shooter will be on target when a projectile leaves the barrel.

Additionally, the FCS compensates in its point of aim according to the elevation of the weapon. For example, if a shooter is firing from or at a position higher or lower than his target, the point of impact will change considerably, especially at longer ranges. Thus, the FCS calculates the angle of the barrel in relation to the target and compensates accordingly—an amazing feat that should pay huge dividends in actual combat, especially in urban settings. It doesn't end there. The FCS even takes into consideration the ambient temperature (which changes the air density and thereby the ballistic arch of a projectile) that moves as the target moves.

The video camera also has a few additional tricks. It can be set in a target-tracking mode that "watches" objects in its field of view. Once acquired, these objects are bracketed in the screen and tracked. If a soldier is faced with multiple targets, he can switch into this mode and then concentrate on dealing with each one, knowing that if one of his foes drops into the rubble or foliage to be lost from view, the FCS will mark his last known position with brackets. This gives a soldier a good idea of where enemies have hidden themselves, allowing him to send a grenade to that point to explode over the position, thereby scoring a hit on an enemy that he most likely would not have even known was still there otherwise.

Many of these features work with both the rifle and grenade portions of the OICW, increasing the likelihood of the hits with both types of fire. While soldiers must still aim (and this may be the one fly in the ointment of the system), the time needed to aim and the skill of judging exactly where to aim has been reduced and simplified.

### The Rifle Half

The rifle half of the OICW is mounted to the grenade launcher with a rigid rail system, a necessity because this portion of the OICW shares the same sight as the grenade launcher. This dictates that the coupling of the whole assembly be tight and precise, which is accomplished with a removable pin.

Although the short barrel of the G36-derived carbine section of the weapon does not have the muzzle velocity of the M16A2, it still is accurate because of the free-floating system used to mount it and the hammer-forged barrel employed by H&K. The barrel consists of a stainless-steel bore (a first for American guns, which at best have either sported a rust-prone standard steel or chrome finish). This thin inner barrel is surrounded by a titanium sleeve that enables it to withstand the pressures generated in firing while keeping the barrel lightweight. The barrel maintains the 1-in-7 twist that has proved so lethal with the M16A2

In the two-round burst mode, the gun cycles at 700 rpm. Since the gas system of the G36 is based on the AR-180, the trigger group remains quite clean even in extended use, a plus for GIs, who traditionally have an aversion to cleaning firearms. Since the Armalite AR-18 system employs a six-lug bolt that mates with the barrel to contain chamber pressures with the bolt and carrier riding during the cycling action on self-contained rods and springs, this means the exterior and receiver of the gun need not be over strong. This permits the use of light carbon-fiber-reinforced polymer for much of the receiver housing without the need for extensive sections of metal in the receiver.

The carbine accepts standard M16 magazines, undoubtedly more a factor of the huge inventory the U.S. military has of these, since more reliable magazine designs are now available.

Because the carbine portion of the OICW can be removed from the other assembles and still function by itself, it may be that eventually a sight system and perhaps a stock may be developed for it. As such, a weapon based on just this part of the OICW would form a short-barreled gun that fits many of the requirements for the PDW, which the U.S. military was earlier hoping to have.

### High-Tech Testing

Some of the testing of the OICW has been about as high-tech as the weapon itself. Given the cost of the 20mm cartridges (somewhere in the neighborhood of $25 per round), anything that can be done to train troops without using large quantities of ammunition is good. But beyond that, it is often impossible to get good records and precise data when testing firearms in the field. Yet until recently, extensive firing was the only reliable way to even come close to simulating combat conditions.

That has changed. Much of the testing in the early stages of the development of the OICW took place with electronic simulators complete with mockup OICWs that recoil and give the feel of the real thing while interacting with computer-generated combat scenarios. The major chunk of this work was done in a special installation at Aberdeen Proving Ground.

There, soldiers involved in testing the guns go through many of their paces in the Small Arms Simulator Testbed (SAST II), a complex "game room" created by the Naval Air Warfare Center Training Systems Directorate and the Army Research Laboratory. This complex offers virtual-reality pictures and sounds to simulate a variety of combat situations. While this isn't real combat, the noise and confusion generated by the system, as well as the tendency of young men and women to get into gaming with a life-or-death level of intensity, have undoubtedly provided a lot of insight into ways that the OICW could be improved as well as how troops might behave in combat.

This virtual testing was just a prelude to the real thing, however. The OICW has undergone testing with the army's famed 25th ("Tropical Lightning") Infantry Division and will see use in all sorts of conditions, from the mud and gunk of jungle warfare, to the desert-like military bases in the West, to the ice and snow of Alaska. That said, it will be interesting to see if much of the training for the OICW—the first truly high-tech firearm to be fielded—is conducted with troops working in an SAST-II-like game room to hone their skills and learn to work effectively with fellow soldiers when engaging an enemy.

### The Money Factor

The hitches in all this technology are expense and weight. The current OICW, even when miniaturized, will weigh between 14 and 12 pounds and carry a price tag of between $10,000 and $12,000. Arguably the lives of soldiers saved with such a weapon would be more than worth the cost, but in reality nations often lack or are unwilling to expend the enormous amounts of money required to arm individual troops. Not surprisingly, then, the current plans are to issue four OICWs per nine-man squad. In the near future at least, it is likely that rather than becoming a standard-issue weapon for combat troops the OICW will be issued to key troops, much as the SAW and M203 grenade launcher are today.

However, the weight and cost of the current system are based on worst-case calculations because, unlike the mechanical side of firearms design, electronics technology is still a maturing science. The electronics for the memory chip, optics, and other key features, as well as the thermal imager and battery packs, are all quickly "shrinking" as new technological breakthroughs occur. This means that the hardware used ın the sighting and range-finding system can be expected to become both smaller and cheaper. Thus, the OICW is likely to become more and more attractive as a choice for a combat weapon in coming years.

That said, the 14-pound weight of the OICW is somewhat misleading in that much of it is in the optical system, as is much of the expense of the weapon. Indeed, retrofitting an M16A2 with a grenade launcher and similar optics results in a weapon that is actually heavier than 14 pounds and costs a bit more than the OICW as it now stands. As advances occur in miniaturization over the next few years, it may be that in time the OICW with its optics and range calculator will actually be lighter than an M16A2 without any optics.

Additionally, because the 20mm grenade is lighter than the current 40mm grenade used by the M203, when one considers both the weight of gun and ammunition, a grenadier armed with the OICW (even in its unrefined, older form) would actually have a lighter load than his counterpart armed with an M203 and a full complement of ammunition. Given the higher hit probability the OICW will most likely afford if it lives up to expectations, it isn't hard to imagine its being the next replacement for the M203, if nothing else.

At the same time, technology such as that used in the OICW is not without pitfalls. Testing demonstrates how a complicated weapon like the OICW might go haywire under adverse conditions (or possibly if "attacked" by a powerful electromagnetic pulse or other forms of counterattacks perhaps not yet dreamed of that will make their appearance on tomorrow's electronic battlefield). In September 1999, during tests at Aberdeen, a 20mm round went off in the weapon's chamber during firing exercises; this caused two injuries, luckily with one person only suffering minor wounds and the other a broken arm.

The cause? Apparently, at least in part, a software miscommunication between the fire control computer and the warhead fuzz of the 20mm cartridge. The HE warhead aimed itself and blew up. This may well be the first gun injury caused by software error, and one saw has suggested that experimenters must be using Windows to run the system.

Design changes and a rewriting of software have undoubtedly cured this problem so it won't be seen in the future. But the incident demonstrates how today's relatively simple firearm may soon be replaced by a complicated combination of electronics and mechanical parts that operate like a "black box," with the shooter having no idea of what actually goes on in the system he is using. That said, accidents have been notably rare, and at this point in testing there's no reason to think the OICW is any more dangerous than weapons of the past. Indeed, both the AR-10 and M14 rifles suffered similar mishaps when first being developed and fielded.

For those who worry about dead batteries in a

complicated system like the OICW, a group of worrywarts of which the author must admit to being a member, provisions have been made for such an event. The final OICW is slated to have emergency, "pop-up" iron sights for use with both the 5.56mm and 20mm parts of the weapon. In this case, the 20mm round can be fired in the point-detonating mode, which is considerably less effective than with the range-laser in use, but still nearly as effective as the current M203. One has to wonder whether this iron sight configuration might be adopted as a general replacement for the M16 rifle, with some key members of a squad then being issued OICWs with the range finder and thermal sights.)

### The 20mm Grenade

The 20mm grenade-launching system is nothing short of amazing when one considers what it is being called upon to do. Throwing an explosive projectile any distance and having it function with any effectiveness calls for the explosive warhead's being very large or placed with pinpoint accuracy. Since the OICW is a hand-held weapon, striving for such accuracy is the only course open to designers, given weight and recoil restrictions.

As noted throughout this book, pinpoint accuracy in combat is an elusive thing that has confounded designers since studies following World War II showed that troops might just as well be firing without aiming (and often did just that) in terms of their chances of hitting a target. So OICW designers knew that they must create a system complex enough that the weapon could place its warhead on target yet so simple to operate that soldiers could actually aim that in the heat of battle rather than squeezing off rounds and hoping to hit something.

The first step in this process came in designing a small but potent grenade system in the 20mm size requirements set forth by the U.S. military. To achieve this, Alliant first developed a tiny computer chip that would act as the multifunction fuse of the weapon; this microchip is rapidly programmed by the range finder of the OICW through electronic signals traveling from the range finder to the an induction coil surrounding the 20mm barrel.

The range finder must calculate the projectile's precise number of revolutions (imparted by the rifled barrel) before reaching the target. When this number is reached, the warhead receives the command to explode. Additionally, the warhead has to be armed as it leaves the weapon to prevent premature detonation when ammunition is being carried or is dropped or struck during the hurried movements of combat. And the microchip itself must withstand all kinds of abuse, including the high gravity force it is subject to when launched from the OICW. All of this is no small order and was impossible to achieve until very recently.

The FCS for the grenade launcher offers four distinct settings for a soldier to choose from according to the conditions he faces. The default setting, "PD" arms the fuse in point-detonation mode, which causes a grenade to explode only when it actually connects with an object. A "Bursting" setting on the FCS panel permits an air burst, good for use against adversaries in the open or hiding in an open-topped foxhole.

The "PDD" (point detonation delay) setting permits a warhead to penetrate a barrier before being ignited. This is useful for dealing with foes protected by light armor, behind a door, or in brush. The forth setting is a "Window" mode, which gives an air burst at a specific distance beyond the range taken by the range finder; in this mode, the user can program the warhead to travel through a window or other thin screen and be detonated a specific distance beyond the barrier. Soldiers have the option (with small "plus" and "minus" buttons located on the trigger guard) of moving the detonation point forward or rearward in 1-meter increments. This might, for example, permit a user to use the laser range finder to measure the distance to the mound of earth in front of a foxhole where a foe has taken shelter and then rapidly program the grenade to explode a meter beyond this point. By aiming slightly above the foxhole, the soldier then places the grenade directly over his enemy, where it would explode and shower the combatant below with shrapnel.

The range finder is considerably more sophisticated and accurate than those of the past, getting the warhead on the mark to within a half-meter or less from a distance of 500 meters and to within 1 meter from 500 to 1,000 meters. And it may be that this accuracy will increase with improvements in technology.

In the past grenades launched from barreled systems had fuses mounted in their tips—a necessity if the warhead was to explode upon hitting the target. But placing a fuse in the nose of a projectile produces a less than ideal bursting pattern. This situation is changed with the OICW's 20mm grenade system that permits placing the fuse in the center of the explosive charge, which is now basically controlled by the microchip inside it that is busy counting the rotations that indicate when the grenade has reached the target.

The projectile weighs 31.4 ounces and has prefragmented metal of various thicknesses surrounding the explosive charge. The projectile fragments itself, unlike most previous designs, and has been carefully crafted by computer design to give a highly efficient distribution pattern guaranteed to create casualties in an oval pattern of about 6 meters in diameter.

Since the recoil even from a semiauto weapon throwing a 31.4-ounce warhead is excessive, the designers pulled off a few tricks inside the OICW to greatly reduce the otherwise punishing force a user would experience. (This is an important consideration, since a soldier may start to flinch in anticipation of heavy recoil and thereby throw off his aim with a weapon.)

The OICW achieves its recoil reduction in firing a grenade with what developers call an "elastomeric recoil mitigation system." Basically, the grenade barrel and bolt remain locked during part of the recoil cycle, moving rearward to be gradually slowed with a system not too dissimilar to the shock absorber on some motor vehicles. So the felt recoil, though lasting longer, doesn't peak with much greater force than that experienced with a standard M16A2 firing a rifle bullet.

### Commitment

At the time of this writing, the OICW program appears to be on the right track. And a lot of people have a lot of money riding on its success, which would not likely be the case had the weapon been failing to live up to expectations. Throughout the U.S. military's Advanced Technology Demonstration (ATD) phase (1994–1999), the companies involved in creating the system have not only worked with government money from contracts, they have also invested more than $12 million of their own in the project. This suggests that they believe there is money to be made in this project and that it will ultimately meet with great success.

In 1999 the proof of principles phase of the OICW was completed, and in August 2000 the 4-year program definition and risk reduction phase began. The latter phase is to refine the system using data on past failures as well as advances in technology. The OICW will see the bulk of its testing during this phase at the Infantry School at Ft. Benning.

During the 4 years, Alliant Technologies is acting as system integrator and is again handling work on the fuzz and 20mm HE cartridge; H&K continues its own work on the weapon system; Pittsburgh-based Brashear LP is working on the fire control system. Additional work is done by Octec (working with target tracking) and Dynamit Nobel (handling work with the "kinetic energy"' projectiles, aka bullets).

At the end of the 4-year phase, assuming that all goes as planned, soldiers will conduct a variety of field tests, both to evaluate the changes made to the OICW system and to make recommendations for the final engineering and manufacturing development phase of production (now slated for 2005 through 2007).

If all goes well, the OICW will then start to be fielded in 2009. It now appears that the OICW will provide combat troops with a precision weapon five times more effective at more than twice the range of existing M203 rifle systems with its 40mm rounds and at least as effective (if not more so) than the M16A2 and M4 carbine now in the hands of most troops. Current U.S. Army plans call for four of the nine soldiers in an infantry squad to carry the OICW, replacing some of today's modular weapon systems, made up of either the M16 rifle or the M4 carbine with an attached M203 grenade launcher.

## THE FRENCH PAPOP

The United States has not been alone in seeking a replacement for the rifle. The French military has also been busy funding research for a similar weapon. The majority of the design work is being handled by several smaller companies and the two big European arms producers, Giat Industries and Fabrique Nationale (the latter undoubtedly adapting its work done early on with the OICW project to this French project). The research has come to be known as the PAPOP (polyarme polyprojectiles, roughly translated as "many arms, many projectiles"), with a view to French sales of the resulting weapon as well as possible adoption by NATO as its future ICW.

This system is very similar to the OICW, with some notable departures. While the gun has both a 5.56mm rifle and grenade-launching submodules, the PAPOP has a considerably larger 35mm grenade, dictated by the French contention (based on computer studies) that this is the smallest projectile that will produce casualties on the battlefield (no doubt news to those designing the OICW in the United States). This larger size does, at least on paper, give the PAPOP a greater potential. However, the trade-off dictates heavier recoil, a heavier barrel on the weapon, and the reduction of magazine capacity to just three grenades. Additionally, the 35mm grenades are carried in a tubular munitions launcher, which suggests that reloading may not be too rapid—a major concern in a weapon whose grenade launcher is the prime system while the rifle acts as a close-combat backup.

In an effort to deal with the recoil of the grenade launcher, the PAPOP has incorporated a buffer and shock-absorbing design coupled with three optional trigger positions that permit the shooter to brace the weapon to minimize its recoil effects. To increase the likelihood of enemy casualties, the weapon also permits grenades to be programmed to explode from one of two fuses, one throwing fragments either forward or in a lateral pattern. This selection is made electronically, the data and arming taking place as the projectile leaves the weapon's barrel.

The video and other sensors of the PAPOP are placed far forward to permit greater ease in peering around corners or from behind cover, with the image transferred to the shooter's eye via a helmet monocle. Like the OICW, the PAPOP has the potential to transfer images via radio to commanders or others needing to assess what is viewed.

The overall design of the PAPOP gives it even less of a rifle look than the OICW. At first glance, the system often brings to mind a soldier carrying some sort of high-tech boom box or briefcase rather than a firearm.

Also, like the OICW, PAPOP is faces two major obstacles that may ultimately lead to its being shelved in favor of a more conventional rifle coupled with updated aiming systems: it is quite heavy (though this is expected to change as the electronic components become more miniaturized), and it is also very expensive. Coupled with the limited magazine capacity for grenades and the recoil they produce, these latter problems suggest that at this point the outlook for its adoption is less than rosy.

### AN AR-15 REPLACEMENT?

Whether the OICW (or the PAPOP or some other system now on the drawing boards) will prove a viable next step in weaponry or an expensive experiment that will be tabled remains to be seen. Most likely, any such system will at least act as an addition to the squad's weaponry, joining specialized weapons like the SAW and replacing the current M203 grenade launcher. Certainly, the success of the army's Land Warrior program suggests that it is possible and economical to simply bolt accessories on an AR-15 to enhance its capability rather than completely replacing the firearm.

The deciding factor will be how much more effective the OICW proves to be in combat when compared with the current battle rifles. If the 20mm grenade proves to be as reliable and lethal as is hoped, then the OICW may become the next general-issue weapon, replacing the M16A2 and M4/M4A1 carbine, along with the M203.

Of course, if this technology becomes cheaper and lighter, one might also argue that it is more cost-effective to simply spiff up the current rifles and carbines with some of the sighting equipment developed for the OICW. The resulting "make do" weapons could serve until technology permits another leap forward, perhaps with something that isn't based on faster burning powders, or bullets, or grenades to provide its effectiveness. And if some genius creates a semiauto, 20mm grenade launcher similar to the M203, then the AR-15 system just might remain in place for some time to come.

Either way, it is likely that the AR-15 rifle will remain the main battle sidearm for U.S. troops and the troops of many other nations through much of the 21st century. It could be that if the OICW proves too expensive or has flaws that have not yet been discovered, the AR-15 will remain in place as the main battle weapon of the foot soldier. Such things have happened in the past, with swords and certain models of muskets staying in use among the best armies with little change in design for centuries. But most of those close to the testing of the OICW wouldn't put any bets on the things remaining static for that long. The initial purchase of 45,000 OICWs is still slated to take place, putting the weapons into the hands of some squads by 2007, starting with elite troop units. To date, the U.S. military has been impressed with these weapons and is investing in them in a big way. At the time of this writing, it appears likely that the OICW, or a lighter weapon very similar to it, will become the workhorse of at least the first half of the 21st century, just as the AR-15 was during the last half of the 20th.

# Chapter 10

# Operation of the AR-15

Shooters of any firearm, including the AR-15, must remember that malfunctions do occur and that the gun might fire unexpectedly. So it's wise to keep the barrel pointed in a safe direction at all times; it should never be pointed at something that isn't meant to be shot. It's also crucial to ensure that the gun is empty before its being stored, cleaned, or worked on.

The floating firing pin of the AR-15 is normally quite safe. But this changes if the firing pin strikes a high or sensitive primer; then it can fire the round as it is chambered. A sensitive primer that causes this slam-fire won't damage the rifle, because the gun is designed so that the pin can't reach the primer unless the bolt is locked in place)—but the bullet zinging from the muzzle can cause unexpected damage if the gun is aimed in the wrong direction. Shooters should be sure to keep the gun aimed in a safe direction even when chambering a cartridge.

A primer not seated to the proper depth can also fire prematurely and may even damage the rifle, shooter, and/or bystanders, since it can be set off by the edge of the bolt as well as the firing pin. The rifle probably won't be damaged beyond repair if this occurs, but it's a good idea to avoid it by using quality ammunition at all times. Those who do their own reloading should inspect every round to ensure that primers are seated to the proper depth. Bullets should also be tightly crimped and cartridges carefully resized and cleaned to prevent other types of malfunctions.

For best results with the AR-15 it is important to use quality ammunition. For those purchasing their own cartridges, best buys are from companies like Federal, Winchester, Black Hills, Action Ammo, and CCI (for pistol-cartridge versions of the carbine). With the 1-in-12 twist, .223 cartridges with 55-grain or smaller bullets are ideal for accuracy; with the faster twists, heavier or lighter bullets can be used with good results. (For a detailed look at the ammunition available for the AR-15 and special combat rounds and reloading techniques, see *Modern Combat Ammo*, available from Paladin Press.)

Another good practice to avoid is locking the bolt open, dropping a round into the chamber, and then releasing the bolt so that it crashes shut. Most often nothing bad will happen, but some cartridges with lighter primers will be fired if this is done. It is always preferable to leave cartridges on the magazine and let the bolt strip and chamber them. (This is also true with cartridge adapters like those designed by Harry Owen, which allow .22 rimfire ammunition to be fired in an AR-15.)

Jams occur with oversized ammunition, dirty ammunition, or a fouled (or too small) chamber. Normally jams can be avoided by *not* using the bolt assist under any conditions. If the round doesn't chamber when the action strips it off the magazine, a shooter is just asking for trouble if he gives a tap to the bolt assist to help the round along. The only time the bolt assist *might* be used without mishap is in extremely cold weather or if quiet chambering is desired, in which case the charging handle can be eased forward and the bolt assist then slides the round into the chamber with a minimum of noise. Otherwise the bolt assist should never be touched.

If a rifle jams with the bolt not closed over the ammunition and the cartridge and chamber are clean, it is likely that the chamber is too small. In this case the firearm should be taken to a gunsmith and the headspace tested. If the chamber is too small, a few turns with a .223 finishing reamer will increase the size by the tiny bit needed to improve the firearm's chambering capabilities.

### Internal Operation of the AR-15

The AR-15 operates in a manner very similar to most other auto-loading rifles. The main difference is in its gas system, which does away with the piston/rod arrangement used of the majority of rifles. Instead, the design funnels the gas from the gas port in the barrel down through the tube above the barrel and into the bolt key of the bolt carrier in the upper receiver. Here the gas forces the bolt to unlock, extract the empty brass, and travel back toward the rear of the receiver.

This system is simple and makes the rifle light. It can also create a lot of problems with dirty or slow-burning powder because unburnt particles are blown directly into the bolt area, where they may accumulate if the weapon isn't cleaned regularly.

Most military versions of the AR-15 can function in either semiauto or automatic mode. Except for a few differences between these two types of fire, the weapon functions almost identically when operated either way. AR-15s that fire only in semiautomatic lack automatic-fire sears and usually have modified disconnectors to prevent their being disengaged if the selector is in the auto position.

Commercial AR-15s are modified further to ensure that if the disconnector is removed, the hammer will be caught by the firing pin (this is why the commercial AR-15 hammer has a notch on its face and the bolt is cut away under the firing pin). Additionally the bolt carrier, rear of the trigger, and selector are generally altered so that they can't be interchanged with automatic parts, making it impossible to construct a selective-fire weapon easily by substituting or removing parts.

Once the shooter has chambered a round in an AR-15, set the selector, and pulled the trigger, the hammer strikes the firing pin, which in turn hits the primer and fires the round. As the gas behind the bullet exiting the barrel rushes back through the gas tube, it forces the bolt carrier backward, causing the bolt cam to rotate and unlock the bolt. The bolt and its carrier then travel to the rear, propelled by the last of the gas coming down the gas tube. The bolt extracts the empty brass casing and hurls out the open ejection port with the spring-loaded ejector.

The bolt carrier cocks the hammer as it travels rearward until the buffer hits the rear of its tube, at which point the rebound of the buffer and the action spring propel the bolt carrier forward. As the bolt travels forward, it strips another cartridge from the magazine and shoves it into the chamber. The final forward action of the carrier engages the cam pin, rotating the bolt and locking it in place over the cartridge.

In the automatic or burst-fire mode, if the trigger is still being held back, the inside rear of the bolt carrier hits the auto sear as the bolt locks, causing the hammer to drop and fire another round. In the burst mode, this cycling continues until only three rounds are fired; then the hammer is engaged by the disconnector and the firearm stops firing. In the auto-fire mode, the firearm continues to fire as long as the magazine has cartridges in it and the hammer is held back.

In semiauto fire, the disconnector holds the hammer back and doesn't release it until the trigger is released. At this point the disconnector drops the hammer, but before the hammer can continue forward the trigger latches onto it. When the shooter pulls the trigger again the hammer drops, firing the rifle and starting the cycle over again.

Anyone who has fired the AR-15 has probably noticed the *ka-whap* feel during recoil. This double-recoil effect is created by the buffer assembly, which has a plastic end cap and is full of loose projectiles (usually disks—or shot in cheap buffers). The disks start to recoil a few moments after the outside of the buffer does, and when they collide with the front of the buffer it creates a "hitch" in the straight rebound. The effect of this is to absorb and disperse some of the recoil as well make the "kick" of the firearm a little less abrupt. The final bump of the buffer pad on the rear of the recoil spring assembly also dampens the recoil and slows the rate of fire.

The principle reason for the complex buffer design is to slow the cycling of the rifle and, in the process, give some extra time for the cartridge to pop up in the magazine and for the various parts and springs in the trigger assembly to bounce around. Additionally, the bounce of the buffer from its plastic end cap propels it forward with extra force to make the rifle chamber rounds more reliably and make the bolt's locking more positive. (Needless to say, a quality buffer is an important feature in an AR-15 because it keeps the firearm running properly.)

For those firing an AR-15 in the auto mode, the cycling rate is too high to compensate for aiming errors. Work has been done toward reducing this rate. The technique with the greatest potential for success is to modify the buffer either by adding a hydraulic system (the Colt's choice) or more moving weights inside the buffer (thereby "pinning" it to the rear of the buffer tube for a longer time as the momentum of the weights is overcome by the recoil spring).

The latter option has been exploited by inventor Max G. Atchisson, whose system was briefly marketed in the late 1990s by Advanced Armament Corporation (AAC). Four models were made and apparently succeeded in reducing the normal auto-mode rate of fire from 600 to 800 rpm to 475 to 600 rpm. It seems likely that in the near future this buffer, or one of similar design, will resurface for enabling shooters to gain more control of the AR-15 when it's fired in auto mode.

An interesting variation on the idea of increasing the buffer weight can be seen in the Counterpoise system marketed by ArmForté. The brainchild of firearms designers Jim Sullivan and Mack W. Gwinn Jr., this system consists of a new buffer assembly, a drive spring, and a counterweight, all of which fits inside the bolt carrier of an AR-15. (The set also includes a "D-Fender" ring extractor booster, described elsewhere in this book). The Counterpoise system reduces the cyclic rate of an AR-15 to 500 to 600 rpm and also increases the forward momentum of the bolt, making chambering more reliable even when the chamber becomes fouled with extensive shooting. About the only major modification to a firearm employing this system is a slight increase in the size of the gas port to move the greater mass of the replacement buffer and counterweight rearward during recoil. Cost of the kit is $194.

Advanced Armament also sells a buffer system that purports to reduce the cycling rate of an AR-15 by 50 percent. This kit comes with a machined-steel buffer (with tungsten weights), buffer spring, insertion/extraction tool, and instructions for use. The rifle and carbine collapsible-stock versions each sell for $149 and are available from Brownells.

### Loading the AR-15

The first step in loading the rifle is to get a magazine full of ammunition. Individual rounds can be chambered by hand in an emergency, but it's a little risky unless the shooter follows the charging handle forward rather than releasing it so he doesn't get a slam-fire as described above.

Magazines can be loaded a round at a time or from stripper clips of rounds. To load one round at a time, remove the magazine from the rifle (if it's there) and hold it in one hand. With the other hand, place a round on top of the magazine follower (the part that moves down into the magazine) with the bullet end of the round toward the front of the magazine. When the cartridge is on the follower, push the round down below the lips of the magazine and then release; the round is held by the lips. Repeat until magazine is loaded.

Stripper clips can enable a shooter to load a magazine in a hurry *if* he's got the clips loaded beforehand and *if* he has a clip guide handy. Stripper clips are not a good substitute for charged magazines but can speed things up if the magazines aren't available. The clips are usually available on the surplus market; one good source for stripper clips and guides is Sierra Supply. Guides usually cost around 50 cents, clips 20 cents each.

Bandoleers are handy for carrying the clips. Even though the cardboard sleeves for the bandoleers only hold two clips, a third clip of 10 rounds can be placed to one side of the sleeve if the shooter wants to carry even more ammunition. The clip guide can then be carried in one of the pockets or—better yet—tied on to one end of a nylon cord and the other end of the cord tied to the bandoleer. Bandoleers cost around $4 each.

The clips hold 10 rounds of ammunition. Metal clips have a brass tag at each end that is bent to a right angle of the clip itself, locking the rounds in the clip. Plastic clips have a small detent dot that holds the shells in place. The clip and rounds can then be carried until they're needed.

When it's time to load an empty magazine, place a clip over the top rear end of the magazine and then a stripper clip in it so that the bullets are pointing in the proper direction. Then push the rounds down into the magazine. With practice this can be done with one smooth motion, but a series of pushes will work almost as well. (Some people find it easier to shove just 4 or 5 rounds into the magazine at a time rather than all 10.) The base of the magazine can be placed against the chest so that both hands can be used to push rounds out of the clip into the magazine.

After using several clips to put the proper number of rounds into the magazine, remove the clip guide (taking care not to loose it) and the magazine is ready.

With the magazine *out* of the rifle and the barrel pointed in a safe direction, pull the charging handle all the way back and release it. This cocks the hammer (and also makes sure the weapon is empty). Next, place the selector in the safe position if it isn't already there.

Shove the magazine into the magazine well until the magazine release clicks shut on it. Military trainers generally have soldiers slap the base of the magazine to be sure it's fully seated; in combat, this is a good idea since it is often impossible to hear the clip of the release popping into the magazine, and dirt may make a magazine seem to be in place even when it is not. Get into the habit of giving the magazine a rap so that it doesn't fall out of the rifle when it's really needed.

With the magazine in place and the barrel pointed in a safe direction, pull the charging handle all the way back again and release it. This causes the bolt to strip a round from the magazine and chamber it. Some shooters prefer to pull the bolt back slightly at this point to be sure a cartridge is in the chamber. If this is done, be sure the bolt is locked back up—perhaps by using the forward assist *if* the rifle and ammunition are clean.

The AR-15 will now fire if the selector is moved from its safe position to a semi, burst, or auto-fire position (depending on the model of the gun, some of these may not be available) and the trigger pulled. The selector positions vary among the models of the AR-15. On the semiauto-only versions, the positions are safe and fire; the auto position is not available. With the M16, M231, M16A1, early Commandos, and other variants of the M16 rifle, the selector positions are usually safe, semi, and auto. With the M16A2 series of guns, the positions are safe, semi, and burst. But among the auto-fire versions these aren't hard and fast rules; a few models may go with the auto or burst options according to the wishes of a government buyer. Furthermore, conversion kits make it possible to transform one configuration to another. And just to keep things confusing, some rifles have a four-position selector with safe, semi, auto, and burst.

If a shooter won't be firing for a while, he should leave the selector in the safe position and close the dust cover over the ejection port. (The dust cover will pop open automatically when the rifle is fired or cycled by hand, but it must be closed manually.)

When all the rounds have been fired, the magazine follower engages the bolt catch and holds the bolt and bolt carrier to the rear. This also keeps the hammer back so that it won't fall on an empty chamber if the trigger is pulled before the shooter realizes his firearm is empty. The bolt catch allows the shooter to do a quick visual check, by turning the rifle on its side and peering through the ejection port, to ensure that the chamber and magazine are empty.

The bolt catch makes it possible to quickly bring the rifle back into action by releasing the empty magazine, placing a full magazine into the well, and pressing the bolt release. This frees the bolt so that it hurtles forward, chambering a round. The hammer is already back, so the rifle is set to fire again. If the shooter may not want to fire right away, he should again move the selector to the safe position.

### The AR-15's Sights

The sights on all AR-15s with the A1-style sights and the front sight on the M16A2 versions can be adjusted by pushing down their detents with the end of a bullet or small punch. Although this is cheap, it isn't too quick. A very useful tool for adjusting the sights is available from Quality Parts for just $8 (one tool for A1-type sights and another for A2-style front sights). The sight adjustment tool can really speed things up with the A1 sights.

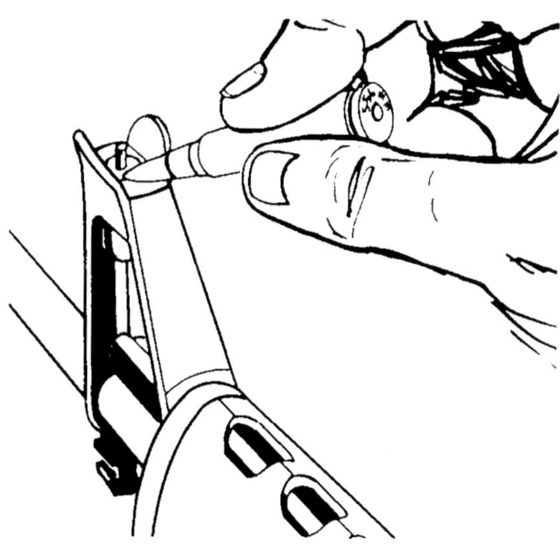

In a pinch, the front sight of an AR-15 can be adjusted with the tip of a bullet or other small tool.

To adjust windage (the horizontal placement of the bullet on target), change the rear sight. Most receivers have markings to show that clockwise movement changes the point of impact to the right. Depress the indent and move the drum as needed. With the full-length-barrel version of the AR-15, turning the A1-style sights one notch changes the point of impact by 1 inch at 100 yards or 2 inches at 200 yards, and so on. (Yes, the sights are designed for English measurements rather than metric; the change in point of impact is 2.8 centimeters at 100 meters for each detent click with the A1 windage sight.) It should be noted that with carbine versions of the AR-15 the horizontal and vertical displacement per click is

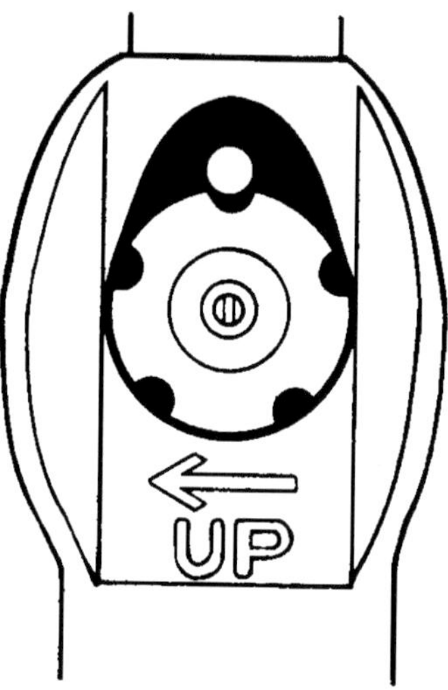


Top view of front sight.

A1 sight adjustment tool.

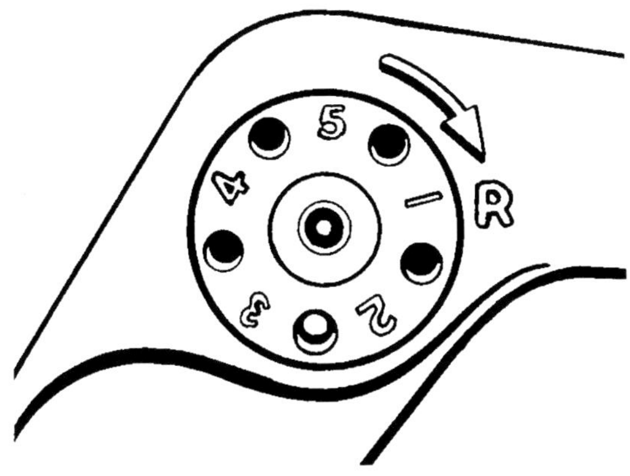


A1 rear sight adjustment wheel.

slightly greater because the sighting radius is shorter between the front and rear sights.

With the A2 sights, each click of the detent moves the point of impact right or left by 1.25 centimeters (1/2 inch) at 100 meters (A2 sights are marked in meters). For greater ranges, the amount of change can be figured by multiplying the number of meters (in hundreds of meters) by 1.25 centimeters. Thus, the shift at 200 meters is 2.5 centimeters; at 300 meters, 3.75 centimeters; at 400 meters, 5 centimeters; and so on. Once the windage knob has been zeroed, it is wise to note the setting in case it is accidentally moved or readjusted later on. Many shooters use a small dab of paint or nail polish to show where the zero should be on the rifle.

On most AR-15s the rear sight has two range apertures. One is for 0 to 300 yards (0 to 300 meters with the A2 sight), and the other, marked with an "L," is the long-range aperture for 300 to 500 yards with the A1 (300 to 800 meters with the A2). On 9mm carbines with A1 sights, the short-range setting is 50 meters, and the "L" setting is gauged for 150 meters. Remember that these figures are approximations, and flipping the long-range sight may or may not allow for accurate long-range shooting; since bullet drop can vary considerably with the actual range and the ammunition used. Nevertheless, the flip sight can be very useful.

The front sight adjusts the elevation, and this is necessary even with the A2 sight when the sights are first zeroed. Be absolutely certain the rifle's chamber is empty when adjusting the front sight, since it is close to the muzzle. There should be an arrow and markings on the front sight to show that clockwise rotation will raise the point of impact. With the A1 guns, one click changes the point of impact 1 inch at 100 yards with the standard-length barrel. With an A2 front sight, one click moves the point of impact by 3.5 cm (1 3/8 inch) at 100 meters.

Once the A2 sight is zeroed, elevation can be handled

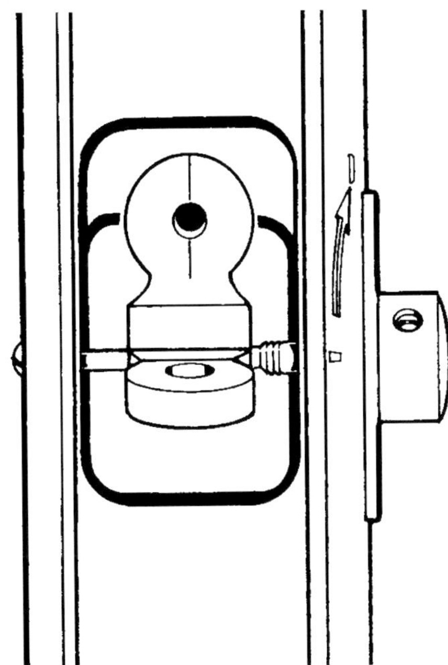

Top view of A1 rear sight.

with the rear sight. With the aperture set to the short-range peep sight, one click raises or lowers elevation by 3.5 cm (1 3/8 inch) at 100 meters. With settings beyond 300 meters, it is quickest to flip to the "L" sight and then use the side markings to "dial up" the zero for the range. To use this sight effectively, spend some time learning to estimate ranges or, if firing from a fixed sight, step off the ranges beforehand and use landmarks to remember what each stepped-off range was (perhaps with a hand-drawn chart to keep track of the ranges).

One "trick" that can be used to sight-in a rifle that has a new barrel is to remove the upper receiver from the lower and pull out the bolt carrier. Place the receiver/barrel on a steady rest, look through the barrel from the receiver end of the gun, and center a sight on some object at 50 meters (with 9mm carbines), 100 yards (with A1 sights), or 100 meters (with A2 sights). Next, without moving the receiver/barrel, look through the sights to see where they are centered and then change them to bring them onto the "target." Continue to zero in the sights until the sights and barrel line up. Even though this visual sight adjustment won't be extremely precise, it will get you into the neighborhood when you finally start firing the rifle to zero it in.

Those who have slower twists on their AR-15 can use a .22 adapter kit for rough sighting in (and .22 CB Caps can be used for very quiet sighting in.) Usually, the zero taken at 30 yards with the .22 will be close to that of most AR-15s firing .223 Remington ammunition.

There is a lot of disagreement about where the zero for an AR-15 should be. Traditionally the 250-yard zero was used for the A1-style AR-15s, using the 0- to 300-range aperture when sighting in the rifle. With A2 sights, the rifle is generally sighted in with a 250-meter zero. According to U.S. Army training manuals, it is impossible to sight in at 25 yards (with the A1) or 25 meters (with the A2) to get very close to a 250-yard or 250-meter zero. Because of the ballistic curve of the bullet, it will be at about the same height at 25 yards (or 25 meters) as it will again be at 250 yards (or 250 meters). That's the theory.

In practice, this close zero is going to be about 7 inches off at the extended range with most rifles and ammunition. (But not only that; the M16A1 will shoot low, while the M16A2 will most likely hit high.) This is close enough for most combat in which soldiers often fail to aim and this extreme of range is seldom used, but it can be a bit aggravating to those who are perplexed about why their rifle doesn't seem to zero in as the military manuals claim it should.

The bottom line here is that if you wish to hit a target dead on at X meters or yards, your best bet is to zero the rifle in at that range, only sight in at 25 or 30 meters to get into the ballpark before zeroing at the longer range. Note that the M16A2 also generally comes closer to a 300-meter zero when zeroed at 30 meters rather than 25 as recommended in most manuals. (Rumor has it that the 25-meter range remains in vogue to help the army avoid the expense of revamping its rifle ranges to the different points).

The proper sight picture is obtained when the front post is in the center of the rear aperture vertically, with its top in the exact center horizontally. The bullet should then strike just a hair above the sight post when the shooter is firing at the distance the rifle is zeroed in.

### Unloading the AR-15

To unload the AR-15 safely, the selector is set to safe, the magazine catch released, and the magazine removed. The charging handle is pulled fully to the rear so that any round in the chamber is ejected and the chamber checked to be sure it's empty (since the rifle might have failed to extract a round). The shooter may or may not want to lock the action open with the bolt stop (to do this, pressure is applied to the bottom of the bolt release button rather than its grooved top). The bolt release can be jarred off with an accidental hit on the rifle, so it should not be depended on as a safety feature. In other words, if the rifle is jarred when a full magazine is in the well and the bolt is held open by the bolt release, the bolt might go forward and chamber a round. So what appeared to be a safe rifle is now ready to fire—or might even fire itself if there is a sensitive primer on the top round in the magazine.

*Remember: All firearms should be pointed in a safe direction and treated as if they are loaded at all times.*

## OPERATING THE M203 GRENADE LAUNCHER

For those with an M203 mounted on their rifle, the operation is pretty simple and straightforward. To load (or reload) the grenade launcher, release the barrel latch on the left side of the receiver (it is about halfway forward to the top and side of launcher's barrel). When the latch is depressed, slide the barrel forward by grasping its ringed area. This automatically cocks the striker and extracts any cartridge in the barrel, since the round or cartridge will be held by the extractor and stay behind on the receiver.

When the barrel is in its forward position, a new cartridge can be inserted into the breech. The barrel is then retracted toward the receiver until it latches. Unless the weapon is to be fired immediately, the safety should be rotated backward toward the trigger.

When the M203 needs to be fired, aim the weapon, push the safety forward (if the safety is engaged), and then pull the trigger. This releases the spring-loaded striker, which will ignite the primer and fire the round.

### M203 Ammunition

The basic 40mm grenade round fired from the M203 is known as a "hi-lo" cartridge because a pistol-cartridge-sized, high-pressure section is first ignited by the weapon's firing pin, after which the gas expands into a larger space, with its pressure lowered as it expands and shoves the projectile out the barrel. These are considerably different from the grenades used with automatic weapons like the Mark 19 grenade launcher, even though the cartridges are very similar. The latter operate at a much higher pressure that would produce recoil forces unmanageable in a weapon like the M203.

A wealth of cartridges is available for the M203. The HE star flare (usually on a parachute), and smoke rounds are the most commonly issued. HE rounds have a maximum range of 400 meters with a casualty radius of 5 meters. They are armed when they achieve a certain number of fast rotations after leaving the barrel—usually at 30 meters from the barrel.

There have been a variety of cartridges created for the M79 and/or M203 over the years, and it isn't rare to see oddball pieces that have been cobbled together by unknown inventors. Likewise, some M203 owners "roll their own" by reloading cartridges or even making rounds from scratch using plastic pipe and other components.

Very short-bodied buckshot rounds (XM576E1 and XM576E2) were seen on occasion in Vietnam. These have a range of only 50 yards for a good hit probability; each round contains 27 pellets of 00 buckshot, making it roughly equivalent to a load of 12-gauge buckshot. Adapters to allow firing shotgun shells in the M203 tube have also been made.

A slightly different approach was taken with some experimental cartridges, including units with eighteen .22 LR shells, all with a "barrel" formed in the body of the cartridge. A large striker plate fired this at the instant the firing pin of the launcher struck it. Lack of rifling made these cartridges less than ideal, and they most likely have not seen use in combat.

Much the same can be said for the flechette cartridges created in 40mm. These seem effective but in reality tend to spread in a pattern that sends some over the target, while others are lost in the ground ahead of the target.

Also seen is the tear gas cartridge, a "silent" DBCATA (Disposable Barrel and Cartridge Area Target Ammunition) round (see Chapter 5) that employs a metal sleeve to contain the discharge of the round. Ahead of the sleeve, a projectile is hurled with some force, almost silently since the report is contained in the cartridge. This makes it possible to launch a grenade without having the enemy easily locate the shooter. Whether these rounds have ever been fielded is unknown.

The XM688 cartridge has a grappling hook on a line. In theory, this should allow the M203 to launch a line that soldiers could use to climb up onto a building. It is doubtful that this is practical or has ever actually been used.

The GR103 cartridge fires a fine coil of wire up into trees, where it can be employed as a long-range antenna. Again, this cartridge has probably seen little actual use, and with new radio technology would seem destined to become obsolete.

Other experimental cartridges produced for the M203 have included miniature mines that can be laid ahead of a position where they wait to be trampled on before going off, rocket-assisted projectiles to create added range, and cartridges with exposed flechettes on which "biological material" could be placed for delivery against a target. The latter projectile doesn't have much of a future in the military: such a round is against the conventions of war, for starters, and is not one a soldier would care to handle, much less have in his possession if captured.

### Aiming Systems for the M203

There are two aiming systems for the M203. One is a sight mounted on the top of the handguard just behind the rifle's front sight; the other is a quadrant sight assembly that mounts on the AR-15's carrying handle. The handguard sight is used in conjunction with the front rifle sight after the ladder sight assembly is erected so that it is at right angles to the barrel. The shooter sights down the aperture using the sight alignment markings calibrated in hundreds of meters (1 being 100 meters, 2 being 200 meters, and so on.). When the target is lined up with the correct range, the weapon is fired.

The quadrant sight is fragile and slower to use but is also more accurate if the shooter can judge ranges well. First, the range is estimated, then it is dialed up on the elevation scale that is marked in 25-meter increments. When the range has been set, sighting is done through the rear aperture of the quadrant sight to the front sight post at the front of the quadrant sight. The front post sight is lined up on the target, and the launcher is fired. Great care has to be exercised not to damage the front sight/elevation screw when carrying an M203 with a quadrant sight.

## SAFETY CONSIDERATIONS

There are a number of safety precautions particular to the AR-15. Even though such problems are not normally encountered in "real life," the unexpected is always possible—and it only takes one anomaly to cause a tragedy with a rifle.

Though many precautions apply to all types of rifles, the AR-15's floating firing pin can cause extra complications. Because the firing pin normally rests against the cartridge when a round is chambered, striking the muzzle or dropping the firearm from a great height onto its muzzle might create enough inertia to fire the cartridge. This is not normally a concern except perhaps for those shinning down ropes on the sides of buildings or from helicopters, but does bear remembering.

What's more important is to avoid firing with an obstruction in the barrel. Before firing a rifle that has been outside for some time or that may have an obstruction in the barrel (e.g., mud, snow, rain, leaves), always check to be sure the barrel is cleared. This is done by removing the magazine and cycling the rifle so that the chamber is cleared. The chamber must be inspected to ensure that it is clear. The bolt carrier is then locked to the rear by pushing on the lower section of the bolt release while the carrier is all the way back. When it is certain that the rifle is empty, the barrel should be examined from the muzzle end. If the barrel is obstructed, it must be cleaned out with a bore brush. Firing the rifle with an obstruction in it will create a bulge in the barrel or blow it up on the spot.

A muzzle cap is useful in keeping "junk" out of the barrel and is readily available from Choate Machine and Tool as well as on the surplus market. If it becomes necessary to fire the rifle in a hurry, it can be fired with the cap in place (provided everything else is as it should be).

The .223 bore is so narrow that it's possible for it to hold a column of water. So if a rifle is dropped into water or has been in heavy rain, it's always wise to remove the muzzle cap, point the muzzle down, pull the charging handle back 2 or 3 inches, and allow a few seconds for the water to drain out of the bore.

The trigger finger should be kept out of the trigger guard until it's time to fire. If the finger is left inside the guard and the shooter falls down or gets excited, it's very easy to fire the rifle accidentally.

When firing the rifle, it's important know what is behind and beyond the target. Even though the AR-15's useful range is only out to between 500 and 800 yards, its bullets can travel up to 3 miles and penetrate a lot of material. Additionally, ricochets from a rock or water can alter the original, intended path of the bullet. *Shooters must think before firing.*

It's wise to always switch the selector from the fire position back to safe if the rifle won't be shot for a while. The shooter should get into the habit of thumbing the safety as the rifle is brought up (so that it isn't discovered that the selector is in the fire position when it isn't supposed to be). The rifle is much less apt to be accidentally fired if the selector is left on safe.

Only the best of ammunition—if possible, factory—should be used. For reloading, full-case resizing is a must, and primers must be fully seated, bullets tightly crimped, and the case free from oil. Corroded, dented, or hot (135+ degrees Fahrenheit) ammunition should never be used.

If a shooter fires a gun extensively and then stops firing, it's wise to eject the round in the chamber within 10 seconds and lock the bolt open with the chamber empty. This will prevent a "cook-off," which can occur when the heat of the chamber causes the powder in a cartridge to ignite.

If it's impossible to eject the round in a hot chamber, a cook-off can occur up to 15 minutes later. The rifle must be kept pointed in a safe direction during this time. If it is necessary to eject a "hot" round, it should not be approached once it is out of the rifle. Even though the bullet isn't dangerous if the round goes off outside the rifle, the small fragments of brass hurled in all directions when the cartridge explodes can cause cuts or eye injury at close ranges.

If you hear a softer than normal discharge or "pop" is heard or reduced recoil is experienced when a round is fired, that may mean that a bad round has been fired and has left a bullet, bullet jacket, or other obstruction in the barrel. If this happens, firing should be stopped immediately, the magazine removed, the charging handle pulled back, and the action locked open. Then the chamber should be visually inspected to be sure it's cleared. Next, the selector should be placed in the safe position and the bore visually inspected and/or a cleaning rod run down it. If a jacketed bullet is wedged in the barrel, it is next to impossible to remove it; this is a job best left to an armorer or gunsmith. If the rifle is necessary in combat and a bullet is stuck in the barrel, it is *possible* to remove it by taking another cartridge *without its bullet but with its powder* and putting it into the chamber and firing it. This is a risky, however, and is recommended *only* as a last resort. This can damage the rifle.

If a cartridge is jammed in the chamber so that it cannot be fired but cannot be extracted, and if the shooter is in combat, then he's in a jam along with his rifle. There are ways to remove the round, but none is safe. One is to put a cleaning rod down the barrel and push downward while pulling back on the charging handle. (This is dangerous because the bore is obstructed by the rod, and *if* the round is accidentally discharged . . .)

Another method is to remove the magazine and reach through the magazine well with a screwdriver and pry the carrier back from the barrel. This may work, or may only break the extractor and/or scar up the receiver and bolt carrier. It's critical to remember that you're working with a live round, which could be set off. Weigh the costs before trying any of this, and be extremely cautious.

### Cold Weather

Firing the AR-15 under extremely cold conditions may dictate the shooter's wearing mittens or large, heavy gloves. In such a case the AR-15 trigger guard can be released to make room. To release it, a cartridge or other small tool is pushed against the spring-loaded pin at the front of the guard/lower receiver hole. When the pin is depressed, the trigger guard is rotated down to where it can be held against the front of the pistol grip (the shooter may wish to tape or wire it in place). It should be remembered that once this is done a safety device has been defeated—any twig, branch, or other obstacle that gets into the trigger area might fire the rifle. To minimize this risk, the safety has to be engaged until it is time to fire the rifle.

Most accidents with the AR-15 can be prevented or minimized by using proper ammunition, keeping the rifle clean, and, most important, always treating the rifle as if it is loaded and might be fired accidentally at any moment. *It must never be pointed at anything that isn't meant to be shot.*

Whether shooting a military rifle with an M203 launcher mounted on it or a semiauto AR-15 Sporter, common sense and good shooting habits can keep the shooter and those around him safe.

# Chapter 11

# Cleaning and Disassembly of the AR-15

Careful cleaning and lubrication of the AR-15 will keep it the most effective and reliable rifle in the world.

It's important to keep any firearm clean so that it will operate at its best and to prevent undue wear caused by grit. However, more than a few AR-15s have been damaged by poor cleaning procedures, so it's a good idea to be careful when cleaning one.

Lubricants like Break Free CLP and Tri-Lube have simplified the chore because they clean and lubricate in one step; it's no longer necessary to use one liquid to clean the gun and a separate one to oil it. The new lubricants/cleaners also stay fluid over a wider temperature range, eliminating the need to use different lubricants for hot and cold weather.

There are several varieties of CLP, formulated for different environmental conditions. However, the standard CLP can be easily employed at any temperature above freezing (at which point it may not flow from its container unless the user gently heats the container up by holding it under an armpit or inside a jacket). As far as providing lubrication, CLP will continue to do the job until the temperature dips to –35 degrees Fahrenheit (–37 degrees Celsius), at which point it will become too congealed to work.

In very warm environments the Grade 2 CLP is preferable to the standard formula; it's also better in humid conditions or when a firearm may be exposed to salty air (with the caveat to also clean the weapon frequently to avoid rust).

In extremely cold temperatures, other precautions are needed. When a gun is brought in from a cold area to a warm area, ideally it should be wrapped in a parka or blanket and allowed to reach room temperature gradually. If condensation forms on the weapon, it should be dried off and lubricated at room temperature before it is returned to cold weather. (Leaving condensation on a gun not only causes rust; it can also result in the formation of ice inside the mechanism, leading to malfunctions.)

Excess lubricant can be as bad as no lubricant at all since it attracts dirt, and the grit may cause more friction and wear to parts than they'd get without any oil. After lubricating an AR-15, it's a good idea to wipe its outside down with a rag to remove any lubricant that might attract sand or dirt.

Good cleaning kits are available from most military surplus stores. These are excellent choices because they were designed specifically for use with the AR-15. Cleaning patches, pipe stem cleaners, and a plastic

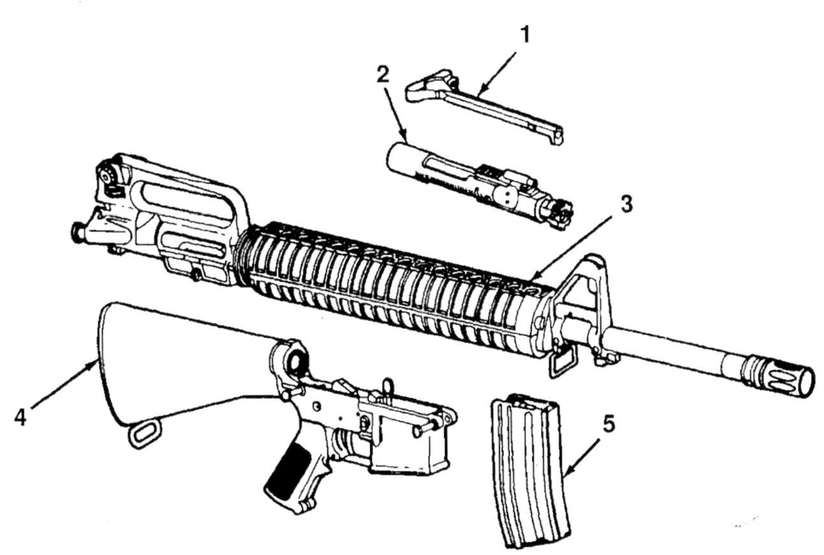


Major assemblies of the AR-15 rifle: 1. charging handle, 2. bolt and bolt carrier, 3. Upper receiver/handguard/barrel, 4. lower receiver/trigger group/stock, 5. magazine.

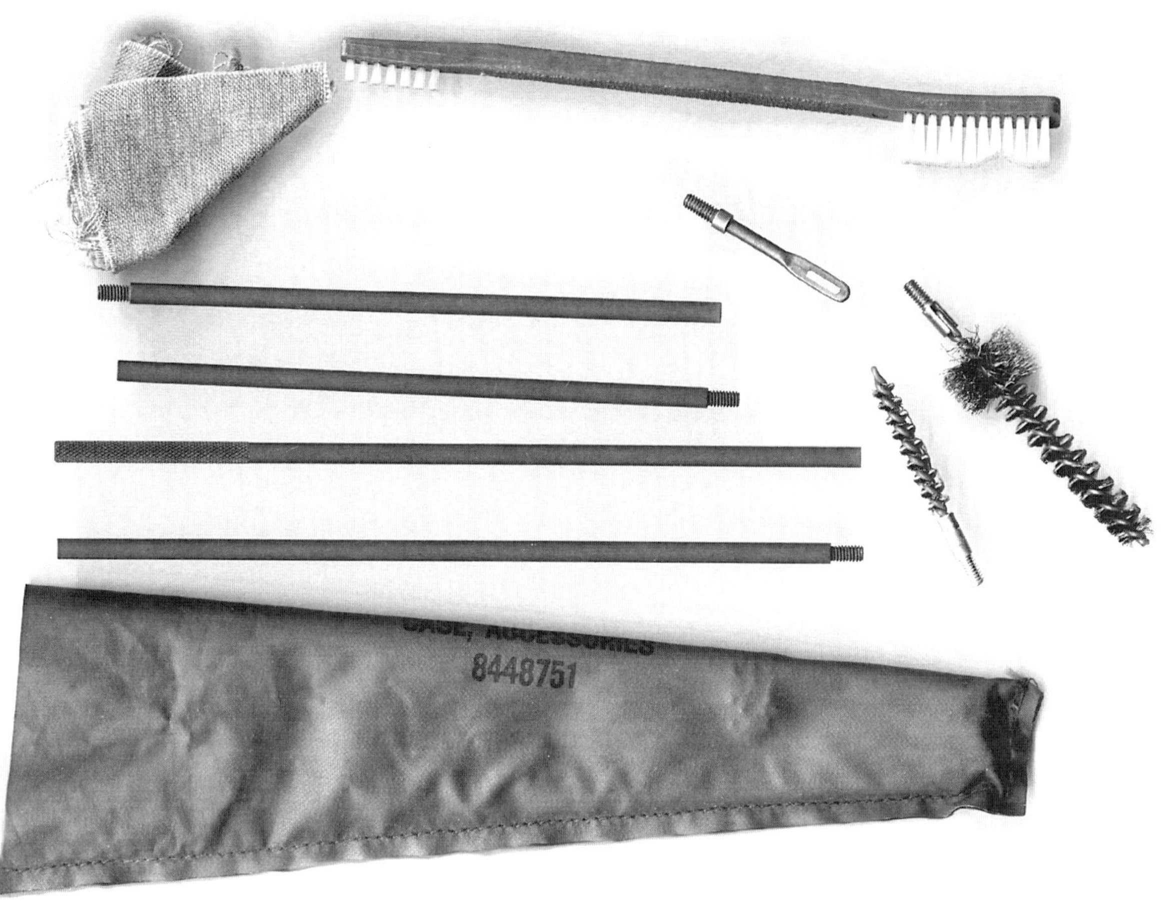


The standard U.S. military cleaning brushes and rods make excellent choices for cleaning an AR-15.

toothbrush will complete a kit if it doesn't include them. If the AR-15 has a trapdoor stock, all the cleaning gear—along with a small bottle of Break Free CLP or other lubricant—will fit into it. Ideally, the gear should be wrapped in a rag with a rubber band so it doesn't rattle.

Many people shy away from the steel cleaning rods in military cleaning kits because they fear the rods may cause extra wear to the bore. In fact, in combat conditions the steel often causes less wear than soft aluminum or brass rods because the latter can pick up grit, which can become imbedded in the soft metal and turn into miniature sand blocks that can quickly damage the bore. Steel rods don't have this problem and will work well if they aren't scraped against the inside of the barrel (something that can be avoided by cleaning the rifle from the receiver end of the barrel).

When cleaning the rifle, avoid using wire brushes on the aluminum receiver; such brushes will take the finish right off. Likewise, wire brushes can damage a night sight.

Brushes and patches are used to maneuver dirt from the chamber to the muzzle. This can't be achieved if they are stroked back and forth, which just shoves the fouling up and down the bore without getting it out of the barrel. Instead, the brush and patches should be pushed through the bore and then removed before the cleaning rod is drawn back toward the receiver.

Start by running a brush soaked in a solvent/lubricant through the bore to loosen dirt. Then shove tight, dry patches through the bore (again, in one direction from the receiver toward the muzzle). Follow these with a patch soaked in solvent, so that the bore is again coated liberally with the liquid. Ideally, set the AR-15 aside for at least a half-hour so the solvent can loosen any fouling that remains.

Next, run a wire brush through the bore again,

followed by alternating solvent-soaked and dry patches. Continue this until the patches come through the bore clean. Then, if the gun has a chromed bore, shove a dry patch through it. If it doesn't have a chrome bore, push an oil-soaked patch through it if it'll be stored for some time, or a dry patch if it will be fired soon.

After cleaning and lubricating the rifle, inspect it to be sure that patch or brush bristles are not trapped anywhere in the bore. Lightly lubricate the barrel and small parts like the windage drum, ejection port cover, detents, charging handle catch, the bolt, and bolt carrier.

Since dirt in the locking area of the barrel behind the chamber can keep an AR-15 from locking up properly, use the large bore brush to carefully clean this area. It's important not to leave the chamber oily; the oil can deactivate the shells or cause a serious pressure problem due to the failure of the brass to be held in place when the cartridge is fired.

The inside of magazines should be cleaned from time to time, but it is best to avoid lubricating them (except in the case of aftermarket steel magazines that have problems with rust). And be aware that lubricants can damage the surface of plastic magazines.

Clean and lubricate the bolt carrier, taking special care to clean the inside of the carrier key and the inside of the carrier where the bolt rides. The charging handle should also be cleaned and lubricated.

Disassemble and thoroughly clean the bolt, especially in the area between the bolt body and the gas rings. The inside of the locking lugs and the hole through which the firing pin runs are often full of carbon deposits, which must be cleaned out along with the surface of the firing pin. Carefully remove any dirt from the lower receiver, buffer, and buffer spring and brush the front and rear sights clean of any sand or dirt with a soft (not wire) brush. After cleaning the bolt, always be sure the splits in the gas rings are *not* aligned; if they are aligned the firearm will fail to function properly.

If time is at a premium, cleaning and lubricating only the most critical parts of the rifle will suffice to keep it functioning well. Since many of the AR-15s have chrome-lined barrels, it is possible to get away with this without having to worry about rust forming inside the bore. Perform the "quick clean" by clearing the rifle, opening up the receiver halves, removing the bolt carrier, and taking out the bolt, firing pin, retaining pin, and cam. Scrape carbon and old lubricant from the firing pin and clean out the bolt and the firing pin hole. Next scour the bolt carrier and the inside of the bolt carrier key with a pipe cleaner. Scrape the chamber first with wire brushes and then with a cleaning pad (on the cleaning rod). If time permits, carefully lubricate and clean the trigger group and buffer tube as well.

In damp or humid environments or regions that are exposed to salt spray, the rifle should be cleaned at least twice a month even if it hasn't been fired. In drier climates, the rifle should be cleaned at least several times a year even if it hasn't been fired, to prevent rust on steel parts. When cleaning and lubricating the weapon, it is wise to inspect all the parts to be sure they are not damaged or excessively worn.

After lightly lubricating all parts of the rifle, add extra lubricant to the bolt, gas rings (which should not have their split areas lined up), cam pin, firing pin hole, and push pins. Put one drop of oil down the carrier key hole and lightly lubricate the lower action.

## CLEANING TARGET RIFLES

or those with a target rifle version of the AR-15 (or AR-10, SR-25, or other spin-off), some extra care must be exercised to maintain accuracy as well as to "break in" the barrel when it is new. Failure to do this can greatly decrease the rifle's potential for accuracy.

Of course, the key is to avoid wear toward the muzzle end of the barrel (as noted above); never let the rod touch the area around the crown of the muzzle. It's also important to use hollow-point bullets rather than full-metal jacket (FMJ) because the exposed lead at the base of the (so-called) FMJ bullet will create a lead vapor when exposed to the heat produced during ignition of the powder. This will gradually create a slight residue in the bore, to the detriment of the rifle's accuracy.

To properly break in the barrel, first fire 10 or 11 single shots, following each discharge by running a solvent-soaked bore brush down the bore from breech to muzzle (three or four times per shot). After using the brush, dry the bore by shoving a clean patch down it; follow this with a patch soaked in solvent (Armalite recommends J-B bore cleaner, which is available from Brownells).

For the next 20 shots, the gun should be cleaned every 3 firings; it should be cleaned every 5 shots for the next 20 shots after that, and every 10 shots for the next 50. After this, the barrel is pretty well broken in. The bore has been "lapped" by the bullets and cleaning, preventing copper from the jackets from fusing to the bore and thereby permanently ruining the gun's potential for the ultimate accuracy.

For optimal accuracy be sure to keep cleaning the bore every 20 shots. Also, be sure to use match ammunition. A quality target barrel calls for quality ammunition. Failure to employ the right cartridge in a target rifle is like using a racehorse to plow a field: it can be done, but the potential of the animal is never realized and the result is less than perfect.

## FIELD-STRIPPING THE AR-15

From time to time you will have to take down the AR-15 to lubricate it or perform routine maintenance; however, do not take the rifle apart any more than is necessary. Each time a part is removed from the lower receiver or other areas not involved in fieldstripping, the part's fit is not as tight when the rifle is reassembled.

The AR-15 rifle is very simple to fieldstrip and, unlike some other battle rifles, has few small parts to be lost in the process. It's a good idea to wear safety glasses when fieldstripping the rifle (just as it is when shooting or assembling the AR-15). The following steps can be used as a guide to fieldstripping most AR-15s. Refer to the exploded diagrams for clarification regarding parts and their locations.

- Remove the magazine from the AR-15 and check the chamber to be sure the action is closed; release the bolt carrier if it's held open so that it is closed.
- Place the selector into SAFE position.
- Push out the rear takedown pin (diagram 1, #35) from the selector side of the lower receiver and pull it out from the opposite side of the receiver until it locks open. This releases the upper receiver so it can be rotated downward. The front pivot pin (diagram 1, #1A) may also be pushed outward if it is necessary to remove the upper receiver from the lower. On AR-15 Sporters, a double screw holds the receivers to the front. To remove the upper receiver from the lower on the Sporter, use two screwdrivers to unscrew the double screw; a drift punch may be needed to push out the inner screw from the outer.
- Pull the charging handle (diagram 3, #14) back; the bolt carrier group (diagram 3, #13A, B, C, D, E) will come back with it. The bolt carrier group should be pulled back so that it can be grasped and removed. After the carrier group is removed, the charging handle can be removed by pulling it back and downward through the slot in the key channel.
- The firing pin retaining pin (diagram 3, #1) can be removed by punching it out with a tip of a small tool. Push from the ejection port side of the carrier.
- Once the retaining pin is removed, the firing pin (diagram 3, #2) can be removed by tilting the carrier up so the bolt faces upward and the firing pin can fall free through the rear of the carrier.
- Twist the bolt assembly (diagram 4, #4) so that the cam pin (diagram 3, #3) is clear of the bolt key (diagram 3, #13C). Now the cam can be lifted free and removed.
- With the cam pin removed, pull the bolt assembly (diagram 3, #4) from the front of the bolt carrier.

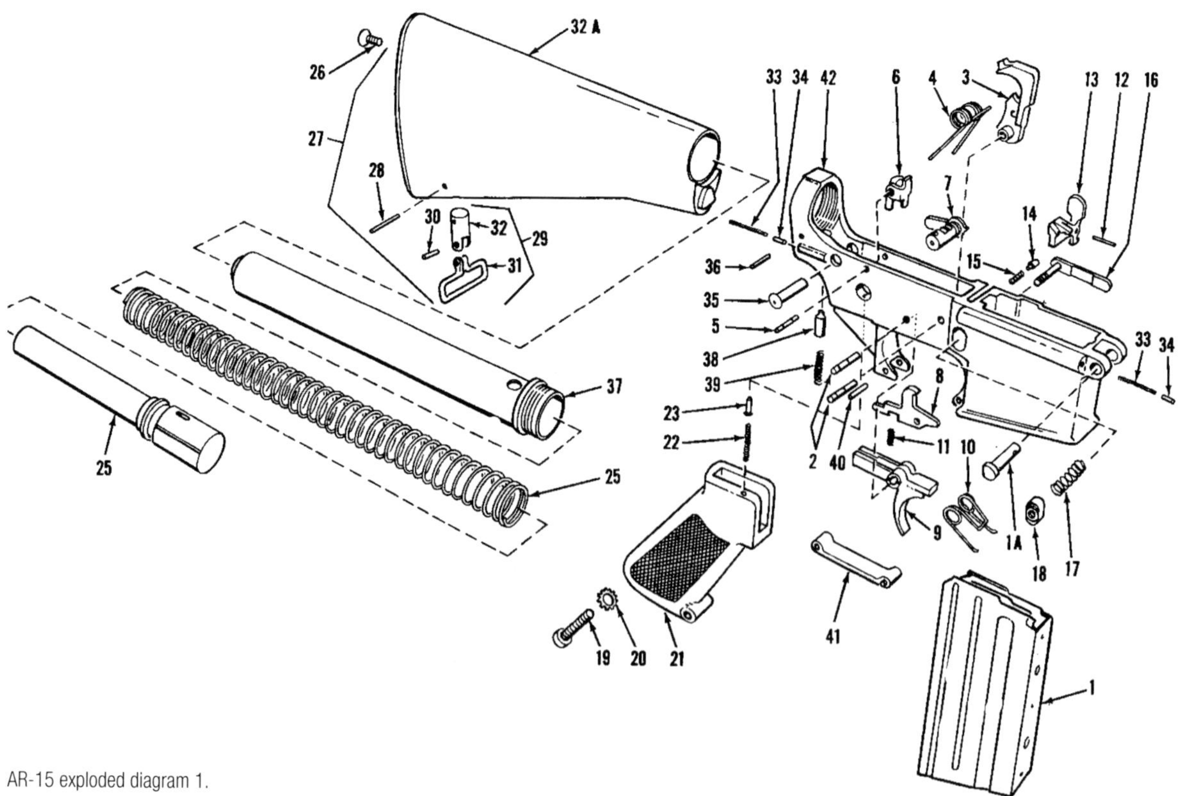


AR-15 exploded diagram 1.

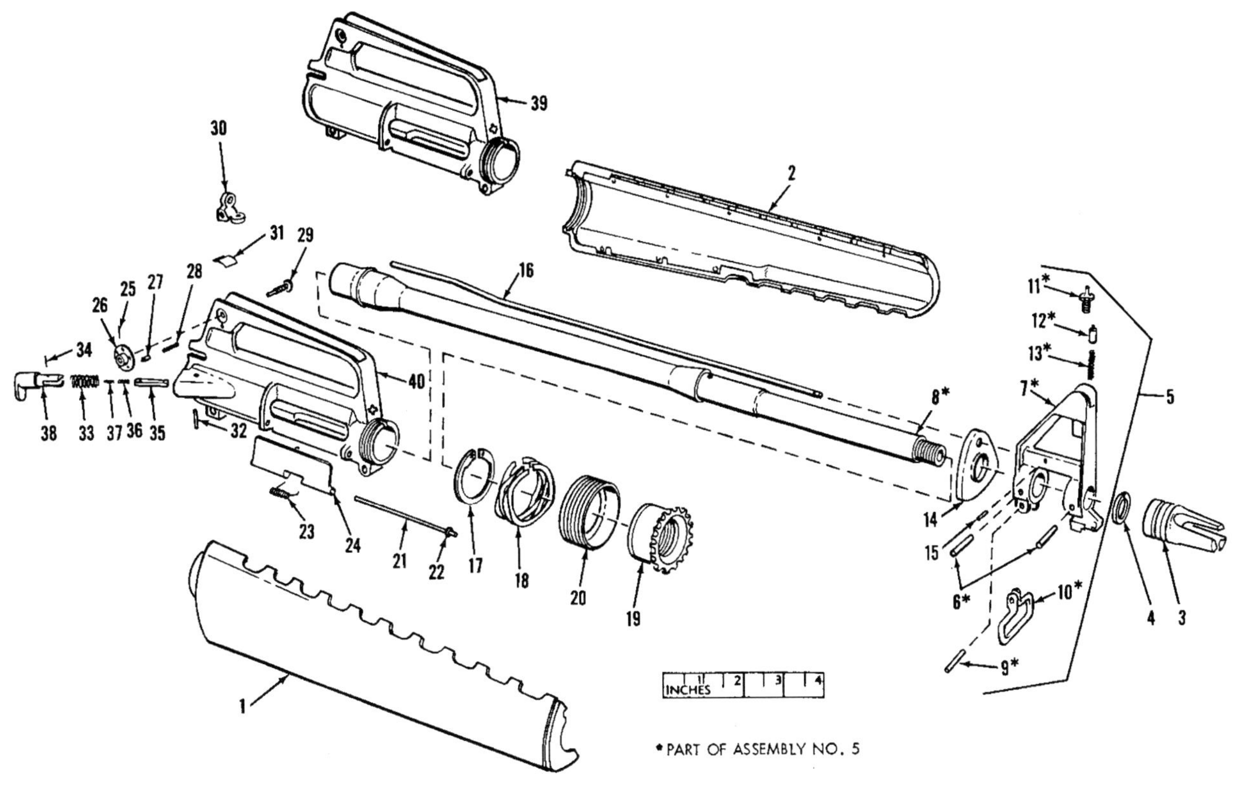


AR-15 exploded diagram 2 (M16 and M16A1 styles), upper receiver/barrel.

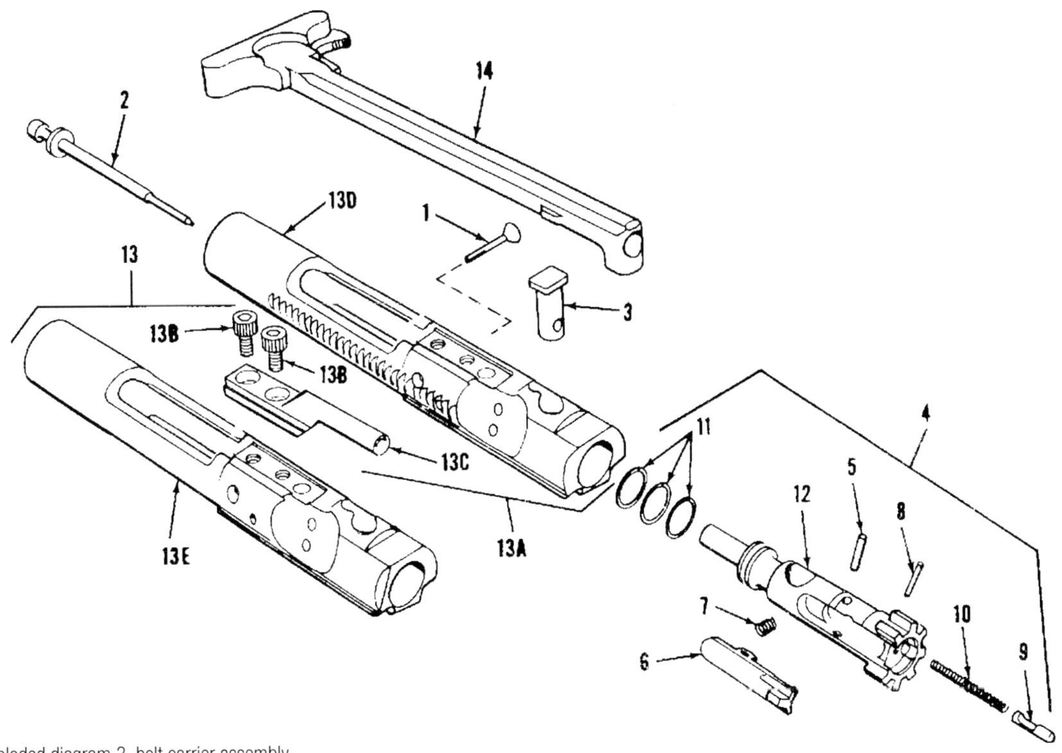


AR-15 exploded diagram 3, bolt carrier assembly.

- Care should be taken in disassembling the bolt, which will free a number of easily lost parts. The extractor spring (diagram 3, #7) is under compression, so be careful not to let the extractor (diagram 3, #6) get away when it is released. While holding the extractor in place, use a small wire or drift punch to push the extractor pin (diagram 3, #5) out of the bolt. Carefully remove the extractor, its spring, and the small nylon plug that is often nestled in the spring.
- The ejector (diagram 3, #9) and its spring (diagram 3, #10) can be removed by drifting out the pin (diagram 3, #8) that retains them. The spring is under tension, so be careful not to let it get away. Placing an empty brass casing into the bolt face and using it to hold the ejector in place can make the removal of the ejector pin easier.
- To remove the buffer and its spring (diagram 1, #25), depress the buffer retainer plunger (diagram 1, #38) while restraining the buffer and its spring. Be sure the hammer is cocked before trying to remove the buffer from its tube. Once the buffer is out, the spring can be wiggled out without holding the plunger down.

It is seldom necessary to remove the handguards (diagram 2, #1, 2) unless they need to be replaced or the weapon is full of mud. Although in theory the handguards are easily removed by pushing the weld ring (diagram 2, #20) toward the receiver, in reality there is often enough tension in the weld spring (diagram 2, #18) to make this hard for most people to do. One solution is to use a screwdriver or other tool to carefully pry the ring away from one half of the handguard until it can be wiggled free. Then repeat the procedure with the other half of the handguard. This will have to be repeated to get the handguards back on if it was necessary to pry them off. Be careful not to scar the finish on the rifle when using a tool as a lever on the weld ring.

Assembly of the rifle is basically the reverse of all the above procedures. Be sure the cam pin and firing pin retaining pin are in place; the rifle would be dangerous to fire without them.

All other disassembly of the AR-15 or any major work on the rifle should be handled by a competent gunsmith. Owners should work on their rifles *only* if they are sure of their abilities to do so; more AR-15 rifles are ruined by amateur work than by accidental breakage. The important rule is: *Do not work on your rifle if you are not sure of what you are doing.*

## DETAIL STRIPPING THE AR-15

Unless he is experienced with working on firearms, the only time a shooter might attempt the following disassembly is in a survival or combat situation where the risk of damaging a gun is worth taking to avoid being without a working weapon.

If a shooter must disassemble the rifle, he should do *only* the following steps that are necessary and skip those not necessary to carry out any work that needs to be done. (Consult Chapter 12 on assembling the rifle before undertaking such procedures; parts listed in parentheses can be located on the charts in Chapter 12.)

- The three gas rings (diagram 3, #11) should be left in place unless they are damaged. Place new rings on the bolt by gently spreading each one enough to get it in place. Don't line up the spaces on the rings. (Note: a single gas ring, known as the McFarland ring, is now available from Competition Specialties for $1.75. This part makes the misalignment problem of the standard rings a thing of the past.)
- When possible, leave the charging handle latch and its spring on the charging handle (diagram 3, #14) when possible. The roll pin holding them can be drifted out of place if necessary.
- The key (diagram 3, #13C) and its bolts (diagram 3, #13B) should be left in place unless they absolutely need to be replaced. On most carriers the bolts are "staked" (a sharp punch has pushed metal onto the bolts to keep them from coming loose), so extra effort will be required to loosen them. A hex wrench will be necessary to remove the two bolts.
- The flash suppresser (diagram 2, #3) or muzzle brake (if present) should screw off unless it's welded to the barrel. Be careful not to lose the lock washer (diagram 2, #4). The flash suppresser is most easily removed by clamping the barrel into place first.
- The front sight assembly (diagram 2, #5) can be removed *with great effort* by drifting out the two pins (diagram 2, #6) from the base. The pins must be pushed out toward the ejection port side of the rifle. This job is best done with a heavy sledge hammer and punch, working on a lead pad. Take great care not to damage the rifle. The base, along with the gas tube (diagram 2, #16), can be moved off the barrel from the muzzle end of the barrel.
- Remove the front swivel (diagram 2, #10) by drifting out the pin holding it. On some AR-15s this is a rivet that must be ground off.
- Release the front sight post (diagram 2, #11), sight detent (diagram 2, #12), and their spring (diagram 2, #13) by depressing the detent and unscrewing the front sight post. (A front/rear sight tool is useful for this.)
- If the front sight has been removed, take off the gas

tube (diagram 2, #16) by drifting out its pin (diagram 2, #15). The gas tube can also be extracted without removing the sight base by drifting out the gas tube pin and pushing the tube to the rear of the upper receiver, then pulling the tube slightly to the side of the front sight base and finally pulling it out of the receiver toward the muzzle.

- With the gas tube removed, unscrew the barrel nut (diagram 2, #19) to remove the barrel. An armorer's wrench is necessary to do this. The barrel can be pulled straight out of the receiver once the nut is removed (it may be necessary to wiggle the barrel a bit to make it creep out).
- The front sight/gas block (diagram 2, #5) is best left on the barrel. It can be removed, however, by drifting out the two pins holding it in place. These pins are tapered and must be removed from left to right. They are usually very tightly installed; it may require a 5-pound hammer and large punch with the sight on a lead or plastic block to drift them out.
- The handguard snap ring (diagram 2, #17) along with the weld ring (diagram 2, #18) and slip ring (diagram 2, #20) will stay on the barrel nut when it is removed. If you wish to remove them, use a pair of needle-nosed pliers to pull the snap ring free of its groove in the barrel nut.
- Remove the ejection port dust cover (diagram 2, #24) along with its spring (diagram 2, #23) and its pin (diagram 2, #21) by sliding the pin toward the barrel side of the receiver *if* the barrel is off. If the barrel is left on the upper receiver, then the C ring (diagram 2, #22) can be popped off the pin and the pin slipped out toward the rear of the receiver, thereby freeing the port cover and its spring. (This is a hassle with receivers that have a bolt assist, but it is possible to do on all AR-15 rifles.)
- Remove the A1- and A2-style rear sight windage drum (diagram 2, #26) by drifting out the windage drum pin (diagram 2, #24) and removing the drum, detent (diagram 2, #27) or ball (on A2), and spring (diagram 2, #28). The spring is under tension, so be careful when freeing the windage drum.
- Remove the rear sight (diagram 2, #30) by unscrewing the rear sight screw (diagram 2, #29). This will free the rear sight leaf spring (diagram 2, #31).
- On A2 rear sights, drifting out the pin (diagram 4, #14) below the elevation knob will free the sight base so the knobs can be screwed to free that part. Be careful to catch the detent ball (diagram 4, #12) and its spring (diagram 4, #11) on the left front edge of the sight. A detent ball and spring under the knobs (diagram 4, #5 and #6) will also be freed along with a spring (diagram 4, #13) below the center post screw of the sight.

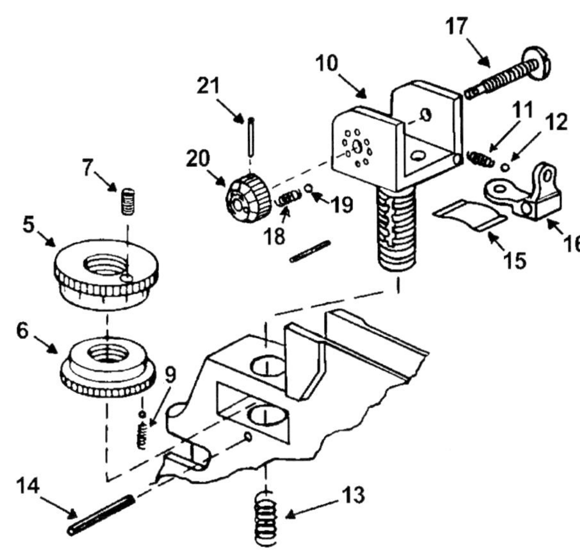

AR-15 exploded diagram 4, A2 rear sight.

- If the rifle has a forward assist, the assembly can be removed by drifting out the pin (diagram 2, #32) that holds it. Generally, it should be drifted out from the top toward the lower part of the receiver.
- The forward-assist assembly can be disassembled by drifting out the pawl pivot pin (diagram 2, #34), but this is generally best left assembled. Drifting the pin out will free the pawl and its spring and detent; they are under pressure, so care must be taken to secure them.
- Remove the pistol grip (diagram 1, #21) and its screw lock ring (diagram 1, #20) by unscrewing its screw (diagram 1, #19). This will also release the selector detent (diagram 1, #23) and its spring (diagram 1, #22).
- Once the pistol grip is off, the selector (diagram 1, #7) can be removed from the bolt release side of the receiver. (The hammer should be cocked to do this.)
- Remove the hammer (diagram 1, #3) and its spring (diagram 1, #4) by drifting out their pin (diagram 1, #2). The spring can be removed by gently pulling one side off the hub. Remember how the spring is positioned on the hammer if you have to remove it.
- Remove the trigger (diagram 1, #9), trigger spring (diagram 1, #10), disconnector (diagram 1, #8), and disconnector spring (diagram 1, #11) by drifting out the pin (diagram 1, #2) holding them. The spring can be removed by gently pulling one side off the hub. Remember how the spring is positioned on the trigger.
- If the rifle has one, the auto sear (diagram 1, #6) can

be removed by drifting out its pin (diagram 1, #5).

- Use a drift punch to removed the bolt release pin (diagram 1, #12). This will free the bolt release (diagram 1, #13), its plunger (diagram 1, #14), and its spring (diagram 1, #15).
- Push the magazine release button (diagram 1, #18) down as far as possible with a small tool and unscrew the magazine catch (diagram 1, #16). This will free the two parts along with their spring (diagram 1, #17).
- The front push pin (diagram 1, #1A) can be removed on most rifles by pulling the pin all the way to its release position and then inserting a small tool or wire from the barrel side of the pin through the hole in it. This will depress the detent (diagram 1, #34) and its spring (diagram 1, #33) and allow you to pull the pin on out. Be careful not to lose the spring and detent; they're under tension. If the push pin does not have a hole in it for the wire to be inserted through, it will be necessary to insert an L-shaped tool down the pin groove and depress the detent so the pin can be pulled free. This tool can be made by grinding a small L wrench down to a flat bar on its short end.
- The stock (diagram 1, #32A) can be removed by unscrewing the screw (diagram 1, #26) at its rear. This will also release the rear pin detent and its spring, which in turn will free the rear push (diagram 1, #35).
- The buffer tube (diagram 1, #37) can be unscrewed on most models of the AR-15. On some rifles (especially military weapons), a pin (diagram 1, #36) may have to be drifted out to allow the tube to be screwed. If the tube has Loctite or similar material on it, it may be necessary to dissolve it with acetone.
- The buffer is best left assembled. However, most buffer caps are held in place with a drift pin. Removal of this pin frees the cap, which can be removed so the rubber pads and metal weights inside can be taken out. Care should be taken in replacing these so the spacers and weights are alternated.
- On old-style rifles (without the trapdoor on the stock), the rear swivel (diagram 1, #31, #32) can be removed and disassembled by drifting out its pins (diagram 1, #28, #30).
- On rifles with a trapdoor stock, the lower screw can be removed to separate the door assembly from the stock and to free the rear swivel.
- On the telescoping stock, the rear of the stock can be removed from the buffer tube by levering up the spring-loaded bolt that holds its release handle down. This will allow the stock to be slid off the buffer. The latch assembly on these rifles is better left in place, but the bolt can be screwed off by drifting out the pin holding it in place. Unscrewing the bolt will free the spring, lever, and screw in the latch.
- To remove the trigger guard (diagram 1, #41), use a small tool to depress the front pin (which is spring loaded) so that it releases the front of the guard. Next, drift out the rear roll pin (diagram 1, #40). Be very gentle in drifting out this pin because the "ears" holding it in place are easily broken.
- The magazines should be disassembled occasionally for cleaning and lubrication. On metal magazines, the metal base on the bottom of the magazine slides out. Some magazines require a small tool to release the plate, which may be held in place by pressure from the spring. Newer plastic magazines generally have a catch somewhere on their sides, which can be released with a screwdriver or similar tool. When removing the bottom plate from a plastic magazine, be careful not to overflex it, which might deform or even crack it.
- The spring inside the magazine is under pressure and will pop partway out after the floorplate is removed. Note the orientation of the spring (it has a front and back, top and bottom) before jiggling it the rest of the way out of the magazine. The follower will come out with the spring and should not be removed from it. Again, carefully note the orientation of the follower and the spring in case the spring comes loose from the follower. The magazine will not feed properly if the spring and/or follower are inserted backward. When reassembling the magazine, jiggle the spring back into place after properly aligning the follower and spring.
- Slide the floorplate back into place so that the printing can be seen on the outside of the bottom of the magazine. Be sure the base is secure and won't come loose.

For reassembly tips, see Chapter 12.

## DISASSEMBLY OF THE M203 GRENADE LAUNCHER

The disassembly of the M203 grenade launcher is pretty straightforward. As with the rifle, the less disassembly done beyond fieldstripping, the better. Proceed as follows to fieldstrip the weapon:

- Loosen the mounting screw and remove the quadrant sight assembly from the carrying handle of the rifle.
- Remove the barrel assembly by pushing the barrel latch and moving the barrel forward until it hits the barrel stop. The barrel can now be freed by shoving a cleaning rod into through a ventilation hole on the

handguard (generally the fourth hole to the rear of the muzzle) and depressing the barrel stop. Once this is done, slide the barrel forward and off its rail.

- Remove the handguard by pulling back on the M16's slip ring and rotating the handguard up and back. (On some rifles, the handguard spring is very tight, dictating the need to employ a screwdriver or similar screw to jockey the ring back enough to free the handguard.)
- This is all the disassembly necessary to clean the weapon. However, it is easy to remove the grenade launcher from the barrel of the rifle by simply cutting the wire at the front of the unit (just behind the rifle's front sight) *if* the wire is present, then unscrewing the two screws, one on the left and the other on the right, which hold the mounting bracket in place just behind the front sight of the rifle. Once these screws are removed, the front of the rail can be rotated downward to go forward under the rifle's front sight assembly and then the unit will come free when the rear of the mount clears the narrower portion of the rifle barrel.

The delicate nature of the trigger group, plus the difficulty in reassembling it (and easily lost parts) dictate that it only be disassembled by a gunsmith or armorer.

Remounting and reassembly is basically a reverse of the above procedures:

- Slide the rail back onto the rifle barrel.
- Secure the rail with the bracket and two screws.
- Install the barrel onto the rail by pressing the barrel stop and sliding the barrel reward toward the receiver.
- Lock the barrel by moving it rearward until it closes with a click.
- Reinstall the handguard by first slipping its forward end under the bracket of the front sight assembly, then pulling back the slip ring and levering the rear of the handguard down. Release the slip ring and it should slide over the handguard (if it doesn't quite clear the handguard, pressing down on the handguard will generally get it positioned so the ring will snap in place over it).
- Place the quadrant sight back onto the rifle.

## CLEANING AND LUBRICATING THE M203

After the grenade launcher has been fired, or if it has been idle for a long time, it should be carefully cleaned and lubricated before being used again or stored away. As with the rifle, the best cleaner and lubricant (and the one used by the U.S. military) is Breakfree CLP. Following are the steps to clean the grenade launcher after fieldstripping it as outlined above (i.e., by removing the barrel; the handguard and rail can be left attached to the rifle if time is limited):

- To clean the bore, attach a clean, dry rag to the cleaning thong and thoroughly moisten the rag with CLP or other cleaner.
- Pull the rag through the bore several times.
- Attach the bore brush to the thong and pull it through the bore several times.
- Follow this with more rags moistened with CLP.

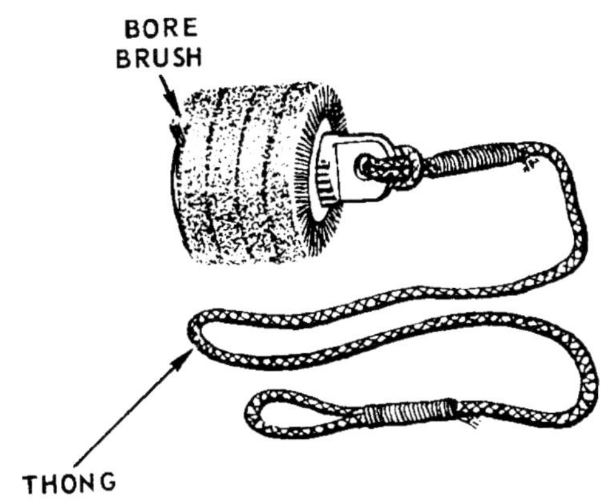


The M203's large, pull-through bore brush.

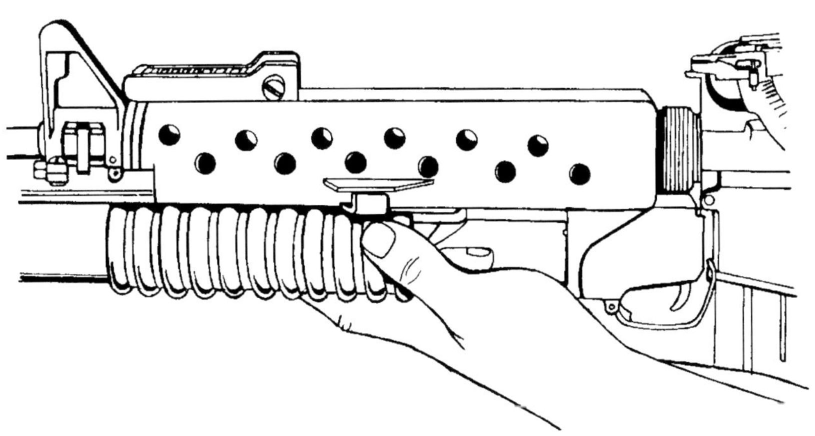

The M203 barrel release is located to the left and above the barrel.

- Pull dry rags through the bore, and inspect each rag as it is removed. The bore is clean when a dry rag remains unfouled after being pulled through.
- Finally, pull a rag lightly moistened with CLP through the bore to leave a light coat of lubricant inside the barrel.
- Clean the face of the breech insert with a patch and CLP.
- Remove excess CLP with dry rags.
- Lubricate the breech with a new, light coat of CLP.
- Use a brush and dry rags to clean all the other parts and surfaces of the grenade launcher.
- Apply a very light coat of CLP to the outside of the launcher. In dusty or desert environments, this step may be skipped in order to avoid contamination of the firearm by grit and dirt.
- Clean the safety mechanism with CLP, rub it clean with rags, then relubricate with a very light application of CLP.

****

With proper maintenance and care, the AR-15 rifle will last longer than its owner.

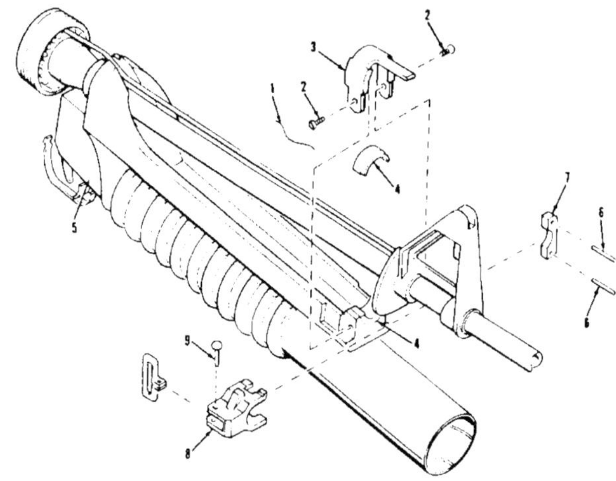

The M203 assembly is held in place by a mounting bracket attached by two screws.

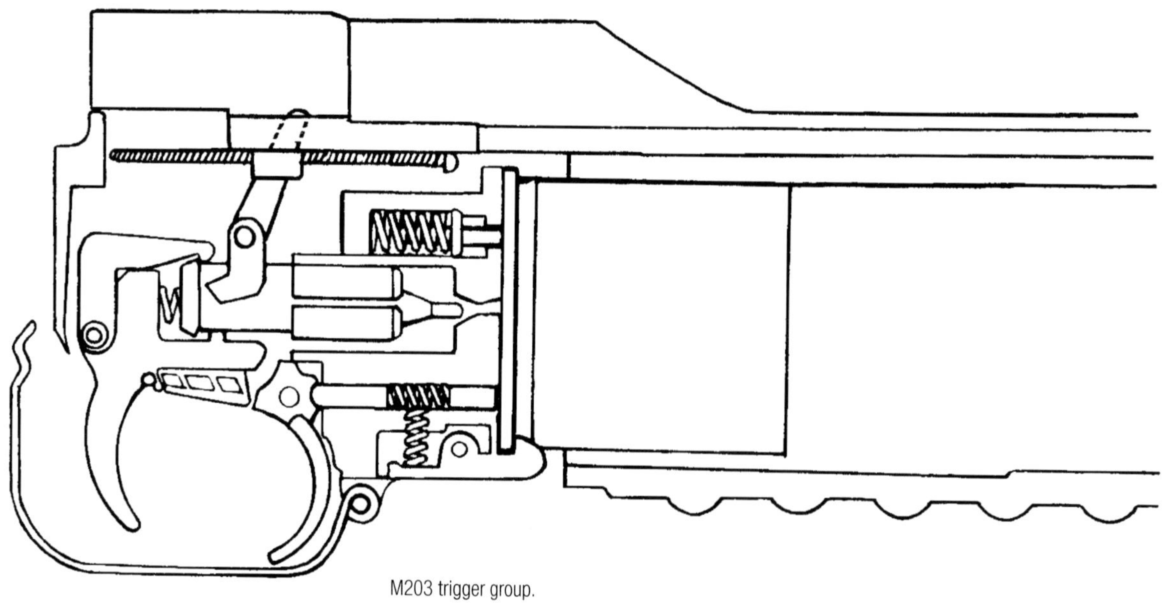

M203 trigger group.

# Chapter 12

# Assembling the AR-15

There are a lot of reasons a shooter might want to build an AR-15. For one, building a gun, especially a one-of-a-kind rifle or a tack-driving target gun, can make a shooter pretty proud of himself. In addition, it's possible to create AR-15 variations that aren't readily available on the market and, in effect, make a custom rifle that's suited to the owner's individual needs rather than a compromise dictated by the greatest number in the marketplace.

Owners of automatic versions of the AR-15 can benefit greatly from a little do-it-yourself work. Since the lower receiver carries the automatic fire mechanism and is the part that must be registered, building a few upper receiver/barrel assemblies can make it possible for the permit holder to "own" the equivalent of several automatic weapons while paying the tax and doing the paperwork for only one selective-fire gun.

One shooter might, for example, own an automatic AR-15 with a regular-length barrel. By building a few upper assemblies he could in effect have six automatic weapons: a short-barreled carbine, a heavy-barreled machine gun, a long-barreled sniper rifle, a submachine gun in 9mm or .45 ACP, and a .22 LR with a conversion kit.

Note that Brownells offers a 9mm magazine adapter that correctly locates Colt 9mm magazines in a .223 lower receiver, thereby doing away with the need to drill and pin an adapter in place (as is done with the standard Colt 9mm guns). This makes it possible to convert a .223 rifle to use a 9mm upper assembly with a minimum of trouble and no gunsmithing work or alterations to the lower receiver for about $120.

Those who own semiauto-only AR-15s can do much the same thing, especially with non-Colt models that have lower receivers with front and rear push pins. Again, shooters can realize quite a lot of savings from what the equivalent arsenal of separate rifles would cost.

Those who build their own rifles will also be able to

Do-it-yourself rifle builders can create one-of-a-kind guns to suit their tastes. This oddity combines an M203 handguard with a 20-inch barrel and a telescoping stock. The upper receiver was originally an A1 surplus part that had part of the carrying handle broken off. The builder cut off the front sight base and mounted a Weaver rail to the gun to complete his "target" rifle.

A do-it-yourself "impossible" gun built by the author. What appears to be a silencer is actually a barrel shroud originally offered by E&L Manufacturing for Heckler & Koch rifles (with an AR-15 barrel now nestled inside it). The stock was created from a Choate M1 carbine stock. Inside is a military .22 LR adapter whose magazine fits inside a standard 20-round magazine. Because the .22 adapter has its own recoil spring, the buffer tube is not needed for the rifle to function.

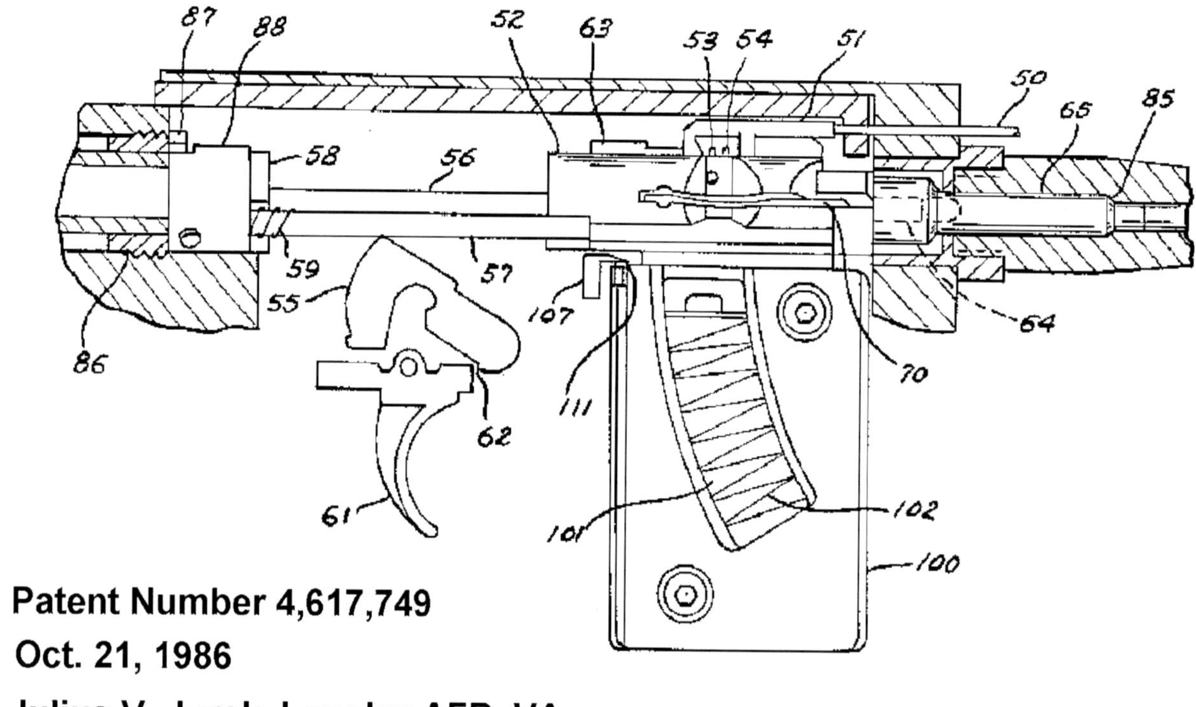


The .22 LR conversion has been popular with inventors and shooters alike. Here's the patent drawing for one such variation created by Julius V. Jurek.

do a lot of the repair work on them when they have to (rare with AR-15s, but it may be called for). Because many parts on the AR-15 are interchangeable, most repair work consists of replacing parts rather than repairing them. Knowing how to do such replacement work can save a lot of money and might be a lifesaver during a battle.

Building a rifle will not save most shooters much, if any, money over purchasing a complete rifle or barrel/receiver assemblies from such companies as SGW, Armalite/Eagle, Bushmaster/Quality, and others offering ready-built rifles or barrel/receiver assemblies. Building an AR-15 should be approached more as a hobby or a way of creating a special AR-15 not otherwise available or to update or modify an existing rifle with new grip, handguards, stock, flash suppresser, heavy barrel, or whatever.

> Is it legal to build a firearm without a permit?
> Usually.
> Maybe.
> You can't be too careful.

The federal government does not place limits on the firearms people can make for themselves provided they are not outside the limits of firearms laws—i.e., minimum barrel length of 16 inches, minimum overall length of 26 inches, and semiautomatic. Armorers working for federal agencies or the military can make a selective-fire weapon; at the time of the writing everyone else is out of luck.

Those building a rifle are wise to check state and local laws because some areas have passed abusive statutes making it illegal to own military-style rifles. A call to city and state attorneys to find out the laws beforehand can save a lot of heartache. (Do not contact the police for such advice. Many departments are ignorant enough of the actual laws applying to firearms and may inadvertently give erroneous information, which can get a person into legal hot water later on).

The firearm should be for the person building it unless he is the holder of a federal firearms license (FFL). This is because the Gun Control Act of 1968 was so poorly written that the term "dealer" is never well defined, nor does the act come to grips with what a firearms manufacturer is. Therefore, a person building a few rifles and selling them to friend might be seen by a gung-ho BATF agent as a dealer operating without a legal license. (Conversely, at the time of this writing, someone probably would not be considered to be a manufacturer or dealer if he just assembled a rifle or two and in a year or so traded them off or sold them at a slight profit.) These rules only apply to someone making a *complete* rifle with a lower receiver. All other parts (except for those used only in an automatic) can be purchased and sold without any special permits.

To build a complete rifle, the lower receiver must be purchased by someone holding an FFL. Most gun shop owners are willing to do this if the builder will pay them a little money for the extra work. For those who don't wish to build many rifles, this is probably the best way to go.

For those who want to make more rifles and possibly even sell some, an FFL is a must, and (according to the current reading of things by BATF) a manufacturer's license may also be needed. Currently these are pretty easy to obtain; contact the BATF office in Washington, D.C., for further information on how to do this.

Because the AR-15 was designed to take advantage of modern manufacturing techniques, it is relatively easy for a person to build an AR-15 or any of its variants from parts. The AR-15 was designed to allow normal manufacturing tolerances without degrading the performance of the rifle when parts are put together without extensive fitting.

Although many people are a little leery of tackling such a project, in fact almost anyone who can chew gum and work a screwdriver at the same time can probably assemble an AR-15 from a pile of parts. All the same, a rifle that doesn't function properly is very, very dangerous. If a person has any doubts about tackling this project, he'd be wise to find someone to help him.

The time it takes to build an AR-15 from parts will vary according to the abilities of the assembler and the extra work required if a few parts have to be hand-fitted together or don't function properly. The main thing is to take enough time to do it right. Anyone who doesn't have the patience to spend several evenings building a rifle should forget it. It isn't a job to rush through; the end result could well be a piece of very dangerous junk.

In general, it's best to allow a week of evenings to get the job done, though experienced or very handy builders can assemble a rifle in an hour or so if they have all the right parts and everything fits the way it should. Those who decide to build a rifle (or a barrel/upper receiver assembly) should first collect the parts they need before the actual assembly begins. Nothing is as frustrating as getting halfway through the building procedure and then having to wait a week for the last part to arrive from a distant mail-order company.

It's wise to avoid "bargain" kits made of military surplus or components of dubious quality. The best bet is to order a complete kit from Bushmaster/Quality, SGW/Olympic, DPMS, Armalite/Eagle, or one of the other companies that carry them. For "bargain basement" kits, check out SARCO; its kits don't offer the range of choices the others do, but it often has a "generic" rifle kit that is less expensive than those from most other sources. For those interested in creating special-purpose rifles, both SARCO and Gun Parts have catalogs worth investigating. For those in a hurry, most of these companies will take credit card orders over the phone. If an FFL is required, it can be mailed overnight for just a little extra, and delivery from the company can be expedited for a bit more as well.

On occasion, parts from military bases are sold as "scrap metal." Although there may be a few parts in such assortments that are in good condition and were perhaps only discarded because they failed to fit some gun an armorer was working on, generally these parts are too worn or otherwise imperfect to be reliable. The bad news is that some unscrupulous folks sell these parts at gun shows or even through shady businesses. Buying one of these "bargain" parts will only cause trouble and headaches; be sure you're buying from a reputable dealer.

Some parts have also been made of stampings that are less than perfect as well. Inspect parts carefully to determine whether they have sharp, machined-looking edges and surfaces. If a part, especially in the trigger group, has less definition in its edges or looks a little melted, has bubbles on its flat surfaces, or is rusty, then it's best avoid purchasing it. Even new-looking parts may be rejects. Be careful what you purchase.

Even though it's wise to stick with factory parts, it is sometimes possible to "self-manufacture" them. This is especially true with the roll pins, push pins, springs, and the like. Small rods can be used to make substitute roll pins, and trigger and hammer springs can easily be fabricated—but parts like firing pins and critical bolt parts should be left to the pros.

Even though it's also possible to leave a few parts out of do-it-yourself rifles, this generally isn't wise, either in terms of safety or ease of use—especially if you're planning to resell the firearm. The rifle will operate without the bolt catch, dust cover, forward- assist assembly, and the front and rear sights (if the shooter uses a scope). Doing without these parts can produce a slight savings, but it's usually cheaper to buy complete kits than a bunch of parts lacking a few of the above, so this isn't as great an option as one might imagine.

Two parts that are best purchased at the same time are the upper and lower receivers. The Colt Sporter semiauto upper and lower receivers don't mate with the military-style receivers, and there is some size difference between various manufacturers. So while it's possible to "mix and match, " it's generally better to buy both at the same time.

Although the rear push-pin hole size is pretty much standard (I say that having spent hours getting various halves to match up properly despite the theoretical "standard" size of 0.250 inch used by all manufacturers of AR-15-style receivers), this isn't the case with the front push-pin holes. A very few early Armalite AR-15s had a front push-pin diameter of 0.315 inch; this was later standardized to Colt's "small hole" front push-pin opening of 0.246 inch in diameter. Many Sporters have a larger hole of 0.316 inch in diameter with both the A1 and A2 receivers; however, this isn't a hard and fast rule (some, apparently made as parts ran out, overlap in the overall types of receivers, including the size of the front push-pin holes). For this reason, a bit of caution must be exercised when exchanging uppers and lowers.

That's not to say it isn't possible to mix the receiver halves. Enterprising AR-15 owners and accessory manufacturers have made it possible to place a military-style upper or lower receiver with the opposite number from a Colt Sporter. The trick is using the right offset adapter pin rather than a front push pin. These are available from several dealers, including Bushmaster.

The offset pin adapts a Colt lower receiver (having a large hole) to a military-specification upper receiver (with a smaller pivot pinhole); these cost $5.95 each, and they have to be positioned just right to work. The reverse offset pin adapts a Colt upper receiver (large hole) to a military-style (small pivot pin) receiver and it has a small metal shim ring that has to be positioned just so; its cost is $15.95.

With one or the other of these pin adapters, it is possible to fit nearly any upper to any lower, though on occasion doing so will require a little hand-fitting work (and there are combinations that don't work due to slight differences in manufacturing tolerances).

For those who want to use several upper barrel/receiver assemblies with one lower, the military-style receiver has an important plus: the forward pushpin. These allow the user to take the gun apart rapidly if he wishes to store or transport it or to quickly place a new upper receiver barrel assembly on the original lower receiver. Even here it is possible to purchase a push pin that replaces the double screw bolt in the front pivot hole on preban Colt Sporter rifles and carbines. This pin isn't "captured" like the M16-style pin; it is held in place by a spring-loaded ball bearing and comes completely free of the gun when pushed out. However, this is still an ideal system that makes quick exchange of receiver uppers possible (with just a bit of care not to lose the pin). These pins are available from Bushmaster and other parts dealers for $9.95.

## PARTS AND TOOLS NEEDED FOR A DO-IT-YOURSELF AR-15

### Parts

To build a complete AR-15, the following parts and assemblies are required:

- Lower receiver (military style with forward push pin is usually best).
- Upper receiver (military style with push pins and forward assist is usually best); A1 styles are cheaper and A2 styles are also a bit harder to assemble.
- Forward-assist assembly (if you have an A1- or A2-style upper receiver). Two types are available—round and teardrop shaped. Both work equally well, so purchasers should get the less expensive one or the one that looks better.
- Lower receiver parts set (semiauto style unless you're working for a government agency).
- Complete bolt.

- Bolt carrier with screws and key.
- Charging handle.
- Firing pin (this part should be chromed).
- Firing pin retaining pin.
- Bolt cam pin.
- Buffer tube (not needed with a Commando or "shorty" telescoping-stock kit that contains this part).
- Buffer spring (this comes with most Commando stock kits).
- Buffer (this usually comes with Commando stock kits; a special one is needed with the standard stock).
- Stock endplate (not needed with Commando stock); this may come with the stock.
- Rear swivel (this may come with the stock; not needed for the Commando stock).
- Rifle stock; several different styles are available, including the telescoping stock, E2 finger hook, thumbhole sport style, and others.
- Pistol grip (standard, A2, trapdoor, and other styles are available).
- Pistol grip screw and lock washer.
- Barrel handguards (of the several styles available, the A2 is generally preferred; handguards with aluminum liners are the best).
- Rear sight assembly (must match the upper receiver).
- Front sight assembly (may already be with the barrel).
- Gas tube and roll pin.
- Barrel (a number of lengths are available, as are heavy barrels and stainless steel barrels; a chrome lining, if available, is a good idea because stainless-steel barrels retain heat and are not ideal for rapid firing or automatic versions of the AR-15).
- Barrel snap ring.
- Barrel weld spring.
- Barrel slip ring (also know as the delta ring); get a tapered ring if possible.
- Flash suppressor (the government style is cheapest and works well, though many prefer those with built-in compensators).
- Flash suppressor lock ring (this may not be necessary with some flash hiders).
- Front swivel (this is unnecessary unless a sling will be used).
- Front swivel roll pin.

For military/law enforcement armorers (or others who can legally create a selective-fire version of the AR-15) or those who need to repair a registered machine gun, most manufacturers, including Colt and Bushmaster, will sell specific parts or kits for these purposes. It should be remembered that for the AR-15 to fire in the auto mode, more than just the burst or automatic fire trigger group and an auto sear are needed. Also required are the proper bolt and firing pin as well as a hole for the auto sear cross pin. Note that BATF rulings sometimes consider these automatic parts, sans rifle, as automatic weapons in and of themselves, especially if the holder also has an AR-15. For this reason, it is unwise to purchase such parts if you do not have a legal reason to own or build a selective-fire weapon.

### Tools

There are few tools that are really required for assembling an AR-15. One handy tool is an M16 armorer's wrench. It allows tightening or loosening the barrel nut, the flash suppressor, some styles of buffer tubes, and a few other odds and ends. This wrench usually can be bought from the place where you buy your parts. The best of these is Peace River Arms' Universal Armorer's Wrench, which costs $25 and is considerably easier to use than most other similar tools. For those assembling telescoping stock versions of the AR-15, the special wrench designed to tighten the buffer tube lock nut in place is also useful.

Barrel vise jaw blocks are very handy. In the past, aluminum blocks were used, but these were poor at keeping the barrel from rotating and also required several different blocks for different barrel sizes. Peace River Arms recently introduced a better solution in the form of a block that mounts on the upper receiver. This does away with the need for several different barrel blocks and

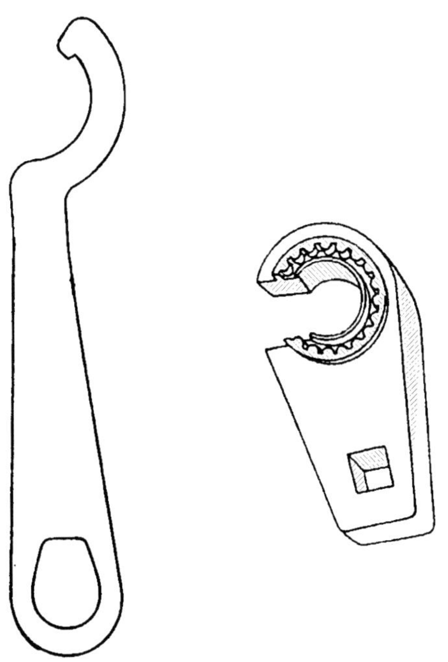

Wrench for tightening buffer tube lock nut on telescoping stock.

Peace River Arms' no-slip armorer's wrench.

Peace River Arms' Universal Armorer's Wrench.

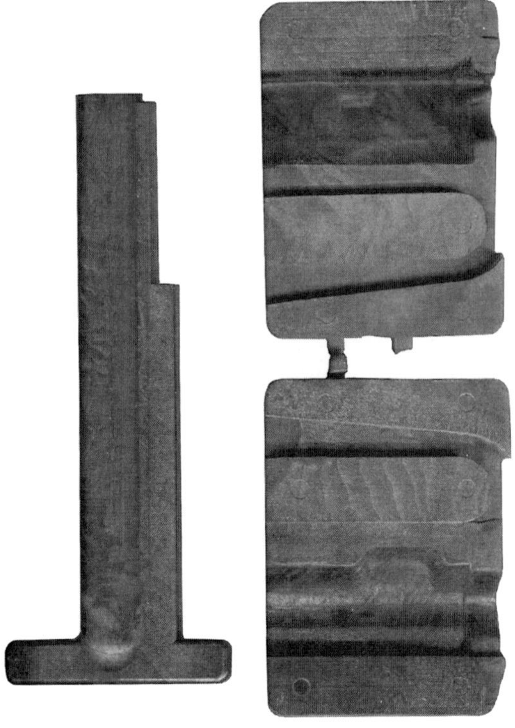

The excellent receiver block and insert marketed by Peace River Arms.

also overcomes all the problems of the barrel rotating as it is tightened to the receiver or flash hiders are mounted on it. For those planning to work on or assemble an AR-15, the $35 price tag on one of these is money well spent.

There aren't many screws in the AR-15, but unlike those on most other guns, standard screwdrivers will work on the few that are there. Take extra care with the screw that mounts the rifle stock to the buffer tube; this one is easy to mess up when tightening.

A set of chamber gauges is practically essential for those buying a barrel, used gun, or reloading ammunition for a rifle. But for those just assembling one AR-15, the easiest route is often to take the gun to a gunsmith and have him check it out; if the chamber is too tight, he'll also be able to ream it out for a small price.

For those assembling several rifles, it's wise to buy a set of headspace gauges from Brownells or Bushmaster/Quality Parts; gauges cost around $20 each, and a set of three is ideal. These gauges can be used to tell whether the chamber is the proper size or not.

When a rifle is fired a number of times the headspace may change, and new rifles often have tight chambers. Normally, the first situation isn't a problem unless hot loads are fired; then the chamber/bolt may become so battered that the chamber actually stretches and the bolt lock-up lugs become deformed. In such a case, excessive headspace may result and a brass may rupture, trashing the rifle and possibly injuring the shooter. Too tight a chamber creates problems in chambering and extraction, resulting in a gun that often jams or otherwise fails to function properly.

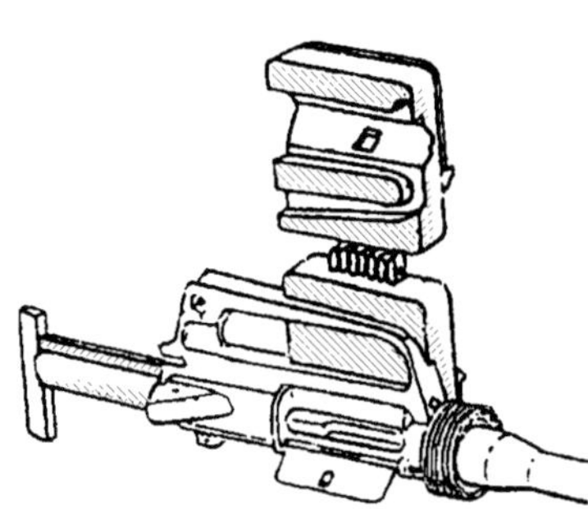

Peace River Arms' receiver clamp wraps around an upper receiver to hold it in place in a vise.

Headspace gauges can be used to discover such problems before they become serious. There are three basic types: GO, NO-GO, and FIELD gauges (some gunsmiths creating target rifles may have additional gauges, but these are not readily available on the market). The GO gauge is cut to the minimum chamber size, the FIELD is the intermediate size that is the upper limit to a

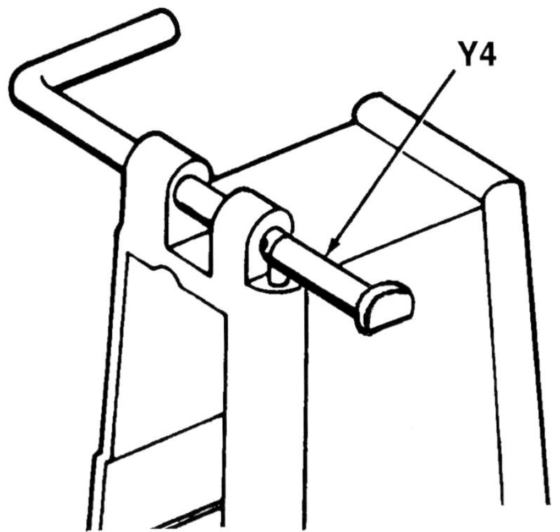


A tool with the diameter of the front pushpin hole can speed up installation of the pushpin by holding the spring and plunger in place as the pin is slid into its hole.

FIELD, GO, and NO-GO gauges.

safe chamber size, and the NO-GO is beyond the safe limit of chamber size. Ideally, a gun only just closes on the GO gauge but not on the other two. A gun is still safe to shoot if it accepts the FIELD gauge but should be monitored with a NO-GO gauge, and hot loads should never be fired in it.

It is important to remember that if a gun accepts the NO-GO gauge, it has excessive headspace and is unsafe to shoot.

To use the gauges, select one and drop it into the rifle chamber and gently push a bolt and bolt carrier over it. By viewing the bolt from the bottom (ideally with the lower receiver removed so that the bolt carrier can be gently pushed forward by hand), it's possible to see whether the lugs rotate into their locked position in the barrel. The bolt should not be forced; only gentle pressure should be applied to see whether or not the bolt will lock with the gauge in place.

With the GO gauge, the bolt should close and lock with the gauge in the chamber. Provided the other two gauges don't permit the bolt to close, this means that the chamber will accommodate any properly sized ammo down to the minimum dimensions for the .223/5.56mm and that the rounds will chamber easily (provided the chamber is reasonably clean when you're shooting).

If the action does not close on the GO gauge, the chamber has not been set to a correct depth or the bolt is oversized. (Changing bolts may help, but generally, the problem will be in the chamber size.) Although the rifle that fails to close over a GO gauge might accept some cartridges when its chamber is clean, chances of its not chambering some rounds are very great. (Note that target guns may shoot very well with such a chamber, but these guns must be cleaned religiously to maintain reliability and cartridges must be carefully resized.)

In general, avoid purchasing a barrel or rifle that does not accept the GO gauge. Such a weapon certainly should not be used in a combat situation, where failure to chamber a round could have fatal consequences. Fortunately, it's easy to ream out the tiny bit of metal left in the chamber of such barrels. This can be done by a gunsmith or, for those with some good metalworking skills, a finish chamber reamer can be purchased from Brownells for $60 (follow the instructions that come with it and take care to work very slowly to avoid removing too much metal from the chamber.)

The NO-GO gauge measures the maximum head space of the chamber. The bolt should *not* close on this gauge. If the bolt does lock, then the chamber is too deep or the bolt is undersized. Generally, it's best to avoid purchasing a barrel that accepts the NO-GO gauge. (Some gunsmiths might be able to correct the problem with an oversized bolt, though the chances of coming across such a bolt are pretty remote unless a large number are available to try out.)

It's also possible that a barrel that chambers the NO-GO gauge is set at the maximum chamber length. This type of barrel could be used by those creating special target ammunition, but such barrels are not ideal for general use, and hot loads should not be fired in them since they might quickly create a dangerous amount of head space in the chamber. Brass fired from a rifle with the maximum headspace will stretch quite a bit, greatly shortening the reloading life of the empties.

If a gun closes on the FIELD gauge, it will generally be safe to fire it with regular loads, and the chances of its jamming because of an oversized brass cartridge are minimal. However, hot loads shouldn't be employed in such a gun; they could slowly cause the dimensions of the chamber and bolt to enlarge. With such a rifle, it's wise to check the chamber with a NO-GO gauge every few hundred rounds to be sure that it hasn't become enlarged enough to be dangerous.

Finally, it should also be noted that it's not wise to switch a bolt from one barrel to another without checking headspace. The changeover might create a dangerous chamber space.

When purchasing a barrel (or a used gun), in addition to checking the head space use a bright light to check for any rust, "dings," craters, or other flaws that don't belong in a good barrel. If the inside of the barrel looks bad, cleaning it will work wonders: more than one nonchromed barrel that has suffered minor rust has proven pretty accurate when cleaned out. Often what looks like a rusted barrel is merely full of dirt and powder residue. It's wise to also sight down a used barrel from several angles to be sure it isn't bent.

Once a barrel is clean, the grooves inside it should be fairly sharp rather than smooth and extremely rounded. If "ballooning" can be seen on the inside of the barrel when peering down it from the muzzle (with the ejection port open in the case of rifles), it's best to avoid purchasing it. It has likely been fired with a bullet or dirt stuck in the barrel, making it almost worthless and probably unsafe.

If the inside of the barrel looks good, the outside can become pretty shabby before it hurt's functioning or accuracy. Minor rust and even major pitting can be removed with a wire brush or steel wool and the exterior repainted or refinished. Handguards will cover much of the barrel as well. Blemishes on the barrel can be used for dickering over the price but shouldn't be a cause for concern unless the barrel is in extremely bad condition.

Chrome lining in the barrel and chamber can make them easier to clean and maintain (it is generally stated that barrels are chromed in the writing that gives the chambering and so forth for AR-15 barrels). The chromed chamber also reduces the chances of rounds jamming in it when it gets dirty from poorly burning ammunition or inadequate cleaning of the rifle.

## OTHER CONSIDERATIONS

### Barrel Lengths

If you're building a carbine version of the AR-15, several styles of 16-inch barrels are available. Those with a permit to own an automatic weapon can usually mount a 10-, 11-, or 14-inch barrel and receiver assembly on their gun without running into more red tape (but they should be sure). For those who want a very compact option, these short barrels may be a boon. However, the short barrels are loud and the bullets don't have nearly as great a velocity, making guns of rather short range for most purposes, especially self-defense. With heavier barrels, some of the handiness of the short barrel is sacrificed, but the barrels also take longer to overheat and therefore may be a useful option with the 10- or 11-inch barrel for those with a selective-fire gun.

Probably the least useful is the 10-1/2- or 11-inch barrel with a flash hider welded to it to bring it to the legal minimum length. The short barrel produces an awful lot of flash and noise, as well as sending the bullet out at a much lower velocity than that of a regular barrel. A better bet is to purchase a 16-inch barrel and (depending on legal considerations) add one of the CAR-15-style flash hiders designed by Choate Machine and Tool and by Quality Parts. These fit down over barrel with only a short flash-hider section over the muzzle, providing the Commando look while retaining the velocity of the 16-inch barrel. (As noted elsewhere in this book, this may no longer be an option due to the federal assault weapon ban.)

Regardless of the barrel length and flash hider, all the Commando and short carbine barrels need a special short handguard and gas tube, so be sure to get the correct handguard when buying one. Note that Quality Parts/Bushmaster and Armalite both depart from the standard Commando handguard size with some or all of these models. Some Bushmaster guns employ a standard-size AR-15 handguard, using a secondary front sight assembly to hold it in place (with a sightless gas block under the handguard in the normal position). Armalite carbines have a unique handguard designed specifically for them; this unit is 2 inches longer than the standard Commando. The plus of the extended handguards is more one of convenience and appearance than actual functioning; however, those with longer arms may appreciate the extra length these afford on carbine versions of the AR-15.

Heavy 20-inch or longer barrels offer a little more accuracy, especially with a bipod, and are a useful option for those building a target or varminting rifle. Remember that even without the "heavy" designation, the extralong 24-inch barrel is heavy and may add several pounds to the rifle, especially with a free-floating metal handguard. Those planning to carry their AR-15s in the field should consider just how much weight they want to add to their firearm. In general, free-floating a standard-weight barrel provides a lot of accuracy while keeping the weight manageable—something those who want accuracy without the feel of an anchor may wish to consider.

### Flash Suppressers and Muzzle Brakes

Some sort of flash suppresser should be mounted on the rifle to protect the muzzle. Government flash suppressers are cheaper than others and work well, but there are some things they don't do well since they're a compromise—provided you have a preban firearm. For those who own a newer gun, it is possible to mount a muzzle brake (which may be nearly identical to previous flash hiders, since the federal law failed to define exactly what a flash hider is, thereby permitting manufacturers to more or less define it themselves). On postban guns lacking a threaded barrel, it is possible to have a gunsmith thread the barrel and then silver-solder the muzzle break in place, thereby avoiding one of the "deciding factors" that limit what hardware and accessories can be used on a postban gun.

Flash suppressers are available with muzzle brake features (and more than a few muzzle brakes also reduce flash). When choosing a unit, it pays to give a bit of thought to what features you do and do not need (see Chapter 13 for more information on flash suppressers/muzzle compensators).

### Bolt Assembly and Carrier

Those building a selective-fire gun or an upper assembly for a selective-fire gun need to purchase an M16-style bolt carrier that has the same length of metal on the rear top and bottom of the carrier so it will trip the auto sear. All other builders should use the Sporter-style carrier designed for semiauto guns.

Chromed firing pins are about the only type on the market. It's best to avoid any others you may see because the firing pin is an area that picks up some heavy carbon deposits, and the chrome makes it easier to clean. For minimum firing pin carbon deposits, shooters should purchase one of Bob Krieger's Self Cleaning firing pins (cost: $20). These have angled cuts in them that let hot gases blow past rather than depositing carbon fouling on the firing pin as is commonly the case. This makes for much easier cleaning of the rifle and, more important, improves the pin's reliability a bit by making it slower to foul. These special pins are ideal for Commandos with 10- or 11-inch barrels because these guns have extra problems with fouling in this area of the firearm.

The tendency of the AR-15 firing pin to indent primers when a round is chambered demonstrates the fine line between safety and potential disaster, especially should a reloader accidentally substitute pistol primers for rifle primers when "rolling his own" cartridges. In such a case it's possible for a round to be fired by the momentum of the firing pin (though one should note that this is very rare). One aftermarket solution to this slight hazard is the titanium firing pin, which is as strong as steel but considerably lighter, lessening the impact of the pin when a cartridge is chambered.

The catch to this is that making firing pins is a very exacting process. Furthermore, titanium doesn't handle impact over time as well as steel does. So this solution may be less than ideal, given the rarity of the problem in the first place. Some sellers of these pins have also claimed that titanium firing pins offer greater accuracy because the lower mass of the titanium firing pin causes it to ignite a primer faster than a steel firing pin. It is very hard to show this in tests: the difference is minute, given the slight difference in mass. And whether a faster primer

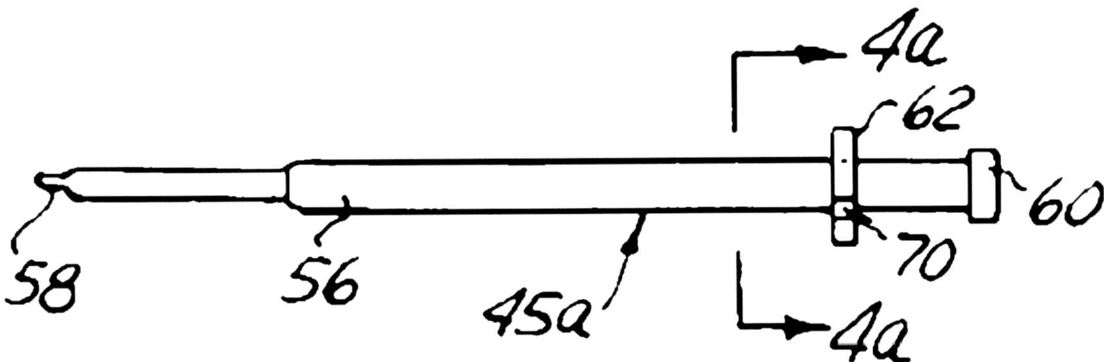


Patent drawing for Bob Krieger's Self Cleaning firing pin design.

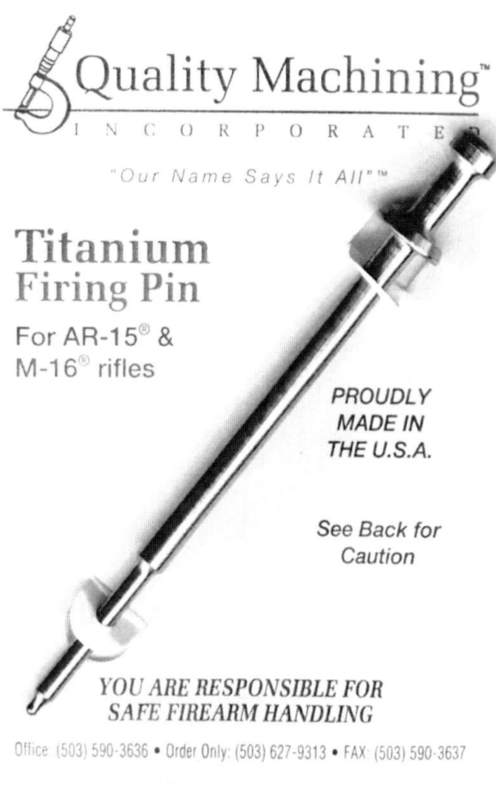


Quality Machining's titanium firing pin.

strike increases accuracy is also a matter for argument. Not surprisingly, then, at least one manufacturer of AR-15-style guns has recommended that buyers avoid the titanium firing pin.

That said, there may be occasions when one would opt for a titanium firing pin, especially if using ammunition with sensitive primers. First choice would be one of the quality titanium firing pins offered by Quality Machining, Inc.

There is some debate as to just how ideal chrome plating is on the exterior of the bolt carrier; many who have worked with chrome carriers suggest that they tend to remove the oil from the grooves in the receiver in which the carrier rides, thereby creating the potential for excess wear or jamming. It seems likely that this is the main reason that military rifles lack chrome plating. (Although I've never seen it, I suspect nickel plating on a bolt carrier would work very well, given the tendency of this material to hold oil in place. Perhaps this is a route to take for those who want to decrease cleaning chores without sacrificing reliability.)

### Receivers

Stainless steel or steel upper/lower receivers are sometimes seen on the market. These are expensive and make the rifle heavier while offering little advantage over the aluminum receivers. Although it seems that a steel receiver would create a safer rifle, this isn't the case with the AR-15 because the bolt locks into the barrel extension. The receivers don't need to be excessively strong to be reliable and, in fact, could probably be made of some new space-age plastic. It's doubtful that this will ever happen in the near future, however: shooters would be a little leery of such a product.

Lefties should consider the Southpaw Receiver offered by Defense Procurement Manufacturing Services for $190. This upper receiver comes with a modified bolt that throws empty brass out the left rather than the right side of the receiver. All other standard parts of the rifle fit onto this receiver, and it's a guaranteed attention getter at most rifle ranges. (Experimenters are talking about the possibility of creating a side-by-side version of the AR-15 rifle with a Southpaw Receiver and a standard receiver, which would enable two rifles to be connected side by side, ejecting their brass in either direction. Such a gun would be heavy and probably would need to be mounted on a tripod due to its weight.)

### Tools and Safety

There are a few other specialized tools for working on the AR-15, but a torque wrench (very useful for mounting the barrel), vise, vise-grip pliers, wire cutter, needle-nosed pliers, regular pliers, files, a wood rasp, drill bits (without the power drill), grinder, hacksaw, small hammer, and a set of files are about the only ones

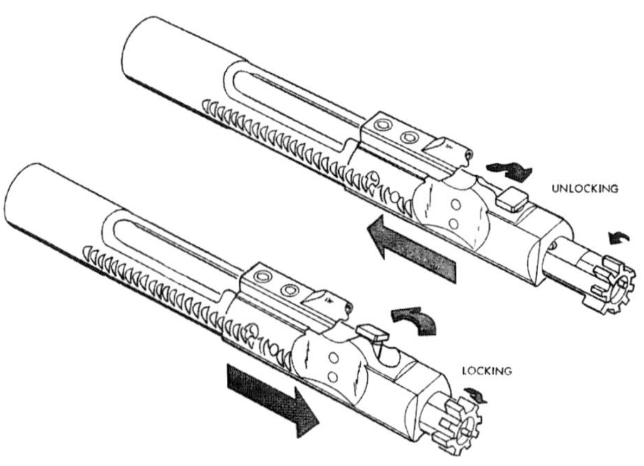


Since the bolt lugs lock into the barrel rather than the receiver itself, an AR-15 can be built around a receiver made of relatively soft material, including aluminum and even plastic.

most hobbyists need. Drift punches are handy to have, but most hobbyists can get by with a nail set and/or several small nails after carefully filing the points flat to create a set of inexpensive drift punches. An ice cube tray or some small plastic containers are a must to keep track of some of the smaller AR-15 parts as the rifle is assembled.

Those who don't wear tempered glasses should invest in safety glasses—and use them rather than losing an eye.

### Fitting and Hole Dimensions

The amount of fitting work needed varies from little to none. Often the worst areas are the small holes in the receiver. Since some manufacturers use a baked-on finish on the receivers, the thickness may vary according to the depth of the finish. This is no big deal except in small holes on the receiver where the finish may make the dimensions small enough to trap a spring or part. Also, these holes are often full of grease and metal chips from the milling done to size the receivers.

Using a small drill bit to ream out the crud in these holes is a good idea so springs and detents don't get trapped in them. Just by holding the drill bit in the fingers, it can be gently rotated to get the dirt out of the holes. A round file is useful for reaming out the pushpin holes in the receiver to get the parts to mate properly: it's very easy to work the soft metal of the receiver with such as file.

Roll pins are often a headache. One good trick is to use oil to coat the hole the pin will be pounded into, reducing the friction enough to make the task easy. If the roll pin is too big, grinding the end to a point may help. On rare occasions it may be necessary to squeeze the pin shut slightly, but this is a tough job, and sometimes pins with a lot of tempering will crack. A small hammer and a drift punch (the type with a small nipple in its center is the best) are good for seating pins.

Care must be exercised to avoid overdoing the hammering, since the receiver is somewhat brittle. That means a mighty Paul Bunyan whack may break off an essential piece of the receiver. A series of gentle taps is preferable, especially with the thin, unsupported metal of the bolt release and trigger guard.

When putting in any pins or roll pins that hold the trigger, hammer, or other parts, one good trick is to use a punch, a nail, or even a part of the rifle that freely fits into the hole. The piece is positioned in place, and the punch (or whatever) is used to hold it there. The pin is then hammered in from the opposite side, securing the part as it pushes out the temporary pin.

### Finish Coats

When working on the rifle, take care not to mar it. Masking or other tape can be put over the surface of the rifle in areas where the tool may mar the finish. A small piece of leather or a plastic bag can also be very useful in protecting parts from being scarred by tools. It's better—and a lot easier in the long run—to take a little time to protect the rifle than to try to touch it up later.

The aluminum in the receiver can't be easily touched up if it gets dinged, but flat paint can make things look a lot better. Most automotive stores have flat black engine paint in spray cans that will work well if the directions on the can are followed carefully. For the best of finishes, Gun Kote is ideal. This produces a good-looking finish and can be applied to the barrel, receiver, or other areas to match them up so that they'll be the same color.

Gun Kote is a phenolic resin base with molybdenum disulfide (a lubricant) suspended in it. It is sprayed on after the metal has been heated to 180 degrees Fahrenheit and then baked in an oven for half an hour at 300 degrees Fahrenheit. This creates a tough coat on the metal similar in appearance to parkerized metal. The real plus is that it can be done in a kitchen without special equipment or working with dangerous chemicals. (The U.S. Navy and Marines often use a material identical to Gun Kote for refinishing their M16 rifles.)

Since the process heats the rifle to a temperature that could melt some plastic parts, it's necessary to remove the stock, pistol grip, handguards, buffer, bolt, and other parts that might be damaged by heat or don't need to be coated. Gun Kote is available from Quality Parts for $10 a can (enough for refinishing three AR-15 rifles).

Steel parts (about everything except the receivers and plastic furniture on the rifle) can be darkened with touch-up gun bluing, also known as cold blue because no heat is needed to use it. Though the color (a dark blue-black) may not match as well as the original, it's generally close enough to hide any scratches or nicks from all but minute inspection. Outers offers the best cold-bluing compound, available in most gun stores. Touch-up blue is especially useful to make the roll pins look right after you've gotten them into place.

After using touch-up bluing, wipe it off carefully and oil the part to prevent rust. The part should be checked several days after its been blued. If there's rust, lightly rubbing the part with some fine steel wool and oil will cure the problem.

Loctite is a slow-setting glue that can be very useful for making sure that parts don't come apart during the hammering of recoil. A drop can be especially useful on the stock screws, buffer tube (on telescoping stocks), and the pistol grip screw. Just a little drop is all that's needed; allow 24 hours for it to harden. Loctite can be dissolved with acetone (nail polish remover), but it's better to avoid using it than to join parts that might need to be taken apart later.

### M16 Parts

Occasionally, a semiauto AR-15 parts kit will come with a military-style hammer (with a hook on its rear spur), which may be coupled with a selective-fire disconnector (with a tail that extends back to the safety) and/or an M16 auto selector rather than a standard safety. Any of these can be dangerous because they may allow a slam-fire to occur, and if BATF is out hunting scalps, the gun may be viewed as an illegal selective-fire weapon. So take care to avoid these parts.

If an M16-style part somehow is received in a semiauto kit, modifying it isn't very complicated, but it does take time, and great care must be taken not to damage it. The modification entails cutting through the hardened surface of the part, making it considerably less durable, so it's generally better have the parts altered by a gunsmith. Or, cheaper yet, simply purchase new parts and then trade the old ones at a gun show. But those who wish to can alter the parts with a grinder wheel, blowtorch, and some other tools found in most shops. The easiest work consists of grinding off the disconnector tail, and in theory this is all that's needed to avoid having a selective-fire rifle. Grind slowly and dip the part in water from time to time to avoid overheating it and ruining the metal's temper.

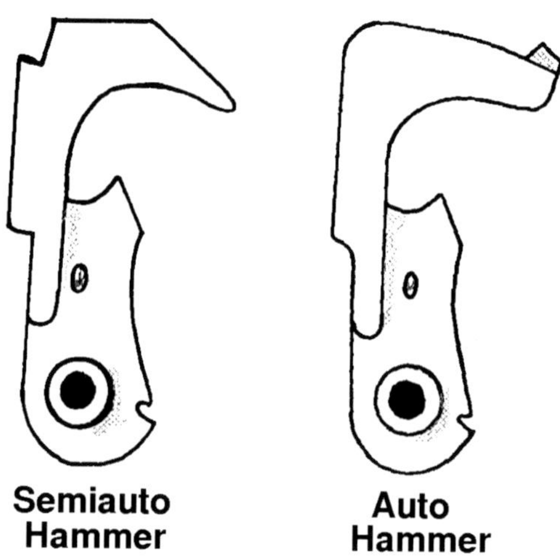


Caption: The difference between the semiauto (left) and automatic (right) versions of the AR-15 hammer are easy to see.

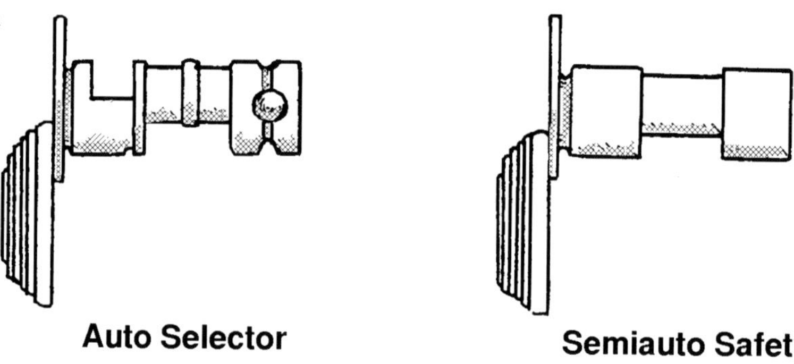


The semiauto (right) and automatic selector.

The next alteration is to grind the rear hook from the hammer's head and add a small—and important—cut into its face. The angle of the new cut isn't extremely critical, but take care to get it as close to the semiauto style as possible so that it functions properly. Having an AR-15 semiauto hammer to copy is a big help for getting this right. Again, be careful not to overheat the part while grinding it.

The safety/selector should have the small ridge in the center of its crossbar ground down or filed away. The rest of it must not be altered, or the safety may fail to function.

Next, a small piece of metal should be soldered over the open rear end of the trigger so that it won't accept an extended M16 disconnector. When this is done, take care once again not to overheat the front of the part; wrapping the nose of the trigger in a wet cloth while the rear is soldered is probably the safest way to do this.

The automatic disconnector is easily modified by simply grinding off its "tail" so that it fits in the semiauto trigger.

The bolt carrier has the rear of the firing pin exposed so that it will catch on the cut in the hammer face, locking the bolt open if the disconnector fails. The bolt carrier is constructed of unhardened steel; removing the metal to expose the rear of the firing pin is easily accomplished with a file.

After these alterations are made test the AR-15 for proper functioning. First remove the magazine (checking the chamber to be sure it's empty), place the safety into its FIRE position, retract the charging handle, ease the charging handle about halfway forward, and hold it there. Then depress the trigger. Release the charging handle and, if the work has been done properly, the carrier will lock partway open. To free the carrier, release the trigger and pull back on the charging handle. The bolt carrier should now go fully forward, and the hammer should remain cocked.

After testing, the parts that have been altered should be hardened or tempered. This is a job for a gunsmith

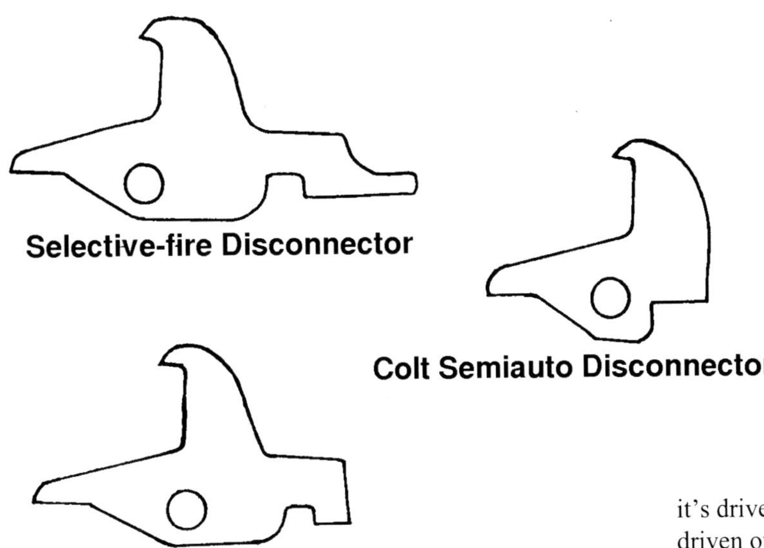


The automatic version of the disconnector can be recognized by its "tail," which is missing from both Colt's as well as non-Colt's semiauto versions of this part.

with a lot of experience—in part because he knows what color indicates a specific hardness of steel parts when they are heated. Most amateurs are just not set up to do this sort of work, so it is best to avoid it if possible.

## ASSEMBLY

The following procedure list will help beginners assemble an AR-15. It's a good idea to check off each completed step to avoid missing an essential procedure. And it's best to follow the steps in order if the rifle is to go together properly. The diagrams can help in orienting parts correctly; even better is to borrow a friend's AR-15 to use as a model.

### Lower Receiver

- Clean out the holes of the lower receiver with small, hand-held drill bits.
- Mount the trigger spring (diagram 1, #10) around the trigger posts (diagram 1, #9). Notice that the spring has its crosspiece to the front and under the front bar of the trigger. Each loop goes around the outside hub on either side of the trigger.
- Set the disconnector spring (diagram 1, #10) in its well in the trigger. The small end of the spring points down toward the trigger.
- Next, put the disconnector (diagram 1, #8) on its spring in the slot of the trigger. To speed up the assembly, temporarily slip the selector lever detent (diagram 1, #23) into the pin hole to hold the disconnector and trigger together. The thickest part of the detent should be inside the center of the disconnector's hole.
- Lower the disconnector and trigger into the lower receiver so that the trigger spur goes through its slot in the base of the receiver.
- Get the pivot hole of the trigger lined up with the hole in the side of the receiver, then drive the trigger pin (diagram 1, #2— it's identical to the hammer pin) in from the side. Gently tap the pin (so the detent doesn't get damaged) until it's driven almost all the way in. The detent will be driven out by the pin (be sure not to let the detent get away). Just before you drive the pin on through the receiver, align the trigger hole with those in the receiver and then tap the pin on through.
- Position the hammer spring (diagram 1, #4) on the hammer (diagram 1, #3). The two legs of the spring should point toward the base of the hammer, and the crosspiece goes behind the neck of the hammer. Check the diagram for proper orientation.
- Shove the hammer into place. The legs of its spring go over each hub of the trigger and the loop of the spring behind the back neck of the hammer. Hold the hammer down and insert a nail or punch through the receiver hole. While the nail holds the hammer and its spring, drive the pin into its hole from the opposite side of the receiver, pushing the nail out and securing the hammer.
- Check the pins holding the hammer and trigger in place by gently pushing them. They should not move out (if they do, they will "walk" out during shooting).

Diagram 5, proper orientation of the trigger spring before the trigger is inserted into the receiver.

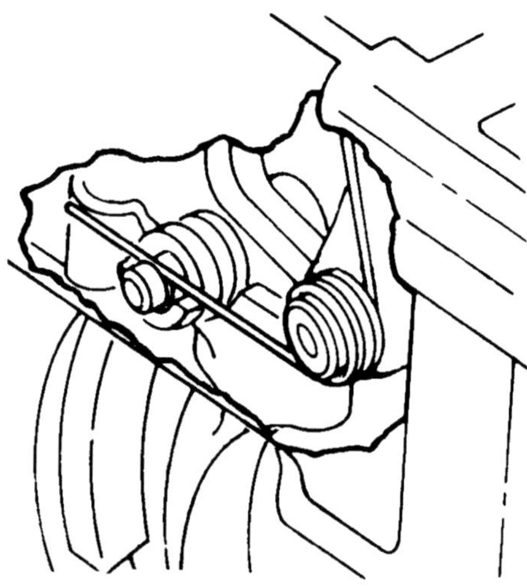

The leg of the hammer spring fits into the notch on the trigger pivot pin to hold it in place. Trigger pins that "walk" can be held in place by deepening the groove that the hammer spring leg fits into.

- The trigger pin should be held by the legs of the hammer spring. If it has a tendency to come loose, it can be modified to stay in place very easily. Remove it and cut its *outer* grooves deeper so that the hammer spring can engage them. This can be done with a file; the more perpendicular the edges of the cut are to the pin, the better it will hold the spring struts. Occasionally, the trigger will need to have the cut deepened so that the struts can reach the pins. If deepening the pin groove doesn't help, check the trigger and remove a tiny bit of metal if necessary. (Antiwalk pins can also be purchased from Bushmaster and other suppliers for around $6. However, these are held in place with a C-spring on the outside of the receiver—not nearly as elegant a solution as some might like.)
- If the hammer pin "walks," it can be modified to stay in place by deepening the groove in its center, which is held by a J-spring in the hammer. This can be done with a file (spinning the pin in a drill bit makes the work uniform). If this doesn't cure the problem, the spring in the hammer should be replaced or bent slightly to tighten its hold on the pin.
- Orient the trigger guard (diagram 1, #41) and depress the spring-loaded pin on its front. This will allow you to slip the guard into its niche behind the magazine well.
- Swivel the rear of the trigger guard into position and drive the roll pin (diagram 1, #40) home to secure it. Use light taps and support the lower side of the receiver "ear" on a surface so it doesn't have pressure against it since the metal on the receiver is quite thin and can be broken with heavy blows. You may wish to grind a slight bevel on the end of the roll pin to help get it started in its hole and be sure to oil it.
- Cock the hammer back so that it's held by the trigger.
- Wiggle the selector (diagram 1, #7) into its hole from the left side of the receiver.
- Fit the pistol grip onto the lower receiver. If it's too tight, it may be necessary to remove plastic from the grip with a file or rasp. Once it fits, set it aside until it's needed.
- Make sure the selector is all the way into the lower receiver and turn the receiver upside down. Drop the selector detent (diagram 1, #23) into its well (pointed end toward the selector) and then slide the detent spring (diagram 1, #23) into the well behind it.
- Lower the grip lock washer (diagram 1, #20) and its grip screw (diagram 1, #19) into the pistol grip (diagram 1, #21) so that the threads extend through the hole. Push a screwdriver into the grip to hold the screw in place as you mount the grip onto the receiver.
- Slide the grip onto the receiver, making sure that the selector detent spring goes into the hole cut in the grip. Take care not to bend the spring between the receiver and grip. When the grip is on the receiver, tighten the grip screw. On some grips, a small space may be left between the rear of the grip and the receiver. Tightening the grip screw an extra bit will help get rid of this space, but be careful not to use excessive pressure; this may break the grip, or the screw may strip the threads of the aluminum receiver.
- If the selector works too stiffly, remove the pistol grip and shorten the selector detent spring a loop or so. If this doesn't help, you may wish to round off the tip of the detent. But don't be tempted to make the selector too easy to work; it might accidentally be slipped into its FIRE position while being carried. You need a positive feel to the selector.
- If the selector rubs against the receiver when it is moved, it may be necessary to remove the selector and grind off part of its lower edge (which can be darkened with touch-up bluing afterward).
- Check the dimensions of the buffer retainer (diagram 1, #38) in its hole. If the hole is too small, ream it out as described above with a file or handheld drill bit.
- Check the buffer tube (diagram 1, #37) by screwing it into the receiver. If the buffer tube has two holes in its side, push a screwdriver through the holes and use it as a lever to screw the tube into place. If the buffer doesn't have side holes, it will probably have a square end that allows you to use the armorer's or

crescent wrench to screw it into the receiver. When the buffer screwed into the rear of the receiver, it should just cover the edge of the buffer retainer hole. If it goes too far into the hole, some of the threaded edge may have to be removed (carefully—you can't put the metal back once it's off!).

- With a telescoping stock, be sure the locking nut is adjusted so that the stock can be positioned correctly. Be sure, too, that the bump on the end plate is forward (it fits into the crater at the rear of the receiver). If you want the telescoping stock to be the minimum length, you will have to carefully remove some of the threaded end and then file the threads back into the end of it where the cut was made. Generally, it's easier to leave the extra length on the telescoping stock, and most shooters find it more comfortable to use with the extra 3/4 to 1 inch of stock left on. With its lock nut tightened against the endplate, the telescoping stock shouldn't rotate when on the rifle. If it does, the simplest solution is to place extra Loctite on the threads—though this may eventually come loose. A better bet is to deepen the groove in the lower front end of the tube and then peen the end of the stockplate where it fits into the cut. The peened surface is then carefully filed so it's tight in the deepened cut. This should secure the stock so that it can't rotate when the nut is tightened.
- When the dimensions of the telescoping stock are correct, insert the buffer retainer spring (diagram 1, #39) and the retainer into their hole.
- With a telescoping stock, place the rear pushpin detent (diagram 1, #34) and its spring (diagram 1, #33) in their holes after checking the dimension of the detent hole to be sure it's big enough.
- With a telescoping stock, be sure the receiver plate is in place. As the telescoping stock is screwed into the receiver, be careful not to pinch the detent spring and be sure the buffer retainer is held under the front edge of the buffer tube.
- With the regular buffer tube, be sure to hold the retainer down as the tube is screwed home.
- If the buffer tube holds the retainer in its hole while still allowing its narrow nub to stick up, then back the buffer up a half-turn or so and apply a small drop of Loctite to the threads of the buffer tube, then tighten it to where it belongs. Be careful not to get Loctite onto the retainer. (Military armorers often drill a hole into the buffer tube/lower receiver and pin the buffer tube into place. Loctite is a lot easier.)
- With a regular stock, set the rear pushpin detent (diagram 1, #34) and its spring (diagram 1, #33) into their hole after checking the dimension of the hole to be sure the detent can move freely in it.
- With longer A2-style stocks, it's necessary to add a small extension to the rear of the buffer tube before shoving the stock over the buffer tube.
- With the regular or A2 stock, push the stock (diagram 1, #32) onto the buffer tube while being careful not to pinch or bend the end of the detent spring sticking out of the back of the receiver.
- With the fixed stock, the trapdoor assembly can now be screwed onto the stock along with the lower swivel. (Many users may prefer to put the swivel on backward so that it's less apt to catch on equipment or jacket "slash" pockets; the swivel can also be cut off, leaving the end to act as a nut to hold the trapdoor in place.)
- If your stock is one of the old-style stocks without a trapdoor, assemble the rear swivel (diagram 1, #31) to its post (diagram 1, #32) with its pin (diagram 1, #30) and then mount the unit in the stock with its pin (diagram 1, #28). Fasten the stock to the buffer tube with the stock screw. Be careful not to pinch or bend the end of the detent spring sticking out of the back of the lower receiver.
- Push the buffer spring (diagram 1, #25) into the buffer tube. Wiggling it as it's snaked into the tube allows it to clear the buffer retainer.
- Slip the buffer (diagram 1, #25) into the buffer tube. The nylon tip goes toward the rear of the stock, and the large flat end toward the barrel end of the stock. You may be able to wiggle the buffer slightly to get it past the buffer retainer, or it may be necessary to depress the retainer. Once the buffer is in the tube, the retainer should hold it in place.

### Automatic Trigger Group

Automatic-fire groups are assembled in basically the same manner as above, and then the auto sear is added. Take care not to mix semiauto-only, automatic, or burst-fire parts; they are not interchangeable.

- The auto sear spring is normally already mounted on the auto sear. If not, it should be placed on the part and the hollow pin holding it mounted in place. Then the assembly (diagram 1, #6) is positioned in the receiver and secured with its pin (diagram 1, #5). This will complete the automatic version of the AR-15.

### Burst-Fire Trigger Group

Burst-fire and four-position (safe/semi/automatic/burst) groups are nearly identical except for the selector and disconnector/counter. On the four-position groups, the selector has a cam and the disconnector/counter a tail that is engaged with the cam, allowing the disconnector/counter to be taken out of

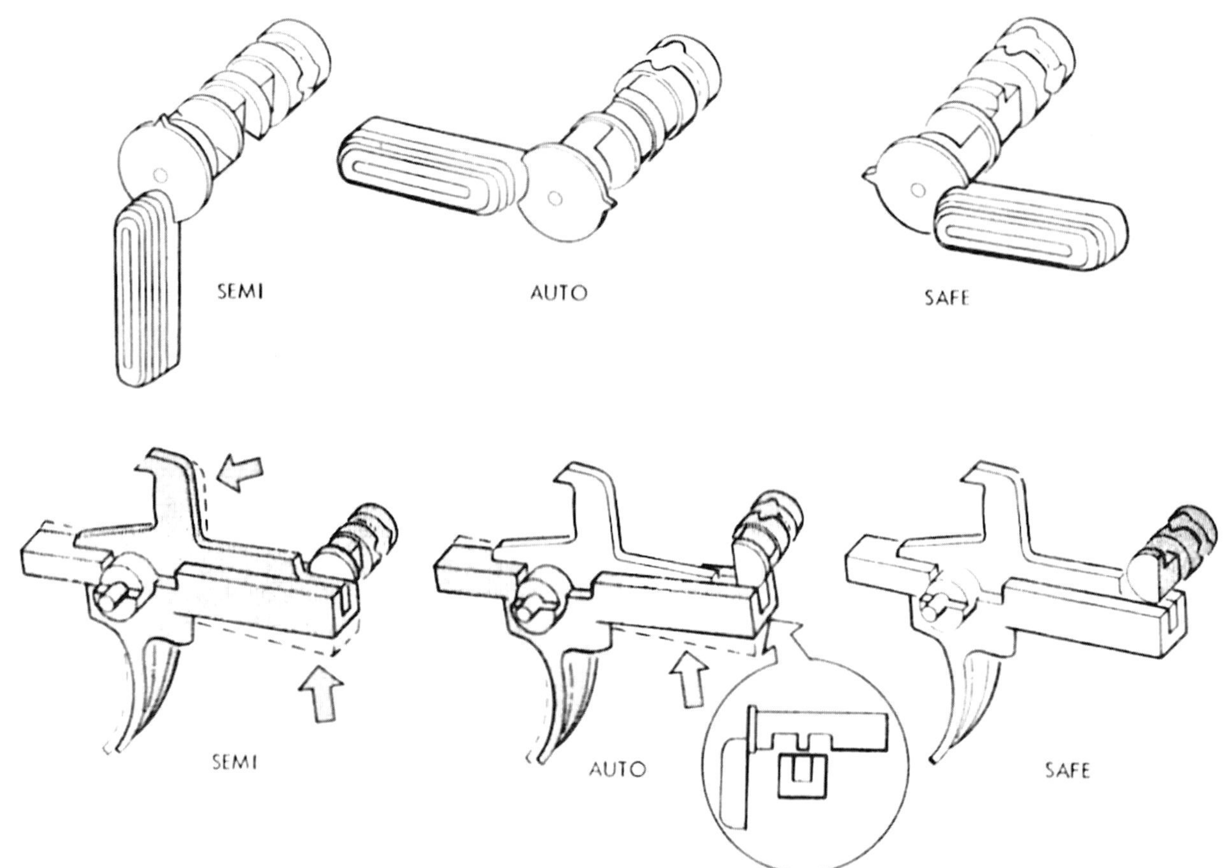


M16/M16A1 automatic-fire trigger group in operation.

operation (just as the standard disconnector is during burst or auto fire). This leaves only the auto sear in operation so that the hammer continues to fall as long as the trigger is back and the bolt forward.

The burst cam (diagram 6, #3) currently in production is for a three-round burst. After the third shot is fired in this burst, the forward hook on the disconnector/counter (diagram 6, #9) is dropped forward by a cam that is lower than the previous two on the rotating cam. This allows the hook on the disconnector/counter to move forward under its spring pressure to clip onto the hook on the side of the trigger, ending the burst and holding the hammer until the trigger is released. The AR-15 can also accommodate double-, four-, or five-round burst cams; these have been made on an experimental basis and might easily be fabricated by a gunsmith.

Assembly of the burst-fire parts is basically the same as with the semiauto version of the rifle, with a few additions. As with other trigger groups, care should be taken not to mix semiauto-only, automatic, or burst-fire parts up; they are not interchangeable.

- Burst-fire trigger groups have a small burst cam (diagram 6, #3) and spring (diagram 6, #4) that go over the right side of the hammer. The hammer spring (diagram 6, #2) then goes over the hammer legs with the crossbar of the spring behind the head of the hammer.
- The trigger (diagram 5) should have its spring placed on its struts with the crosspiece of the spring below the nose of the trigger.
- The two sear springs (diagram 6, #10) are nestled in the single well in the top of the trigger; the sear/counter (diagram 6, #9) goes on the right side of the trigger, and the sear (diagram 6, #8) goes on the left. A slave pin or small length of wire no wider than the trigger should be placed in the trigger's shaft to secure the sear/counter and sear.
- Place the trigger assembly in the receiver and drive its cross pin through (driving out the slave pin) to hold it in place.
- Lower the hammer assembly into the receiver with the two spring legs over the struts of the trigger. Once the hammer assembly is in place, drive the

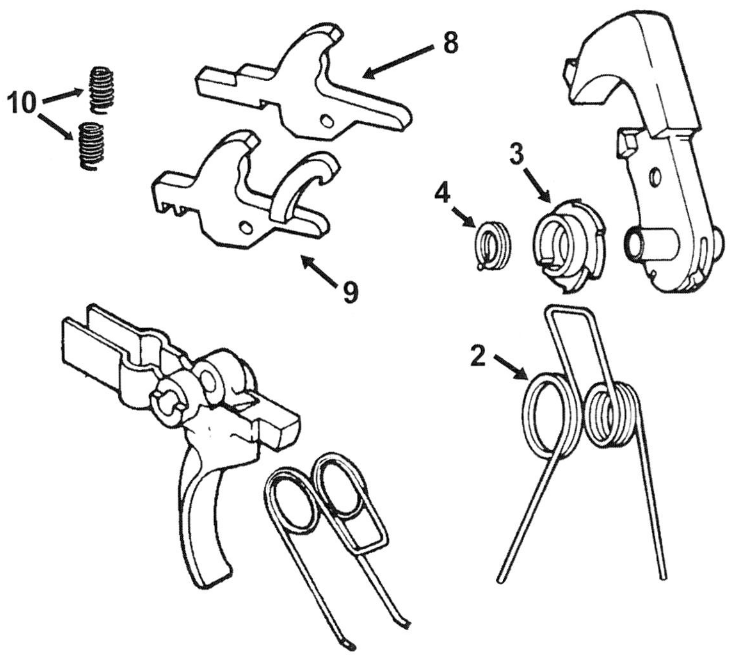


Diagram 6, burst-fire trigger assembly.

cross pin through to secure it. Then cock the hammer and insert the selector.

- The auto sear spring is normally already mounted on the auto sear. If not, place it there, using the hollow pin to hold it in place. Then position the assembly (diagram 1, #6) and secure it with its pin (diagram 1, #5). This will complete the automatic version of the AR-15.

### Bolt Carrier

If the bolt carrier (diagram 3, #13D or 13E) does not have the key (diagram 3, #13C) mounted on it, position it on the bolt and screw in the two hex bolts (diagram 3, #13B). Use a punch to stake the bolt carrier metal over the edge of each hex bolt; it's essential that the bolts not come loose. If they do, the pressure of the key will shear them off very quickly.

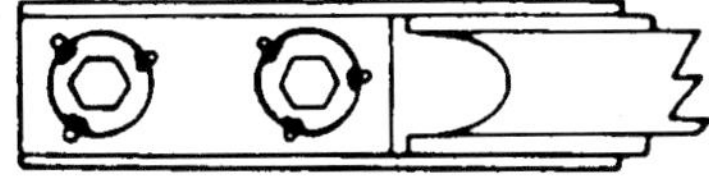

Top view of carrier key showing metal "staked" over the heads of the hex bolts.

- If the bolt (diagram 3, #4) is not assembled, slip the three bolt rings (diagram 3, #11) onto it. Do not line up the rings' spaces; that would allow gas to seep through the spaces and hinder the action of the rifle.
- Set the extractor spring (diagram 3, #7) in its well. Many kits have a small silicon insert that goes inside the spring to aid in its functioning.
- Put the extractor (diagram 3, #6) in its proper location and slide its pin (diagram 3, #5) into its hole.
- Notice that the ejector (diagram 3, #9) has a slot in it. The longer end above the slot goes toward the face of the bolt, and the slot lines up so that the roll pin (diagram 3, #8) can go through the slot. Put the ejector spring (diagram 3, #9) into its well and follow with the ejector, aligning it properly. (An empty cartridge can be used to hold the ejector down.) Push a drift punch into the roll-pin hole to retain the ejector. Now drive the roll pin into the bolt from the side opposite the punch.
- Be sure the extractor is aligned so that it's on the same side as the bolt carrier's two oil holes (and bolt-assist grooves), and push the bolt into the bolt carrier. (If you don't align the bolt properly, it's impossible to push the cam into place in the next step.)
- Push the bolt cam (diagram 3, #3) into the bolt and bolt carrier. Then turn the cam so that it's under the bolt key.
- Slide the firing pin (diagram 3, #2) into the bolt by inserting it into the rear of the bolt carrier and bolt.
- The firing pin retaining pin is now slipped into the bolt carrier from the side opposite the bolt's extractor. Do not spread the feet of this cotter pin. If the bolt carrier is turned with the bolt face up, the firing pin should not fall out. If it does, remove the retaining pin and reinsert the firing pin.

### Forward Assist and Ejection Port Cover

Not all upper receivers have a forward assist. Therefore you may need to skip the next few steps if your rifle doesn't have this feature.

- The forward-assist assembly (diagram 2, #32–38) is generally together when purchased. If not, note the alignment of parts on the diagram and assemble them accordingly, pushing the spring and its detent into their hole, placing the pawl in place, and drifting in the pin to hold it in place.

- Check that the cross pin holding the pawl in place is smooth and then push the plunger spring (diagram 2, #33) around the forward assist and shove the forward-assist assembly into its well. If the forward assist is the round style, be sure that the slot on the assembly is positioned so that the retaining pin (diagram 2, #32) can go by it; teardrop forward assists should have their rounded, large portion pointing down and the assembly temporarily secured with a drift punch.
- Drive the retaining roll pin (diagram 2, #32) into its hole from the lower side of the receiver. Properly orienting the ejection port cover and its spring is very awkward and will probably require several tries. The assistance of a "helper" can greatly simplify matters at this point.
- Snap the C-spring (diagram 2, #22) onto the ejection port cover pin (diagram 2, #21) if it isn't already on the pin.
- Run the cover pin into the receiver from the barrel end of the receiver and into the right half of the ejection port cover (diagram 2, #24).
- Position the spring (diagram 2, #23) so that its long tail is on the barrel end of the inside of the port cover (the side with the latch on it).
- Using a pair of needle-nosed pliers, twist the spring an extra turn so that it's tighter. It should end with its tail on the stock end against the receiver. Hold it in this location and slide the pin on through the cover and the hole on the opposite side of the port.

### A-1 Style Rear Sight

- Set the rear-sight leaf spring (diagram 2, #31) into its well in the receiver. The convex side of the spring should be upward with its two ends pointing downward toward the receiver cut it fits into. Occasionally the spring will be too large or the cut too small; grinding the edges off the spring will bring it to size. Be careful not to overheat the spring; this will ruin its temper.
- Hold the rear sight (diagram 2, #30) down on the rear sight spring and push the windage screw (diagram 2, #29) through the windage screw and receiver holes until the screw's threading reaches the center of the sight. Then use a screwdriver to screw it all the way into the sight base. When the sight base has moved all the way to the left, tap the screw so that it pops past its threaded portion toward the sight. Now the screw will stay in when turned counterclockwise to center the rear sight halfway between the receiver ears.
- Oil the hole for the roll pin (diagram 2, #25) and drive it into the windage knob (diagram 2, #26); the pin should not interfere with placing the knob on the sight screw.
- Place a drop of oil on the detent spring (diagram 2, #28) and put it and its detent (diagram 2, #27) into their well. Then push the windage knob over them and temporarily secure the knob to the screw with a small punch or wire pushed in from the open side of the knob.
- Finish drifting the cross pin into the knob to secure it in place; this can be done with a pair of large pliers or (very carefully) with a small punch and hammer.

### A2-Style Rear Sight

- The elevation knob (diagram 4, #5) and elevation index (diagram 4, #6) should be joined with their index screw (diagram 4, #7). Use a 1/16 Allen wrench to tighten the screw, and do not over tighten it. It will need to be adjusted later. (Note: all springs in the A2 sight assembly should be interchangeable.)
- Put a drop of oil into the ball-bearing spring hole and drop the spring (diagram 4, #9) into the hole following with the ball bearing. While holding them down with a small drift punch, shove the elevation assembly into place, taking care to keep the ball bearing under it.
- Place a drop of oil into the hole in the front of the rear sight base (diagram 4, #10) and then insert it into the elevation knobs and turn them until the base is all the way down. Next, back the elevation knob up 22 clicks and place the spring (diagram 4, #11) followed by its ball bearing (diagram 4, #12) into the hole. Carefully retain them in the hole as the elevation knob is turned, pulling the sight base downward into the receiver until the ball and spring are held in place.
- Start the helical-spring roll pin (diagram 4, #14) into its hole and then turn the upper receiver upside down and place the helical spring (diagram 4, #13) into the hole under the rear sight. While carefully holding the spring down, drive the roll pin the rest of the way into the receiver and check to be sure the spring is secure and completely under the roll pin.
- Rotate the elevation knob all the way down and back it up one click. Now loosen the screw holding the elevation index so the index can be rotated so that its "3/8" position is flush with the left side of the sight assembly. Retighten the screw.
- Set the rear-sight leaf spring (diagram 4, #15) into its well in the rear sight assembly. The convex side of the spring should be upward with its two ends pointing downward toward the receiver cut it fits into. Occasionally the spring will be too large or the

cut too small; grinding the edges off the spring will bring it to size. Care should be taken not to overheat the spring; this will ruin its temper.

- Hold down the rear sight (diagram 4, #16) on the rear sight spring and push the windage screw (diagram 4, #17) through the windage screw hole and rear sight assembly, using a screwdriver to tighten it all the way into the sight base. When the sight base has moved all the way to the left, tap the screw so that it pops into place past its threaded section. Now you can turn the screw counterclockwise to center the sight without having the screw come out. Back the sight into its center position about halfway between the receiver ears.
- Oil the hole for the roll pin (diagram 4, #21) and drive it partway into the windage knob (diagram 4, 20)—but do not drive it so far into the knob that it won't slip onto the rear sight screw.
- Place a drop of oil on the detent spring (diagram 4, #18) and put it and its detent (diagram 4, #19) into their well in the windage knob. Then secure the detent and slide the windage knob over the sight screw. Secure the knob to the screw with a small punch or wire pushed into the open side of the sight and finish drifting the roll pin into place to secure the knob. This can be done with a pair of large pliers or (very carefully) with a small punch and hammer.

### Barrel and Gas Tube

The front sight (diagram 2, #5) will usually be mounted on the barrel along with barrel nut (diagram 2, #19), handguard cap (diagram 2, #14), sight pins (diagram 2, #6), and possibly the front sight post (diagram 2, #11), its spring and detent, and the front swivel. If these parts are on the barrel, some of the following steps may be omitted.

- Slide the barrel nut (diagram 2, #19) onto the barrel from the muzzle end of the barrel. Be sure the teeth end of the nut is toward the muzzle.
- Slide the handguard cap (diagram 2, #14) onto the barrel from the muzzle end.
- Slide the front sight (2, #7) onto the barrel from the muzzle end.
- Tap the front sight pins (diagram 2, #6) into the sight base from the right side of the sight. The tapered end of the pins goes in first.
- Set the front swivel (diagram 2, #10) into the proper location and drive its roll pin (diagram 2, #9) home. If the swivel is held in place by a rivet, you'll need to peen the rivet closed.
- Drop the front sight spring (diagram 2, #13) into its well.
- Push the front sight detent (diagram 2, #12) into the well and screw the front sight post (diagram 2, #11) into position.
- After putting the flash suppresser lock ring (diagram 2, #4) onto the muzzle, screw the flash suppresser (diagram 2, #3) onto the muzzle.
- Slide the slip ring (diagram 2, #20) over the end of the barrel. It should have room for the weld ring (diagram 2, #18). If it does not, it's on backward.
- Insert the weld ring (diagram 2, #20) into the slip ring.
- Use needle-nosed pliers and/or a screwdriver to pull the C-ring (diagram 2, #17) onto the barrel nut. Start on one side of the spring, placing it into the slot that will retain it, and work the rest of it around the slot, finally levering the other end into place. Check to be sure the ring is in the slot of the barrel nut.
- Oil the rear of the barrel nut (which will be touching the barrel) and the threads inside the barrel nut. Then wiggle the barrel into the receiver, aligning the barrel indexing stub into the slot of the receiver (a tight fit is desirable here; if the barrel doesn't want to be fully seated, use a rubber mallet to tap it into the receiver).
- If the index stub won't go into the slot even with some gentle hammering on the barrel, the slot may need to be enlarged with a file. Don't remove too much; a tight fit is desirable.
- If the barrel is too loose in the slot, use a small wire to make a shim that fills the space so that the barrel will be tight when it's pushed onto the receiver. There should be no play in the barrel when it's twisted after the index stub is in its slot.
- Check to be sure the ejection port cover is positioned

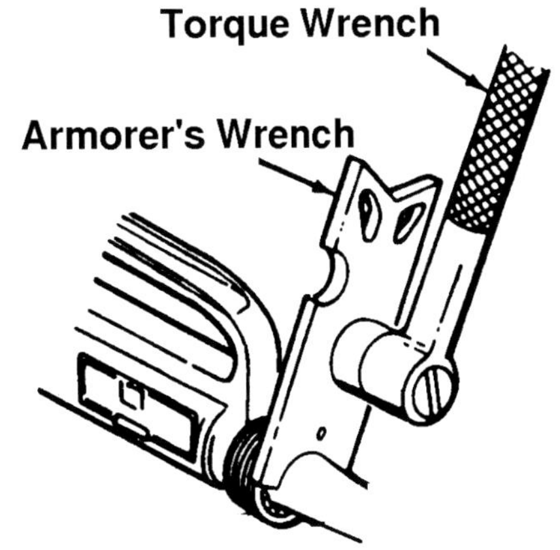

Armorer's wrench used with torque wrench to tighten barrel nut.

on the receiver properly. It isn't fastened on (the barrel will secure it), so don't let it slide off the front of its pivot holes.

- Screw the barrel nut onto the receiver loosely by hand and then finish the job with an armorer's wrench. The wrench is almost essential for this, and a barrel clamp or receiver block clamp mounted in a vise is also nearly indispensable. The nut should be tight but not extremely so; torque wrenches should be adjusted to 35 to 45 foot-pounds. Do not tighten fully until the next step has been completed.
- Use a small tool to align the slip ring, C-ring, and weld spring slots so that they are even with the gas tube hole on front of the receiver.
- Now carefully tighten the nut so that the receiver hole is lined up with one of the notches of the nut. A small tool may be useful to check the alignment (or you can carefully stick the gas tube into the hole from the receiver side to check the alignment). It's essential to line up the receiver hole and a notch for the gas tube to connect with the carrier key so that the rifle will function properly.
- Carefully position the gas tube (diagram 2, #16) alongside the front sight with the solid end toward the muzzle and the open end of the gas tube toward the receiver. Wiggle the gas tube through the nut, slip ring, weld spring, and C-spring and through the hole in the receiver. This is a tight fit, and care must be taken not to bend the gas tube. Push it into the receiver until the solid end clears the front sight base.
- Check the position of the holes of the gas tube and align it if necessary so that the hole going through it points to the left and right of the barrel and the gas hole points toward the barrel. Once it's aligned, shove the gas tube into the front sight base, wiggling it until the cross pin is lined up with the hole in the sight base (a small punch may help in lining it up). Be careful not to bend the gas tube.
- When the holes of the tube are lined up with the holes in the front sight, drive the roll pin (diagram 2, #15) through the sight base and tube.
- Push the bolt carrier and bolt into the upper receiver. The bolt carrier key should slide over the gas tube with very little resistance or friction. If the key doesn't go around the tube without binding, check the alignment of the tube. A screwdriver can be used to very slightly bend the end of the gas tube to align it with the gas key. Also check the key if there is binding; sometimes it's necessary to give a slight polish to the inside of the key with a file to make it go over the gas tube smoothly. Do not try to fire the rifle if the key doesn't go on and off the gas tube loosely. After the tube is aligned remove the carrier.
- Insert the front of one of the handguard halves (diagram 2, #1 or #2) into the front handguard cap. Keep in mind that with some handguards there are right/left or upper/lower halves that can't be substituted for each other.
- Push the slip right back toward the receiver and then pull the handguard half into position. It may be necessary to use a screwdriver to lever the slip ring back from the handguard. If the handguard is a little too big to fit, use a file or wood rasp to remove a tiny portion from the outside edge of the areas that seem too big.
- Repeat the above two steps to get the other handguard half into position.

### Final Assembly

- Pull the two pushpins (diagram 1, #35 and #1) out on M16-style lower receivers or the rear push pins on Sporter-style receivers. Put the upper receiver into position and shove the front push pin through the two receiver halves or, with the Sporter, join the two screws that connect through the front receiver hole.
- Push the upper receiver down and push the rear push pin through if possible. If the rear push pin doesn't go through the rear receiver easily, it will be necessary to use a round file to remove metal from the rear push pin hole of the upper receiver. Be sure to check where the holes fail to line up and remove minimal amounts of metal, checking the fit often to see whether the job is completed. Remember that it is impossible to put the metal back if you file off too much.
- When the rear push pin fits, leave the halves open and slide the charging handle (diagram 3, #14) into the upper receiver by pushing it into the large tubular hole and then moving the lugs on the inside of the receiver up through the two cut-out grooves in the receiver slot. Don't push the charging handle all the way in.
- Insert the bolt carrier into the upper receiver and then shove it and the charging handle all the way in.
- Close the receivers together and push in the rear push pin. The rifle is now assembled.
- To give a professional finish to the rifle, touch-up bluing can be used on exposed steel parts. For the aluminum receiver halves, carefully degrease the metal with acetone and apply a light coat of black engine block paint or Gun Kote, taking care not to get the material on the bolt or bolt carrier or in the trigger group.

## TESTING THE RIFLE

- Insert an empty magazine into the magazine well and be sure that it's locked into place.
- Pull back the charging handle and release it. The

bolt should be held back, and the charging handle should not be carried forward unless the bolt release on the side of the receiver is pushed. If the action closes rather than staying open, pull the charging handle all the way back again and look into the ejection port while the action is being held back. The bolt should be behind the bolt catch. If it isn't, then the buffer spring needs to be shortened.

- If the buffer spring needs to be shortened, open the receiver halves by pushing out the rear push pin and then hold the buffer in its location while you depress the retainer (diagram 1, #38) to free it. When the buffer is released, carefully remove it and its spring. Cut off a quarter-turn of the spring and replace it and the buffer and repeat the above step. Don't take off too much of the spring without testing it for the proper length; it won't grow back if you cut off too much.
- After the bolt is held back on an empty magazine, try cycling some dummy rounds through the rifle to be sure it chambers them correctly.
- Check the chamber with head space gauges before firing.
- Test the hammer/carrier lockup to be sure it's working. This will prevent a slam-fire if the trigger or disconnector fails.
- Pull the trigger to let the hammer drop on the firing pin. Then, while holding the trigger down, retract the charging lever fully with the other hand and release it. Now release the trigger (a click should be heard as the hammer is released by the disconnector and caught by the nose of the trigger). Pull on the trigger; the hammer should be heard dropping at this point. If instead the hammer follows the bolt forward while the trigger is being held, the disconnector and/or its spring is not functioning properly and should be replaced. Do not fire a rifle that fails this test: it may be very dangerous.
- Before firing the rifle, lightly lubricate the bolt and all moving parts as outlined above. This is essential for proper functioning and to prevent undue wear.
- If there are any doubts about the safety of the rifle because it fails to pass any tests or for some other reason does not seem right, have a gunsmith inspect it. It's better to spend a few dollars for a gunsmith than have the gun fail and have to spend thousands for a doctor—or a mortician.
- Once the rifle has been checked out, the next step is to test-fire it. Avoid using maximum loads until you have test-fired your rifle a number of times. Start out by just placing a single round in the magazine and cycling it into the chamber. As always, keep the rifle pointed in a safe direction; it might fire the round if the firing pin is too long, the hammer drops or something else unforeseen occurs.
- Examine the empty brass casing after the first firing. Is it ruptured? Does the head (primer end) appear deformed?
- If all seems right, try placing two or three rounds in the magazine and firing them. Again, examine the brass casing to be sure that it isn't showing problems that may be developing with the rifle.
- If all seems normal, try firing a full magazine through the rifle, checking the brass afterward and carefully inspecting the rifle for loose or broken parts. If all is as it should be, the rifle is ready for service.

## MOUNTING AN M203 ASSEMBLY ON AN AR-15

An M203 launcher can be mounted on a standard-barrel AR-15, many Commando-style guns, and M16A2-style guns. It will not fit on most H-BARs without altering the launcher assembly so that it will fit on the thicker barrel. With the 20-inch barrel, the M203 handguard can be used; with the Commandos, usually the top handguard half is left over the gas tube to protect it. Currently Bushmaster is working on a handguard cover for the M4, which would work on most Commandos having an M203 added to them.

To mount an M203 on a suitable AR-15, first remove the rifle's handguards and slide the M203 onto the barrel by placing the open, upper rear end of the launcher onto the middle portion of the barrel (where it's narrow enough for the M203 to fit over it). Once the slot of the M203 is on either side of the rifle's gas tube, shove the M203 toward the rifle's receiver.

Once the launcher is in position, place an insert between the forward end of the rifle's gas tube and the launcher's barrel. Then place the bracket over the gas tube and fasten it to the top front of the M203 body. This will completely fasten the M203 in place.

If desired, the sling mount can be put on the right or left of the barrel by placing it around the barrel inside either leg of the front sight base. The mount is held in place with two roll pins, which should be drifted into position. (Many M203 users prefer the "assault carry" sling arrangement described in Chapter 13.)

Slip the M203 handguard, which protects the user's fingers and the rifle's gas tube, into place over the rifle gas tube and barrel, and mount the quadrant sight if desired. The weapon is now ready to be used.

Disassembly of the M203 is basically a reversal of the above procedure.

*****

If problems develop with the AR-15, it should be checked by a competent gunsmith, who can make it serviceable for a small sum. Again, spending a little money to make a rifle safe and usable is better than causing injuries or death because the rifle isn't functioning properly.

# Chapter 13

# Accessories for the AR-15

There is an almost endless array of accessories for the AR-15, both in the form of military and aftermarket offerings, and it appears that new products will continue to be developed for some time. It's safe to say that there are more accessories and gadgets made for this rifle than any other firearm. This makes it almost impossible to be familiar with what's available.

AR-15 owners will do well not to get overburdened with gadgets. It's so easy to get taken by advertising hype and posed pictures in combat magazines of young, burly guys with 120-pound packs. People who acquire the gadgets find that they have a rifle that's impossible to use quickly and a load of gear that's hard to carry. Nothing can get a person killed more quickly in combat or be more uncomfortable on a day in the field (not to mention getting a guy laughed off the rifle range).

Those who are facing combat would do well to talk to people who have spent some time in combat and speak candidly about their experience. These veterans generally have one thing in common: in combat they got rid of about half the junk they carried during training so that they could move quickly if they had to and could keep going a lot longer. It's wise to save time and money and avoid superfluous gear. The guys who don't usually don't live to tell about it.

Only those who collect military gadgets will want to buy a lot of the stuff offered to AR-15 owners. Most shooters can get by with very little: an AR-15, a load of magazines filled with ammo, a good pocket knife, odds and ends of a first-aid kit, a canteen, suitable clothing, and maybe a butt-pack with a few necessities are sufficient for anything from combat to hunting.

Some gadgets are, after all, little more than adult toys. Of course there's nothing wrong with this; shooting has become an enjoyable recreation for many gun owners and is certainly safer than some other sports. But shooters must take care not to confuse entertainment with the moment they pick up their firearm to use it for self-defense.

Sometimes even the best of accessories and gear aren't compatible. Discovering that a beautiful pistol harness makes it impossible to shoulder and aim an AR-15 or that the rifle won't fire with a high-tech night-vision scope bolted on can be frustrating —or even life threatening. Shooters should try every item to be sure it works as it should with everything else.

Sometimes, otherwise excellent equipment has screws or bolts that require a hex driver (L-wrench). These drivers are easy to use, but it's impossible to "improvise" an L-wrench in the field; either a shooter has one or he's out of luck. Now, a shooter may carry all the wrenches needed for the accessories. I If there aren't many accessories, this isn't too much of a problem (and they can be fitted into the trapdoor on many AR-15 stocks or grips). But when many different sizes are needed, it can become a problem. And if a wrench is lost in the field . . .

Rather than suffering the cost of not carrying essentials (like candy bars), shooters should replace the hex-head screws or bolts with slot-head screws or bolts. The latter are often available in hardware stores or, if they have the smaller threads used on some gun parts, from Brownell's. For slot-head screws and bolts, a shooter just needs a screwdriver or maybe a pocket knife—or even the edge of another piece of equipment or piece of junk found in the field.

A hex-head screw or bolt can often be slotted by first cutting a shallow slash in it with a triangular file to get the slot started and then slowly proceeding with a hacksaw to make a groove for a large screwdriver. Cold bluing will make everything look like new again, only now the screw can be tightened in the field. (If care is taken, the slot can be made narrow enough to allow the L-wrench or whatever to be used as well as the screwdriver, giving the best of both worlds.)

Even better is to replace screws and bolts with wing-head screws so that the piece can be tightened without using any tool. Fashion-conscious shooters can even finish these with cold bluing.

## COMPANIES MAKING ACCESSORIES

Although major manufacturers and government entities may design and create accessories for the AR-15, many accessories are produced by "mom and pop" operations, often based on a product or products thought up by the creative mind at the helm of the small business.

Good examples—chosen only because of my knowledge of the business's history and its fine products—are cheek rests, bipods, and other accessories produced by Cherokee Accessories.

The company was started by a gentleman whom I'll call "Ben" (He asked that his family name be kept out of this book to avoid troubles from liberal neighbors who don't know he's producing gun accessories and, in fact, started his business with such products). Ben was a teacher of an industrial plastics class. One relevant lesson dealt with the techniques that graduates might employ to start their own business, using what they had learned in Ben's class. Wanting to demonstrate to the class just how such a thing could actually be done, he created some prototype cheek rests for the AR-15, based on an idea he had apparently been thinking over. He sent photos of them to *Guns and Ammo* magazine along with the name he'd come up with, Cherokee Accessories, and then promptly forgot about them.

Six months later a student came into his class, opened up the annual product review issue of *Guns and Ammo,* and asked, "Professor, aren't these your ideas?"

They were, to his surprise. Studying the magazine, he discovered that he had more pages and photos devoted to his cheek rests than did Colt or almost any other operation.

And then the orders started coming in. What had been a demonstration of how to create a business became more than an exercise. As Ben later put it, "When people started sending money, I had to make parts." Being skilled at making moldings and dealing with plastics, he figured this wouldn't be much of a problem and planned on creating his hobby business to fill the few orders that he was receiving.

Individual readers weren't the only ones interested in Ben's design, however. Dick Swan of Atlantic Research Marketing System had created a scope mount and telescope that would be sold with Colt's new Delta rifle. All that was missing was the selection of the cheekpiece to complete the gun. Swan saw Ben's cheek rests in *Guns and Ammo*, made a call to the inventor, and soon three different sample prototypes were headed to Atlantic Research Marketing and from there to Colt.

Cherokee Accessories might have remained more or less a hobby business had there not been two more twists to the story in September of 1984.

First, because of some internal squabble at the school over EPA regulations, Ben abruptly found himself unemployed with only a few hours' notice.

Next, Colt Firearms placed an order for one of the cheek rests that Ben had designed and submitted to Swan. This was a sort of good news-bad news event. It is one thing to build a prototype, but quite another to create a series of inexpensive copies that can be sold at a profit. Because Ben didn't have a lot of working capital, he knew he would be hard-pressed to create a large number of plastic moldings without a hefty investment in both equipment and staff.

"With no money and a hungry family," Ben later told me, "I had to fill that order. So I made eight silicone molds and began casting parts out of tough urethanes. I could only make 32 parts a day, and the production was a sticky, gummy mess. But since the wholesale price was high and no one else had anything like it, we were in business. Positive cash flow was $625 a day."

But there was a catch. Soon Colt wanted even more cheek rests—more than Ben could produce without a hefty investment in a mold. Despite the money coming in, he didn't have that investment money available. With the Colt order exceeding Ben's frantic efforts to produce more, a situation was developing that undoubtedly would have led to Colt's finding a new supplier if Ben failed to increase his production.

Next came another bit of fortune: While attending an inventors' meeting, Ben met a gentleman who manufactured printed circuit boards and asked Ben to create an injection mold for him. Ben was surprised because he knew the inventor had all the equipment on hand to make the molds but didn't realize it. Sitting down with his fellow inventor, Ben quickly explained how to set up electroform molds. The two soon struck a business arrangement that would result in the Delta cheek rest.

Creating molds is not an easy task. Often several stabs are necessary before a designer gets the shell right. However, Ben's skill permitted him to produce a viable mold with his first try. Now the owner of a new mold, Ben and his son, Gordon, carefully placed the assembly into an old mold base, set it on blankets in the back of the family truck, and drove it to a molding plant that they had access to over the weekend. They then ran the mold for 33 hours straight, producing Delta cheek rests at a phenomenal rate, taking turns sleeping in the back of the truck when they became too exhausted to work any longer.

At the end of the marathon production run, the mold collapsed, totally worn out. But the two had produced 1,000 cheek rests, all of which were purchased by Colt. Using the proceeds as seed money, Ben created an aluminum mold that his company uses to this day to produce some of its cheek rests.

Keeping up with all that technology has to offer, Ben

recently started exploiting low-cost silicone molds. This has enabled him to add a variety of products to his line without hefty investments in products that might—or might not—be well received by potential buyers. These molds have proven to be good for producing 4,000 or more parts, thereby giving a good indication of whether or not there's a need to produce a more durable mold.

(Interestingly enough, Ben has produced a video and book set, *Reproduce Almost Anything*, that shows how to create such molds. As Ben notes, "Third world countries could easily start making basic molded parts and bring a lot of people up by their bootstraps.")

Today both father and son are busy creating new products and refining their earlier products as well; Gordon is also busy working as an animator for a nationally syndicated TV cartoon series when he's not working on three-dimensional graphics or on moldings for the family business.

In addition to the products currently marketed by Cherokee Accessories, there are a lot of prototypes and projects in the works that may be marketed, including a cheekpiece with a built-in laser designator.

Ben's story may not be typical. Many gun accessory businesses aren't nearly this successful, and quite a few fail either due to poor design or simply because there is not a big enough market available for them. Yet many of these companies are quite similar to Ben's and in many ways typify both American ingenuity and the strong individualism, idealism, and bootstraps spirit that has made our nation great.

## FEDERAL CONSIDERATIONS

Before an owner of an AR-15 or one of its spinoffs starts bolting accessories onto a gun willy-nilly, it is important to realize that some modifications can transform a standard firearm into an illegal weapon. Being aware of these laws and obeying them to the letter is important if you are to avoid having a gun confiscated and/or receiving jail time and stiff fines. When in doubt, err on the side of caution. Also be sure to direct questions to a lawyer rather than law enforcement personnel, who are notorious for giving bad legal advice.

One of the more recent laws that affects how a firearm can be configured is the 1994 federal assault weapon ban, which is part of the modification made to the Gun Control Act of 1968. This amended law defines the cosmetic features that can transform a firearm from a regular gun into something that, at least according to the gun grabbers in Washington, D.C., who were behind this legislation, "is the weapon of choice for drug dealers."

Although this legislation claims to "ban" specific guns, in fact it is only a ban on the manufacture of military-style guns for sale to civilians. That means that preban guns can still be purchased and owned in most areas of the United States (though this varies according to local and state laws). Postban guns that are identical, save for when they were made, are illegal for civilians to own without a special permit or other government waiver.

Obviously this raises the following important points:

- You can own a preban gun if you're willing to pay extra for it. This then permits a variety of modifications that would otherwise be impossible to carry out.
- It is possible to transform almost any postban gun into an illegal weapon simply by changing a few cosmetic features on it.
- It is easy to buy a gun that is claimed to be preban by an unethical person when, in fact, the gun is postban. This leaves the buyer not only out of money after paying a preban price tag but with an illegal firearm.

All the specifications of what constitutes an "assault weapon" as defined by this law are cosmetic. That means a postban gun will do almost anything a preban gun will do, will function just as well, and will be every bit as deadly. For all purposes, the difference between these guns, like the law itself, is simply a matter of looks, with nothing of real substance other than in the legal arena.

There are also older federal laws that should be kept in mind. The basic federal rules are that rifles (as well as shotguns) must have an overall length of over 26 inches to be legal to own without a special federal permit. Additionally, a rifle must have a barrel length of at least 16 inches (with 18 inches required for shotguns). This length is determined by measuring the inside of the barrel from the muzzle to the bolt face when the bolt is in battery. That means that most barrels are actually shorter, legally, than they really are physically.

### Assault Weapon Specifications

The provisions of the assault weapon ban can be a legal and intellectual quagmire if not read carefully. The law makes it possible to transform a regular semiauto rifle with a detachable magazine into an assault weapon if it has two of the following:

- A threaded barrel that accepts a flash hider or silencer, a flash hider, and a bayonet mount
- A folding or telescoping stock
- A pistol grip
- The ability to accept a grenade launcher

Up front there are some legal angles that you may

come across. Probably the best advice is to see your lawyer if you have questions. Generally, it is also wise to avoid taking seriously the talk of gunshop commandos.

One oddity is in the wording of the law, which says that to be an assault weapon the gun must have "any two" of the items listed above. A literal reading thus means that a gun has to have two threaded barrels, two folding stocks, two pistol grips, or the ability to accept two grenade launchers to be an assault weapon. My advice, however, is not to plan on this saving your bacon if you get dragged into court for owning an illegal assault weapon.

A second point is that virtually any rifle, especially the AR-15, can accept a grenade launcher with little or no modification. Currently the law is interpreted to mean that a grenade launcher must actually be mounted on the rifle, but one can see that a change in BATF policy could quickly make almost all postban AR-15 rifles illegal because most have a pistol grip in place. While it is doubtful that this will occur, it isn't hard to imagine a liberal in the White House and the same ilk controlling Congress coming up with such a policy while the mainstream media whip little old ladies of both sexes into a ban-the-guns frenzy.

These soapbox statements aside, you can easily break the law by doing something as simple as putting a postban AR-15 telescoping stock on the rifle. Ditto with something like replacing the front sight assembly with one that has a bayonet lug, having a gunsmith thread the barrel, and so on. Obviously great care has to be taken to avoid running afoul of this legislation.

Since there are "pistol" versions of the AR-15 available, it is also important to note that there are slightly different specifications in this law as to what constitutes an illegal assault weapon in relation to a semiauto pistol. A pistol with two of any of the following features is legally considered an assault weapon:

- An ammunition magazine that isn't contained in the pistol grip
- A threaded barrel capable of accepting a barrel extender or flash suppressor
- A forward handgrip
- A silencer
- A shroud that is attached to, or partly or completely encircles the barrel
- A manufactured weight of 50 ounces or more when the pistol is unloaded
- A semiautomatic version of an automatic firearm

Accidentally transforming a perfectly legal AR-15 pistol into an assault weapon is not too likely , but it's wise to keep these provisions in mind before making any modifications to your pistol. Since the AR-15 pistol already has a magazine that isn't in the grip, there is no room for another of these options. That means adding a barrel shroud or forward grip, for example, will automatically make the gun illegal to own. Probably the best advice with a pistol is to just leave well enough alone and make no modifications to it at all, other than perhaps mounting a scope on it.

While most of the firearms covered in this book are rifles, there are a few semiauto shotguns, so the assault weapon ban as it pertains to shotguns should be mentioned as well. Having two of the following transforms the shotgun into an assault weapon:

- A folding or telescoping stock
- A pistol grip that protrudes conspicuously beneath the action of the weapon
- A fixed magazine capacity in excess of five rounds or the ability to accept a detachable magazine

Finally, it should be noted that the assault weapon provisions apply only to semiauto firearms. This means that removal of the gas tube from an AR-15 so that the gun functions only when cycled by the charging handle (or perhaps a handguard pump action, should one be inventive) would transform the firearm from one covered by this law to one that is not. That said, the actual test of this conjecture has not been seen, so one is well advised to make such modifications with caution and only after receiving legal advice on the matter.

As things now stand, the assault weapon ban as well as the 10-round magazine maximum (covered below) are slated to cease in 2004. Whether the political climate will permit these ill-advised laws to quickly go out of existence or become renewed will depend in large part in how unified gun owners are in their voting against antigun politicians as well as who is in the White House.

There's one more area in the assault weapon ban as it now stands.Although it is true that guns made and assembled before the ban and that had an assault weapon configuration are grandfathered in the bill and therefore not illegal, this is not so for guns or receivers that were made *before* the ban but that did not have the assault weapon configuration. This means that simply looking at the serial number and date of manufacture on a gun doesn't mean that you can tell whether or not it is a legal preban gun or an illegally converted firearm.

This is a letter sent out by Edward M. Owen, Jr., chief of the Firearms Technology Branch of the BATF:

> Semiautomatic pistols and rifles assembled after September 13, 1994, and possessing two or more of the features listed in [Section 921 (a)

> (30), Title 18 U.S.C.] are semiautomatic assault weapons as defined. The fact that the receiver may have been manufactured prior to September 13, 1994, is immaterial to classification of a weapon as a semiautomatic assault weapon. Additionally, payment or non-payment of excise tax is also immaterial to classification of a firearm as a semiautomatic assault weapon.

Many gun owners don't understand this fact, and undoubtedly more than a few illegal guns have been created because of this (though by the same token, the BATF would undoubtedly be hard-pressed to prove this point in many cases).

Suppose, for example, that you owned a preban AR-15 that had been built with a target barrel lacking a flash hider and bayonet lug. As such, the gun would only possess one of the "no-nos" that creates an assault weapon. Now after the ban, you put a standard upper receiver on the gun with a barrel having a flash hider and/or a bayonet lug.

Illegal.

Even though the gun was built before the ban, it would be illegal to so modify it.

Likewise a gun built on a receiver manufactured before the ban would still need to conform to the new law or be an illegal conversion of a firearm (which is what the BATF has declared a bare lower receiver to be) into one of those dreaded assault weapons.

The bottom line is that if a gun was in the assault weapon configuration before September 13, 1994, it is perfectly legal. If it was given an assault weapon configuration after September 13, 1994, even if manufactured long before then, then it is an illegal conversion.

Finally, it is important to be aware of local and state laws in addition to the federal ones. Covering these is outside the scope of this book; a quick call to city and state attorneys' offices will generally give you the information you need.

### The Law and High-Capacity Magazines

The assault weapon ban made it illegal to manufacture magazines or other feeding devices with capacities of over 10 rounds for semiauto guns, both rifles and pistols. However, due to the lag between the time that the bill was passed by Congress and signed into law by President Clinton, a huge number of high-capacity magazines were manufactured during the last weeks before the law went into effect. Coupled with the large number of military surplus magazines made for various AR-15 rifles worldwide, there is a large supply of preban magazines that promise to keep most shooters well supplied if they are willing to pay a small premium.

These preban magazines are legal to buy and own. However, it is illegal to modify postban magazines to hold more than 10 rounds. As noted elsewhere in this book, law enforcement and government agencies can purchase postban magazines of greater capacity. Whether these can then be resold or given to others is a legally dubious proposition at best, though more than a few have turned up in civilian hands (arguing that such bans are less than effective). The best advice is that if you're in law enforcement work, don't yield to the temptation to sell these to civilians; if you are not technically a law enforcement officer or serving in any other capacity that entitles you to legally possess one of these magazines, don't be tempted to receive one, even from a well-meaning friend.

All of these legalese preambles out of the way, let's take a look at just a few of the many accessories available to those who own a variant of the AR-15 rifle.

## BAYONETS

Bayonets for any modern rifle are arguably useless on the barrel; AR-15 bayonets are no exception to this rule. Since the end of the Korean War, bayonets have not been important to U.S. soldiers except for parading, building confidence through mock bayonet fights, guarding prisoners, and controlling crowds.

Looking through records of war wounds from World War II to the present, it is hard to find even a single casualty resulting from a bayonet mounted on the end of a rifle. Little wonder then that many seasoned troops toss their bayonet when entering combat, carrying instead a pocketknife or sheath knife to actually handle the chores that a bayonet is supposed to perform.

Of course, a bayonet on the end of a rifle might save you if your gun has jammed or you're out of ammo. Yet, in reality, the chances are nearly 100 percent that if either happens to you, neither will happen to your enemy at that same moment. Thus, he will shoot you long before can reach him with a bayonet should you be foolish or unfortunate enough not to get to a safer place.

Even if you meet a foe who's out of ammunition, most combat takes place in rough terrain, rubble, or close quarters that don't lend themselves to the fancy footwork needed to actually bayonet a foe. Furthermore, should you jab an enemy, chances are good the blade will lodge permanently in flesh and bone, due to both the friction on the blade and the depth afforded by a two-hand hold on a rifle.

Now ask yourself: What are the chances of your fighting one on one with an enemy who lacks ammunition and is by himself? Perhaps in the days of the Civil War this happened. But in these days of lightweight ammunition that can engage an enemy at a hundred yards, a day when highly reliable firearms are the norm, and a time when semiauto fire is common to combat weapons, the chances are slim to none that a bayonet will ever save a life on any contemporary battlefield. Even the current M9 "Bowie knife" design, which makes an excellent field knife, is totally ineffective as a weapon when mounted on a rifle.

There is no sign that this conflict between military wants and actual combat effectiveness will end any time soon, no matter whether soldiers are equipped with firearms or some yet unimagined weapon of destruction. During recent staged photo shoots of the new urban combat gear the U.S. Army is fielding, troops were

Staged bayonet charge during World War I. In fact, the heavy firepower in the trenches made such tactics suicidal at best and marked the end of the bayonet as a serious weapon on the modern battlefield. (Courtesy of U.S. Army.)

The M7 (bottom) was modeled after earlier M1 carbine bayonet (top).

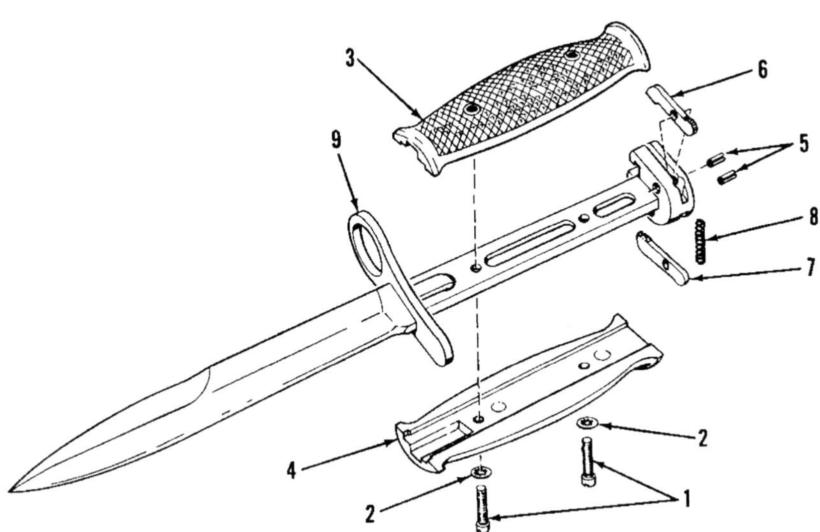


Exploded drawing of the M7 bayonet.

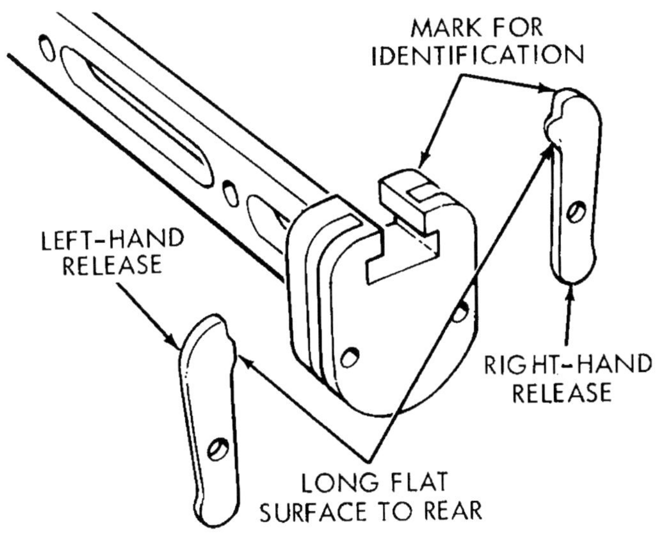


Bayonets lock onto the AR-15 with two spring-loaded release catches. Pressure applied with the fingertips makes it possible to slide the bayonet back off the rifle.

asked to place bayonets on rifles already laden with night-vision scopes, lasers, and other equipment, no doubt endangering each other as they huddled in "storm-the-building" poses.

For those who want to buy either the M7 or M9 (one hopes as a camp knife or as a piece of history rather than to place on the barrel of an AR-15), they are available from a number of suppliers, including DPMS, for $29.95 for the older model and $129.95 for the M9.

One of the oddest bayonets to come down the pike in recent years is the G.R.A.D. RS-1, which has a five-round revolver mechanism in its grip. By loading the cylinders and releasing a trigger that normally is hidden in the handle of this bayonet, the user can fire a .22 LR cartridge. Because the weapon lacks a regular pistol grip/barrel configuration, BATF has classified it as "any other weapon" under title II of the National Firearms Act. As such it takes a bit of special paperwork to own. How practical such a bayonet would be in real life is one for gunsmith commandos to debate for years to come. In addition to the firing version, G.R.A.D. also offers blank and nonfunctional versions of the bayonet. And yes, it will mount on an AR-15 with the standard flash hider and bayonet lug.

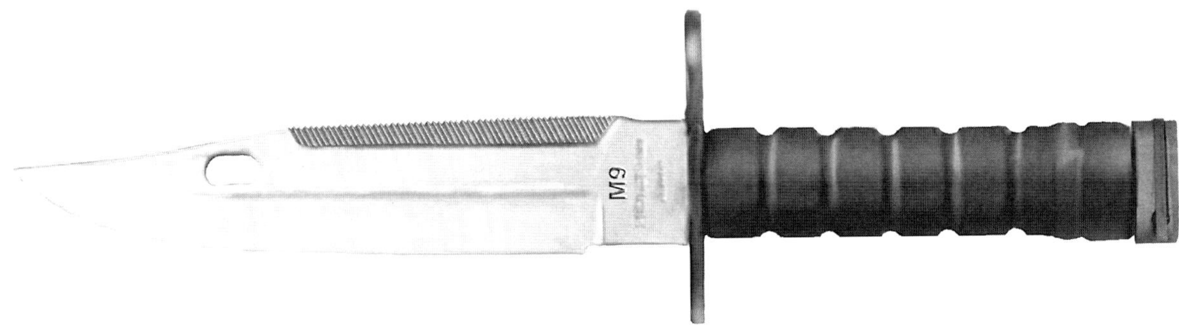


While a great camp knife, the M9 bayonet would perform poorly on the end of a rifle in actual combat. Cutout in the blade locks into the sheath to create wire cutters.

U.S. Army Sergeant 1st Class Burnham explains M9 wire cutting technique to a Royal Thai Army soldier. (Courtesy of U.S. Department of Defense.)

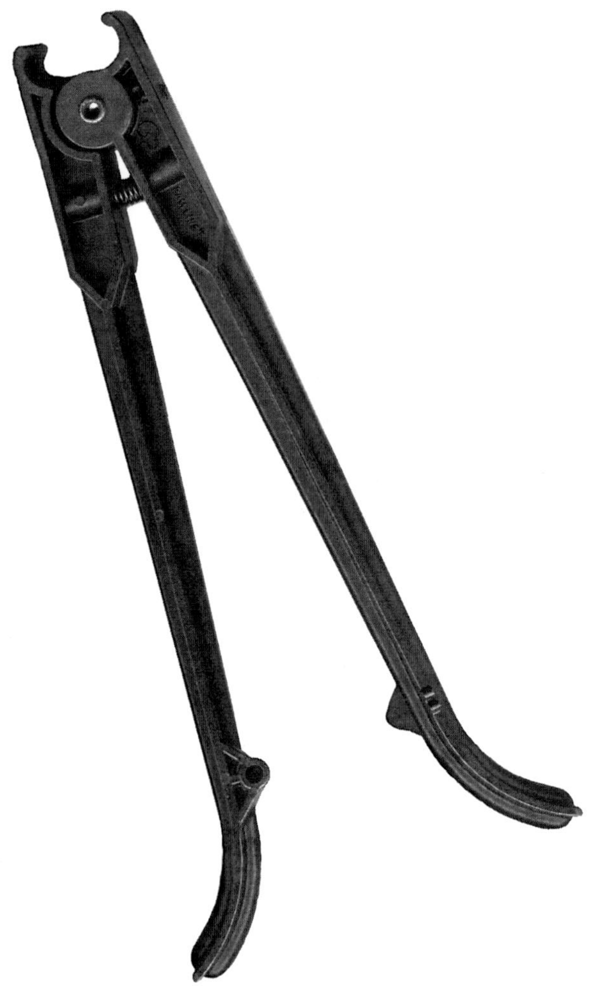

Ram-Line's tough plastic Universal bipod.

## BIPODS

If an owner is shooting an AR-15 at the target range or some other prepared, fixed position with a clear field of fire or using an AR-15 on an H-BAR SAW, then a bipod might be useful. However, many shooters discover that a twig, backpack, binocular case, or some other improvised system works just as well. Many areas have so much brush and obstructions on the ground that prone shooting is impossible, which makes bipods useless; in such areas shooters can get along fine by resting a hand on a stationery rest and placing the rifle against the hand. This allows for improved accuracy without the hassle of carrying a bipod around.

(A rather strange product that was also marketed for a short time was a rod that the user fastened to his belt and then extended upward to the handguard of his rifle. This allowed for a steadier shot because of the support offered by the shooter's waist. The device worked fine but was somewhat awkward and has since gone to whatever place accessories go to when they die.)

Bipods can add insult to injury with light-barreled AR-15s since the point of impact may change slightly with the bipod mounted, especially when some shooting is done standing with the bipod on the barrel and some of it with the bipod resting on the ground. The change of impact isn't too great, but it can be disconcerting. So rule number one is to place bipods only on AR-15s with free-floated barrels (and then place the bipod on the handguard, not the barrel) or on H-BARs that don't suffer from barrel flex.

Metal "clothespin" bipods developed by Colt as the M3 bipod for the military are usable and quick to put on

Harris Bipod. (Courtesy of Harris Gunworks.)

B-Square's Rigid Service bipod.

and take off but they are rust prone and hard to carry when not in use; these are still available from DPMS (for $12.95).

A clothespin design variant, which is better than the Colt product, is Ram-Line's tough plastic Universal bipod, which costs only $19.96 and can be quickly mounted on or taken off the rifle. Made of 66 percent nylon and 33 percent glass fiber, it's quite strong and the locking lugs on its feet make it practical to carry in a pocket. (These are available from CIE Global.)

One popular bipod with target shooters (and the one found on many AR-15 sniper rifles) is the lightweight aluminum Harris bipod (made by Harris Gunworks). Looking somewhat like Rube Goldberg contraptions due to their external springs, the Harris bipods actually work well; they also come in a huge variety of models, including the Model 25 (which has legs that are adjustable from 12 to 25 inches), the Model L (9 to 13 inches), the Model LM (9 to 13 inches with its legs ejected by spring action rather than retracted by spring action as with the other models), the Model H (13.5 to 23 inches), Model 25C (13.5 to 27 inches), and Model BR (6 to 9 inches). Additionally, each of these models comes in two styles, a standard stationary bipod or the S-style 45-degree swivel model. Costs range from $60 for the smaller standard models to $82.95 or more for the longer S styles. A universal adapter to mount a Harris bipod on the AR-15 costs an additional $15; this can be purchased from a number of dealers that carry target-style versions of the AR-15.

One of my favorite permanently attachable bipods is B-Square's Rigid Service bipod (which is very much like the company's earlier Ultimate bipod). Made of aluminum and weighing only 8 ounces, this bipod is lightweight and has no exposed springs or levers; the latter feature helps minimize capturing dirt or vegetation when the bipod is mounted on the rifle. The self-leveling, spring-locking legs can be quickly folded up or deployed and come in both black and stainless finishes. The B-Square Ultimate bipod can be attached to an AR-15 by simply tightening the two bolts on the bipod's bracket assembly on either side of the barrel, securing the bipod tightly in place. It costs $59.95.

The company now offers a second, similar model that is mounted to the AR-15 handguard; for those with a free-floated barrel, this is arguably a better system because it won't interfere with accuracy. The Rigid Sporter bipod (part number 6002) can be attached to a swivel stud or the handguard with a special mount (costing an additional $14.95). Cost is $59.95 for the stainless-steel-finish version (6003).

Another fine bipod is the Cherokee Featherweight. As its name suggests, it's lightweight and tips the scales at only 5.7 ounces. It is made of steel and epoxy-fiberglass so that it's strong enough to take a lot of abuse. The bipod legs fold under the rifle when not in use and can be deployed quickly and noiselessly with one hand. The standard black version of the Featherweight is $65, with a stainless-steel version costing $100.

Cherokee has taken the Featherweight and created the only AR-15 bipod to date that not only works well but also appears to be part of the firearm rather than something tacked on as an afterthought. This is done by creating a replacement for the lower half of an A2 handguard, with space for the bipod to fit into when it is in the folded position (creating the feel of a regular handguard). Marketed as the Featherweight Bipod/AR-15 Forearm, this is an excellent system for anyone who needs a bipod but wants to shoot from the standing position comfortably. The bipod can be fastened to either

Cherokee's Featherweight Bipod/AR-15 Forearm folds into a special handguard when not in use (top); the feet snap down quickly and can be mounted in either forward or rear positions according to the preference of the shooter.

end of the handguard, making it possible to have it near the receiver just ahead of the magazine well or out toward the front sight handing from the other end of the handguard. It costs $170.

Heavy steel M14 and M60 bipods are available from Gun Parts, SARCO, and Springfield Armory. While these are too heavy for most shooters, those who want an SAW-style setup and a reduction of recoil may find these bipods useful. The bipods' individually adjustable legs may be another desirable feature.

Lightweight extendable bipod legs are offered by Harris; these are often found on police countersniper AR-15s due to their low weight. These cost around $50 for units designed for the AR-15 bipod, with an additional $16.50 for a barrel mount adapter or $8 for a handguard adapter.

## BLANK-FIRING DEVICES

Although most training on the AR-15 can be better done with cartridge conversion kits, there may be an occasional need for a blank adapter, especially for war games or reenactment groups. Since a blank cartridge doesn't develop as much recoil as a normal round does (which is why Hollywood heroes have such great control over automatic weapons held in the most casual way), an AR-15 will fire only single shots if a blank adapter isn't used to plug most of the barrel and force more gas through the gas tube rather than allowing it to exit the muzzle.

Currently there are two types of blank adapters available for the AR-15. One is the "Hollywood-type," which rides inside the flash suppressor of the rifle and is all but unseen from the outside of the rifle; this is useful for making things very realistic but can also be dangerous since the adapter is easily forgotten and left in the rifle when switching to regular ammunition—with disastrous results! Too, it's hard to tell whether a rifle is really safe or not for those being shot at with blanks—a disconcerting or even dangerous proposition.

Better are the military type of blank adapters available on the surplus market. These fasten to the flash suppressor and have a bolt that screws into the muzzle of the suppressor. These adapters are generally painted red so that they're easily spotted and are available from most surplus dealers; Sierra Surplus sells them for $8.

Even though most blanks are loaded with smokeless powder, occasionally blanks are sold with black powder in them. For those fortunate enough never to have worked with black powder, it is hygroscopic and promotes rust and corrosion in any firearm that has been fired with it. Alhough the chrome-lined barrel of most AR-15s isn't harmed by black powder, the same isn't true of the gas tube, bolt, bolt carrier, or inner mechanism of the rifle, which are all exposed to the powder residue. Blanks loaded with black powder must be avoided at all costs.

## BRASS CATCHERS

A brass catcher that traps empty cartridges as they spill out the ejection port can save a shooter's having to search and pick up his empty cartridges after a day at the range, and it keeps the environment cleaner. Needless to say, brass catchers are a real boon for reloaders since they help keep brass clean and in one place. A brass catcher isn't a good idea for combat, and it can be noisy in the brush ( where the plastic unit sounds positively drum like), but it is ideal for target shooting or plinking.

The best brass catcher for the AR-15 is from E&L Manufacturing; it's made of rigid plastic and it clips onto the receiver of the standard AR-15. The E&L catcher rarely if ever causes a jam and holds up to 50 casings before it needs to be emptied. The standard model 103 fits the A1/A2 variants in .223 as well as 7.62x39mm; the 103A is designed for the Sporter in 9mm; the 103B will also work with the A3 if the detachable carrying handle is mounted on the rifle. It costs $29.95.

DPMS offers four brass catchers that have cloth bags rather than a plastic container (this makes for quieter brass catching, but the catchers aren't as easy to use as the snap-on E&L catcher). The WOOK Flat Top Brass Catcher is designed for A3-style receivers and costs $39.95.

The Levang Mag Brass Catcher connects to the rifle's magazine and then is adjusted to the ejection port, making it capable of working with virtually any model of AR-15 using an extended .223 magazine. Its price is $43.95. The Quiet Catcher goes for $14.95, while a similar unit that attaches to a scope costs $19.95.

## CARRYING CASES

Carrying cases protect AR-15s from getting scuffed and nicked in a vehicle and are also useful for storing guns. For those who have to carry an AR-15 to a gunsmith or through a populated area to a rifle range, a storage case is ideal since media hoopla has branded even semiauto-only AR-15s as "criminal's machine guns."

Ideally, a case allows air to circulate through it to minimize condensation in the case (and rusting of steel parts on the gun). Among the best are Uncle Mike's cases, which are readily available at most gun stores. Their excellent Sidekick carrier is sized for the AR-15

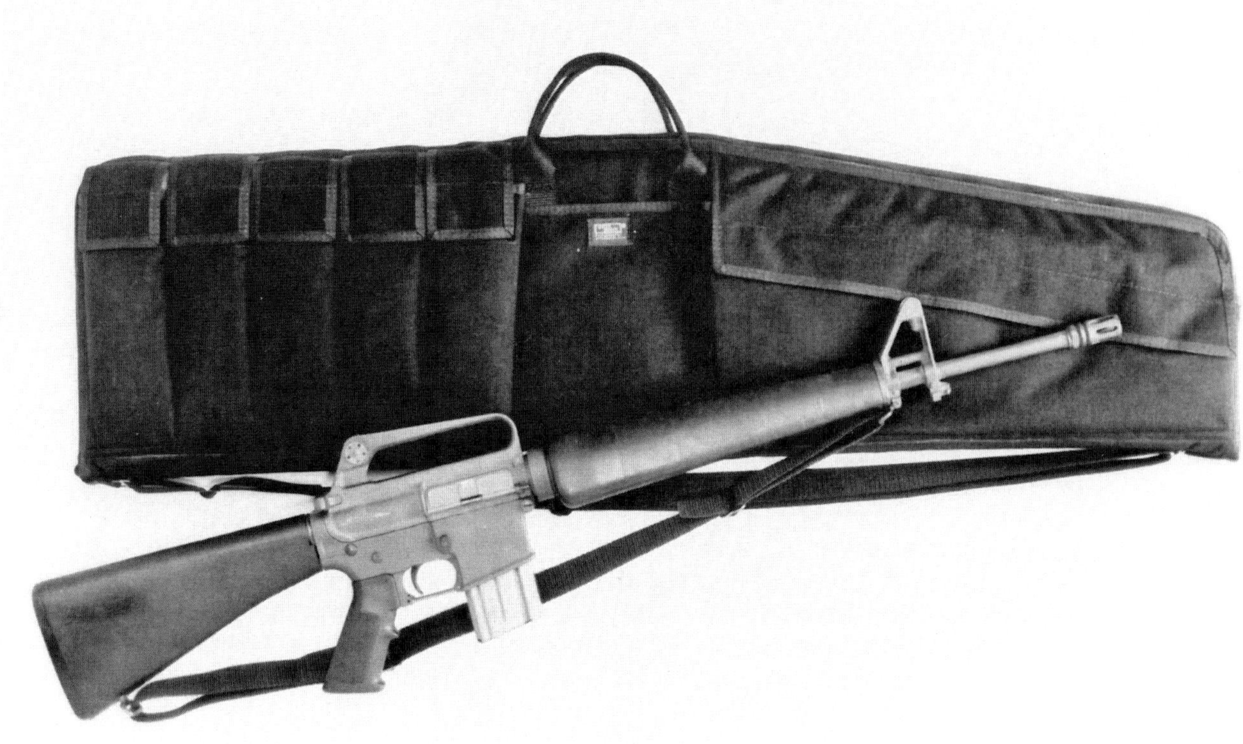

Uncle Mike's excellent Sidekick carrying/storage case. (Courtesy of Michael's of Oregon.)

and has pockets for spare magazines and the like. Bushmaster offers several excellent soft cases for the AR-15 (with solid as well as camouflage finishes). Prices for the Bushmaster soft cases range from $79 to $99. Also offered is a tough plastic "hardside" case for just $15, which is ideal for shipping a gun or carrying it in the back of a jeep or the like, thanks to the foam padding inside the case.

## CARTRIDGE CONVERSION KITS

During the mid-1970s, the U.S. Army started work on the creation of a .22 LR adapter for the M16A1 rifle. Versions of these were created by Colt, the U.S. Rock Island Small Arms Laboratory, the U.S. Military Armament Corporation, and Saco Defense Systems (a division of the Maremont Corporation). Of these, the one designed by John Foote for the U.S. Military Armament Corporation was finally selected to become the XM261 and was later finalized after a few modifications as the M261. The U.S. Air Force adopted a slightly different conversion unit designed by Julius Jurek at Langley Air Force Base in Virginia, and these are also sold on the surplus market. In addition, several commercial adapters have been created and are currently available.

All these .22 LR conversion actions, like most semiauto .22 rifles, are semiauto in action and contain their own bolt, recoil spring, and guide assembly that replaces the standard bolt of the AR-15. On the front of the adapter, a chamber insert shaped like the end an empty .223 cartridge insert fills the space in the rifle's chamber, while the inside of the insert becomes the new chamber for the .22 rounds. The conversion units carry fairly low price tags and can quickly pay for themselves for those who like to plink. The devices also allow hunting small game that would be vaporized by the standard .223 bullet.

Not all inserts extend into the area of the chamber where the rim of the neck on a .223 cartridge normally reaches but instead end in the area occupied by the .223 brass's shoulder. This can create leading problems as bullets collide with the small edge before they reach the rifling. Consequently, adapters with the "short neck" should be relegated to use in barrels that will only be fired with the .22 LR, or the shooter should be prepared to do some serious cleaning before firing a .223 cartridge in the gun.

As noted elsewhere, the .22 LR creates excessive

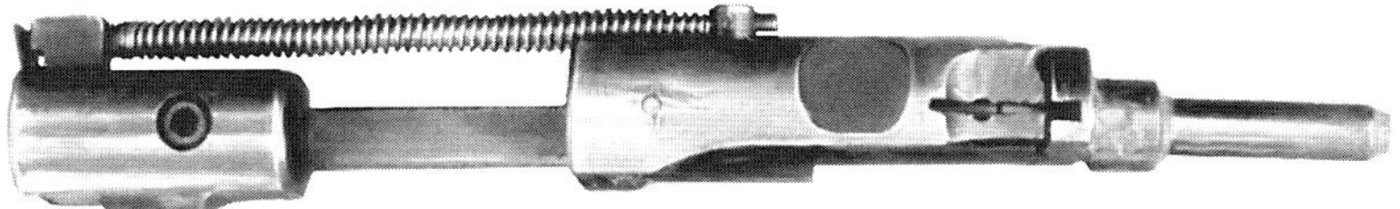

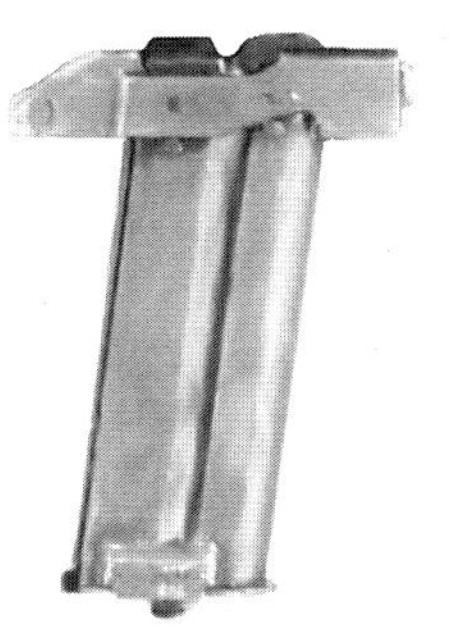

Military .22 adapter assembly. Magazine fits inside standard rifle magazine.

fouling in barrels with faster twists. Therefore these units are best used in 1-in-12-twist guns. Owners with fast-twist AR-15s may wish to purchase a barrel/receiver assembly with a slower twist or simply buy a .22 rifle like those listed earlier in this book.

Military surplus conversion units sometimes suffer from reliability problems. From a training standpoint this is perhaps not all bad: it forces the user to learn to recover quickly from problems that might occur in the worst of circumstances. If the rifle is used for hunting small game or the like, functioning problems can be aggravating, to say the least.

The M261 unit fires only in the semiauto mode and uses magazines that are nestled inside stock AR-15 magazines (you furnish the AR-15 magazine for the .22 magazines to go in). The .22 magazine units can be placed in or out of the standard magazines so that the magazines can still be used with the 5.56mm rounds, but this is a bit of a hassle. A better practice is to use defective 5.56mm magazines and put the .22 magazine inserts into the defective magazines and leave the inserts them there.

The M261 unit is currently available from SARCO for $125. The kit comes with three 10-round magazine inserts and a few spare parts. The M261 can be made considerably more reliable by keeping it religiously clean (especially the chamber) and by modifying the firing pin by grinding the point down so an I-shaped area (rather than O-shaped) hits the edge of the rim-fire round. Care must be taken when changing the firing pin so that it doesn't puncture the brass (which might cause gas to escape back into the action) or make the firing pin miss the primer area in the rim of the round.

At least two commercial .22 LR conversion kits have also been marketed. Colt offered a .22 LR adapter kit for $120 (this has since gone out of production); the company also offered the kit with some of its rifles. The kit came with a full-size plastic magazine that gave the "look" of the 20-round magazine. Spare magazines could also be purchased from Colt.

Colt .22 LR conversion kit, shown here in its blister pack. (Courtesy of Colt Firearms.)

The second unit is still available at the time of this writing. Max Atchisson, a noted firearms designer in his own right, created the runner-up .22 conversion kit in the U.S. Army trials. After the design he created for Military Armament Corporation was rejected by the army, he apparently remained fascinated by the concept and went on to create a totally new unit that employed elements of the military adapters coupled with several refinements of his own. This unit became the Atchisson MKIII, which is now offered by Jonathan Arthur Ciener; this adapter is superreliable and is the first choice for those wanting to convert an AR-15 to .22 LR use.

The Atchisson MKIII offers greater magazine capacity and generally functions better than the other .22 conversion units. Unlike the other .22 LR conversion kits, the Atchisson MKIII can function in selective-fire guns and comes with the hardware to convert it to this use (it will not fire in the auto mode with semiauto-only rifles).

As noted elsewhere, SGW/Olympic Arms has .45 ACP, 9mm Luger, and 7.62x39mm conversion kits; and Dalphon offers conversion kits in .50 AE, .45 ACP, .40 S&W, and 9mm Luger, as well as 7.62x39. Additionally, Colt has recently fielded a drop-in 9mm magazine unit, making it practical to purchase this adapter along with the company's upper barrel/receiver assembly to convert a rifle to 9mm use without the need to drill and pin the lower receiver as is currently done with 9mm Colt AR-15 carbines and submachine guns.

Ciener .22 LR adapter, shown here in a carbine.

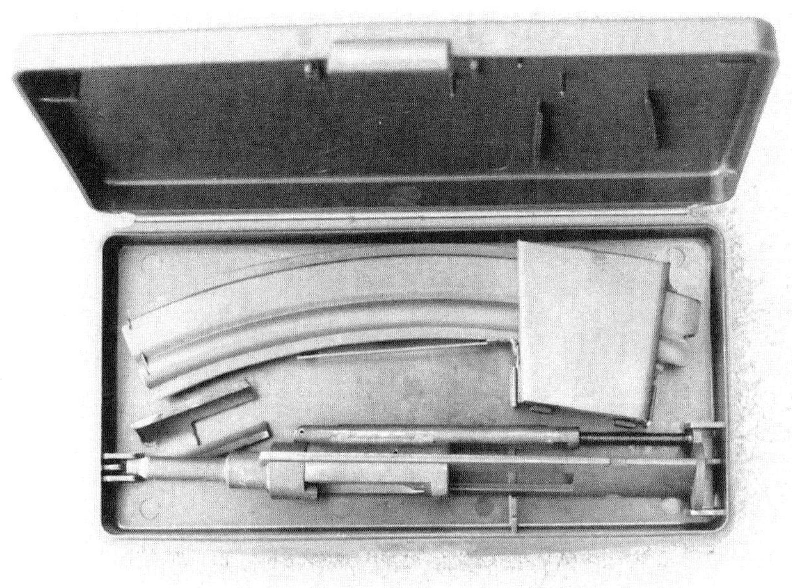

Ciener's 22 LR adapter kit comes in a box (upper left) and can quickly transform an AR-15 into the equivalent of a .22 trainer.

## M2 BOLT ADAPTER

Because the fast twist of the M16A2/M4 carbine precluded employment of .22 LR training devices (since the soft lead bullets quickly coated the inside of the barrel when the faster twist cut into each bullet's surface), the U.S. military took a different route than the Canadians (who opted for the .22 LR C10 training rifle). Instead the U.S. military adopted plastic ammunition coupled with the M2 practice bolt system created in 1986 for the M16 rifle.

Designated the Training Bolt, M2 (Rifles and Carbine Team, AMSTA-LC-CSIR), this carrier and bolt lack a gas key and a locking lugs on the bolt. Instead the unit operates in a straight blowback mode with the blue-cased M862 plastic training ammunition. This allows standard rifles to be used by simply exchanging the bolt in the rifle. The plastic ammunition has plastic and metal bullets that have a high muzzle velocity but that quickly drop in speed, giving the projectiles a maximum range of only 250 meters. (Because of the high muzzle velocity and short range of such bullets, there has been talk of using this or similar ammunition against terrorists or in general law enforcement work; but there appears to be no actual use of such cartridges at the time of this writing.)

Another useful training device employed by the army is the Multiple Integrated Laser Engagement System (MILES) that permits a variety of weapons, including the M16, to fire blanks as well as an invisible laser beam. Each member of the training exercise wears helmet and

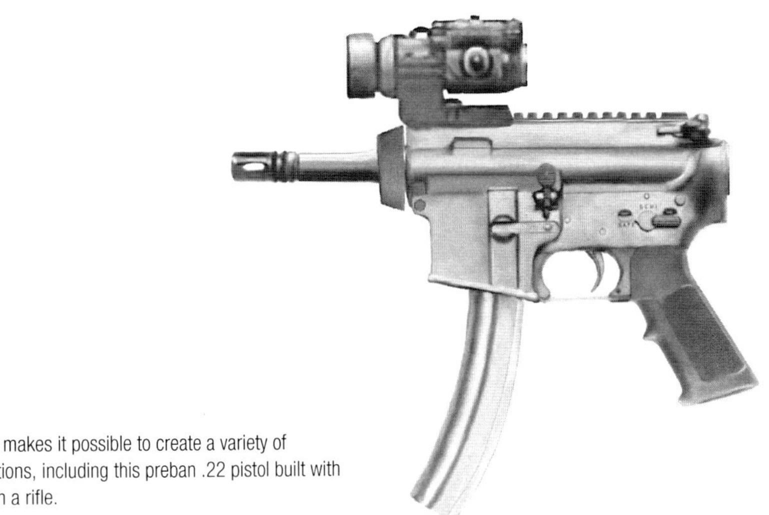

The Ciener .22 LR adapter also makes it possible to create a variety of otherwise impossible configurations, including this preban .22 pistol built with new parts not previously used in a rifle.

MILES training equipment in action, with Pfc. Brian Ashavranner of Bravo Company, 1st Battalion, 8th Marines. (Courtesy of U.S. Department of Defense.)

torso sensors that register a "hit" when a laser beam hits them. This makes it possible for soldiers to engage in training exercises that resemble Laser Tag in concept—but involve the weapons they'd actually be using in combat. This translates into a realistic battlefield environment for soldiers using the MILES.

The MILES lasers register near misses as well as hits, so soldiers become aware if an enemy is shooting at them but missing, much as in actual combat. Similar MILES devices are mounted on tanks, helicopters, and other vehicles; these systems remain insensitive to laser hits from small-arms fire while reacting to the coded lasers employed with antitank and antiair weapons in these exercises.

## CARTRIDGE ADAPTER INSERTS

For a time, Harry Owen offered special inserts that allowed .22 CB Cap, .22 Short, .22 Long, .22 Long Rifle, or (with a second adapter) .22 Magnum cartridges to be fired—single shot—from the AR-15. These inserts are shaped on the outside like an empty 5.56mm round (complete with the extractor groove) with a chamber on the inside of the insert. A small striker/insert is placed into the adapter behind the round; this striker transfers the firing pin's force to the rim of the round in the adapter.

The .22 rimfire is placed in the appropriate adapter, the action of the AR-15 is pulled open, the adapter with the round is placed in the chamber of the rifle, and the action eased shut. Care *must* be exercised to avoid letting the action slam shut on the round—it may be fired by the AR-15's floating firing pin: instead ease the bolt forward by maintaining the grip on the charging handle as it goes forward, then fully seat the bolt with the forward assist.

Once the adapter and cartridge are chambered, the shooter can fire the single round. Pulling the action open after firing extracts the adapter, and a small stick or nail can be used to push out the empty cartridge and striker from the adapter so that it's ready to be reloaded.

One of the nice features of the single-shot adapter is that it allows the shooter to go from .223 Remington to a smaller cartridge and back without opening the receiver and pulling out the bolt carrier, as is the case with the semiauto adapter kits. This can be a real plus when the smaller cartridge is suddenly needed—as might be so in a hunting or survival situation. The flip side of this is that it takes forever to get off a second shot unless you have more than one adapter (and even then they have to be individually fed by hand into the chamber). Currently no one seems to be making these single-shot adapters, though they can sometimes be found at gun shows. It seems likely that they will be available again in the near future, and those handy with tools can create these on a lathe.

In both semiauto adapters as well as the Harry Owen-style single shots, there are some types of ammunition that add to the flexibility of the rifle. For instance, there are standard lead bullets, which are usually available at discount stores at a low price that makes practice cheap. And there are high-velocity .22 rounds like CCI's Stinger, which is ideal for varminting at close ranges.

For very quiet shots (and even nearly unnoticeable varminting or target practice indoors or in the backyard), the new .22 Long CB Caps (offered by Remington, CCI, and Federal) are especially useful and can be cycled by hand through the action of the .22 semiauto conversion kits as well as in the single-shot adapters. These cartridges are also ideal in adapters for training beginners because, unlike standard .22 LR cartridges, the CB caps don't cycle the action, so it becomes a "bolt action" for all practical purposes.

## FLASHLIGHT MOUNTS

While a flashlight mounted on a rifle can turn it into a dandy target at night, a flashlight does have some advantages, especially if it is one of the newer, bright lights capable of identifying a target (so the shooter isn't firing blindly) and for showing approximately where the bullet will hit (thereby acting as an aiming device). A flashlight mounted on a gun must have a momentary switch so that it can be quickly turned on and off. Such a switch guarantees that the light is automatically shut off if it is dropped—or is downed by a shot. Having the light go off in such a case can be a lifesaver.

Powerful flashlights with halogen or xenon bulbs can create enough light to dazzle an opponent. This gives the user of a firearm an intimidating edge, especially indoors. Most flashlights suitable for mounting on an AR-15 will accept a xenon or krypton bulb (available at most large electronics stores); bulbs should be matched to the type of batteries that work best with them and the manufacturer's recommended voltage/amperage and specifications adhered to carefully (by matching the bulb with the correct batteries, the life of the two can be boosted by up to 20 percent). For a time, B-Square manufactured a Mag Lite Saddle that mounted a standard-sized D-cell flashlight to most of the B-Square scope mounts. The lighter weight of flashlights has now made this mount more or less obsolete, so it is no longer found in the company's catalog.

It's now possible to mount a flashlight directly in scope rings. All that's needed is a flashlight with a 1-inch-diameter body (or smaller, since electrician's tape can be used to "shim" fit it). Of course, ideally, the flashlight would also have a momentary switch on a cord—not standard fare.

Fortunately, you can buy a flashlight designed specifically for use on a rifle like the AR-15. The unit is marketed by Applied Laser as the Beamshot Tactical. The flashlight is powered by two CR123 3-volt lithium batteries for a 20-hour continuous/2- to 3-year battery life. The flashlight costs $78, with a remote cord switch for mounting on the handguard of an AR-15 running an additional $10.95. This can be mounted on a 1-inch scope with the company's RF4 mount or to the rifle's barrel with the RF3 mount, either of which costs $10.95. The "WLS Light System 2000," available from CIE Global, features a xenon lamp powered by two 3-volt lithium batteries to deliver up to 6,000 candlepower light output from one very small flashlight with an adjustable beam.

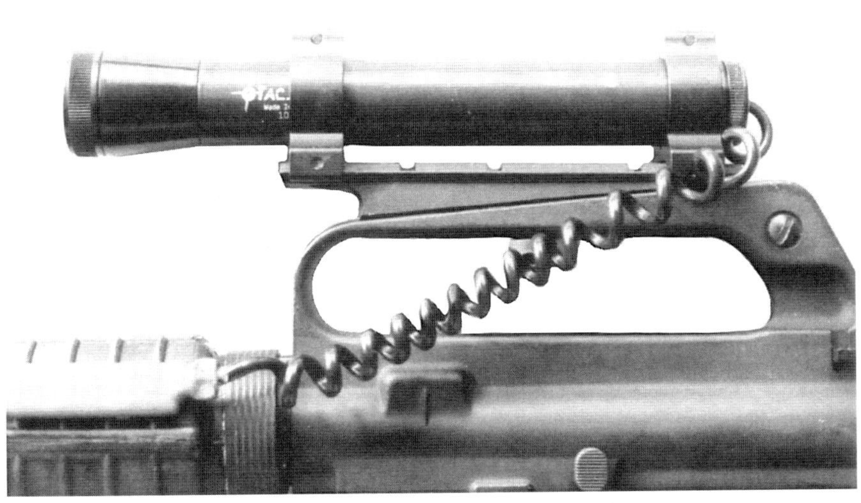

Powerful flashlights with a 1-inch body can be easily mounted in scope rings, as shown here with a (now discontinued) Tac-Star flashlight.

Clamps can also be employed to mount a flashlight to the barrel of an AR-15. A remote momentary switch attached to the handguard makes this very convenient to use.

The flashlight also comes with a pressure-sensitive on/off switch at the end of a curly cord that is easily attached to an AR-15 handguard. A precision mount secures the flashlight to the barrel of a firearm.The cost is $119.95

The Surefire M-500A is a set of M4 carbine handguards with built-in light and switches, giving the user a flashlight mount that has no exposed wires and buttons that won't shift position. One button is a momentary on switch, another a rocker off/on switch, and the third disables the light so it remains off while in storage. The light is powered by three lithium batteries, with the case machined from aircraft aluminum and anodized black. Available from Brownells, the M-500A is not cheap; the cost of the unit is $481.

The TACM III (also from Brownells) is a compact 30,000-candlepower flashlight that comes with a barrel mount and a momentary switch on a short cord. Mounting it on an AR-15 makes it easy to bathe an area in light with a little pressure on the handguard-mounted switch. The flashlight is powered by two 3-volt lithium batteries and costs $131.85.

It should be noted that in many areas of the United States using flashlights on firearms when hunting is illegal. However, there are parts of the country where hunting raccoons or other animals with a flashlight is legal. In such areas, the flashlight mount systems discussed above may be an ideal way to engage in the hunt.

## FLASH SUPPRESSORS AND MUZZLE BRAKES

Flash suppressors minimize the muzzle flash that can give away a position of a rifleman in combat; consequently, most modern military and police rifles have flash hiders (also called flash suppressors) attached to their muzzles. These devices don't completely eliminate muzzle flash, but they do reduce it, especially with ammunition designed for minimal flash and with rifles having longer barrels.

Muzzle brakes reduce felt recoil and make shooting a more enjoyable experience. Compensators help prevent recoil forces from pushing the barrel upward off target and are generally the same as muzzle brakes with most modern designs that both reduce recoil and compensate for recoil. The frequent trade-off for reduced recoil and compensation is added noise and flash, although some muzzle brakes do a pretty good job of keeping them to a minimum so that the brake isn't too noisy. Some modern systems try to combine the muzzle brake and the flash hider to have the best of both systems.

A flash hider or muzzle brake has an added plus of protecting a barrel from dings and damage; this is important because damage to the muzzle can quickly ruin accuracy. Consequently, even sport shooters who don't need to reduce flash will discover that a flash hider or muzzle brake makes good sense on an AR-15.

Oddly enough, many flash hiders also reduce bullet dispersion, to make a barrel more accurate, and may even increase muzzle velocity by a few feet per second. (The increased accuracy is a good reason for target

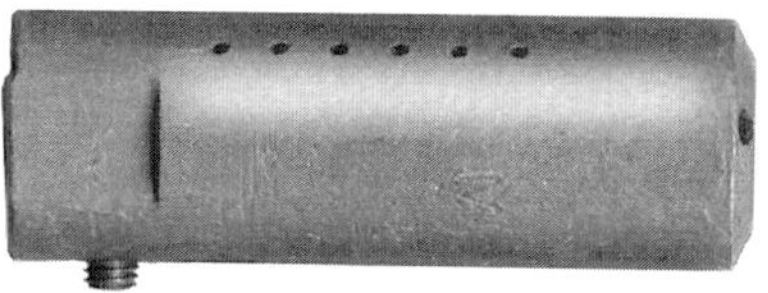

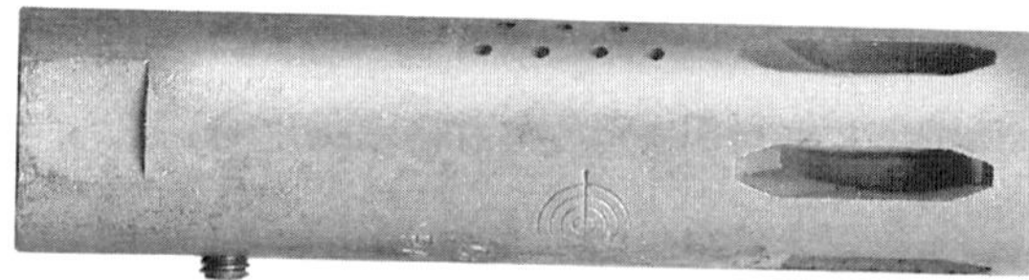

Just a handful of the many, many flash hiders and muzzle brakes that have been created for the AR-15.

shooters to purchase barrels threaded for a flash hider or muzzle brake.)

The A1-style birdcage hider is cheap and works well; the A2-style is nearly as effective and has the lower cutouts missing, so it acts as a compensator to keep the barrel on target during strings of fire (and also keeps from raising a dust cloud during prone shooting). These two hiders may be all most shooters need.

For maximum flash hiding, the open-prong flash hider is hard to beat. One modern version of this, which almost completely eliminates flash on 20-inch barrels and comes close to this with 16-inch or shorter barrels, is the Sommers Vortex, invented, designed, and refined by Sonja Sommers (working for Smith Enterprise, Inc.). Currently Smith Enterprise sells this flash hider for $40. Two and a quarter inches long, the Vortex has computer-designed prongs that are slightly offset to create a swirl of gas that ignites any burning powder residue. Originally the unit was designed just for hiding flash, but it was also found to reduce the size of groups being fired and to reduce recoil somewhat. (The trade-off here is a loss in velocity of a few feet per second—something most shooters won't be able to detect.) Because of all the enhancements the Vortex offers, it's now its being sold more or less as a multipurpose device, though it is illegal for civilian use on postban AR-15s.

For those who hated the original duckbill flash hiders on the AR-15, the Vortex has a feature to help avoid the device's getting caught on vegetation: a groove around its prongs that permits wrapping a small piece of wire around it to make a birdcage hider. Provided just a small wire is used, the increase in flash is imperceptible.

The now-discontinued Fabian Brothers' muzzle brake is most ideal when it can be located; the final model dropped felt recoil by around 44 percent and stabilized the muzzle to put bursts of automatic fire in one spot with just a bit of practice with the stabilizer on a selective-fire rifle. The original design for this brake (sold as the DTA Mil/Brake) didn't do much to suppress flash, but the design was revamped when it was sold to Fabian Brothers and became the Muzzle Stabilizer after being reworked to have birdcage-style A1-type slits at its front, which greatly reduced the flash. The result was both a muzzle brake and a flash hider in one very effective unit. In addition to the standard .223 Muzzle Stabilizer, Fabian Brothers also makes a 9mm version for carbine models of the AR-15.

Sadly, the manufacturing rights for the Fabian Brothers' muzzle brake were sold to L.L. Baston, which soon after went out of business. With the assault weapon ban currently limiting the potential sales of flash-hider-equipped muzzle brakes, it seems doubtful that the new owner of L.L. Baston's machinery will go to the trouble of reviving it, which is a shame. One can always hope that the time will come when the assault weapon ban will be allowed to expire and the Mil-Brake will again be marketed.

Another good compensator/muzzle brake, used by Jerry Miculek to win the 1989 steel challenge, is the Clark/Miculek muzzle brake. This unit is modeled after the style of brake used by artillery and tank cannon, with twin holes on either side of its cylinder. These openings quickly bleed gas to the side to eliminate almost all muzzle rise. There are models to fit an AR-15 in the standard .223 as well as a second version for 7.62x39mm; unfortunately, these are available only with the preban threading, so even though technically you might mount one on a postban gun, you'd need a gunsmith to thread the barrel and then permanently weld the brake in place.The cost is $45 from Clark Custom Guns, Inc.

The EGW compensator from Brownells has A2 styling with a small hole in an otherwise solid front that captures a large share of the muzzle blast to counter the recoil a shot produces. Like the A2 hider, the lower slot in this compensator is missing, thereby eliminating dust signature during prone shooting. This unit requires that the muzzle be threaded and employs a "peel" washer to properly index the compensator. Its cost is $50.

The Cav Comp from Brownells also has the look of an A2 flash hider but again is actually a brake and can even be employed on a postban gun provided its barrel is threaded and the unit welded in place. The Cav Comp sells for $25.

The JP Enterprises Recoil Eliminator is another brake that employs the same engineering found on tank gun barrels. It employs two curved restrictor plates that capture muzzle gas and act like sails to shove the gun forward, thereby countering recoil and muzzle flip. The preban version ( $79.95) screws onto standard threading, while the postban version ($89.95) mounts on a barrel with set screws that hold the compensator in place. Both are available from Brownells.

## FREE-FLOAT HANDGUARDS

Because pressure on an AR-15 handguard, especially when exerted by a sling or bipod, can change the point of impact with the barrel, many target and sniper rifles have a free-floated barrel to improve (often dramatically) their accuracy. Often free-floating a standard barrel will give it the ability to shoot 1-inch or smaller groups at 100 yards; sometimes even greater accuracy can be enjoyed with the addition of a quality heavy barrel—though many shooters aren't able to realize this accuracy without a lot of practice. (The name "free-float handguard" has been adopted for handguards that free-float the barrel—somewhat confusing since it sounds as if the handguard, not the barrel, is being free-floated.)

To mount a free-floating handguard on a rifle is no easy task with many AR-15s, due to the tightness of the pins holding the gas block (and front sight with those barrels having them) in place. As noted elsewhere in this book , the front sight assembly on a gun that has been fired often can be removed only with great effort by drifting out the two pins securing the base of the assembly out. Also important is that these pins are tapered and can only be removed by pushing them out from left to right (i.e., toward the ejection port side of the rifle). This job is best done with a heavy sledgehammer held with a very short grip near the head of the hammer and a large punch, working on a lead pad. Great care must be taken not to damage the rifle. (Once you've done this, you'll understand why most people opt to buy a free-floated barrel on a factory-assembled target rifle rather than create one on their own.)

Once the gas block is removed from a barrel and the barrel nut holding the barrel to the receiver removed (also outlined elsewhere in this book), the floating handguard can be placed over the barrel with its send, which is threaded to form a barrel nut and screwed onto the upper receiver to hold the barrel in place, taking care to align one of the holes at the handguard's rear end to accommodate the gas tube.

With the new handguard in place, the barrel block (or a new one without a front sight base if the gun will be used with a scope) is then replaced and the pins pounded back in to secure it, a process that doesn't call for a sledgehammer because the pins will soon tighten up as they become heated after the rifle has been fired a few times—though they should be quite tight after a drift punch and regular hammer have been employed to slip them into the gas block base.

A number of companies offer free-float handguards. DPMS has one of the best assortments, with both carbine and rifle lengths. The company also offers a DCM National Match handguard for $151 and a Hotrod handguard with 19 steel rods inserted into two aluminum end caps for a superventilated, free-floating handguard; the latter model's cost is $89.95. The company's H. Merchant DCM Free Float Tube is a tube that accepts A2 handguards, giving the look of a regular rifle while actually having a free-floating barrel; the price for this system is $149.95 (without the A2 handguard).

The JP Enterprises High Grade Free Float Tube (available from Brownells) is a two-piece handguard with an internally threaded tube and separate barrel nut. The handguard section has 20 elongated slots to aid barrel cooling as well as affording a more secure grip. The standard model extends from the front of the receiver to the rear of the front gas block; the long version extends past the gas block to cover it (and obviously must therefore be used with a low-mount gas block without a front sight). Either version sells for $150.

Brownells offers low-profile gas port assemblies for use with scoped AR-15s (and that will go under the JP Enterprises extended handguard). One is Smith's low-profile gas port assembly to replace the front sight/gas port for $46.66. The aluminum unit comes with dual set screws to provide positive attachment and has a black anodized finish. The second gas block assembly is made by GB Systems and comes in two versions, one for 0.75-inch diameter barrels and the other for 0.94-inch diameter barrels. Either sells for $39.95.

Brownells also offers the EGW free-float handguards, which are formed from a single piece of extruded-aluminum tubing coupled with a machined barrel nut. These come in black ($60), blue ($68), or red ($68) anodized finishes with the rifle models and black for the carbine ($60).

Also available from Brownells is the Rock River Arms free-float barrel, which is "DCM legal" since it holds A2 handguards in place over its tube while keeping them free of the front sight/gas port assembly. This kit comes with A2 handguards, sling swivel and gas tube. It costs $125.

## HANDGUARD VERTICAL GRIPS

The vertical handguard grip has been seen off and on with weapons at least as far back as the Thompson submachine gun. These offer a bit more stability and certainly place the forward hand at a more natural angle. At the same time, they add one more component to the weapon, hanging down where they can get caught on objects, as well as complicating storage. So there are minuses that often completely offset any gain offered by these additions to a carbine or rifle.

However, when scope systems like those seen with the Land Warrior and OICW programs are used to enable shooters to "look over walls and around corners" by putting the rifle in harm's way while the image is piped back to a helmet-mounted viewer, then the forward grip can be a great aid (if not essential) in maneuvering and aiming the weapon.Once in place, it makes possible a variety of holds that are useful—and nearly impossible without the forward vertical grip in place. Little wonder, then, that the new modular systems being created for use by the U.S. military include a detachable grip that mounts on the Picatinny rail system (more on this system later).

Of course, there are grips and there are grips. For years, experimenters have bolted AR-15 pistol grips to the handguard (the vent holes of the A2 handguard making this an easy task) or to the bayonet lug. The catch with these is that the off hand comes to the forward grip at an angle, making the pistol grip less than ideal for a secure hold. (These grips are still being marketed by Bushmaster and Laser Sales for those who wish to try one of these.) Consequently most new systems use the H&K-style grip with a tubular profile. This design can be securely gripped from a variety of angles and remain comfortable to use.

For those with access to a rail-mount handguard and one of the vertical grips in the SOPMOD kit, all that's necessary is to put the grip where it is needed. These parts can also be purchased from Knight's, probably the best route for those who aren't on a limited budget (the vertical grip costs $50 and a rifle rail handguard system $335, with an M4 rail system for a handguard going for $287). These rail systems simply replace the handguard of the rifle or carbine, and then the grip attaches to the lower (or side if a user so desired) on the Weaver rail at whatever distance from the receiver feels most comfortable. Once the screws are tightened on the grip, it is securely attached to the handguard.

I have seen do-it-yourselfers create much the same feel for considerably less. One unit that makes this quick work is the grip that E&L Manufacturing offered on its barrel shrouds. This unit is a near-duplicate of the H&K grip and ends in a steel bolt; by adding a washer and nut inside the handguard, a shooter can then screw this grip

The Knight's rail mount system and sling mount accessories make it possible to easily modify the M4 carbine.

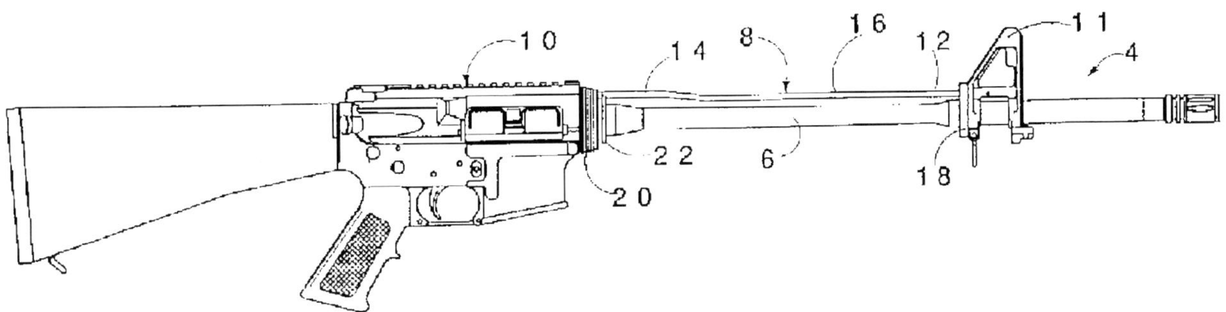

**RAIL ADAPTER HANDGUARD SYSTEMS FOR FIREARMS**

Inventor: **Douglas D. Olson**, Vero Beach, Fla.

Assignee: **Knights Armament Company**, Vero Beach, Fla.

**Patent Number:** **5,826,363**

**Date of Patent:** **Oct. 27, 1998**

One of the patent drawings for what would eventually become Knight's rail mount system.

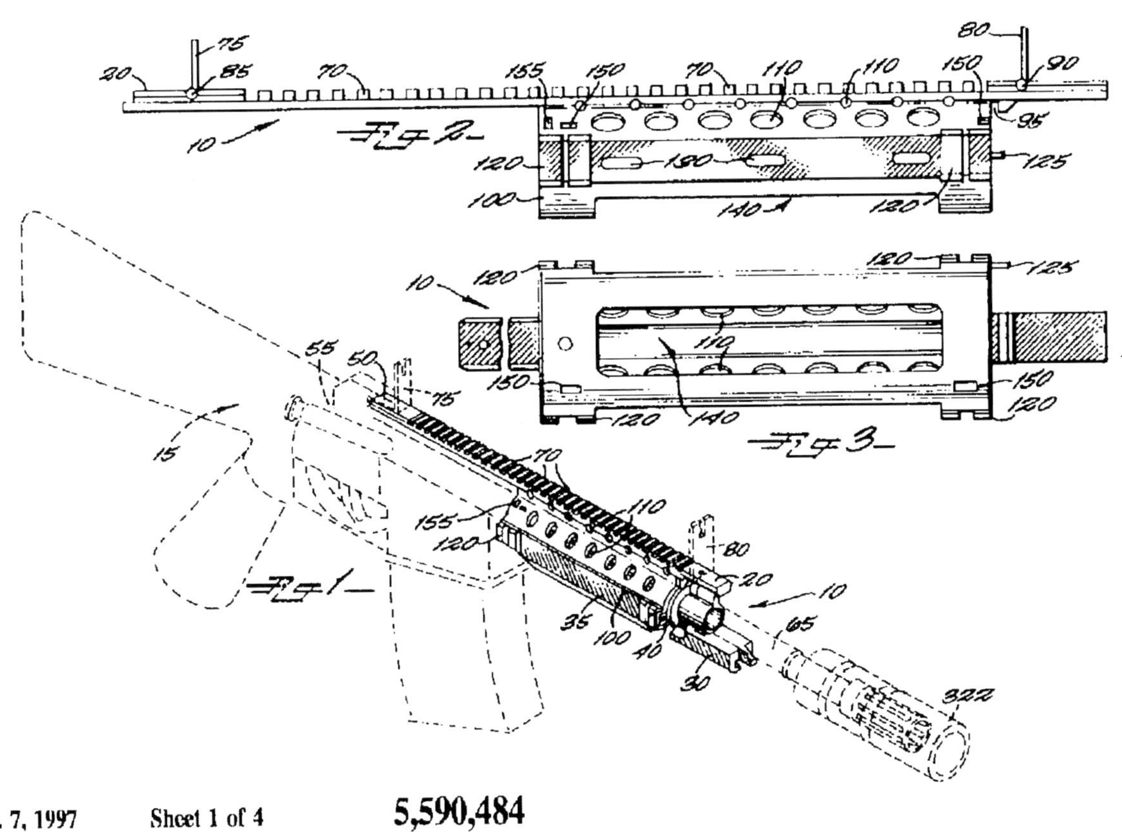


Patent drawing for rail mount system.

into place. About the only drawbacks are that it is not as strong as the Knight's system and it not as easy to mount and remove.

I have also seen handy forward grips created with bicycle and motorcycle handlebar grips, placed over the appropriately sized pipe that was welded to a bolt. This was then secured with a washer and nut to an A2-style handguard. This is a lot of work, but if you have access to some welding equipment it is undoubtedly a cheaper—though admittedly not quite as convenient or strong—alternative to the rail mount.

## LASER SIGHTS

Technology has transformed the laser sight from a huge system that was both expensive and impractical to a tiny unit that sells at very affordable prices. Keeping up with models and prices is nearly impossible; it can be said with some certainty that by the time this edition gets to print, some of the data about specific sights will be out of date. With that in mind, treat this section as an overview, and perhaps a short history, rather than the definitive writing about laser sights.

Some of the first laser sights for hand-held firearms were created for the AR-15, not surprising given its military use as well as a lot of room in its hollow stock for a massive battery pack to power the early monstrosities. The laser itself looked like a huge scope mounted on the top of the gun or under the barrel. The cost ran into the thousands of dollars, and batteries quickly added to the hemorrhage of money when the units were used for practice. But these lasers proved the practicality of such systems as a nighttime aiming system and paved the way for more modern—and much smaller—laser sights. So while modern laser sights have the limitations of the originals in many ways (more on this in a moment), thanks to today's electronics, they are now tiny and reasonably priced.

Lasers create a tight beam of red coherent light that appears as a bright red dot up to one or two hundred yards away in dim light. Although this beam is straight and a ballistic arch is curved, the two are close enough that that the beam from a laser mounted parallel to a bore will coincide within several inches to the impact of a bullet over several hundred yards. This makes it practical to pinpoint targets without using an AR-15's standard sights.

There are drawbacks with laser sights. One is that unless the light is in the proper spectrum, it's useful only in dim light because sunlight hides the beam's red dot. A few companies now offer "daylight" lasers, but unfortunately, due to the federal regulations that limit the brightness of lasers ( to protect eyesight from damage from the beam), their red dots are still a tad hard to pick out on targets in bright sunlight.

At the other extreme, when a laser sight is employed in a really dark environment, the laser is readily seen but it doesn't illuminate the target. Therefore, either a light source has to be added or the shooter will end up firing more or less blindly (which is practical if returning fire toward muzzle flashes). The laser beam can also be seen as a bright red light by anyone facing the muzzle of an AR-15 with a laser on it, and in fog, rain, or smoke, the beam becomes a beacon leading to the shooter's position. Military users sometimes use a laser that puts out a beam that can't be seen by the naked eye—but can be seen by night-vision equipment. Obviously, this is great if your side has the night-vision equipment, but not so wise should both groups have this night-vision equipment.

A shooter with a team of members similarly equipped with laser sights will also quickly discover that it is hard to tell which bouncing laser dot is which member's. Consequently, a squad generally uses a laser on the leader's rifle, which can act as a designator, directing bullet traffic as it were. However, it is possible to key a laser to special electronic visors that differentiate between the user's laser and those of his team; at this point, it becomes possible (albeit expensive) to equip each member of an assault team with laser sights.

There are times when the laser shines (so to speak). In dim light and indoor day conditions, the laser works very well to quickly point out a target so a shooter can be "on target" in only a moment without shouldering and aiming his AR-15. For those who can operate within the parameters of a laser sight, it can be a very useful aiming device, especially when operated with a momentary switch left on only long enough to acquire a target and fire.

Prices for good lasers at the time of this writing range from \$200 to \$350; the units have shelf lives of at least 10 years, and their operational life is 10,000 or more hours. The life of batteries ranges from 30 minutes to several hours depending on the laser and whether it's flashed on and off or left on continuously (which is harder on the batteries). Newer lasers have a flickering strobe beam that makes the batteries last even longer.

Some newer lasers can be mounted in Weaver rings, within 1-inch scope rings, or in Adventurer Outpost's flashlight barrel mounts created for the Tac-Star. Most manufacturers also offer a "clamp" mount that couples their laser to a scope, making it possible to have an optical system mounted to take over when the environment is too bright for a laser.

(For those who want to mount a laser or other scope on a Weaver rail, see the rail mounting systems section in this chapter.)

Most laser sights have elevation and windage screws making zeroing simple (just use the iron sights or rifle scope and adjust the laser so it's in the center of the sight picture). Since most laser sights for firearms have a pressure switch on the end of a cord for activation with the thumb or fingers, care must also be taken to avoid snagging the cord.

These are the key points to keep in mind when shopping for a laser sight:

- Be sure the mount is stable and the laser easily zeroed to your rifle.
- Be sure the unit uses standard batteries that are easy to find
- Be sure the laser has a momentary switch so it will shut down if you are injured, drop the weapon, or forget to turn the unit off when you store it.

Mounting a small laser on an AR-15 is a snap, thanks to mounting brackets that connect it to the barrel. Coiled cord and momentary switch fastened to the handguard complete the system.

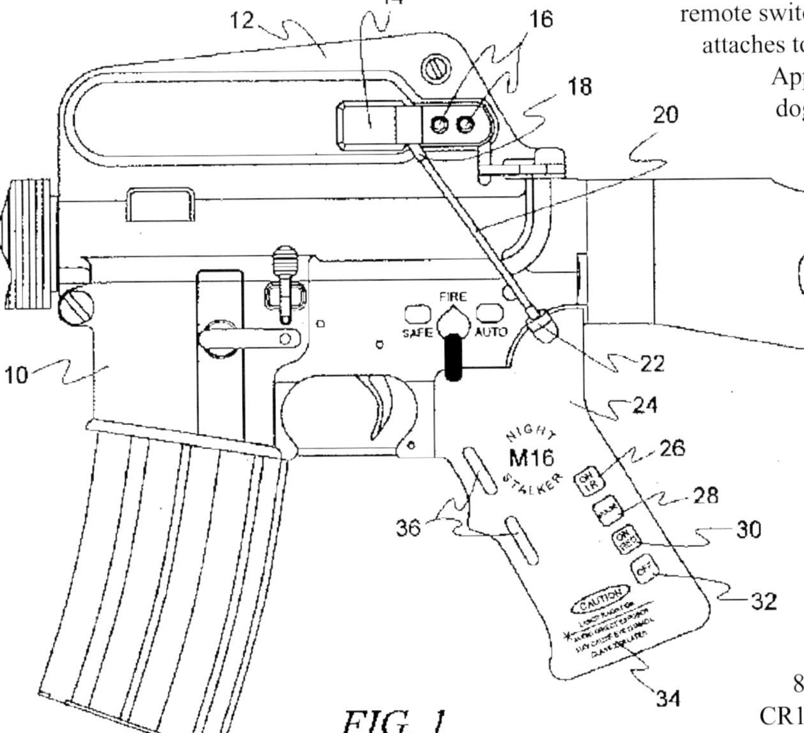


Patent drawing for a laser sight not yet marketed, with its controls conveniently mounted in the pistol grip of the AR-15.

It should be noted that at this writing Colt is producing an AR-15 sight for its rifles. Marketed as the Integrated Laser, the unit attaches to the front leg of the front sight post and sits ahead of the sight, below the sight picture. It is activated by a pressure switch mounted to the handguard. Its Cost is $299.95, making it less than competitive with some other models.

Another popular unit is the Lasersight, which mounts to the barrel of an AR-15 with a mounting bracket. A remote switch on an expandable "curly-cue" cord then attaches to the handguard. It costs $169.95.

Applied Laser currently appears to be the top dog in the civilian and police marketplace with several models of laser sights available. One of the more popular models with the AR-15 is the Beamshot 1000 Super (costing $58), which manages to be about five times brighter than older, similar laser sights and can be used out to 500 yards in dim light. This laser uses three SR44 or LR44 batteries for up to three hours of continuous use with batteries having a battery shelf life of two to three years.

Applied Laser's Ultra ($78) has a wavelength of 635nm, making it easier to see, and although in daylight the beam is easily lost except at closer ranges, at night the bright beam can be employed out to 800 yards or more. This laser uses a single CR123 3-volt lithium battery to give it 20 hours of continuous use with a 2- to 3-year battery shelf life. A remote cord switch for mounting on the handguard of an AR-15 (or elsewhere, depending on the laser sight placement) runs an additional $10.95. Lasers can be mounted on a 1-inch scope with the company's RF4 mount or to the rifle's barrel with the RF3 mount, either of which costs $10.95.

One of the newer innovations in civilian/police laser sights is Applied Laser's Beamshot Greenbeam 2000, which uses a greenish laser operating at 532nm to produce a dot that is visible in daylight. This unit carries a hefty price tag, however, currently $499 (though this is likely to drop in the future). This laser will operate for four hours with a single battery and fits the company's other mounts.

Another popular civilian/police laser site is the Universal Rifle Laser available from CIE Global. This unit comes with a remote switch with expandable curly cord along with the hardware to mount the aimer on an AR-15 barrel. Its cost is $119.95.

The U.S. military has developed several laser aiming systems that operate outside the spectrum that the eye can see but can be spotted by night-vision equipment. This makes a system ideal for use against an enemy that doesn't have the latest technology. This type of laser can also be used to designate targets or draw the attention of fellow soldiers to a specific location. Of course, like the standard laser, such a system becomes a ready target if an enemy also has night-vision equipment. In such a case, a false sense of superiority might mean the undoing of a user equipped with such a laser sight.

The standard laser aiming system currently issued to U.S. military units is the AN/PAQ-4C Infrared Aiming Light manufactured by Insight Technology (of Manchester, New Hampshire). This unit is a bit over 1.5 inches in diameter and 6.1 inches long, weighing 9 ounces with batteries (two AA size). It has a range of 100 to 300 meters, depending on the environment it is used in. Cost is in the neighborhood of $400. In addition to mounting on the AR-15 rifles, mounts are available for use on the M60, M249, and M2 machine gun.

## LEFTY AND OFFHAND AIDS

In addition to helping left-handed users, levers, buttons, and other controls on a firearm can be a big asset for house-to-house fighting or other situations where a rifle needs to be switched from one side to another to negotiate building corners, room entries, and the like. For this reason, in addition to being a boon for left-handed shooters, ambidextrous controls can be a lifesaver in the field.

Another plus starting with the A2 version of the AR-15 is the shell deflector hump behind the ejection port that guarantees that no longer will an occasional hot brass cartridge be spit into a lefty's face while he tries to concentrate on his target. (And for those lefties using the A1 model, all is not lost. Uncle Sam created the "cartridge deflector," which snaps into the carrying handle ahead of the sight and acts in the same manner as the hump does on the A2 models. The only catch is that these are getting hard to find. Good places to check are Sierra Supply and other military surplus dealers.)

One excellent ambidextrous device to hit the market recently is the Ambi-Catch, an ambidextrous magazine release that permits dropping a magazine by touching the same spot on the left side of the receiver occupied by the release button on the right side, for true ambidextrous operation. This device shows some slick engineering; it replaces the magazine catch on the left of the receiver with a new unit having a rocker design; once the substitution is made, depressing the rear of the rocker lifts the magazine catch to release the magazine. Currently this device is in use by members of the army Special Forces

House-to-house fighting often entails switching the rifle from one side to the other to negotiate corners of buildings and doorways. In such cases the bullpup is at a disadvantage. (Courtesy of U.S. Department of Defense.)

The Ambi-Catch permits lefties to release the magazine with an index finger. (Courtesy of Norgon LLC.)

An ambidextrous selector makes life easier for lefties. A C-clip secures the lever.

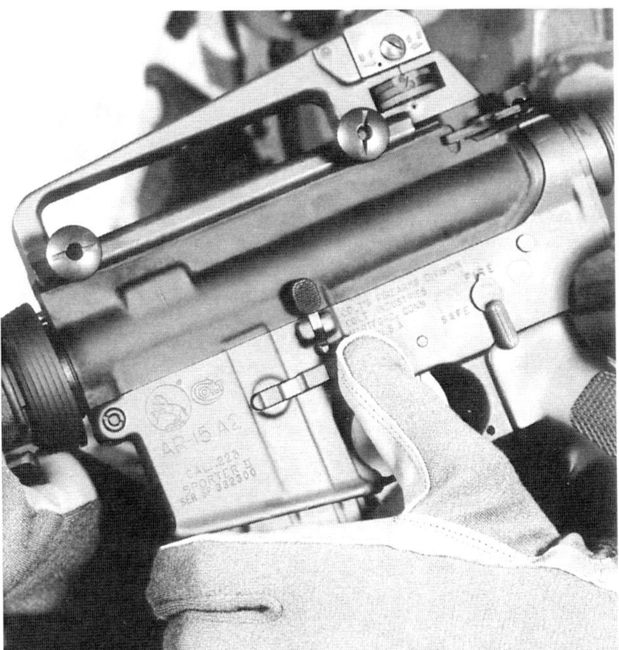

The Ambi-Catch also allows the release of a magazine with the thumb of the off-hand, something many shooters find more convenient for a magazine exchange. (Courtesy of Norgon LLC.)

and navy SEALs, and it wouldn't be surprising if it becomes a standard part of new AR-15s.

The Ambi-Catch also permits releasing a magazine with the thumb of the left hand as the catch is depressed with the thumb. This leaves the right hand free to keep its position on the trigger and also makes exchanging magazines without dropping the empty possible. This may be a mode many right-handers want to adopt with this catch. The Ambi-Catch is available from Norgon LLC for $89.95 (with discounts for law enforcement and government groups buying in quantity).

The charging handle is pretty much ambidextrous, and the magazine release can be hit with the thumb of the right hand to drop it as the new magazine is brought up (maybe grabbing the empty in the process—those living in a right-handers' world get pretty skillful at juggling-like maneuvers).

The selector of the AR-15 can be manipulated with the trigger finger (if the shooter is left-handed). But an ambidextrous safety makes the task easier since the shooter can just thumb the safety off like his right-handed friends do. The ambidextrous safety is available from Quality Parts (Bushmaster) for $35.

And of course there's the "true lefty" version of the AR-15 upper receiver offered by DPMS. This receiver has the ejection port cut into the left side of the receiver (and the right side left solid without the usual port cut out) and comes with a modified bolt that sits "upside down" to flip brass toward the left and out the ejection port. With one of these receivers and modified bolt (and an ambidextrous safety), a shooter can transform an AR-15 into a real lefty gun that ejects brass out its left side. Then the owner's right-handed friends can take a try at firing the gun to see what it's like to get hot brass thrown into their shirt pocket from time to time.

## MAGAZINES

This is one of the most important parts of the AR-15. It's also one of the parts that users often skimp on: this is a mistake because poor magazines guarantee failure to feed sooner or later and may do so when the shooter's life is on the line. It's worth a few dollars to purchase quality magazines so a rifle will function properly when it's really needed.

One of the most fragile systems with the AR-15 is its magazine. Damage to the magazine due to dropping or misuse can quickly make the firearm malfunction when cartridges fail to feed properly. Always take care not to drop loaded magazines, and be especially careful with the "lips" at the top of the magazine that hold the cartridges in. Damage to this area of the magazine will make cartridges fail to feed properly.

It's wise to purchase extra spare magazines in case one or more of those you own become damaged. While the current ban against manufacture of magazines with a capacity greater than 10 rounds is still in effect in the United States, high-capacity magazines manufactured before the ban are legal and widely available. These cost a pretty penny, but the added capacity can be important in a gun used for self-defense or in other shooting where high-capacity magazines are a plus.

If you are in law enforcement work, you may be able to obtain extended-round magazines made exclusively for government use. These carry a low price tag and are very reliable, making them a first choice if you can legally obtain them. Just don't be tempted to resell or give them to others who are not in law enforcement. This has become a common practice in some police departments, but these black-market magazines could get you into very serious trouble, possibly ending your career and most certainly causing a lot of expense and embarrassment.

Since the most sensitive parts of a metal magazine are the lips, again, take care not to drop magazines on their lips or allow them to scrape or bump into other objects. Loaded magazines should be carried in pouches designed for them, not cloth military bandoleers or the like.

Probably the best way to carry spare magazines is in some of the newer SWAT-style vests on the market. Some give good access to the magazines carried in them. "Six-pack" pouches are also seen from time to time. These have six 30-round magazine pouches arranged in a purse-like configuration with a strap. The real plus of this design is that it can quickly be plucked from a closet or car trunk along with a rifle, and then the shooter is ready to go without a lot of fastening of belts and adjusting of gear. These are sometimes available from surplus dealers.

Sierra Supply also sells U.S. GI 20-round magazine carriers (holding four magazines) for $4 and a carrier for three 30-round magazines for $8. These are well designed and work fine with standard-issue aluminum magazines as well as many others listed in this section.

To speed up the removal of magazines from pouches that hold three magazines, some users put a tape tab on the magazine so that it can be pulled out by the tab. Care must be taken that the tape is really secure or else the magazine will fail to come out or, worse yet, be dropped after clearing the pouch. In pouches that hold groups of two or three magazines, only one magazine needs to be taped provided a spare container is used for the empties (a wise procedure). After the first magazine is drawn from a pack, the other one or two can be removed easily. It's also sometimes helpful to cut out part of the magazine pouch so that the cover on it will get out of the way when opened. (This also means the pouch needs to be replaced much sooner and that magazines can spill out if the latch on the pouch comes loose.)

Magazines should be carried in a pouch with their lips down and—if possible—the ammunition pointing in a direction that will enable a shooter to get it into the rifle without fumbling. Generally, this means the bullets are pointing out and the primer side of the rounds are toward the user's body. A good pouch should be rigid enough to give protection to the magazines' lips.

If a magazine becomes damaged or fails to feed properly, it should be destroyed. Parts should be salvaged from it only if the lips are bent or if it's obvious what is wrong. If the shooter is unsure, he should discard all the parts; it's better to have only working spare parts rather than a lot of parts that may be defective.

In the past, the U.S. military has used the Adventure Line brand of magazines (a name that undoubtedly has caused a lot of snickers on the battlefield and during training exercises) and Colt magazines. Of these the Colt magazines are the most reliable, although older ones were often plagued with too-loose floorplates that occasionally left the user with an empty magazine in his rifle after the plate slid out and the spring, ammunition, and magazine

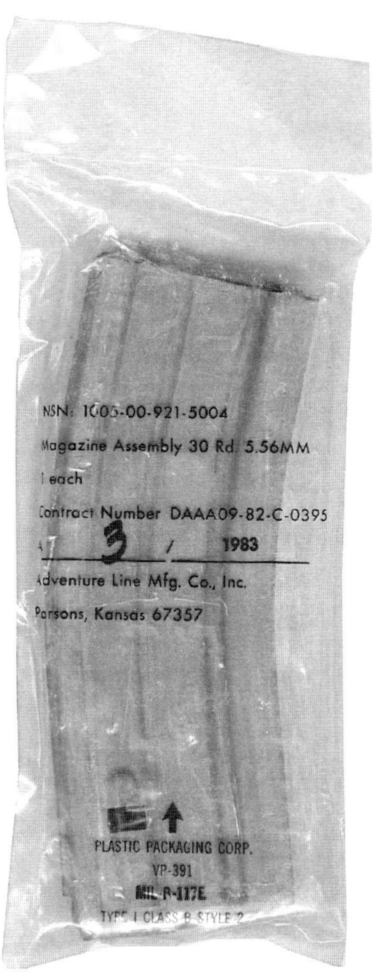

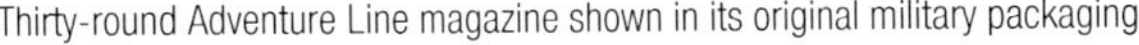

Thirty-round Adventure Line magazine shown in its original military packaging.

Colt steel "waffle" 20-round magazine.

follower popped out. The moral of the story is to always check to be sure that all the floorplates of magazines (regardless of the brand) are tight or taped so they won't come loose.

There are also collector's magazines that shouldn't be used, both because of their rarity and because they became collector's items after they worked so poorly that few of them were made. One of these is the waffle-pattern 20-round magazine originally made for the first military AR-15s. Another is the 20-round disposable plastic magazine (not to be confused with the modern ones). Both are rare and could be traded for a number of good modern magazines. Also among the collector's magazines is the red 20-round magazine for blanks with a spacer bar in its front so that only blanks can be used in it. (A brief guide to the various magazines made by different manufacturers appears earlier in this book.)

Regular 20-round magazines are available for the AR-15 and are acceptable but are nearly as expensive and nearly as large as the 30-round magazines but with only two-thirds the capacity. The added firepower of the 30-round magazine makes it a better buy for most purposes. That said, those shooting the rifle from the prone position (which is often done in various contests) may find the shorter profile of the 20-round magazine more ideal. And some shooters just prefer its handier size.

Until 1991, the AR-15 Sporter rifles were sold with two 20-round magazines with a block that allowed only 5 rounds to be placed in the rifle (a hunting restriction in many states). Those not wanting the limited capacity could slide out the floorplate, remove the metal "U," and have a good 20-round magazine. That changed after 1991 and the Colt 20-round magazines have a limiter riveted into them. It isn't too hard to cut these rivets off with a drill press or file, but it's easier to purchase new

Standard U.S. military issue 20- and 30-round metal magazines.

Aftermarket 40-round metal magazine (left) and plastic 30-round Thermold magazine (right).

magazines from one of the aftermarket suppliers and save the five-round magazines, for hunting or other uses.

Several companies manufacture plastic magazines for the AR-15. These function very smoothly because the plastic-on-plastic moving parts tend to be self-lubricating. The feed lips on plastic magazines also hold their shape very well and aren't sensitive to bumps or bending of the lips or body of the magazine. Often a serious crunch that would put a metal magazine out of commission will not even hurt a plastic magazine. And since this is how most magazines meet their end, the plastic magazines last quite a while longer than the metal ones under most circumstances.

Although some users claim that plastic magazines sometimes have trouble with particles of grit that get embedded in the plastic and create a magazine that works poorly, most shooters don't have this problem. For those working in a desert, the plastic magazines might be a second choice behind the aluminum magazines but otherwise they seem pretty hard to beat. (It should be noted that the Israelis use plastic magazines with AR-15 rifles and don't seem to have this problem.)

Among the best magazines are the excellent black plastic Thermold 30- and 45-round magazines developed for the Canadian military and often seen on the surplus market. Interestingly, the 45-round magazine can be collapsed to 30-round capacity; this makes it possible to store the magazine with ammunition in it indefinitely without worrying about the spring's "setting." When the magazine is needed, it's compressed and ready to go with 30 rounds in place. (While most magazines don't take a "spring set" and work fine if stored indefinitely while loaded to maximum capacity, some shooters worry about this—including the Canadian military, apparently.)

Ram-Line offered a smoked plastic 30-round magazine that allows a shooter to see how much ammunition is in the magazine. An added benefit is that the magazine fits in either the AR-15 or other rifles, including the AR-18 (or AR-180) and the Mini-14, making it ideal for shooters with different kinds of rifles. The original cost for these was $17, but this price has slowly risen because the company discontinued making them due to the federal ban on high-capacity magazines.

The Israeli Orlite M16 magazines are also appearing on the U.S. surplus market. SARCO sells used, 30-round Orlite magazines in excellent condition for $5 each at the time of this writing.

The MWG 90 Round Magazine that Colt offers with its H-BAR light machine guns is also available to owners of the AR-15, though sales of new units made after the assault weapons ban are now—ironically, since the

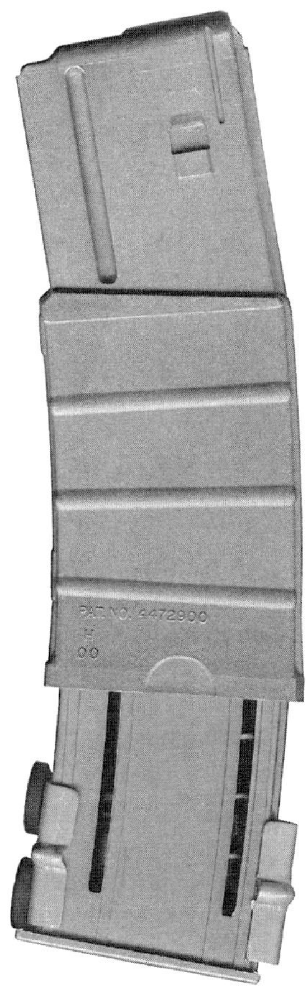


Thermold 45-round magazine with the spring assembly in its extended position.

Ram-Line 30-round magazine works in the AR-15, AR-180, or Mini-14.

argument was that these were only of use to criminals—available only to law enforcement or military buyers (and currently offered by Mounting Solution Plus).

The MWG magazine was apparently designed at least in part by Mack W. Gwinn, Jr. (who also created the Bushmaster pistol and rifle). The magazine has an offset snail drum that rides to the left of the receiver. The big plus of this unit is that it doesn't lie any lower than a 20-round magazine, so the user can stay low when firing from a prone position. The offset design has the added plus of causing the drum to try to tilt in the magazine well; this takes some of the pressure off the magazine catch so that it doesn't bear the full weight of a loaded magazine. A transparent plastic panel on the rear of the magazine allows the user to tell at a glance how many rounds are in the magazine.

A special loading tool is needed to stuff the last cartridges into the Ninety Rounder (one comes with the magazine), and the manufacturer recommends that fewer than the full 90 cartridges be left in the magazine for long-term storage. Cost for government buyers is $96, with preban magazines (when you can find them) running a bit more depending on the demand.

The Beta C-Mag uses dual drums on either side of the magazine well to create a 100-round magazine with the same low profile as a 20-round box magazine. For the duel magazines to work, they have special plastic spacers shaped like rounds of ammunition; this enables each drum to feed into the central section leading up the magazine well.

Like the Ninety Rounder, the C-Mag is made of tough plastic and gives a shooter a lot of bangs before reloading. Currently sales of the C-Mag are restricted to military and police users and both the U.S. Air Force and Marines have placed small orders for these devices (with the marines ordering 5,000 for their H-BARs). The company also offers a special pouch for the magazine.

Since the Chinese are busy trying to market their CQ

AR-15 look-alike, it isn't surprising that they've utilized the drum design of the Type 81 SAW for use with the AR-15. These steel drum magazines hold 120 cartridges and fit all AR-15s. The Chinese drum magazine has a hinged back that allows it to be pulled back and the magazine quickly loaded. Then the spring is wound up with a key or left unwound if the magazine is to be stored. The drum hangs directly below the magazine well, making it less ideal than the MWG unit for prone shooting, but many shooters may wish to put up with this for the added capacity the magazine offers. These drums have proven over time to be not overly reliable; therefore shooters are generally wise to steer clear of them.

The Ninety Rounder and C-Mag challenge the idea that belt feed systems are needed with today's light machine gun. It will be interesting to see whether this trend toward drum magazines continues in the near future (though, sadly, the current ban on the manufacture of magazines with greater than 10-round capacity for semiauto rifles for civilian ownership has greatly reduced the incentive to produce such a magazine).

Whether it's a drum magazine or a conventional box design, new magazines should always be carefully tested to be sure they work. Due to slight deviations in tolerances, magazines and some AR-15s don't always work together even if they are both in good working order. Just because the magazine works in one rifle or is new does not guarantee that it will work in another firearm. It's better to find that out before investing too much in the magazines' working properly.

Thermold magazines, for example, may fit too tightly in some non-Colt guns. In such a case, a little judicious sanding on the exterior of the magazine may help: inserting the magazine several times will show wear marks on it to point out tight spots needing to be sanded. Rarely will the lower rib on the magazine need to be cut

MWG 90-round magazine. (Courtesy of MWG.)

High-capacity magazines, coupled with the compact size of a pistol or carbine version of the AR-15, result in a potent weapon for hostage rescue or other tactical situations.

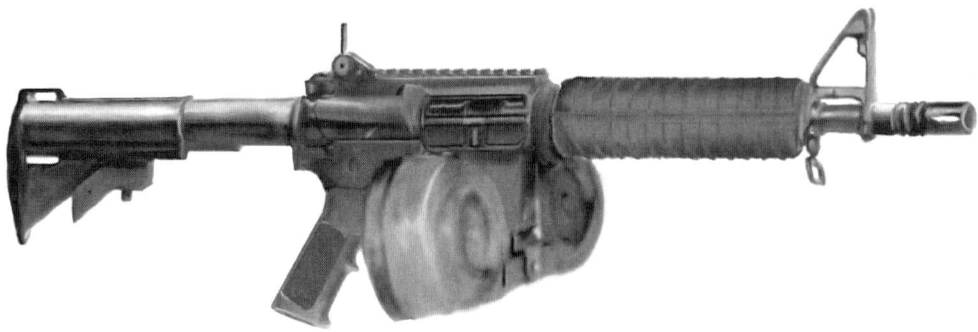

Beta "C-Mag" employs dual drums for a 100-round capacity.

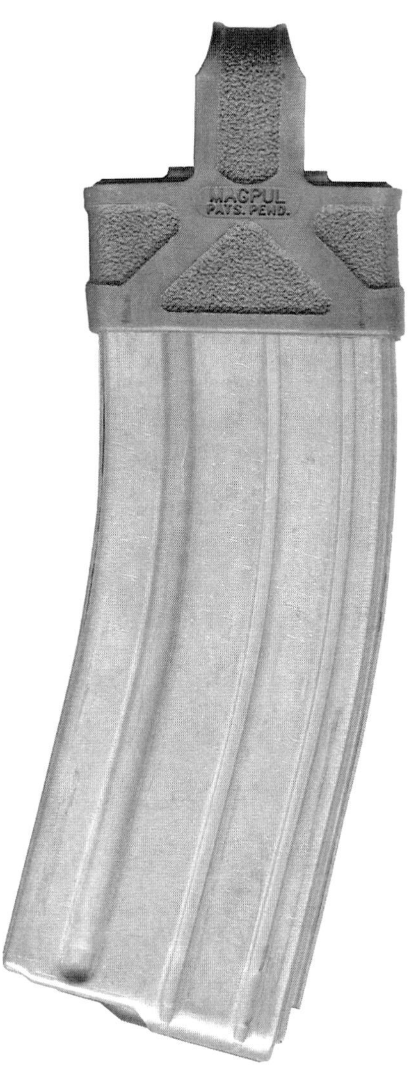


Magpul on magazine.

or filed to go into the magazine and lock consistently. Fortunately, these tasks are easy with the plastic Thermold magazines. New metal magazines often come from the factory with a sharp edge on their upper front rims over which the cartridges are stripped and pushed into the chamber. Often a round hangs up on this edge. Though this edge will gradually wear off, it's often a good idea to *gently* round it off with a file, removing only enough metal to get rid of the burr and make it smooth. (Another practice is to be sure that reloaded rounds have their exterior edges chamfered—rounded off—so they won't hang up on the feed edge of the magazine.)

Unlike drum magazines, box magazines can be stored for years fully loaded without the spring's "setting," just as the hammer and trigger spring in the rifle will not set even if they are left in their same positions all the time. However, some magazines may work a little better if once in a while the springs are allowed to move to their fully expanded point. But shooters shouldn't worry unduly about leaving the magazines loaded for 6 months to a year—they'll still work just fine if they worked well before.

A magazine is one of the most important parts of an AR-15 and should be treated with the care a very important part deserves so that it won't fail it's really needed.

## THE MAGPUL

Regardless of what magazine you select for your AR-15, there's one accessory that will make any of the box magazines mentioned above much more convenient to use. Marketed as the Magpul, it consists of a thermoplastic loop with a ring that fits around the base of a magazine. Once in place, the ring can serve several important functions, the foremost being that it gives the user a handle to grab when pulling a magazine out of a pouch or other carrier. Rather than fumbling in getting a new magazine (often a panic proposition in combat or contests), a shooter can grasp the plastic loop and pull the magazine free.

Additionally, the Magpul loop can be placed over a finger, making it possible to carry an empty or full magazine at the ready if it isn't convenient at the moment to replace it in a pouch. In fact, a shooter facing the need for rapid firepower could juggle two or three magazines on his off hand, keeping them ready for a fast reload as the need arose.

There are different sizes of Magpuls available, including a model for the AR-10, AR-15 (in .223 or 7.62x45mm), and 9mm. These are available from Magpul Industries and priced from $2.50 to $2.85 per pull. A shooter would do well to buy one for each AR-15 magazine he owns.

## MAGAZINE CONNECTORS

Spring clips, tape, and various other systems of clamping two magazines together to increase capacity are often tried. In general the tape and spring clips don't work well (and the practice of taping two magazines together with the lips of one down is a guaranteed way to get dirt into one and probably bend its feed lips, creating a jam when it's shoved into the rifle). Some newer magazines have been fielded, such as those for the Heckler & Koch C-41, which have snap sections molded into their bodies permitting magazines to be connected somewhat like Lego blocks.

For magazines lacking such built-in aids, the best method for holding magazines together is the metal or metal-and-plastic connectors that hold magazines parallel to each other. Several types are offered, including the Mag-Pac by ARMS (which works on Thermold magazines as well as metal magazines and costs $29—*when* you can locate these, since they're becoming hard to find), the Choate Machine and Tool connector (which works only on metal magazines and costs $36), and Buffer Technologies' Mag Cinch (which works on a variety of magazines and costs $20).

All these units hold two magazines very rigidly at just the right space apart to work in the AR-15, making them ideal for those wanting a lot of ammunition available in a hurry—and there can be a lot. With two Thermold 45-round magazines, for example, a shooter can have 90 rounds riding with his rifle. When using these pairs of magazines, care must be taken to start with the spare magazine on the selector side of the rifle, otherwise it's possible to block the ejection port cover so that it can't open. And when the empty magazine is on that side of the firearm, the ejection port cover must be left down.

DPMS has gone the dual magazine connector one better, offering a TM-01 tri-connector that unites three magazines, holding them side by side. It costs $20 per connector, and the result is quite a bit of ammunition right at a shooter's disposal. With a quick reindexing of the magazines, for example one could use 45-round Thermold magazines to have 135 rounds ready to go—more than even a drum magazine holds.

Of course, the catch is that they add a lot of weight to that of the rifle. Ninety or 135 rounds on a belt carried at the hips seems like almost nothing even after hours of travel. That same amount on a rifle makes it seem like a very great burden. Of course, for those setting up a system that will sit in place, this may not be a consideration, especially given the fast reloading made possible.

Another interesting solution to carrying several magazines at once in the rifle is the Redi-Mag. This device allows carrying regular magazines with a spare one to the selector side of the rifle. It has one plus: regular magazines can be placed in it easily so that regular web gear can be used to carry the spares. The Redi-Mag weighs 8 ounces and is attached to the rifle with two clamp screws. The rifle is not altered; rather, a clever latch allows the magazine release on the AR-15 to also release the spare magazine when the empty is released. This makes it very quick and simple to change magazines. When the full magazine has been placed into the rifle, the shooter can slip a new spare magazine into the holder by just pushing it into place. The Redi-Mag is available from Advanced Specialty Products, Inc. for $29.95.

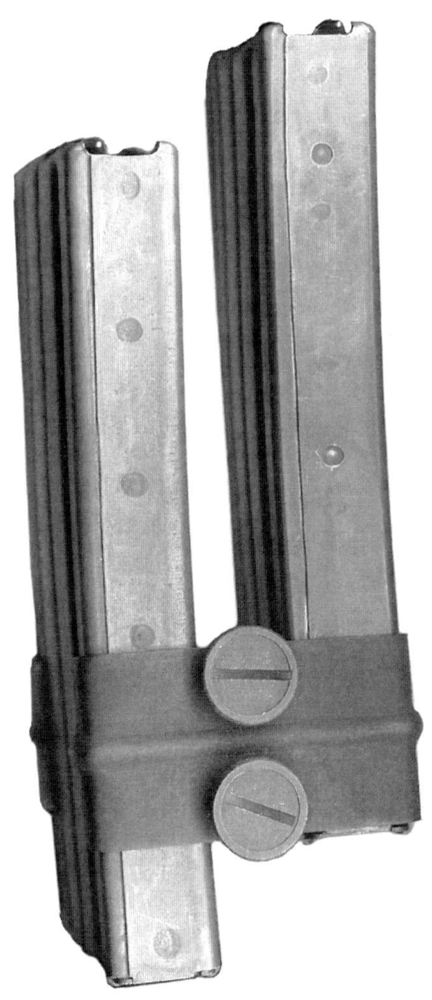

Choate Machine and Tool magazine connector.

## MWG ACCURIZER

The MWG Accurizer is in a category all its own, even though the concept is to be found on guns other than the AR-15, with the Bushmaster M17S as well as some sniper rifles created by Heckler & Koch being prime examples of this system. Basically the device is a shroud that attaches over a barrel to increase the tension on it, reducing the barrel flex and vibration when the bullet travels down the bore. One might think that such an oddity would not do much to change the accuracy from one round to the next, but (when properly tensioned) it does.

MWG claims a reduction of group sizes by one-half when the Accurizer is in place; those who use this device generally find that this promise is fulfilled. Models are available for both 16- and 20-inch barrels; however, the units are held in place with the threading for the rifle's flash hider, making this suitable only for postban guns. (Finding an Accurizer to purchase is not easy; it may be that it's currently out of production.)

## NIGHT SIGHTS

The U.S. military developed a very good night sight system that consisted of a front sight containing a tiny glass vial of radioactive promethium 147 and a modified rear sight with an extralarge 7mm aperture for nighttime use. The front sight was screwed into the sight base just like a regular sight, and sighting in was only a little different since the front sight had only four detent positions (like the M16A2 sight). Care had to be taken not to damage the somewhat fragile glass vial, but the unit worked well. During the day, the 2mm "L" sight is used and zeroed in at 250 yards. Beyond 300 yards, it's necessary to practice hold over (aiming above the target) rather than switching sights as is normally done with regular AR-15 sights. With nightfall the sight was changed to the 7mm aperture.

Since then several similar nighttime sights have also been marketed, usually with tritium gas (an isotope of hydrogen) in the vial rather than promethium 147; it's a bit safer should the glass accidentally be broken. Should a vial of a tritium sight break indoors, it's prudent to evacuate the area and open windows to allow the radioactive gas to escape. But the amount of exposure is minuscule as long as the vial remains unbroken, with radioactive emissions virtually nonexistent and no more dangerous than glow-in-the-dark wristwatches or similar devices. In fact, with tritium night sights, the radiation exposure is quite low even if the vial containing the gas does break. Kerry Kinder of Meprolight has remarked that inhaling the gas from three of the vials in his night sights would amount to less radiation exposure than one dental X-ray.

One manufacturer of the new night sight is Trijicon; its AR-15 front sight post is virtually identical to the original army sight with a vertical glowing post encased in the front sight blade. These are offered both as a single front sight with a glow-in-the-dark insert (for $26) as well as a separate large-aperture rear sight with luminous elements (which costs $17). Shooters would do well to get both rather than to try to operate at night with just one or the other.

The Israeli military developed a similar system for their M16A1 rifles; these sights are available for a time in the United States from Hesco as the Meprolight sights (which are available for a wide range of firearms including the AR-15). Four sight kits are offered for the AR-15 by the company. One (the ML115P) is a glow-in-the-dark insert front post, another (the ML115P) is the glowing post with a nonglowing "ghost ring" rear sight coupled with the standard peephole so that the two apertures can be flipped back and forth for day or night use. (The Meprolight is now manufactured by Scopus Light, a subsidiary of ADSI, based in the Philippines.)

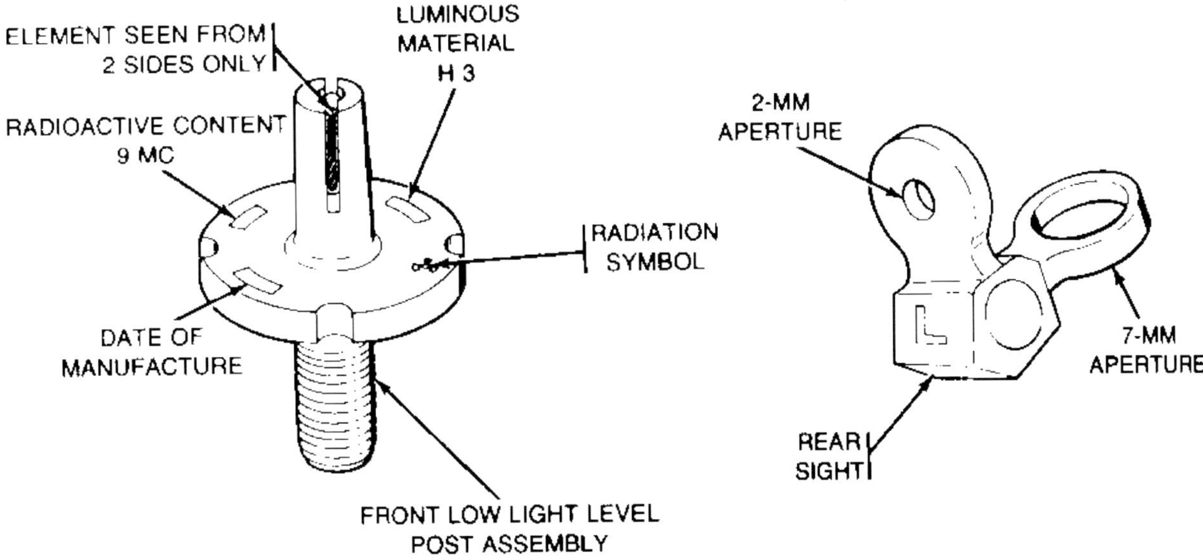


Military tritium night sight parts set. In these kits, only the front sight has a tritium element, making them less than perfect in very dark light.

The other two styles of Meprolights have a standard aperture for daytime shooting with a notch sight on its second position; this notch sight is quick to use at night, thanks to glow-in-the-dark inserts on either side of it that make it quick to line up with the glowing front sight. The ML1150 is designed for A1-style sights, while the ML1160 is for A2-style sights; both are ideal for nighttime use. The cost is $80 for each of the kits or $33 for the sight post alone.

U.S.-based Innovative Weaponry has produced a similar system for the AR-15 that has quickly gained acceptance by many police and other law enforcement agencies, as well as the military. Innovative Weaponry sights are now found on the guns issued by the U.S. Customs, DEA, Navy SEALS, Delta Force, and Air Force.

The company's P-T sight has two dots on either side of one of the rear apertures and a line post on the front that make it very quick to get onto target. It costs $90. (In addition to the standard greenish light that appears in night sights, Innovative Weaponry has been experimenting with other phosphors in its sights to create red, yellow, and other possibilities in an effort to see whether target acquisition can be speeded up. Consequently, the future may see a number of "Christmas tree" effects, though currently these aren't offered for sights designed for the AR-15 series of firearms.)

Early in 1992, Colt introduced the (what else would it be named?) Tritium Night Sight developed by Randall A. Allen. The rear sight is the now conventional large peep sight with a single insert at the bottom of its ring. This single insert at the base of the peep sight has dictated a complicated front sight: centering a glowing front sight with this system would be next to impossible. Consequently, the front night sight has a large clamp that goes around the rear strut of the iron sight's base with six different glowing inserts in it, four in a straight line leading up to the sight and two on either side of the sight post.

Meprolight sights, shown here in a display bubble pack.

Those who have seen Colt's sight are a bit perplexed by this complicated arrangement and, in addition to its being rather expensive due to the number of inserts in the front sight, the sight seems to be both more fragile and slower to use than the post/dot systems of either the Meprolight or the P-T sights. Unless the Colt system proves to have some advantage that has not been readily apparent with the first demonstrations, it seems likely that it will take a back seat to the other two designs.

As for the original single-post system without any glow element in the rear sight assembly, it works *only if* the user practices diligently. But there is little doubt that for the surest sight acquisition at night glowing elements in both the front and rear sight are a big plus. For even though it's possible to practice aiming the AR-15 during the daytime until the point of aim can be found through habit, it's disconcerting to aim at a target and only be sure of where the front sight is. And in fact, it's probable that this insecurity in itself could cause hesitation that may be fatal for those using the AR-15 for self-defense.

For maintenance of the tritium sights, care only needs to be taken not to expose them to excessive heat (from soldering irons, flames, or the like), and the glues used to secure the vials in the sights should not be exposed to cleaning solvents like acetone, ethanol, or other strong solvents since they can be dissolved by these liquids; ultrasonic cleaning systems also can damage the adhesives.

Like old soldiers, tritium sights don't die; they only fade away. The tritium "glow" doesn't go out all a sudden but gradually dims with a useful life of 8 to 12 years, depending on the brightness the user desires. At the point where the sights are too dim to suit their owner, they should be returned to the manufacturer for proper disposal and replacement.

Other night sight systems have been created using light-emitting diodes (LEDs), but these are generally a second choice after tritium night sights for the simple reason that they are bulkier and must be turned on and off, and there is always a chance that the battery or device will fail at a critical moment.

The exception to this might be the dot sights listed below; these can be used both day and night. The shooter will have some carryover with his abilities to find the target at night, and this might give him an edge in such a case.

## NIGHT-VISION SCOPES

Being able to strike out at enemies with supernatural accuracy has been the dream of most warriors since the first combatant threw a stone. Today's night-vision equipment realizes this dream by making it possible for a soldier to see in the dark and shoot at enemies while they are all but blind at night.

There are three types of night-vision devices: passive, active, and thermal imagers. Active night-vision devices date back to World War II when both the United States and Germany produced infrared night-vision equipment. The Americans created the M3 Sniperscope, while the Germans made the *Vampir* sight; both were of short range but effective and took their toll of helpless troops on both sides.

Active devices tend to be heavier and have a smaller range than other night viewing devices since they require a source of infrared light to illuminate the area being viewed. Because the light source and the optical system that turns the reflected infrared light into a visible image both need a lot of battery power, the equipment is weighty and needs large amounts of energy with a huge battery to power them. Too, in the past battery life was short and, perhaps worst of all, the infrared light source was visible to other active or passive night viewing equipment, so the hunter could quickly become the hunted.

Active equipment is still in use for the simple reason that it's less expensive than passive equipment. Some work is being done to use divergent-beam infrared lasers to extend the range of the units and limit the chance of their being detected by enemy troops with passive viewers.

Passive devices use available light: city glow, moonlight, starlight, or any other dim light sources that are enough to allow the units to create pictures of what is being viewed. These units' big asset is that their range is not as limited as that of active devices, and because passive equipment doesn't need its own source of light, it's impossible to detect. Passive devices were created during the Vietnam era to enable U.S. snipers to kill enemy soldiers.

These units are built around an image intensifier, which is much like a TV camera; the circuits inside the device take small contrasts in light and dark patterns of whatever the front lens is pointed at and boost the lighted portions to perhaps 64,000 times the brightness of the original picture. This image is placed on a TV-style screen at the back of the scope so that the user can view what the device is pointed toward.

The passive system must have at least a tiny bit of light to work. On an extremely cloudy night when the moon isn't out or there are no city lights, the scopes won't create a usable picture. But such occasions are rare, and in most areas of the world there is always enough ambient light to allow the passive scopes to create an image. Additionally, many passive systems now have a small infrared LED to provide light in totally dark environments (the only catch is that these are easily spotted by an enemy with night-vision gear).

Presently there are two generations of passive night-vision devices. The first generation is good if there's no need to view areas that are partly lit. In such a case, streaking and blooming can result. Streaking is caused when a light is viewed directly, causing the circuits to overload and create a streak of light on the viewing screen for as much as a full second. Blooming happens when a lit area is viewed so as to create a flaring effect around the object inspected. Even though first-generation passive equipment suffers from streaking and blooming, it's less expensive and works well in nonurban areas.

Second-generation scopes are quite good, and the third-generation scopes are even better in many ways (and accordingly more expensive).

Mounted on a rifle, a passive scope can work as a sighting system both in the daytime (with the use of a filter to restrict the light entering the system) and at night. Second-generation night-vision goggles are also available that enable the user to see in the dark and use regular high-quality binoculars or rifle scopes and see through them practically as if it were daytime (except for the eerie green glow they give the viewing area).

Most passive scopes can be quickly put out of action by exposing the lens to a bright light with the unit on, and all are sensitive to mishandling and use expensive batteries. So care has to be taken not to trash the scope.

There are a number of good systems that are easily mounted on an AR-15 rifle. Among these are ITT's Night Enforcer AG6015 and Night Enforcer F7201A (both of the third generation); the ATN MK7700 and TS-3; Newcon DN 300 and DN 510; Litton's Raptor 6X, AN/PVS-4, and Aquilla III; and US Night Vision's D 242, Falcon, and D 441 scopes. (These are the top-of-the-line presently; for those with more limited budgets, these companies also offer first- and second-generation units that are considerably less expensive.)

The cost of third-generation equipment is high, often in the $3,000 to $4,000 range. However, the cost for first- and second-generation equipment has dropped to the point that units can sometimes be purchased for a few hundred dollars.

New thermal imaging units are showing up on the market along with the passive and active devices. One of the first of these is Magnavox's Short Range Thermal Sight. This 4-pound unit demonstrated that it was practical to pick up an image on a small screen, displaying the heat signature of an enemy soldier in total darkness.

Since then thermal imagers, too, have dropped in price and become much smaller. While they're still too expensive for most individuals to purchase without fainting, government agencies have been buying them. And no wonder, since these units can do a lot that night-vision scopes cannot. Since the thermal or infrared band is actually the same as radiated heat, anything that gives off heat can be seen with a thermal imaging system even if it isn't visible to the naked eyes or is behind a light cover, fog, or smoke. Too, these sights can be used in nighttime or daytime, making it practical to leave the unit in place for use around the clock.

The U.S. OICW, as well as the Land Warrior equipment, has demonstrated that it is practical to field a thermal imager on a rifle, thereby greatly enhancing the abilities of a fighter. Whether the price of these units will drop enough to make them practical for civilian and police use remains to be seen, however. But if the trends displayed by laser sight as well as passive equipment are any indication, it may be that the thermal scope will become a viable consumer item in the near future.

Regardless of how high-tech these scopes are, they all run on batteries. And it pays to purchase units that run on commonly found batteries. Because even if price is not a consideration, discovering that the rare battery needed to power a scope has to be ordered from some specialty house and will take next to forever to get to you turns your prized scope into a useless paperweight when it is in need of power.

## PISTOL GRIPS

Like the "floating handguard," the term "pistol grip" is confusing since the grip is on the AR-15 *rifle* and not a pistol (unless, of course, we're talking AR-15 *pisto,* in which case the confusion can be compounded to the point that it may resemble an Abbot and Costello routine). The pistol grip is only called this because its shape resembles that of a pistol, thereby distinguishing it from the previous more conventional rifles used by the U.S. military as well by hunters before the AR-15 made its appearance.

That bit of confusion (we hope) out of the way, there is a wealth of pistol grips available for the AR-15. Without a doubt, the A2 style is superior to the original style; for those wanting to upgrade an older gun to the A2 grips, Colt, Bushmaster, and others offer these for a modest sum.

Over the years, several companies have also sold "stow-away" grips of one sort or another; these have a trapdoor in the base of a grip in which odds and ends may be stored. One asset of these is that they also keep mud from getting into the grip during prone shooting.

Peace River Arms also offers an extension pad that goes over the back of an AR-15 pistol grip to lengthen the distance the finger needs to reach forward to the trigger. The contoured plastic pad looks like part of the rifle and can be screwed into place, glued, or just secured with a rubber band for temporary use. Shooters with larger hands often find that this makes the rifle considerably more comfortable to fire, and many target shooters prefer it as well. Its cost is just $5.

Cherokee offers its excellent TacGrip that replaces the standard stock with a grip having finger swells down its front (giving a bit better control when holding the rifle). But the real feature of this grip is the choice of three different-size sections that go down the back of it,

Two of a number of "stowaway" grips with storage compartments. Left is from Ram-Line, while the right was made by SGW.

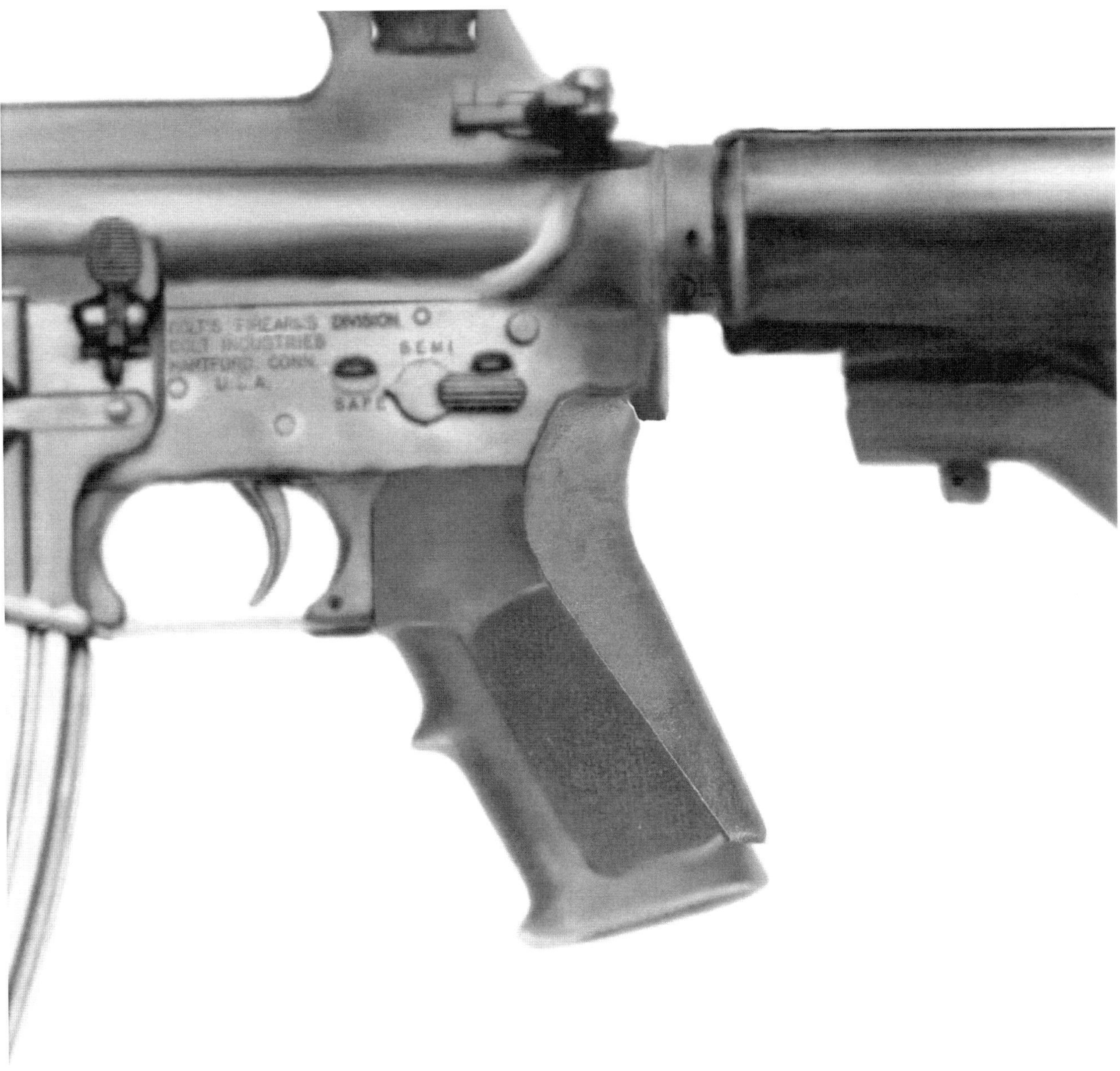


Peace River Arms grip adapter for the AR-15.

permitting the user to chose how "fat" he wants the grip to be. This makes it possible to select anything from a short reach to the trigger to a longer one, whose need may be dictated by a larger hand. In effect, the TacGrip permits a shooter to customize the grip to his hand, rather than having to make do with the standard grip, which is somewhat of a compromise to accommodate both small and large users. The TacGrip is $49.95.

A slightly more complicated way to move the trigger finger position back is offered by Injection Plastics Manufacturing with its Rite Pull Adapter, a plastic insert that goes between the pistol grip (which must first be removed) and the receiver. Once this space is in place, an additional 0.75 inch is added to the grip length, giving a long reach to place just the pad of the finger on the trigger (for those with normal-sized hands). The Rite Pull Adapter is available from Brownells for $27.50. Speedlock Systems Slipgrip is very similar to the Rite Pull Adapter but consists of two parts rather than one. Also from Brownclls, it rctails for $35.85.

For those doing target work with the AR-15, DPMS offers several interesting variations in pistol grips. One is the Panther Pistol/Palm Grip, which is made of black plastic with an adjustable palm stop (similar to that used on H&K target rifles). The unit mounts to a rifle like a standard grip and costs $49.95.

Clip-A-Grip (also available from DPMS) is a black polyurethane molding that goes around a standard A2 grip to create a target pistol configuration; the attachment can be easily removed or placed back on without tools, or permanently attached with epoxy glue. Its cost is $24.99.

DPMS also offers the Royal Arms Sniper Grip with a real "race gun" that looks at home on a contest gun that isn't restricted to a "military look." The styling of this grip makes it suitable only for right-handed use; it retails for $54.95.

The Hogue AR-15 OM Rubber Grip maintains the traditional look of the AR-16/M16 grip but adds palm swells and finger grooves, along with the rubbery surface that gives a very firm grip even when the weapon is wet. Hogue also offers a matching AR-15 Rubber Forend handguard that free-floats the barrel for improved accuracy; it also has Hogue's rubbery finish and is available in rifle and carbine lengths. The OM grip runs for $ 21.95 with the Rubber Forend in either length costing $89.95 (both the grip and handguard in either size are also available in a kit for a total of $99.95).

The Pearce Grip gives an AR-15 the grip angle of a 1911 semiauto .45 pistol, and even accepts grip panels designed for the .45. Some shooters find this reduced wrist angle considerably more comfortable for consistent shot placement. In addition to this grip, buyers will need to buy grip panels for it—ideally the same ones they employ on their pistol to "feel right at home" with either gun. It is possible to buy the grips with standard .45 panels as well. The cost is $20 for the grip without panels and $36 with standard grips. These can be ordered from Brownells.

TacGrip gives the shooter a better feel for the trigger, making it ideal for target shooters as well as those with large hands. (Courtesy of Cherokee Accessories.)

## RAIL MOUNTING SYSTEMS

In addition to the more or less standard Weaver rails and such mentioned previously, there has been a wealth of Weaver rails sprouting up in various spots on the AR-15, almost like mushrooms after a spring rain (in fact, all that is missing is a rail mount for the AR-15 magazine and stock—perhaps along with one for the rifleman's chin).

The key need for this to work properly is that the systems are steady

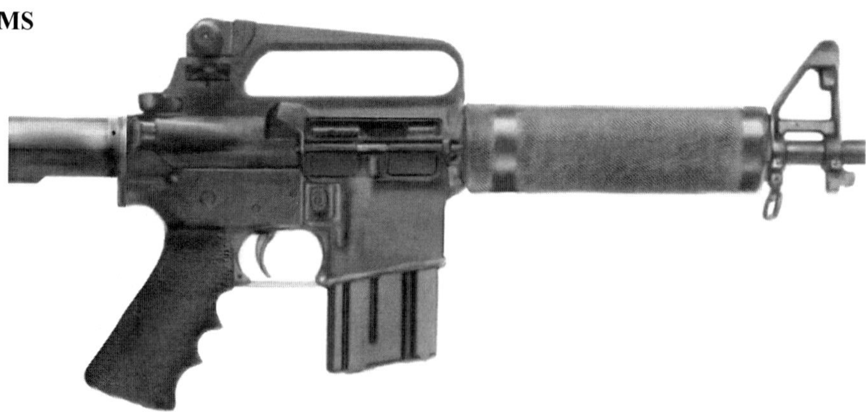

Hogue AR-15 pistol grip and fore end.

Rail mount systems on the handguard of an AR-15 make mounting a variety of accessories, such as this vertical grip, a snap.

and can be aligned with the rifle's barrel. That said, the tight tolerances in the manufacture of the AR-15 have almost any part attached to the upper receiver or barrel meet this condition.

I suspect that such parts and/or systems have been pretty common from about the time the first AR-15s were fielded, given that the carrying handles of these rifles have universally had a hole drilled into them specifically for mounting either a scope or a rail system.

And several patents have been granted for rail systems that extend from the upper receiver down the length of the top of the gun as well as down the sides of the handguard and so forth. The system that uses this configuration most successfully is Knight's FIRM-style rail mounting system, originally created for the M4 carbine and since spreading to the military rifle as part of the modular weapon system; Knight's Rail Integration System puts four evenly spaced rails around the handguard of an M-4 carbine. These units are capable of adapting a wealth of accessories to a carbine or rifle having the basic rail system, including the scopes, forward grip, lasers, and other accessories covered elsewhere in this manual.

Of course, a lot of "rail mounting" can take place right from the carrying handle if you have DPMS's Tri-Mount (covered more fully in the scope mount section). This accessory provides a wide range of mounting options and might even be exploited for a "quick on, quick off" assembly of flashlight, laser, and scope to quickly transform a standard AR-15 to a specialized "night shooter." One might, for example, mount a small laser on one side, a flashlight on the other, and a dot scope on the top—or any of a multitude of other accessories and combinations.

DPMS's 4-Rail Gas Block carries this same idea to the front of the rifle, replacing the standard front sight assembly with a gas block having four short Weaver/Picatinny rails. These permit the attachment of a laser, flashlight, grip, or other accessory that has a rail mount system. The DPMS block is black anodized aluminum with a matte finish; it retails for $49.95.

For those needing only a single rail to which to fix a detachable iron sight, JP Enterprises offers its Adjustable Gasblock (mentioned in more detail elsewhere in this book). This unit is available for standard (0.750-inch) and (0.936-inch) barrels for $69.95 and $79.95, respectively.

As one might expect, Bushmaster also offers a number of accessories that mount on the Weaver/Picatinny rails, many of them as part of its Bushmaster Modular Accessories System (BMAS) group of products. One of these is the 3-Rail Gas Block (similar in concept to the DPMS four-rail system—but obviously with one fewer rail); costing $52.95, the unit can be purchased with a new barrel from Bushmaster or purchased for retrofit on barrels with standard 0.750-inch-diameter barrels. The three-rail block is milled from steel and finished in black manganese phosphate. It has rails on the top and each side and is drilled and tapped for the addition of a sling swivel stud if a user so desires.

Bushmaster's Detachable Front Flip Sight is another part of the BMAS system. This sight clamps to the top rail of the company's Flat Top Gas Block or other Picatinny rails with Allen screws holding it in alignment. The sight locks up or flips down by releasing its lock button and presents a standard A2 front sight post for aiming when in the upper position. It costs $72.95.

Also available from Bushmaster is the Mark Brown Custom Flat-top Mount ($195.95), which fits the receiver rails of the company's V Match rifle as well as any A3 flat-top model made by Bushmaster or other manufacturers. This unit lacks a carrying handle, instead having a rail that rests just over the flat-top rail and to the rear sports an A2 rear sight that is adjustable for both windage and elevation, making it an excellent backup sight to a dot scope or other device.

Another rear sight designed for mounting on a flat-top receiver is the BMAS AR Flat Top Rear Sight ($89.95), which attaches directly to the receiver. This A2-style rear sight has both windage and elevation adjustments and makes an ideal backup sight for other optics mounted on the rail.

ARMS makes its own rear sight that mounts on the A3 flat-top with a slight twist to the idea. The #40 Low Profile Stand Alone Flip up Rear Sight does just what its name suggests, flipping up for use or capable of being folded out of the way when not needed. Its cost is $99.95, and it is available from Bushmaster and other suppliers. The dipolar sight has a 250- to 300-meter close-combat aperture and a 500- to 600-meter aperture.

Since scopes and other accessories mounted on the flat-top receiver, as well as on other rails, have an ugly way of being just a tad too short for ideal viewing (or whatever), part of the BMAS includes Mini Risers, which are rails with Weaver rings, designed simply to raise an accessory by a half-inch when mounted between it and another rail. Costing $14.95 each, a pair or two of these can cure some otherwise serious problems in getting scopes or other equipment aligned properly.

The ARMS Multibase ($59.95) available from Bushmaster is a quick-detach rail that can hold a scope or other device using Weaver rings to it, coupling the unit to another Weaver rail or a flat-top AR-5 receiver. The good point of this is that the unit can be quickly removed or reattached, a plus if the original rings or equipment is slow to mount or remove from a rail.

For those wanting to add more rail mount areas to an A1 or A2 carrying handle and handguard, the ARMS #39A2 Bi-Level Rail ($125.00) is ideal. The unit attaches to the upper carrying handle with a knob that extends through the hole in the carrying handle. Once in place, the user has a rail in the top of the carrying handle to which a scope or other equipment can be attached as well as a rail that extends from the front of the unit, just a short distance above the top of the handguard. This latter rail permits mounting a dot scope so that it is lined up with the iron sights, making it possible to quickly aim the gun and have the iron sights lined up in the same plane (a great benefit for developing innate aiming habits as well as providing an instant backup with the iron sights should the scope unexpectedly fail).

As more and more accessories are mounted on rails along the handguard, barrel, or gas block, some AR-15s will have enough barrel flex to change the point of impact with all that gear attached (and depending somewhat on the hold on the gun). To prevent this from happening, several companies have introduced free-floating handguards with rail systems on them.

One of these is C-MORE's Quad-Rail Handguard, which free-floats the barrel and also presents a rail down the top, bottom, and each side of the assembly. This gives a shooter a wealth of points to attach accessories to a rifle. The handguard is ventilated and constructed of aircraft aluminum alloy.

Olympic Arms has fielded a similar system, the F8Max, which is designed for carbine versions of the AR-15, including the M4 carbine. The F8Max handguard is made from solid extruded aluminum with its Picatinny rails being an integral part of the primary tube; an inner tube acts as a heat shield.

## SCOPE MOUNTS

Many AR-15s come out of the box shooting like target rifles thanks to the "bolt-action"-style lockup of the bolt to the barrel as well as high quality control among barrel manufacturers. With or without free-floated barrels, a scope mount makes a lot of sense for many of the owners of these guns.

While placing a scope on a target model of the AR-15 that already has a mounting block on its receiver is no problem, it's a bit more work with the standard "carrying handle" rear sight style of upper receivers. The AR-15 has been designed with scope mounting in mind, and the handle is grooved on the top with a hole in it just for the purpose of mounting a scope (and Colt even offers a Sporter model that comes with a scope-mount block).

Armalite offers an improved scope mount that extends over the handguards to offer longer eye relief; two models are available, one for 1-inch scopes and the other for 30mm. The mount costs $89.

The best known maker of mounts for the AR-15 series is ARMS, whose products have been used for years by police and the U.S. military, as well as by civilians. This company has a well-earned reputation for quality mounts and has extended its line to cover most of the AR-15 variants.

The original and most popular of the ARMS mounts fits into the carrying handle of the standard A1/A2 guns and features the Swan system, allowing for universal mounting of Weaver scope rings and most military and police systems, including NATO STANAG, and doing away with the need for any special adapters). The mount also has a "see-through" design that permits seeing iron sights, a good way to do a rough check of a scope's zero as well as to provide emergency aiming should the scope become damaged. The mount is held in place in the hole in the carrying handle of the AR-15 with a self-locking thumbnut. The cost is $59.95.

ARMS also offers a low-profile #15 mount for the Trijicon reflex sight that has become popular with police and military users. The #15 attaches to the bottom of the reflex sight with three screws, and then uses locking levers to hold the scope in place. The precision of the manufacturing and locking system permits scopes to be removed and replaced without the loss of zero, for all practical purposes. It costs $120.

The ARMS #19a and #19acog are similar to the #15 but designed to provide a universal platform for NATO STANAG, Weaver rings, and many infrared and night-vision optical systems ($140 for the #19a and $150 for the #19acog).

The #38 Swan Sleeve from ARMS fastens to the AR-15 flat-top receiver, thereby providing an extended mounting surface over the upper handguard to secure several mil-spec systems in place. Additionally, the unit has a flip-up rear sight that aligns with the existing front sight of the rifle while boasting an A2-style windage and drop adjustments. The #38 is available in three lengths, including the #38 STD (standard) selling for $150, the 8.46-inch #38 EX (extended) for $165, and the #38 S-EX (superextended) with a 14-inch length that sells for $180.

B-Square offers several popular mounts for the AR-15. The company's QD/Return to Zero 18526 system is designed to fit into A1/A2-style carrying handles and attaches to the gun with a large thumbscrew knob. As its name suggests, the mount is precise enough to remove and remount the scope while keeping pretty close to zero. The unit also has a see-through slot so the iron sights can be used in a pinch with the scope mounted. The cost is $64.95.

There are also two B-Square scope mounts for the flat-top receiver. The QD/Return to Zero 15150 is nearly identical to the company's handle-style system, again permitting detachment and reattachment of a scope while maintaining zero ($74.95). The other mount for the flat-top is the 15100, which is a base that fits atop the rail of the receiver, raising a scope placed on it high enough to see over the front sight, thereby giving a brighter sight picture. While it is possible to "see through" the front sight because of the way most optical scopes work, this cuts down on the light-gathering quality—and with dot scopes the actual picture of the target can be blocked by the front sight ($54.95).

Other fine mounts for Weaver-style rings are offered by SGW, Tasco, Aimpoint, K-Loc, and SARCO (with K-Loc and Aimpoint mounts having a U-channel in them so that the iron sights can still be used). For those planning on mounting large high-magnification varminter scopes on a rifle, the extra long "GI"-style mount from SARCO for $15 is ideal; this is modeled on the scope mount pioneered in Vietnam.

Shooters needing to mount a scope in conjunction with a laser, flashlight, or other hardware that normally fits in a scope mount can do so by using the Tri-Mount, marketed by DPMS. This system has three Weaver bases that mount in the handle of an AR-15, placing one base alongside the carrying handle, one on top, and one on the other side of the carrying handle. Additionally, the center of the base is grooved so that the iron sights can still be used! This makes a range of mounting systems possible: one might, for example, mount a small laser on one side, a flashlight on the other, and a dot scope on the top—or any of an array of accessories and their combinations. The mount's cost is around $49.

A few plastic scope mounts have been made in the past, and this is a good idea for making a light assembly, but many have some noticeable flex that can change the zero of the scope if pressure is changed on the bolt holding the unit to the rifle. Consequently, while the plastic scope base is undoubtedly what everyone will be using in decades to come, there may still be some bugs in it. (For those who enjoy tackling simple gunsmithing tasks—or want to hire a gunsmith to do the work—it's possible to cut off the carrying handle/rear sight of the rifle and replace it with a scope rail. This procedure basically consists of milling off the top of the receiver, squaring it, and then mounting a rail on its top with epoxy followed with drilling and tapping screws to mount it permanently in place. This procedure is covered in *AR-15/M16: Super Systems,* available from Paladin Press.)

Scopes are mounted onto the base or mount with scope rings. There are all types of rings. Because of the wide selection, it's possible to greatly vary the height of the scope as well as use scopes of different diameters. Ordering rings through the mail can be a little frustrating when the owner doesn't know exactly what size is needed. And getting the right height of rings with larger-than-normal scopes or scopes having eye-relief distances greater or less than normal is tricky. In such cases it's wise for a shooter to visit a gunshop along with the rifle, mount, and scope to discover which rings will work with his rifle and mount.

## SCOPES AND CHEEK RESTS

Since a proper cheek weld is conducive to proper scope use, and since a scope mount placed in the carrying handle places the scope pretty high above the rifle, a cheek rest of some type is mandatory on such an AR-15.

Fortunately there are several companies that offer excellent cheek rests ideal for this purpose.

Arguably the most versatile lineup, and perhaps the best cheek rests, are those being marketed by Cherokee Accessories, with models that vary from entire stocks with adjustable heights to snap-on, snap-off assemblies. Most of these models come in the standard "AR-15 Black" as well as "Desert Tan, Arctic White, and Jungle Green." All the rifle stocks fit both the A1 and A2 models of AR-15s.

Cherokee's Hawk Delta Pro is one of the the cheekpieces that is easy to use cheekpiece because it simply snaps on or off the stock, making it easy to switch to iron sights (provided the scope rides on a see-through mount)—and weighs only 7 ounces. If this isn't enough, it has a small, watertight storage chamber molded into the cheek pad. Its price is $75.

The company's Delta Cheekpiece is, as its name suggests, a refinement of the basic system the company created for Colt to employ on its Delta H-BAR. The unit weighs 9.5 ounces, attaches with a "clamshell" system that takes only a few minutes to fasten in place, and costs $69.95.

The CAR-15/16 Cheekpiece fits AR-15 shorty stocks that include the M4 carbine. As such, it provides a much needed accessory that brings the eye right into line with scopes mounted in the carrying handle of these guns. This has an additional benefit of bringing the stock lower on the shoulder, giving the stock a firmer positioning rather than having it try to ride nearly on top of the shoulder. The 4.3-ounce unit snaps on or off instantly, has a cubic inch of watertight storage space in its pad (which is a good place for spare batteries for those using an electric scope), and retails for $34.95.

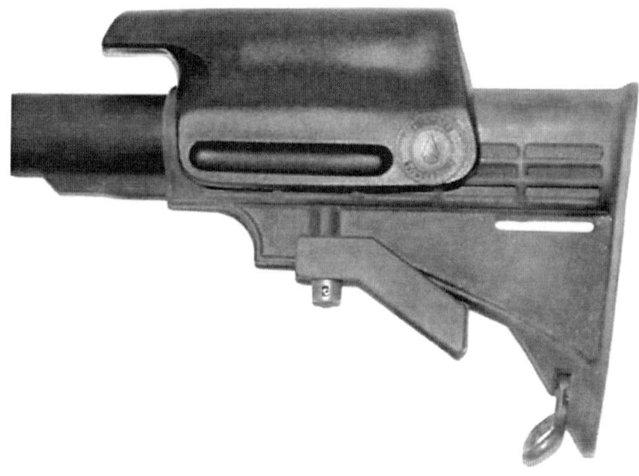

The Cherokee CAR-14/M-4 is designed for the newer M4 stock.

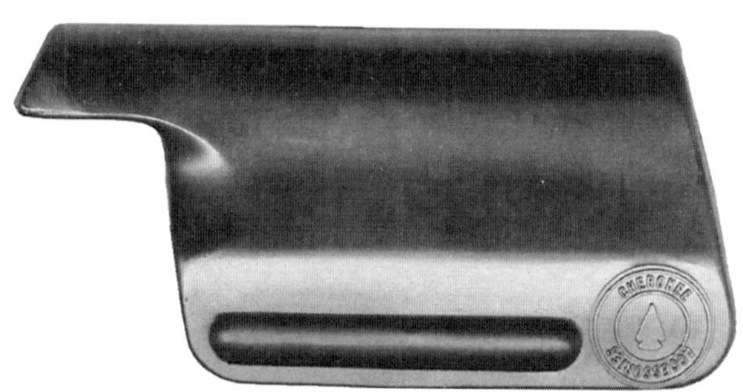

Cherokee CAR-15/16 Cheekpiece.

Cherokee CAR-15/16 Cheekpiece shown on telescoping stock.

Original Cherokee Delta cheek rest. (Courtesy of Cherokee Accessories.)

Cherokee replacement stock has a cheekpiece that can be "dialed" to create a custom fit for the shooter. (Courtesy of Cherokee Accessories.)

The CAR-14/M-4 Cheekpiece (retailing for $36.80) is similar to the standard model but designed to fit into the grooves molded into the M4 Rock River Arms collapsible stock (the cheek rest is snapped off by simply prying up on its cantilevered portion). Its weight is only 3.5 ounces and, like other cheekpieces from Cherokee, it has a watertight compartment for the storage of spare parts, extra batteries, or whatever.

The Cherokee Delta-Star cheekpiece has an extrahigh pad to bring the eye into alignment with a night-vision scope or other large, high-riding devices; the unit is otherwise identical to

Cherokee replacement stock with cheekpiece in upper position to accommodate large night-vision scope. (Courtesy of Cherokee Accessories.)

the Delta model. Like other of the company's products, this one has a number of military and police users, including those in the Israeli military. The retail price is $69.95.

Cherokee also offers an adjustable stock assembly that has a built-in cheek rest that can be "dialed" to the proper height to suit the user's needs by twisting a screw assembly in the stock that raises or lowers the cheek rest. The stock is a replacement for the standard stock and requires only a screwdriver in order to replace the original on an AR-15. The cost is $150.

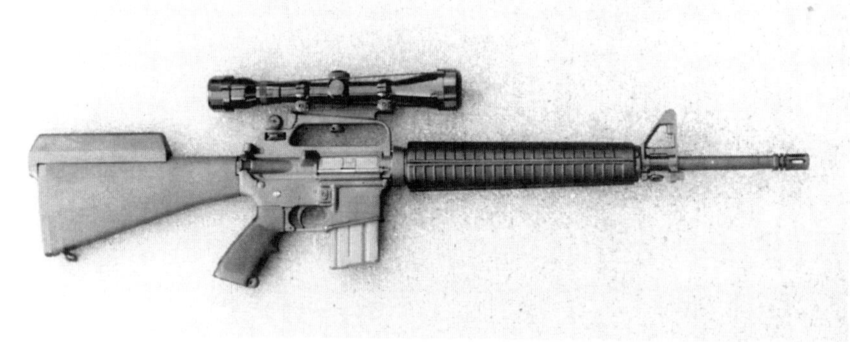

The E&L Manufacturing cheek rest shown here on an AR-15 Sporter II.

E&L Manufacturing offers a tough plastic cheekpiece that matches the standard AR-15 stock and is held in place with the rear buffer screw for a secure fit. It costs only $19.95. This unit isn't a quick-on, quick-off system, but it is inexpensive and works well.

For those having a scope that is offset to the left side of the receiver (as would be the case with a scope in the left position of the Tri-Mount), DPMS offers a quality leather cheekpiece. This mounts to the stock using the rear sling swivel and Velcro to hold the cheekrest in place. The cost is $25.

It should be noted that a carrying-handle-scoped AR-15 can be used without a cheek rest, but with most optical systems, especially telescopic sights, parallax can become a serious problem. Additionally, getting the sight aligned with the eye is slower because the shooter has to "bob and weave" a bit to locate the picture. A good cheek rest cures both problems, bring the eye into proper alignment for a faster and more accurate shot. As noted above, a cheek rest and scope also lowers the rifle on the shooter's shoulder, often making for a more natural feel and better recoil control as well.

## SCOPES FOR THE AR-15

The commercial marketplace offers a huge assortment of scopes that will serve the owner of an AR-15 well. For instance, Beeman, Tasco, Unertl, Armson, Redfield, Leupold, Simmons, Bushnell, and Shepherd all have fine scopes that are tough and backed by excellent service and warranties. Given the reasonable cost of these scopes and their high quality, shooters do well to avoid little-known "bargain" scopes, since the money saved isn't very much and the quality can be quite poor. (The exception to this is models being discontinued by brand-name manufacturers, which can carry low tags and be of high quality.)

Variable scopes have traditionally been plagued with points of aim that wander as the power is changed; consequently, most military or police personnel, as well as gamers and hunters, use fixed scopes, the only exception being range-finding sniper scopes issued to troops who are trained to be extra careful not to damage their equipment.

And even many snipers prefer the ruggedness of a fixed scope. The 4X and, to some extent, 6X scopes seem to be the best compromises available in terms of power and field of view with rifles. For faster shooting at closer ranges, 1X or 1.5X scopes are sometimes seen; these allow the shooter to aim with both eyes open.

Scopes with more than 6X of magnification have narrow fields of view that make it hard to follow moving targets, and the wobble introduced by the human nervous system dictates using a bipod or other system to keep the rifle stationary. Consequently, most high-power scopes should be reserved for varminting. The only other time a high-power scope has an advantage is at dusk or at night, when they may be capable of better light gathering than lower-power scopes.

Range-finding scopes are variable scopes that also move the zero up or down according to a range scale on the scope. These probably aren't needed within 300 yards, though those who need a sniper rifle might arguably be making longer shots. Range-finding scopes are usually a little bit more sensitive to abuse, cost more, and have to be compatible with the ammunition the owner uses—so care needs to be exercised in investing in one of these scopes.

Most range-finding scopes work by having the owner bracket some object of known size between two crosshairs (with hunting scopes, the known size object is usually the animal's body; with combat scopes, a man's body. With a little figuring the owner can adapt the hunting scope to combat use or vice versa.) Once the object of known size is bracketed by the crosshairs, the shooter checks the scale on the variable magnification control to see what the range is and then adjusts the bullet drop compensator scale so that it reads the same distance as the scale on the magnification control. Finally, the owner adjusts his magnification to suit his needs and then fires the shot. Obviously this isn't the quickest system in the world, but shooters can become fairly quick with practice.

In the past, the U.S. military used commercial scopes for snipers but soon created the automatic ranging telescope (ART), system which was quicker to adjust and capable of judging ranges (later the commercial scopes followed the military's lead). The first scopes produced during the Vietnam War were quite good and soon led to a second generation of ART scopes. These ART II scopes had the range scale and magnification adjustment coupled together so when the two crosshairs bracket an 18-inch object, the range compensation is right and the shot can be fired. This makes for very quick shooting.

The only bad thing about this is that the scope is locked into a fixed amount of magnification in order to have the correct range. This isn't as bad as it might seem, however, since greater magnification is needed for farther ranges to bracket the target. ART II scopes carried a $600-plus price tag and are now out of production.

Springfield Armory (the company, not the government entity) recently released its 4-14x40 Tactical Government Model, which has a scope that employs a range finder to zero the scope for the bullet drop of .223 match ammo out to 700 meters, and also has a level to help the shooter avoid canting his gun, thereby assuring the greatest possible accuracy in ranging the target. This system greatly increases the accuracy of a first shot made in the field. Springfield also offers an optional flip-up lens cover and 80mm sunshade for this scope, making it a good choice for those needing to extract the maximum long-range accuracy from an AR-15.

It should be noted that Colt chose Tasco scopes for the expensive countersniper "Delta" version of the AR-15, and many shooters find the low price tags of these Japanese-made optical systems attractive. Among the Tasco scopes suitable for mounting on an AR-15 are the World Class series (fixed and variable powers with lower price tags) and the Compact series (which are small but have narrower fields of view).

Regardless of the scope selected, if a shooter opts for a full-size detachable scope, then he would be wise to also invest in the Cherokee Scope Holster, which is a tough plastic molding with a padded interior and an exterior with a belt loop and web gear attachment points on the outside. This container is designed to carry not only the scope but also the mount, making it simple to remove the scope from an AR-15 and slip the scope into the Scope Holster—or to remove the scope and mount it on the gun again. The cost of the Scope Holster is $80.

"Combat" scopes of abbreviated size have recently become popular with military users as well as sportsmen. These scopes are designed only for daytime use (due to their poor twilight factors) and have rather narrow fields of view. But they are light and compact and therefore ideal for some shooters carrying an AR-15. In the past, several scopes blazed the trail in the direction of compact but efficient scopes; among the most notable of these were the Beeman SS-2, SS-2L, and SS-3 series, and Colt offered a 4X combat scope for some time as an accessory but has since discontinued it.

There are a few very expensive combat scopes that combine a small size with wide optics and good light-gathering capability. Among the best of these is the 4X Trijicon Advanced Combat Optical Gunsight (ACOG), which was developed specifically for modern military rifles like the AR-15; this site has been adopted by the U.S. Special Operations Command as a part of its Special Operations Peculiar Modification (SOPMOD) kit.

The big plus of the ACOG is that it doesn't need batteries to operate, employing instead ambient light to illuminate its aiming cross-hair reticle (or dot, depending on the model) in the daylight and using a Tritium insert to create its aiming point at night. It is also relatively light in weight, tipping the scales at only 8 ounces, even with its

Cherokee Scope Holster. (Courtesy of Cherokee Accessories.)

M4 flat-top with ACOG scope mounted on it.

AR-15 mount. Cost is steep for this sight, running at $623 as this is written.

The ACOG 4 x 32 is the unit employed by U.S. troops; it is slightly shorter than its sister model and has an aluminum body built to take a beating without failing to function properly. The black daytime reticle in the ACOG 4 x 32 glows red at night and in low light due to its tritium composition; ranging is adjusted by the reticle pattern with the width of the horizontal lines in the reticle corresponding to the width of a man at any given range. The optics are parallax free along the vertical axis of the scope. This unit is designed to fit in the carrying handle of an AR-15 and has a see-through base permitting iron sights to be used should the scope fail.

Trijicon ACOG TA01NSN is basically the same as the ACOG 4 x 32 but designed for mounting on A3 flat-top receivers. This model has some modifications created for U.S. special forces buyers, including an integral rear ghost ring aperture and a tritium glow-in-the-dark front sight that can be employed as emergency or close-quarter sights. This scope is available from Bushmaster for $795.

The ACOG 3.3 x 35 is a bit longer and also ports a slightly larger field of view and less magnification, making it suitable in the eyes of some both as a close-combat dot scope and a suitable long-range sniper scope.

The Trijicon TA44-5 Compact ACOG was also created for special forces use and is basically a more compact version of the ACOG 4 x 32. This TA44-5 has an aiming dot that uses either available light or a tritium element for dark environments. Its price is $595.

The 3.5X Ernst Leitz (of Canada) has also established a good reputation; Colt's ACR candidate rifle uses it. This scope has a tritium illuminating device for periods of reduced light.

The Trilux scope (aka the SUIT—Sightunit, Infantry, Trilux) was originally created for the FN FAL in the 1950s. The units were used by Israeli, Canadian, and British troops on that rifle. When the M16 rifle was adopted by the Israeli and Canadian forces, the scope was also modified and a new cam created to calibrate it to the .223 cartridge along with an adapter to mount it on the AR-15. Although no longer manufactured, these scopes often are found in the used and surplus market with varying costs. Their rugged construction generally makes them a good buy.

The reticle is an unusual inverted post that can take some getting used to but that some shooters feel is faster in finding a target. The original 4X scope had a tritium insert for night use that is missing from most units sold as surplus to civilian buyers. However, Enterprise Arms offers a battery-powered insert that makes the reticle glow just as it did with the original tritium insert (the cost for this addition is $49.99).

SARCO has added the Marksman Elite combat scope to its line of products. The scope is designed for use with the AR-15 and has a built-in bullet drop compensator calibrated to the .223 cartridge; once the rifle is zeroed in at 100 meters, the range can then be

Colt ACR with Ernst Leitz scope. (Courtesy of U.S. Army.)

U.S. Marine demonstrates the plus of scopes over iron sites; the scope permits a "heads up" view of the target with both eyes open, giving a wider field of view. (Courtesy of U.S. Department of Defense.)

dialed up anywhere from 100 to 500 meters and the shooter can place the crosshairs on the target without having to worry about bullet drop.

The Marksman Elite also has a sight reticle that can be illuminated by daylight or moonlight or with an optional battery-powered light system. The 15.2-ounce, 7.75-inch-long scope presents a bright picture and has an integral mount that allows quick attachment or removal to the AR-15 carrying handle (no other mount or rings are needed). The price is $269 for the scope, with an additional $21 for the battery attachment.

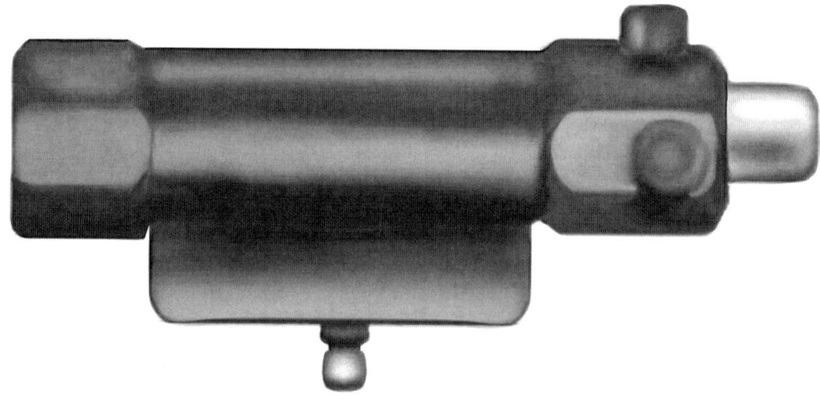

Trijicon's Armson OEG sight is simple and reliable, operating without batteries.

Gun South offers the Blits Optics System that has a quick-detach mounting system for the AR-15. The high-quality optics of the Hedsoldt 4X scope are said to have good light-gathering qualities that make this unit useful in dim light.

A different optical aiming system that comes in sizes as small as the combat scopes are what have become known as dot scopes. Each of these creates a small red dot in the shooter's sight picture and has the added benefit of being capable of nighttime use. Unlike most optical systems, most dot scopes offer no magnification, thus making them quick to use at close ranges. In addition to speed, the dot scopes allow shooters to aim with both eyes left open when firing so as to keep a wider field of view. This has made these scopes popular with military and police users as well as combat "gamesmen."

Two distinct varieties of dot scopes are made. The easiest to maintain are those that use available light; some of these are useless in dim light, while others use a radioactive tritium insert to give a green dot picture at night. The most successful of these is Armson's Occluded Eye Gunsight (OEGG), which is still available for as low as $168 from some suppliers. The version designed for the AR-15 comes complete with its own mounting system that fits into the rifle's carrying handle, and the base has a sight tunnel so that the iron sights can still be used with the scope in place.

The OEG scope is only as bright as the light around it; firing from a hidden position that is dark toward one that is brightly lit creates problems for some shooters because the aiming dot will be weak. Another consideration is that with these scopes both eyes must be kept open; shooters who can see from only one eye or who have trouble with both eyes tracking will not have much luck with the OEG.

The brightness of the tritium insert in the scope will eventually run down and have to be replaced; this is a job for the factory because handling the radioactive inserts can be hazardous. However, the inserts remain usable for up to 10 years, so this is a minor problem. The big plus is the OEG doesn't need batteries and is tougher than electric dot systems.

Electronic dot scopes use a small LED and optics to create a red aiming dot in the center of the scope's field of view. Since the shooter can see through the scope, it gives a better view of the target area and can be used by those who can see well from only one eye. The tiny battery powering the electric dot scope must be turned on and off or it will run down. But the battery will give hundreds of hours of use before it's time to change batteries—which are readily available at Radio Shack or similar stores carrying the hearing aid or watch batteries. And shooters using an electric dot scope in cold weather should invest in lithium batteries, which will continue to function when the temperature dips.

The brightness of the dot can be adjusted from a very dim point for night use to a brilliant ball for daytime shooting. Most electric dot scopes have polarizing filters available for very bright daytime sunlight (this requires the use of both eyes since the view through the scope becomes limited). Aimpoint and Tasco offer 3X optical attachments for their scopes so that they can be converted for long-range use. Aimpoint also makes a 2X red dot scope, fittingly named the "2 Power" for shooters who want a very compact unit with a small amount of magnification.

Among the best "civilian" electric dot scopes are the Action Arms Ultra-Dot; Tasco Pro-Point series; and Aimpoint 3000 series (available in black or stainless finishes and several sizes). All three manufacturers have mounts that either accommodate Weaver mounting bases or take 1-inch scope rings—except for the Aimpoint 5000 series and all of the Tasco red dot scopes, which have 30mm tubes ( generally supplied with mounting rings for standard-size Weaver mounts).

Currently the Aimpoint Comp M has a slight lead on other dot scopes, at least in terms of good press. This has come about because the army decided to buy 80,000 to 100,000 of the scopes along with the company's mounts for the M16A2 rifle and M4A1 carbine. Needless to say, police SWAT teams and civilian shooters, who often take their cue from what the military selects, have been buying these scopes in droves.

During the ACR trials, Colt's entry had a 3.5X scope manufactured by Ernst Leitz of Canada mounted on the rifle; this scope has a tritium illuminating device for

For a time Colt offered a dot scope with the company logo on it. This scope has since been discontinued. (Courtesy of Colt Firearms.)

Aimpoint scopes have proved popular with the U.S. Army—here shown from the business end of things. (Courtesy of U.S. Department of Defense.)

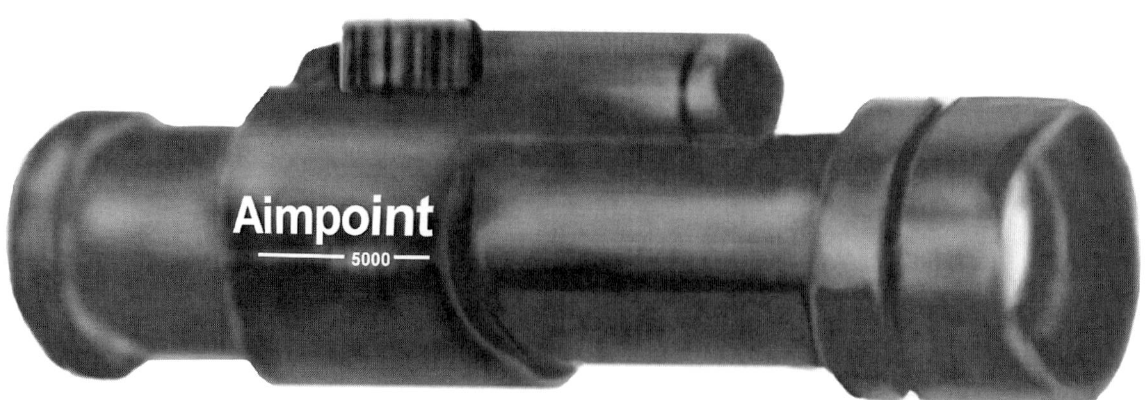


Aimpoint 5000 series dot scope.

C-MORE Systems railway dot scope.

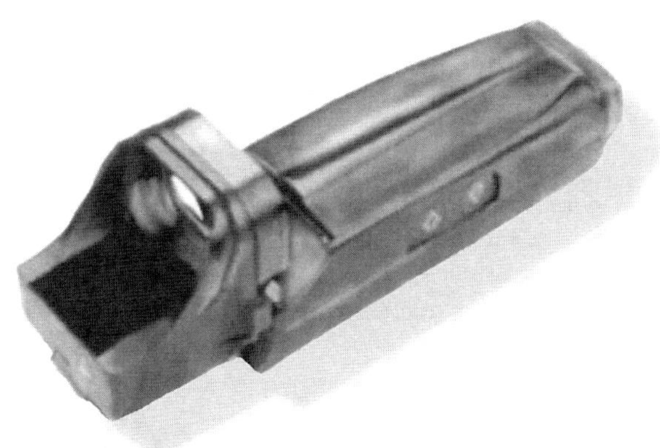

Bushnell HOLOsight.

periods of reduced light. With the current search by the U.S. military for an M16A3 rifle scope, it's possible that the military may have a scope for every soldier on the front line. How this affects the shooting abilities of the average soldier remains to be seen, but a new doctrine stressing hiding and sniping from longer ranges might have a profound effect on battlefield tactics.

The Israeli army has issued a reflexive sight system that is rather large but presents a larger sight picture that undoubtedly makes it fast in acquiring targets. Manufactured by International Technologies Lasers, the multipurpose aiming reflex sight boasts a built-in laser that can operate in either the infrared or visual mode for use in aiming at and designating targets, with or without night-vision gear. This makes for a complete system in one very tough unit.

The Israeli-made Meprolight Mepor 21 reflex sight is also becoming common on Israeli-issued M16 rifles and M4 carbines and is most commonly seen with special forces units. The scope weighs 7 ounces with its mounting adapter.

The C-MORE Systems railway dot scope is a reflexive sight designed to attach to any Weaver or Picatinny, rail, making it ideal for use with the AR-15 flat-top receiver, although it can also be mounted on other rail systems on an A2 or A1 receiver as well. The sight has a tubeless, heads-up display that is powered by an LED (with interchangeable dots so the user can change the dot size). The Railway is constructed of polymer with an aircraft alloy base that fastens to a rail with three clamps. The scope also boasts positive locking windage and elevation controls. Its cost is $249.

Colt teamed up with C-MORE to produce the Scout, which is nearly identical to the Railway but uses a mount that fits an A1 or A2 carrying handle, placing the site just above the handguard and in line with the iron sights so that the red aiming dot lines up with the front sight. This makes an ideal system because the shooter has his iron sights ready should he need them for backup; it also helps a shooter learn to instinctively bring his rifle onto a target as he works with the scope and rifle. The cost for this sight is $368.

C-MORE and Colt also teamed up to create the Tactical Sight, which is designed for the AR-15 flat-top, having an iron sight at its rear and the basic railway system ahead of that. The benefit of this system is that it too puts the dot in line with the iron sights to give the shooter an instant backup aiming system as well as improving his instinctive shooting skills. The cost for this sight is $444.

Bushnell has introduced a reflexive sight that is very similar to the C-MORE systems. Dubbed the HOLOsight, the Bushnell unit attaches to a standard Weaver rail to produce what appears to be an illuminated dot inside ringed crosshairs floating 50 yards in front of the user's gun. This has a slight advantage over a dot because if the shooter's eye is grossly misaligned with the sight, he is more apt to spot a corner or outer ring of the crosshairs than he would with a lone dot in a similar sight. The HOLOsight runs on standard N alkaline batteries (available in most hardware and discount stores for a few dollars); battery life is about 30 hours, and the unit is designed to shut itself off after 8 hours to prevent draining the battery completely if the user forgets to shut the sight off. This sight costs $265, making it very competitive as well. Bushnell also markets a 2X attachment to give magnification to the unit.

The U.S. military's Military Operations in Urban Terrain (MOUNT) testing and training has demonstrated the usefulness of the Picatinny Arsenal's M68 Sight, Reflex with Mount designed for use with the M16A2 and M4/M4A1 carbines. The M68 sight is a more or less conventional red dot scope that has demonstrated the superiority of being able to fire with both eyes open instead of squinting down an iron sight, increasing hit probability while reducing engagement time. This sight has become one of the key components of the military's Land Warrior and MOUNT operations, proving to be a quick way to increase the capability of troops to use the range and accuracy afforded by the AR-15 rifle. The overall length of the M68 is 5 inches with a weight of 9.6 ounces (for a total of 13.9 ounces with the MIL STD 1913 Interface mount).

The Trijicon Reflex Gunsight 4 MoA uses a fluorescent fiber-optic system to collect available light and a tritium element for nighttime illumination, thereby doing away with the need for batteries. The sight creates an amber aiming dot, which some feel is more easily seen than the red that has become common with many sights. The price is $369.95 with an A1/A2 carrying handle mount or $359 for a unit that fits onto a Weaver or flat-top rail. These scopes are available from Bushmaster and other suppliers.

The EOTech Holographic Diffraction Sight (HDS) is offered by Bushmaster for $299.95. This tubeless sight makes the claim of being the first "holographic" sight on the market. That said, the sight picture is pretty much the conventional red dot, with a few additional technological tricks, including a small "brain" that adjusts the brightness of the dot to the ambient light levels. The unit operates on N alkaline batteries that keep it going for 70 hours of continuous use. The HDS mounts on any Weaver rail.

Although not currently in production, the Israeli-made Falcon dot scope is sometimes still seen on military or police rifles in the United States as well as Israel and elsewhere. This scope has a large, heads-up display and with a bright dot in its center; power is provided by a 3.6-volt lithium battery. The unit can be mounted in the carrying handle of an A1/A2 rifle or on a rail system. Thanks to an aluminum body, the Falcon is rugged but on the heavy side and is expensive to manufacture. Consequently, this dot scope has slowly lost favor to newer, lighter units.

The Optima 2000 dot sight is compact enough to use on handguns but can also be employed on an AR-15. The catch is that the device doesn't have an off/on switch, instead using a cover that causes it to go into a "sleep mode" and shut down when the available light drops to zero. This sounds like an inconvenience—but it is more than that. The sight will also shut down in a very dark environment. Since it is conceivable that this may happen in combat, this sight is best employed only for target or recreational shooting, not for combat.

## SIGHTS

The peep sight on the AR-15 is excellent, and many people do excellent shooting with the sights "as are." Those who achieve this are probably best advised to leave well enough alone and not change anything.

However, there are replacement sights and odds and ends that can create a slightly improved sight picture for some shooters. That said, probably the quickest fix for precision work is to mount a quality scope on the rifle. But this is not always practical or even possible for some target matches that require iron sights.

One inexpensive trick is to place the front sight into a mandrel on a lathe or drill press and turn the post so that it is square without a taper. Some shooters find that the lack of taper is conducive to a more accurate sight pattern. Reducing the width of the front blade also makes for a slightly more accurate picture; however, target acquisition may suffer—which may be a consideration depending on how much speed the shooter is afforded to find the target in a contest.

The accuracy of zeroing in can also be (at least in theory) improved by cutting an extra notch between each standard notch in the sight adjustment sections of the front sight, as well as on the rear sight. This gives a finer adjustment and makes it possible to zero in with greater position "between the clicks" with such modifications. That said, such modifications call for machining skills that put them out of the range of many shooters.

Bushmaster offers a hooded front sight, the KNS Precision Front Sight, with a tiny crosshair in it. This sells for $35.95. The company also offers a Tactical model (for $49.95), which has a tiny bead on the vertical crosspiece; this can be moved up or down with an Allen wrench to give a second zero mark or for greater clarity in dimmer light.

For shooters who lack a front sight on an AR-15 (but would like to have one) on the Bushmaster V Match rifle, the company also offers the Front Flip-Up Sight that clamps around a milled gas block base to offer an iron sight alternative to a V Match. It is designed to be used with any open iron rear sight that can be attached to the flat-top upper receiver, such as the ARMS Swan Sleeve, the ARMS # 40 Flip-Up Rear Sight, the GG&G Rear Flip-Up Sight, or the A3 Type Removable Carrying Handle. The BMAS Front Flip-Up Sight is machined from quality-billet aircraft aluminum to strict military standards. It locks up or down with the push of a button and installs with an Allen Wrench. It is elevation adjustable and includes a MIL SPEC front sight post installed. In addition, the base is drilled and threaded to accept sling swivel mounts or bipod attachment lugs. Cost of the BMAS AR Flat-Top Rear Sight is $89.95.

GG&G offers its Fully Integrated Rifle Enhancement (FIRE) system, which is designed to be used with the rail systems on flat-top receivers as well as on gas blocks. The company's rear backup iron sight is known as the Multiple Aperture Device (MAD); it attaches to the rear of a flat-top rail, with its apertures safely tucked in a folded position or rapidly brought up should they be needed; cost is $141.95. The company also offers a similar A2-style sight that flips up and down; the cost is $125.95. To use with either of these sights, GG&G also offers a flip-up front sight that mounts on a rail gas block.

## SINGLE-SHOT ADAPTER

Some target shooters, as well as beginning shooters, can profit from using a rifle in the single-shot mode. The AR-15 can be modified by blocking the gas port in one way or another to achieve this end. However a simpler method is to modify a magazine so that it holds the bolt open after a shot, thereby presenting an open port that a shell can be slipped into for the next shot. Again, a shooter must exercise caution to avoid letting the action fling itself shut on a round because this may cause a slam-fire when the AR-15's floating firing pin strikes the primer. Instead, a shooter should ease the bolt forward by maintaining the grip on the charging handle as it goes forward, then fully seat the bolt with the forward assist. For this reason rifle—not pistol—primers must be used when reloading ammunition: the more sensitive pistol primer might be ignited when a bolt chambers a cartridge stripped from the magazine.

Saturn Custom Machining offers a single-shot adapter that replaces the follower in a standard magazine. Once this Delrin follower is in place, it engages the bolt hold-open lever after a shot and permits loading even cartridges with long-seated bullets into the firearm. This accessory is available from Brownells for $22.50.

## SILENCERS

Some may argue with the name "silencer," but that was what the inventor, Hiram Percy Maxim {spelling check: Hiram Percy Maxim], called the first such devices and that's the name that has stuck with the public. As will be seen, however, the "silencer" is far from silent when used with the AR-15; consequently, these devices are probably better called sound suppressors with this firearm.

Silencers have a "forbidden fruit" attraction to many in the public, partly because Hollywood gives them abilities that aren't possible in real life and partly because some states have outlawed them. Folks from other nations can often buy silencers without red tape, even in countries with otherwise strict gun laws, and are frequently amazed (to the point of laughing) that the United States should have such laws. Nevertheless, the federal government has continued to tax and red tape suppressors nearly out of existence. Even so, shooters in many parts of the country can own these if they go through a little paper work and pay a $200 federal tax, provided the states they live in haven't displayed their ignorance of real life by banning outright the ownership of silencers.

The report from an AR-15 firing standard ammunition through a silencer is not silent for the simple reason that the bullet's supersonic crack makes almost as much noise as normal discharge at the muzzle. With heavy bullets that are subsonic, things are better, though the ammunition may not be as effective unless it has been carefully tailored for the task.

An AR-15 with a 20-inch barrel creates a peak sound level of 165 dB 1 yard from the rifle (and a bit more noise is made with a shorter barrel). An average conversation reaches 50 dB; heavy traffic, 80 dB; a thunder clap, 110dB; the threshold of pain (where the ear starts to suffer damage) is 120 dB—which is why shooting an AR-15 without hearing protection damages the ears and is painful to boot, especially if it has a short barrel.

Needless to say, it would take a very effective device to soak up the 165-dB sound of an AR-15 muzzle blast. And there are other sounds to be taken care of, including the expanding gases hissing through the ejection port, the clattering of the action, and that supersonic crack of the bullet.

So, about the best that today's technology can do is make the muzzle blast sound "only" as loud as a .22 LR bullet—about 135 dB, which is above the threshold of pain and far from quiet (especially compared with what is achieved with those bogus little Hollywood silencers).

This is not to say that a sound suppressor cannot be useful to a military snipers operating at long range. In such a case, lowering the muzzle sound of an AR-15 to that of a .22 LR will enable the sound to be absorbed by vegetation and terrain so that a target several hundred yards away will be unable to discern where the shot came from. Because there is no muzzle blast, so the crack of the bullet and its echoes will actually be more confusing than otherwise, making it nearly impossible to tell where the shot came from.

Mitchell WerBell III was instrumental in developing and demonstrating just how effective a sound suppressor on an AR-15 could be. During the Vietnam War, WerBell's Military Armaments Corporation created a series of Sionics sound suppressors that the inventor and businessman introduced to U.S. special forces as well as special South Vietnamese troops. Eventually, the M16A1 with a Sionics suppressor mounted on it was classified as a special missions assault rifle by the U.S. Army, and it undoubtedly took more than its fair share of North Vietnamese soldiers and Vietcong.

For those who want more silence than can be created by using the .223, an alternative is to adopt a different cartridge that fires a heavier bullet that travels at subsonic speed. In the past about the only such option was to use a carbine chambered in .45 ACP. However, more recently manufacturers and inventors have created some AR-15 conversions chambered for the .300 Whisper, 6.5 Whisper, or 7mm Whisper, all of which employ heavy

An M4 carbine decked out with some of the SOPMOD bells and whistles, including a quick-detach M4-96D suppressor.

Gemtech Predator silencer mounted on an AR-15 carbine.

bullets traveling at a subsonic speed to put a lot of energy on a target while avoiding supersonic speed and the crack that speed can produce.

One of the more common silencers for U.S. military users is Knight's M4-96D Suppressor (also manufactured by Gemtech). Provided that special subsonic ammunition is employed with the M4-96D, this unit is capable of reducing the noise signature by 30dB, with no degradation of the weapon's accuracy. This silencer is also equipped with a special quick-detach system that replaces the standard birdcage flash hider on the carbine; in effect, when the silencer is removed, the shooter has a flash hider in place on his gun.

The M4-96D is a step up in silencer design, having been optimized by computer to cut down on design costs and being manufactured to high tolerances on CNC machinery. Suppressor life is known to exceed 15,000 rounds. The M4-96D is 7.75 inches long with a diameter of 1.5 inches and a weight of 24.7 ounces.

A spinoff of the military design is offered by Gemtech as its Predator M4-96C suppressor, which exploits the same computer-optimized baffle stack of the M4-96D. The Predator mounts on the threads normally employed for the flash hider; the sound signature is said to be similar to that of a rimfire rifle shooting .22 Shorts. Made mainly of stainless steel and alloys, the unit is 6.2 inches long and 1.5 inches in diameter, with a weight of 20 ounces. Gemtech also offers the Raptor 2L for use with 9mm versions of the AR-15 and markets an integral silencer/barrel system for 9mm guns as the Talon SD-R.

## SIMON BREACHING LAUNCHER SYSTEM

The Simon Breaching Launcher System, developed by Israel, enables an M16 rifleman to blow open a door or breach a window from up to 40 meters away. This system was adopted by the U.S. military through the Warfighter Rapid Acquisition Program—in turn an outgrowth of the Military Operations in Urban Terrain Advanced Concept Technology Demonstration, which was initiated in the late 1990s to locate and incorporate existing technology from sources outside the military for possible use rather than waste resources and time trying to develop similar equipment.

The business part of this system is affixed to the muzzle of the M16 and then launched with a grenade-

Gemtech Raptor silencer.

Gemtech Talon-SD-R.

launching blank cartridge (current work is being done to permit launching the projectile with a standard round). The projectile contains a shaped charge at its rear that is set off when the tip of the projectile hits a surface a short distance from the door to be entered. The impact creates a blast wave that breaks the door away without creating projectiles that could wound civilians or hostages that might be behind the door (even though it's likely that the concussion produced and the velocity of the door itself would injure anyone within a few yards). Most of the projectile is plastic, making it light and portable.

## SLINGS

At first glance, the standard AR-15 has sling swivels that seem to have been designed for marching rather than carrying a rifle. A lot of times this doesn't make much difference since the rifle will be carried without a sling. Slings need to come off whenever they become a problem, such as when a shooter has to travel through heavy brush; then being able to detach the slings in a hurry can be a big plus. The first rule with slings is to be able to detach them quickly.

Some front swivels (or movable rear swivels on some aftermarket stocks) make a lot of racket without their slings. For those who won't be using a sling, it's often a good idea to drift out the pin holding the swivel units, grind out the rivet that fastens them, or unscrew them. Or if they will be used only occasionally, a bit of tape or cloth can be wrapped around them to cure their rattling.

It should also be noted that the barrel on many of the AR-15s is not supported by the handguards; this means that it flexes slightly if a lot of pressure is placed on it. Normally this isn't a problem, but it does become one if a sling is tightened on the barrel to steady a shooter's aim. When a lot of pressure is put on the barrel with the sling, the impact of the bullets will drift to the side as much as 3 inches at 100 yards. This is different with the H-BAR versions of the rifle and target rifles offered by SGW, Insight Systems, and other companies that free-float the barrel inside the handguard. Unless it is attached to a floating-barrel handguard, a sling should be employed only for carrying an AR-15, not for steadying the rifle when firing.

Whenever an AR-15 is carried with a sling, it's wise to keep the safety on until the rifle is brought up to fire. A muzzle cap on the barrel is also a good idea; it keeps dirt and moisture out of the bore. The plastic muzzle caps are available from Choate Machine and Tool, as well as most surplus companies, for less than 50 cents each and are well worth the buy. And if the rifle is needed in a hurry, the cap can be fired through—without having to worry about whether there is dirt in the bore.

Most new AR-15s and military rifles come with a sling that is just fine for a walk in the forest or marching. Sometimes that's all that's needed, and the tough nylon found on most of these slings will last a long time, too.

But there are some options. Probably at the head of the list for comfort and carrying ease are the numerous styles of Uncle Mike's slings available from Michaels of Oregon (and sold in most guns stores). These run the gamut from the basket-weave leather Cobra Straps to inexpensive nylon slings in camouflage, brown, black, and white (for use in snow). The nylon slings come either with padded "shoulder savers" or as plain straps. In general these slings can't be beat for carrying a rifle for extended periods.

Some shooters prefer what has come to be known as the "assault carry," in which the sling is placed over a shoulder and the rifle held at the hip ready to be brought up rapidly to the shoulder. Aside from the rifle's being quickly brought into play, many people find this method of carry easier than the old "marching" style with the rifles simply slung over the shoulder.

The assault carry is pretty easy to achieve with the Commando-style telescoping stock: just thread the sling through the front sight mount (rather than the front swivel) and then push the other end of the sling through the holes on either side of the buffer tube toward the rear of the stock. Adjust the sling so that the rifle can be shouldered, and you're ready to go. If a standard-size sling is being used and it's too short, a pair of nylon shoelaces can extend it.

Although there have been endless modifications and field-expedient devices created to allow the assault carry with the AR-15, the best of these is simply the shoelace tied to a good sling. The secret is create a large loop for the rear swivel and run the shoelace over either side of the stock after looping it through the rear swivel. When the rifle is brought up to shoulder, the loop flops off the back of the stock and lies under the shooter's arm. This is quick, efficient, and cheap, and permits using a quality sling with a shoulder pad (like those from Michaels of Oregon).

A kit that helps accomplish the assault carry just like many field-expedient systems is the top sling adapter kit issued by the U.S. military. It's available on the surplus market from Sierra Supply and other suppliers for under $10 and works fine with the black generic sling that comes with many AR-15s.

Six-foot-long nylon straps are available from a number of companies that carry AR-15 accessories. With a strap this long and a couple of extra slide buckles, it's possible to improvise a sling system similar to that used on Heckler & Koch combat rifles. This system has a lot of advantages, one being that the weapon can be worn

One solution to obtaining an assault carry with an AR-15 stock: an aftermarket sling swivel has been screwed into a standard stock, while the lower sling swivel has been ground off at the stock's base.

very close to the body at a port arms position and will stay there without the user's having to hold it. This leaves the user's hands free for other tasks while the weapon remains ready for quick use; if the rifle is needed, it can be quickly swung up to the shoulder and fired since the sling adjusts with the movement.

The H&K sling arrangement is created with a 6-foot-long sling with a slide double-O fastener on its end, like those on most slings, and an extra slide fastener threaded on so that the sling runs through one of the two spaces on it while leaving the other hole free. Also, the stock needs to have a nylon cord run through the rear swivel and up over the top of the stock and tightened so that there is little slack.

One end of the sling is fastened to the front sight assembly and then the length is run back along the selector side of the rifle with the free sliding fastener's empty half pointing outward toward the person doing the work. The sling is threaded through the cord tied around the stock and then brought back toward the front sight and the free end fastened to the open slot of the spare slide fastener.

Now if this complicated procedure is done correctly, the sling will have one part running the length of the rifle, doubling under the cord on the stock, and then moving along its own first half to end on a slide that can move freely either toward the front sight or toward the stock.

To wear it properly, the shooter puts the outside loop of the sling around his back and left shoulder (if he's right-handed), while the half of the sling next to the rifle goes across his chest. The rifle can then be slung up so that it's across his chest or pulled out and down into a firing position. It can also be slung back and up to be carried behind the wearer with the barrel down (a muzzle cap is recommended for this). The AR-15 can also be taken off and carried with both straps together in the regular "marching" style or worn on the back with an arm through each loop of the sling. The H&K carry is a very versatile system.

For traditionalists who want a military-style leather sling, even these are available for the AR-15 from Defense Procurement Manufacturing Services.

The U.S. military has issued a variety of slings for the M16 and its variants. At the time of this writing, one of the better of these is the "Sling, Close Quarter Combat (Rifles and Carbine Team, AMSTA-LC-CSIR), which is currently in use. It is most often found on the M4 Carbine with a shoestring-like bit of nylon twine on the buttstock securing one end of the sling in place. This makes it possible for the sling to drop away when the rifle is raised from the assault carry to the shoulder. The front of the sling can be secured in several ways, from a quick-disconnect swivel designed for this system to a wire lanyard that attaches to the front sight. Either of these helps keep the sling away from the sight picture when the gun is brought up to fire.

## STOCKS

Tall, thin shooters find the stock of the A1 models of the AR-15 to be about an inch too short to be comfortable; the A2 model is longer and generally makes a good replacement stock for such shooters. In addition to the Colt A2 stocks, Choate Machine and Tool offers an E2 stock that is 3/4 inch longer than the standard stock (the E2's cost is $33) and has a neat hook that allows those firing with a bipod to hold the stock against their shoulder with their off hand.

Of course, those who live in areas that have both

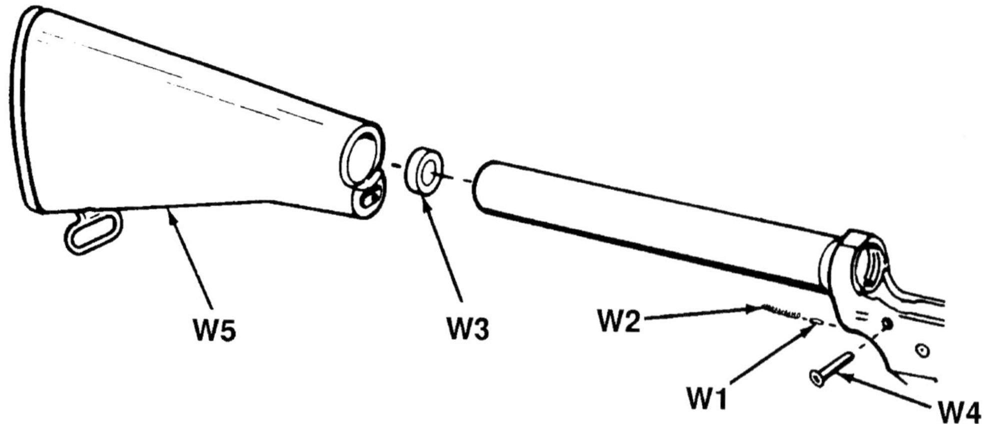

A2 or other extended stocks require a spacer insert (W3) to be placed between the buffer tube and stock.

very hot and very cold weather are going to have their length of pull change with the seasons due to the varying bulk of the clothes worn in different seasons. One quick solution is to use a shorty stock with extra "stop" holes drilled in its rail (as is now done with newer stocks—and an easy job for a gunsmith). With these holes in the rail, the shooter can shorten the length of pull very easily to accommodate the greater bulk of a cold-weather coat. Regrettably, this can only be done with a preban gun now.

Side view of A2 spacer next to buffer tube and the screw that holds the stock to the two parts.

Z-M Weapons has a variation on the shorty theme. By incorporating its design for the upper receiver that lacks a buffer tube (instead having an over-the-barrel spring system), the company has been able to market a part of the folding stock for use on preban guns or by law enforcement personnel. One of these folders also incorporates a shorty-style latch system, thereby making it possible to adjust the length of pull to five different positions as well as fold the stock to the side of the rifle for more compact storage. Its cost is $340. Z-M Weapons also offers the fixed stock found on its sporter. Both of these stocks require that the Z-M Weapons upper receiver system be placed on an AR-15 as well, otherwise there's no way to fire the weapon—at least not more than once.

Choate offers an extended butt plate that replaces the trapdoor of the AR-15 ($15) and SGW offers a stock spacer kit that achieves the same end by filling the space between the stock and the receiver with a longer screw and internal spacer to take up the slack at the rear of the buffer tube (the cost for this assembly is $9).

On the flip side, stocky shooters may desire a shorter length of pull than the new A2 stock offers; these shooters often get the length of pull more to their liking by placing old stocks on their rifles. These stocks are still plentiful and are available from Gun Parts and SARCO. To place one of these stocks on an A2 rifle, the buffer tube extension must first be slipped off and the new stock slid on, with care being taken not to bend the detent pin that the stock holds in place in the rear of the receiver.

Rock River Arms offers several innovative stocks that many shooters may wish to consider. Most welcome the company's CAR Buttstock, which sports a much-needed lower heel on the butt of the stock, making a shorter stock considerably more comfortable when shouldered. The six-position telescoping stock gives an extra 3/4 inch in length when fully extended and has a distinctive corrugated section down its side for added strength and durability. A pivoting steel swivel is located at the heel of the stock for added flexibility with sling

Rock River Arms' CAR Buttstock sports a lower heel that most shooters will find more comfortable than the older shorty telescoping stock.

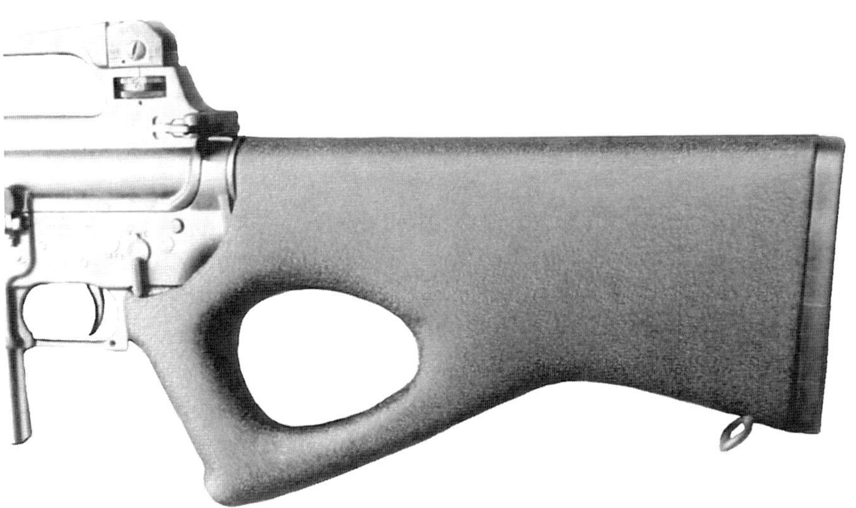

SGW thumbhole stock.

use. The price of the stock (which comes with its own buffer and spring) is $90. Rock River Arms also offers a nonretractable, fixed version of this stock for use on postban guns for $95.

The Rock River Arms LE Entry Tactical Buttstock also comes with an aluminum buffer and spring. This unit is a more or less standard stock with one important difference: it is only about half as long as a standard stock. This makes it ideal for SWAT teams and others working at close quarters with a carbine version of the AR-15 (and perhaps wearing a flak vest to boot).The cost for this stock is $55.

E&L Manufacturing offers an adjustable slip-on recoil pad with a butt designed to fit the curvature of the shooter's shoulder. The interior waffle design of the pad reduces felt recoil while adding only 1/4 inch to the length of the stock. An additional 1/4-inch removable foam insert is included with the recoil pad if added length is desired. In conjunction with an A1 stock, this makes it practical to change the length of the stock when going from summer to winter clothing, wearing a ballistic vest, or making other changes that dictate shorter or longer lengths of pull. The slip-on/slip-off capability of the E&L recoil pad makes this practical. Its cost is $11.95.

Shooters who want to depart from the military look of the AR-15 should replace the standard stock with a thumbhole stock. For a time SGW offered a black plastic stock for $55; currently this is not in the company's catalog. The thumbhole stock is a little tricky to install on an AR-15 because the springs holding the selector and rear push pin detent get in the way. One solution is to drill out the safety detent/spring hole so that the spring and detent can be dropped in and the selector wiggled into place after the stock is fastened in place.

Currently Brownells offers two thumbhole stocks. One is the very comfortable Bell & Carlson fiberglass-Kevlar thumbhole stock (for $120.20); this unit accepts the standard A2 buttplate to complete its assembly. The other is the JP Enterprises laminated- wood thumbhole stock that is designed for use with a scope mounted on an AR-15 flat-top receiver; this stock has a Monte Carlo-style cheekpiece with a high-contoured finish and is available in midnight gray, black/natural gray, coffee brown, or light-brown/dark-brown finishes. This stock includes a rubber recoil pad and goes for $199.95.

TAPCO offers an M231-style telescoping stock like that originally created for the guns used in Bradley fighting vehicles. This stock comes complete with a special buffer, buffer spring, and aluminum buffer tube; the buffer systems rides inside a short, black anodized-aluminum housing with a steel rod stock that extends 5 inches when released by the button catch. The stock costs $59.99 and should be placed only on preban guns or law enforcement carbines in order to avoid breaking current assault weapon laws. The stock might also be modified so that it stays only in its extended position; however, this modification would need to be permanent and not easily altered to be legal.

Target shooters often add shot or other weights to the hollow stock of an AR-15. This helps stabilize the rifle for rapid firing, reduces recoil, and also reduces the "shooter shakes" that occur naturally when a firearm is being aligned on a target. The catch to lead shot is that in addition to the irritating rattling it produces, there is a lot of space between between the individual spheres, making it less dense than a solid chunk of lead.

With this in mind, Brownells also offers the Georgia Precision Shooters Buttstock Weight, which is made to conform exactly to the inside of an A1 or A2 stock. This ingot can be cut, drilled, or trimmed to achieve the required balance. The A1 version weighs 2 pounds, 14 ounces (and costs $26), while the A2 version weighs 3 pounds, 11 ounces and sells for $22.75.

## "TACTICAL CHARGING HANDLE" LATCH

The charging handle on the AR-15 is sometimes a bit hard to operate. On occasion, a shooter will think the action is jammed because he's pulling with all his finger pressure on the right side of the handle and with no pressure on the latch, thereby making it impossible to move and giving the illusion that the action is "frozen." One solution is the "tactical charging handle," which is basically an extension to the release. The only downside is that the extension can also cause irritation, if not injury, to those carrying the rifle for any time on a sling, especially if they are right-handed.

Currently Brownells offers two versions of the tactical latch. One is the Alchemy Arms Tactical Charging Handle Release (what else could they name it?) for $19.95, and the other is the Badger Ordnance Tactical Latch, which sells for $18.95 and has a right-angled ring that makes it ideal for rifles with scopes mounted on them. These latches simply replace the standard release on the charging handle of the AR-15.

## TARGET AND MATCH TRIGGERS

The AR-15 is blessed with a very good trigger, especially in contrast to that of European military rifles, which often have a long, grating pull. However, for those engaged in target shooting, varminting, sniping, or other shooting where the utmost precision is required, the standard pull may not be quite good enough.

Occasionally, one sees a trigger and hammer that match up very well and give an almost perfect pull on an AR-15 right out of the box. And if a gunsmith has a box of trigger group parts, often he can scrounge through it and hand-match a pair that will give a great pull. This is probably the best route to take: the parts are standard but offer the feel a precision shooter needs (albeit one with the standard weight of pull).

This same end can be met by polishing the bearing areas of the hammer and trigger *but* not without one major drawback. Because the surface hardening on the trigger and hammer is very thin (which is ideal for overall strength), any polishing almost always cuts through this surface and leaves the user with a part that will wear out in a hurry. Target shooters and others who want great precision often achieve it through extended practice with the single gun they'll use when a precise shot is needed. So, the prospect of yanking out and replacing the trigger and hammer, and thereby creating a totally new feel for the gun, is not pleasant to contemplate.

That said, if a hammer and trigger already have a good feel, a few strokes with a very fine whetstone may give the feel a target shooter wants. But more than the very lightest work is apt to destroy the surface and, in the long run, make what was once good inferior. This work should be approached only by a seasoned gunsmith who knows exactly what he's doing.

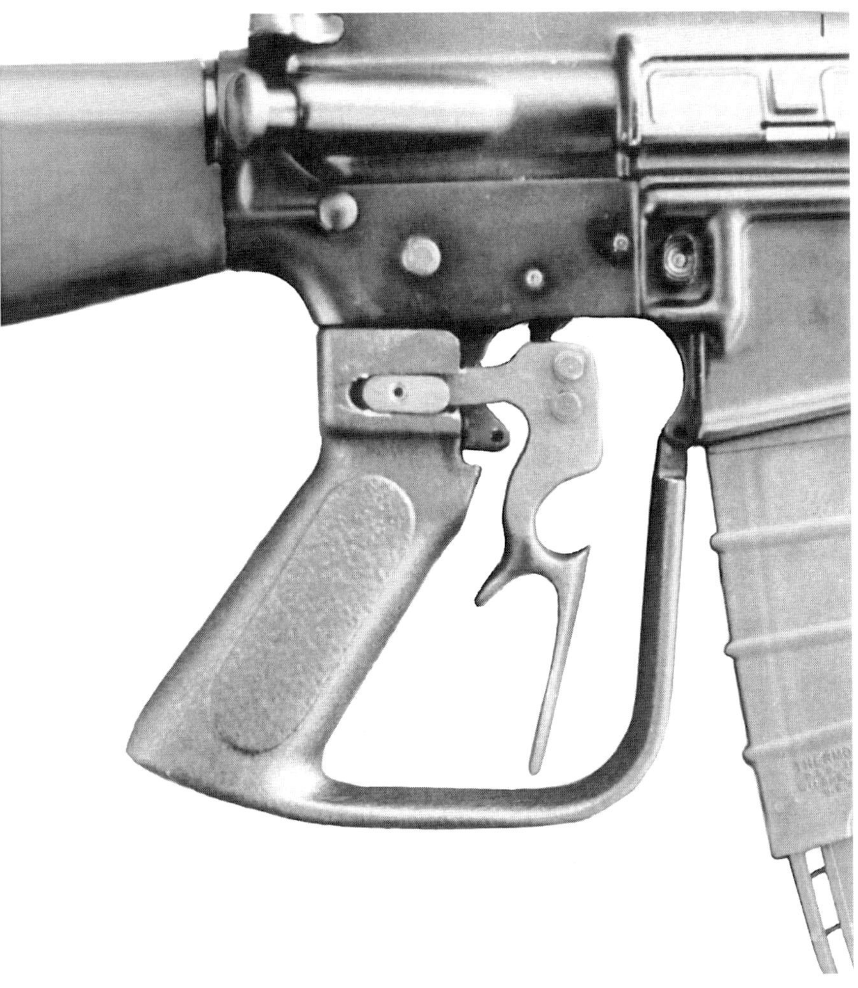

The Ultimate rapid fire mechanism.

For most of those who need precision and a nice light pull, a better solution is to purchase a match trigger group and place that in the gun. A number of companies offer these. One good bet is Bushmaster's parts set, which was created for its target rifles. Costing $119, this set has a modified selector and hammer spring that can be set for a pull of 3.5 pounds at the first stage and a light 1 pound at the second, letoff, stage. (The only catch with the Bushmaster target trigger set is that it won't work in Colt lowers with the politically correct "block" over the safety—something to keep in mind if you own one of these rifles.)

Brownells offers a stainless-steel match trigger set of parts that fit the AR-15 Match Target Competition H-BAR and AR-15 Match Target Competition H-BAR II, as well as other Colt rifles. This set costs $86.25. Brownells also offers a J P Enterprises Low Mass Hammer, which is 36-percent lighter than the standard hammer: in theory this gives a faster ignition of a primer; easier to notice is the crisper trigger pull. The cost is $44.95.

## TRIGGER ACTUATOR

Inventive activities are often spawned by government restrictions, and this most certainly has been true with the current ban on manufacturing automatic weapons for private citizens and the tight restrictions on ownership of such firearms in many states. This has led to hand-cranked trigger pushers, trigger group inserts, and other devices that make rapid fire possible without technically converting an AR-15 to what is legally a selective-fire configuration.

The B.M.F. Activator was one of the first of these devices and is still available used if a person shops around on the Internet. While arguably an adult toy rather than a serious combat device or the like, its Gatling gun-like action can be a lot of fun when plinking with a rifle. The unit clamps to the trigger guard of the AR-15; cranking its handle causes a cam to cycle in and out, toggling the trigger and causing the rifle to fire each time the cam comes out, four times for each rotation of the handle, with the action happening according to the speed with which the crank is turned. The big shortcoming of the B.M.F. Activator is that its plastic body warps if it's left on the rifle for any length of time. But it does create bursts of fire. (One has to wonder why no one has created a metal version of this device; it might become a "serious" tool if it were a tad more robust and reliable.)

A similar mechanism is the Ultimate, which consists of a pistol grip that replaced the standard grip. Once in place, a long lever on the unit is cycled by the shooter's fingers, causing the trigger to be tripped by a small cam in the mechanism both when pulled and pushed, firing two shots during the time one normally takes place. By cycling the lever quickly, short bursts can be fired. The Ultimate originally sold for $130 but is now out of production.

The Tri-Burst was another device like the two above that employed a ring outside the trigger guard to activate a lever with three cams that tapped the trigger each time the external ring was pulled. This created a three-round burst of sorts, though it was a bit awkward due to the long arch of the ring. Perhaps more troubling was an external trigger that might cause the rifle to fire if it was dropped. Perhaps it's fortunate this device is no longer marketed.

Of course, a motor or wind-up clockwork spring system might be attached to a BTF or other system to create automatic fire with a press of a button. And that's just what it would be considered legally as well: automatic. And illegal. Therefore, no one should be tempted to create such a device: it would undoubtedly be awkward, heavy, and illegal.

Much the same effect, also generally illegal, can be created by shortening the reach of the disconnector in the trigger group of an AR-15. The hammer will then drop from the disconnector hook when the trigger is released but will not be caught by the nose of the trigger, thereby causing a second shot to be fired. (Since an automatic weapon must legally fire more than one shot with each *pull* of the trigger, this is technically still a semiauto rifle, though I would not recommend attempting to claim innocence by arguing this fine point in court.)

It might even be possible to add a lever to a disconnector and connect it to a cam on the selector to create a "two-round burst" position in the rear position of the selector.

But . . .

There's a big catch. It creates a potentially very dangerous situation for anyone picking up the rifle and trying it out—who probably won't expect a second shot when the trigger is released. Also, if a shooter "freezes" and hangs onto the trigger when he fires, he is left with a gun that will go off the moment he releases the trigger—again very possibly with disastrous results. All in all, it's better to avoid creating a dangerous situation like this, legalities aside. (For those who might be otherwise tempted to create such a modification, it is my understanding that this too has been ruled illegal by the BATF.) Another gadget that creates the illusion of automatic fire is the Hell-Fire, a device that fits onto the AR-15's trigger guard. The device uses a spring mechanism that reduces the pull on the trigger so that the trigger can be pulled very easily with the lever on the Hell-Fire system. Once the shooter becomes familiar with the device, the trigger finger can be held more or less stationary with the hand alongside the gun. This allows the recoil to push the shooter backward, and his stance and the internal recoil spring, bolt, and carrier then propel the firearm forward slightly after recoil. As the gun goes forward, the trigger finger lightly touches the trigger, tripping it, and again firing the gun. This continues, creating the effect of automatic fire even though the AR-15 is actually firing in a semiauto fashion. The end result is what looks and sounds like automatic fire—but under conditions that make it nearly impossible to aim the gun with any reliability.

For those into lots of bangs at a time, the Hell-Fire system is fun to shoot. It can also be dangerous if the user is unfamiliar with it, so it's wise to practice with only a few cartridges in a magazine until controlling the recoil is learned. And, for safety reasons, when the Hell-Fire is attached to the trigger guard, the chamber of the rifle is best left empty until just before firing.

A few small nations are said to have purchased these units for use with their armies. And the Branch Davidians apparently invested in some of these devices. Perhaps this tells you something. It is best to use these devices only for entertainment, and only when you're being very careful to avoid accidents.

****

As mentioned at the beginning of this chapter, new accessories and modifications for the AR-15 are continually coming out. Just don't get caught up in trying to get the perfect rifle and accessories . . . you never will. Always look at things as a compromise. Once an owner finds a setup that works for his needs, he should stick with it and practice with his gear.

A person who's familiar with his equipment and operates it well can almost always outperform the guy with the "state-of-the-art" equipment who's bogged down by too much and hampered by his ignorance.

Shooters should purchase only the essentials and then practice and practice some more until their shooting skills are honed to perfection.

# Chapter 14

# Selective-Fire Conversions

Selective-fire weapons have always been controversial. One side of the argument is that if bursts of ammunition are needed, either the cartridge being fired is too mild or the shooter needs better shooting skills (with one gun guru calling the submachine gun a "slob's weapon"). The other side is that in combat there is little time for aiming and bursts are needed to compensate for the loss of abilities under the stress of combat—in which everyone becomes a slob trying to survive.

Probably the truth lies somewhere in between.

Often the less a person knows about combat, the more effective he thinks automatic fire will be. Film As film footage of soldiers in Vietnam and Lebanon who fired long bursts over barricades without even seeing a target shows, that automatic fire can turn a rifle into something akin to a one-shot, sightless weapon, as soldiers hope they can hose an area and accidentally hit an enemy in the process. Such sites certainly bolster the slob theory of automatic weapons use.

But sometimes automatic fire is effective, and on the battlefield there is little doubt that automatic weapons totally changed the face and tactics of combat when they appeared at the end of the 1800s. Abruptly, the number of men a commander had behind bolt-action guns with long bayonets didn't matter as much as how many machine guns the enemy had.

In addition, the AR-15 is more controllable during automatic fire than older, larger-caliber rifles. In the hands of an experienced shooter, an AR-15 with good muzzle brake is every bit as controllable as a submachine gun and has a range that rivals that of the heavier machine guns. And three-round burst modification, coupled with lightweight ammunition (in contrast to cartridges like the .30-06), does a lot to extend the amount of ammunition the shooter of a selective-fire AR-15 has on hand.

To the detriment of civilians, many U.S. politicians and their staffs apparently do their legislation research in front of the silver screen. But this is nothing new. When movie gangsters started being portrayed with "Tommy guns," the politicians became convinced that only gangsters bought automatic weapons and the 1930s saw restrictions placed on such guns, with some states all but banning automatic weapons.

Much the same thing happened in the 1980s as shows like "Miami Vice" showed drug dealers using all kinds of high-tech guns rather than the revolver most criminals still carry. Soon the hue and cry against certain types of guns was heard in Washington, D.C. Despite the fact that only one registered machine gun had ever been used to commit murder since the restrictive laws of the 1930s, and then only by a jealous spouse rather than a hardened criminal, a move was soon afoot to fight crime by banning the manufacture of automatic firearms (for everyone but government users, of course). By 1990, the manufacture of new selective-fire guns for citizen purchase had been banned in the United States.

## PURCHASE AND REGISTRATION

For those who were still living in states where automatic weapons could be purchased and owned (albeit after fingerprinting, red tape, and transfer taxes), some manufacturers went all out to produce selective-fire weapons before the manufacturing ban. Furthermore, many automatic AR-15s were already in private ownership. Consequently, those who want such guns for recreational shooting, self-defense, or whatever can still purchase them in many states—although the prices are climbing as more and more people decide to purchase the guns but fewer and fewer guns are there to be sold due to the ban.

Once a gun is registered as a machine gun, its basic configuration can be changed: this includes the various parts in it because only the lower receiver of an AR-15 has a serial number. Therefore, it is likely that many of today's AR-15s could have long lives as selective-fire rifles. Such firearms can be "upgraded" by adding burst-fire parts or even modifying them to fire from an open bolt or other configuration that may be developed in the future. Also enabled is the creation of upper receiver assemblies in other calibers or with different barrel lengths that can be quickly mounted on the lower receiver; as noted earlier, these give the owner of such a rifle a number of automatic weapons for the price of one.

In the interest of history, and to allow government organizations to see what is still available for them in the way of selective-fire weapons, this chapter examines the various parts, modifications, and conversions that have been created and are possible with an AR-15. It should be noted, however, that converting a semiauto-only rifle to a selective-fire weapon without prior approval by the BATF is illegal and is permitted only when the work is done for government agencies. Anyone else who does such conversions faces heavy fines and/or imprisonment and confiscation of his firearm. Given the availability of selective-fire AR-15s already available and the quasi-selective fire gadgets like the Hell-Fire (described in the previous chapter), an illegal conversion is not worth the humiliation or the price that will be paid in terms of both money and freedom.

## CONVERSIONS

That said there are a number of ways to convert an AR-15 to auto fire. Some are much better than others. Most people assume that semiauto rifles are hard to convert to selective fire, but in fact this isn't so for most firearms—and the AR-15 is no exception. In fact, Browning made his first machine gun with a lever-action rifle coupled with a flap arrangement at the barrel, thereby demonstrating that not even a semiauto action is necessary to create a selective-fire weapon. (In fact, such "conversions" happen by chance; most gunsmiths admit that people often bring guns in for repair that have become automatic weapons due to stuck firing pins, broken parts, and so on. These weapons are seldom turned over to the BATF but, rather, repaired and given back to their owners.)

The catch to this is that not all selective-fire conversions are good and some of the accidental ones created by part failure as well as those made illegally can be extremely dangerous. That said, it is good to examine some of the poor ones first to see what should never be done in the way of modifications. And again, a warning:

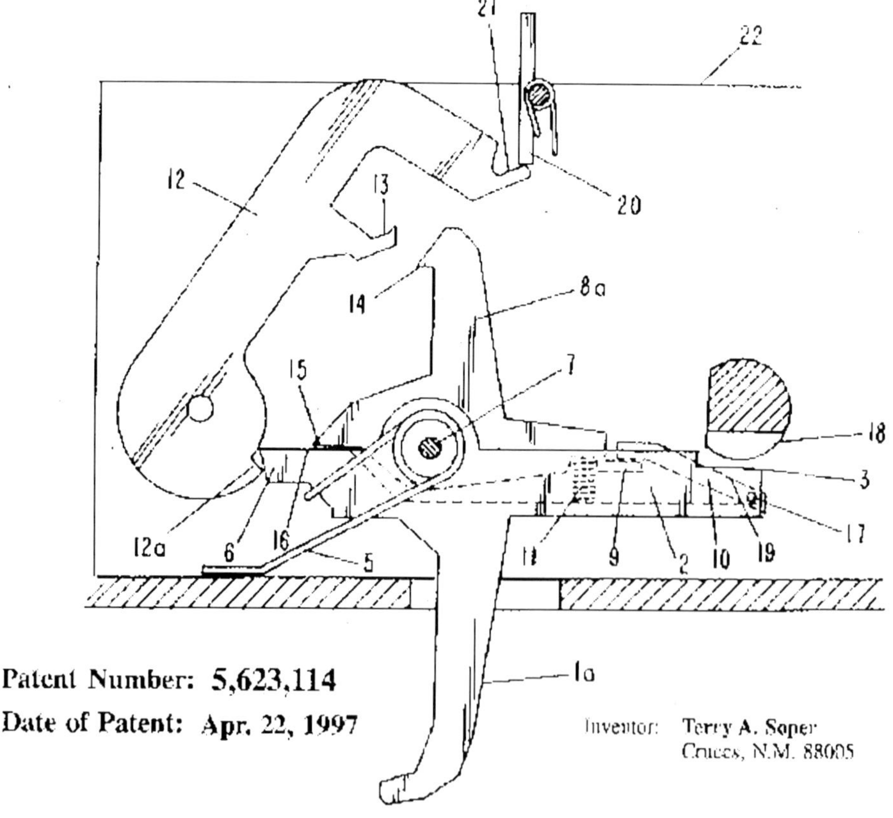


Patent drawing for a selective-fire mechanism unlike the one that has become more or less standard with automatic versions of the AR-15.

*It is against the law to alter a semiauto weapon to fire in a full-auto mode without the appropriate approval from federal, state, and local authorities. Severe penalties are prescribed for violations of these laws*

One way to convert an AR-15 to auto fire is to place an automatic rifle disconnector, safety selector, hammer, and trigger into a commercial semiauto AR-15 or to remove the selector and grind off the catch in the face of the hammer. This will enable some slam-fires when the selector is placed in the auto mode with the auto parts or, in the case of removing the sear, whenever the trigger is pulled. As mentioned elsewhere in this book, this is nearly suicidal because, sooner or later, one of the primers will fail to fully ignite and a bullet will be lodged in the barrel. At this point another bullet might follow the first one, or the shooter might assume that the problem is mechanical rather than with the ammunition and then chamber and fire another round. This will blow up the barrel and quite possibly injure the shooter and/or those around him.

Pistol primers might improve this situation somewhat, giving a greater chance for full ignition, but they might also fire a round every time a round is chambered since the floating firing pin of the AR-15 is too rough for pistol primers. In this case, the gun might start firing when a round is simply chambered and continue to do so until the magazine is emptied. Certainly, a weapon that starts firing in full automatic on its own when a round is chambered is far from ideal for anyone but the criminally insane.

Another full-auto conversion that overrides the semiauto control can be created by locking the hammer back and putting the selector in the safe position. Once this is done, the receiver halves are opened and the striker (a rod that moves freely in the bolt carrier so that it can strike the rear of the firing pin) goes inside the bolt carrier; the striker is held in place because it's large enough to be retained by the curve of the bolt carrier.Once this is done, the user then closes the receiver halves, pulls back the carrier and locks it in place with the bolt hold-open latch, and then places a full magazine—of however many rounds he wishes to fire—into the rifle.

At this point, hitting the hold-open release so that the bolt goes forward will fire the cartridge that's chambered when the striker hits the firing pin. This most likely will cause the rifle to cycle, strip off another round from the magazine, and fire it when the striker hits the firing pin. This probably will continue until something breaks or jams or the magazine is emptied. In theory this action can be stopped by pushing the bolt hold-open latch down to catch the bolt—but by the time the shooter accomplishes this, the gun is probably empty. Again, a system only Charles Manson would like.

This last system is about as bad as removing the disconnector and—like the other—not recommended. However, we'll see later that the striker itself can be used to create an automatic version of the AR-15 that fires from an open bolt.

### The Automatic Disconnector

Perhaps the strangest "machine gun" ever created was the Automatic Disconnector marketed by S.W.D. in 1985. This device consists of two sheet-metal parts that were capable of transforming a standard Colt Sporter from semiauto to auto-only fire. The BATF ruled that the parts themselves were the machine gun (a ruling that may seem odd to most people but that had a precedent dating back to 1968 when the Gun Control Act passed by Congress classified parts made only for machine guns as machine guns). So the Automatic Disconnector parts became, as gun writer Nolan Wilson put it, "a submachine gun to fit every wallet"—because it fit *into* a wallet.

The system was ingeniously simple. The connector link (stamped from 0.050-inch-thick steel) fit around an AR-15 disconnector and extended back in the receiver to sit under the rear takedown pin. The pivot plate (stamped from 0.30-inch-thick steel) extended into a notch in the rear of the connector link and extended upward behind the rear takedown pin.

When a Sporter was fired with these two additional parts in it, the disconnector operated in the usual manner, holding the hammer back when the trigger remained pulled. But when the bolt carrier slammed the bolt into place, chambering a round and locking the bolt, the rear of the carrier also hit the pivot plate. This in turn levered around the rear push pin, pulling back on the connector link, which jerked back the disconnector, releasing the hammer, which continued forward, striking the firing pin and firing the cartridge. (This gadget is why the newer Colt Sporters have a bolt carrier with its lower rear surface completely milled out.)

The drawbacks to the Automatic Disconnector are that it fires only in auto mode and requires quite a bit of energy to force the pivot plate forward. It's probable that a dirty rifle would have problems with the bolt's failing to lock. Nevertheless, it is a display of the inventiveness that made the country great and now, more often than not, is stymied by bureaucrats and lawmakers.

### Motorized Firepower

Although a motor-driven rifle is not suitable for combat, such a device might have some very limited use on a vehicle or airplane, or with remote-controlled "robots." In theory, it is possible to connect an assembly similar to the B.M.F. Activator (covered in the previous chapter) to a motor. Adjusting the motor speed would control the rate of fire.

Also, a solenoid might be connected to the trigger to create similar effects. Using various electronic counters and timers could make it possible to fire bursts of various counts and speeds.

Of course, such modifications are considered illegal unless done under the cover of government work.

### Finding the Right Parts

The most practical conversion of an AR-15 to auto-fire is simply employ the auto-fire parts designed by Colt (or, better yet, by buying one of the company's automatic rifles). For older guns, the semiauto can be transformed by drilling a hole for the auto sear in the proper place; newer ones require milling out metal sections of the receiver because the parts and receiver have purposely been designed not to match so as to discourage unauthorized conversions. Placement of the auto-sear hole is critical, requiring very careful measurement, and, if possible, a drilling jig created from a previously converted gun should be used. (This is not a job for an amateur and to be legal must be done on a weapon preapproved for government or law enforcement work.)

As for the auto sear and other parts, they can generally be purchased from dealers like Quality (Bushmaster), Jonathan Arthur Ciener, or others, *only* if the proper paper work is supplied by the purchaser to prove that he has a legitimate need for the parts. Among the necessary parts, assuming that a semiauto-only gun is being converted, are an M16A1-style bolt carrier, trigger, hammer, sear, selector, and disconnector.

It is possible to convert a rifle to three-round burst fire once the auto-sear hole is made and the piece fitted to the rifle. The burst-fire parts are also available from some sources, with TAPCO and SARCO currently offering them at the lowest prices. Currently users have the choice of two three-position selector kits (safe-semi-auto or safe-semi-burst) or a four-position kit (safe-semi-burst-auto).

Rather than replacing the semiauto bolt carrier, it is possible to get a metal insert for the rear of the carrier. It generally works well but has a tendency to come loose over time. For better results the conversion plate should be welded in place or—better yet—an M16-style bolt carrier purchased.

### The Drop-in Sear

Those who don't want a hole drilled into the receiver to accommodate an auto sear pin may convert it to selective fire by using the so-called drop-in auto sear and then replacing the semiauto parts listed above for

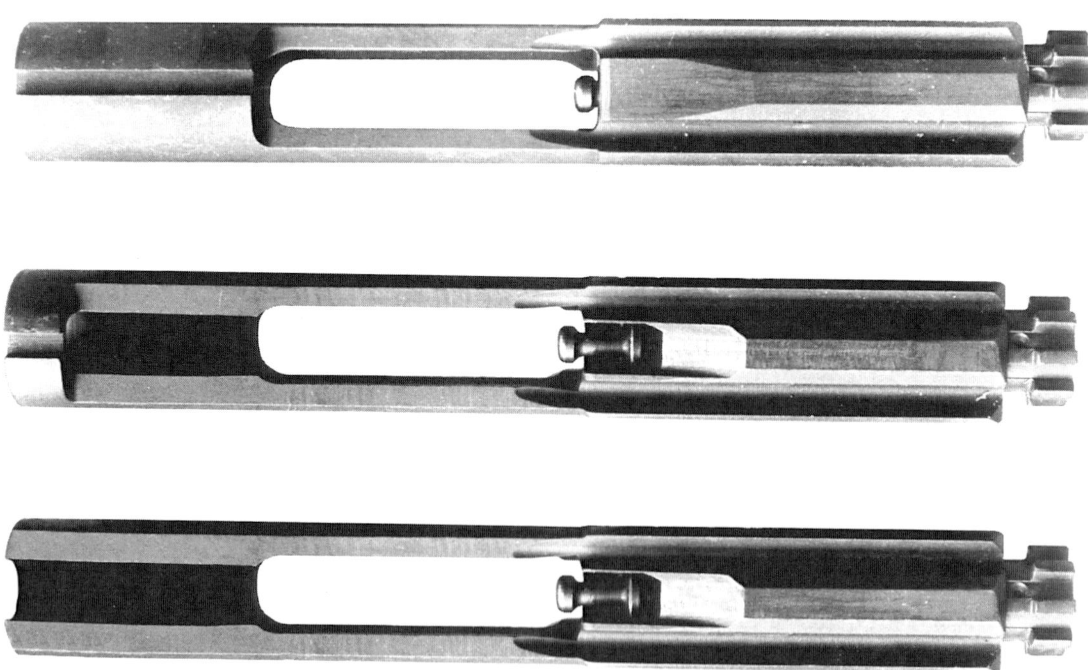

The different types of bolt carriers can be readily identified by viewing them from their lower side. Top is an M16 carrier, center is the first production-style AR-15 Sporter (semiauto only), and the bottom is the later-production Colt semiauto bolt carrier.

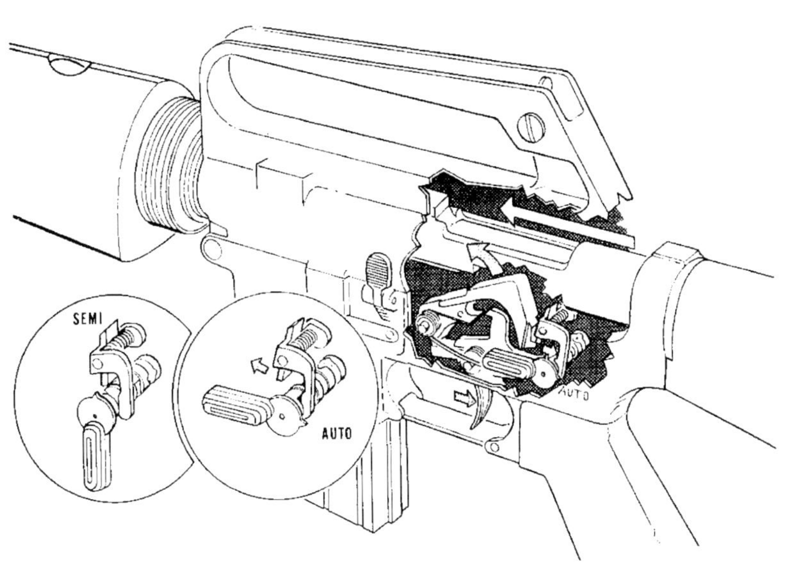


Original disconnector mechanism employed with the AR-15.

or a roll pin and should not easily drift out of place while still allowing the sear to move freely. Usually a pin .470 inch long and .093 inch in diameter works well.

The drop-in sear's housing must fit tightly into the space behind the safety selector; extra metal should be left on the finished sear body so that it can then be tightly hand-fitted into its space. The sear should then be tested by cycling an empty firearm by hand a number of times *before* trying to actually fire it with live ammunition.

selective fire. But this is generally a lot of work and offers little in the way of advantages.

Like the Automatic Disconnector, the drop-in auto sear has itself—by bureaucratic magic—been classed as an automatic weapon. Consequently it is sometimes possible to buy one of these sears as a machine gun. This raises the sticky question of whether it can actually be *used* in what was originally a semiauto-only rifle. At the time of this writing the answer appears to be no. So one should be careful about purchasing even a drop-in sear made before the automatic weapons manufacturing ban because the sear might be used to illegally convert a sporter into a selective-fire rifle.

The drop-in sear works just like the standard auto sear except that it has its own body that contains the trip lever/sear and its spring and pin. The sear assembly is pretty easy to make, though careful measurements must be taken because the dimensions of many rifles, especially those not originally designed for automatic fire, can vary considerably.

The body of the drop-in sear housing can be aluminum. The sear and its cross pin must be steel, and the sear should be heat-treated to minimize wear. The spring size is not critical, but it must be strong enough to quickly position the sear to trap the hammer within the cycling rate of the bolt. The best results are generally gotten from a spring in the neighborhood of number 18 music wire about .500 inch long with an outward diameter of .125 inch; 10 turns of the wire should give the spring the tension needed. The pivot pin can be either solid pin

### Open-Bolt Firing

Another possible auto conversion allows the rifle to be fired from an open bolt. The main consideration with this system is fashioning a striker that's heavy enough to give consistent ignition of the primer even when the firearm gets dirty, yet make it light enough to avoid undue wear or even breakage of parts. Care must also be taken to keep the cyclic rate low, or the weapon will become uncontrollable. This can generally be done with both the selection of ammunition and by adding weight to the buffer assembly and, perhaps, to the bolt carrier. Again, experimentation is called for to create the correct combination.

The drawbacks to open-bolt firing are the somewhat reduced accuracy (the bolt travels forward and locks shut as it fires, jarring the aiming point considerably on all but the most securely held rifles) and the decreased safety of the rifle. Probably the greatest concern should be safety.

A problem arises from the fact that the rifle will fire when a loaded magazine is in the well and the bolt slams forward. This means that if the bolt is held by the hold-open lever, for example, releasing the bolt on a poorly designed system can cause the rifle to fire. Likewise, dropping a rifle with a closed bolt and a full magazine in place might cause the bolt to cycle back and then slam forward, firing a round. The same would take place if a weapon with the bolt locked back and the safety on was dropped: the fall might jar the sear loose and cause the rifle to fire.

The best solution to these problems is to put a second sear notch on the lower side of the bolt carrier, locating the notch so that it prevents the bolt from traveling forward if the trigger isn't pulling the sear down. The notch should be located so that the sear catches the bolt carrier before it retracts far enough to strip a cartridge from a magazine on a return trip.

This, and proper safety measures, should prevent any accidental discharge. Of course, it's essential that anyone performing this conversion fully tests the components to ensure that they actually do prevent accidental discharges and that parts will not fail and thus produce injuries or worse.

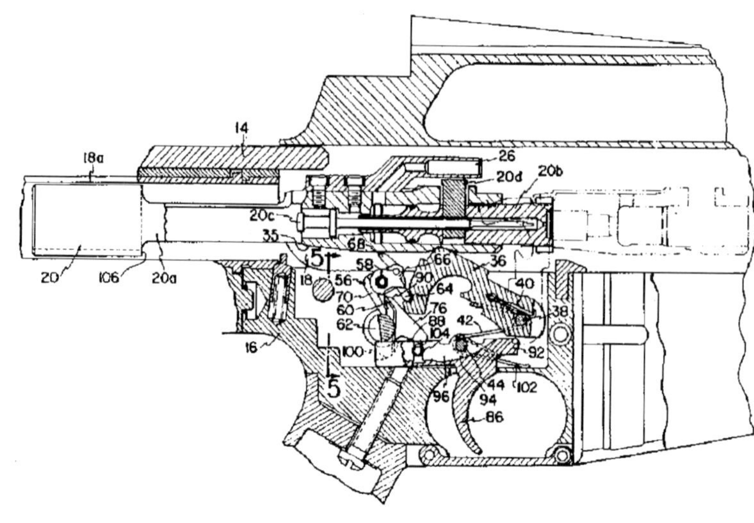


**OPEN BOLT FIRING MECHANISM FOR AUTOMATIC FIREARM**

Inventor: **Henry J. Tatro**, Westfield, Mass.

Assignee: **Colt Industries Operating Corp.**, West Hartford, Conn.

**4,433,610**

**Feb. 28, 1984**

Open-bolt firing mechanism for the AR-15 (patent number US-04433610).

Even though selective-fire rifles are relatively safe, the bottom line is that they are not as safe as most commercial semiauto rifles. Users should beware of any lack of redundant safety devices and be very, very careful when using such firearms. In short, the open-bolt modification can produce a weapon considerably less safe than the regular AR-15. It is possible to create an open-bolt firing system by modifying the hammer to act as a sear, but this creates a very heavy trigger pull. It's better to drill the extra holes in the lower receiver to accommodate the sear or construct a subassembly similar to the auto sear discussed above into which the open-bolt sear can be placed.

A trigger group system can be created to do this by slightly modifying the M231 open-bolt system. Other conversion arrangements are possible, but this is one of the easier ones. The new sear and trigger extension (which sits in the disconnector slot) should both be made of steel, as should the sear cross pins. The piano wire used to construct the sear spring should be similar to that used for the standard hammer spring (some experimentation will be called for). Two new pins and holes are necessary to hold the auto sear in place. The forward pin goes between the C-shaped opening at the front of the sear to limit its travel; the rear pin acts as pivot point for the sear and retains its spring as well.

The striker should be made of steel, and it needs to be to be sized according to the considerations listed above. In general, this is in the neighborhood of .575 inch in diameter and 3 inches or less in length. The striker must fit inside the rear half of the bolt carrier, where it should move freely inside the carrier. It is essential that the striker hit the firing pin with enough force to fully fire the cartridge's primer—a misfire could leave a bullet in the barrel, which can be disastrous during full-auto fire.

A number of other auto conversions of the AR-15 are undoubtedly possible, and it seems likely that inventors will continue to come up with new systems. But the most important consideration will always be the quality of the work: failure of parts can lead to dangerous operation, even damaging the weapon, and cause grave injury to the shooter or those around him. Converting a firearm to automatic fire is not a job for the novice.

### The TAC Trigger Mechanism

The TAC trigger system makes it possible to select auto or semiauto fire through the amount of pressure applied to the trigger of a selective-fire AR-15. This system releases the semiauto's sear with a 5-pound trigger pull; when the pull is increased to 8 pounds, the system automatically goes into its selective-fire mode. This system does away with the need to fool with the selector and seems ideal for close-quarter combat when a "panic pull" would give a full-auto response to a threat.

The trigger assembly fits and functions in AR-15s with standard "M16" and three-round-burst selective-fire modifications. And, it is not considered to be a machine gun in itself since it can't be employed to convert a

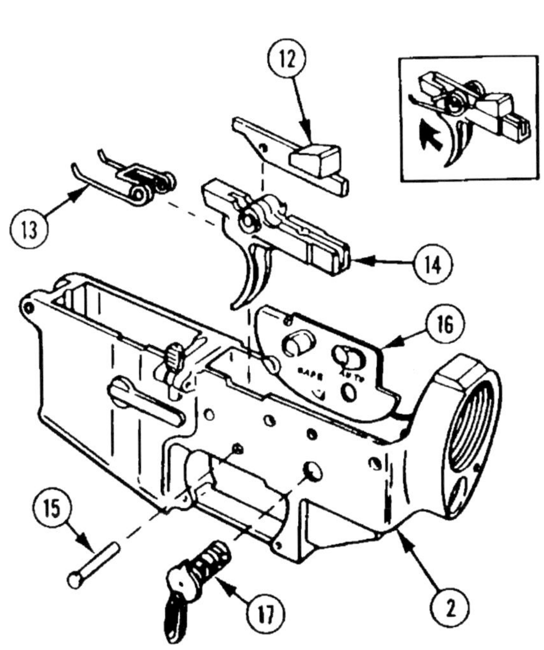


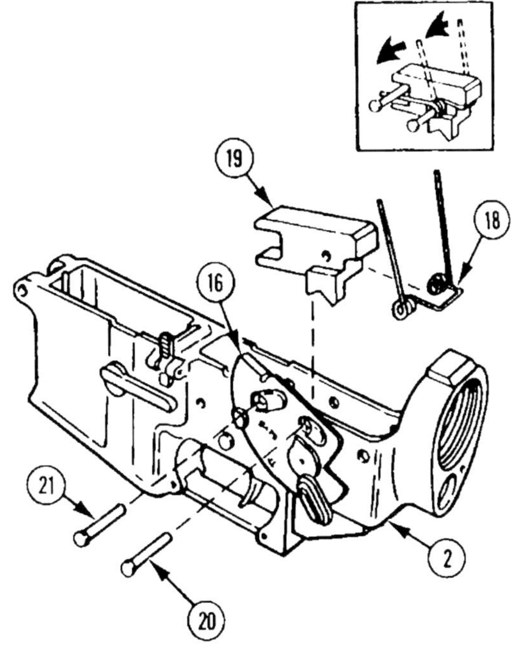


The M231 trigger group design lends itself to use in open-bolt auto fire systems.

semiautomatic into a full-automatic without the addition of other automatic parts. The TAC mechanism works with a drop-in auto sear, though a lot depends on the quality of the drop-in sear itself.

The TAC mechanism works in .223 and 9mm guns as well as most .22 conversion kits, thus giving it some added flexibility for owners of an automatic version of the AR-15.

### Adjusting Ejected Cartridge Arc

For everyone who fires an automatic weapon, not only those who are left-handed, nothing is quite as irritating as an AR-15's throwing its cartridges straight back from the ejection port, showering especially the left-handed shooter with hot brass—and denting cartridges so they are harder to reload. Fortunately, there are a few tricks that can be employed to reduce or even eliminate this nuisance.

For lefties, the solution may simply be to get an upper receiver with the deflector "bump" in it. This will cause most brass ejected rearward to bounce away and thereby miss the shooter.

However there's a more elegant solution that also will save brass from getting dinged up when it leaves the ejection port. This is done by replacing a few key parts. That said, it is important to remember that the ejection angle varies greatly with the ammunition used. This is because the speed with which the carrier travels rearward also determines how violently cartridges are extracted and tossed from the gun. In general, the more powerful the ammunition, the greater the likelihood for the empties to be thrown forward, rather than rearward, when ejected from the port.

But just using hotter ammunition is not the best cure for the problem, for the simple reason that it adds wear and tear to the gun—and there are also upper limits to how "hot" ammunition can be before it presents a danger to gun and shooter. So the other solution should also be explored, perhaps first if a gun has gradually started throwing empties rearward.

This solution is pretty simple: replace the ejector and extractor springs with new ones, and also add the D-fender buffer around the extractor spring when performing this job (more on the D-fender buffer elsewhere in this book). Doing this usually shifts the ejection pattern forward so that it is no longer a problem.

Of course, once the springs are replaced, the shooter may discover that shells are being tossed too far forward and getting dented on the front of the ejection port, or even threatening to jam the rifle. In this case, removing the D-fender buffer or shortening the extractor spring by just a coil or two (removing just one link at a time) should cure this problem.

## TROUBLESHOOTING AUTOMATIC WEAPONS

In addition to the steps given elsewhere in this book, there are a few things you can do to improve the reliability of an automatic AR-15. Keep in mind that many failures are created because of inferior parts. Buying a quality, new selective-fire trigger group often cures a problem, especially if the previous owner decided to "tune" his weapon to improve its performance. Check the barrel markings to be sure the right barrel is on your automatic weapon; sometimes previous owners have replaced a good barrel with an inferior one before trading the gun off; buying a quality barrel from Colt or whoever manufactured the original weapon will often greatly improve things. Also check for dings in the gas tube; these are rare but are detrimental to performance, and they might be overlooked with the handguards in place.

Of course, dirt and grime negatively affect performance. Automatic fire pushes a lot of unburned powder into the trigger group and firing pin of an AR-15, so cleaning the weapon regularly and thoroughly is essential for optimal performance.

Often, reducing the cyclic rate also helps reliability. There's more than one way to do this, and one good way for those using a carbine, especially one with a shorter barrel (such as the 11.5-inch version) is with the La France Twin Tube. This replaces the standard gas tube with one that has some extra tubing, thereby increasing the flow time of gas ported from the barrel to the carrier key. This may not seem that it would make much difference to the operation of a machine gun, but in fact it does on many guns, often improving their performance greatly.

Another route to slowing the cyclic rate is to place a heavy buffer into the gun. Currently Colt offers an H Buffer for AR-15 carbines (the "H" stands for "heavy," and this buffer is marked with an H as well). Unless such a buffer is already in place, most shooters will see a marked reduction in the rate of fire by putting an H buffer in the carbine.

Extraction problems may be helped, if not cured by installing the D-fender buffer discussed above and replacing the extractor and its spring with good-quality ones made by Colt or Bushmaster.

Sometimes the gas port size is wrong in an automatic weapon, and this produces problems. Usually a failure to cycle properly is caused by a barrel or port vent that is too small. It is possible to overenlarge a port hole (and really hard to replace the metal once it is reamed out—as many a do-it-yourselfer has discovered). Fortunately, there's a solution for this latter problem in the form of the ArmForté Regulated Gas Tube. This unit replaces the standard gas tube (with both carbine and rifle versions available). The key feature is a small valve that can be adjusted with an Allen wrench to regulate the amount of gas traveling through the tube. This means that a shooter can compensate for an oversized gas port caused by erosion—or an inept resizing of the port—and enables a shooter to adjust his rate of fire somewhat, as well. This system also permits totally shutting off the gas tube to transform the rifle into a single-shot, manually loaded rifle, making it ideal for training or use with a silencer. This unit's cost is $59.95.

JP Enterprises offers a slightly different way to adjust gas flow through the port with its Adjustable Gasblock, which has a single rail to which the user can affix a detachable iron sight. This unit is available for standard (0.750-inch) and (0.936-inch) barrels for $69.95 and $79.95, respectively.

There's more than a little debate over exactly what the correct gas port size should be. And, in truth, the "correct" size varies with the firearm because the mass of the bolt, bolt carrier, firing pin, buffer, and buffer spring, as well as the power of the spring on the hammer, are all going to affect how much gas is needed to cycle the firearm. In addition, some ammunition produces a higher pressure level at the port. So, while there is undoubtedly an ideal gas port size for any given AR-15, knowing what that might be is another matter.

Fortunately, most longer barrel lengths are pretty forgiving of this. Problems are generally seen with shorter barrels (which is why the U.S. military has gradually lengthened the shorty until it finally reached the longer dimension of the current M4 carbine). That said, guns with shorter barrels often work more efficiently if the port size is in the 0.086- to 0.093-inch range, but this is not a hard and fast rule.

If you run into problems with an automatic version of the AR-15 (or have more general questions about an AR-15), an excellent online source of information is found at <http://www.biggerhammer.net>. In addition to a wealth of data about the AR-15 and its variants, there is a message board at this site where AR-15 owners can ask or answer questions about these firearms. It can be an important resource.

*****

An automatic AR-15 is not as effective in combat as many people might think. Shooters of selective-fire weapons must be skillful and must learn to maximize the effectiveness of their fire through the use of short bursts and judicious periods without firing to avoid overheating the barrel. Nothing demands more skill than the skillful use of an automatic AR-15.

# Chapter 15

# Troubleshooting the AR-15

So many of the problems with the AR-15 can be traced to the use of poor ammunition, improperly cleaned rifles, or magazine failure. Paying attention to these areas of concern can save a lot of headaches.

Most important is that substantive repairs should not be undertaken by anyone other than a gunsmith. Although the chart below shows that replacing some parts offers a "quick fix," it should be noted that a skilled gunsmith can often repair or modify parts so that replacement may not be necessary. However, replacing crucial parts, is generally a better policy, especially those that receive a lot of wear. A firearm is always potentially dangerous, particularly one that malfunctions. If an AR-15 isn't working right, it should be taken to an expert repairman as soon as possible.

If an individual has to work on his own rifle, he must unload it first. He should stay clear of the muzzle and keep it pointed in a safe direction at all times.

If a round is jammed in the rifle, he must remember that it could go off at any moment. If, for example, a cartridge gets only partway into the chamber, it must be treated very cautiously; if it goes off it will pepper anyone nearby with brass fragments (another reason shooters should always wear safety glasses and be very gentle when live rounds are involved).

Because many of the parts in the AR-15 are under spring tension or are themselves springs, some in blind holes, it is essential to wear safety glasses. Even when the gun is unloaded, great care must be taken to avoid injury.

*Unless a shooter is really sure of what he's doing, he should not attempt troubleshooting*

The only exception to this rule *might* be if a person is in combat with his life on the line because of a malfunctioning rifle. Then, and only then, should an attempt be made to get the rifle functioning again with the following procedures. Whenever possible, these steps should be taken with an *unloaded* AR-15, with both the magazine removed and the chamber empty.

As a final caution, even though it is logical that simply replacing a part is the quickest and cheapest way to repair the malfunctions listed below, too often the temptation is to tinker and try to fix something to save a few bucks. The latter seldom works, and a shooter, whether making the repairs himself or having a gunsmith make them, will almost always save time and money by buying a quality replacement and will have a much, much more reliable firearm.

Most extraction problems are caused by a chamber

**Troubleshooting Procedures for AR-15**

| Problem | Check For | Repair Procedure |
|---|---|---|
| AR-15 won't fire | Selector on safe | Place in fire position |
| | Firing pin in wrong position | Reassemble so that retaining pin is between the shoulder and head of firing pin |
| | Too much oil in firing pin recess | Wipe/clean firing pin recess |
| | Dirt in firing pin recess | Wipe/clean firing pin recess |
| | Poor ammo | Remove/discard |
| | Firing pin broken | Remove/replace |
| | Lower receiver parts defective/worn or broken | Remove, clean, and/or replace |
| Bolt won't unlock | Dirty or burred bolt | Clean or replace |

| Problem | Check For | Repair Procedure |
|---|---|---|
| Rounds won't extract | Charging handle bent | Replace charging handle |
| | Broken extractor | Replace |
| | Dirty/corroded ammunition | Remove (may have to be carefully pushed out with cleaning rod) |
| | Carbon/fouling in chamber or extractor lip | Clean chamber and lip |
| | Broken or bad extractor spring | Replace |
| | Badly pitted bolt | Replace |
| Rounds won't eject | Broken ejector | Replace |
| | Frozen ejector | Clean/lubricate |
| | Bad ejector spring | Replace |
| Rounds won't feed | Dirty or corroded ammunition | Clean or replace ammuniton |
| | Defective magazine | Replace magazine |
| | Dirt in magazine | Clean and lubricate magazine |
| | Too many rounds in magazine | Remove several rounds from magazine |
| | Poor buffer movement | Remove buffer/spring and clean and lubricate |
| | Magazine not seated | Magazine catch may need to be tightened (push release button down and tighten or loosen the catch by turning it) |
| Bolt carrier travels over magazine without chambering round | Magazine catch hole too low | Discard and replace magazine |
| | Magazine spring reversed | Disassemble magazine and place the "front" of the spring toward the rear of the magazine |
| | Broken magazine | Replace |
| | Broken or warn catch | Replace |
| Double feeding of rounds causing a jam | Defective magazine | Replace |
| Round won't chamber completely | Dirty or corroded ammunition | Clean or replace ammuntion |
| | Oversized rounds | Replace ammunition |
| | Damaged ammunition | Replace ammunition |
| | Fouling in chamber | Clean with chamber brush |
| | Undersized/too tight chamber | Have gunsmith ream to specifications |
| Bolt won't lock | Fouling in locking lugs | Clean and lubricate lugs |
| | Frozen extractor | Remove and clean extractor |
| | Buffer/spring are not moving freely | Remove, clean, and lubricate |
| | Bolt/bolt carrier not moving freely | Remove, clean, and lubricate |
| | Gas tube bent | Check to be sure key goes over gas tube; if not, straighten or replace tube |
| | Inside of gas tube fouled | Replace gas tube |
| | Loose carrier key | Tighten and peen screws |
| | Damaged carrier key | Replace carrier key |
| Short recoil (new rounds aren't feeding into chamber) | Gaps in bolt rings aligned | Remove bolt and unalign ring spaces |
| | Fouling in carrier key or outside of gas tube | Clean key and end of gas tube and then lubricate |
| | Missing or broken gas rings | Replace rings |
| | Broken or loose gas tube | Replace or resecure with new cross pin |

| Problem | Check For | Repair Procedure |
|---|---|---|
| | Fouling in gas port | Remove gas tube; clean port and gas hole in barrel |
| Bolt does not lock open after last round fired | Fouled bolt latch | Clean |
| | Bad magazine | Discard and replace magazine |
| | Broken or missing bolt catch, plunger, and/or spring | Replace |
| | Selector lever binds | Fouling/lacks lubrication; if it still binds, disassemble and clean |
| Bolt carrier hung up | Round jammed between bolt and inside of receiver | If round has not been fired, be very careful; this is a potentially dangerous situation. *Stay clear of muzzle and keep gun pointed in safe direction.* Remove the magazine; hold the charging handle back and slam the butt of the rifle against the ground. CAUTION: when round is freed, the bolt will remain under tension. While bolt is held back, push charging handle forward and let the round fall through the magazine well opening. |
| Rifle won't cock | Worn or broken trigger spring, or broken hammer | Replace |
| | Worn or broken disconnector hook(s) | Replace disconnector(s) |
| | Missing auto sear or weak or broken spring | Replace sear or spring |
| | Long leg of auto sear in wrong position | Remove and assemble correctly |
| Magazine won't lock into magazine catch | Dirty, broken, or corroded magazine or catch spring | Clean or replace if necessary |
| Failure to cycle in burst mode | Broken, dirty, or faulty trigger group parts | Clean or replace |
| Fires two rounds in semiauto mode | Worn disconnector, hammer, or trigger | Replace |
| | Missing disconnector | Replace |
| | Misaligned or loose receiver | Replace or exchange parts |
| | Worn trigger pin hole | Replace lower receiver or (if possible) redrill hole and replace with larger pin and hammer made for it |
| Hammer pin "walks" out of receiver | J-spring in hammer not holding pin in place | Replace hammer or cut deeper center groove in pin |
| Trigger pin "walks" out of receiver | Hammer spring not engaging groove in pin | Replace hammer spring and/or cut grooves deeper in pin |
| Bolt locked halfway forward | Dirt in disconnector spring | Clean and oil |
| | Disconnector broken or missing (semiauto-only guns) | Replace disconnector |
| | Firing pin shoulder too long (semiauto-only guns) | Replace with standard semiauto firing pin rather than "M16" style |

that's too small (a problem usually cured by having a gunsmith ream it with a finishing reamer), by a broken or defective extractor spring, or by a broken claw on an extractor. However, some selective-fire versions of the AR-15 do have extraction problems largely because the weapon may be cycling faster than is ideal. Selection of the proper powder or ammunition may help this situation, but not always.

Buffer Technologies' D-Fender offers one fix for this. The D-Fender is a composite D-shaped ring that fits around the standard extractor spring, creating extra push when the extractor is in place. This small addition actually increases the pressure of the extractor claw holding a brass rim by a factor of four. The D-Fender is a simple fix for this problem—and is considerably cheaper than trying to modify the gas system in any variety of (expensive) ways. For those having extraction troubles with an AR-15, it pays to be sure that the chamber is properly sized and clean—and if there's still a problem, then the D-Fender may be a quick fix (for $12.95).

An interesting component that does a lot to reduce the play between receiver halves with a springy bit of plastic is the Accu-Wedge offered by Z-M Performance Systems. This small component fits between the upper and lower receiver halves, where it is compressed, making the two halves fit tightly. It prevents the rattling noise that some AR-15s make. For just $4.95, this provides another quick and inexpensive fix for a problem that could otherwise cost a bundle to remedy.

(Play between the receiver halves isn't detrimental *as long as the gun still functions properly.* That said, the author once test-fired an experimental AR-15 that had so much slop between the upper and lower halves that if a little downward pressure was applied, the disconnector failed to function properly and the gun would fire two- and three-round bursts—in the semiauto mode—before it finally stopped. Needless to say, ultimately this condition is both unsafe and illegal if not corrected.)

Finally, if you run into problems with an AR-15 that have you stumped, there's often an owner "out there somewhere" who can help you. The key is finding that person. One excellent online source of information is at <http://www.biggerhammer.net>, which has a message board where AR-15 owners can ask or answer questions about these firearms.

A hangfire occurs when a round's primer fails to

**Troubleshooting the M203**

| Problem | Check For | Repair Procedure |
|---|---|---|
| Failure to fire* | Safety on | Rotate safety to fire position |
| | Empty chamber | Open barrel and load (after waiting 30 seconds) |
| | Faulty ammunition | Wait 30 seconds, then remove cartridge and reload |
| | Water or excess lubricant in firing pin well | Wait 30 seconds, then recycle weapon and pull trigger again |
| | Worn or broken firing pin | Replace firing pin |
| | Dirt or residue in firing pin recess | Clean |
| | Burred sear or firing pin | Repair |
| | Weak or broken firing pin spring | Repair |
| Failure to extract | Defective extractor on spring or spring pin | Repair |
| | Ruptured cartridge case | Recycle barrel and/or pry empty from barrel with a tool |
| Failure to eject | Worn, broken, or missing ejector spring or retainer | Repair |
| Failure to chamber | Faulty ammunition | Try another round |
| | Dirty chamber | Clean bore and chamber |
| Safety fails to stay in position | Broken or worn safety or missing spring pin | Repair |
| Failure to cock | Broken sear | Repair |
| | Improper assembly of cocking lever | Repair |

| Problem | Check For | Repair Procedure |
|---|---|---|
| | Loose, broken, or missing cocking lever spring pin | Repair |
| Failure to lock | Excess plastic or debris on breech end of barrel assembly | Clean breech |

* Any failure to fire should be treated as a hangfire, as outlined below.

properly ignite the powder charge, which causes a failure of the round to fire. What's dangerous here is that the round may have enough primer explode to cause a few powder grains to burn in a very slow fire that grows until the round then actually fires. If this happens when the round is in the barrel, the gun may fire unexpectedly. Or, if the round has already been extracted, it may explode and send fragments of the brass casing in all directions and cause injuries.

Even though hangfires are relatively rare, care must be taken to avoid an injury. Since most hangfires take place within 30 seconds of the primer's being struck, keeping a firearm pointed in a safe direction for this time is essential. Avoid extracting a shell during this time: it might explode with the breech only partway open, which will cause damage to the weapon and serious injury to the shooter.

After 30 seconds, extract the shell and then get well away from it. After an hour or more has passed, retrieve the cartridge and dispose of it properly, remembering that the exploding shell could produce grave injury if exposed to heat or other detonation-causing factors.

Most failures to fire are really misfires in which either the primer or powder fails to ignite. The most probable cause is ammunition that has become wet or deactivated by water, grease, or oil. Therefore, it is essential to keep ammunition clean and dry and to take special care to not get oil on a cartridge immediately after the M203 has been cleaned.

# Appendix

**ADSI, Inc.**
2/F NE Section, Topy Main Building
#3 Economia Street, Bagumbayan
Libis, Quezon City 1110, Philippines
www.marieatchada@adsi-inc.com

**Advanced Specialty Products Inc.**
P.O. Box 5010
Woodland Hills, CA 91365
www.aspila.com

**Aimpoint AB (Sweden)**
Headquarters Jägershillgatan 15
SE-213 75 Malmö
www.aimpoint.com

**Aimpoint, Inc. (North American Sales)**
7702 Leesburg Pike
Suite 304
Falls Church, VA 22043

**Alliant Techsystems**
600 Second Street NE, MN11-2015
Hopkins, MN 55343-8384

**American Spirit Arms, Corp.**
15001 N. Hayden Road
Suite 112
Scottsdale, AZ 85260
www.gunkits.com

**Applied Laser**
2245 East Colorado Boulevard
Suite 104-120
Pasadena, CA 91107
www.appliedlaser.com

**AR-7 Industries, LLC**
998 North Colony Road
Meriden, CT 06450
www.ar-7.com

**Armalite, Inc.**
P.O. Box 299
Geneseo, IL. 61254
www.armalite.com

**ArmForté**
P.O. Box 61
Levant, ME 04456
www.armforte.com

**B-Square Company**
P.O. Box 11281
Fort Worth, TX 76110
www.b-square.com

**Big Hammer**
www.biggerhammer.net

**Birdman Weapons Systems, Inc.**
P.O. Box 76063
Highland Heights, KY 41076
www.birdman.org

**Brownells, Inc.**
200 South Front Street
Montezuma, IA 50171
www.brownells.com

**Boderman's Sports**
RR4 Box 131 Halls Road
Kutztown, PA 19530

**Buffer Technologies**
P.O. Box 104903
Jefferson City, MO 65110
www.buffertech.com

**Bushmaster Firearms, Inc.**
999 Roosevelt Trail
P.O. Box 1479
Windham, ME 04062
www.bushmaster.com

**C-MORE Systems**
P.O. Box 1750
7553 Gary Road
Manassas, VA 22110
www.cmore.com

**Carl Zeiss Optical**
1015 Commerce
Petersburg, VA 23803

**Cherokee Accessories**
2128 Farrol Avenue
Union City, CA 94587
www.cheekpieces.com

**Choate Machine & Tool, Inc.**
P.O. Box 218
116 Lovers Lane
Bald Knob, AR 72010
www.RifleStock.com

**CIE Global**
P.O. Box 2490
Indian Trail, NC 2807
www.gunaccessories.com

**Clark Custom Guns, Inc.**
336 Shootout Lane
Princeton, LA 71067
www.clarkcustomguns.com

**Colt's Manufacturing Company, Inc.**
P.O. Box 1868
Hartford, CT 06144-1868
www.colt.com

**Combat Military Optics, Ltd.**
3900 Hopkins Street
Savannah, GA 31405

**Combined Tactical Systems, Inc.**
388 Kinsman Road
Jamestown, PA 16134
www.less-lethal.com/

**Competition Specialties**
P.O. Box 451
105 E. Cass
Osceola, IA 50213

**Dalphon**
P.O. Box 2215
Shelton, WA 98584
www.dalphon.com

**Defense Procurement Manufacuring Services, Inc. (DPMS, aka Panther Arms)**
13983 Industry Avenue
Becker, MN 55308

**E&L Manufacturing, Inc.**
4177 Riddle Bypass Road
Riddle, OR 97469
www.elmfg.com

**Entréprise Arms**
15861 Business Center Drive
Irwindale, CA 91706-2062
www.entreprise.com

**Fabrique Nationale Manufacturing, Inc.**
P.O. Box 24257
Columbia, SC 29224
www.fnmfg.com

**Firequest International, Inc.**
P.O. Box 315
El Dorado, AR 71731
www.firequest.com

**Fulton Armory**
8725 Bollman Place #1
Savage, MD 20763
www.fulton-armory.com

**Gemtech**
P.O. Box 3538
Boise, ID 83703
www.gem-tech.com

**GG&G**
3602 East 42nd Stravenue
Tucson, AZ 85713
www.gggaz.com

**Global Outlet Night Vision Gear**
5907 West Irving Park Road
Chicago, IL 60634
www.night-vision-gear.com

**G.R.A.D.**
6280 South Valley Boulevard #120
Las Vegas, NV 89118
www.grad22.com

**Gun Parts Corporation**
226 Williams Lane
W. Hurley, NY 12491
www.gunpartscorp.com

**Gunsite Training Center**
P.O. Box 700
Paulden, AZ 86334
www.gunsite.com

**Gunsmoke Enterprises, Inc.**
P.O. Box 2537
Okeechobee, FL 34973
www.gunsmoke-inc.com

**Harris Gunworks**
20813 North 19th Avenue
Phoenix, AZ 85027-9002

**Hesse Arms**
9487 Inver Grove Trail
Inver Grove, MN 55076
www.hessearms.com

**Holmes Firearms Company**
Route 6, Box 242
Fayetteville, AR 72701

**Hogue**
P.O. Box 1138
Paso Robles, CA 93447-1138
www.getgrip.com/main.html

**JLM & Sons**
P.O. Box 33
Londonderry, NH. 03053
www.gunsnh.com/jlm&sons.html

**Impact Tactical Weapons Systems**
1569 West 2650 South #7
Ogden, UT 84401
www.impactguns.com

**Innovative Weaponry, Inc.**
2513 East Loop 820 North
Fort Worth, TX 76118
www.ptnightsights.com

**ITT Night Vision**
7671 Enon Drive
Roanoke, VA 24019

**J&T Distributing** (AR-15 parts and accessories)
Box 430
Winchester, KY 40391
www.jtdistributing.com

**Jonathan Arthur Ciener, Inc.**
8700 Commerce Street
Cape Canaveral, FL 32920
www.22lrconversions.com

**Knight's Manufacturing Company**
7750 9th Street Southwest
Vero Beach, FL 32968
www.knightsarmament.com

**Laser Sales**
P.O. Box 599
Springfield, OH 45504
www.lasersales.com

**Leitner-Wise Rifle Company**
1033 North Fairfax Street, Suite 402
Alexandria, VA 22314
www.leitner-wise.com

**Lonegun Wholesalers**
9391 South Tilly's Hill Road
Gentry, AR 72734
lonegun.safeshopper.com

**Magpul Industries Corp.**
P.O. Box 17697
Boulder, CO 80308-0697
www.norgon.com

**MK Ballistic Systems**
2707 Santa Ana Valley Road
Hollister, CA 95023
www.mkballisticsystems.com

**Military Manufacturing Corp. M2**
P.O. Box 96207
Las Vegas, NV 89193-6207
www.m2corp.com

**MFI**
563 Via San Miguel Lane
Liberty, KY 42539
www.mfiap.com/airsoft/acce/rail_m16.htm

**Mounting Solution Plus**
P.O. Box 971202
Miami, FL 33197

**Mr. 40mm**
Randall R. Shivak
1455 Lowell Street, Rear
Elyria, OH 44035
www.40mm.simplenet.com

**MWG Company**
10655 Southwest 185th Terrace
Miami, FL 33157

**Night Scopes International**
P.O. Box 8
Clinton, OK 73601

**Norgon, LLC**
7518 K Fullerton Road
Springfield, VA 22153
www.norgon.com

**North American Integrated Technologies (distributor for La France MK16K-45)**
P.O. Box 82049
San Diego, CA 92138-2049

**Olympic Arms, Inc.**
620-626 Old Pacific Hwy Southeast
Olympia, WA 98513
www.olyarms.com

**Pachmayr, Ltd.**
1875 South Mountain Avenue
Monrovia, CA 91016
www.pachmayr.com

**Paladin Press**
Gunbarrel Tech Center
7077 Winchester Circle
Boulder, CO 80301
www.paladin-press.com

**Peace River Arms**
3515 Reynolds Road
Lakeland, FL 33803

**Professional Ordnance**
1070 Metric Drive
Lake Havasu City, AZ 86403
www.professional-ordnance.com

**Quality Cartridge**
P.O. Box 445
Hollywood, MD 20636
www.owlnet.com/quality

**Quality Machining, Inc.**
P.O. Box 129
Sherwood, OR 97140

**Ramo Defense Systems**
450 Allied Drive
Nashville, TN 37211
www.ramo.com

**Rigel Optics** (night-vision and hunting optics)
1851 335th Avenue
Goose Lake, IA 52750

**Remcon/North Corp.**
P.O. Box 957
7 Enterprise Court
Meredith, NH 03253
www.remcon-north.com

**Rite-Pull**
P.O. Box 811
Noblesville, IN 46061
www.suresite.com/in/r/ritepull

**Rock River Arms**
101 Noble Street
Cleveland, IL 61241
www.rockriverarms.com

**Rocky Mountain Arms**
P.O. Box 329
Longmont, CO 80502-0329
www.rockymountainarms.com

**SARCO Inc.**
P.O. Box 98
323 Union Street
Stirling NJ 07980
www.sarcoinc.com/guns.html

**Sherluk Marketing & Trading** (AR-15/M16 parts)
P.O. Box 6991
Toledo, OH 43612
www.sherluk.com

**Sierra Supply**
P.O. Box 1390
Durango, CO 81302
www.sierra-supply.com

**Smith Enterprise, Inc.**
1701 West 10th Street #14
Tempe, AZ 85281
www.smithenterprise.com/vortex.html

**Soundtech**
Box 391
Pelham, AL 35124
www.hypercon.com/soundtech

**Springfield Armory**
420 West Main Street
Geneseo, IL 61254
www.springfield-armory.com

**Swarovski Optik North America, Ltd.**
2 Slater Road
Cranston, RI 02920
www.swarovskioptik.com

**SSK Industries**
590 Woodvue Lane
Wintersville, OH 43953
E-mail: info@sskindustries.com
www.sskindustries.com

**TAC, Inc.**
2501 Walter Lane
Las Cruces, NM 88005
www.zianet.com/tsoper/wizze.html

**TAPCO, Inc.,**
P.O. Box 2408
3615 Kennesaw
North Industrial Parkway
Kennesaw, GA 30144
www.tapco.com

**Trijicon, Inc.**
P.O. Box 930059
49385 Shafer Avenue
Wixom, MI 48393-0059
www.trijicon-inc.com

**Unertl Optical Company**
P.O. Box 895
310 Clay Avenue
Mars, PA 16046

**Victor Arms**
2610 Bycreek
Houston, TX 77068
www.victorarms.com

**Wilson Combat**
2234 CR 719
Berryville, AR 72616

**Z-M Weapons**
203 South Street
Bernardston, MA 01337
www.zmweapons.com/index.ht